About the Author

Mike Mayo writes mostly about Hollywood and film. A print and broadcast journalist, he hosted the nationally syndicated *Movie Show on Radio* from 2001–06 (it was renamed *Max and Mike on the Movies* after ownership changes in 2005 and will eventually return as a podcast). Mayo continues to do weekly radio reports with stations in Richmond; Lynchburg, Virginia; Atlanta; and Detroit/Windsor, Ontario; and is a frequent guest on Wisconsin Public Radio to talk about movies. His work also appears in the *Washington Post*.

For Marcia,
As Always

American Murder:

Criminals, Crime, and the Media

Scurrilous Cutthroats,
Marauding Desperadoes, Demented Psychopaths,
Deluded Assassins, Serial Widows, Ruthless Gangsters,
Angels of Death, and Hardened Hitmen
from Colonial Times to the Present,
and the Songs, Books, Plays, and Films They Have Inspired

By

Mike Mayo

AMERICAN MURDER:

Criminals, Crime, and the Media

Visible Ink Press
43311 Joy Road #414
Canton, MI 48187-2075

Visible Ink Press is a registered trademark of Visible Ink Press LLC.

Most Visible Ink Press books are available at special quantity discounts when purchased in bulk by corporations, organizations, or groups. Customized printings, special imprints, messages, and excerpts can be produced to meet your needs. For more information, contact Special Markets Director, Visible Ink Press, at www.visibleink.com or (734) 667-3211.

Art Director: Mary Claire Krzewinski
Typesetting: Graphix Group

ISBN-13: 978-1-57859-196-1

Mayo, Mike, 1948-
    American murder : criminals, crime, and the media / Mike Mayo.
        p. cm.
    ISBN-13: 978-1-57859-191-6
    ISBN-10: 1-57859-191-0
    1. Crime in popular culture--United States--Case studies. 2. Crime in mass media--United States--Case studies. 3. Murder in mass media--United States--Case studies. I. Title.
    HV6789.M36 2008   364.1092'273--dc22
                                                   2007047626

Front and back cover images used by permission of AP/WIDE WORLD PHOTOS except "Body with Toe Tag" used by permission of iStockphoto.com, Bonnie Jacobs

Printed in the United States of America
All rights reserved
10 9 8 7 6 5 4 3 2 1

Table of Contents

L

M

N

O

P

Q

R

AMERICAN MURDER

Introduction

"The Americans certainly are great hero-worshippers, and always take their heroes from the criminal classes."

When Oscar Wilde wrote these words in a letter on April 19, 1882, he was referring to Jesse James. Wilde was in Missouri on a coast-to-coast lecture tour of the country and, to judge by the other letters he wrote then, was having a whale of a good time. Jesse had been shot a few weeks before, just a few blocks from where he was staying. By the time la belle Oscar hit town, the locals were stealing everything that had any connection to the famous outlaw and selling the items at public auction.

Wilde marveled at the prices they were getting for Jesse's coal scuttle, dust bin, and boot scraper, and he was delighted by the excitement Jesse's murder had generated. Perhaps the famous writer and future jailbird (they nailed him on a "gross indecency" rap in 1895) recognized a kindred spirit. The "great train-robber and murderer," as Wilde referred to him, had been famous for years, and for good reason. Jesse was no slouch when it came to self-promotion, and he had legions of defenders both locally and nationally. In death, though, he was transformed into something much greater and Wilde was on hand to witness it.

Jesse was one of the first celebrity murderers. Over the years, he became such an icon in American popular culture that the truth of his many crimes has largely been forgotten. Perhaps more accurately, the truth has been eclipsed by stories—stories people want to hear and see again and again.

The simple truth is that the idea of murder fascinates us.

I came to this book as a writer, film reviewer, and omnivorous consumer of crime fiction. I knew a little about almost all of these cases. I knew a lot about a few of them. Almost all of it was wrong. The difference between historical truth and what we assume to be true about the past is vast. What do you think when you hear these names?

- Charlie Starkweather and Caril Ann Fugate: Most people probably imagine two good-looking misunderstood kids in love who somehow went wrong and spun out of control. Don't believe it. They killed one of Charlie's friends who had helped them hide out and Caril Ann's baby sister because she wouldn't stop crying.

- Bruno Hauptmann: Revisionists have cast him as an innocent carpenter who was framed by the powerful men who supported Charles Lindbergh. Not a chance. There isn't a single piece of hard evidence anyone else had anything to do with the kidnapping and murder.

- Lizzie Borden: No nice middle-class girl could savagely slaughter her upstanding parents. If they made her miserable enough, she could.

Deliberately taking a life is the ultimate crime. It happens a lot in this country, and it's mostly men who do it. But all murders are not created equal, either in the eyes of the law or for the purposes of this book. If one drug dealer kills another drug dealer, for example, nobody but their families is likely to care. If a guy gets liquored up and goes home and kills his wife, it is sad but unremarkable. If she fights back and kills him, then we've got one less drunken jerk to deal with.

But when a murder is really significant, for any number of reasons, it acquires more weight and importance. When, let's say, the victim is famous, or when there are great numbers of victims, or when the victim or the murderer is unusually attractive or wealthy, or when the method of the murder is particularly horrifying, well, everything changes. The whole country takes notice and we pay attention to each step of the process.

It begins with the first reporting of the crime and the revelation of the details. If those details are sufficiently shocking, our interest is piqued. Then the evidence accumulates as more clues are revealed. By this point, we are actively trying to learn the most recent revelation. We want to know more, and the media—print, broadcast, Web—all want to be the first to pass along those precious bits of information.

At some point, law enforcement will identify a suspect and attention will focus on that person. Usually, the next steps are arrest, indictment, and trial, though if the suspect is wealthy or famous, he may be able to prolong those phases.

We tend to think the trial and verdict—or verdicts when appeals or civil trials follow—are the end of the story, but they're not. The stories in this book rarely end neatly. There are few clear-cut cases here, though many of these murderers are pretty damn rotten. Even if the trial ends with a conviction and the sentence is carried out, more stories are going to be told about the murder and the murderer. As time passes, those stories can take several forms because the major players can be cast in widely different stereotypical roles.

Murderers, even the sickest serial killers, may be perceived as a glamorous, romantic figures. Or, if they're unattractive, they may be seen as brutish villains. Victims may be completely blameless and sympathetic, but if the case involves sex and the victim is a woman, she may be perceived as somehow deserving what she got.

The cops can be portrayed as dedicated, hard-working law enforcement professionals or bumbling, corrupt flatfoots.

The prosecutor may be a four square crime-busting DA, or perhaps a politically ambitious weasel who uses trumped up charges to further his or her upcoming campaign for mayor, senate, whatever.

The defense attorney may be an utter slimeball who knows the client is guilty and will still use any loophole or unscrupulous tactic to get him/her off, or the counselor may be a valiant crusader for an unjustly accused innocent.

In the biggest, most important cases, one strong narrative line tends to gain more currency than others. It comes to be accepted as the truth, or the true myth, as it were. That's the process that gives us Jesse James as the American Robin Hood, standing up for poor folks against the godless bankers. It transforms John Dillinger from an accomplished bank robber into a dashing rebel, capable of breaking out of any jail, and who might, in the end, have eluded the feds and cops who claimed to have gunned him down.

This book, then, is about the murders who have captivated and fascinated us the most intensely. The ones who have demonstrated such long-lasting importance that their names still evoke an immediate reaction and recognition: Manson, Capone, O.J.

Most entries begin with a description of what happened, who the key participants were, where and when people were killed, and how it was done. But even those simple facts are often in dispute. When that's the case, I've gone with what seems to be the most logical sequence of events. If there are significant unresolved contradictions or questions, both versions are included. (Did Pretty Boy Floyd participate in the Kansas City Massacre? He strenuously denied it, and many writers have accepted this denial. Still, honest readers can disagree.)

After the facts have been laid out, we turn to the stories. With the most notorious murderers, these stories start almost immediately and spread swiftly if they touch the right chord in the public consciousness. It can be as difficult to sort through as it is to figure out the facts, because stories take on a life of their own, or a reality of their own, and then they become part of the larger story too. Rule of thumb: the more famous the murder, the more rich and varied the stories. I'm sure there are some I've missed, but I have searched diligently among the most scurrilous rumors, tawdry exploitation, and bad movies I could find. I've tried to point out where they stray from the historical record, particularly the movies.

In some cases, the murder has not generated any wild tales, folk songs, novels, or films. But these "unknown" crimes are so wild and unusual they must be mentioned, if only briefly.

Not to be too crass and flippant (and this book is often crass, flippant, and in very poor taste) but to earn a place in these pages, the American murderer must have killed either a large number of normal people or one relatively famous person, or he or she must have pulled it off with real drama and audacity. Also included are several notable nonmurderers. They're the cops and writers whose careers are so inextricably linked with the killers, and the criminals who stopped short of murder but still pulled off something out of the ordinary.

Among the other lesser known killers are some incredible tales. Consider the following:

- "Baron" Lamm, whose contributions to the craft of bank robbery and heist movies are incalculable.
- The still-unsolved Cleveland Torso Killings and New Orleans "Axeman" murders.
- Joe Ball—what went on in the pit behind his Texas roadhouse was bad enough, but what he did was worse.
- Albert Fish, probably the most vicious and depraved serial murderer this country has ever produced.
- "Trigger" Burke, the hitman who viewed World War II as practice.
- Salvatore Cardinella and Robert McConaghy, two men who came this-close to cheating the executioner.
- Theodore Coneys, the real Denver "Spider Man."
- "Two-Gun" Crowley, one of the first killers to claim "the movies made me do it."
- T. Cullen Davis, the Texas millionaire who provided the model for TV's J.R. Ewing and got away with more than J.R. ever dreamed.
- George Rogers, the porcine pyromaniac who set a luxury liner ablaze, killed 134 people, and was proclaimed a hero.
- Adolph Luetgert, who definitely did not grind his wife up in his sausage factory.
- Ed Morrell, the forgotten California outlaw whose life was far more eventful and bizarre than any fiction.
- Edmund Kemper, who told the parole board and doctors he was truly sorry for murdering his grandparents. The board members didn't know what he had in the trunk of his car.
- Ronald DeFeo, Jr., the real Amityville horror.
- Albert Terrell, who claimed he was sleepwalking when he slashed his mistress' throat and set her bed on fire.

And let's not forget the ladies:

- Barbara Graham, who talked her way into the gas chamber.
- The "Bloody" Benders of Kansas, whose daughter Kate was "a beautiful voluptuous girl with tigerish grace."
- Nannie Doss and Lydia Sherman, serial widows.
- Libby Holman, the Broadway sex symbol who shocked the world even more after she was charged with the murder of her wealthy husband.

• Winnie Ruth Judd—yes, she was the notorious "trunk murderess" but everyone said she was a real sweetheart.

• Beulah Annan, who has been the subject of two movies, one of them a Best Picture Oscar winner.

• Bathsheba Spooner, the Revolutionary War wife who found herself with an inconvenient older hubby and a handsome 16-year-old soldier on the front porch.

With the more famous killers, it is often difficult to separate fact, fiction, lies, and exaggerations. That's particularly true of the Old West outlaws and the 20th century mob guys. Both groups found eager accomplices in the media who wanted to turn them into popular heroes. In post-Civil War America, eastern newspaper and magazine readers devoured stories about frontier adventures. A few years later when the movies were born, those same desperados were further romanticized on screen. The motion picture industry actually matured at the same time organized crime rose to power during Prohibition. On screen and in real life, gangsters and bootleggers became sympathetic figures who provided a valuable service. Besides, as Bugsy Siegel put it, they only killed each other.

With the outlaw cowboys and the mobsters, good writers, editors, and filmmakers knew the unvarnished truth wouldn't sell nearly as well as a great story, and so they told the best stories they could. This book attempts to look at those large gray areas between the historical truth of these murders and the stories that have flourished as time passed. With each entry, I have tried to point out the best books and websites that go into more detail.

All forms of popular entertainment have been quick to exploit or adapt real crimes while the public is still interested. The murder of Mary Rogers in 1841 was one of the first cases to attract wide attention. New York newspapers were intensely interested in the killing of the pretty young woman, who had worked in a tobacco shop where she was particular favorite of the local politicos and literati. The press actually forced the authorities to investigate the murder more thoroughly than they had wanted to (or were able, given their lack of resources). A year later, the perpetually impoverished Edgar Allan Poe decided to cash in. He changed the setting to Paris and the name to Marie Roget, but everyone knew what he was writing about.

Only a few weeks after John Wilkes Booth was killed, Dion Haco, a 19th century Robert Ludlum, produced a fact-based (sort of) fictional account entitled *J. Wilkes Booth: The Assassinator of President Lincoln.* Chapter One, "The Mysterious Meetings and Their Special Object," begins:

At one of the most fashionable houses in Monument Square, Baltimore, a number of persons were seen gathering together during the month of June, 1860. There was nothing extraordinary in the outward appearance of these men, nor did their actions excite any special attention; but had a detective been on their track he would have soon discovered that beneath that gentlemanly exterior lurked something far more malevolent than usually engages the attention of ordinary citizens.

But movies have created the deepest and most pervasive transformations of murderers and other criminals into heroes. The protagonist of an American movie—from silent one-reelers until today—is usually a man with a gun. In most cases, the hero is justified in the use of his weapon, be he cowboy, detective, soldier, or cop. But not always. If the ticket-buying public is interested in Billy the Kid or Al Capone, somebody's going to make a movie about him. And in the process, that character is going to become attractive, glamorous, and seductive. It's simply the nature of the medium; it always has been, and it is more true now than ever.

There was a time when it was almost not true, in Hollywood's "Golden Age" when the studio system was in full force, from roughly the mid-1930s to 1950. During those years, a few large studios produced virtually all of the feature films shown in the country and owned large chains of theaters. They controlled the business completely. They decided which subjects would be addressed; who would write, direct, and star; what the movies would look like; where they would be shown; how much a ticket would cost; and what kind of popcorn would be sold at the concession stand. The studios had a captive audience. The only competition outside of the largest cities was radio. In those years, sixty to ninety million Americans went to the movies at least once a week.

Despite such popularity, and because of it, the movies had vocal critics. Conservative political and religious groups objected to the depictions of sin, sex, and violence they saw on the screen, and to the licentious lives of the people who made movies. (Those same forces also railed against communism, black people, women, Jews, Chinese, Italians, Irish, gays, etc. etc. Some things don't change.) Various legions of decency and state censorship boards had the power to keep certain films from being shown and to edit "offensive" scenes at will. In the wake of such Hollywood scandals as the Fatty Arbuckle rape trial—though he was never convicted of anything—and the success of films like *Scarface* (1932), *The Public Enemy* (1931), and *Little Caesar* (1931), these pillars of rectitude demanded something be done about the tidal wave of sex and violence corrupting our great nation.

In response, the industry agreed to a strict form of self-censorship called the Hays Code. Named for Motion Picture Producers and Directors Association Board President Will Hays, it was a list of rules defining which activities could and could not be shown on screen. Right up front, the Code's purpose was boldly stated: "No picture shall be produced that will lower the moral standards of those who see it. Hence, the sympathy of the audience should never be thrown to the side of crime, wrongdoing, evil or sin."

To that end, violence was not to be presented in detail; drug traffic and drug use were not to be shown; revenge was not to be justified; and the use of firearms was to be restricted to the essentials.

The studios agreed to the restrictions because they had such a tight monopoly on visual narrative entertainment. They realized that if they could rein in their most adventurous elements—those writers, directors, and actors who wanted to tell the most lurid, challenging stories—they could continue to make middle-of-the-road, highly polished comedies, dramas, and musicals, and their theaters would still be filled every week. Problem solved. Such an attitude made it tough for realistic crime films, and so none of the great 1930s outlaws—Pretty Boy Floyd, Machine Gun Kelly, Baby Face Nelson—

appeared on screen except in newsreels. Hays also specifically ordered the studios not to make films about John Dillinger.

Once the Code was in force, the studios submitted their scripts to the board for approval. They made the movies with occasional trims and cuts here and there to satisfy the keepers of the Code. True government censorship was avoided, and the studios prospered. Then, in 1948, two things happened that profoundly changed the movie business: the first was the Supreme Court's Paramount Consent Decree, which broke up the major studios' monopoly on the business by ordering them to sell their theaters and eliminate the "block booking" that forced theaters to take titles they didn't want in order to get the ones they did. The decision opened the door for independent producers and foreign films that embraced more adventurous material.

The second change was the arrival of television. The TV networks immediately began to churn out the kind of comedies, melodramas, and music shows that had been the studios' bread and butter. Movie attendance plummeted. The Code remained in place until 1968 when it was replaced by the Motion Picture Association of America (MPAA) ratings system. President Jack Valenti realized it was time for the movies to grow up a little, and to let the marketplace decide what kind of stories would be told. The ratings would describe the content of individual films and people could make up their own minds about what they and their kids would see.

Under the new regime, one of the first true crime films to be produced was *Bonnie and Clyde* (1967) and its glamorization of criminality was both complicated and blatant. The filmmakers claimed they didn't mean to romanticize the title characters. Look, they said, see how these two misguided kids die horrible deaths at the end—they're not rewarded for their crimes. But Warren Beatty (who was also a producer) and Faye Dunaway were two of the most popular and attractive stars of their day, and the sharp clothes they wore inspired a retro fashion trend. It was impossible for them not to make the characters seem exotic and alluring.

Since then, even more power has shifted to actors and they now make important decisions about which films will be made and how the characters will be portrayed. They're not going to play hideous, unsympathetic, sadistic beasts, not if they want people to pay to see their next movie. (The exception is Charlize Theron who copped an Oscar for *Monster* in 2003 when she uglied up to play serial killer Aileen Wuornos and convinced Hollywood she was a serious actress and not just another glamourpuss.)

Finally, it is not the filmmaker's job to recreate objective, historical truth. It's the filmmaker's job to tell a good story. People ought to understand this better than they do. Any adult who goes to a Hollywood movie expecting to see historical truth deserves to be lied to. When the studios or, more often, independent producers have tried to address real murderers, the results have generally been poor. But not always. Some films stick close to the gruesome facts and reveal something about their subjects.

The Honeymoon Killers (1970) changes some key facts about Martha Beck and Ray Fernandez, but it is psychologically accurate with excellent performances and a properly sordid atmosphere.

In *Summer of Sam* (1999), Spike Lee cares more about the effects of serial murders on a community than he does about David Berkowitz. The result feels completely authentic, while David Fincher's *Zodiac* (2007) is less about the San Francisco killings than the obsessive forces that drive the people who become fascinated by certain crimes.

Martin Scorsese's masterpiece *Goodfellas* (1990) is still the most detailed examination of day-to-day life in the mob, and the details of the Lufthansa heist are right, right enough, anyway. Both *Mobsters* (1991), about Lucky Luciano's creation of the Mafia, and *Tombstone* (1993), about the gunfight at the O.K. Corral, take liberties, but they get the key details right, and they are gloriously entertaining.

In *Breach* (2007), the filmmakers invent some scenes, but star Chris Cooper makes spy Robert Hanssen's dark inner world seem completely real. *Reversal of Fortune* (1990) is a film about uncertainty. The evidence in the case of Claus Von Bülow can be interpreted two ways. Director Barbet Schroeder and actors Jeremy Irons and Ron Silver make the most of challenging, intelligent material.

Gus Van Sant turns murder into black comedy in *To Die For* (1995), and in her portrayal of a woman who was consumed by ambition, Nicole Kidman is letter perfect. Even so, the conclusion is whole cloth. In *Elephant* (2003), Van Sant takes a completely different approach to the killings at Columbine High School. Filmed in a real school, it's told as an eerily dreamlike documentary with young unprofessional actors.

Siege at Ruby Ridge (1996) succeeds in making its characters believably flawed. It shows Randy Weaver and his family warts and all, but does nothing to diminish the horrors they experienced.

By telling the story of *United 93* (2006) with the techniques of a documentary, director Paul Greengrass comes closer to the horrible truths of 9/11 than any other feature has to date.

Documentaries, for the most part, generally fare better than their glossy screen counterparts when retelling crimes. These are the best: In *The Thin Blue Line* (1988), director Errol Morris combines recreations with interviews to show how justice was twisted in the Randall Adams murder case. David Wolper's *Four Days in November* (1964) has little to say about Lee Harvey Oswald, but because it was made while memories were still fresh, it powerfully recreates the stunned mood of the nation immediately after the assassination of John Kennedy. *Paradise Lost: The Child Murders at Robin Hood Hills* (1996) was instrumental in bringing the West Memphis Three to public attention. It details what may well be a mistaken conviction.

Before the days of film, our most famous murderers were often celebrated in song. Though the tradition has largely died out in this country, a few diehards still hang on to the form. In the early and middle parts of his career, Bob Dylan was fond of writing lengthy hymns to various killers, and he was usually romanticizing very bad people. Bruce Springsteen was much more tough-minded and accurate in "Nebraska." The grim song comes closer to the truth of Charlie Starkweather than any of the films ever made about him. In their ambitious musical play *Assassins* (1991, 2004), Stephen Sondheim and John Weidman cut to the central truth shared by presidential assassins—that they're angry unstable men whose political motivations are not nearly as important as their inner demons.

Today, most people probably go to the Web for information about crime and criminals. They may well start at Wikipedia (wikipedia.org), but by far the best site is the Crime Library (crimelibrary.com). It covers a wide range of subjects and the writers are careful and list their sources. Crime Magazine (crimemagazine.com) is more limited in scope, but is filled with good material.

The best way, however, to find good, detailed, reliable information about America's great murderers is to go to the books written about them. There are thousands, if not millions of them out there. In creating this book, I read a lot of them. My favorites include three very fine overviews, Carl Sifakis' *The Encyclopedia of American Crime* (1982, 2001); Robert Jay Nash's *Bloodletters and Bad Men* (1973), and Richard Hammer's *Playboy's Illustrated History of Organized Crime* (1975).

Bryan Burrough's *Public Enemies* (2004) and John Toland's *The Dillinger Days* (1963) tell the stories of the great 1930s outlaws as one smooth fast-paced narrative. I disagree with some of their analyses, but still recommend both books.

James L. Swanson's Manhunt: *The 12-Day Chase for Lincoln's Killer* (2006) is another fast read, cutting down the pursuit of John Wilkes Booth to its essentials. Rick Geary has written and illustrated six wonderful books about American murders: *The Mystery of Mary Rogers* (2001), *The Murder of Abraham Lincoln* (2005), *The Borden Tragedy* (1997), *The Beast of Chicago* (2003, about Herman Mudgett), *The Bloody Benders* (2007), and *The Fatal Bullet: The Assassination of President James A. Garfield* (1999). His black and white illustrations are particularly effective in revealing important details of place and dress. The books are scrupulously researched and Geary tells the stories economically and vividly.

The Stranger Beside Me (1980) established Ann Rule in the field of crime writing. She was closer to Ted Bundy than anyone else who has tried to tell his story, and her portrait of him is intimately detailed. Truman Capote's *In Cold Blood* (1966) is so beautifully written it transformed the brutal murder of a Kansas farm family into a new art form, the nonfiction novel. It's also a first-rate piece of crime writing.

Carlos Clarens' *Crime Movies: An Illustrated History* (1980) is a brilliant work of criticism, particularly in its analysis of the early gangster films. It's even more impressive when you realize Clarens was working before the days of home video.

Today, few people outside of San Francisco know about Theo Durrant, and much of his story has been wrongly reported for years. Virginia McConnell corrects the mistakes in *Sympathy for the Devil* (2001). Some may question her conclusions but she makes a strong case. As does Jerry Bledsoe in *Bitter Blood* (1988). The Lynch-Klenner murders don't really fit within the limitations of this book but Bledsoe tells the story in all its fantastic, unbelievable detail. For my money, it belongs on the shelf with *The Stranger Beside Me* and *In Cold Blood.*

In their books *Billy the Kid: The Endless Ride* (2007), and *Billy the Kid: A Short and Violent Life* (1989), Michael Wallis and Robert Utley successfully separate the hundreds of myths about the Kid from the reality of young Henry McCarty. T. J. Stiles does the same in *Jesse James: Last Rebel of the Civil War* (2002), though his approach is more academic. In *Inventing Wyatt Earp* (1998), Allen Bara focuses more on the 20th century stories about the lawman, particularly the ones on television and film.

As for mobsters, the *Last Testament of Lucky Luciano* (1974) is simply one of the greatest titles ever. Yes, the book is self-serving and probably contains at least one inaccuracy or exaggeration on every page, but as he's portrayed by authors Martin Gosch and Richard Hammer, Charlie Lucky is a charmer and it's hard not to like him.

Jim Fisher's *The Lindbergh Case* (1999) and the *Ghosts of Hopewell* (1994) will not put an end to the conspiracy theories still surrounding the famous kidnapping and murder, though they should. Fisher has studied the case thoroughly, and these are two of the best books on the subject.

Though it has been fictionalized several times, the Massie Case is not well known outside Hawaii. David Stannard recounts the shameful episode with an academician's depth in *Honor Killing: How the Infamous "Massie Affair" Transformed Hawai'i* (2005). Another controversial figure, Bathsheba Spooner, is covered in Deborah Navas' *Murdered by His Wife* (1999). Both Bathsheba's crime and her punishment are detailed and Navas tries not to take sides. The book is fascinating.

These writers have done the real heavy lifting. They tell terrific stories with the depth of detail they deserve. Still, as good as these books are, they're probably not going to uproot any of our cherished myths. Millions of people are going to continue to believe that John Kennedy was killed by a CIA-Cuban-Mafia-Illuminati-Rotarian conspiracy. The story of a single unimportant guy with a rifle shooting a president is somehow harder to believe, and less entertaining than a story about shadowy forces with godlike powers.

In the end, these glamorous gangsters and noble outlaws and seductive serial killers are the stories we want to believe. And, true or not, a story that people want to believe is a powerful thing. Consider, for example, the famous myth of John Dillinger's legendary endowment. It can probably be traced back to a post-mortem photograph where the bank robber's arm, stiff with rigor mortis, prominently and impressively tents the sheet covering the body. The picture led to stories that boys and men have told each other for generations. But if the same photograph had been taken of, say, Baby Face Nelson, the story would never have gained any currency. Nelson was a needlessly violent, insecure little thug. The public didn't love him.

But people did love Dillinger. He was good looking, cocky, and in the latter days of the Depression, he was seen as a guy who robbed banks, not people. It was widely reported he wouldn't take cash from people who happened to be in a bank lobby when he knocked over the joint. It might have been true, but it doesn't matter. People wanted to believe it, and the myth of the heroic Dillinger was born and the enormous accoutrement was part of it.

As we were finishing work on this book in the spring of 2007, two murder cases made the news. In Blacksburg, Virginia, college student Cho Seung-hui went on a rampage and killed 32 people before he shot himself. A week later in New Jersey, fertility clinic nurse Melanie McGuire was found guilty of killing her husband. The state argued she drugged him, shot him, and sliced up the body in the bathroom of their townhouse. After wrapping the parts in plastic bags, she packed them up in three pieces of designer luggage and ditched them in the Chesapeake Bay. She did it because she was having an affair with a doctor at the clinic. She was a petite, attractive young woman with a high-powered defense team, and the whole state was riveted by the case.

It's too early to say what paths their stories will take. Cho has already entered the pantheon of sorehead spree killers. In the wake of McGuire's lengthy trial with its mountain of circumstantial evidence, people in New Jersey were stunned by the cold brutality of the murder, and most felt the jury reached the proper verdict. But Melanie McGuire continued to proclaim her complete innocence and some believe her. If the story is ever filmed and she is played by a hot young actress and the filmmakers take her side, what will people conclude about her? Which story will they believe?

Mike Mayo
Chatham, New Jersey

Acknowledgements

M any thanks to the staff of the Library of the Chathams for their help in finding so many older books. Their work reminded me of my own days as a librarian, where I discovered Carl Sifakis' *The Encyclopedia of American Crime*, Jay Robert Nash's *Bloodletters and Bad Men*, and Richard Hamner's *Playboy's Illustrated History of Organized Crime*, still three of the most enjoyable books I've ever read.

Additional thanks to Roger Jänecke at Visible Ink Press, Marco Di Vita at Graphix Group, Joanne Lewis (design), Bob Huffman (photos), Jane Hoehner (proofreading), Larry Baker (indexing), and Taryn Pfalzgraf (project management). Last but certainly not least, Marcia Schiff and Regalle Asuncion of Associated Press, for photo research and the use of their photos (all photos are from AP with the exception the movie stills or posters— *Roscoe "Fatty" Arbuckle*, *The Assassination of Jesse James By the Coward Robert Ford*, *The Boston Strangler*, *Butch Cassidy and the Sundance Kid*, *The Party*, *The Seven Year Itch*, and *The Valley of the Dolls* provided courtesy of the Kobal Collection).

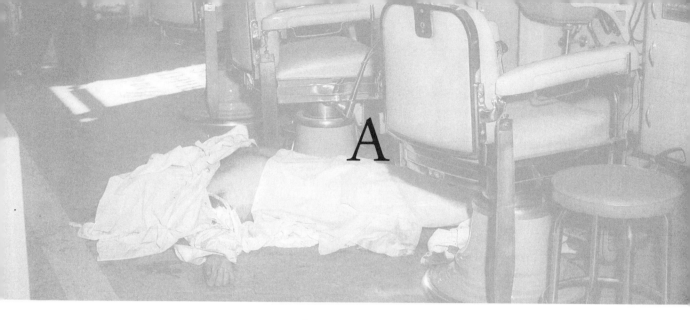

Abbott, Burton W.

The thing about Burton "Bud" Abbott is that he wanted to be caught.

On April 28, 1955 in Berkeley, California he kidnapped and killed fourteen-year-old Stephanie Bryan. Somehow, this unassuming married college student persuaded the girl to get into his car and drove her up to his cabin, little more than a shack, in Weaverville, almost 300 miles north of San Francisco. They fought on the way. Two people saw them but were not able to reach Abbott's car and could provide no useful identification. Two weeks after the kidnapping, Stephanie's French textbook was found, but beyond that, nothing. The case attracted nationwide attention.

On the night of July 15, while rummaging through some boxes of old clothes in the basement of her house, Georgia Abbott found a purse and wallet with Stephanie's identification. Naturally, she was shocked and took the things upstairs to her husband and some visiting friends. Abbott was curiously uninterested. Even after they had called the police, he appeared to pay little attention to the matter, playing chess while the cops conducted their initial search. They came back the next day for a more thorough examination of the house and found

more of Stephanie's stuff—books, brassiere—buried in the sandy floor of the basement. Abbott claimed he had no idea how they got there. His garage had been used as polling place in May; anyone could have gone down there and planted the evidence. The cops didn't buy it and arrested him.

The police learned about Abbott's cabin and searched the area with dogs. They found Stephanie's body, panties tied around her neck, up a steep slope from the place. The circumstantial case against him was strong, and Abbott admitted having driven to the cabin on the day of the kidnapping. But why? What was his motive? Because the body was so badly decomposed, there was no evidence of a sexual element. Was Abbott, a slight man who had suffered tuberculosis, physically capable of such a crime?

At his trial, the final piece of evidence that persuaded the jury was the testimony of criminologist Dr. Paul I. Kirk, who found four matching samples of hair and fabric fibers from Stephanie's clothes in the back seat of Abbott's car. Even so, it took more than 50 hours of deliberation to find Abbott guilty of kidnapping and murder, and because of the lengthy time frame, many people believed he might be innocent.

Before Abbott's execution, though, something else emerged. During the trial, Abbott had shared a cell in the Alameda county jail with John Douglas Cober, who was serving a stretch for writing bad checks. They talked a lot about the case. According to Cober, Abbott said that he simply wanted to be famous. The best way he could see to do this was to commit a pointless crime, allow himself to be arrested for it, and then be found not guilty. To accomplish this goal, Abbott deliberately left the purse in the basement where he knew his wife would find it. During the commission of the kidnapping, he created false, contradictory evidence, burying the body first in one location and then moving it to the grave near the cabin. There was no sexual motivation, he allegedly said—though he had tied the dead girl's panties around her neck to create that impression.

Cober's story not withstanding, Abbott never confessed. The day before his execution, he did tell a psychiatrist he couldn't confess because he knew how hard that would be on his mother. He went to gas chamber on March 14, 1957.

Abbott's story has never made it to the small or large screen, though elements of it have been appropriated in countless formula mysteries. *San Francisco Chronicle* reporter Bernice Freeman Davis wrote about Abbott's trial in detail in her book *The Desperate and the Damned.*

Abbott, Jack

Norman Mailer probably regretted the day he learned about Jack Abbott.

Abbott was a jailbird who had first run afoul of the law as a kid. He came from an unstable home and had been in and out of foster care. He worked his way up from juvenile detention to reform school to the Utah State Prison where he stabbed a fellow inmate to death in 1965. Six years later, he escaped and robbed a bank in Colorado before they caught him again and sent him back.

In the late 1970s the self-educated Abbott learned that Norman Mailer was working on a book about murderer Gary Gilmore. Abbott wrote to the famous literary lion and offered to help with the book, providing details of his extensive involvement with the penal system.

Impressed with Abbott's language, Mailer corresponded with him. Their letters eventually formed Abbott's book, *In the Belly of the Beast.* As it was being readied for publication, Mailer supported Abbott's efforts to obtain parole. In June 1980, they were successful.

Abbott's book was published to universal critical acclaim and a high-powered publicity campaign including an appearance on the *Today Show*, a *People* magazine story, an interview in *Rolling Stone*—the works. To meet the terms of his parole, Abbott lived in a halfway house in New York.

On July 18, 1981 Abbott went out drinking and picked up a couple of girls. Early in the morning, they stopped off at an all-night restaurant, Binibon, for breakfast. Their waiter was Richard Adan, a young writer and actor who was also the son-in-law of Binibon's owner. When Abbott asked to use the men's room, Adan told him it was for staff only. Abbott became angry and they argued about it.

Abbott asked Adan to step outside and the argument continued on Fifth Street. It ended when Abbott pulled a knife. Adan turned and tried to run but the ex-con reached around and stabbed him in the chest.

Racing back inside, Abbott told the girls they had to leave—he had just killed a man. He picked up his stuff and caught a bus out of town. He made it as far as Mexico, but returned to the United States. He went to work in the Louisiana oil fields, where U.S. marshals caught him in September.

At his trial, Abbott attempted to claim self-defense and blamed the prison system and society in general for everything he had done. Not a single bit of it was really his fault, he said. That didn't fly: he was found guilty of manslaughter, given 15 years to life, with the sentence to be served after he had finished the eight years left in Utah.

Convict/author Jack Henry Abbott, handcuffed, on his way to jail in New Orleans, September 24, 1981. (AP Photo)

In 1987 Abbott's second book, *My Return*, was published to universal critical contempt. In 2002 Jack Abbott hanged himself with a noose fashioned from shoe laces and bed sheets in his cell at the Wende Correctional Facility in upstate New York.

To date, no one has expressed any interest in adapting his second work to the screen.

Abu-Jamal, Mumia

The facts of the case could hardly be simpler.

Around 4:00 a.m. December 9, 1981 veteran Philadelphia police officer Daniel Faulkner pulled over a light blue Volkswagen driven by William Cook. It had been going the wrong direction on a one-way street. The stop took place in a rough part of town, so Faulkner called for backup. Even at that hour of the morning, there were a number of eye-witnesses to what happened next.

As Cook got out of his car, he sucker-punched Officer Faulkner. Faulkner fought back, striking Cook with his flashlight. Cook's brother Wesley, aka Mumia Abu-Jamal, was watching from his cab, parked nearby. He pulled his .38 from a holster and ran over. He shot Officer Faulkner once in the back.

Faulkner turned, pulled his service revolver and, before he fell to the sidewalk, shot Abu-Jamal in the abdomen. Abu-Jamal stood over him and continued to fire. Though he missed with three shots, he killed

Curiously, throughout his career as one of the mob's top executives, Adonis maintained an involvement with jewelry theft and fencing. He just wanted to keep his hand in and, according to Luciano, Adonis always liked flashy rocks.

Officer Faulkner with a bullet to the head. Police found the wounded Abu-Jamal at the scene and took him to the hospital where he angrily boasted of what he had just done.

Six months later, Abu-Jamal went to trial where, for a time, he served as his own lawyer. Neither he nor his brother testified. A jury of two blacks and ten whites found him guilty. In a separate sentencing phase, they sentenced him to death.

That might have been the end of a sad story but the combination of Abu-Jamal's striking dreadlocked appearance and his experience as a radio reporter made him "mediagenic," so he managed to persuade many on the left he not only had been the victim of racism but that the "real killer" was still out there. A federal judge overturned the death penalty in 2001, and this decision is being appealed. As of this writing, legal wrangling continues.

Rallies and marches have been held to refocus attention on Abu-Jamal's case, and filmmaker John Edginton made a documentary about the murder and the trial called *Mumia: A Case for Reasonable Doubt?* The answer to the question posed in the subtitle, however, is a resounding "Guilty! Guilty! Guilty!" The film may be the least persuasive bit of propaganda ever produced. It ignores or discounts the overwhelming evidence of Abu-Jamal's guilt, focusing instead on less reliable testimony and the minor contradictions found in any investigation.

Adonis, Joe

Even though he was one of the founding members of the **Syndicate**, Joe Adonis remains relatively unknown compared to his friends and contemporaries **Charlie "Lucky" Luciano** and **Bugsy Siegel**.

Born Giuseppe Antonio Doto in Italy, he stowed away on an ocean liner and snuck into America in 1915. He went to work as muscle for mobster Frankie Yale in Brooklyn. He found his greatest success through Luciano. At first, Doto was completely loyal to Charlie Lucky.

It was some time in the 1920s that Doto decided to change his name to Joe Adonis because he found himself so physically attractive. Not everyone shared that opinion. In 1922 he was arrested for rape and always had a reputation as a womanizer. By the late 1920s Adonis controlled bootlegging in Brooklyn, having taken over after Frankie Yale was rubbed out in a drive-by shooting.

In 1931 when Luciano decided to consolidate his power and end the Castellamarrese War by killing his boss **Joe Masseria**, Adonis was part of the handpicked four-man hit team put together to do the job. The others were **Albert Anastasia**, **Vito Genovese**, and Bugsy Siegel. After they got rid of another old boss, Salvatore Maranzano, five months later, Adonis took a place on the Board of Directors of the newly formed Syndicate. He and the other new bosses prospered. They paid off the cops, judges, and politicians to leave them alone, and made millions in booze, drugs, prostitution, loan sharking, protection, the numbers, and union racketeering. Life was good.

Adonis stayed in the background. When Luciano was deported to Italy after World War II, he looked after his friend's interests. He didn't really come to the attention of the law until Abe "Kid Twist" Reles decided to leave the mob's assassination bureau, **Murder, Inc.**, and tell all he knew to the New York D.A. in 1948. By then, Adonis had expanded into New Jersey.

Curiously, throughout his career as one of the mob's top executives, Adonis maintained an involvement with jewelry theft and fencing. He just wanted to keep his hand in and, according to Luciano, Adonis always liked flashy rocks.

In the early 1950s Adonis was called to testify before the Kefauver Committee on Organized Crime and was charged with violating New Jersey gambling laws. He was facing a federal perjury rap, too, when they learned Adonis was an illegal alien. On August 5, 1953 he was deported to Italy and moved to Naples where he lived near Luciano. By then, the two men were no longer close. Luciano thought Adonis had sided, at least tacitly, with his rival Vito Genovese. Charlie Lucky died in 1962, Adonis a decade later when he suffered a heart attack while being questioned by Italian police.

Befitting his low public profile, Adonis appeared in only one mob movie, *Lansky* (1999), as a minor character.

Allen, Floyd

The 1912 murders in the Carroll County, Virginia Courthouse remain the most deadly ever to occur in an American courtroom. The shootout took more lives than the 1970 hostage incident in Marin County, California.

Today, almost a century later, people in the mountains of Southwest Virginia still argue over and dispute key details of the matter. Those details are wrapped up in a sticky web of family loyalties, politics, and long-simmering personal animosities. This much is reasonably certain: the Allens were Democrats in a solidly Republican county.

Floyd Allen was suspected of being a moonshiner. He was hot tempered and had stated publicly that he would never spend a day in jail. Two of Floyd's nephews, Wesley and Sidna Edwards, had been involved in a fight with some other youths over a girl. When charges were filed against them, they fled to neighboring North Carolina where they were caught.

Deputy Sheriff Thomas Samuels brought them back. On the way to Hillsville, Virginia they passed a store run by Sidna Allen, Floyd's brother. Floyd was there. Objecting to the way his nephews were being treated, he pistol-whipped the deputy and took custody of the boys. Floyd turned the boys in later that week, and eventually, they served short jail sentences.

Floyd was also charged in the beating of the deputy. The situation in Hillsville was so polarized that a jury could not be seated. Rather than move the proceedings, the Commonwealth of Virginia decided to import a jury from outside the region. Floyd was promptly found guilty. On March 14, 1912 court reconvened for sentencing, with Judge Thornton L. Massie presiding. A large crowd gathered in the courtroom, including various Allens and other family members. Several of them were armed, Floyd and Sidna Allen among them.

When Judge Massie announced the sentence of one year, Floyd stood and replied "Gentlemen, I ain't a'going." That's when the shooting started.

Who fired first?

Some say it began when Floyd pulled a pistol, or a brace of pistols, from his pockets. Others say Sheriff Lewis Webb accidentally fired a .38 automatic which he had borrowed and was not familiar with. It really makes little difference.

The place erupted in gunfire as more than a dozen men fired more than 100 rounds. When the gunsmoke had cleared, five people were dead or dying, including Judge Massie, the Commonwealth's Attorney and Sheriff Webb. Many more were wounded. Floyd and Sidna Allen were among the most seriously hurt. Others who had been involved ran for the hills and beyond.

Due to a quirk in Virginia law, after a Sheriff has been killed, his deputies lose their legal authority. The governor had to hire the Baldwin-Felts Detective Agency in Roanoke, the largest city in that part of the state, to restore order and, as a local newspaper account put it, to "take charge of the whole situ-

Former CIA agent Aldrich Ames leaving court after pleading guilty to espionage and tax evasion charges, 1994.

ation and handle it in a way to save the honor of Virginia and bring the desperados to justice."

Within a few months, the detectives had rounded up everyone who had taken part in the court shooting. Floyd Allen and his son Claude were sentenced to death and were electrocuted a year later. Four others were sentenced to long prison terms but were pardoned in the 1920s.

At least one film project has been talked about in recent years, along with a full-length book, but none have come to fruition.

Ames, Aldrich

He was the most murderous traitor ever to work against America, or at least the most murderous we know about. His work led directly to the deaths of at least 25 people, probably many more. Perhaps the worst part is that Aldrich Ames was born to the business. His father had been a spy in Burma in the 1950s for the CIA. When the family returned stateside, young Aldrich attended Langley High School in Virginia.

After college, Ames used his family connections to find a position at the Agency. He was a poor recruiter in his overseas postings and was passed over for promotions. At the same time, his marriage was falling apart and he was drinking heavily.

While on assignment in Mexico City, he met Rosario Casas Dupuy, a Colombian working for her embassy there. They became lovers and when he finally got a promotion and a transfer back to headquarters in 1983, she followed. In short order, Ames divorced his wife and the lovely Rosario embarked on an epic spending spree. In less than a year, she had maxed out all his plastic.

What to do?

In his new position in Soviet counterintelligence, Ames had access to the names of all the CIA's "human assets," including Russians and others who were working for America.

On May 17, 1985 Ames made contact with a Soviet agent in Washington and started selling names. Before it was over, he would be paid $2 million with the promise of more and a riverside dacha after he retired to Mother Russia.

When all of their double agents disappeared, the CIA became suspicious, but for more than a year refused to believe they had a mole in their midst. In November 1986 they assigned veteran Jeanne Vertefeuille to look into the matter. One of her mole whackers noticed Ames was driving a Jaguar XJ6 that cost more than he made in a year, and that he had just paid more than half a million in cash for a new home Rosario was refurnishing top to bottom.

Hmmm?

When asked, Ames lied and said Rosario came from a wealthy Colombian family. Even though

Ames had flunked three polygraphs, he somehow managed to explain those away, too. The mole whackers kept digging and found more problems with Ames' explanations. In 1993 they bugged his house and got the dirt they needed.

Ames and Rosario were arrested on February 21, 1994. Rosario sang like a canary but still got five years. Paroled in 1999, she took a powder back to Colombia.

Ames remains locked up in the Federal Corrections Complex in Butner, North Carolina.

Several books have been written about Ames and one fairly well-regarded film was made for television in 1998, *Aldrich Ames: Traitor Within*. It starred Timothy Hutton, who also played another much less important Russian spy in *The Falcon and the Snowman* in 1985. The Ames film was directed by John Mackenzie, who also made *Ruby* about Oswald assassin Jack Ruby in 1992.

Anastasia, Albert

He was called the "Lord High Executioner" and the "Mad Hatter," and nobody doubted he deserved the nicknames. Albert Anastasia was one of the most murderous of the old-school gangsters. He killed a lot of people, and generally seems to have enjoyed killing. He also ordered the deaths of many more.

Born in Italy, Anastasia jumped ship in New York sometime around 1920 and went to work on the Brooklyn docks. He rose to power in the longshoremen's union and killed one of his fellow workers. He served 18 months for the murder in Sing Sing, but was released early after he was granted a new trial. It never happened. Four key witnesses vanished, establishing a pattern that would follow Anastasia and his crimes for years to come.

In 1931 when **Charles "Lucky" Luciano** decided it was time for a changing of the guard, he chose Anastasia to be part of the four-man hit team that killed their boss **Joe Masseria**. Anastasia knew Luciano had the brains and the leadership skills to run things, so he always followed Charlie Lucky's lead

as the Syndicate or Commission was formed to keep gang members from killing each other whenever they wanted. The bosses would decide who was to be killed, and so they established **Murder, Inc.** as their enforcement division. When they put the Mad Hatter and the equally sadistic **Louis "Lepke" Buchalter** in charge of it, they knew what they were doing. If aptitude tests had been available for assassins, Anastasia and Lepke would have scored off the charts.

Murder, Inc. was in operation for almost a decade and got rid of hundreds of hoodlums who stepped too far out of line, witnesses who were willing to testify about mob crimes, and the occasional honest citizen who somehow got in the way. In 1940, when high-level hitman Abe "Kid Twist" Reles realized he was being set up for elimination, he agreed to talk to New York District Attorney Burton Yurkus.

Reles made the details of Murder, Inc.'s operations public and testified against a few of his fellow mobsters before Anastasia had him thrown out a sixth floor window—while he was supposedly in police protective custody.

When World War II started, Luciano was in prison but was still running things. Anastasia came up with the idea of causing trouble on the New York docks and then convincing the feds the only way security could be guaranteed was through the mob. His brother "Tough" Tony Anastasio (different spelling) set fire to the *Normandie*, a French liner being turned into a troop ship. After it burned, the feds, fearing it might have been sabotage, agreed to accept Luciano's help in securing the New York docks. In return, he was moved to a country club prison for the duration of his sentence. After the war, he was deported to Italy but still remained top dog.

By then Anastasia had taken control of the Mangano family operations, much to the displeasure of longtime rival **Vito Genovese**. One Mangano brother, Vincent, disappeared; the other, Phil, was killed. Luciano and boss **Frank Costello** reasoned that the Manganos had been planning to kill Anastasio and so he was merely acting in self-defense. Case closed.

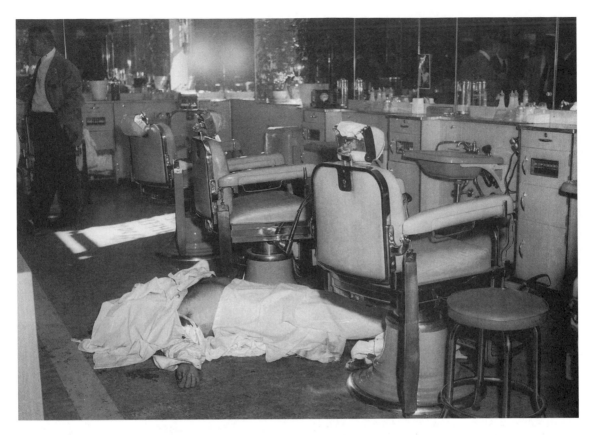

Albert Anastasia meets his end at the Park Sheraton Hotel's barber shop, 1957. (AP Photo)

In the mid-1950s the feds went after Anastasia on income tax evasion charges. One trial ended in a hung jury. Before the second trial, one witness and his wife vanished from their blood-soaked Miami home. Another's body was found in the trunk of a car and a third witness disappeared. Anastasia copped a plea and served one year.

Finally, Anastasia went too far. First, he ordered a hit on a tailor's assistant who recognized bank robber Willie Sutton and told the cops. When the man was killed, the other bosses were horrified. Civilians who didn't threaten them in any way were off limits. Sutton was a freelance thief with no mob connections. Anastasia had ordered the killing simply because he didn't like squealers. A serious breach of mob etiquette.

The capper came when he tried to muscle in on **Meyer Lansky**'s Cuban gambling operation. Meyer, Luciano's right-hand man, had a rock solid agreement with Cuban dictator Fulgencio Batista. Meyer ran all of the gambling on the island and split the proceeds fifty-fifty. There was no room for Anastasia, but he wouldn't take "screw off" for an answer.

The next time Genovese wanted to get rid of the Executioner, Meyer agreed.

On October 25, 1957 Anastasia went to the barbershop in the New York Sheraton Park Hotel for a shave. Somehow, his bodyguard was otherwise occupied. When the barber wrapped Anastasia's face in a hot towel, two masked men slipped in, shoved the barber aside and opened up. The Mad Hatter went down in the proverbial hail of gunfire.

Because he remained so unrepentantly old-school throughout his long career, Anastasia has always been a secondary character in mob books and movies. He figures more prominently in documentaries.

Anderson, William

"Bloody Bill" Anderson never commanded a force as large as **William Quantrill**'s, and he didn't slaughter as many defenseless victims, but, pound for pound, he was just as sadistic and dangerous.

Like Quantrill, before the Civil War Anderson was a thief and murderer. He greeted the outbreak of hostilities in Kansas and Missouri as a career opportunity. He led a band of about 65 cutthroats in attacks on antislavery towns. They also engaged in ambushes against Union troops. For a time, **Jesse** and Frank **James** rode with him.

They fought the war on a personal level. In 1863 two of Anderson's sisters, Mary and Josephine, were rounded up by Union forces. Accused of assisting the Confederates, they were imprisoned with nine other women at a building in Kansas City, Missouri. When the building collapsed on August 13, Josephine was killed and Mary was crippled. Thereafter, Anderson claimed the incident as justification for his crimes.

He and his men were famous for not taking prisoners. They killed everyone they encountered, scalped many of them, and displayed the scalps on their horses' bridles. Anderson himself was a fearsome figure with a full beard and long tangled hair.

On September 27, 1864 he and his men attacked the town of Centralia, Missouri. They stole everything they wanted, raped, murdered, and burned. When Anderson learned a train was due at noon, he ordered a barricade be erected across the tracks at the depot. The train was forced to stop and Anderson's men ordered everyone off—including 28 Union soldiers heading for leave in Iowa and northern Missouri. Anderson spared one, Sgt. Thomas

M. Goodman, saying he planned to use him in a prisoner exchange for one of his men who had been captured. The rest were shot, scalped, and mutilated. That night, Anderson's outfit attacked a larger but less experienced Union force that was following them. They killed more than 120 men. A few days later, Sgt. Goodman escaped and told Union forces what had happened.

About a month later, Anderson's men came up against a more seasoned Union militia unit under the command of veteran Col. Samuel P. Cox. Using Anderson's own tactics, Cox sent a few of his troops on horseback to engage Bloody Bill. After firing a few shots, the Yankees turned and fled, appearing to be panicked. Anderson ordered his men to mount up and give chase. He led the charge himself, racing in pursuit at full gallop. Straight into a trap.

The bulk of Cox's force was hidden in a grove of trees. As soon as their fellow soldiers reached them, they opened fire. By then Anderson was close and he was hit. His bullet-riddled body fell from his horse behind the Union lines.

According to one version of the story, the Yankees found a silk cord with 53 knots on Anderson's body. It was thought to be a count of his personal kills.

Anderson is a minor character in some of the Jesse James films. He also shows up in Clint Eastwood's *The Outlaw Josey Wales* (1976). The film is based on a novel by Forrest Carter, the pen name of Asa Carter. In the 1950s and '60s, Asa Carter was an active racist who wrote speeches for Governor George Wallace.

Annan, Beulah

Today, nobody remembers Beulah Annan, but everybody knows her fictional incarnation Roxie Hart, the heartless but still sexy and somehow loveable killer. To date, Roxie has been seen in two moderately successful Broadway plays, one smash hit revival, two touring shows, and three films, one of them picking up a Best Picture Oscar. Not bad for a gal who plugged her lover in 1926.

Roxie was the creation of Maurine Dallas Watkins. In Jazz Age Chicago, newly liberated women, many of them "flappers," created a virtual female crime wave. The Cook County jail really did have a "Murderess Row" for these lethal ladies. The *Chicago Tribune* decided it needed a woman's perspective on the courts, and so they brought in the young Ms. Watkins. She covered two stories that particularly struck her.

One was Beulah Annan. When her lover Harry Kalstedt told her he was moving on, she shot him. As he lay bleeding on the floor, she spent a few hours listening to her favorite jazz record, "Hula Lou," and drinking cheap gin before she called her husband Albert, a mechanic, and told him she had killed a burglar. By the time the cops arrived, she was so soused that she told them the truth.

In jail, Beulah met Belva Gaertner, another dame who, a few weeks earlier, had killed her lover. Maurine Watkins had covered that case too and labeled them "the prettiest" and "the most stylish" inmates on Murderess Row. Soon after she was locked up, Beulah and her lawyers came up with the lie that she was pregnant, leading to the famous headline: "Beulah Annan Awaits Stork, Murder Trial."

Maurine Watkins' fresh, funny stories about the two, along with all the other newspaper and radio coverage turned them into minor celebrities. Coincidentally, at the same time that the murders and the trials took place, Chicago was also transfixed by the kidnapping and murder of Bobby Franks by **Leopold and Loeb.** Maurine Watkins covered their trial, too, though her stories were more serious, analyzing the psychology of the two young killers.

Beulah and Belva made dramatically effective courtroom appearances and were acquitted by all-male juries. After the trials, Watkins left Chicago and went to the Yale Drama School where she turned the material into a play, originally called *The Brave Little Woman,* but soon retitled it *Chicago.*

Beulah and Belva became Roxie Hart and Velma Kelly. The lawyers morphed into Billy Flynn and Maurine herself became columnist Mary Sunshine. In 1927 the play had a good run on Broadway and

was filmed for the first time. The silent version has never been released on home video. The only known print appears to be in the UCLA film archives, and it reportedly sticks close to Watkins' original story. When it was filmed again in 1942, under the title *Roxie Hart,* Hollywood was under the strict rules of the Hays Office which forbid anyone portrayed on the silver screen from getting away with a crime. So, Ginger Rogers' Roxie was innocent.

Maurine Watkins continued to work occasionally in the film business, but her later years were marked by poor health. She also found religion, and came to be ashamed of the bracing gallows humor that drives *Chicago.* When choreographer Bob Fosse and dancer Gwen Verdon first approached her about transforming the story into a musical in the 1950s, Watkins rebuffed them. Fosse never lost interest and continued to ask. It was only after her death in 1969 that he secured the rights.

Fosse collaborated with songwriters John Kander and Fred Ebb to create the 1975 show. It was a hit, but not as big a hit as another musical that opened about the same time, *A Chorus Line.* The 1996 revival of *Chicago* was much more successful and led directly to the 2002 Oscar-winning film. By the mid-'90s, everyone understood the strong connections between crime and entertainment in American culture, and so the story's jaundiced appraisal of our justice system found a larger and more appreciative audience.

Arbuckle, Roscoe "Fatty"

Though his name conjures up images of Hollywood decadence and depravity, Roscoe "Fatty" Arbuckle was never convicted of a serious crime. Two juries could not reach a verdict. A third acquitted him and even added a lengthy statement to their verdict calling the comedian "entirely innocent and free from all blame." Not that it mattered; by then, the damage had been done.

In his day, Arbuckle was one of the silent screen's most successful stars, right up there with Charlie Chaplin and Harold Lloyd. He invented the pie in the face, and Paramount paid him a cool million dollars a year. He worked hard for the money, cranking out six pictures a year at the height of his popularity.

Over Labor Day, 1921, Arbuckle decided to take some time off from work, with friends director Fred Fishbach and actor Lowell Sherman. They left in Arbuckle's luxurious Pierce-Arrow for a weekend of partying in San Francisco. For Arbuckle, it was a less than perfect trip. He had suffered burns to his leg and butt right before they left (cause unknown), and was forced to sit on a rubber donut, which they had to stop and buy on the way.

They settled into three adjoining rooms in the swanky St. Francis Hotel, ordered a few cases of bootleg booze and invited a bunch of girls up to help them drink it. Among the young lovelies was Virginia Rappe (pronounced rap-PAY after she added the "e"), and her acquaintance Bambina Maude Delmont. Rappe was an unstable starlet known to sleep around. She had had several abortions and, at the time of the party, she may have been in search of another. Delmont had an even shadier reputation that included arrests for extortion and fraud.

Around three o'clock on the afternoon of September 5, Arbuckle got ready to leave the hotel with a friend and went to his room to change clothes. He claimed that he found Rappe passed out in his bathroom. When he tried to move her, she puked on him. He put her on his bed but she rolled off and became hysterical, so he called Delmont and another woman to help.

They put Rappe in a tub of cold water and called a doctor who diagnosed her as drunk. A few hours later another doctor took a look and gave her a shot of morphine. The next day, he gave her a second shot and inserted a catheter because he was told that she had not urinated for some time. Then Delmont called her pal Dr. Melville "Rummy" Rumwell, and told him that Arbuckle had raped Rappe. The good doctor found no evidence of it, but Rappe's fever did not abate. She was taken to a hospital where she died on September 9. The cause of death was a peritonitis infection caused by a ruptured bladder.

Roscoe "Fatty" Arbuckle in happier days (1917), before his rape trial.

How was her bladder ruptured?

Politically ambitious D.A. Matthew Brady decided it had happened when the extra-large comedian raped her, as Delmont alleged. He had Arbuckle arrested on first-degree murder charges, later changed to manslaughter. Arbuckle steadfastly denied that anything untoward had happened.

Newspapers, particularly those owned by William Randolph Hearst, disagreed. They essentially convicted Arbuckle and printed every salacious detail they could unearth. Rumors held that Rappe had been raped with a Coke bottle or a champagne bottle or other objects. The jolly fat man everyone had seen on the screen was transformed into a massive hulking predatory beast.

Public criticism of filmmakers' private lives and proclivities had been going on for years. It coalesced around Arbuckle and the mysterious murder of director **William Desmond Taylor** that occurred during the trial. Eventually, those cases and others led to the creation of the Hays Office, Hollywood's official institution of self-regulation. (As restrictive as the organization was, it did prevent true federal censorship.)

Arbuckle's trials were torturous affairs despite the fact that there was no real evidence—physical or eye witness—against him. Maude Delmont never testified. When Arbuckle took the stand, his testimony was strong, even when Virginia Rappe's bladder was displayed in open court. Curiously, the other internal organs that would have revealed a pregnancy were destroyed after the autopsy. Could Dr. "Rummy," who was said to perform illegal abortions, have had a hand in that?

The last jury finally found that Arbuckle had nothing to do with Rappe's death, but by then, his career had been destroyed. Despite the verdicts, the Hays Office banned him from the screen for ten years, though he continued to direct under the pseudonym William B. Goodrich. Just before his death in 1933, Arbuckle made some two-reel comedies for Warner Bros. Moviegoers liked them but he never found the large appreciative audience he had once enjoyed. In later years, his name became synonymous with Hollywood excess.

Joseph Moncure March's 1928 narrative poem "The Wild Party" really has nothing to do with the case, but nevertheless became the basis for a 1975 film adaptation where James Coco and Raquel Welch play characters loosely based on Arbuckle and Virginia Rappe. (March's work is terrific in its own right; it is now available in a 1994 edition illustrated by Art Spiegelman.) Jerry Stahl's 2004 novel, *I, Fatty*, attempts to set the record straight about the rape.

Some of Arbuckle's films survive on DVD. One of the best collections is *The Forgotten Films of Roscoe "Fatty" Arbuckle* (Laughsmith Entertainment/Mackinac Media, 2005). The four-disc set contains an excellent, unbiased booklet on the man's life and work.

Archer-Gilligan, Amy

She was not America's first angel of mercy turned angel of death, but she was an efficient, ruthless killer with more than 40 victims to her credit.

Though "Sister" Amy Archer had no training or official qualifications, she opened a nursing home in Windsor, Connecticut in 1901. Her husband James funded the enterprise and it did so well they moved up the road to Newington, where they started the "Archer Home for the Elderly and Infirm" with 14 beds. They thrived for three years, but in 1910 James died. Attending physician and family friend Dr. Howard King attributed the death to "natural" causes. Apparently the senile medico would write "natural" under "cause of death" on any piece of paper Amy put in front of him.

Sister Amy cashed in James' insurance policy and continued her good works for another three years. There were 12 more deaths in her establishment in those years, about average for the times. In 1913 she remarried. Michael Gilligan was a well-to-do widower who happily joined his fortune to hers. A year later he, too, succumbed to those pesky "natural" causes. At least, that's what Dr. King said.

Sometime while she was running her Home for the Elderly, Amy devised an early form of long-term care insurance, though the "long-term" part turned out to be a bit dicey. For $1,000—or full access to your bank account—she would guarantee a lifetime of care for a client with "nutritional" meals and the best healthcare Dr. King and Sister Amy could deliver. From a strictly legal point of view, they delivered.

By then, though, the death rate was climbing to about ten a year, and people were starting to get suspicious. If they had known about the amount of arsenic Amy was buying to control rats, they would have been even more suspicious. Over the next five years, Dr. King wrote "natural causes" on no less than 48 death certificates. Eventually, the newspapers took an interest in the unusually high turnover rate at the widow Archer-Gilligan's establishment. Her final victim was Franklin Andrews who had been the picture of health on May 29, 1914 and was found dead on the 30th.

Police finally exhumed the bodies of Sister Amy's charges and found evidence of arsenic poisoning.

Initially, Amy was charged with five counts of murder. She swore she was innocent, and Dr. King bizarrely claimed that the bodies had been tampered with by "ghouls," and the poison added after death. At the trial, Amy's lawyers objected strenuously, and finally the five charges were reduced to one, Mr. Andrews. That proved to be enough. She was convicted and sentenced to life.

While in prison, Sister Amy's behavior became increasingly unhinged. She was transferred to an asylum where she died in 1928.

Arnold, Stephen

If he were alive today and appearing on any of the cable TV shows, Stephen Arnold would certainly be described as having anger management issues. Such terms did not exist when he was a schoolteacher in Cooperstown, New York, in 1805. It was a position for which he was uniquely unqualified.

If one of his young charges made an error, Arnold would become angry to the point of rage. He lost it completely when his six-year-old niece missed a particularly easy one. She misspelled "gig." He hit her over the head with a club and killed her. Realizing that he had gone too far, he took a powder

to Pittsburgh. Within months, he was caught and returned to Cooperstown for trial. It was something of a formality and Arnold was sentenced to hang.

Things were slow in the backwater burg and so the execution was promoted as the event of the season. They had a parade with marching bands and infantry and artillery to escort the hair-triggered Mr. Arnold to the gallows. A massive crowd gathered to soak it all in.

The preacher who had been engaged to comfort the soon-to-be-deceased made the most of his moment in the spotlight by launching into an hour-long sermon on the deadly sin of anger.

Arnold piped up, too, citing examples from his own sorry state to illustrate the minister's points. Then, at long last when the reverend finally wound down, they reached the moment everyone had been waiting for. The hangman readied the noose, a hush fell over the crowd, and... the sheriff stepped forward and called it off.

He said he had received a reprieve from the governor that very morning. He himself did not agree with letting the miscreant off, but there was nothing he could do—nothing but let things go to the last second to put the fear of God into Arnold, so to speak. Of course, by waiting so long, he also made sure the crowds stayed in town, which didn't hurt business at the local bars and stores. But that had absolutely nothing to do with his decision or his timing.

The grounds for the reprieve were temporary insanity and Arnold was later paroled for the same reason. Today, his story has been forgotten, but it has everything tabloid journalism has always loved.

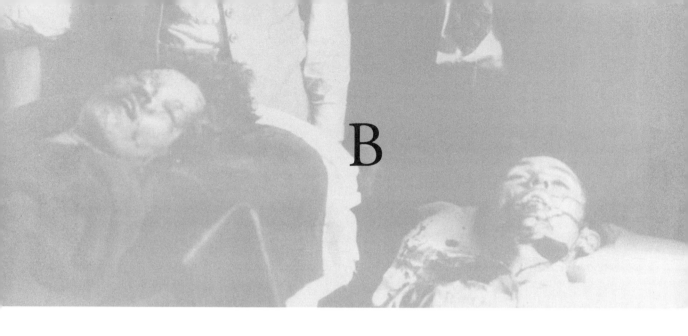

B

Bailey, Harvey

Had you been of a mind to rob a bank in the 1920s, Harvey Bailey was the guy you wanted to work with. He was simply the best in the business—smart, patient, cautious... well, usually cautious.

Bailey was born in 1887 and grew up in the Midwest. Got married, had kids, and turned to bootlegging. By 1920 he had been arrested for burglary and jumped bond. Two years later, he hit the big time when he went to work with the famous **Baron Lamm**, the gang that knocked over the Denver Mint. Actually, the Mint was serving as a vault for the Federal Reserve Bank of Denver. On December 18th the Mint transferred $200,000 in crisp new $5 bills and $65,000 in negotiable securities to the Bank a few blocks away. It was transported in a pickup truck with a wire cage over the bed and armed guards for protection.

The gang had rented an apartment nearby and cased the job carefully. That morning, they cut off the pickup with a stolen Buick as it neared the Mint. A brief, intense gunfight ensued. When it was over, one guard was dead, one gang member was seriously wounded, and the gang got away with the loot. No one was ever arrested for the heist; no one even knows exactly how many people were involved, though a few months later $80,000 was recovered in St. Paul, Minnesota.

Old Harve, as he was known, continued to work when he had to throughout the 1920s, seldom staying with any one gang for very long. Realizing his fellow crooks were a largely unreliable lot prone to doing stupid things with their swag (buying fancy, highly noticeable cars, for example), he avoided them whenever possible. Instead, he opened a couple of gas stations in Indiana and invested in real estate. But the stock market crash brought hard times, and Old Harve had to go back to a business that paid well.

His mistake came in 1932 when he threw in with the **Barker-Karpis** gang to stick up a bank in Fort Scott, Arkansas. It was a poorly organized job that ended with a police chase. Bailey's cut was a measly $4,000. Fed up, he left the gang and, breaking his own rule, went to Kansas City to play golf with a couple of fellow bank robbers. The feds nabbed him on the first tee of the Old Mission Golf Course and sent him to the Kansas State pen.

Less than a year later, he busted out with ten hard cases. Though he was shot in the knee during the breakout, Bailey hit a few small banks for operating capital. By that time, the national "war on crime" was in full swing and Old Harve realized it was time to get out of the game. On the way to Mexico, he stopped to rest and recuperate at "Boss" Shannon's ranch in Paradise, Texas. His timing could not have been worse.

Shannon was **"Machine Gun" Kelly**'s father-in-law, and just a few days before, Kelly had used the ranch to hide his kidnap victim Charles Urschel. By the time Harve got there, Urshel had been released. He was describing the ranch in rich detail to the FBI, and a nationwide manhunt was under way for Kelly.

Bailey knew he should hightail it out of there but he was too tired and in too much pain. The G-men found him asleep on a porch. That should have been the end of the story, but they sent Old Harve to the "escape-proof" Dallas County jail where he promptly bribed a guard to bring him a hacksaw. On September 5th he busted out yet again, but this time a massive manhunt came after him and he was arrested in Oklahoma without putting up a fight.

He was sent to Leavenworth and later to Alcatraz until he was paroled in the mid 1960s. Harvey Bailey died in 1979.

Compared to the generation of bank robbers who came after him, Harvey Bailey was a quiet, even conservative outlaw. Consequently, he has never been a significant figure in popular culture or entertainment. His story would still make a great movie.

Ball, Joe

In Texas, Joe Ball is the subject of campfire stories, and the details surrounding his crimes are so outlandish the truth is readily embellished into legendary horror. In the end, though, it's impossible to say exactly how many people he killed.

We do know Ball was born in 1896 and grew up the son of a wealthy family in Elmendorf, Texas, just south of San Antonio. As a young man, he was considered something of a gun nut. He enlisted in the Army and served in World War I, returned home, and became a bootlegger. When Prohibition was repealed in 1933, he opened a roadhouse, the Sociable Inn, out on Highway 181. Two bedrooms for whatever and a bar big enough to accommodate the occasional cockfight.

The main attraction was the alligator pit out back, a cement pond with one big gator and four little ones. Feeding time on Saturday night was the highpoint of the week, and Joe drew big crowds when he tossed in live puppies, kittens, raccoons… anything he could get his hands on.

The other distinguishing feature of the Sociable was its staff. Joe always seemed to hire the prettiest waitresses, despite his reputation as a creepy kind of guy. Perhaps it explained the rapid turnover, too. The girls came and went rather quickly.

But when "Big Minnie" Gotthardt disappeared in 1938, her family asked questions at the local sheriff's office. They went to see Joe and he claimed she had left because she had a black baby. They accepted the explanation, but what about Dolores Goodwin? And "Schatzi" Brown? They had all just left, Joe said.

A few months later Big Minnie's family still hadn't been able to locate her and Joe was questioned again. Then Julia Turner's family came to the Bexar County sheriff with a similar complaint. The last they had heard from her, she was working for Joe Ball. Finally, a neighbor told the deputies that he had seen Joe cutting up a body and feeding it to the gators, and another man said Ball had stored a barrel of something that reeked most foully in his sister's barn. By the time the deputies got to the barn, the barrel was gone, but they decided to question Joe again and found him at the Sociable.

They told him this time it was more serious and he would have to come with them to San Antonio. Joe said he needed a minute to close things up. They agreed. He went behind the bar, chugged a cold beer, and rang up "No Sale" on the register. The cash drawer popped open. He pulled out a .45 and briefly threatened the deputies before he shot himself in the heart. Dead.

As investigators looked into Joe's activities, they got help from his longtime handyman, Clifton Wheeler, who told them Ball had forced him to help get rid of "Schatzi" Brown's body. According to Wheeler, she was going to leave, and Ball killed her in anger. They dismembered the body and buried it near the San Antonio River. He said Ball had acted alone when he took Big Minnie to a remote part of Ingleside, Texas and shot her. Again, Wheeler helped him bury the body. And why had he killed Minnie? Because she was pregnant with his child and refused to leave. So, apparently with Ball's women, it was damned if you did, damned if you didn't.

As for the other 12 to 14 women who had passed through the Sociable and the teenaged boy who used to hang around, who knew? There was, however, an ax clotted with blood and hair out by the alligator pit.

The only real proof the police ever found of Ball's crimes were the two bodies. In the end, Clifford Wheeler served two years for helping dispose of them. The five alligators went to the San Antonio Zoo and stories about Joe Ball are still told over campfires and on home video.

Tobe Hooper, Texas filmmaker of *Chainsaw Massacre* fame also made the lesser-known but equally gut-churning *Eaten Alive,* a surreal ultraviolent Southern gothic tale with veteran character actor Neville Brand turning in a disturbingly believable performance as a "Joe Ball" character.

Barker, Kate "Ma"

"Ma" Barker loved not wisely but too well. In Ma's eyes, her four precious but mostly lethal sons could do no wrong. In truth, the Barker boys— Doc, Fred, Herman, and Lloyd—did an awful lot wrong: armed robbery, murder, and kidnapping being the most serious.

The boys grew up in Missouri in the 1910s and '20s, and were all in trouble with the law from an early age. Whenever one of her brood got into a scrape, Ma would cajole, whine, and bully the authorities into letting him go. She was definitely

Ma Barker, not just another pretty face, circa 1935. (AP Photo)

the alpha female of the household. When it came to the kids, her husband George, a sharecropper, didn't even try to do anything.

The family moved to Tulsa, where the boys and their doting mom eased their way into more profitable crime by setting up their house as a hideout and gathering place for local gangsters to meet and plan their work. Herman was the first to branch out on his own. In 1922 Lloyd was involved in a post office robbery. He was caught and sentenced to 25 years in Leavenworth. Doc was nabbed stealing a government car, then was later convicted of killing a night watchman. He got life in Oklahoma State Prison. Freddie drew a 5-to-10 stretch in Kansas State Prison for a variety of offenses.

Herman was killed in a shootout with the police after he robbed a Missouri bank. The cops claimed

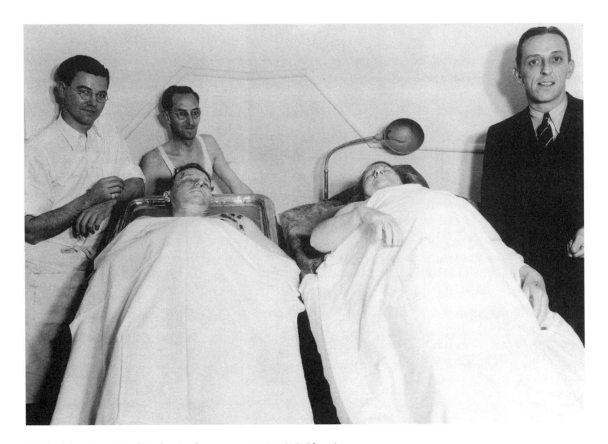

Ma Barker and son Fred Barker in the morgue, 1935. (AP Photo)

that he killed himself to avoid capture. Ma said her boys would never do anything like that. She worked tirelessly to get the rest of her sons out of jail, pestering parole boards and prison officials. It paid off in 1931 when Freddie was released with his new-found friend, **Alvin Karpis.**

Some say Karpis was the real organizational brains behind Ma Barker's gang, and it's probably the truth. He was a more experienced and imaginative criminal, and the Barker family fortunes changed dramatically after he entered the picture. As Karpis wrote in his autobiography, "It wouldn't have occurred to her to get involved in our business, and we always made a point of discussing our scores when Ma wasn't around. We'd leave her at home when we were

arranging a job, or we'd send her to the movies. Ma saw a lot of movies."

Indeed. The gang relocated to St. Paul, Minnesota, where they were protected by Harry Sawyer who oversaw all criminal activities in the area. He also introduced them to others who took part in their jobs. The gang pulled off several Midwestern bank robberies that netted them around $500,000 total.

Then they decided the risk-reward ratio was better for kidnapping than in robbing banks. They got $100,000 for brewer William Hamm, Jr., and twice that for banker Edward G. Bremer. Flush with success, they became too famous for their own good. Freddie and Karpis underwent painful plastic surgery with negligible results, and the Barker mob moved to Toledo, Ohio where Doc and Freddie killed the doctor who had botched their makeover. That's when the gang broke up.

Karpis split off on his own. Shortly thereafter, Doc was captured in Chicago by famous G-man Melvin Purvis without a shot being fired, and was sent to Alcatraz straightaway. The feds found a Florida map in Doc's place and used it to trace Ma and Freddie to a cottage in Lake Weir, Florida. The FBI surrounded the place. The gunfight that followed lasted between 45 minutes and four hours, depending on whose account you believe. When it was over, Freddie and Ma were dead. According to the G-men, she had a Tommy gun clutched in her mitts. Four years later, Doc was killed trying to escape from Alcatraz.

It is altogether appropriate that the Barker gang's exploits have been immortalized on film in 1970's *Bloody Mama,* by the king of B-movies, Roger Corman. It was certainly an inspired moment in casting when Corman hired Shelley Winters, at her full-throated, blowsiest best, to portray Ma. And yes, that's a young Robert DeNiro as Lloyd.

Barnes, LeRoy "Nicky"

"Nicky" Barnes provided the prototype for Hollywood's modern black gangster. A new Robin Hood, he was the cool, handsome "drug kingpin" who lived large with the most expensive cars, the finest threads, the most luxurious apartments, the sexiest women—the portrait painted by the famous 1977 *New York Times Magazine* cover story entitled "Mr. Untouchable."

Barnes' rise to such rarified heights began when he met **"Crazy Joe" Gallo** in Greenhaven Prison in the late 1960s. That's where they agreed to take over the Harlem drug trade. Gallo used his connections to deliver large amounts of pure heroin to Barnes, after he was released. Barnes, in turn, set up a system of workers and apartments where the dope was diluted with other substances and packaged for

retail sale. He also provided the black "muscle" to run things in his neighborhoods. It was a profitable setup for both of them.

It was profitable for Gallo until 1972 when he was gunned down by rival Mafiosi. Barnes continued to prosper until the *Times* magazine piece was printed. Rumors within criminal circles had it President Jimmy Carter was so incensed and affronted by the article that he personally ordered the Justice Department to take Barnes down.

Whatever the reason, after several arrests and unsuccessful prosecutions, Barnes was convicted on federal drug charges and sentenced to life without parole. But in 1981, upon learning that a rival was shacking up with his squeeze, he agreed to cooperate. He ratted out his former partners and more than a dozen were sent up the river on his information, while he was released to the witness protection program.

Barnes was at least a partial inspiration for the character Frank White, played by Christopher Walken, in the 1990 film *King of New York.* He was evoked more explicitly a year later in *New Jack City* where Wesley Snipes played a charismatic drug lord named Nino Brown. In 2005's *Carlito's Way: Rise to Power,* Sean "P. Diddy" Combs played "Hollywood Nikki," while in 2007's *American Gangster,* directed by Ridley Scott, Barnes is only a supporting character, played by Cuba Gooding, Jr. Barnes tells his own story in *Mr. Untouchable,* his 2007 autobiography. His influence on "gangsta" rap is deep and pervasive.

Barrow, Clyde and Bonnie Parker

"Bonnie and Clyde." You can't hear the names and not see Faye Dunaway and Warren Beatty—young, beautiful, sleek, and sexy.

The 1967 groundbreaking film, directed by Arthur Penn, has completely overshadowed the reality of these pint-sized killers. **John Dillinger** reportedly called them "a couple of punks" and he was right. The biggest haul they ever took in was $1,500. They usually stuck up mom & pop stores, lunch counters, and jerkwater banks. Strictly small time.

Faye Dunaway and Warren Beatty at the 1968 premiere of *Bonnie & Clyde*. (AP Photo)

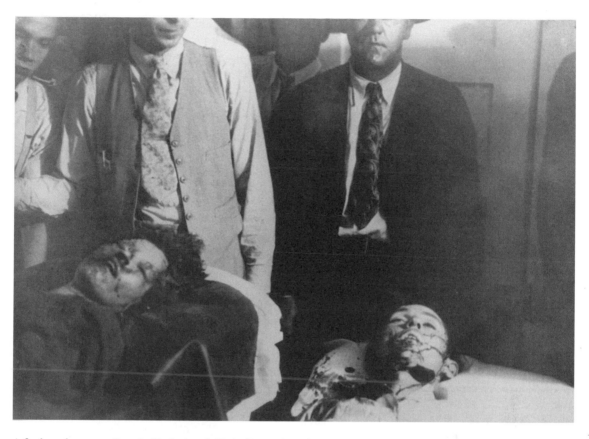

A far less glamorous Bonnie (Parker) and Clyde (Barrow) in the morgue, 1934. (AP Photo)

But they were relentless self-promoters—particularly Bonnie—who reveled in the newspaper coverage of their crimes, where they were dubbed the "Texas Rattlesnake" and "Suicide Sal." The strange sexual dynamics of their gang also set them apart from your run-of-the-mill 1930s outlaws.

Clyde Barrow met Bonnie Parker in late 1929 in Dallas. She was sort of married, but so what? She was also "bored crapless." As the Depression closed in on Texas, Clyde's past caught up with him and he was sent to the Waco County jail. Bonnie helped him escape but he was quickly recaptured and sent to the Eastham Prison Farm, an institution proud of its reputation for sadistic brutality and torture. According to some sources,

Clyde became a dedicated homosexual during his two years there.

Whatever his inclination, after he got out, he and Bonnie hit the road in a stolen car. For the next two years with various associates they stole stuff, murdered, and kidnapped people throughout Texas, Missouri, Oklahoma, and Arkansas, and made regular visits to visit their kinfolk. Eventually, Clyde's jailbird brother Buck and his wife Blanche joined "the Barrow Gang." They were fairly successful at stealing weapons and amassed a formidable arsenal of pistols, submachine guns, and Browning Automatic Rifles. They used them to shoot their way out of several tight spots where law enforcement agencies had identified them, but did not close in with enough fire power to take the gang. Their escapes from Dexter, Iowa and Joplin and Platte City, Missouri were incredibly violent and provided the factual basis for Penn's 1967 film, which shattered the rules for Hollywood's conventional depictions of gun violence.

Frank Hamer, a bounty hunter and ex-Texas Ranger, put together a posse with the sole purpose of getting rid of the pair. The relative of a young gang member had provided a hideout for Bonnie and Clyde after their last shootout, but realized how hot they were. He contacted Hamer and an ambush was set up on a lonely country road. It worked. On May 23, 1934 Bonnie and Clyde were caught in a deadly crossfire and got what was coming to them.

But the story of ruthless rat-faced young punks doesn't sell movie tickets, so they became misunderstood, unconventional, rebellious young lovers. They first appeared on screen in the superb 1949 film noir *Gun Crazy*. Plot details have little to do with the real characters' crimes but their fascination with firearms and the doomed nature of the relationship are emotionally accurate. The rarely-seen, low-budget 1958 *Bonnie Parker Story* stars Dorothy Provine and curiously changes Clyde's name to Guy Darrow.

Neither of these even came close to the importance of *Bonnie and Clyde,* a rare landmark film that changed the movies. Under the then-new MPAA ratings system, it was one of the first films to receive an "R" rating. Though many other films had portrayed outlaws in a flattering light, none had done it so audaciously or explicitly.

Barrows, Sydney Biddle

In 1984 "lifestyles of the rich and famous" became an all-purpose catchphrase for the widening field of celebrity gossip. Of course, people had been paying attention to the misdeeds and excesses of blue bloods for centuries, but in the Reagan years, it all reached new heights, or lows, depending on your point of view. Nowhere was it more apparent than in the case of the "Mayflower Madam."

Sydney Biddle Barrows—what a wonderfully proper and evocative name!—was descended from two of the Mayflower pilgrim families. Though her family was not particularly wealthy, she never planned on entering the sex trade. After high school, she studied merchandizing and fashion buying at New York's Fashion Institute of Technology, and won the Bergdorf-Goodman Award when she graduated in 1972. She went to work for Abraham & Straus, a department store, then went to another smaller buying company which she left after disagreeing with her new boss.

While looking for work, she ran into a similarly unemployed friend who confided that she was making ends meet by answering phones for an escort service. She was knocking down $50 a night, tax free, for getting the right girl to the right guy. Not bad. Before long, Sydney too was working the phones for Eddie's Executive Escorts. When she realized how poorly Eddie ran things, Sydney and her friend decided to go into business for themselves—as management, not labor. No matter how busy things got, Ms. Barrows never pitched in personally to help tickle the pickles.

In May 1979 they started Cachet. As an escort service, Cachet employed women who claimed to want only part-time work. In their day jobs, they were teachers, lawyers, whatever, and moonlighted for the extra money, or for the thrill of it. Sydney and company worked only with clients they knew or with new ones who were referred by existing clients. Eventually, they ran ads in the *International Herald-Tribune* and *Village Voice.* They operated in Manhattan, only at the better hotels and apartments. Working out of an Upper West Side apartment, Cachet fielded phone calls from clients then got in touch with the appropriate gal and gave her an address. Off the young lady would go in a cab to her assignation, to return a few hours later a few hundred dollars richer.

As Barrows describes it in her scrupulously PG-rated book *Mayflower Madam,* the sex biz was downright wholesome. As she puts it, there was vir-

Sydney Biddle Barrows (aka the Mayflower Madam) with attorney Robert Halmi and a mysterious unidentified hand at a New York City news conference, 1985. (AP Photo).

tually no touching below the waist. In her initial interviews with prospective "escorts," she assured them they would not have to do anything too kinky, but that particular part of the pitch was left a little vague. She does admit, though, near the end, that she really didn't want to know everything that went on between the girls and the guys even though she was curious about it.

Given her background, she was a stickler for fashion and made sure her girls dressed well. She learned that clients liked busty blondes, Southern accents, and tasteful hats. Go figure on the hats thing, but the formula worked. Hers was one of the most expensive services in the city.

For five years, everything was just ducky. The girls were happy in their work. As a boss, Barrows was kind and forgiving. Clients included well-heeled locals, visiting businessmen, Saudi oil princes, and a large number of United Nations staffers. Business was so good Barrows was able to open a second service, Finesse, even more expensive and exclusive.

Alas, it all came to an end in 1984 when the cops busted Cachet, literally breaking the door down with a sledgehammer. Why did they choose Sydney's operation? She believes it had to do with a dispute with her landlord, a disgruntled former employee, and an overzealous cop.

> *"I killed Leigh Ann because she was one of the reasons for my demise... I really wish I hadn't killed her now. She really couldn't help it and I love her so much anyway... I give you my wife Leigh Ann Barton, my honey, my precious love. Please take care of her. I will love her forever."*

Whatever the reason, after the bust, the authorities realized the procuress they knew as Sheila Devlin was the socially-connected Sydney Biddle Barrows. When the two local tabloids, the *Post* and *Daily News,* discovered that little nugget of information, they went into a feeding frenzy and the "Mayflower Madam" was born.

Because the case became so prominent, it could not be swept under the rug, much as the DA might have wanted to forget the whole thing. Our girl quickly became a local hero and used her notoriety to every advantage. To raise money to pay her lawyers, she threw the "Mayflower Defense Fund Ball" at a hot disco: ticket price, $40 a head. She wore Tracy Mills; it was the event of the season.

When Barrows finally went to trial, the charges were reduced. She pled guilty to a misdemeanor and paid a $5,000 fine. As her lawyer reportedly said, it wasn't even a slap on the wrist, it was a kiss on the wrist. Since then Sydney Biddle Barrows has parlayed her celebrity into three books. On the small screen, she was the subject of an A&E biography and Candice Bergen played her in the 1987 adaptation of *Mayflower Madam.*

Barton, Mark

In the ugly roll call of modern mass murderers, Mark Barton, the Atlanta day trader, can't claim the highest body count but he is certainly one of the most grotesque. He killed his own children as they slept and then wrote a self-pitying, horribly sentimental explanation.

Barton grew up in an Air Force family. An intelligent loner, he became heavily involved with drugs in high school and college. Plagued by emotional problems and overdoses, he finally received psychiatric care and managed to graduate with a degree in chemistry from the University of South Carolina in 1979. A series of jobs followed with marriage to Debra Spivey, and two kids, Matthew and Mychelle. At the same time, Barton's mental state was beginning to deteriorate again. Abusive at home and paranoid at work, Barton was fired in 1990.

The family moved to Georgia where Barton began an affair with Leigh Ann Lang, more than ten years his junior. Then in 1993, while on a camping trip, Debra and her mother were beaten to death. Since Barton had recently purchased a $500,000 life insurance policy on his wife, he was the primary suspect in the murders. But he had an alibi, and police were not able to find enough evidence to bring charges.

Instead, a few weeks later, Leigh Ann moved in. They married in 1995. Barton's emotional and mental problems remained. With the insurance money, he embarked on a new career playing the stock market as a day trader at Momentum Securities and All-Tech Investment Group. Bad choice.

By 1999 Barton had lost huge amounts of money and was deeply in debt. He had done so poorly that his trading privileges had been revoked. He decided to end it all on the morning of July 27th, when he beat Leigh Ann to death with a hammer. Immediately, he was filled with remorse and wrote, "I killed Leigh Ann because she was one of the reasons for my demise as I planned to kill the others. I really wish I hadn't killed her now. She really couldn't help it and I love her so much anyway... I give you my wife

Leigh Ann Barton, my honey, my precious love. Please take care of her. I will love her forever."

The next night, he did the same to Matthew and Mychelle.

On Thursday, the 29th, Barton went to a meeting arranged with the management of Momentum Securities to regain his trading privileges. To accomplish this goal, he needed to come up with $50,000 cash. That's what everyone thought he was there to do—but the manager he was meeting with was late. While he waited, Barton chatted with other traders and staff members he knew. He chatted until his patience ran out. Then he produced two pistols, a 9mm and a .45 and said, "It's a bad trading day and it's about to get worse." He opened up, point blank, at the people closest to him. By the time the police got there, four were dead, many more were wounded, and Barton was gone. He had slipped out and walked across the street to All-Tech Investment.

Again, he was cheerful and pleasant as he made his way to a manager's office. Again, he opened fire on the staff. At All-Tech, he killed five and wounded about a dozen. And again, he was able to walk away in the panic and confusion he had created.

Barton was identified fairly quickly, and police discovered the carnage in his apartment. Several hours later, his van was seen and police were called in to follow. They held back in unmarked cars until Barton pulled in to a gas station. They quickly surrounded the van and ordered Barton to surrender. He responded by shooting himself in the head, several years too late.

Beck, Martha and Raymond Fernandez

Lonely Hearts Killers

The story of Martha Beck and Raymond Fernandez has been filmed twice in America, as *The Honeymoon Killers* in 1970 and, much less successfully as *Lonely Hearts* in 2007. The story turns on three perennially popular subjects: sex, murder, and weight loss.

In 1947 Martha Beck was a divorced mother of two children. She had been an early bloomer, sexually mature at the age of ten, who had filled out to a hefty 250 lbs. She had a good job as a nurse superintendent at a Pensacola, Florida hospital, but neither her kids nor her work gave her the emotional fulfillment she so desperately craved. For that, she needed romantic love, the kind she read about in magazines and saw in movies, the kind she hoped to find when she placed an ad in "Mother Dinene's Family Club for Lonely Hearts."

Martha's ad was answered by Raymond Fernandez. By all accounts, Raymond had once been a normal, personable young man. He suffered an unfortunate accident in 1945, when on board a freighter, he was smashed on the head by a falling hatch. The heavy steel creased his skull so severely that it damaged his frontal lobe and put him in the hospital for months.

After he was released, Ray was a different man. He stole things for no reason, served a stretch in the pen where he converted to Haitian voodoo, and became convinced he had supernatural power over women. Abandoning his wife and family, he preyed on women he met through lonely hearts clubs. After exchanging increasingly affectionate letters to ascertain his marks' financial worth, he would arrange to meet them. He then turned on that old voodoo charm and connived to separate them from their cash and valuables before he vamoosed. Most were so embarrassed they did nothing.

Jane Thompson was different. She traveled with him to Spain where his wife still lived. Fernandez killed Jane there—no one knows exactly how—and returned to New York where he installed himself in her apartment. That's where he was living when he first contacted Martha. After a couple weeks of passionate correspondence, he caught a southbound train and arrived in Florida on December 28, 1947.

Martha was immediately smitten by this sweet-talking hunk… all right, a hunk with a misshapen head, but a hunk nonetheless. They were hot and heavy between the sheets that very night, and for the first time in her unhappy life, Martha really got her rocks off. She was a new woman, she was Raymond's woman.

But Raymond didn't really want a woman, at least not a full-time woman. Martha was ready to get married right away but he put her off and returned to New York. Distraught, she attempted suicide and was fired from her job. On January 18, 1948, kids in tow, she showed up on Raymond's doorstep. Over the next week, something developed between the two. He came to need her or to see a use for her, and she fell even harder for him. But, he said, her children were not to be a part of it. On January 25th, she took them to the Salvation Army and left them there.

Martha then joined Raymond in his pursuit of lonely women and helped him to fleece several. When one of them, Myrtle Young, proved troublesome, they drugged her and managed to put her on a bus back home to Arkansas where she died.

Their next victim was 66-year-old Janet Fay, a widow who lived in Albany. Posing as sister and brother, Martha and Raymond met her there at the end of 1948. By January of '49, they had persuaded her to empty her bank accounts and move to Long Island with them. But things just didn't work out between Martha and Janet.

One night, there was a disagreement. As is so often the case in these matters, Martha would later claim she "blacked out" and couldn't remember exactly what happened. She just knew that when she came to, there on the floor was Janet, bleeding from a head wound. There was a bloody ball peen hammer and a scarf tightly wound and knotted around Janet's neck. After several days of indecision, the lovers buried the body in the basement of a rented house and forged breathless letters to Janet's family describing her connubial bliss.

Oops! Martha and Raymond typed the letters and Janet's family knew she couldn't type. They called the police.

By this time, the lonely hearts killers had set their sights on Delphine Downing, a widow who lived in Grand Rapids, Michigan, with her two-year-old daughter Rainelle. They went out to meet her and, once again, the plan worked. For a time. When Delphine caught Raymond without his toupee one day and got a good look at his dented dome, she was horrified.

Somehow, Martha got a fistful of sleeping pills inside Delphine. While she was out cold, Raymond shot her in the head. For the next two days, they raided Delphine's checking account and tried to decide what to do next. As they saw it, there was no choice. They simply had to drown the little girl, bury her in the basement beside her mother, and then cover both graves with fresh cement—which is exactly what they did.

Then, exhausted from a hard day's work, they went to the movies. Soon after they got back, the cops knocked on the door. Perhaps relieved it was over, Martha and Raymond spilled their guts without reservation. Or perhaps it was the D.A.'s promise they would not be extradited to New York, and, with good behavior, they could expect to get out of a Michigan prison in a relatively few years.

Their confession ran 73 pages. As for the nonextradition stuff, crime-busting New York governor Thomas Dewey was having none of it. Their trial opened in the Bronx on June 29, 1949 in the middle of a record-breaking heat wave.

Raymond tried to deny his confession but it didn't wash. For her part, Martha settled on a defense that would become much more popular decades later. She claimed she had been the victim of sexual abuse as a child. The real highlights of the trial, though, were the intimately detailed descriptions both Martha and Raymond provided about their various sexual acts. More than 20 cops were called in to deal with the crowds mobbing the courthouse. The New York tabloids went berserk with the material and the verdict was inevitable.

They were executed—Raymond first, Martha second—at Sing Sing on March 8, 1951.

Leonard Kastle's black and white *The Honeymoon Killers* has become an enduring cult favorite and rightly so. It is one of the most accurate true crime films ever made. Some important details are changed—Martha's kids become her mother—but the rest is mostly right. The real keys, though, are the low-budget shot-on-location atmosphere that creates a tone of sweaty desperation, and the completely believable relationship between Martha (Shirley Stoler) and Raymond (Tony Lo Bianco). The story was also the basis for the 1996 Mexican film *Profundo carmesí (Deep Crimson).*

Martha and Raymond returned to the screen in *Lonely Hearts* but the filmmakers were not attempting the "realism" Kastle had achieved. The new version of the story starred the tiny but voluptuous Salma Hayek who probably weighed as much as the real Martha's leg. Never in the long and rich history of Hollywood's glamorizing of unattractive historical figures have such liberties been taken. Filmmaker Todd Robinson obviously had other interests in the story. His grandfather Elmer Robinson (played by John Travolta) was one of the New York detectives who investigated the case. The focus is as much on him as it is on the killers, portrayed as psychopaths who become increasingly unhinged.

Becker, Charles

Charles Becker was a tough corrupt cop in a tough corrupt town, New York, at the turn of the twentieth century. He may also have been a murderer; or he may have been the victim of a zealous, politically ambitious prosecutor. With this story, you have to choose your villain.

By 1912 Becker was a lieutenant with a mixed record. One innocent bystander had been killed by Becker and his partner while they were chasing a burglar, and there had been other incidents. Even so, the big cop was personable enough that when Rhinelander Waldo was appointed Deputy Police Commissioner, he put Becker in charge of the unit to clamp down on illegal gambling establishments in the city's Tenderloin district, now Times Square.

It was a sweet deal. Under Becker's watch the gamblers had a choice: they paid him a portion of their take or he closed them down and destroyed their equipment with an ax. The system wasn't perfect. Sometimes places had to be shut down temporarily, but things blew over soon enough.

Becker became a wealthy man. He was courted by the press, rode in a limo, and hung around with the famous Bat Masterson, then sports editor of the *Morning Telegraph.* One of Becker's "clients" was gambler Herman Rosenthal, a loudmouth who, as an associate put it, didn't know the rules. Herman complained to the mayor after his thoroughly illegal establishment was closed. (The mayor threw him out.) When his joint was closed again, Herman wound up in the office of crusading Manhattan district attorney Charles Whitman, where he spilled his guts. His accusations were splashed all over the front pages of the newpapers.

That night, while having a brandy at the Metropole Hotel, Rosenthal stepped outside and caught three bullets in head, one in the neck.

The cops found the shooters quickly enough—Gyp the Blood, Lefty Louie, Whitey Lewis and "Dago" Frank Cirofici. They claimed to have been hired by Bald Jack Rose and Ridgey Webber, the notorious dognapper. Rose and Webber quickly ratted out Big Jack Zelig, saying he had hired them to do the job for Becker. Zelig backed them up and was killed before he could testify in court.

Whitman went after Becker and got a conviction. After it was overturned, he got a second conviction. Neither of them meant very much to Becker's defenders who claimed all of the colorfully named crooks who eventually got the chair had reasons of their own to want Becker dead.

Not that it mattered. In 1915 Becker's appeals ran out and the only hope he had to avoid the electric chair was clemency from the governor. By then, that was Charles Whitman, who had ridden his prosecution of the cop all the way to the governor's mansion.

The final insult was a botched execution. Apparently they underestimated Becker's considerable bulk and set the voltage improperly. It took three separate jolts to do the job. To date, Charles Becker is the only New York policeman to have been convicted of murder and executed for it.

In F. Scott Fitzgerald's *The Great Gatsby*, Meyer Wolfsheim, a fictionalized **Arnold Rothstein**, tells the story of Becker and Rosenthal to Nick Carraway over drinks at lunch.

Stephen Crane's novella *Maggie: A Girl of the Streets* was inspired when he saw Becker beating up a prostitute who hadn't sufficiently paid him off. Becker's partisans say the cop busted the writer and a hooker.

D.W. Griffith's *The Musketeers of Pig Alley*, sometimes called the "first" gangster movie, was loosely inspired by the first part of the story. The 18-minute film was made and released while the news of Rosenthal's death was still fresh.

Rhinelander Waldo was a supporting character in E.L. Doctorow's brilliant novel *Ragtime*. In the screen adaptation, he was portrayed by James Cagney, in his final film.

Beckwith, Byron de La

Medgar Evers

The assassination of Medgar Evers in 1963 set the stage for the political violence that would follow in the tumultuous decade.

His story is the archetypal American Dream. Born into a poor Mississippi family, he served in the Army in World War II and took part in the invasion of Normandy. After the war, he went to college, married, started a family, and went to work for a black-owned insurance company. He quit that job to become the first NAACP field officer in Mississippi, among the most racist states in the union.

Evers knew he was a target. In May 1963 his carport was firebombed. On the night of June 12th, he came home from a meeting with NAACP lawyers. He had just gotten out of his car when he was shot in the back. He died three hours later.

Byron de La Beckwith, a lowlife fertilizer salesman and Klansman, was the killer. He had set up a sniper's nest about 200 feet away. Apparently unconcerned about prosecution, he left his 30.06 rifle, complete with telescopic sight and fingerprints, at the site. When he was arrested eleven days later, he said the weapon had been stolen. In 1964 two all-male, all-white juries claimed to believe him. Governor Ross Barnett and Gen. Edwin Walker, a prominent segregationist who had been a target of Lee Harvey Oswald, visited to show their support.

In 1993 the Mississippi Supreme Court ruled that Beckwith could be tried again. Finally, justice prevailed. Beckwith was sentenced to life and died in prison in 2001.

The assassination and the third trial are the subject of both the 1983 made-for-television film *For Us the Living*, and the 1996 theatrical release, *Ghosts of Mississippi*. Bob Dylan sings about Evers and Beckwith in his song "Only a Pawn in the Game."

Bembenek, Lawrencia

Strip away the sexy sensationalism that has nothing to do with the facts of the case, and it's clear Lawrencia Bembenek was railroaded. She was guilty of being an outspoken, attractive blonde. Her problems began when she tried to do what was considered to be "man's work" in the early 1980s. She wanted to be a cop, like her father.

In those days, the Milwaukee police department didn't want women on the force. It did want the affirmative action funds it received for hiring women and minorities, but that didn't mean they had to stay hired. Laurie, as she was known, sixth in her class at the police academy, was fired on August 25, 1980 after only one month on the job for no real reason. She promptly filed a discrimination suit, and gave evidence concerning other misconduct and corruption within the department to Internal Affairs. At around the same time, she worked briefly as a waitress at a Playboy Club and posed in a sexy dress for a beer calendar.

In December 1980 she met police officer Fred Schultz. They were married a month later even though Fred had only recently gone through a divorce. His ex, Christine, lived with their sons Sean and Shannon in the house Schultz had built.

On May 28, 1981 around two-thirty in the morning, someone got into that house and shot Christine. The person or persons had tied her hands in front of her and gagged her with a bandanna. The assailant(s) then woke up the boys, possibly while attempting to tie them up. Sean was able to describe the intruder as a tall man with long reddish hair in a ponytail, wearing an army field jacket, green jogging suit, and low-top black shoes, the kind favored by cops. After the boys woke up, struggling and screaming, their mother was shot.

The intruder fled. Sean called his mother's boyfriend, Stewart Honeck, another cop. Fred Schultz, on duty that night, was called, too. Having these two men—both so personally involved with the victim they had to be considered as potential suspects—at the crime scene was the beginning of a series of official mistakes and errors in judgment.

That same night, Schultz and his partner Michael Durfee went to his apartment and examined Schultz's off-duty pistol. They determined that the dusty revolver had not been fired or cleaned recently. They also neglected to write down the serial number. Later, the pistol would be identified as the murder weapon, though it was not turned in as evidence for another two weeks.

Suspicion immediately fell on Laurie and Schultz because he was angry at the amount of alimony he had to pay. But Schultz had an alibi and passed a lie detector test. Laurie was advised by her attorney not to take one and she didn't. She was finally charged with murder on the grounds that she had access to the weapon and a key to Christine Schultz's house. Several other people, including an ex-roommate, had equally easy access to both the weapon and the key.

There was physical evidence: two blonde hairs allegedly found on Christine's body. But those mys-

Lawrencia "Bambi" Bembenek, in court, 1986. (AP Photo)

teriously appeared sometime later. Dr. Elaine Samuels, the first expert to examine the hair evidence, stated she had found no blonde hairs and that all of the samples she tested were from the victim.

When she was arrested in June, Laurie claimed she was being set up by the police, and given the flimsiness of the case against her, it wasn't completely farfetched. The prosecution claimed she went to Christine's house intending to frighten the woman so she and Fred could move back in. Then something went wrong… and of course, she was a feminist.

Astonishingly, the jury found her guilty. She was sentenced to life, and then her celebrity really began.

Naturally, she appealed her conviction. When that failed, she tried to get a new trial. In 1984 Schultz filed for divorce. On July 15, 1990 she escaped.

Dominic Gugliatto, brother of a fellow inmate, helped after Laurie climbed out a window in the laundry. She soon became something of a national folk hero and "Run, Bambi, Run!" became a catchphrase. ("Bambi" was an unwanted nickname she had acquired as a cop.) By then, she was famous and fame changes everything.

The star-crossed lovers made it as far as Thunder Bay, Ontario, before a piece on *America's Most Wanted* generated a tip she was waiting tables at a local restaurant.

Laurie fought extradition, claiming refugee status under the Geneva Convention. The Canadian government finally agreed to return her but noted several legal errors in her trial. It was enough to spur a judicial inquiry into the murder investigation and the trial. Several glaring and embarrassing errors surfaced. Among them:

- The careless treatment of the murder weapon, which might not even be the murder weapon;

- Questions about the authenticity of the bullet removed from Christine Schultz's body: initials carved on the bullet by the experts who identified it did not match the initials on the bullet presented as evidence;

- Witnesses who said career criminal Frederick Horenberger, whose MO included wearing a wig as a disguise, claimed he had been paid $10,000 by Fred Schultz to kill Christine; and

- Failure to examine blood found beneath Christine's fingernails.

The state offered a face-saving deal. If Laurie pleaded guilty to second-degree murder, the sentence would be reduced to time served, plus parole. In short, she would be free. She accepted.

Several books were written about the case, including Laurie's own account, *Woman On Trial.* It became the basis for the miniseries *Woman On the Run* with Tatum O'Neal. Its competition was the weirdly titled *Calendar Girl, Cop Killer? The Bambi Bembenek Story* with Lindsay Frost. Of course, Laurie was also a guest on *Oprah.*

Only a few years after her trial, the film *Fatal Attraction* became a phenomenal hit in 1987. The story of a career woman who attempts to destroy a family certainly borrowed something from Bembenek.

Finally, Laurie agreed to an ill-fated appearance on *Dr. Phil* that once again provided fodder for the tabloids. She claimed that while Dr. Phil's staffers were awaiting the results of DNA tests that would finally prove her innocence, they virtually held her captive in a Marina Del Ray apartment building. No phone, no radio, no television. She tied bed sheets together and tried to escape out a window. In the attempt, she fell and broke her leg so severely it was amputated below the knee. She sued.

In 2004 the Los Angeles Superior Court dismissed the suit without prejudice, meaning Dr. Phil had not imprisoned her and she could not refile the suit. It's a suitably bizarre postscript.

Bender Family

There is one "official" version of the Bender family story—sometimes called the "Hell Benders," America's first mass murderers—and there are several variations on the more colorful legends. Details and motivations vary considerably but they all agree on the basics.

The family consisted of Old Man William John, Ma, John the younger, and sister Kate. (According to some, Ma and Kate were mother and daughter but the guys were not even Benders.) They arrived in the township of Cherryvale, Kansas in 1870 as part of a small cult of spiritualists. The other families involved in the group moved on but the Benders stayed on a 160-acre spread near the well-traveled Osage Trail. They built a small house where they sold groceries and rented out beds for the night.

Kate also moonlighted as "Professor Miss Kate Bender" who led public séances, healings, and spiritualist performances. Apparently, the act was a hit. A road marker later erected in Labette County by the Kansas Historical Society and State Highway Commission described Kate as "a beautiful, voluptuous girl with tigerish grace."

Kate also performed smaller private séances back at her little house on the prairie. Some of her clients never left. Likewise, some luckless travelers spent their last nights at the Benders' roadside inn. The house was divided by a canvas partition made from a wagon cover. The public room was on one side; the family's living quarters on the other.

A visitor who appeared to be sufficiently well-heeled would be seated with his or her back to the canvas. Pa or John, a mental defective, would lurk on the other side with a sledgehammer. The Benders would then smash their victims' heads and slit their throats before dumping the bodies down a trapdoor to the cellar. Later, after all the valuables had been sorted through, the bodies were buried in the orchard out back.

The Benders operated their bloody business from the winter of 1871 until the spring of 1873. How did it end?

The official version has it that as word of the mysteriously vanished travelers spread, suspicion was centered on Osage township. The most recent disappearance appeared to be Dr. William York. Aware they were the focus of these stories, the locals held a meeting at the Harmony Grove schoolhouse. About 75 people showed up, the two John Benders among them. All agreed to obtain a search warrant and to go through every farm and building in the community to put an end to the rumors.

Three days later, the Benders had vanished. A party was organized to search the farm. The first thing they noticed was a foul smell from the basement, coming through a trapdoor that had been nailed shut. Gaining entrance, they found it covered with partially dried blood. There was nothing else in the house, but Col. Ed York, brother of the missing doctor, noticed mounded dirt in the orchard. That's where they found the graves.

Dr. York was one of nine victims, one of them a little girl who may have been buried alive. Several unidentified dismembered body parts were found, too.

According to one unofficial legend, Col. York was searching for his brother alone, and went to the Bender house because he knew the doctor had stayed there before. The Benders told him they had not seen his brother. Perhaps he had been waylaid by wild Indians or even the outlaw **Jesse James**. Why didn't the Colonel come inside and take a load off? Would he care for a cup of tea or a glass of cider? Have a seat right here...

The Colonel declined and pressed on with his search and then returned to the place with a posse. Other more fanciful versions have him finding a locket on the floor that had belonged to his brother. In any case, by the time he returned with his companions, the Benders were long gone.

After their disappearance, the official story and the legends go in different directions. Officially, the family caught a train to Humboldt, Kansas where they split up; Kate and young John heading to an outlaw stronghold in Texas or New Mexico while Ma and Pa went on to Kansas City and St. Louis. All four vanished.

According to the legend, a posse set out in search of the Benders and returned, unsuccessful, some time later. But no one who had been part of the posse would say much of anything about what had happened. In 1909, though, one man made a deathbed confession in Chicago that the posse had found the family. They shot Ma, Pa, and young John, and burned Kate alive before they threw the bodies down a 20-foot well. A year later, another man, dying in New Mexico, told the same story with the same 20-foot well. He also said the Benders had been carrying several thousand dollars and the posse had split the money.

Whatever the truth, the Benders were never heard from again.

In their day, the bloody Benders became celebrities after word of their crimes spread. The curious descended upon their farm and took away everything as souvenirs. In 1961 a replica of the house was constructed for the Kansas Centennial Celebration. It was run as a museum until 1978 when the citizens of Cherryvale decided they would rather have a fire station where the museum stood.

The Benders' story has been told in fiction by Manly Wade Wellman in his 1960 novel *A Candle of the Wicked,* and by Robert H. Alderman in *The Bloody Benders* (1970). The Benders make a brief, uncredited appearance in Neil Gaiman's novel *American Gods* and are the subject of Rick Geary's illustrated book, *Bloody Benders.*

Two obscure low-budget horror movies have been produced, *Bloody Bender* (2002) and *Bloody Bender's Return* (2003). And, of course, the murderous innkeeper is a stereotype in hodophobic (fear of road travel) horror and suspense novels and films.

Berkowitz, David "Son of Sam"

As serial killers go, David Berkowitz is really not very interesting.

He did not torture his victims; his crimes were poorly planned; his weapon of choice was a pistol; and he was a lousy shot. But he committed his crimes in New York City, the media center of the known universe, so he attracted infinitely more attention than he deserved. For a serial killer, his background was unusually ordinary. There was no abuse. He later blamed his hatred and fear of women on the mother who had given him up for adoption, but it doesn't really explain anything.

He was raised by Pearl and Nat Berkowitz in the Bronx. A large kid, he was something of a bully. Pearl died when he was a teenager and he took it badly. In 1971 he joined the Army and was sent to Korea where his only sexual experience with a hooker resulted in a dose of the clap. About the same time, his adoptive father remarried and moved to Florida.

Berkowitz returned to New York, lived alone in Yonkers, and became a prolific arsonist. He may have attacked two women with a knife, but only

one, whom he wounded, has been confirmed. He worked as a security guard and his mental condition deteriorated. Later, he would make many outlandish claims—he was receiving orders from a neighbor's dog, he was part of a satanic conspiracy—but he also denied them.

The facts are simple enough. Beginning on the night of July 29, 1976 he walked the streets in the Bronx, Queens, and other boroughs looking for women to kill. He used a .44 magnum pistol. Initially, his nickname was "the .44 killer." His first victims were two girls who were talking in a parked car. That night, he killed Konna Lauria and wounded Jody Valentini. He continued, picking random targets of opportunity. By April 1977 he had killed or wounded six people, mostly women, and was attracting considerable attention in the local print and television news. He started writing crude, nutty anonymous letters to the cops, to columnist Jimmy Breslin, and to his neighbors. He signed the first missive to the police with "Son of Sam" and the name stuck. Short and punchy, it was perfect for a tabloid headline.

During the summer of 1977 Berkowitz picked up the pace, and the police task force investigating the killings was literally flooded with tips and clues. Among those were the strange letters and notes (one including a confession) Berkowitz was still firing off to his neighbors, a parking ticket he had received in the neighborhood on the night of one of his murders, and an eyewitness description.

All of the dots were finally connected on August 10, 1977 and Berkowitz was arrested as he went to his car. He gave up without a fight and freely confessed. At trial, he pleaded guilty and was sentenced to 365 years for killing six people and wounding several others.

Berkowitz inspired several rock bands to write songs about him: the Talking Heads' "Psycho Killer" (1977), Dead Boys' "Son of Sam" (1978), the Beastie Boys' "Looking Down the Barrel of a Gun" (1989), and many others. He's also a supporting character in the ESPN miniseries *The Bronx Is Burn-*

ing (2007). Among the better books are David Abrahamsen's interviews, *Confessions of Son of Sam* (1985) and the 1978 novel *.44* by Breslin and Dick Schaap.

But the best examination of what Berkowitz's crimes really meant to New York and New Yorkers is Spike Lee's film *Summer of Sam.* Berkowitz is a minor character in a story that focuses primarily on two young men, played by John Leguizamo and Adrien Brody, who live in a neighborhood where one of the killings takes place and are affected by the community's reaction to the crimes in extremely personal ways. Lee's intimate understanding of his native city, the times, and the generation make it one of the best and most carefully layered American crime films.

Billington, John

They never should have let the son of a bitch on the boat.

John Billington was a mean-tempered bully, and his fellow colonists would have been better off if he hadn't set foot on the *Mayflower.* But he did. Billington, his wife Ellen, and their sons Francis and John the younger were aboard when the *Mayflower* dropped anchor at Provincetown harbor. Straightaway, the Billingtons started causing trouble. Even before the newly arrived immigrants could move on to Plymouth Rock, Francis almost sank the ship when he fired a gun near an uncovered barrel of gunpowder and set fire to a cabin.

Soon after they settled in Plymouth, Billington the elder insulted the settlement's head honcho Miles Standish, and was sentenced to public humiliation by having his neck and heels tied together. Billington quickly made nice and they let him off with a warning.

Some months later, John the younger went out wandering in the woods, got lost and was taken by a group of Nauset Indians. They gave him to another tribe who took him Cape Cod and put up with him for a few weeks before they let him go. If he was anything like his old man, who can blame them? Actual-

> *John Billington was the continent's first English murderer on record. He was hanged in September 1630.*

ly, his release had to do with the political instability that existed between the natives and the new arrivals.

Four years after his son's return, Billington had something to do with a series of letters sent back to England and meant to undermine the colony, but he pleaded ignorance of the whole matter, and, since nobody had any proof, again he walked. More important, at the same time, Billington was involved in a bitter dispute with his neighbor John Newcomen. It lasted until the day in 1630 when Billington bushwacked him: he hid behind a boulder and shot Newcomen with a musket. In no time flat, a jury found him guilty of murder "by plain and notorious evidence" and ordered him strung up.

Doubtless, the resident Native Americans had dealt with many murders, but John Billington was the continent's first English murderer on record. He was hanged in September 1630.

Bjorkland, Rosemarie "Penny"

Why did she do it?

There is no question Penny Bjorkland murdered August Norry. Was it a completely random, unplanned act—as she claimed—or was there something else to it?

In 1959 Rosemarie Diane Bjorkland, called Penny, was a clerk at a publisher's service bureau in Daly City, near San Francisco. Only 18 years old, she was considered a good worker. On the morning of Sunday, February 1, she woke up and decided she was going to kill somebody. Why? "Just to see if I could and not worry about it," she said later.

She packed a .38 and a box of bullets and set off into the hills to find someone to shoot. Landscape gardener August Norry had been dumping grass clippings from his truck when Penny happened upon him. He offered her a ride. Aiming through the passenger door, she emptied the revolver into him, reloaded, and went around to the driver's side. She put six more shots through Norry's body, pulled him out onto the road, reloaded again, and shot him six times more.

She jumped behind the wheel and peeled out. Somewhere in the process, she dropped the box of ammo. Later, a witness claimed he saw a freckle-faced blonde driving like crazy in a truck that matched Norry's. It was soon found parked in a lover's lane.

The Daly City and San Mateo County authorities went to work on the box of bullets and caught a break. The slugs were wadcutters, a particular kind of bullet favored by target shooters. When they took one of the unfired rounds apart, they learned the shells had been hand-loaded with extra gunpowder, making them "hot loads." The shells were unusual, too, with three distinctive grooves or cannelures for lubrication. They came from a Connecticut manufacturer who was able to provide them with the names of four local distributors. After questioning gunshop owners, they came up with a list of five men who regularly hot-loaded their wadcutters.

One of them was Lawrence Schultze, already known to the cops for his association with an auto theft ring. Initially, he claimed some boxes of his bullets had been stolen, but when a spectrographic analysis proved his bullets had been used in the Norry killing, Schultze, on the advice of his attorney, had a change of heart. He admitted he had sold the bullets to Penny Bjorkland, and he still had a copy of the receipt.

For her part, Penny had been trying to get caught. She had sent a handwritten anonymous letter to a local newspaper claiming a "girl friend" of hers had killed Norry. She told her co-workers she had done it; they laughed it off.

Penny was arrested on April 15th. She confessed immediately, waived a jury trial, and asked to be tried and sentenced by a judge. Seven psychiatrists examined her; six said she was legally sane though severely emotionally disturbed. The judge gave her life.

But was it really that simple?

Penny's problems had been building. She had been in trouble in high school, caught with vodka in her locker. She had a love/hate relationship with her gorgeous mother, and scornfully dismissed her 13-year-old brother as "a square." Two weeks before the killing, she stole the pistol from a friend in San Francisco. After buying wadcutters from Schultze, she had asked him along for a little target practice up in the hills.

And it turned out that Norry wasn't a complete stranger, either. She had met him at least once before, and he had driven her home. What about his reputation as a ladies man? Penny had let it be known she felt "cheated" when she found out Norry had lied claiming to be 23 and unmarried. He was 27 and married but, she said, it meant nothing to her.

Was there more to their relationship? Was it an adolescent *Fatal Attraction*? Did Penny say in effect "I won't be ignored?"

Black Hand

In a way, the Black Hand was a precursor to the **Mafia** in America. It was not a highly organized group, but rather a badge of intimidation used by Italian extortionists who worked the urban ghettos in the early years of the twentieth century.

A note bearing a drawing of a black hand or a black handprint would be passed to a prosperous merchant or shopkeeper with a demand for money. If he didn't pony up, he or a member of his family would be harmed, kidnapped, or killed.

In 1908 there were 242 Black Hand extortion attempts reported to New York cops who estimated that for each one they learned about, 250 were unreported. (How they came up with this amazing and possibly invented figure is unknown.) Virtually anyone in the community was a potential victim. Even opera star Enrico Caruso was tapped. At first, he paid a fairly modest $2,000, but when they came back and asked for $15,000 he balked and called the police.

The cops set a trap and caught a couple of businessmen who had figured it was an easy way to make a buck. Even so, Caruso's family maintained private security and police protection from then on.

In New York, the big cheese of the Black Hand was Ignazio Saietta or "Lupo the Wolf." Saietta was famous for maintaining a "murder stable" deep in what was then Italian Harlem on 107th Street. It was a place where they tortured, murdered, burned, and/or buried both their victims and gang members who fell out of favor. One-stop shopping. When the cops raided the place, they dug up 60 bodies, but, somehow, no arrests were made. Saietta said he had rented the property out and had no idea what his tenants had done. His gang continued to use the facility until 1917.

The house of horrors was uncovered by NYPD detective Joseph Petrosino. He was the first cop to infiltrate the Italian gangs and alert the public and the Congress about criminals who were coming into America on phony papers. Petrosino was so effective that New York Police Commissioner Theodore Bingham sent him to Palermo, Sicily, to get the goods on gangsters who could be deported. Though the mission was supposed to be secret, word got out and Petrosino was gunned down in Sicily on March 11, 1909. Back home, he was given a hero's funeral with crowds jamming the streets of Little Italy.

No one was ever charged with Petrosino's murder, but it was generally agreed to be the work of Don Vito Cascio Ferro, a powerful Sicilian Mafia leader who had been kicked out of New York by Petrosino.

Black Hand extortion died out when Prohibition came in and the gangs turned to the more profitable business of illicit hooch.

Petrosino's story was dramatized first in a 1912 silent film, *The Adventures of Lt. Petrosino*. In the

1950 Gene Kelly vehicle, *Black Hand,* Petrosino's name was changed to Lewis Lorelli and he was played by J. Carrol Naish. *In Pay or Die* (1960), he was played by Ernest Borgnine. Two Italian miniseries were made about him in 1972 and 2006.

Ignazio Saietta provided the model for Don Fanucci, the old guy in the white suit who was bumped off by a young Vito Corleone in *The Godfather, Part II*.

Blackbeard

Edward Teach (or Thack or Titche) was America's first famous outlaw. He was probably born in England around 1680, but since he ended his bloody career in the colonies, he was considered one of ours.

Teach sailed with English privateers (licensed pirates) in Queen Anne's War (1702–13) and then set out on his own. Commanding several ships, he preyed on merchant shipping and towns on the Atlantic coast of America and the West Indies.

Teach cut a fearsome figure with the bushy black beard that gave him his nickname. He braided it with hemp and lit matches, and sported knives, swords, and three braces of pistols. He earned a reputation for ruthless violence. If a ship offered any resistance, all aboard would be killed, or so the stories went. Others said he never killed anyone who wasn't trying to kill or capture him. His most famous act of piracy may have been his blockade of the port of Charleston. It ended when he was paid off with drugs and medicine.

Blackbeard got away with it for years because he paid off the governor of North Carolina and bought an official pardon. He and his men were notorious bullies and Teach had as many as a dozen wives in various ports.

The citizens of North Carolina finally got fed up and petitioned Governor Alexander Spotswood of neighboring Virginia for help. He said he would help and gave the job to doughty young lieutenant Robert Maynard.

Because Blackbeard operated in the shallows, where large warships could not go, Maynard took two ships, *HMS Pearl* and *HMS Lyme,* and two hired sloops, the *Jane* and the *Ranger,* and set off from the James River on November 17, 1718.

Four days later, they found Teach on his ship, the *Adventure,* off Okracoke Island on North Carolina's outer banks. The ships fought with cannon for a time and seven of Maynard's men were killed. Finally, they managed to board the *Adventure* and went at it hand to hand. The good guys prevailed, though the pirate proved hard to kill. It took five bullet wounds, twenty lacerations, and one beheading to do the job. By then, he was not only merely dead, he was really most sincerely dead.

Maynard sailed home with Teach's head hanging from the bowspit.

Tales of Blackbeard's buried treasure sprang up immediately, though there is absolutely no evidence to support it. A ship that may have been his was discovered in 1996. It is the subject of an exhibit at the North Carolina Maritime Museum in Beaufort.

The pirate has inspired dozens of fanciful supernatural tales, including Disney's 1968 *Blackbeard's Ghost* with Peter Ustinov. Raoul Walsh's 1952 *Blackbeard, the Pirate* is standard Hollywood swashbuckling. More recently, there have been a 2005 BBC film and a 2006 Hallmark miniseries, both titled simply *Blackbeard.*

Blake, Robert

Bonny Lee Bakley was a cut-rate little grifter. Until she married actor Robert Blake, her closest brush with fame had been nude photos published in *Hustler* magazine. She craved recognition and wealth, and that's what got her killed.

Bakley sold nudie pictures of herself and contacted men through personal ads in sex magazines. She would string them along with promises of a personal visit if they'd provide cash for travel, usually around $40. If they couldn't manage that, she

would try to wheedle stamps and phone cards. Not exactly a master criminal.

She was actually more interested in hooking up with a celebrity. By the time she met Blake, she had already been linked with aging bad boy rocker Jerry Lee Lewis and Marlon Brando's troubled son **Christian**, who had killed his half-sister's boyfriend.

Robert Blake had gained his first fame as a child actor in the *Our Gang* comedies, beginning in the late 1930s. He also appeared in the *Red Ryder* series, and had a small role in *Treasure of the Sierra Madre.* As an adult, he attracted national attention for his portrayal of murderer **Perry Smith** in *In Cold Blood.* (Curiously, *Sierra Madre* was one of the real Perry Smith's favorite films.) Blake was nominated for an Emmy for his portrayal of another real family murderer, **John List**, in *Judgment Day.* His last major role was as a raccoon-eyed spectral figure of death in David Lynch's hallucinatory *Lost Highway.*

Bonny did not believe life could imitate art. She met Blake at a Hollywood party and ingratiated herself to him in the backseat of his SUV that very night in the parking lot of a Holiday Inn. At the time, she was living in Arkansas and was on probation for possession of stolen credit cards, but she managed to slip away to L.A. occasionally, and in September, 1999, her efforts bore fruit, as it were. But when she tried to share the joyful news of her pregnancy with Blake, he hung up on her and changed his phone number.

Bakley then tried to persuade **Christian Brando** the impending bundle of joy was his, but that didn't work, either. After the baby was born in June 2000, Blake said yes to a DNA test to settle the paternity question. He invited Bakley to bring the infant to L.A., she did, and agreed to leave the child with a nanny while she and an attentive Blake went out to lunch. But at the restaurant, she was braced by two big guys who claimed to be cops and said they knew she was breaking her probation. They were taking her downtown. As they hustled her away, Blake told her not to worry; he would handle everything and the baby would be fine.

Robert Blake, former *Baretta* star, accused of his wife's murder and writer Dominick Dunne. (AP Photo)

Out in the car, one of the cops gave her a choice: go to jail or go home. If she agreed to fly back to Arkansas and save them endless paperwork, they would take her to the airport. Bonny agreed and didn't realize Blake had conned the conwoman until she talked to her parole officer. Threatening legal action, she changed her mind when Blake proposed marriage, and went back to L.A. for the ceremony. Alas, things did not go well for the star-crossed lovers.

Blake had unusual ideas about connubial living arrangements. Bonny slept out in the guest house and the baby stayed with Blake's adult daughter from a previous marriage in another neighborhood.

Less than six months after the wedding, on May 4, 2001, the unhappy couple went out to dinner at an Italian restaurant. Blake parked around the corner, next to a dumpster. After eating, they went back to the car and Blake claimed he had left something in the restaurant—a .38 pistol. While he went back to retrieve it, someone shot Bonny twice, killing her. Blake claims he returned to the car and found her covered with blood. No one actually saw him go into the restaurant for the pistol, though several people did notice him after he saw the body. They commented on his unbelievable, phony grief.

A few weeks after the killing, a retired stuntman who had worked with Blake went to the police and told them the actor had approached him to kill his wife.

A year later, Blake and his bodyguard Earle Caldwell were charged with murder and conspiracy. By the standards recently set by **O.J. Simpson** and the **Menendez brothers**, it was a fairly tame Hollywood trial.

Defense lawyers put the victim on trial—Bonny had certainly left them with a wealth of raw material—and they attacked the investigation. Despite the overwhelming evidence, the jury found reasonable doubt and Blake walked. A few months later, a civil jury reached the opposite conclusion, finding him responsible for the wrongful death of his wife, and ordered him to cough up $30 million. Fat chance.

So far, two books have been written about the sordid case, *Murder in Hollywood* by Gary King and *Blood Cold* by Dennis McDougal and Mary Murphy. The latter chapters of Miles Corwin's fine book *Homicide Special* examine the killing from the point of view of the detectives who investigated it.

Perhaps it's too early (and too close to home) for anyone in Hollywood to bring the story to the screen, but all the elements are there for an updated *Day of the Locust*.

Bledsoe, Jerry

Jerry Bledsoe had been a newspaper writer for many years before he ran into what may well be the most bizarre series of killings ever committed in America. The Lynch-Klenner murders of 1985 claimed the lives of nine men, women, and children in and around North Carolina. Bledsoe first wrote about them in a series of articles for the *Greensboro News & Record*.

The newspaper wasn't the right medium to tell the whole story. Bledsoe's book, *Bitter Blood* (1988), fills in the gaps—most of them, anyway; there's more than nobody will ever know—in a tale so psychologically and physically complex as to be almost incomprehensible. But Bledsoe made it understandable and compelling by sticking with the main char-

acters and their families, and, finally, he found the internal logic behind the madness and self-destruction. Along with **Ann Rule**'s *The Stranger Beside Me*, it is a masterpiece of true crime writing.

Since then, Bledsoe has written three other books about North Carolina crimes. *Blood Games* (1991) follows a college student who plotted to kill his mother and stepfather, and involved his friends who were fellow *Dungeons and Dragons* players. *Before He Wakes* (1994) is about a seemingly normal middle class woman who lost not one but two husbands to "accidental" shootings. *Death Sentence* (1998) focuses on the crimes and redemption of poisoner Velma Barfield, the first woman to be executed in America following the reinstatement of the death penalty.

In all of his books, Bledsoe is less interested in the whodunit aspects than in the larger effects of serious crimes not only on the lives of those who are touched by them but their communities as well.

He left newspaper work in 1989 and founded the Down Home Press, specializing in books about the South. His recent books have branched out into other fields.

Three of Bledsoe's books became television movies: *Bitter Blood* aired in 1994 as *In the Best of Families: Marriage, Pride, and Madness. Blood Games* became *Honor Thy Mother* in 1992, and *Before He Wakes* made it to the screen in 1998.

Bonanno, Joseph

Joseph "Joe Bananas" Bonanno certainly had the strangest career of any of the original Mafia dons. (Given that hated nickname, how could he not?) He was also the most nakedly ambitious of the bunch, though he titled his autobiography *A Man of Honor*.

Born in Sicily in 1905, Bonanno moved to America as a child, but his family returned home and he learned the ways of the traditional Italian **Mafia**. He also became an anti-Fascist and returned to America after Mussolini took over in 1922.

Back in Brooklyn, Bonanno joined the Castellammarese gang and signed on as a loyal soldier in 1927 when **Salvatore Maranzano** arrived in New York from Sicily and attempted to take over all the gangs. That meant unseating **Joe "the Boss" Masseria.** The Castellammarese War lasted several years and was settled only when **Lucky Luciano** decided to betray his boss, Masseria. Luciano put together a team with representatives from four of the major groups involved to spread responsibility for the killing.

Maranzano promptly proclaimed himself to be the new boss. Five months later, Luciano turned on his new boss and had him killed, too. He replaced the Sicilian hierarchy with a more open command structure based on cooperation among the gangs and respect for each other's territories. Luciano's motto might have been "Make money, not war" and so he left Bonanno in charge of Maranzano's men.

Joe Bananas did well and branched out into other legitimate businesses, most famously funeral homes. He bought several and used them to solve that perennial Mafia problem—what to do with the dead bodies? Bonanno came up with the double coffin in which the unwanted stiff was placed beneath a false bottom of a casket's intended resident.

In the 1960s Bonanno extended his operations into Arizona, Canada, California, Haiti, and Cuba, then moved to Tucson to oversee them. The other bosses worried Joe Bananas was moving too fast and taking more than his share. Angered by their resistance, Bonanno called his friend and fellow boss Joe Magliocco and ordered him to kill four of the other bosses, including **Carlo Gambino.** Even though the idea of whacking these top men violated everything the organization stood for, Magliocco agreed, and gave the job to hit man **Joe Colombo.**

Columbo immediately ratted out Bonanno and Magliocco to Gambino and the rest. They ordered the two men to appear before them. Bonanno refused. Magliocco, in extremely poor health, acquiesced. Because he was so ill—he would die within months—they fined him $43,000, allowed him to retire, and replaced him with Colombo.

They replaced the still recalcitrant Bonanno in absentia with one of his former aides, Gaspar DeGregorio. Bonanno refused to accept it and the "Bananas War" broke out within his gang. By the fall of 1964 the other bosses had had enough. On the night of October 20th, while Bonanno was exiting a taxi with his lawyer, he was snatched off the street in New York. They held him for more than a year at a Catskills resort while they tried to figure out what to do with the old-time boss.

Joe Bananas argued he still had enough supporters that his death or disappearance would result in all-out war, a coast-to-coast bloodbath. Finally, Bonanno agreed to hand over his operations and accept forced retirement. Others have suggested that perhaps the banana man staged the whole thing and was simply hiding out. Whatever, he went back to his Tucson estate and the Bananas War continued sporadically until 1968 when Bonanno was slowed down by a heart attack.

In 1983 he published *A Man of Honor* and prosecutors tried to use portions of it to get him to admit to his criminal activities. He pleaded the fifth, said he had been mistaken in the book, that he couldn't recall, etc. The evasion got him a 14-month stretch for obstruction of justice, but they couldn't hold him. In 2002, at age 97, he died of heart failure.

The only dramatization of Bonanno's story was the 1999 hard-to-find cable adaptation of his book, *Bonanno: A Godfather's Story.* Some parallels can be found between his activities and the elder Michael Corleone's in the second and third parts of *The Godfather* series.

Booth, John Wilkes

Though he was from Maryland, a mid-Atlantic border state during the Civil War, John Wilkes Booth held views about slavery that sound particularly backward and evil today. Booth was a proud, unapologetic racist who believed black people were inferior beings, less than fully human, and were lucky to have been brought to America. Slavery, he argued, was good for them and good for white people, a win-win proposition, as it were. (To be fair, such beliefs were shared by many, North and South.)

Booth also bought into the romantic myth of the antebellum South, and used his position as one of America's most popular actors to champion his political beliefs. (Some things don't change.) Even though Southern states had begun the war by attacking American soldiers at Fort Sumter, South Carolina, Booth saw President Abraham Lincoln as the great villain, a "tyrant." As the war was winding down, with more Union victories and the defeat of the South became more imminent, Booth's hatred grew to overpowering dimensions and he hatched several nutty schemes.

During the war, Booth had been involved with Southern sympathizers and intelligence operations through the Knights of the Golden Circle, and Confederate spy John Surratt. He traveled to Canada to meet with them and transported badly needed medicine to the South. In 1864 he and a handful of conspirators planned to kidnap Lincoln with the idea of spiriting him away to Richmond, Virginia, and ransoming him back to the Union for prisoners of war and medical supplies. Some have proposed that officials of the Confederate government were actively involved in this part of Booth's machinations. Booth and his people were actually in position to ambush the poorly protected president, but Lincoln changed his plans and they did not make the attempt.

As the war came to a close with the fall of Richmond and Lee's surrender at Appomattox, their plotting seemed to be over. But in April 1865 Booth learned that Lincoln was going to attend a play, *Our American Cousin*, at Ford's Theatre in Washington, D.C. Seizing the moment, he decided to kill the president while other members of his cabal attacked Vice President Andrew Johnson and Secretary of State William Seward, a vocal proponent of equal rights.

Joining Booth were Lewis Powell (aka Lewis Paine), a fellow racist and Confederate deserter and borderline nutcase; George Atzerodt, a notorious drunk; David Herold, a dimwitted kid who idolized the actor; and Samuel Arnold and Michael O'Laughlin, two childhood friends. Also involved were Mary Surratt, the spy's mother, who ran a rooming house where the conspirators sometimes met, and Dr. Samuel Mudd.

How did Booth gather and control this band of motley louts? Simple: money. Then, as now, popular actors were extremely well paid and, at age 27, Booth was a rich man. Whenever these guys got together to plot, Wilkes picked up the tab for plentiful food and drink.

The plan was to attack the three men simultaneously around 10:15 p.m. on the night of April 14th. Booth, who was intimately familiar with Ford's Theatre, would take the President. Atzerodt's target was the Vice President in his rooming house. Powell went after the Secretary of State, who had been seriously injured a few days before in a carriage accident.

Atzerod never even tried to do his part. He pawned his pistol for $10, got drunk, and skulked out of town. Powell came within inches of killing Seward. Claiming to have medicine for the Secretary, he got inside the house where he attacked Seward's oldest son and a male nurse. Powell actually got into Seward's bedroom and stabbed him with a Bowie knife before he was chased away. The neck brace Seward was wearing saved his life.

Booth took a horse to a stage door behind the theatre and called to stagehand Edman Spangler to take care of it for him. Booth went backstage, cut through a passage beneath the stage, and entered a bar next door where he had a quick whiskey.

Returning to the theatre, he made his way up the stairs to the corridor leading to the presidential box and waited for his moment. Booth knew the play had one guaranteed laugh, a line that always brought down the house, and it was delivered by an actor who was alone on the stage. Earlier in the day, Booth had fashioned a brace to block the vestibule door, and he had drilled a small hole in the door leading to the presidential box. He was able to look inside and see that the President was there with his wife and another couple. (No, the door was not locked and Lincoln's only guard had decided to either move to a better seat or have a drink next door. In either case, the man was never reprimanded or punished in any way.)

As the sellout crowd of 1,700 erupted in laughter, Booth slipped into the box and shot Mr. Lincoln at point blank with a single-shot .44 caliber Derringer. He yelled "Sic semper tyrannis"—"Thus always to tyrants," the state motto of Virginia. Major Henry Rathbone, who was sitting near the President, tried to stop the killer. Booth pulled out a knife and slashed open the Major's arm. He then leapt from the box to the nearly empty stage below. In the process, his spur caught in a decorative flag and he broke his leg as he landed. He screamed out "The South is avenged!" before he ran, limping, for his horse.

The President was carried to a nearby rooming house where he died at 7:22 a.m. the next morning.

With young Herold's help, Booth rode southeast into rural Maryland where they stopped at Dr. Mudd's house. He splinted Booth's leg and sheltered them for the night. The next day Booth and Herold moved on and wound up hiding in a pine thicket while news of the assassination spread, and the hunt for the conspirators widened.

Most of the others, including Mary Surratt, were quickly arrested. For more than a week, Booth and Herold laid low and tried to find a way to cross the Potomac River into Virginia, where they hoped to be received by a more sympathetic audience.

While hiding in the thicket, Booth read newspapers brought by a former Confederate agent, and learned about the law of unintended consequences. The resurgence of war that Booth had hoped to inspire by killing the President did not occur. Instead, Lincoln, who had been a controversial and often unpopular leader, even among his supporters, was transformed. As our first assassinated president, he became a beloved martyr overnight. At the same time, Booth, who had been known as "the handsomest man

in America" had a $100,000 bounty placed on his head and was vilified in the North and South.

Twelve days after the assassination, Booth and the boy were trapped in a small tobacco barn near Port Royal, Virginia, by Union troops. Herold surrendered but Booth remained defiant until the end. The barn was set afire. Booth was seen moving around inside. He was shot by Sgt. Boston Corbett who claimed Booth was about to open fire on the Union soldiers with a carbine.

The bullet hit Booth in the throat and effectively paralyzed him. As he lay suffering that night, he asked soldiers to hold up his hands so he could see them. Near death, he muttered what would be his last words in a faint, hoarse whisper: "Useless, useless."

They carried him to the front porch of a nearby house where he died at dawn the next morning. The rest of the conspirators—most of them anyway—were tried by a military commission and found guilty, pdq.

On July 7, 1865 Mrs. Surratt, Lewis Powell, George Atzerod, and David Herold were hanged. Dr. Mudd, Michael O'Laughlin, and Samuel Arnold were sentenced to life. Edward Spangler got six years. O'Laughlin died in prison, but Mudd and Arnold were later pardoned by President Andrew Johnson.

On the day of the assassination, John Surratt had been in Elmira, New York, spying on a prisoner of war camp. When he learned what had happened, he made his way to Canada and to Italy. He was found serving in the Swiss Guard there, but escaped. He was finally caught in Egypt and was returned to America in 1867. He was eventually found not guilty in a curiously bungled trial. Surratt and the trial have featured prominently in the more outlandish theories generated by the real conspiracy; those fantasies finger everyone from Vice President Andrew Johnson, Secretary of War Edwin Stanton, international bankers, and the Catholic Church.

The story of the murder quickly became an important element of American popular culture. Mere weeks after Booth's death, the first fictional account appeared, a novel called *J. Wilkes Booth: The Assassinator* (1865) by Dion Haco. Hundreds if not thousands of books followed. Perhaps the most widely read is Jim Bishop's 1955 *The Day Lincoln Was Shot.* The phenomenal bestseller was filmed for cable television in 1998 with Rob Morrow as an acceptable Booth, and charismatic character actor Lance Henriksen as Lincoln. The adaptation takes relatively few liberties with the facts, though one invented scene has Booth practicing with his Derringer before a mirror—a moment clearly meant to recall Robert DeNiro's "Are you talking to me?" scene in *Taxi Driver.*

The most recent mainstream book on the subject is James L. Swanson's fast-moving *Manhunt: The 12-Day Chase for Lincoln's Killer* (2006). As of this writing, it was being prepared for the screen with Harrison Ford as Col. Everton Conger, the leader of the Union force that pursued Booth.

The History Channel's documentary *The Lincoln Assassination* (1995) uses historians and commentators to tell the story. Similar material is handled much more forcefully in part of Ken Burns' *Civil War* miniseries.

Booth is one of the central characters in John Weidman and Stephen Sondheim's musical *Assassins* (1991, 2004). Though they portray his death as a suicide—widely rumored at the time—they get his anger and frustration absolutely right, along with the anger and frustration the nation felt in the wake of the assassination. It is fitting they end his long song with their narrator, the Balladeer, singing "Damn you, Booth!"

Perhaps the best visual depiction of the assassination is Rick Geary's 2005 graphic novel, *The Murder of Abraham Lincoln.* Using carefully researched black and white drawings, he presents the major characters and provides the key details of Ford's Theatre in a clear, straightforward manner.

Geary also examines the contradictions and many unanswered questions still surrounding the assassination. Why was President Lincoln so lightly guarded, particularly after he had asked Secretary of War Edwin Stanton to provide more protection? More importantly, Geary describes the horror and sadness that swept the country after its first presidential assassination.

Borden, Lizzie

Lizzie Borden almost certainly killed her father and stepmother. Almost. She had motive ($500,000 inheritance, a huge fortune in the day), means (several handy hatchets), and opportunity (a quiet summer day when her sister was off visiting friends). Lizzie got away with it for two reasons: first, she had excellent legal counsel, the best money could buy; and second, she was incredibly lucky.

The basics of the killings are pretty straightforward: Andrew Borden was a pillar of the Falls River, Massachusetts business community. He owned considerable property and was known not to part easily with a nickel. He lived in a modest house in a modest part of town with Abby, his second wife of 36 years; the two daughters of his first marriage, Emma and Lizzie; and the family maid, Bridget Sullivan. It was oppressively hot on Thursday, August 4, 1892. Emma was seeing friends in Fairhaven, gone for about a week. A visiting uncle, John Morse, who had arrived the day before, was off with other family members across town on Weybosset Street.

Around nine o'clock in the morning, Andrew left the house to take care of various business matters.

About a half hour later, Mrs. Borden ordered Bridget to clean the windows and went upstairs. Mr. Borden returned about 10:45 a.m. Bridget had to unlock the front door to let him in. At 10:55 Bridget went to her room to take a nap, and Mr. Borden did the same in the sitting room.

At 11:10 a.m., Lizzie went into the sitting room where, she said later, she found her father dead, his head bashed in and sliced open by 19 hatchet wounds. Lizzie yelled for Bridget to get the doctor who lived close by. In the next frantic minutes, another friend, Mrs. Churchill, arrived.

Lizzie Borden had an ax... Actually, it was a handleless hatchet believed to be the murder weapon in the 1892 Borden murders (on display at the Fall River Historical Society in Fall River, Massachusetts). (AP Photo/Charles Krupa)

They all wondered where Mrs. Borden was. Lizzie said she had heard her stepmother come in and asked Bridget to go upstairs and find her. Mrs. Churchill went up the front stairs and found Mrs. Borden dead, killed with the same savagery. By noon, the house was filled with police, and the story was well on its way to becoming a national incident.

Suspicion fell on Lizzie right away.

Her statements about where she had been at the time of the murders didn't make complete sense. Was she out back in the barn? In the barn loft? Or upstairs in the house? And what about the curious events of the day before, on August 3rd? Mrs. Borden, who had never been particularly warm with Lizzie, had complained to the doctor of violent nausea and claimed she was being poisoned. (The doctor believed a mutton roast, which had been left unrefrigerated for days, was the likely cause.)

Yet why had Lizzie tried to buy prussic acid, a poison, from the drugstore? And what about the hatchet with the broken handle found in a bed of ashes? And was Lizzie really seen on the following Sunday burning a piece of clothing? It was a dress, she said, a paint-stained dress.

A coroner's inquest was held on the next Monday and Tuesday. Lizzie testified, and when it was over, they charged her with the murder of her father. The case went to a grand jury in November.

It ended with Lizzie being charged, curiously, with three counts, one for killing her father, one for her stepmother, and one for both.

The trial began in June 1893, almost a year later. By then, everyone who could read a newspaper or magazine was following the case, and everyone had an opinion, mostly divided by gender. Women tended to see Lizzie as innocent, while men thought she did it. The jury, of course, was all-white, all-male. So was Lizzie's "dream team" defense. It was led by Andrew Jennings, another of Fall River's most prominent men. He had represented Lizzie's father. Along with him came a younger lawyer, Melvin Adams. They thought they needed a third, so they brought in another veteran, George Robinson. Robinson, as it happened, had appointed Justice Justin Dewey to the bench. Dewey was presiding over Lizzie's trial.

Early on, the defense won two key points. They kept Lizzie's unhelpful inquest testimony from being introduced as evidence on the grounds she had not been officially charged when it was given. Second, they objected to the whole matter of her attempting to buy poison as irrelevant, and the judge agreed.

Finally, just before the trial was to begin, when interest in the case was at its peak, they caught an incredible break. Amazingly, there was a third ax murder in Falls River! Portuguese immigrant Jose Corriera killed Bertha Manchester. It didn't matter that Jose hadn't even been in the country when Mr. and Mrs. Borden were killed; a third horrific murder added yet another element of doubt. It took the jury all of 68 minutes to find Lizzie not guilty.

After the trial Lizzie and her sister Emma moved into a much nicer house and lived together until they had a falling out in 1904, possibly over Lizzie's involvement with a young actress. Emma eventually moved to New Hampshire. Both she and Lizzie died in 1927 and left their estates to charity. Bridget Sullivan returned to her native Ireland, but soon returned to the United States. She married and moved to Butte, Montana. She died in 1948 with none of the trappings of wealth.

So what really happened? No one will ever be able to say with certainty, though countless theories have been presented, most of them blaming the three young women involved. Perhaps a better question is: why does Lizzie Borden remain so controversial and intriguing more than a century after the murders?

The crime has the combination of bloody brutality and a mundane, familiar setting that people always find irresistible. It is also filled with the most deliciously grotesque details, including the fact that the first autopsy of Mr. and Mrs. Borden was done on their dining room table. Then the funeral was interrupted when the authorities realized they needed their heads for further examination. The skulls were displayed at the trial. Lizzie fainted when she saw them.

Finally, it's still difficult to believe this well-bred young woman could have behaved in such a normal unassuming manner for 32 years, indulged in one ultraviolent episode, and lived another 35 uneventful years. It doesn't add up.

Which is why the story has been translated into every conceivable form of entertainment from the 1970 made-for-television movie *The Legend of Lizzie Borden* with Elizabeth Montgomery in the title role, to an Agnes DeMille ballet. In his novel, *Lizzie,* Evan Hunter (aka Ed McBain) theorized a sexual encounter witnessed by Mrs. Borden precipitated the killings.

Rick Geary's superb graphic novel, *The Borden Tragedy,* coolly presents the most pertinent facts and unanswered questions, and leaves conclusions to the reader. A century's worth of more speculative nonfiction books would fill several shelves. Everyone connected with the family has been accused, and the various imaginative scenarios range far afield. Lizzie herself and the murders remain as enigmatic as ever.

Boston Strangler

Albert DeSalvo

It's difficult to say exactly how deeply Albert DeSalvo was involved in the Boston Strangler murders.

"Come in." He did. Thirteen times.

20th Century-Fox presents

THE BOSTON STRANGLER X

Panavision® Colour by De Luxe   The people and events depicted are based on fact!

TONY CURTIS · HENRY FONDA · GEORGE KENNEDY

Mike Kellin   Murray Hamilton   Robert Fryer · Richard Fleischer · Edward Anhalt · Gerold Frank

Hollywood's version of *The Boston Strangler*, starring Tony Curtis, 1968. (Kobal)

He confessed to all of them, along with two more. Details suggest two different killers might well have been at work, and that's what forensics experts believed at the time. Between June 1962 and January 1964 eleven women were killed in and around Boston. They lived in the apartments where they were murdered and there was no evidence of forced entry, suggesting they knew their killer or willingly let him in. The murders took place in daylight. The women were bound, strangled, and some were sexually assaulted. Some bodies were placed in graphically sexual positions. Six were 55 to 75 years old; five were 19 to 23 years of age.

Two other women may have been victims of the same killer or killers. They were 69 and 85 years old. One of the younger women was black; the rest

were white. One victim was stabbed repeatedly. The rest were strangled with their own clothing or other belongings.

The murders took place before and after the assassination of John Kennedy and thoroughly panicked the city. A task force was formed to lead the investigation; it was headed by Massachusetts Attorney General Edward Brooke.

DeSalvo came from an abusive family. His father had been arrested twice for beating his mother and the kids weren't spared, either. While in the Army in Germany, DeSalvo married. Back home in America, his wife had to put up with demands for sex several times a day. In 1955 DeSalvo was charged with molesting a nine-year-old girl but the mother decided not to press charges. Afterwards, he worked a series of jobs and supplemented his income with breaking and entering and burglary. He was busted twice but got off with suspended sentences.

At the same time, he was living out his sexual fantasies as the "Measuring Man." DeSalvo developed a smooth pitch, approaching women at their homes and telling them they had been recommended for a modeling agency he represented. It was all going to be above board, he said, nothing suggestive and the pay was $40 an hour. All he needed to do was to take down their measurements and someone from the agency would be in touch. He got off on the groping that followed. Some women complained to the police and when DeSalvo was caught breaking into a house in March 1960 he confessed to being the "Measuring Man" as well. He was sentenced to 18 months but they released him in under a year. When he got out, his wife would have nothing to do with him, and DeSalvo's predatory sexual activities escalated.

His next incarnation was the "Green Man" for the color of the work clothes he wore. He committed crimes throughout New England, breaking into houses and tying up the women he found. His proclivities ranged from fondling to rape. It is impossible to know exactly what he did or how many women he attacked, because he later lied and exaggerated everything he said to the police.

The Strangler's murders began two months after DeSalvo's release on the Measuring Man charges. In October 1964 a Green Man victim gave police such a good description of her assailant that the artist's sketch reminded them of Measuring Man. She identified DeSalvo, and so did other Green Man victims. He was arrested and sent to the Bridgewater State Hospital for psychiatric evaluation.

At Bridgewater, DeSalvo met murderer George Nassar, a brilliant and manipulative con who was being defended by rising legal star F. Lee Bailey. The young lawyer was making a name for himself with successful appeals for **Dr. Sam Sheppard**. This is where the story gets complicated.

After he was charged with rape in the Green Man matter, DeSalvo confessed to the Strangler murders. Some who have gone over his confession claim it contains nothing he could not have learned from the extensive newspaper reports. But why would he have lied?

DeSalvo might have thought that with the high-profile Strangler charges, he could attract equally high-powered counsel in the form of Bailey. DeSalvo already knew he would be incarcerated for the rest of his life, but if he cooperated with authorities on the Strangler murders, he might get to serve his time in a hospital, not a prison. And, he might be able to arrange a book deal to take care of his family financially. That's one theory.

On the other hand, the Strangler's MO was not dissimilar from his other crimes, and DeSalvo might have been telling the truth, at least about some of the murders. The fact remains, though, that there was no physical evidence linking him to the killings; DNA tests performed on one of the victims in 2001 still were not conclusive.

DeSalvo did not get the hospital confinement he wanted, but was sent to Walpole State Prison where he was stabbed to death by unknown parties in 1973.

The 1968 film, *The Boston Strangler,* is based on DeSalvo's confessions but takes many liberties with the facts. The killings also provided the inspiration for William Goldman's *No Way to Treat a Lady* and, loosely, for the 1964 thriller, *The Strangler*. William Landay's dense crime novel, *The Strangler,* uses the case to examine larger issues of police work and family in Boston.

One of the best books on the subject is Sebastian Junger's 2006 *A Death in Belmont*. When Junger was a baby, DeSalvo worked with a builder who constructed a studio for Junger's mother, who taught art classes. One morning DeSalvo acted in an odd, somewhat threatening way toward her, though she never mentioned it to anyone, and on another day, he made a creepy, discomforting advance to one of her students.

Christian Brando, son of screen legend Marlon Brando, consults with attorney Robert Shapiro (of O.J. fame) in Los Angeles, July 1990. (AP Photo)

Some weeks later an older woman, Bessie Goldberg, was murdered in a nearby neighborhood. Though the MO fit the Strangler's, a man named Roy Smith was arrested for the crime. Smith was a black man who had been in trouble with the law for minor stuff, and he had spent part of the afternoon working in the Goldberg home. Despite his denials, Smith was convicted. Later, after DeSalvo confessed to the other killings, he was questioned about Mrs. Goldberg, but denied having anything to do with it.

Junger examines evidence and makes a strong case for Smith's innocence. Throughout his version of the story, though, he understands how complicated it was and avoids sweeping certainties.

Brando, Christian

The killing of Dag Drollet is a simple sad story, remarkable only for the celebrity of the supporting cast of characters.

Christian Brando was the first child of star Marlon Brando and his first wife, actress Anna Kashfi. Their relationship, like so many in Hollywood, was passionate and short. The marriage ended angrily in 1959, a year after Christian was born. He grew up shuttling between his mother, whose career floundered as she sank into drug and alcohol abuse, and his father, whose career flourished so spectacularly that he bought an entire island in the South Pacific.

Brando finally won sole custody when his son was 13 years old.

Brando's fifth child, Cheyenne, Christian's half-sister, was 11 years younger. Raised primarily in Tahiti, she was a beautiful, unstable young woman whose emotional problems were exacerbated by a terrible automobile accident when she was a teenager. Even before the single-car crash, she had had problems with alcohol, drugs, and depression. Afterwards, as she was recovering, she became pregnant by her longtime live-in boyfriend, Dag Drollet.

The son of an influential Tahitian family, Drollet was devoted to Cheyenne though their relationship was understandably shaky and he had considered ending it. Still, he accompanied her when she moved to Los Angeles, where her father thought she and the baby would receive better medical care. They moved into his compound high atop Mulholland Drive where her half-brother Christian was a frequent visitor.

Christian's demons included basic drugs and alcohol with the dangerous addition of firearms. He was something of a gun nut, a gun nut devoted to his little sister. On the night of May 16, 1990 Christian and Cheyenne went out to dinner at a trendy L.A. beanery while Brando and Dag Drollet stayed in. Over the meal, Cheyenne told increasingly vivid and fanciful tales of Dag's terrible behavior toward her. These were almost certainly schizophrenic fantasies, but to Christian, who was drunk and getting drunker, the stories were evidence of abuse.

The siblings got back to the compound around 11:00 p.m. Christian grabbed a .45 revolver, found Dag, and shot him in the back of the head. He died instantly. Later, Christian would say he only meant to scare him, that they fought over the gun—all the usual excuses.

The cops took Christian into custody that night. Some weeks later, Brando had Cheyenne taken to Tahiti and placed in a hospital where she could not be subpoenaed to testify.

Lawyers were able to get Christian's initial confession thrown out on a technicality and eventually plea-bargained the charge down to voluntary manslaughter. He served six years. After his release, he became involved with Bonny Lee Bakley. She tried to persuade Christian he was the father of the child she had conceived with actor **Robert Blake.**

Cheyenne gave birth to a son in Tahiti and soon attempted suicide with sleeping pills. She tried other methods, too, and was finally successful, hanging herself in 1995.

Bremer, Arthur

As the would-be assassin of a fringe presidential candidate, Arthur Bremer is not particularly important politically. He was a self-described "little fat noise." But that has not stopped the conspiracy theorists.

Bremer was the archetypal misfit loner. He had worked as a busboy and janitor until his irrational behavior got him sacked. He then decided to impress everybody by doing something big. He went out and bought a pistol. When he was caught carrying it in Milwaukee in 1971, the cops confiscated it. He went out and bought two more.

After a brief failed relationship with a 15-year-old girl, the 21-year-old loser settled on President Richard Nixon as his target. When Nixon proved too difficult to approach, he shifted his focus to George Wallace, the Alabama governor who was seeking the Democratic presidential nomination.

Bremer followed him at campaign stops beginning in Michigan. On May 15, 1972 after a speech in a shopping center parking lot in Laurel, Maryland, Wallace stepped from behind his bulletproof protection to press the flesh with his supporters. Bremer called out to him, and when the candidate approached, he opened fire. Wallace was hit four times and paralyzed from the waist down. Three others were wounded.

Bremer was sentenced to 63 years. He served them in the Maryland Correctional Institute where he declined to participate in any mental health programs or treatment, but in other respects has been a model prisoner. He was released in late 2007.

Though his pathetic story has never been filmed, Bremer became a significant cultural influence, albeit second hand. His memoirs, published as *An Assassin's Diary*, were a partial basis for Paul Schrader's character Travis Bickle in *Taxi Driver*. And *Taxi Driver* provided an early role for Jodie Foster. Her character, Iris, had such a profound effect on **John Hinckley Jr.** that he attempted to kill Ronald Reagan in the belief it would impress the actress.

Buchalter, Louis "Lepke"

If **Charlie "Lucky" Luciano** was the most famous of the early gangsters, Louis Buchalter was equally powerful and perhaps as wealthy with a vast criminal empire under his control.

The nickname "Lepke" was given to Louis by his mother, from the Yiddish diminutive "Lepkeleh," meaning "Little Louis." Buchalter was a short (five-feet, seven inches), slight man, but he was also a cold-blooded sadist who enjoyed inflicting pain.

In the early 1920s Lepke was a protégé of New York gambler **Arnold Rothstein.** Lepke's first break came with unions. Using murder and intimidation, he and his men placed themselves in key positions in the garment industry, particularly the cutter's union, which controlled the manufacture of men's suits and had been run by Lepke's boss "Little Augie" Ogden. In 1926 Lepke machinegunned him in the back seat of a cab and took over the operation. He expanded it, adding the much larger Amalgamated Clothing Workers Union, truckers unions (which had nothing to do with the Teamsters in those days), and the motion picture projectors union.

In the early 1930s Lepke aligned himself with Luciano because Charlie Lucky, unlike the older Italian gangsters, wasn't a raging anti-Semite. Luciano had been working with **Meyer Lansky** and **Ben "Bugsy" Siegel** since they were boys and was happy to deal with anyone interested in making money. When Luciano took control in 1931, following the murders of his bosses **Joe Masseria** and **Salvatore**

Maranzano, Lepke was invited to join in the Syndicate or Commission the hoodlums had organized.

The goal was to establish boundaries so no one poached on anyone else's territories. As part of the deal, Lepke and the equally vicious **Albert "Lord High Executioner" Anastasia** were given control of **Murder, Inc.,** the group of hitmen who maintained the uneasy cooperation among the greedy and notoriously impolite thugs.

His many enterprises thrived, and Lepke became fantastically wealthy. He lived large with a luxurious midtown Manhattan apartment, chauffeur-driven limos, bespoke suits, winter vacations in Florida and Hot Springs, Arkansas—perhaps the wildest, most open city in America at the time.

The elevated public profile brought Lepke to the attention of hard-charging crime buster Thomas Dewey. The district attorney went after Lepke on the union extortion angle. At the same time, federal prosecutors were trying to bust him on an antitrust restraint of trade rap. They made the restraint of trade rap stick in 1933, but Lepke served only two weeks in jail before a friendly judge reversed his conviction.

By 1937 the heat was hotter than ever. With new racketeering charges and a massive narcotics investigation underway, the high-rolling Lepke decided it was time to take a powder. For two years, he vanished.

Anastasia squirreled him away in a series of "safe" Brooklyn apartments while Dewey put a $25,000 dead-or-alive price on his head. The DA said he had enough evidence to put Little Lewis away for 500 years. Not to be outdone, the FBI kicked in an extra $5,000 to the reward.

At the same time, one of Murder, Inc.'s top men, Abe "Kid Twist" Reles, was singing like a soloist in the Vienna Boys Choir to another New York DA. Still in hiding, Lepke started ordering hits on anyone who could connect him with his most serious crimes.

It all got to be too much for the other bosses. They argued that either Lepke should turn himself in or they would kill him. The only dissenting voice was Anastasia's. The mobsters took the problem to Luciano, who was running the show from a prison cell in those years, and Charlie Lucky arranged a compromise.

What if Lepke turned himself in to the FBI? The worst federal charges would get him only a couple of years. Luciano assured the reluctant Lepke that the fix was in, and the feds wouldn't turn him over to Dewey. Lepke and the even more reluctant Anastasia finally agreed.

The mob guys got in touch with columnist and radio star Walter Winchell. He was tight with **J. Edgar Hoover.** On August 24, 1939 Anastasia and Lepke drove across the Brooklyn Bridge to Fifth Avenue and 28th Street in Manhattan where they pulled up next to a parked car. Winchell was behind the wheel. Hoover was waiting in the backseat to make the collar personally. Lepke got in, sat next to him, and they discussed the terms of the deal.

By the time Lepke realized there was no deal—they planned to bust him on the drug rap and then turn him over to Dewey—it was too late. The car was surrounded by FBI agents.

Lepke got 14 years on the narcotics charge, 30-to-life on the state racketeering, and the New York boys weren't close to being finished with him.

Even though Abe Reles was killed while in "protective" custody, he and two other informants fingered Lepke, Mendy Weiss, and Louis Capone (no relation to Al) for the 1936 murder of ex-trucker Joseph Rosen. Lepke had put the man out of business and when he complained, they hit him.

Lepke, Capone, and Weiss were convicted of murder. All three were sent to Sing Sing where they went to the chair on March 4, 1944. Lepke has the dubious distinction of being the only high-level mobster ever to be executed.

Only one film has been made about Buchalter, the hard-to-find *Lepke* (1975) with Tony Curtis. Lepke is one of the main characters in *Murder, Inc.* (1961) and had a recurring, supporting role on the original *Untouchables* television series in the 1950s and '60s.

Bundy, Ted

Why, so many years after his execution, does Ted Bundy still fascinate us? He was neither the most brutal nor the most prolific serial killer. He was, perhaps, the most charismatic, attractive, manipulative, and sly. His affable smile was a perfect mask of white middle-class normality hiding a sadistic sexual predator.

He was also the subject of one of the finest true crime books, **Ann Rule**'s *Stranger Beside Me*. Theories about the source of his murderous depravity abound. The facts, as they're known, are pretty straightforward.

Bundy was the product of a brief 1946 union between Louise Cowell and some guy (which is about as definitive as anyone can be on this fact.) Bundy spent his early years in Philadelphia where he was raised by his grandfather, a fierce racist and sadist. Bundy was told the man was his father and that his mother was his sister. (He didn't learn the truth until he was 22.) Signs that something was wrong with little Ted appeared as early as age three, when a teenaged aunt awoke to find the weird smiling boy standing by her bed, placing butcher knives underneath the blankets.

In 1951 Louise and Ted moved to Tacoma, Washington where she married John Culpepper Bundy. Though Ted took the man's name, he never got along with his stepfather. He seldom got close to anyone for very long because he was a true psychopath. He could appear to be completely engaged and sympathetic to others while he really felt no emotion, no connection of any sort.

He did well academically in high school and college and participated in organized activities. Politically, he was a conservative, and was even named "Mr. Up and Coming Republican" by the Washington state GOP. At the same time, though, he was engaged in shoplifting and theft, both large and petty, breaking into homes to take things he wanted.

The same dark side was much more violent and dangerous when women were concerned. In the early 1970s Bundy met and apparently fell in love with a bright, pretty, wealthy young woman from California. She was not as taken with him and broke off the relationship. Later, Bundy wooed her again, but when she responded, he abruptly cut off all contact. Later, some would say she provided the model for his victims—attractive, white, long straight hair. As a predator, though, Bundy was voracious.

Though he may have begun killing earlier, his first victim was probably 18-year-old Joni Lenz. On January 4, 1974 he crept quietly into her bedroom where he beat and sexually assaulted her with uncontrolled savagery. She lived but suffered horrible permanent damage. Less than a month later, he abducted Lynda Ann Healy from her room. (Her decapitated, dismembered body was found a year later.) When not attacking sleeping women, he used a fake plaster cast on his arm or leg and asked sympathetic young women to help him with something, often involving his VW Bug.

At other times, he impersonated a law enforcement officer. In 1974 he killed more than ten women in Washington, Utah, and Colorado. During those same months, he was working at a Seattle suicide crisis center where he shared a shift with fledgling writer Ann Rule.

It's impossible to say exactly how many women he stalked and killed, or what he did to them before and after death. Dozens have come forth with stories about the young man with the cast and the VW Bug who almost kidnapped or attacked them. We do know that on July 14, 1974 Bundy killed two women in full daylight at the crowded Lake Sammamish State Park.

Then on November 8th, in Murray, Utah, he attempted to abduct Carol DaRonch from a bookstore. She fought her way free, but not before he had tried to handcuff her, and threatened her with a pistol and crowbar. More importantly, she was with him for several minutes and knew exactly what he looked like. That same night, he found another victim, and in the following month, he continued to kill.

Ted Bundy, seeming to enjoy jury selection in a Miami courtroom, 1979. (AP Photo)

Police in the various jurisdictions came to realize they were dealing with a suspect who drove a light brownish VW and had been referred to as "Ted."

On August 16, 1975 Salt Lake County police sergeant Bob Hayward spotted a light colored VW. He knew it didn't belong to anyone in the neighborhood. When he approached, the Bug took off. He gave chase and when he stopped the suspect, he found the passenger seat had been removed. Inside were handcuffs, an ice pick, crowbar, and ski mask.

Bundy was arrested and later picked out of a lineup by Carol DaRonch. He was convicted of aggravated abduction, and evidence was piling up in the other killings and disappearances. In April 1977 he was transferred to the Garfield County Jail in Colorado to be tried for a murder there. He chose to act as his own attorney and was given access to

Aspen's courthouse law library to work on his case. He escaped by jumping from a second story window. He was caught trying to get out of town in a stolen car, and brought back.

At the end of December, Bundy escaped again. He made his way out of the Garfield County Jail by crawling up into the ceiling and out through a jailer's apartment. After stealing a car, he made it as far as Chicago and then, under the name Chris Hagen, to the campus of Florida State University in Tallahassee.

He lived on stolen goods and credit cards. On the night of January 14, 1978 Bundy reverted to his original MO. He crept into the Chi Omega sorority house where he beat two women to death in their sleep and seriously wounded two others before attacking a fifth woman in a nearby apartment. A few weeks later, he abducted and murdered a 12-year-old girl. Days later, while driving a stolen VW, Bundy was approached by a patrolman. Again he tried to run, and again he was caught. Finally, he was caught for good.

Throughout the trials that followed, Bundy maintained his complete innocence. Strong eyewitness testimony, fiber and blood evidence, and bite marks from the Chi Omega murders matching his teeth convicted him.

During the extended appeals process, Bundy became famous. The 1980 publication of Rule's *Stranger Beside Me* certainly played a part in his celebrity, but Bundy continued to find ways to surprise. While questioning friendly witness Carole Ann Boone at a 1980 trial, Bundy exchanged vows with her. Since a promise made while under oath is considered legally binding in Florida, they were married in the eyes of the state. (They had a child, a girl, but Boone divorced him and changed her name.)

Bundy managed to keep the wheels of justice turning until 1989. During those prison years, he became a pen pal to **John Hinckley Jr.**, would-be assassin of Ronald Reagan, and **David Berkowitz**, New York's "Son of Sam."

Bundy went to the chair on January 24, 1989. A few weeks later, the supermarket tabloid *Weekly*

World News published a post-autopsy photo of Ted with the top of his skull stitched back on after his brain had been removed.

One miniseries, *The Deliberate Stranger* (1986), and two films, *The Stranger Beside Me* (2003) and *Ted Bundy* (2002), have told the story of his murders with a fair degree of accuracy. Thomas Harris appropriated several of Bundy's tactics and experiences in his Hannibal Lecter novels.

Buntline, Ned

(Edward Zane Carroll Judson)

Ned Buntline was a scoundrel. As such, he was the right man to propagate the tall tales and outright lies that make the Old West so popular.

He was born Edward Zane Carroll Judson in New York, 1823. As a youth, he joined the Navy and traveled a good bit. He never really gave up his wanderlust.

After he left the Navy, he became a writer. To avoid confusion with his father, also a writer, he took the nom de plume Ned Buntline. (A buntline is used to tie a square sail.) Finding it difficult to persuade publishers to print his autobiographical yarns, he founded several short-lived magazines and newspapers to bring his work to the public. Moving frequently, he championed an assortment of causes—temperance (even though he had a well-developed taste for the grape) spiritualism, nativism, etc. He was a proud founder of the Know-Nothing political party and was instrumental in fomenting the 1849 Astor Place riot.

The riot was a ridiculous affair, begun after an English actor was cast in a New York City production of *Macbeth*. As is so often the case in the Big Apple, it all had to do with complicated local politics. When it was over, 23 people were dead and more than 120 were injured in mob violence. Buntline was fined $250 and got a year in the pen for his part. In another nasty bit of business, he killed a lover's husband and barely escaped being shot himself by the man's brother.

Throughout, Buntline continued to write fiction, mostly shilling shockers and dime novels. He loved to dress the part of the writer/adventurer with elaborate "frontier" outfits, hats and medals. He was particularly fond of medals, sometimes festooning his chest with 20 or more. Always on the lookout for new material, he headed west with the opening of the transcontinental railroad. After his arrival in the West, he met a cavalry scout named William Cody. The two hit it off and Buntline gave his new friend a nickname and a starring role in his new dime novel, *Buffalo Bill—King of the Border Men.*

The book was a hit. To capitalize on its resounding success, Buntline came up with the idea of a Wild West play. Cody reluctantly agreed to star, and Buntline dashed off *Scouts of the Plains.* It debuted in Chicago in 1872 and was a sensation, both there and on the road. A year later, Cody went off on his own with Buffalo Bill's Wild West Show.

Buntline continued to crank out hundreds of widely read bad books, making heroes of most of the now-famous Western characters, including **Wyatt Earp**. There is, however, no strong evidence to prove the writer actually invented or designed the Buntline Special pistol—a Colt .45 revolver with a 12-inch barrel, removable shoulder stock, and the name "Ned" carved into the handle. According to the story, Buntline had five of the pistols manufactured by Colt and presented them to Earp and four other lawmen.

The weapons have featured prominently in several books and films and the 1950s television series starring Hugh O'Brian. If they ever existed, none are known to have survived.

Buntline himself has been portrayed on film by Dick Elliott in *Annie Oakley* (1935), Thomas Mitchell in William Wellman's *Buffalo Bill* (1944) and by Burt Lancaster in Robert Altman's *Buffalo Bill and the Indians,* or *Sitting Bull's History Lesson* (1976).

Burke, David

Among American mass murderers (subset "disgruntled workers") David Burke was something of a

> *On the way out, Thompson's secretary absently told Burke to have a nice day. He stopped and said deliberately, "I intend on having a very nice day."*

rarity for two reasons: first, he was black in a field dominated by white men; and second, though he used a revolver, his primary weapon was an airplane.

Burke, an employee of USAir, got into trouble when he was caught dipping into the flight attendants' beer fund to the tune of $68. For that trifle, he was placed on unpaid leave. At a hearing on the case, Burke admitted his guilt and asked for mercy. He didn't get it. His supervisor, Raymond Thompson, dismissed him on the spot. On the way out, Thompson's secretary absently told Burke to have a nice day. He stopped and said deliberately, "I intend on having a very nice day."

Burke went home and wrote a goodbye note to his friends. He also picked up his .44 Magnum pistol, "the most powerful handgun in the world," as Dirty Harry Callahan so memorably put it.

Burke bought a ticket on Pacific Southwest Airline's flight 1771, the nonstop shuttle between Los Angeles and San Francisco, the same shuttle Thompson took every day. Since Burke's employee badge had not been confiscated after the hearing, he was able to skip security and board the airplane with his weapon. What happened afterwards has been reconstructed through recovered evidence, ground witnesses, and the cockpit voice recorder.

After being seated, Burke scribbled a note on an air sickness bag: "It's kind of ironical, isn't it? I asked for leniency for my family, remember? Well, I got none, and now you'll get none."

As the plane leveled off at 29,000 feet, Burke got up from his seat. He may have handed Thompson the note and gone on to the restroom. A few moments later, he shot Thompson. A flight attendant dashed forward and opened the cockpit door. "We have a problem," she said. The captain radioed that he had an emergency and asked "What kind of problem?"

Burke then forced his way into the cockpit and announced, "I'm the problem," before he shot the two pilots. They fell forward and as the plane pitched into a steep dive, Burke shot himself.

Plunging straight down, the airplane broke apart at 13,000 feet when it reached a velocity of Mach 1.2 and the flight recorders ceased to function. The wreckage landed on a hillside in rural San Luis Obispo County. Two days later, FBI investigators found a piece of the barrel and trigger of Burke's pistol with a small piece of skin wedged in the broken metal.

Forty-three people died in the crash. In the aftermath, federal laws were passed requiring "immediate seizure of all airline employee credentials" upon firing and subjecting all crew members to security screening.

Burke, Elmer "Trigger"

Elmer "Trigger" Burke was a hot-tempered hitman who adored his work. More specifically, he said there were only two things he loved—machine guns and money.

Elmer grew up in New York's Hell's Kitchen neighborhood, where he was raised by his older brother Charlie, a street thug who showed him the ropes. Predictably, young Elmer got into trouble with the law and wound up enlisting in the army to avoid prison for a grocery store stickup. It was in the service that Elmer first demonstrated his proficiency with a Tommy gun and earned the nickname "Trigger." He distinguished himself at the Anzio invasion by taking out a German machine gun nest by himself. He killed all eight of the Nazis inside and was still pouring on the lead until his lieutenant arrived on the scene and told him to stop firing because they were dead.

"You're goddamned right they are," Trigger answered.

After the war, he continued to ply his chosen trade of armed robbery and branched out into assassination, charging a flat fee of $1,000 per hit, real money in the late 1940s and early 1950s.

Oddly, he missed on his most famous assignment. When mob bosses worried that Joseph "Specs" O'Keefe was about to spill his guts to the feds about his role in the famous 1950 Brink's job in Boston, they gave the contract to Trigger.

On June 10, 1954 the happy hitman tracked his target to the Dorchester neighborhood where he unlimbered his trusty chopper. He chased O'Keefe through the streets, spraying bullets everywhere, and seriously wounded Specs in the chest and arm. Thinking he had killed the man, Trigger calmly disassembled his piece, put it in its case, and sauntered away as cops converged on the source of the gunfire. O'Keefe, still alive, was able to name his attacker.

Burke was arrested the next day and escaped from an ancient jail a few months later. He was recaptured in Charleston, South Carolina and extradited to New York where he was wanted for the murder of bartender Edward "Poochy" Walsh. Ironically, he had popped Poochy in anger when the barkeep objected to the way Burke was kicking a colleague. The Pookster thought fists would have been sufficient. Enraged at his impudence, Burke shot him in the head.

Poochy's murder was the one that sent the Triggerman to the electric chair on January 8, 1958, after his final meal of a big steak and six cigars. Astonishingly, his story has never made the movies. It should.

Burke, Jimmy "the Gent"

Back in the day, the Lufthansa heist was famous for being the biggest stickup in the history of American crime, $6 million, give or take, in cold cash and jewels. Today, it's best known from Martin Scorsese's masterpiece, *Goodfellas*.

Basically, it was a simple inside job.

In 1978 Louis Werner was a cargo agent at Lufthansa Airlines at New York's Kennedy Airport. He knew when large amounts of money were scheduled to move through the facility, from continent to continent. He also had a gambling problem that put him heavily into debt to mob guys. He decided to square his IOUs by telling them what they needed to know—how to knock over his employer.

Jimmy "the Gent" Burke (Robert De Niro on screen) was the perfect guy to put it all together. He specialized in air cargo theft with more than a hundred jobs to his credit. One problem: he was in jail. Sort of.

Actually, he was in a New York halfway house and was free to "work" during the day. His friend Henry Hill (Ray Liotta) brought the job to him and they recruited half a dozen other guys.

Just before 3:00 a.m. on December 11th, they cut through a chain link fence at the airport and disabled an electronic alarm. They overpowered a guard and moved on to the loading dock at Building 261. It took a little more than an hour to go through the high-value vault, where they ran into their first problem.

The guy in charge of transportation had been ordered to get two vans. Instead, he got one, which meant they had to squeeze all six guys and the swag into one vehicle. They may have left half of what they could have taken on the dock.

Once they had made their getaway and moved the loot to another car, they gave the van to Stacks Edwards (Samuel L. Jackson) and told him to dispose of it. But Stacks got high and left the van on the street. A week later, he got whacked in his apartment for that little error in judgment.

The top mob guys then decided they didn't want to play nice with their little friends. The low-level guys got just enough to keep them happy for a time, then they started to disappear.

The cops knew precisely who had pulled off the score, but they couldn't prove squat. Hill had not yet turned informant and everyone was so scared nobody would talk. The FBI finally arrested Werner, who went to jail refusing to name names. The only part of the stolen money ever recovered came from him.

Another reason for the minimal arrests was the lack of cooperation among the seven—count 'em, seven—local and federal law enforcement agencies investigating the heist.

Sometime later, after he had been busted on a separate drug charge, Henry Hill ratted out his remaining pals. His testimony helped nail Burke on a murder charge for Angelo John Sepe, one the Lufthansa guys. Burke died in prison in 1996.

Henry Hill's story became the basis for Nicholas Pileggi's book *Wiseguy*, and Scorsese's adaptation, *Goodfellas*. For a better understanding of the differences between fact and film, listen to one of the commentary tracks on the special edition DVD.

The real Henry Hill and Edward MacDonald, the FBI agent who brought him in, provide an enlightening and comfortably chummy perspective on an important film. The story of their relationship after Hill's defection is continued in the misfire comedy *My Blue Heaven* (1990) where a variation on Hill is portrayed by Steve Martin and Rick Moranis takes the MacDonald role.

The story of the Lufthansa heist is also told in the rarely seen 1991 made-for-television film *The $10 Million Getaway*.

Burns, Robert Elliott

I Am a Fugitive from a Chain Gang is one of the most famous of the "serious" Warner Bros. crime films. Lurid and violent (for its time) with a wonderfully melodramatic fatalism, it paved the way for the films noir that would follow decades later.

The film is based on the eventful life of Robert Elliott Burns. In 1922 he was an unemployed

World War I vet. With two other guys, he stole $5 and change from a grocery store. For that, the great state of Georgia sentenced him to six-to-ten years of hard labor on a chain gang. After a few weeks, he persuaded a fellow inmate to smash his shackles with a sledge hammer and bend them enough to slip off his feet. He then escaped and headed north.

Burns started a new life in Chicago and made a go of it, becoming a successful magazine editor. Things would have been fine, but his estranged first wife learned where he was and ratted him out to the Georgia law.

Promised a pardon, Burns went back to Georgia voluntarily, only to be locked up again and sent back to the chain gang. This time, his brother Vincent made his case a national issue. Vincent, a minister, managed to arrange a hearing with the Georgia governor. But, having been fooled once, Burns took matters into his own hands.

Miraculously (well, perhaps not so miraculously; he had help from a friendly farmer), Burns escaped again and went north again, this time to New Jersey where his brother and widowed mother lived. There he wrote a series of magazine stories about his experiences in the South. Those were collected into a book, *I Am a Fugitive From a Georgia Chain Gang!* and formed the basis for the 1932 Paul Muni film, which omitted the state name and exclamation point from the title. Its depictions of the brutal conditions of the prison system actually caused some states to make changes.

Burns' problems, however, were not over.

Georgia officials were embarrassed and angry about the film. When they learned Burns was living in West Orange under an assumed name, they demanded New Jersey extradite him. Governor A. Harry Moore said no. He called a special hearing at the state capitol in Trenton where Burns was represented by **Clarence Darrow.** Typically, Darrow used the occasion to call attention to the inhuman, overcrowded conditions in Georgia prisons. Several other governors backed up Moore in his refusal to give up Burns.

Even so, the Georgia people weren't finished: they sent a telegram to the West Orange police chief requesting he arrest the escapee. The chief tore it up.

In 1941 a new Georgia governor made yet another attempt to coax Burns back by claiming conditions were much improved. Prison reformers disagreed loudly and Burns stayed put. Finally, in 1945, Governor Ellis Arnall abolished chain gangs in Georgia and commuted Burns' sentence.

The book and film of Burns' experiences may not be well remembered today, but they were touchstones of the 1930s, works that touched large appreciative audiences, and brought real changes to the legal system. The story was retold as a television movie in 1987, *The Man Who Broke 1,000 Chains* with Val Kilmer in the title role.

Burns' story was more fully fictionalized in the seminal 1960s film *Cool Hand Luke,* where Paul Newman's "failure to communicate" created a memorable hero for another generation.

Capone, Alphonse

Al "Scarface" Capone was the complete gangster—ruthless, brutally violent when necessary, but also well-organized, personable, and focused on profits. In the 1920s and early '30s, he became the personification of organized crime, profiled in the *New Yorker,* his mug even on the cover of *Time* magazine.

Though he will forever be associated with Chicago, Capone was born and raised in New York. He came to the Windy City at the urging of his mentor and friend Johnny Torrio. The silky smooth Torrio had moved to Chicago years before to work for Big Jim Colosimo, one of the city's most powerful whoremasters. In 1920, when Prohibition went into effect, Torrio realized an enormously rich market was about to open and urged Colosimo to seize the moment. Big Jim said no, he was happy with what he was doing. Torrio had him shot and brought in Capone as his partner.

In the wild days of his youth, Capone had worked as a bouncer in the Harvard Club brothel where he got his nickname of Scarface, and contracted the syphilis that would eventually kill him. By 1920, though, he had put that life behind him; he had married, had a son, and was working in legitimate business. But when Torrio called, Al said yes and set off on a different path.

The first thing Al and Torrio had to do was to reach some kind of accord with the city's other major bootleggers, Dion O'Banion, the two O'Donnell gangs, the Genna brothers, and others. They all met, divided up the city and suburbs, and set about making money with beer, liquor, prostitutes, and gambling. All was right with the world for three years. Then William "Decent" Dever, a reform Democrat, was elected mayor and started cleaning things up.

Torrio and Capone promptly decamped to nearby Cicero and set up shop there. At the same time, hostilities erupted among the other gangs. In May 1924 O'Banion told Torrio he was retiring and offered to sell Torrio the Sieben Brewery. Torrio agreed, but there was a catch—O'Banion knew the place was about to be raided. It was and Torrio was caught red-handed. A few months later, he and Capone sent two torpedos—John Scalise and Albert Anselmi—to O'Banion's flower shop. They put six slugs into the Irishman.

Ten thousand people showed up for the funeral, and O'Banion's friend Hymie Weiss (a Catholic despite the name) vowed vengeance. Three months

**Al Capone, enjoying Chicago football in 1931.
(AP Photo)**

later, Weiss and two henchmen attacked Torrio with shotguns, seriously wounding him. That was enough for Johnny. He and his wife retired to Italy, leaving the field open for Capone.

Before Big Al could retaliate, Weiss struck again. One morning he led a ten-car convoy into Cicero. He drove past Capone's headquarters, the Hawthorn Hotel. They sprayed the building with machinegun fire, shattering every window in the place but hitting none of the hundred or so of Al's men who were inside. Weiss and company went home to dust off their marksmanship medals and Al got serious. Weiss was gunned down outside O'Banion's flower shop.

As boss of Chicago, Capone was as visible and gregarious as Torrio had been discreet. He loved seeing himself in the papers and always had a snappy

line for reporters ("You can get more with a kind word and a gun than with a kind word alone."). The last of Al's major enemies was Weiss' partner Bugs Moran, and the **St. Valentine's Day Massacre** was arranged to take care of him. Moran was late and survived the massacre, but in the uproar that followed, Capone's enemies redoubled their efforts. They bribed three of his closest associates—Giuseppe "Hop Toad" Giunta, Scalise, and Anselmi—to betray their boss, which led to the most notorious moment in Capone's career.

Capone threw a big dinner for his crew in a private dining room at the Hawthorn. At the end of the evening when they were all stuffed and satiated, Capone's bodyguards grabbed the three men and wired them to the arms of their chairs. Capone pulled out a baseball bat, strode up behind the traitors, and personally beat each of them to death as an object lesson to everyone else.

Soon after, Capone was whipsawed by two federal investigations. G-man Eliot Ness and his "Untouchables" attacked Al's bootlegging operations, while Elmer Irey of the IRS went after him for unpaid income taxes. How could he afford a mansion on Palm Island, Florida, the armor-plated limos, etc.?

In the end, it was the taxes that got Capone. Big Al tried to cut a deal with the feds, even tried to bribe the jury, both to no avail. He was fined $80,000 and sentenced to 11 years, served in Atlanta, Leavenworth, and Alcatraz.

When he was paroled eight years later, Capone was a broken man. He went back to his family in Florida and lived the rest of his days as an invalid. The syphilis became paresis. He died in 1947 at the age of 48.

Not surprisingly, Capone has been a perennial favorite for Hollywood. He figured in many low-budget gangster flicks and attracted some of the best actors—Rod Steiger (*Al Capone,* 1959), Ben Gazarra (*Capone,* 1975), and Jason Robards (*St. Valentine's Day Massacre,* 1967). His most famous

Capone mug shot. (AP Photo)

incarnation came in 1987's *The Untouchables,* where writer David Mamet, director Brian DePalma, and star Robert De Niro made the most of the ultraviolent, mythic qualities of the character.

Capone was more fully fictionalized in Howard Hawks' 1932 *Scarface,* while in 1959's *Some Like It Hot,* George Raft's character Spats is a thinly disguised Capone.

Cardinella, Salvatore ("Sam the Devil")

Before Al Capone took over, Salvatore (sometimes known as "Samuele") Cardinella was the toughest mug in Chicago.

Cardinella's gang ran a "**Black Hand**" extortion racket. They threatened the wealthy and powerful within the Italian community with violence, then went away once they were paid off. They did pretty well on a local level until the feds got interested because they were using the U.S. mail system. Cardinella and his mob then switched to robbery and other strong-arm tactics.

The obese Salvatore was so sadistic he was known as "Il Diavola" or "Sam the Devil." He and his thugs, equally feared killers, were said to have been responsible for more than 20 murders. In 1921 Cardinella and two of his henchmen were convicted of one of those murders and sentenced to hang. Here's where the story gets really weird.

Cardinella came up with a scheme.

Declaring the Cook County jail's food to be crap, he went on a hunger strike. Authorities in those days being less concerned with public relations than they are now, said, 'fine, you don't want to eat, don't eat.'

By the time he had his date with the gallows, Sam the Devil had shed some 40 pounds. On that very day, Chicago police lieutenant John Norton got an anonymous phone call saying Cardinella's guys had a plan to revive him. Norton gathered a group of cops and headed out to the jail. At the rear entrance, they found a hearse sent to collect the body. Inside the hearse they found a doctor, a nurse, a full complement of stimulants and syringes to inject them, and a rubber mattress filled with hot water.

Inside the Cook County jail, they found that skinny Sam had kept his appointment with the hangman. His body was stretched out on a slab and his family was hurriedly filling out all of the necessary paperwork to take possession of the svelte deceased. Smelling a rat, Norton declared the corpse would not be released for 24 hours.

The Cardinella clan howled in protest but to no avail.

When doctors examined the body, they learned that with his dramatic weight loss, Cardinella's neck had not been broken by the fall. He had been strangled to death and so it wasn't impossible that by quickly warming the body and zapping it with the right drugs, he might have been revived and reborn, as it were. (Think John Travolta and Eric Stoltz giving the chest pop to Uma Thurman in *Pulp Fiction*.)

But it didn't happen. Instead, Cardinella is remembered by the few who know him as the main inspiration for Rico Bandello in the famous 1931 film *Little Caesar*. (No, it wasn't Capone.) Cardinella's death is also mentioned in a couple of Ernest Hemingway's short stories, and his fate may have been something of an inspiration for the various gangsters-cheating-the-executioner B-movies popular from the 1930s to the '50s.

The unfortunate demise of **Thomas "Black Jack" Ketchum**, some 20 years before, is an example of the opposite extreme in gallows mishaps.

Carpenter, Richard

He was a small-time Chicago crook with more persistence than ambition, and it was really just bad luck that made Richard Carpenter so famous, albeit briefly.

Born in 1929, he pulled a few petty robberies until he was arrested in 1951 for stealing $8 from a cabbie. That earned him a year in jail and he came out vowing to keep to the straight and narrow and make his mama proud. For a year, he did just that, but then he ran off the rails.

On December 4, 1953 Carpenter stuck up a grocery store for $100. Carrying two pistols, he robbed bars, mom-and-pop markets, and Laundromats. He usually waited until closing time when the till was full, then calmly demand the cash. He seldom got much money but he stuck to it. Over the next 18 months, he pulled 70 jobs.

Then in August, 1955, Carpenter was recognized on the subway by a policeman named Murphy who nabbed him. When they got off the train, Carpenter pulled a piece and killed the cop. That changed everything.

Three days later, off-duty policeman Clarence Kerr was at the movies with his wife to see *Call Me Lucky*. He recognized Carpenter slouched sleeping in a seat. After telling Mrs. Kerr to leave, he pulled his pistol on the drowsy killer and ordered him out. Carpenter complied, then pretended to stumble in the lobby and again drew his weapon. He shot officer Kerr in the chest and ran, but this time, his aim was off. He barely missed the policeman's heart. Kerr was rushed to the hospital where a surgeon saved his life.

On the run, Carpenter made it to the back door of truck driver Leonard Powell's house. He forced his way into the kitchen as the two Powell children were watching a news report about him on television: the biggest manhunt in Chicago history was under way. Fearing for their children, Mr. and Mrs. Powell told them Carpenter was a friend.

He held the family hostage through the night. All the while, Powell talked to him and pretended to be sympathetic with his predicament. He managed to sell the sincerity so well that the next morning Carpenter allowed the family to go outside for some fresh air. As soon as they were clear, they ran and yelled for their neighbors to stay inside.

Minutes later, Chicago's finest surrounded the Powell house. Carpenter managed to get to the roof and, from there, to jump to another building where he was captured by patrolman Ted Louis Sparrow.

Carpenter was electrocuted in Joliet State Prison on March 16, 1956. He lived long enough to know that his home invasion and hostage-taking were the inspiration for Joseph Hayes' novel and play *The Desperate Hours*. It became a fine William Wyler film with Humphrey Bogart and Frederic March in the Carpenter and Powell roles. It was remade, with considerably less success, in 1990 by Michael Cimino with Mickey Rourke, who actually bore a strong resemblance to Carpenter, and Anthony Hopkins as Powell.

Carter, Rubin "Hurricane"

The truth of Rubin "Hurricane" Carter's guilt or innocence is lost behind countless lies, fictions, pop songs, dramatic inventions, and recantations.

Some believe the 1999 film *Hurricane* tells the emotional truth about a proud man who was unjustly persecuted. Others see the film as a complete whitewash based on a violent conman's self-serving memoirs.

This much is true:

Carter, born in 1937, had a troubled childhood in Paterson, New Jersey. He had a juvenile record and was convicted of assault and robbery when he was 14. He ran away from the reformatory, enlisted in the army, and did poorly there. He was discharged in 1956 as "unfit for military service" and sent back to reform school. A couple of months after his release,

he beat and robbed three people, one a middle-aged woman, and was sent up again for four years.

After his second release in 1961, he turned his attention to boxing. He had a relatively successful middleweight career, and actually fought for the title on December 14, 1964 against Joey Giardello. He lost a unanimous decision. This was his high point; by 1966, he was out of the top ten.

At 2:30 a.m. on the morning of June 17, 1966, two black men walked into the Lafayette Bar and Grill in Paterson. They opened up with a shotgun and a pistol. Bartender Jim Oliver and customer Fred Nauyoks were killed right away. Customer Hazel Tanis was seriously wounded and died a month later. Customer Willie Marins was shot in the eye and blinded, but survived. Patty Valentine, who lived above the bar, provided an identification of the white getaway car.

Within an hour, cops had pulled over Carter's white Dodge and questioned him and his acquaintance John Artis.

Later, two eyewitnesses, Alfred Bello and Arthur Bradley, who had been in the neighborhood that morning to commit a burglary, identified Carter and Artis as the shooters. A grand jury indicted them for murder. The motive: revenge. A black bartender, the stepfather of a friend, had been killed by a white man six hours before. Carter and Artis were convicted by an all-white jury and sentenced to life.

In prison in 1974 Carter wrote the first part of his autobiography, *The Sixteenth Round*. Bob Dylan was inspired to compose his song "Hurricane" a year later. That got the ball rolling and soon Carter became a true *cause célèbre* as the wealthy and famous demonstrated on his behalf for a new trial.

They got their wish in 1976 when the New Jersey Supreme Court overturned the first conviction on a technicality and Carter was released. While he was preparing for his new trial, he was involved in an assault on a woman who had been fundraising for him. His celebrity support dried up and Carter was convicted a second time by a mixed-race jury.

Rubin "Hurricane" Carter on death row at the Trenton State Prison, 1974. (AP Photo)

His remaining supporters were undeterred and continued to press their appeals. In 1985 a federal district court judge ordered a third trial. New Jersey prosecutors appealed all the way to the Supreme Court, but to no avail. In 1988, with the remaining witnesses then dead, they elected not to pursue a third trial. Freed, Carter moved to Toronto, Canada.

In 1999 Denzel Washington received an Oscar nomination for his portrayal of Carter in *Hurricane*. The film, based on the autobiography and *Lazarus and the Hurricane* by Sam Chaiton and Terry Swinton, presents Carter as the completely innocent victim of a conspiracy of racist cops. A foreword admits the filmmakers made up characters and

actions. It essentially ignores the real weaknesses in the state's case and replaces them with conventional Hollywood stereotypes.

Denzel Washington did not win an Academy Award for his work, and many people in the film business suspected the reason, at least in part, was that the film took too many liberties and the Academy of Motion Picture Arts and Sciences did not want to give their highest award and an endorsement to a man who might well be a murderer. (No jury has ever found Carter not guilty.) Ticket buyers were not overwhelmed, either. The film was only moderately successful. Washington would win his Oscar two years later for his work as a charismatic, corrupt—and thoroughly fictional—cop in *Training Day*.

Butch Cassidy and the Sundance Kid (Paul Newman and Robert Redford), Hollywood-style, 1969. (Kobal)

Cassidy, Butch

More than any other figure of the Old West, Butch Cassidy is associated with a single film. It's one of the best and is more accurate than you might guess. When he wrote *Butch Cassidy and the Sundance Kid*, William Goldman built his story around real events, and, as he put it in *Adventures in the Screen Trade*, "the personal story of these two unusual outlaws."

Butch was born Robert LeRoy Parker and, by all accounts, was a good natured, amiable sort who boasted he had never killed anyone, despite a long career on the wrong side of the law. He took the name Cassidy from his mentor Mike Cassidy, a rustler who had showed the young teenager how to steal horses and cows in 1880s Colorado.

Butch had come from a brief stint of honest labor as a butcher, but it didn't last, and he and a few friends turned to bank robbery. In 1894 Butch was caught stealing horses in Wyoming and sentenced to two years in the state prison. One story, possibly apocryphal, holds that right before he was to be sent to prison in Laramie, he told his jailers he needed a night off on his own. He promised he would come back in time for the transfer, and, since he was such a nice guy, they agreed and let him go. Butch was as good as his word; the next morning, there he was.

Eighteen months later, according to a story that is almost certainly true, Governor William Alfred Richards offered Butch a pardon if he swore he would never break the law again. Butch answered he couldn't go that far, but he would promise to never commit any crimes in Wyoming, and that was good enough for the governor.

That's when Butch founded the Wild Bunch, or the Hole in the Wall gang with his friends the Sundance Kid (Harry Longbaugh or Longabaugh), Elza Lay, the real brains of the outfit, and several others.

The gang's MO was to strike at banks, trains, and cattle herds in neighboring states and then return to either Hole in the Wall, Wyoming, or Brown's Hole or Robber's Roost in Utah where they could spot approaching posses.

They were so successful in their endeavors that they pissed off the management of the Union Pacific railroad who hired Pinkertons and other lawmen outfitted in a special train car to chase down the gang. As soon as Butch learned how serious the forces of civilization and commerce had become, he did the only sane thing—he ran.

In 1901 Butch, Sundance, and Sundance's sweetie, Etta Place, who was either a hooker or a school teacher, went to New York where they caught a steamer for South America.

For a time the two prospered as bank robbers in Argentina, but the law stayed on their trail and they took off for Chile. After that, details become uncertain. In 1906 or 1907, Etta returned to the United States for health reasons. Butch and Sundance hired on as armed guards for a tin mine in Bolivia for a short while before they returned to their bank-robbing roots.

The "official" version of their demise has them surrounded by a regiment of the Bolivian army after they had pulled off a payroll job. The two gringos were trapped and gunned down in a fusillade of fire in the little town of San Vincente. Another version has Sundance killed there, while Butch escaped and returned to America where he lived until 1937.

Whatever the truth of the story, the real Butch and Sundance have been replaced as popular culture icons by Paul Newman and Robert Redford. The film they made with Goldman and director George Roy Hill is one of the last great westerns and a superbly crafted piece of entertainment, regardless of genre. Of the 1979 prequel, *Butch and Sundance: The Early Days,* the less said the better.

Redford's portrayal of Sundance made him an international star, and so is directly responsible for his involvement with the Sundance Film Festival and the ski resort in Utah.

Castellano, Paul

"Big Paul" Castellano had a relatively brief tenure as the boss of New York's Gambino crime family.

He went to work for his cousin **Carlo Gambino** in the early 1930s. Castellano's ascension through the ranks wasn't harmed when Carlo married his sister Katherine. When Don Carlo died in 1976, he passed the crown to Castellano, though it probably should have gone to underboss Aniello Dellacroce. To keep the peace, Gambino gave Dellacroce the mob business in Manhattan and ensured his loyalty to Castellano.

The new boss bought a mansion on Staten Island and tried to change the mob's direction. He wanted to get out of the most dangerous and controversial areas, namely narcotics, and do more work with union corruption, inflated construction contracts, and stolen luxury cars. It worked for a time, but Castellano was apparently not well liked by his troops, particularly **John Gotti**.

As a leader, he was distant and aloof, and other factions within the Mafia families were against him. He had also been targeted by the FBI, who had managed to bug his palatial 17-room home. The wiretap led to his arrest, along with several other bosses in 1985. Discontent over his management style deepened.

On December 2nd, Dellacroce died of cancer. Castellano did not go to the funeral, and this was interpreted as blatant disrespect by many of his associates. Then he named Thomas Bilotti as a new underboss. Until then, Bilotti had been his bodyguard, and so his promotion was seen as a second slap in the face. Finally, there were concerns about jail. If convicted on the charges he faced, Big Paul could have been sent up for more than 100 years. The man was 70 years old. Who could say he wouldn't rat out everyone else to save himself?

Despite such widespread discontent, Castellano and Bilotti did not take even the most basic security precautions.

On the evening of December 16th, they drove to a meeting at Sparks Steakhouse in midtown Manhattan. They were unarmed and had no bodyguards. As Bilotti got out from behind the wheel of the limo, three men approached and opened up with semiautomatics. Bilotti and Big Paul were shot repeatedly. Before the killers ran away, one took time to put one more bullet into Castellano's head. Seven years later, Gotti was convicted of ordering Castellano's murder and on several other charges. Sentenced to life, he died in prison.

Castellano got the standard gangland biopic treatment in the TNT production *Boss of Bosses,* based on Joseph O'Brien's book. Chazz Palminteri portrayed him as a sensitive, caring kind of guy who virtually wanted to turn the Mafia into a Montessori school but just couldn't get the kids to play well with each other. Castellano also showed up as a supporting character in *The Big Heist* (2001) and *Witness to the Mob* (1998), and was a villain—surprise, surprise—in *Gotti* (1996).

Chapman, Gerald

If gentleman bandit Gerald Chapman had not existed, F. Scott Fitzgerald might have invented him. He was a perfect crook for the Roaring '20s: a dapper little dude who sported tailored suits, spats, homburg, walking cane, and a fake British accent, he became the first Public Enemy Number One.

Born in 1888, he had been a common crook until he was assigned to a cell in New York's Auburn Prison with Dutch Andersen. Dutch was Danish, from a wealthy family. He also had the polish and the experience young Gerald lacked. The kid became his protégé and learned all that Dutch could teach him about cons, swindles, and embezzlement.

When Gerald was released, he cleaned up his act and waited for Dutch to be paroled. The two of them headed west to Chicago where they worked all of Dutch's con games.

They moved back to New York $100,000 richer, where they rented a ritzy Gramercy Park apartment and thoroughly enjoyed their ill-gotten gains with actresses, floozies, and bootleg booze. They burned through the loot quickly and were on the lookout for another job when their old pal Charles Lorber, from Auburn, showed up. He had a great idea.

Lorber had figured out the routes that mail trucks took at the end of the day from Wall Street to the post office. They carried sacks of registered mail stuffed with cash, bonds, money orders, and negotiable securities.

On Monday, October 24, 1921 they pulled off a daring heist. The three of them tailed the money truck up Broadway in a car. At the right moment, Chapman sprang from the back seat of the moving convertible. He landed on the running board of the truck and stuck a pistol in the driver's face. He told him to pull into a side street where they blindfolded the man and made off with five bags containing nearly $1.5 million. It was the largest mail robbery in U.S. history.

The problem was that most of it was in securities and those were difficult to turn into cash. Chapman and Dutch realized they would have had a better chance of getting away with it in Chicago and went back there. It worked, but back in the Big Apple, Lorber got greedy and was caught. He ratted out his pals who were picked up right away.

Chapman made a remarkable escape attempt before the trial in New York, when he seemed to leap from a high window in the Post Office building. He actually crept onto a decorative ledge and then into a vacant office. It was dramatic but pointless. He was quickly caught and then tried, convicted, and sent to the federal prison in Atlanta.

By then, Chapman had become quite the celebrity and boasted he would escape from Atlanta, too.

He did, using the tried-and-true sheets-tied-together bit, but again, he was quickly caught and was shot three times in the process.

Undeterred, six days later, he tried it again. Third time lucky: it worked.

A couple of months later Dutch escaped, employing the other prison cliché, the tunnel. But before he and his old partner could get back together, Chapman fell in with thief Walter Shean. Together, in October 1924, they tried to knock over a department store in New Britain, Connecticut.

The job went sour and a cop was killed. Shean was captured, and he fingered Chapman as the shooter. In December, Chapman was caught a second time. By then, though, he was a full-fledged celebrity with his own fan clubs, and the trial was a media event. Even the *New York Times* had expressed grudging admiration for his courage, persistence, and ingenuity. Chapman claimed complete and perfect innocence. Never been to New Britain, didn't know this guy. It didn't fly.

Convicted and sentenced to the gallows, Chapman dryly told reporters, "Death itself isn't dreadful, but hanging seems an awkward way of entering the adventure."

He found out on April 5, 1926.

At the same time, Dutch Anderson had been driven mad. He came to believe that one of their Midwest contacts had betrayed Chapman and he killed the man and his wife. A cop in Muskegon, Michigan recognized Dutch and they killed each other in a shootout.

Chapman and Anderson may have been a partial inspiration for the Paul Newman and Robert Redford characters in *The Sting*. The best book on the subject is H. Paul Jeffries' nonfiction novel *Gentleman Gerald*.

Chapman, Mark David

Most members of a certain generation can remember where they were when they learned about three things—President Kennedy's assassination, 9/11, and the death of John Lennon. He was that important.

Perhaps there is some karmic balance at work. Lennon's killer suffered virtually all of the excesses and sins of the 1960s. His insanity, however, was his own.

Born in 1955 to a middle class family, Mark David Chapman was caught up in the first heady wave of Beatlemania. At the same time, he was a misfit who constructed an elaborate fantasy life, hammered booze and drugs, experienced a charismatic evangelical religious transformation, and attempted suicide. His life had been a series of personal and professional failures that led him from Decatur, Georgia to Beirut, Hawaii, and finally, to the Dakota apartment building in New York.

Later, Chapman would be diagnosed as a pathological narcissist, obsessed at various times with Lennon and J.D. Salinger's novel *The Catcher in the Rye*. Periods of lucidity were punctuated by episodes of suicidal depression. Chapman worked as a security guard and at other low-level jobs. He also got married. But in the fall of 1980 his insanity deepened. After contacting the Federal Aviation Authority to learn the particulars of traveling with a firearm, he packed his .38 in his luggage and flew from Honolulu to New York. Following federal guidelines, he did not bring bullets (he had been told they could be damaged by changes in air pressure) so he had to look up an old friend in Atlanta to secure some hollow points. He started stalking Lennon, but the dark madness lifted briefly. Chapman attributed it to watching the film *Ordinary People,* in which Timothy Hutton played a young man overcoming strong suicidal impulses. Chapman returned to Hawaii.

Less than a month later, Chapman was back outside the Dakota where John Lennon and Yoko Ono lived.

On Monday, December 8th, Chapman finally met John Lennon. Twice. In the afternoon, he spotted John and Yoko leaving the building. He thrust out a copy of Lennon's new *Double Fantasy* album, and asked him to sign it. Lennon did, then climbed into a limo and headed off to a recording studio.

When the singer returned at 10:50 p.m. that night, Chapman was still waiting for him. As Lennon got out of his car and headed for the door, Chapman pulled the revolver out of his coat pocket and fired five shots. Four hit Lennon. He managed to stagger into the concierge station where he collapsed. Chapman took off his coat, so the police would be able to see he was unarmed, and sat down on the sidewalk to read *Catcher*.

Two patrolmen rushed Lennon to an emergency room where he died.

Chapman surrendered, declaring himself to be "Holden Caulfield, the *Catcher in the Rye* of the present generation."

As ceremonies, services, and concerts marked Lennon's passing over the following weeks, a young **John Hinckley Jr.** told his tape recorder, "I just want to say goodbye to the old year, which was nothing but total mystery, total death. John Lennon is dead, the world is over, forget it. Anything I might do in 1981 would be solely for Jodie Foster's sake. Just tell the world in some way that I worship and idolize her." Three months later, he would shoot President Ronald Reagan.

Chapman ignored lawyers' advice to use the insanity defense and pled guilty. He was sentenced to 20 years to life and is incarcerated at Attica.

Several books have been written about Chapman. The character Rupert Pupkin in Martin Scorsese's film *The King of Comedy* is based in part on Chapman and other celebrity stalkers. In the 2007 film *Chapter 27*, Jared Leto plays Chapman. It debuted at the 2006 Sundance Film Festival.

Chessman, Caryl

"Red Light Bandit"

Caryl Chessman is remembered for his punishment, not for his crimes. He went to the gas cham-

Mark David Chapman, before he became known as John Lennon's killer. (AP Photo)

ber for a series of robberies, kidnapping, and two violent rapes, but he did not kill anyone, and so his execution became a cause célèbre rivaling the protests that surrounded **Sacco and Vanzetti**. He spent 11 years and 10 months—to the day—on California's Death Row and became the most famous inmate of his era, earning a place on the cover of *Time* magazine on March 21, 1960.

Born in 1921, Chessman began his criminal career in high school where he learned to hotwire cars. That led to other thefts. At 16, he was caught breaking into a drugstore and entered into a lifelong relationship with the California penal system. He progressed steadily from the Little Tujunga Foresty Camp to the Whittier School for Boys, to the Preston Industrial School, to San Quentin. His various incarcerations were the result of armed robbery,

Caryl Chessman: Who Me? He was a robber and rapist, but not a killer. (AP Photo)

auto theft, assault with a deadly weapon, and attempted murder. He and assorted gangs were involved with more than 50 jobs.

At each of these institutions, Chessman's intelligence and charm persuaded authorities that he was seriously interested in rehabilitation, and people went out of their way to help him. At San Quentin, Chessman rose through the ranks to work as a clerk in the warden's office. This led to a transfer to an experimental "prison without walls" in Chino where inmates took a large degree of responsibility for their own behavior. Chessman followed the rules for 10 weeks before he walked away and went back to a life of crime with another ex-con, stealing cars and breaking into homes in Southern California.

Chessman was caught again fairly quickly and sent to Folsom where he did hard time in a special punishment unit. Four years later, he convinced the parole board he was a changed man and they let him out. About a month later, the "Red Light Bandit" appeared in Los Angeles.

Chessman used a red spotlight on a stolen car and khaki clothing to intimidate motorists he found parked in out-of-the-way places. He impersonated a policeman and threatened his victims with a loaded automatic, stole money, and, in two cases, kidnapped women long enough to rape them. (The technical charge in both cases was "forcible oral sex.")

Chessman was caught on January 23, 1948 after he had robbed a clothing store at gunpoint, and eluded police on a wild high speed chase. It ended with a patrol car ramming Chessman's stolen Ford. In the car, they found physical evidence linking him directly to one rape victim. Later, both women identified him.

The most serious of the charges brought against Chessman came from California's "Little Lindbergh" laws that called for the death penalty or life in prison without the possibility of parole if a kidnapping also involved robbery and bodily harm to the victim. The DA decided to go for the maximum penalty and assigned one of his best lawyers, J. Miller Leavy, to the Red Light Bandit case. Chessman elected to represent himself. Eventually he accepted a public defender as an advisor, but throughout the proceedings, he did himself more harm than good. It may not have mattered, because the state's case was so strong. After hearing the evidence, the jury of 11 women and one man deliberated for two days.

Early on, they asked the judge if "life without the possibility of parole" really meant what it said. The judge answered that it did not. Commutations and pardons could be granted; laws could be changed. With that in mind, the jury found Chessman guilty of all of the most serious charges and on June 25, 1948 he was sentenced to death and sent back to San Quentin.

From cell 2455, he initiated a series of appeals based partly on the fact that the court stenographer had died before he could finish transcribing his notes into a full trial transcript. After another stenographer finished the job, Chessman challenged his work. More appeals to state and federal courts followed, and death penalty opponents gravitated to Chessman's side. Appeals went to the Supreme Court more than once. In short, it was the process that has become so familiar with any high-profile case.

Through it all, Chessman found time to write a book. *Cell 2455 Death Row* became a dubious bestseller in 1954. (Here's a typically fervid passage: "Evil seeks but the opportunity and the means to destroy itself; only when frustrated and denied its birthright does it turn with savage violence against its tormentors.") Its success was due in no small way to its author's impending demise. But once again, it was postponed. Chessman continued to write, even though the Board of Corrections forbade it. A second book, *Trial by Ordeal*, a prolonged argument against the death penalty, was smuggled out and published, then a third, *The Face of Justice*, again claiming his innocence.

Neither of the later books did particularly well, though Chessman's public support continued to grow—Albert Schweitzer, Steve Allen, Brigitte Bardot, Eleanor Roosevelt, Shirley MacLaine, and thousands more all lent their voices to Chessman's cause.

Caryl's string finally ran out on May 2, 1960 when they broke the pellets in the gas chamber. To the end, Chessman stuck to the con's favorite excuse—some other guy did it—though his guilt was never really in question. The justice of his sentence was in question, as it still is in many death-penalty cases.

If a state declares it has the right to put one of its citizens to death, what are the rules? Which crimes deserve the ultimate punishment? Is there a real alternative, another method of keeping the most dangerous predators away from the rest of us? Given Chessman's history of incarceration—where he sharpened his criminal skills—alternating with periods of freedom where he committed steadily escalating crimes, there is every reason to believe he would have been more dangerous than before if he had ever been released. The Chessman case brought these questions into sharp focus in the 1950s. Half a century later, we're no closer to real answers.

Chessman's story has been dramatized on film twice. In 1955, *Cell 2455 Death Row* was turned into a film noir focusing on his crimes. Then in 1977, Alan Alda starred as Chessman in a made-for-television movie about his appeals, *Kill Me If You Can*. Neither has ever been available on any form of home video and given their undistinguished reputations, they will likely remain largely unseen.

Chowchilla School Bus Kidnapping

In 1975 Fred Woods and brothers Jim and Rick Schoenfeld were three slackers who still lived with their parents near San Francisco. They had big ideas about striking it rich but never really did anything. Then—nobody's sure how it happened—they came up with the notion of a kidnapping. Why not? Just a year before, the Patty Hearst story had been all over the news, and before that, Clint Eastwood's hit *Dirty Harry* ended with the bad guy snatching a school bus full of kids.

Somehow, the idle speculation became a scheme that became a plan that became a crime.

Fred Woods' father owned a rock quarry in Livermore, California. In December, using his own name, Woods bought a used moving van and they buried it in a remote corner of the quarry. They equipped it with mattresses, battery-powered ventilation fans, and a portable toilet.

On the afternoon of July 15, 1976, pretending to have car trouble, they flagged down a school bus driven by Ed Ray near the central California town of Chowchilla. The bus carried 27 kids, ages 5 to 14. The kidnappers had guns and wore stocking masks. They took control of the bus and drove it into a drainage ditch. A white van with blacked-out windows pulled up to the door of the bus and half the kids were loaded into the back. A few minutes later, the rest were herded into a second van.

The vans took a meandering course lasting about 11 hours and finally ended at the buried moving van. Ed Ray and the boys and girls climbed down into the eight-by-twenty-five-foot box through an opening in the roof. Each kid's name was noted down and an article of clothing taken as proof of possession. Ed Ray's boots and trousers were taken. They were given bread, water, cereal, and potato chips. The roof hatch was closed and they were left in the dark.

Chowchilla police had realized something was wrong within hours of the kidnapping and had found the bus by eight o' clock that night. Having no clues and no ransom note, they could do little. As word of the crime spread, reporters descended upon the town and frantic parents worked the phones. This was where the kidnappers' careful plan first went awry. They tried to call in their $5 million ransom demand to the Chowchilla police but kept getting a busy signal. After repeated efforts, they decided to take a break, get some sleep, and try the next day.

After about 12 hours locked in the moving van, Ed Ray and some of the bigger boys piled mattresses up and were able to reach the hatch. By wedging a wooden beam at its edge, they were able to lift it enough for Ed to reach out. He found it was weighed down by two heavy batteries. With more work, they removed those and more dirt that blocked the way. Then they could crawl out.

When all the kids were free, they walked toward a distant light and were met by two astonished quarry workers. After questioning by the FBI, the kids got home early on the morning of July 17th.

Not long after, the kidnappers woke up and learned their perfect crime had not gone so well. Fred Woods and Jim Schoenfeld elected to run for it and headed for Canada. Rick Schoenfeld went home and confessed all.

The police investigation quickly turned toward Fred. They even found a handwritten outline of the plan at his house.

Rick turned himself in; Fred and Jim were caught a couple of weeks later, and were taken without incident.

The three pleaded guilty and opted for a trial by a judge rather than a jury. They got life without the possibility of parole, but in 1981 it was changed to life with the possibility of parole. All three have been model prisoners but, at this writing, have not been granted parole.

Two books have been written about the case and it was the subject of a 1993 made-for-TV movie, *They've Taken Our Children*, with Karl Malden as Ed Ray.

Cleveland Torso Killings

As the name suggests, the Cleveland "torso killings" are among the grisliest unsolved murders in the annals of American crime.

They probably began in September 1934, when part of a woman's torso was found near the Euclid Bay amusement park on the shore of Lake Erie. The legs had been cut off at the knees, and the body had been treated with some chemical that discolored it. The upper part of the torso had been found several miles away two weeks before. She was never identified. The newspapers called her "the lady of the lake." Later, she would be known as Victim Zero.

A year later, two decapitated male corpses were found in Kingsbury Run, a hobo jungle that thrived—if that's the right word—in the dark days of the Depression. It was a junky, weed-choked ravine in downtown Cleveland where the unemployed had built a rough shantytown. Both of the victims had been castrated. The genitals were found nearby with one of the heads. One of the men was identified; the other remains unknown.

Four months later in January 1936, parts of Florence Polillo were found in a half-bushel basket behind a meat market. Four months after that, another severed head and its heavily tattooed body turned up in Kingsbury Run. Another decapitated male corpse was found in July in the southwest part of the city. Evidence suggested he had been killed before Tattooed Man.

On September 10, 1936 a bisected torso and parts of the legs were found in a stagnant Kingsbury Run pond. By then, the papers were calling the killer "the mad butcher" and newly appointed safety director Eliot Ness knew the cops had a problem. He had been brought in to control police corruption and gambling, but the killings weren't making his job any easier. Twenty detectives were assigned to the gruesome murders.

By February 1937 another part of a woman's torso washed up on Euclid Beach. The other half was found in Lake Erie three months later. No head was ever found.

Another body, the partial skeleton of a black woman, was found under a bridge on June 6th. She might have been dead for a year. A month later, on July 6th, the upper part of a man's torso and thigh were discovered floating in the Cuyahoga River near Kingsbury Run. Other parts, but not the head, were found in the water over the next few days.

On April 8, 1938 parts of a woman's leg were found in the river. Other body parts were wrapped in burlap. Again, no head. Four months later, on August 16th, parts of two skeletons—a man and a woman—were uncovered in a dump. The victims had been dead for several months and even though the skulls were found, they were never identified.

A few days later, reacting to heavy public pressure, Ness ordered police raids on the hobo jungle in Kingsbury Run. The cops rousted all of the unfortunates and burned down their shacks and shanties.

It may have marked the end of the killings. Or not.

On May 3, 1940 three decapitated and mutilated men's bodies were found in boxcars near Pittsburgh. Railroad records placed the cars in Youngstown, Ohio roughly between Cleveland and Pittsburgh, in December, 1939.

Then, ten years later in July 1950, another dismembered decapitated body was discovered in a lumberyard a few miles from Kingsbury Run. The head was found later and the victim was identified. Otherwise, the crime was identical to the first of the mad butcher's killings.

Several suspects were identified at various stages of the investigation but no one was ever charged. Experts have never even agreed on the number of murders that might have been committed. Could more than one person have been responsible? Why did the killings stop? Or did they?

In January 1939 the *Cleveland Press* received an anonymous letter, postmarked from Los Angeles, claiming to be from the butcher. He bragged about his accomplishments and claimed to be continuing his experiments in "sunny California." Eight years later, in 1947, **Elizabeth Short**, the "Black Dahlia," was murdered and dismembered in a manner echoing the Cleveland killings. Any direct connection would seem to be impossible, but nothing about either case has ever been explained logically.

The unsolved murders have largely been forgotten, though at this writing, a feature film to be directed by David Fincher was in production. The best book on the subject, James Jessen Badal's *In the Wake of the Butcher*, covers the case with a wealth of detail.

Cline, Alfred

In his day, the 1940s, Albert Cline was an "American Bluebeard." He made a prosperous little career of marrying and killing women, after they had rewritten their wills making him the beneficiary.

He pulled it off eight times. His ninth victim was a man, evangelist Ernest Jones, who also put his trust in Cline.

The ladykiller's MO was effectively simple. After the wedding, he and the new Mrs. Cline would honeymoon at a distant hotel where she was not known. He'd lace a drink with sedatives, powerful enough to knock the bride out, but not kill her. A doctor would be summoned and told she was suffering "another heart attack." Soon thereafter, Cline would kill her with a stronger dose. The doctor would list heart failure as the cause of death. The grief-stricken widower would have the poor woman's body cremated, and then move on to his next target.

Cline's victims included Elizabeth Hurt of San Francisco who succumbed at the Hotel Windsor in Jacksonville, Florida and Alice Carpenter of Jacksonville, who made it as far as the Hotel Lanier in Macon, Georgia. Cline continued until 1944 when he met and wed Delora Kreb, a widow from Chicago.

Kreb's family grew suspicious after she and Cline went west to Portland, Oregon for the honeymoon. He killed her there, and forged her signature on annuity documents to keep her monthly $500 checks coming in. The annuity ended on November 15, 1945. On November 29th, he informed the family she had died after a weeklong illness. They didn't buy it.

California authorities investigated and learned of his serial marriages, but since Cline had had all of the bodies cremated, they had no evidence or proof. They were, however, able to nail him on a forgery rap. He was sentenced to 126 years in Folsom, but died after three years from a heart attack.

The Bluebeard character has been a staple of popular entertainment in the nineteenth and early twentieth centuries. Cline may have been a partial inspiration for the 1947 film, *Love from a Stranger*.

Cohen, Mickey

Meyer Harris "Mickey" Cohen grew up in the mob. As a seven-year-old in Los Angeles when Prohibition became law, young Mickey delivered alcohol made at his family's pharmacy. As a teenager, he traveled east where he met and worked with the likes of **Owney Madden** and **Al Capone**. He went back home when **Ben "Bugsy" Siegel** took over the mob's operations in the City of Angels. Mickey worked with gambling and took over after the Bugster was killed in 1947 when Mickey achieved his greatest fame as a colorful character.

Mickey was always a tough nut, known for his violent ways. His mansion, surrounded by flood lights and an electric fence, was bombed twice. He survived, though his collection of expensive suits took quite a hit in one attack. For a time, gangster Johnny Stompanato was his bodyguard. After Stompanato fatally found himself on the pointy end of nine-inch carving knife wielded by **Cheryl Crane**, daughter of his paramour Lana Turner, Mickey paid for his funeral.

Around the same time, Cohen became a secret banker of fellow crook and Californian Richard Nixon. But it wasn't enough to keep the feds at bay; like most major mobsters of his time, Mickey testified before the Kefauver Committee. He was finally nailed on a couple of IRS beefs, and served time in Atlanta and Alcatraz. He died peacefully in 1976.

Johnny Stompanato, left, who was later stabbed to death by Cheryl Crane (daughter of Lana Turner) and reputed mobster Mickey Cohen at a trial in the 1950s. (AP Photo)

Cohen has been a supporting character in two excellent films, *Bugsy* (1991), where he's played by Harvey Keitel, and *L.A. Confidential* (1997) by Paul Guilfoyle. Cohen also appears in several of James Ellroy's crime novels where the mobster's reveries on Lana Turner's beauty and sexual prowess are brilliant.

Coll, Vincent
"Mad Dog," or "Mad Mick"

Vincent Coll earned the nickname "Mad Dog" on July 28, 1931 when he machinegunned a five-year-old boy. Until then, he had been known as the "Mad Mick," an immigrant Irish kid from New York's Hell's Kitchen neighborhood.

Born in 1909, Coll and his older brother Peter grew up on the streets and had impressive rap sheets for breaking and entering and grand larceny before they turned 21. Afterwards, they worked briefly for **Dutch Schultz**'s bootlegging operation. Vinnie's specialty was intimidating bartenders into taking the Dutchman's brew. But the Mad Mick was as ambitious as he was sadistic; he also tried to recruit Dutch's men to join him in his own booze business.

Once Vinnie's operation was up and running, he taunted Dutch by opening his headquarters half a block away from Dutch's office. When Dutch's lieutenant Vincent Barelli refused to join the new mob, Coll killed him and his girlfriend Mary Smith. By

> *Vincent Coll earned the nickname "Mad Dog" on July 28, 1931 when he machinegunned a five-year-old boy. Until then, he had been known as the "Mad Mick," an immigrant Irish kid from New York's Hell's Kitchen neighborhood.*

then, a full scale war had broken out between the two bootleggers, but it was a comparatively small conflict compared to the Castellammarese War going on between **Joe "the Boss" Masseria** and **Salvatore Maranzano** at the same time.

Coll was recruited to take part in that one, too. Maranzano reportedly paid him $25 grand to hit **Lucky Luciano**, **Frank Costello**, **Joe Adonis**, and **Vito Genovese**. But Luciano's men got to Maranzano first. Coll kept the money and continued to piss off everyone else in the New York underworld.

He raised money by kidnapping gangsters' aides and ransoming them back to their bosses. He reasoned they were the people with ready cash and wouldn't go to the cops because they'd have to explain the source of their money to the IRS. The tactic worked well enough to keep his war against the Dutchman's larger gang going.

Dutch escalated the feud by killing Peter Coll and putting a $50,000 bounty on Vinnie's head—dead only. He sent his top enforcer, Joey Rao, after the Mad Mick. Then one day in July 1931, Coll spotted Rao walking down 107th Street in Spanish Harlem. It was a hot day. Lots of kids were playing in the street as Coll slowly cruised by and opened up with a Tommy gun. Four kids were wounded

and young Michael Vengali was killed. Coll was quickly identified.

The mayor and the papers dubbed him the "Mad Dog" and demanded justice be done, PDQ. Coll responded by kidnapping one of gangster **Owney Madden**'s men and demanding $30,000. He got it and used the money to retain mouthpiece Sam Leibowitz, the hottest defense lawyer in town.

Leibowitz made mincemeat of the government's open-and-shut case and Mad Dog walked. But not for long: the Dutchman and Rao weren't finished.

As the possibly apocryphal story goes, Coll called Madden again to browbeat and threaten him. Madden kept him on the line long enough for the call to be traced to a telephone booth in a drug store on West 23rd Street—where Rao and associates found him and riddled his body with .45 slugs. Other sources claim it was **Bugsy Siegel** who tracked down the Mad Dog and finished him off.

On screen, Coll has been portrayed by Nicholas Sadler in *Mobsters* (1991) as a ferocious homicidal lunatic. Nic Cage is more restrained as a renamed Coll in *The Cotton Club* (1984). Two biopics, both titled *Mad Dog Coll* and both hard to find, were made in 1961 and 1993. The particular method of his demise—shot while using a pay phone—has become a convention of the genre. In most crime movies, a character is in greater peril in a phone booth than in a school of ravenous piranha.

Collins, John Norman

The grisly murders of Michigan coeds in the late 1960s provided a rough preview of **Ted Bundy**'s crimes a few years later. John Norman Collins never captured the public imagination as Bundy did, but his crimes were gruesomely similar. Both were clean-cut, outwardly respectable young men. Both were considered suspects but dismissed because they seemed so normal. But even a scratch of that "normal" surface revealed a dark interior.

Seven young women were murdered in the Ypsilanti/Ann Arbor area between 1967 and 1969, with five of the murders taking place in March and August of '69. Additionally, a girl was killed in California while Collins visited there in June 1969. Circumstantial evidence strongly suggests he killed her, but he was never charged with the crime.

Actually, Collins was convicted on only one of the Michigan murders, the only one with very strong blood and hair evidence—even though he had been under suspicion for some time.

The victims' bodies were found in remote rural areas. At least two of them were moved before they were found. Evidence suggested the killer visited them before placing them where they would be found. All had been sexually assaulted, beaten, and mutilated. One victim's feet and one hand had been cut off. Another had 47 stab wounds. Most of the girls were college students; the youngest was 13. One of the final victims, Karen Sue Beineman, was last seen getting on a motorcycle with a man she did not know.

At the time, Collins was living in the area. He'd been kicked out of his fraternity house for stealing, and had purchased a travel trailer with a hot check and fake ID. He owned several motorcycles. That fact, along with eyewitness descriptions, brought him to the attention of police for a second time. An inexperienced cop interviewed him but did nothing more, giving Collins the opportunity to get rid of a cardboard box filled with stuff. One of his housemates said the items included a woman's shoe and handbag. About the same time another policeman, David Liek, who was also Collins' uncle, learned his nephew was a suspect. Collins had been housesitting for Liek while the family was on vacation.

When he learned what was going on, Liek became suspicious of fresh paint on the concrete floor of his basement. A thorough examination revealed bloodstains matching Karen Beineman, and hair clippings that matched ones found in her panties. (Mrs. Liek trimmed her sons' hair in the basement.) Later, blood and fabric evidence from two other victims was found in Collins' car.

But because the evidence was so strong in the Karen Beineman case, prosecutors elected to try Collins on only the one charge. Throughout the trial, and to this day, Collins professed complete innocence. The jury disagreed and sentenced him to life without the possibility of parole.

The story did not end there, though.

In October 1988 Collins appeared on a Detroit talk show and restated his innocence. Again, he was so charming and persuasive some viewers believed there had been a miscarriage of justice. Those feelings were reinforced in 2004 when another man was charged with one of the murders based on new DNA evidence. But that case, the Jane L. Mixer murder, had not really fit the rest of the 1960s killings. She had been shot, but not mutilated or molested, and her body was found, fully clothed, in a different area from the others. The DNA match was found after a 2002 conviction on prescription fraud.

Collins' possible connection to the unsolved murder of the Robison family in 1968 is the subject of Judith Guest's 2004 novel, *The Tarnished Eye*, and he provided the name for the self-described Michigan Heavy/Death/Speed Metal band John Norman Collins.

Colombo, Joseph Sr.

In the early 1960s when **Joe Bonanno** ordered Joe Colombo to kill **Carlo Gambino** and three other Mafia Dons, Colombo did the smart thing: he ratted out his boss. It was simple insanity to try to hit four of the top Mafiosi. But others in the Bonanno-Profaci crime family didn't see it that way and the Banana War broke out between the rival factions.

Colombo had worked with gambling, loan sharking, and airport hijacking before he graduated and joined a hit squad with Crazy **Joe Gallo** and his brothers Larry and Albert "Kid Blast." Police figured they made at least 15 kills.

After Bonanno was removed, Gambino placed Colombo in charge of the divided family. By then, Crazy Joe was in jail and Colombo set out on a quixotic quest to create a better image for organized crime, particularly Italian organized crime.

He demanded that the men who worked in his crew have real jobs. He himself was a real estate salesman, but his most important work was more public.

Years before, an organized boycott by the Italian-American community against Chesterfield cigarettes had caused the tobacco company to withdraw its sponsorship of the television show *The Untouchables*, where all of the villains were Italians. They were successful. The show was cancelled.

Colombo decided to adopt the tactics used so successfully by Jewish, black and anti-Vietnam war organizations. He formed the Italian-American Civil Rights League to eliminate the stereotyping of upstanding Italian-American citizens as gangsters in popular entertainment, and to end the FBI's unwarranted harassment of the same. Tapping into the anti-establishment zeitgeist, he too was successful.

Frank Sinatra sang at a benefit that knocked down $500,000. The 1970 Unity Day Rally in Columbus Circle drew a crowd of 50,000. Governor Nelson Rockefeller gave the group his blessing.

Reaction was not so positive in the top echelons of mob leadership. Carlo Gambino supported his boy Joe at the first rally but grew increasingly uncomfortable with all of the attention. Colombo was going too far.

Things were just getting warmed up at the second Unity Day Rally on June 28, 1971 when Colombo showed up surrounded by bodyguards. A black man with a camera and a statuesque black woman, both with press credentials around their necks, approached the young mobster. The woman yelled out "Hello, Joe!" As the mobster turned toward her, the man pulled out a .32 semiautomatic and pumped three bullets into Colombo's head.

Bodyguards and cops swarmed over the shooter and in the confusion put three .38 slugs into his back. The black man was Jerome Johnson, a 24-year-old petty criminal. He died there in Columbus Circle. Colombo lapsed into a vegetative coma and was technically alive for another seven years. The woman who had accompanied Johnson and the pistol that fired the fatal shots both vanished.

The most likely explanation is that the gullible Johnson was promised a big payday and an escape route by rivals within Colombo's organization. But who? Some reports claim Gambino ordered the hit. Others say Joey Gallo, who had been released from jail and had made strong connections with black gangs while he was in the joint, was behind it. No one believed Johnson was working alone.

Given Colombo's eventful but brief career, he is a fairly minor figure in mob lore. An HBO special on him was broadcast in 2005. He is a supporting character in the 1999 film *Bonanno*.

Coneys, Theodore

It certainly was a strange murder, much too strange for fiction.

In September 1941 Philip Peters was temporarily living alone in his bungalow on Moncrieff Place in Denver, Colorado. His wife was in the hospital with a broken hip. One day while he was visiting her, Theodore Coneys came by the house.

Coneys was an old acquaintance, once a fellow member of the West Denver Mandolin Society which had met regularly at Peters' house. But that had been years ago. Since then, Coneys had fallen on hard times and was hoping for a handout from Peters. Instead, finding the house unlocked, he went inside and helped himself to whatever he could find.

Poking around, he noticed a tiny trapdoor in the ceiling of an upstairs closet that opened on to a minuscule attic room, little more than a spiderhole. The door was much too small for most people, but Coneys was a slightly built little guy and could wriggle through it. Upon reflection, he decided the attic room wasn't much, but it was better than spending a winter outdoors, and it could be home. He fixed up some makeshift bedding and moved in. Over the next few weeks, he'd wait for Peters to go out before he emerged to eat, clean up, etc.

Everything went fine until October 17th, when Coneys was rustling up some grub. He thought Peters had left, but the older man had just been taking a nap and surprised Coneys in the kitchen. Not recognizing his uninvited guest, he yelled. Coneys snapped and attacked him with an old pistol normally used as a hammer. Peters fell down dead.

Anyone else might have thought it was a good time to take a powder, but Coneys decided to maintain his new living arrangement. After dragging the body to a bedroom, he simply locked up and retired to his tiny digs. When neighbors and then the police came to look in on Peters, they were confronted with a classic "locked room" mystery. There was the body with every door and window locked from the inside. They saw the little door but couldn't believe a human being could fit through it.

Sometime later, Mrs. Peters was released from the hospital and came home. She and a couple of housekeepers came to believe the house was haunted, probably by Philip. Eventually, she moved in with her son.

Still, people continued to see strange lights in the house at night, and to hear odd noises, but whenever the cops searched it, Coneys eluded them. Not buying the supernatural explanations, police set up surveillance on the bungalow and waited.

On July 30, 1942 they saw a curtain move and caught a glimpse of a face. They dashed across the street and into the house. Hearing a sound from upstairs, they gave chase and arrived in time to see Coneys' tiny feet disappearing through the little door. When they pulled him out, he fainted. He spent the rest of his life in the Colorado State Penitentiary for the murder of Philip Peters.

"The Spiderman," as he was dubbed for his long prehensile fingers and wild-eyed look, became locally famous as a campfire horror tale. He may have been an inspiration for the 1989 made-for-TV horror movie *Hider in the House.*

Cook, William

William Cook might be better known today if his senseless kidnap/murders hadn't been eclipsed by the more handsome and charismatic **Charlie Starkweather**. Both were 1950s thrill killers but where

Starkweather had James Dean looks and a cute girlfriend, Cook had a bad eye that scared people and a prison tattoo spelling out HARD LUCK on his fingers. It was not completely inaccurate.

Cook was one of seven children born into crushing poverty in Depression-era Missouri. His mother died when he was a little kid, and his alcoholic father abandoned his offspring, leaving them to live in an abandoned mineshaft. William had a tough time in foster care and got into trouble with the law at an early age. Petty crime led to robbery and auto theft, and he went straight from reform school to the Missouri State pen where he earned a reputation as a tough customer. Released in 1950, he briefly reconciled with his dad before he set out drifting, hitching rides across the West and Southwest. In El Paso, he bought a short-barreled .32 pistol and decided he was ready to take what he wanted.

On December 30, 1950 in Lubbock, Texas, Cook managed to catch a ride heading back toward Missouri. That night on the road, he pulled his gun on the driver, took his wallet, and ordered the man into the trunk. Some miles down the road, the captive managed to pry the trunk lid open and made a break. Cook kept driving until the car ran out of gas east of Tulsa, Oklahoma.

That's where he flagged down Carl Mosser.

Mosser, his wife Thelma and their children Ronald, Gary, and Pamela (ages 7, 5, and 3) were on their way from Illinois to visit Carl's twin brother in Albuquerque, New Mexico. Cook forced his way into their car and told Mosser to drive around. They headed west and south, through Oklahoma City to Wichita Falls, Texas, where Mosser attempted to overpower Cook when they stopped for gas and food. It didn't work and an angry Cook kept the family at gunpoint. For three days, they drove west to Carlsbad, New Mexico, then turned back east, crossing Texas again, then north into Missouri.

Somewhere along the way, Cook slaughtered all five of the Mossers and their dog. He dumped the bodies in a mineshaft near Joplin, and abandoned the car not far from where he had first seen it near Tulsa.

Police found the Mossers' bodies and the car. And in the blood-stained, bullet-holed vehicle, they found a sales receipt for Cook's .32. The manhunt was on.

In Osage County, Oklahoma Cook was able to overpower a deputy sheriff and steal his car. He threatened to kill the man but didn't. His next luckless victim was Robert H. Dewey. Cook shot him in the head and headed south into Mexico. Despite the country's reputation in popular mythology as a refuge for outlaws, it wasn't the place for Cook. He kidnapped two other men and made it as far as the little town of Santa Rosalía where he was recognized by Police Chief Francisco Morales on January 15, 1951. Chief Morales simply walked up to Cook and yanked the pistol from his belt. The Mexican authorities hustled him back to the border, where they turned him over to the Americans.

On December 12, 1952 Cook was executed in San Quentin's gas chamber for the murder of Robert Dewey.

Cook's one-man crime wave provided the inspiration for the little-known but excellent 1953 film noir, *The Hitch-Hiker*, directed by Ida Lupino. She and her co-writers wisely limited the story to the last chapter, Cook's kidnapping of two men out for a fishing trip. The most vicious crimes occur off camera. William Talman, best known for his television role as Perry Mason's hapless opponent Hamilton Burger, is spookily believable as the psycho.

Cooper, Dan "D.B."

Deep within even the most law-abiding soul lies the hope that Dan Cooper (aka "D.B.") is alive and well. And we also hope he invested his somewhat ill-gotten $200,000 wisely and is now enjoying a serene retirement on a beach somewhere. Who can say? Maybe he is.

On the afternoon of November 24, 1971, Thanksgiving eve, a man who gave the name Dan Cooper bought a ticket on Northwest Orient flight 305 at the Portland, Oregon airport, bound for Seattle-Tacoma.

He wore a dark suit and a narrow tie. Judging by the composite sketch drawn later, he was about the most average-looking average white guy imaginable. Your basic six-footer, 175 pounds, give or take.

As soon as the plane was in the air, he handed flight attendant Florence Schaffner a note. It said he had a bomb in his briefcase. He wanted $200,000 in used $20s, two parachutes, and two backup chutes ready at Sea-Tac before the plane landed. If not...

The crew and the airline obeyed his instructions. While the 727 circled the airport, Cooper had a bourbon and water. After the plane landed and parked on a remote part of the field, Cooper asked that the passengers and Ms. Schaffner disembark, leaving three flight officers and another flight attendant on the plane with him. He requested meals be brought for them. When an FAA official wanted to come aboard, Cooper told him to forget it.

Instead, he asked for his note back and studied the instruction card for operating the aft stairs of a Boeing 727.

Initially, he told the pilot he wanted to go to Mexico. The plane was to stay below 10,000 feet (he claimed to have a wrist altimeter) and to fly no faster than 150 mph with the flaps set at 15 degrees. The pilot said they couldn't make it to Mexico under those conditions without refueling in Reno, Nevada. Cooper agreed, and they left Sea-Tac on Vector 23, a standard low-altitude route. They took off at 7:46 p.m., a little more than two hours after they had landed.

As soon as they were airborne, Cooper ordered the flight attendant into the cockpit, leaving him alone in the cabin. Around 8:00 p.m., a light on the instrument panel indicated the door to the aft stairs had been opened. About 20 minutes later, the crew noticed a slight change in the plane's attitude. First the nose dipped, then the tail—which happens if the aft stairs are lowered.

When they landed in Reno, the cabin was empty.

If Cooper indeed jumped out where they thought he did, he would have come down in the

Artist's rendering of "D.B. Cooper," 1971. (AP Photo/FBI)

forest near the Lewis River, north of Portland. It was, at best, a guess. The area was thoroughly searched in the following weeks and nobody found anything—no bright red and yellow parachute, no body, no money. Not then, anyway.

In February 1980 a boy playing on the bank of the Columbia River found $5,800 of the payoff money. (The FBI had written down the serial numbers.) Beyond the cash, the only physical evidence was eight Raleigh cigarette butts, a black tie, and a tie tack left on the plane.

Dan Cooper became known as D.B. Cooper when the FBI investigated a man by that name who turned out to have nothing to do with the hijacking. Four months later, in April 1972, an almost identical

job was pulled on a United flight over Utah. Richard F. McCoy, Jr., an ex-Green Beret helicopter pilot and skydiver got $500,000. The married father of two was also a student at Brigham Young University and a Sunday school teacher who had described his plan to a pal who ratted him out. McCoy was arrested and convicted on the United job, and was sent to the slammer for 45 years. He escaped in 1974 and was killed in a shootout with the FBI. Some have suspected he was also Dan Cooper.

Retired FBI agent Russell Calame wrote a book claiming that to be the case, *D.B. Cooper: The Real McCoy*. McCoy's widow, Karen Burns McCoy, disagreed and successfully sued Calame, his coauthor, and the publisher.

Others have offered similar theories but that's all they are—theories.

Whatever happened, you've got to admire Cooper's thoughtfulness and attention to detail. First, he demanded a reasonable amount of money. Then by asking for two parachutes, he suggested he might be planning to take a hostage, so the cops could not give him one rigged to fail. The specificity of his instructions to the crew strongly suggests familiarity with aviation and skydiving.

All of this and the sheer audacity of his plan, along with the fact no one was harmed, turned D.B. Cooper into an instant folk hero.

The 1981 film *The Pursuit of D.B. Cooper* treats the whole affair fairly lightly. He has been the subject of countless songs, too, but Cooper's lasting cultural importance is more tangible. His crime and those of more other more violent and dangerous hijackers caused significant changes in air travel from aircraft design (doors can no longer be opened in flight) to airport security.

Although we may idealize him as a "good" Robin Hood outlaw, remember Cooper the next time you get wanded at an airport.

Corll, Dean "Candyman"

No one will ever know exactly what went on in the suburban house of horrors created by Dean Corll. The details provided by his accomplices are frightening enough.

Born in 1939 into a highly unstable family, Corll appeared to be a normal, extremely likable young man. Virtually everyone who knew him noted how polite and helpful he was. His mother Mary was a high-maintenance woman who married his father twice. (Her final husband total was five.) In the 1950s she founded a candy business, making pecan confections in her Houston, Texas home. Dean lived in an apartment above the garage and worked in the family business. Drafted in 1964, he spent a year in the army and was given a hardship discharge after Mary divorced again and needed his help with

the candy biz. At the same time, Corll worked as an electrician with Houston Lighting and Power.

In 1964 the candy company had outgrown Mary's facilities and moved to the rundown Heights neighborhood near an elementary school. That's when Corll picked up the nickname "Candyman" because he gave away so many free samples to the local kids. All the while, Corll was dealing with his hidden homosexuality.

His mother relocated the business to Denver in 1968. Corll stayed in Houston in an unremarkable little frame house in the suburb of Pasadena. Around the same time, he became friendly with two dimwitted teenagers. Wayne Henley was a junior high school dropout druggie. David Brooks was a fellow slacker interested mostly in getting high. Corll, a large man at six-feet, 200 pounds, gave the boys what they wanted.

His house was party central for booze, beer, pot, and glue-sniffing. All he asked for in return was an introduction to their friends or any other young men they could inveigle over to his place. When he got them alone, things turned nasty. Very nasty.

The identity of his first victim is unclear. It might have been Jeffrey Konen who disappeared while hitchhiking in 1970, or it might have been David Hilligiest or Gregory Winkle, who vanished a year later.

No matter who was first, after years of being the good boy, Corll had given in to his darkest, most violent sexual fantasies. He paid Henley and Brooks to bring young men—even children as young as nine—to his house. After getting them so high they were helpless, he would introduce them to the torture board in a back bedroom. It was a piece of plywood rigged with handcuffs and ropes for restraint. The floor was covered with plastic sheeting to make cleanup easier. Corll's sadistic kicks came from an evil assortment of glass pipettes, dildos, and knives. Many of his victims were mutilated, beaten, strangled, and stabbed.

During the next two years Corll, Henley, and Brooks killed at least 27 people. They disposed of most bodies beneath a boat shack outside of town, where they were buried and covered with lime. When parents of the missing boys went to the Houston police, they were invariably told their children had run away, probably to join those damn hippies out in California. Many of the victims came from the Heights.

As the killings went on, Corll became more violent, unstable, and unpredictable. On August 8, 1973 he snapped when Henley brought a girl, young Rhonda Williams, to one of their little gatherings. Another boy, Tim Kerley, had tagged along, but the presence of a girl ruined everything for Corll. Henley talked to him and thought he had placated the older man. Corll calmed down and passed around more beer and dope.

Henley and the other kids overindulged and fell asleep. He awakened to find Corll snapping on handcuffs. His feet had already been tied. His friends were tightly bound and gagged. Brandishing a .22 pistol and knife Corll claimed he was going to kill them all, but not before he enjoyed a session with the torture board. Henley, who had not been gagged, tried to talk him out of it. He was sorry he had brought a girl, it was the wrong thing to do, he knew it. If Corll would just set him free, he'd make up for it. He'd rape Rhonda; Corll would rape Tim, and then they'd kill them both. Wouldn't that be great?

Corll agreed. While he was trying to assault Tim, Henley picked up the pistol. Corll, he said later, came at him. Henley put six slugs into him and called the police. He took them to the boat shack. The police brought along prison "trustees" to do the dirty digging. Over the next several days they found 17 bodies there and 10 more at other sites.

For a time, Henley and Brooks claimed their participation had been limited to procuring the boys, but they finally admitted they'd been involved in the killings, too. Both were found guilty and sentenced to life.

In the pantheon of modern serial killers, Corll is not particularly well known. He's overshadowed by higher body counts and more dynamic personalities. His story is not the stuff of popular entertainment, though Jack Olsen's book about him, *The Man With the Candy* (2000), is one of the fine writer's better books.

Wayne Henley has made something of a name for himself with stylized paintings he creates in jail. He and other serial killer-artists and the people who buy their work are the subject of the 2001 documentary *Collectors*. The film follows two of these specialized fans as they travel to Houston for an exhibition of Henley's work and visit with his mom.

Corona, Juan

The first body was found on May 19, 1971 when a farmer noticed a filled in, grave-sized hole in his peach orchard near Yuba City, California. He called the police. The last body was found less than a month later on June 4th—there were 25 of them.

They were all grown men; farm workers and migrants aged 40 to 68. All had been stabbed and slashed with a heavy blade, possibly a machete; some had also been shot. Receipts and deposit slips for labor contractor Juan Corona were found in some of the graves, so he was the first suspect. He had also been seen near some of the gravesites and with some of the victims shortly before their deaths.

When a search of his house and property turned up a ledger with many of the victims' names and bloodstains in his car and truck, Corona was arrested and charged.

Corona, 37, had been diagnosed as a schizophrenic in the 1950s and given more than 20 electroshock treatments as therapy. He had also come to the attention of police before, regarding an assault in nearby Marysville. A man had been attacked in a café, owned by Corona's half-brother Natividad. The wounds were similar to those of the dead men, and the victim of the café attack had named Natividad as his assailant. Natividad, known to be gay, fled back to Mexico, but Juan had been at the café that evening.

At trial, the physical evidence was not thoroughly persuasive. Questions were raised about blood types, tire tracks, and the handling of key pieces of evidence that had been mislabeled. Even so, it was enough. In January 1973 Corona was found guilty on 25 counts and was sentenced to life. A second trial nine years later had the same result.

Throughout, Corona has maintained his innocence. At the time of the crimes, he was America's most prolific serial killer. Four books have been written about the case, foremost among them Tracy Kidder's *The Road to Yuba City* (1974).

Corona's story has not been dramatized as a film, but included in the History Channel series *History's Mysteries: Infamous Murderers*.

Costello, Frank

Though he was never as famous as his colorful contemporaries **Lucky Luciano** and **Meyer Lansky**, Frank Costello was equally important to organized crime. While Lansky and Meyer worked with the gangs who ran the criminal enterprises, Costello, a decade older, cultivated and bribed the politicians, judges, and policemen who allowed them to say in operation in New York. They called him "the Prime Minister of the Mob" and if it makes him sound too polite and antiseptic, it is not completely inaccurate. As Luciano said, Costello was a man who knew how to keep his mouth shut and tend to business.

Born in Italy, Costello and his family moved to New York around the turn of the century. He joined a gang and pulled a stretch in jail for carrying a concealed weapon. After he got out, he went to work with "Big Bill" Dwyer, the politically connected boss of the docks, which brought him into contact with Luciano, Meyer, gangsters **Owney Madden** and Frenchy DeMange, and the big wheels in the Tammany Hall political machine. As Luciano and Lansky gained more and more power, Costello was there with them, always in the background, never

doing anything to call attention to himself. True, he liked to dress well, but he avoided the spotlight as assiduously as some others—**Bugsy Siegel**, **Al Capone**, and **Legs Diamond**—courted it.

Costello's areas of expertise were jewel smuggling and gambling in Louisiana and Florida with an emphasis on the slots.

It's hard to say exactly how high his political connections went on a national level, but Costello had some influence there. During the 1920s and 1930s, **J. Edgar Hoover** steadfastly denied the Mafia or organized crime even existed. Rooting out those sneaky communists, he said, was much more important. But in those same years, Hoover played the horses. Everyone knew he liked to go to the races and place the occasional $2 wager. Everyone didn't know he had FBI agents place $100 bets for him. And they didn't know he sometimes got hot tips on sure things from his good friend, columnist Walter Winchell. And Winchell got his tips from Costello. It was a good system; everybody won, everybody went away happy.

When Luciano was deported to Italy after World War II, Costello looked after his interests and made sure Charlie Lucky got his share of the profits.

Costello also used his contacts and acted when hitman Abe "Kid Twist" Reles spilled his guts to the New York cops about **Murder, Inc.**, the syndicate's enforcement arm. Costello shelled out big bucks to learn the hotel where Reles was being held and the names of the cops who were guarding him. Some $100,000 later, Reles mysteriously plunged from a sixth floor window.

Luciano's absence deepened the already existing enmity between Costello and ambitious boss **Vito Genovese**.

The only thing keeping Don Vito from open rebellion was the presence of Willie Moretti, who ran rackets in New Jersey and parts of Manhattan and had a tough, extremely devoted army of more than 250 "soliders." As long as he was on Costello's side, Genovese couldn't make any big moves. Unfortunately, Moretti was losing his mind. The syphilis he had contracted years before was driving him mad. The Kefauver Committee on organized crime was trying to get Moretti to testify and so Costello moved him from one hideout to the next to keep him safe from both the feds and Don Vito.

Eventually, Moretti did testify before the committee, but, by then, the old man was so far gone he revealed nothing. Costello was forced to testify, too, in 1951, and gave away zilch. None of that mattered to Vito Genovese. He still lobbied the other bosses to approve his removal of Moretti, and he got it in October 1951. After Moretti was gone, Genovese moved quickly to take over parts of his operations and to position himself to attack Costello more directly.

The attempt took place on May 2, 1957 in New York. After dinner at a swell French restaurant, Costello returned to his apartment building to find Vincente "the Chin" Gigante waiting in the lobby.

The humungous hit man pulled out a piece, yelled "This is for you, Frank," and squeezed off a quick shot before he dashed out the door. His aim was less than perfect. The bullet only grazed Costello's head, though he did bleed all over the tasteful lobby.

When the cops questioned him, Costello refused to say anything, either about the shooter or what those receipts from the Las Vegas Tropicana Casino were doing in his pocket. They leaned on him for a while and threatened more tax charges. Costello had nothing to say.

He did, however, understand his time was up. Rather than go to war with Genovese, he retired, dividing his time between Manhattan digs and his Long Island mansion. He died of natural causes in 1973.

Given the low profile Costello so studiously maintained, it's no surprise he hasn't played a significant role in gangster films, at least not under his own name. Parts of his career and demeanor were certainly on Mario Puzo's mind when he created Don Vito Corleone in *The Godfather*, the sleek mobster who has important political connections and survives an assassination attempt.

Costello is also a minor character in *The Gangster Chronicles* (1981), *Gangster Wars* (1981), *Kingfish* (1995), *Bugsy* (1991) and *Mobsters* (1991).

Cowley, Samuel

Though his name is virtually unknown outside the FBI, Samuel Cowley was one of the most important men in the bureau in the early days of its "war on crime." By 1934 Director **J. Edgar Hoover** had become dissatisfied with **Melvin Purvis'** performance as Special Agent in Charge of the Chicago office. **John Dillinger, Pretty Boy Floyd, Alvin Karpis**, and the Barker gang were on the loose and making headlines every day. Purvis was responsible for their capture and seemed to be making little headway, though he lost no opportunity to step into the spotlight.

Cowley had come to the FBI in 1929 from Utah by way of George Washington University. He bounced around several offices and built a reputation as a solid administrator, particularly skilled in the organization of paperwork—in short, he was a hard-driving desk jockey. He wound up in Washington where he was promoted to director of investigations, and then was transferred to Chicago. Though he was routinely referred to as Purvis' second in command, he was actually put in charge of the office. Not surprisingly, with such an unorthodox chain of command, morale suffered.

Cowley settled down, did his job organizing tips and personnel, and successfully avoided publicity. After the shooting of Dillinger (if, indeed, he was killed) the relationship between Hoover and Purvis deteriorated futher, and in September Cowley was officially put in charge. As it happened, the office was short-staffed on Tuesday, November 27, 1934, when the manhunt for **Baby Face Nelson** went into its final act.

Cowley was at his desk when a call came in from Agent Jim Metcalfe, who had spotted Nelson and his pal John Paul Chase on a stakeout. Metcalfe said Baby Face was headed for Lake Geneva. Cowley immediately dispatched two other agents to help, then decided to join the hunt himself. Without taking time to put on a bulletproof vest—he found them too heavy—he and Agent Ed Hollis picked up weapons and steered their Hudson out to Highway 12 where they found Nelson already trading shots with the other two agents some distance away. Nelson's car had been disabled at the side of the road. Cowley and Hollis skidded to a stop. All of the participants whipped out weapons—automatic rifles, machine guns, and sawed-off shotguns.

The desk jockey put six shots into Nelson but it wasn't enough. Baby Face charged maniacally ahead with his Tommy gun and unloaded on the two agents, hitting them both. Hollis died right there. Cowley was taken to a hospital, where he died early the next morning. A few hours later, Nelson's naked body was found in a ditch.

Cowley was given a hero's funeral in Salt Lake City. He is still the most senior agent killed in the line of duty.

Cowley never received the attention of his contemporaries in popular entertainment, and it is probably what he would have wanted. He did receive long overdue recognition for his contributions in Bryan Burrough's fine 2005 book *Public Enemies*.

Crane, Bob

Bob Crane became famous for portraying a smart, cocky World War II POW in the sitcom *Hogan's Heroes*. It ran for six successful years from 1965 to 1971. Crane had come to acting by way of radio, where his sunny style made him the most popular on-air personality in Los Angeles.

Beyond the easygoing smile, there was another side he didn't really try to hide. Crane was a compulsive womanizer. His many affairs broke up two marriages. When home video made its first ripple in the consumer market, he was an early adapter. He used still and video cameras to record his sexual exploits, sometimes without the consent or knowledge of the women involved.

It was his interest in video that introduced him to John Carpenter (not the film director). Carpenter was an electronics technician who helped Crane with the equipment and shared his proclivities. They recorded their extensive extracurricular activities.

After *Hogan* ended, Crane couldn't find any important work in film or television, so he took to the dinner theater circuit with the sex farce *Beginner's Luck*. He was appearing in it in Scottsdale, Arizona, when he was killed.

On the afternoon of June 29, 1978 a fellow cast member came to his unlocked apartment after Crane had missed a lunch meeting. She found him in bed, dead. He had been struck twice on the temple with a heavy object. A cord cut from a VCR had been tied around his neck after he died.

Suspicion immediately fell on Carpenter, who had been in Scottsdale until that morning when he'd flown back to Los Angeles. But there was no evidence linking Carpenter to the killing and he cooperated fully with police, answering questions without a lawyer after he had been read his rights.

More than a decade later, in 1992, Carpenter was finally charged with murder. The ostensible reason was that Crane had broken off with him, and an angry Carpenter retaliated by killing him. The thin motive and lack of physical evidence led to an acquittal. Carpenter died in 1998.

Given the number of Crane's partners and their potentially angry boyfriends, fathers, husbands, etc., there were any number of people who might have wished the actor harm.

Crane's compulsions and his death are the subject of Paul Schrader's perceptive and underrated *Auto Focus* (2002). It's a sympathetic portrayal of a self-described "nice guy" who couldn't control his sexual life and never understood how he was viewed by other people. As Crane and Carpenter, Greg Kinnear and Willem Dafoe make a properly bizarre odd couple. Though the film suggests Carpenter might have killed Crane, it does not identify a murderer.

Crane, Cheryl

Lana Turner and Johnny Stompanato were tempestuous lovers. Their relationship was a series of passionate sexual encounters and equally violent fights.

In the mid-1950s, Turner, the one-time "sweater girl" was still one of Hollywood's most popular leading ladies. Stompanato was a World War II veteran with an adventurous life that took him to California where he worked as bodyguard and bagman for mobster **Mickey Cohen**. When Turner's marriage to actor Lex Barker broke up in 1957, Stompanato (a.k.a. Johnny Valentine or Johnny Steel) made his move.

The actress already had a reputation as a serial bride—she eventually walked down the aisle eight times with seven men—so Stompanato acted quickly: flowers, phone calls, expensive dinners, a fancy portrait, and an invitation for her teenaged daughter Cheryl Crane to ride his new horse. And then there was Stompanato's other nickname, "Oscar," in honor of his award-worthy endowment. Lana was swept off her feet and into the sack.

Problems soon surfaced. Though Lana loved the tingly excitement of going out with a "gangster," she really didn't want to be seen with him in public or photographed on his arm, for example, at the Academy Awards.

The snubs didn't sit well with the hot-tempered Lothario, and he expressed his anger with his fists. But Lana always came back. When she got lonely shooting a movie in England, she invited him to join her. When he became too obstreperous, she and the studio had him deported. Upon her return, ready for a quick Mexican vacation, Johnny was at the airport, happy to join her in Acapulco.

The big finish came on Good Friday, April 4, 1958.

Lana and Johnny were yelling at each other in her bedroom in her Beverly Hills mansion. He threatened her, saying that he would disfigure her, and kill her mother and her daughter. Cheryl heard

Lana Turner, looking much like *Madame X* at her daughter Cheryl Crane's trial, 1958. (AP Photo)

them and called out through the closed door for them to stop. Lana told her to leave.

Cheryl went as far as the kitchen where she found a 9-inch carving knife, and came back. Again, Cheryl asked her mother to open the door. She did. Stompanato was on the other side holding some clothes on coat hangers over his shoulder.

Cheryl would say later that she thought he had a weapon. Whatever the truth of it, she stabbed him once, quickly and efficiently. With that single stroke, she punctured his aorta, sliced a kidney, and cut into a vertebra. He collapsed.

Lana called her mother. She came over right away with a doctor in tow. He gave Stompanato a shot of adrenaline through his chest, directly into the heart. (So that's where Quentin Tarantino found his inspiration for *Pulp Fiction*!) All to no use. "Oscar" was a goner.

Lana's next call was to lawyer Jerry Geisler, mouthpiece to the stars, the man who had gotten Charlie Chaplin and Errol Flynn off on rape charges. Geisler called the cops and orchestrated everything thereafter. The most dramatic moment came at the Coroner's Inquest where Lana, mirroring a moment from her Oscar-nominated performance in *Peyton Place*, gave a riveting performance before a packed courtroom. She told how Stompanato had treated her, and then gave a detailed description of her brave daughter's actions on the night in question. It worked. In less than 30 minutes, the jury came back with a verdict of justifiable homicide.

The matter wasn't yet over. Mickey Cohen made an attempt at blackmail with some nude photographs Stompanato had taken while Lana was asleep, but the Mickster didn't have the negatives—Lana did—so the threat went nowhere. Instead, he gave the gushing love letters she'd written to her inamorato to the newspapers. She was also embarrassed by the DA's questioning of her fitness as a mother, which led to Cheryl pulling a stretch at the El Retiro Institution.

The case immediately achieved a place of honor in Hollywood mythology. Novelist Harold Robbins based his 1962 novel *Where Love Has Gone* on the story. It was filmed in 1964 with Susan Hayward (who had previously played murderess Barbara Graham in 1958's *I Want To Live*) in the lead, Bette Davis as Lana's mother, and young Joey Heatherton as Cheryl.

Several other attempts to bring the lurid story to the screen have been made in recent years, but all have floundered at some point in the production process. Enquiring minds continue to wait.

Crater, Joseph Force

The spring and summer of 1930 were eventful for Joseph Crater.

In April, New York governor Franklin D. Roosevelt appointed Crater to the state Supreme Court.

He and his wife Stella spent part of July on vacation in Maine, but the judge was called back to New York City on pressing business. His girlfriend—rather, one of his girlfriends, to be completely accurate—decided to meet him for a little tryst in Atlantic City and he couldn't refuse.

By August, Crater was back in Maine, but no sooner had he arrived than he had to leave again for the city. He was in his court chambers on August 6th when he had his assistant John Mara cash two checks for him totaling $5,150. He also destroyed some papers and had Mara help him carry six portfolios full of documents to his apartment. He then told Mara to take the rest of the day off.

That afternoon, Crater ordered a ticket for the Broadway show *Dancing Partner* and said he would pick it up at the theater. Around 8:00 p.m., he went to Billy Haas' restaurant on West 44th Street where he dined with lawyer William Klein and Klein's date, showgirl Sally Lou Ritz. They finished up around 9:15 p.m. Klein and Ritz caught a cab for Coney Island and left Judge Crater walking toward Broadway, possibly hailing a cab, though he wasn't far from the theater. In either case, nobody ever saw him again, though someone picked up the ticket waiting for him at the box office.

He had told Mrs. Crater he would be back for her birthday on August 9th. A few days after, when he still hadn't shown up, she became worried and called some of his friends and associates. They began to look for him, but kept things on the QT, reasoning that if word got out, it would hurt the judge's chances when he came up for election in the fall.

When the story finally broke on September 3rd in the *New York World*, it was big news. Even in New York City, judges are generally not misplaced. Investigators found the papers Mara had helped carry to Crater's apartment were gone, but the portfolios were still there.

Several of the women Crater was involved with either came forward or were revealed, adding a sexual element to the already intriguing mystery. Crater sightings were regular occurrences from Los Angeles to Havana. One widely circulated rumor was that the judge had had a heart attack while visiting one of the city's classier bordellos and his body had been taken care of by gangsters. Actually, Crater's fate almost certainly had something to do with his association with the corrupt Tammany Hall political machine that ran the city and was under investigation at the time.

The judge was declared legally dead in 1937, but he became so famous in his 15 minutes that his name was a punch line for decades. Curiously, his story has never been filmed. The best book on the subject is Richard Tofel's *Vanishing Point* (2004).

Crowley, Francis "Two-Gun"

"I hadn't anything else to do, that's why I went around bumping off cops," so said Francis "Two-Gun" Crowley, justifying his 1931 New York crime wave, in a note written as police closed in on him.

The dim-witted teenager had a fetishistic love of pistols, and a troubled relationship with authority figures. Not surprising. His mother abandoned her illegitimate son early on, and his poverty-stricken foster mother had to put him to work at age 12.

Crowley's brief, violent life was a prototype for the most dangerous juvenile criminals who would emerge later in the twentieth century. The second grade dropout started with car theft, having been taught the skill by his foster brother John, who was shot and killed in a 1925 confrontation with a police officer that took both their lives. This is where Crowley's hatred of cops took root.

The diminutive thug—he barely cleared 5 feet and weighed 110 lbs. with bricks in his pockets—learned that with a pistol and a hot car, he got some respect. He started hanging out with Bronx gangs and in February 1931, at the tender age of 19, was part of a shootout at an American Legion club. Soon after, Crowley wounded a cop in a Manhattan gunfight, and upgraded to bank robbery in New Rochelle. Afterwards, he got serious.

Crowley and his pal "Fat" Rudy Duringer were habitués of a dance hall called the Primrose Club. Rudy fell for a girl who worked there, Virginia Brannen. Alas, his affections were not returned. One night while the three of them were driving around with some friends, she told Fat Rudy she was going to marry someone else. Heartbroken, he shot her. The two friends then stashed the body at St. Joseph's Catholic Seminary.

A week later Crowley had found a girlfriend of his own, 16-year-old Helen Walsh. They were parked at a Long Island lover's lane late one night when Patrolmen Fred Hirsch and Peter Eudyce approached the car. When Hirsch asked to see a license, Crowley pulled out a .38 and shot him three times. Hirsch managed to return fire, but Crowley jumped out of the car, stole the service revolver from the dying policeman, put two more bullets into him, and roared away.

But not before Eudyce got a good look at the young killer and his sweetie. Ballistics linked the bullets that had killed Hirsch with other crimes. On this evidence and Eudyce's description, a massive manhunt was set in motion. As one newspaper put it, "the most dangerous criminal at large was hunted through the city last night." The cops knew who they were dealing with and had unequivocal "shoot to kill" orders, from the very top, Commissioner Edward Mulrooney himself.

A media storm followed. Newspapers dug into the story as eagerly as the police. New York *Journal* police reporter Joe O'Connor followed a series of unpromising leads to dance hall girl Billie Dunne, who told him Crowley had showed up at her apartment with his girlfriend and Fat Rudy. Then, with questionable intelligence, the fugitive ordered Billie from her own apartment. And where, the reporter casually inquired, might that apartment be? The miffed and temporarily homeless dancer told him it was 303 West 90th Street.

O'Connor called detectives to tell them what he had learned, then got in touch with *Journal* photographer Jerry Frankel. They staked out the place,

Francis "Two-Gun" Crowley, on his way to trial, 1931. (AP Photo)

waiting most of the afternoon until Frankel finally decided to go into the building and check out the apartment.

The photographer schlepped his gear to the third floor and knocked. Inside the apartment, Crowley told him to scram. Before Frankel could do anything, he was pulled away by cops who had been holed up in the hallway. That's when Crowley threw open the door. The cop killer stood there, simultaneously threatening and ridiculous with his trousers rolled to his knees, two pistols strapped to his shins, two more on his belt, and another in a shoulder holster. He opened fire; the cops responded and the Siege of West 90th Street had begun.

Hundreds of police officers, including Commissioner Mulrooney and assorted brass, assembled and cordoned off the area. A crowd that grew to 15,000 gaped from the barricades and neighboring buildings as the cops blazed away with rifles, shotguns, machine guns, and tear gas.

For hours, Crowley dashed from window to door to window, and fired outside. Cops cut through the roof and ceiling and dropped in tear gas canisters. Crowley tossed them out, while Helen and Fat Rudy cowered together under a narrow day bed. When the cops finally kicked down the door and disarmed the kid—who had been blinded by the gas—they found wounds from several bullets. They also found a self-pitying note he had written, saying the movies had made him do it.

It took a jury all of 25 minutes to disagree. Helen testified against him. Both Two-Gun and Fat Rudy got the chair. Throughout the trial, the cocky kid joked with reporters and smirked at the judge's sentence.

At first, after he was sent up the river to Sing Sing for execution, Crowley maintained the tough-guy pose. He tried to escape and made as much trouble for everyone as he could, setting fire to his mattress and flooding his cell. But in the few weeks and months that followed, Crowley changed. Away from the glare of the public spotlight and, perhaps aware of his mortality, he calmed down. The outlaw bravado

disappeared and he even had several serious conversations with Warden Lewis Lawes who found him to be properly behaved and a bit studious, but with a mental age of 10. That was one side of Francis Crowley. "Two-Gun," the other side, reappeared whenever he was with the general population of prisoners.

Duringer was executed in the electric chair on December 13, 1931. Crowley's date was January 21, 1932. When they tied the hood over his head, he said, "My last wish is to send my love to my mother."

Francis Crowley was one of the first to blame the media for his crimes, and he was certainly entranced by glamorized violence. He was a slender reed easily bent by any breeze. It's also clear he basked in his brief celebrity, and that newspapers and radio were happy to exploit him. It was the same symbiotic relationship the popular press would experience with **Charles Starkweather** and Caril Ann Fugate half a century later.

Crowley is largely forgotten today, but he was immortalized on film by James Cagney as Cody Jarrett in Raoul Walsh's *White Heat* (1949). As all Hollywood films do, it takes countless liberties with Crowley's story, but it makes use of many key details, primarily the criminal's obsessive devotion to his mother and the importance of forensic evidence in the efforts to catch him.

Crowley's police standoff may also have been a partial inspiration for Luc Besson's fine action film, *Leon, the Professional* (1994).

Cullen, Charles

Among killer nurses, Charles Cullen is notable mostly for his cooperation with authorities after he was caught. Beyond that, his homicidal career follows familiar patterns.

Born in 1960, he grew up in working-class New Jersey and Pennsylvania. His troubled family was devoutly Catholic. By the time Cullen was a teenager, both of his parents and two siblings had died and he had attempted suicide. Another suicide attempt ended his Navy service. He graduated from nursing school, found a job at a hospital, and killed his first victim. It was 1988.

Cullen's mental condition continued to deteriorate despite marriage and children. He divorced, declared bankruptcy, attempted suicide several more times, and moved from job to job, hospital to hospital. Patients died wherever he went.

He murdered with drug overdoses, usually digoxin or insulin. Hospital executives were aware of these "clusters" of deaths and Cullen came under suspicion more than once. But there was a severe shortage of nurses and so even with his history of emotional problems, Cullen was able to find work throughout New Jersey and Pennsylvania. It ended in December 2003, when he was arrested for attempted murder.

Cullen confessed right away and promised to reveal everything if he were spared the death penalty. Prosecutors agreed, and he is now serving life.

The final count of his victims appears to be around 30. When asked why, Cullen replied with the standard answers: he thought they were going to die soon and he was easing their suffering. At other times, though, he claimed not to have been in control of his actions, not even remembering the actual killings. Whatever the truth, his 15-year reign of quiet terror is proof the medical system is still not equipped to deal with in-house killers.

Cunanan, Andrew

Andrew Cunanan is often inaccurately described as a gay serial killer. He was gay, but as these crimes are defined, he was actually a "spree" killer, closer to **Charlie Starkweather** than to **John Wayne Gacy**. Like Starkweather, he was a flashy, good-looking young guy who decided to go out in a blaze of violent glory.

Cunanan's upbringing in middle-class San Diego was free from egregious abuse. He came out as a teenager and immersed himself in gay nightlife, playing several different roles in the culture and eventually moving to San Francisco. He was the tasteful paid companion (glorified boytoy) of a wealthy older man who maintained him in fancy

digs until Cunanan became too pushy and sugar daddy kissed him goodbye.

At the same time, he was heavily involved in gay sadomasochistic porn, both as a consumer and a participant, and in illegal drugs, particularly crystal meth. Throughout his early 20s, Cunanan was able to keep the two sides of his life separate and in balance. But as he got older and thicker he saw it all starting to slide away and seems to have realized he hadn't really done anything with his life.

In April 1997 he made arrangements to leave California and visit a friend, David Madson, in Minneapolis. Even though Cunanan was broke, with his credit cards maxed out at $40,000-plus, he gave away most of his best stuff to friends and threw a big going-away party for himself.

He'd been in Minneapolis only a few days when something went terribly wrong. Either acting alone or with Madson, he killed Jeff Trail, another friend he had known in California. In Madson's apartment, Cunanan attacked Trail with a clawhammer. He rolled the body up in a rug, and he and Madson took off in Madson's Jeep. Madson's body was found a few days later on a country road north of Minneapolis. He'd been shot three times in the head.

Less than a week later, Cunanan had made his way to Chicago where he encountered 72-year-old real estate developer Lee Miglin. He may have seen Miglin puttering around in his open garage and decided he wanted Miglin's Lexus. Or he may have already known Miglin, though there is no direct evidence to support it (some have suggested Miglin's son Duke was gay and knew Cunanan, though Duke denied it.)

Miglin's wife Marilyn, famous for her role on the Home Shopping Network, was away for the weekend. Whatever the circumstances, Cunanan made his way into Miglin's home. Once he had overpowered the older man in the closed garage, Cunanan went totally medieval. He wrapped Miglin's head in duct tape, and savagely tortured him, stabbing him with a screwdriver, and cutting his throat with a saw. He then spent the night in Miglin's townhouse, had a meal and a bath before he stole some gold coins and made off in the Lexus.

When he learned the cops knew about his new ride—based on their tracking him with the car's cell phone—Cunanan ditched it near Philadelphia. His next victim was William Reese, custodian at the historic Finn's Point Cemetery in Pennsville, New Jersey. Cunanan forced him into the basement of the caretaker's house, and shot him execution-style in the back of the head. He stole Reese's pickup and drove south.

Cunanan's last stop was Miami Beach, where he stashed the truck in a public garage and checked into a cheap hotel on May 10th. For the next two months, he lived openly, hanging out at gay clubs, even though a national manhunt for him was taking place.

Cunanan had a purpose for going to Miami. For reasons no one understands, he was hunting fashion designer Gianni Versace, world famous for his silly clothes and conspicuous wealth. They had crossed paths once before, when Versace mistook Cunanan for someone else, but that appears to have been the extent of their contact.

Even though Versace was an icon of the gay community and was known for his wild parties with younger men who were paid to attend, there is no evidence the fashion maven and the psycho killer ever met in that context. Perhaps Cunanan was simply jealous of the other man's wealth and status— the mansions, the entourage, the hobnobbing with Princess Di. Versace had everything; Cunanan had a stolen .40 caliber pistol. It just wasn't fair.

Versace was routinely accompanied by bodyguards whenever he was in public, but he felt so safe in the neighborhood of his gated Miami estate he went out alone each morning to buy coffee, newspapers, and magazines at a café on Ocean Drive. On July 15th, Cunanan followed him back to his mansion and shot him twice in the head as he opened the gate. Versace was dead before he fell to the marble steps.

Again, Cunanan vanished. For eight days, the FBI and local police searched for him. The killer

Andrew Cunanan's FBI Most Wanted poster, 1997. (AP Photo)

was holed up on a luxurious houseboat whose owner was in Las Vegas.

On the afternoon of July 23rd, the boat's caretaker and his wife came by to check on the place. They found it unlocked and when they went in, saw signs someone had been living there. As they were looking around, they heard a loud shot. They hustled out and called the police. The cops went into full TV-ready SWAT team frenzy, surrounding the boat with helicopters, car lights, and snipers.

The shot heard by the caretakers had been the one that Cunanan put through his brain. He wasn't going to answer any questions.

Cunanan's story has been the subject of several books. The most detailed is Maureen Orth's *Vulgar Favors* (2000). Hollywood has not shown any interest, but *Fashion Victim: The Killing of Gianni Versace*

Princess Diana, Elton John, and others attend Gianni Versace's funeral in Milan, 1997. (AP Photo)

(2002) is a straightforward documentary focusing more on Versace and his gaudy creations than on Cunanan.

Czolgosz, Leon

Armed with screwy politics, mental instability, a .32 pistol, and an unpronounceable name, Leon Czolgosz decided to make his mark.

At the turn of the twentieth century, he was one of seven children of impoverished Polish immigrants in Detroit, Michigan. He grew up to be a factory worker in an era of bitter labor-management conflict, which led him to the anarchist movement and the writings of "Red" Emma Goldman.

As an offshoot of socialism, anarchists were against all governments and supported their over-

throw by any means necessary. In essence, they were libertarian terrorists. Like so many other radical movements, they were splintered into dozens if not hundreds of groups in the Midwest.

Czolgosz's activism seems to have been checkered. He was denounced by other anarchists and may have suffered a breakdown in 1898. The 20-something moved back in with his father and withdrew from the world.

Then he learned of the assassination of Italy's King Humbert I by Gaetano Bresci, a fellow anarchist who had the courage of his convictions. Leon was inspired. He had been shown the one true path.

Less than a month later, he moved to Buffalo, New York, where the magnificent Pan-American

Exposition was taking place. He rented a room for $2 a week over a noisy saloon and haunted the Exposition. He knew President William McKinley would visit, so Czolgosz bought an Iver-Johnson revolver.

The next day, he wrapped the pistol in a towel, put it in his pocket and set off in search of the President. Czolgosz found him that afternoon shaking hands with well-wishers in the Temple of Music. Mr. McKinley was guarded by local police, Secret Service officers, and a squad of soldiers from the 73rd Company.

Czolgosz waited in line. When he reached the President, he shot twice. One bullet was deflected by a button. The other cut through McKinley's abdomen and lodged in his pancreas. The assembled "guards" immediately set upon the shooter and might have beaten him to death on the spot, had not the President told them not to hurt the guy.

His wound was serious, but, like James Garfield 20 years before, McKinley succumbed several days later to an infection—gangrene—brought on by unsanitary treatment by his doctors.

Czolgosz confessed fully and immediately. Like Bresci, he was proud of what he had done. The trial began less than a month after the shooting. It took eight hours and 26 minutes from jury selection to guilty verdict. The assassin died in the New York electric chair on October 29, 1901.

The changes Czolgosz effected are arguably as great as those brought about by any of the American presidential assassins. Though they mean to bring down or cripple the government, they actually strengthen it. McKinley's death brought Theodore Roosevelt to the presidency.

Czolgosz is a minor character in Stephen Sondheim and John Wideman's musical *Assassins* (1991, 2004). Beyond it, he is largely forgotten.

D, E, F

Dahmer, Jeffrey

Even among serial killers, who tend to come from troubled homes, Jeffrey Dahmer had a tough childhood.

He was born in 1960 to two parents who hated each other, fought constantly, and divorced when Dahmer was 17. His mother split, taking his brother and assuming her fundamentalist husband would take care of Jeffrey. Wrong. Dad had decided to depart, too, with the same assumption, abandoning the boy. By then, Dahmer was already in pretty bad shape.

At age 8, he had been molested by another child. Picked on mercilessly in high school, he regularly got drunk on beer before classes began. After school, he liked to "experiment" on small animals, killing and skinning them and preserving their remains. He once mounted the head of a dog on a post in the woods near his house.

His first murder took place while he was left alone at his parents' place. He picked up 19-year-old Stephen Hicks who was hitchhiking. Back at Dahmer's home, they got a little drunk and had sex. When Hicks wanted to leave, Dahmer bashed his head in with a barbell and strangled him. He dismembered the body, and later broke up the bones and scattered them in the woods.

Dahmer tried college and the military but didn't last long in either. He moved in with his grandmother in West Allis, Wisconsin in 1982. During the next five years, he was picked up on various sex-related charges—disorderly conduct, fondling a 13-year-old. His killings did not resume until 1987 when he lured another young man to his death. The alcoholism continued, along with the "experiments." His grandmother, unaware of the killings, got fed up and kicked him out in the spring of 1988.

Dahmer moved to an apartment in Milwaukee where the homicidal madness became uncontrollable. His MO didn't vary. Most of his victims were black or Asian young men picked up in gay bars. At his house, they were rendered helpless with drugs or drink, and killed. Dahmer's lust descended into necrophilia and cannibalism.

The most famous incident in his sick career occurred on May 16, 1991 when 14-year-old Konerak Sinthasomphone escaped from Dahmer's trap. Neighbors saw him dazed, naked, and bleeding on the street and called the cops. The Laotian boy did not speak English, and Dahmer was able to persuade police they were just having a little lovers' spat and everything was really okay. They led the kid back to Dahmer's apartment and left. (Sinthasomphone was the younger brother of a boy Dahmer had molested

Jeffrey Dahmer in a Milwaukee courtroom, facing first-degree murder charges, 1991. (AP Photo)

three years before.) Dahmer killed him that night and kept his head as a souvenir. He kept a lot of souvenirs, and killed at least 17 men and boys.

It ended in 1989 when another of his victims, Tracy Edwards, managed to escape and ran into the street with handcuffs clamped to one wrist. He flagged down a police car and told the officers he had met this guy in a bar and gone back to his place where the guy turned into a monster and threatened him with a knife. When the cops got into Dahmer's apartment, they found a chamber of horrors that rivaled **Ed Gein**'s. Polaroids of body parts and mutilations, human heads, other organs, electric saws.

An insanity defense went nowhere and Dahmer was sentenced to 15 life sentences with a minimum of 936 years (Wisconsin does not have the death penalty).

Dahmer was locked up in the Columbia Correctional Institute where he refused to accept any sort of protective custody. He survived one murder attempt and refused to press charges against his attacker. Four months later another inmate, murderer Christopher Scarver, killed Dahmer and fellow inmate Jesse Anderson by attacking them with a metal bar from an exercise machine.

In 1994 Dahmer's father published his version of things in *A Father's Story*. Dahmer has also been the subject of an album by the metal band Macabre. Three low-budget horror films have been made about him, *Jeffrey Dahmer: The Secret Life* (1993), *Dahmer* (2002), and *Raising Jeffrey Dahmer* (2006).

Dalton Gang

As an outlaw, Bob Dalton was a big idea kind of guy. He didn't sweat the little details and that's what did him in. His brothers, too.

They came from Missouri and were distantly related to the Younger brothers who had ridden with **Jesse James**. The oldest of the several Dalton sons, Frank, became a U.S. Marshal and was killed in the line of duty in Oklahoma 1887. Following his lead, three of his brothers—Grat, Bob, and Emmett—signed on as lawmen, too. But things didn't work out for them and they started stealing horses. When warrants were issued for their arrest, they headed west to California where their brother Bill lived.

The Daltons attempted their first train robbery in California on February 6, 1891. It was a disaster. They killed the engineer, George Radcliff, but got no money when the guard of the express car, where valuables were kept, refused to unlock the door and peppered them with shotgun fire. Then during the getaway, Bill and Grat were captured.

At trial, Bill was acquitted and stayed in California. Grat was convicted but managed to escape and went east to join his brothers in the Oklahoma and Indian Territories. Their lack of success at train robbery not withstanding, they persuaded other men, including Dick Broadwell, **Bill Doolin**, and Bill Powers, to join the gang.

For a time they were moderately successful bandits, but it wasn't enough for Bob. He wanted to pull off a big job, one that would give them the recognition they deserved. But what?

Finally, it came to him—they would rob two banks at once! Not even the James gang had attempted that. And he knew just the place where they could find two banks conveniently located right across the street from each other. In Coffeyville, Kansas.

Emmett argued against it. They were well-known in Coffeyville, people would recognize them. Bob said they would wear wigs and false beards, and he was not to be denied. Off they went.

On the way into town on the morning of October 5, 1892 Bill Doolin's horse came up lame and he excused himself to steal another while the three Dalton boys, Dick Broadwell, and Bill Powers continued on. Some sources suggest the lame horse was an excuse and Doolin had some idea of what was coming. In any case, he and Bill Dalton later reformed the gang and were killed by lawmen.

The five outlaws ran into their first problems as they entered Coffeyville. Alec McKenna, a childhood acquaintance, recognized them right away and noticed the weapons under their coats. Then they ran into the second problem. the hitching posts in front of the banks had been removed so the street could be repaired. The only place they could tie their horses was in a nearby alley. Details, details.

They left the horses in the alley. Grat Dalton, Powers, and Broadwell went into the C.M. Condon bank, while Emmett and Bob Dalton took the First National. Meanwhile, McKenna was alerting the townspeople they were being robbed. Dozens of citizens grabbed rifles, shotguns, and pistols. They converged on the street and opened fire.

Emmett and Bob realized what was happening and tried to get out the back door of the First National. Grat, Broadwell, and Power went back out the front door of the Condon bank straight into a hail of bullets. Powers was cut down right there.

Grat was wounded but managed to kill Marshal Charley Connelly before he died. Broadwell was wounded but mounted his horse and tried to ride out. He was hit two more times. His body was later found outside town. Emmett, seriously wounded, made it onto his horse, too, but when he went back for his dying brother, Bob, he was hit by two more shotgun blasts.

The famous photograph taken later that day shows the bodies of Bill Powers, Bob and Grat Dalton, and Dick Broadwell laid out in a row, hands crossed, propped against rough wooden siding.

Miraculously, Emmett survived. He was sentenced to life in prison, though eyewitnesses said he didn't kill anyone. A model prisoner, he was released in 1907 and married his childhood sweetheart. He then moved to California where he worked in real estate and served as a technical advisor in the early days of movies.

Emmett actually played himself (and his brothers!) in the 1918 silent film *Beyond the Law*. An adaptation of his book *When the Daltons Rode* (1937) was made in 1940. The Dalton brothers appeared in a few of the standard 1950s westerns. Dan Curtis' *Last Ride of the Dalton Gang* (1979) treats the story as light comedy. The rarely seen made-for-television film *The Last Day* (1975) with Richard Widmark is regarded as the most accurate account.

Darrow, Clarence

Clarence Darrow was America's first celebrity lawyer. He was involved in many of the most important criminal cases of his time (1857–1938) and he won a lot of them. With a carefully contrived image based on rumpled clothing and unkempt hair, he was an intelligent, eloquent, fierce advocate for his clients. Perhaps as significantly, he was also a skillful manipulator of the national press, who realized the importance early on of the "court of public opinion."

Largely self-educated, Darrow believed most of his cases were won and lost in jury selection and he was famous for his research into potential jurors. "Get the right men in the box and the rest is window dressing," he reportedly uttered, believing the Irish and Jews as the most easily swayed by his emotional appeals. He was also quoted as often saying (in *The Encyclopedia of American Crime*, 2001), "Give me that combination in the box and I could get Judas Iscariot off with a $5 fine."

Among his clients were several labor leaders, including Big Bill Hayward and Eugene V. Debs, who was later a partner in his firm. Darrow successfully defended Ossian Sweet, the black Detroit doctor who killed a white man—part of a mob attacking his home—and **Robert Elliott Burns**, the famous fugitive from the Georgia chain gang.

Darrow's most famous case was probably the Scopes Monkey Trial where he defended a Tennessee public school teacher who taught evolution. His opponent was William Jennings Bryan who argued for the literal truth of the Bible. Though Darrow made Bryan look narrow-minded, he actually lost the case.

Darrow's unconventional defense of murders **Leopold and Loeb** in 1924 was just as impressive. He did not deny their guilt or try to mitigate it with an insanity defense. Instead, he decided to have their case heard by a single judge—not a jury—and essentially put the death penalty on trial. It worked. The judge spared the boys' lives.

Given his affinity for unpopular causes, it's no surprise Darrow was constantly in financial straits. Late in his career he was so impoverished he accepted a role in the disgraceful **Massie Case** and represented four white defendants who had kidnapped and murdered a Hawaiian man. The legendary lawyer seems to have enjoyed the islands and was not his usual fiery self in court. His clients were found guilty, but they managed to escape punishment when the President intervened.

Darrow was a true larger-than-life figure with a taste for the grape and other pleasures of the flesh. His autobiography is a fairly tame look at his event-

ful life. The best biographies are by Irving Stone and Kevin Tierney. On screen, Orson Welles played a slightly fictionalized Darrow in *Compulsion* (1959). So did Spencer Tracy and Jack Lemmon in the 1960 and 1999 screen versions of *Inherit the Wind* (Jason Robards and Melvyn Douglas also played the role in other TV adaptations of the play by Jerome Lawrence and Robert E. Lee.) In the 1970s Henry Fonda played Darrow in a memorable one-man stage show broadcast on television, and Kevin Spacey starred in a rarely seen 1991 made-for-TV movie about Darrow.

Davis, T. Cullen

Killing your ex-wife's boyfriend and her daughter: $1,000,000.

Assassinating a judge: $2,000,000.

Getting away with it: Priceless.

That's exactly what many people think happened with T. Cullen Davis. Even though he was identified by eyewitnesses in the first crime and was recorded on tape ordering the second, a pit bull of a lawyer was able to persuade two Texas juries otherwise.

In the early 1970s Davis was a wealthy Texas oilman, rumored to be the model for the wily and duplicitous J.R. Ewing on the TV series *Dallas* (1978–91).

Davis had married Priscilla Wilborn, a well stacked high-maintenance blonde. Their blessed union ended in a nasty divorce that took several angry years to work out. In the process, Priscilla got Davis' mansion and substantial alimony. Davis was incensed.

On the night of August 2, 1976 someone broke into the mansion and executed 12-year-old Andrea Wilborn, Priscilla's daughter from her first marriage. The killer probably didn't expect to find her there. She wasn't supposed to be in the house that night. Her mother was out celebrating a victory in the divorce proceedings with her boyfriend Stan Farr. When they returned, the killer attacked them with a pistol.

Wounded, Priscilla yelled, "Stan, run! It's Cullen!" She broke loose and fled. The killer shot Farr four times, killing him. The gunman gave chase and caught Priscilla just as another couple drove up. Beverly Bass recognized Cullen Davis and said so to her companion "Bubba" Gavrel, Jr. The gunman fired at them and wounded young Gavrel. He was crippled for life. Both Priscilla and Beverly escaped and identified Davis as their assailant.

When the police picked him up early the next morning, Davis did not resist. One of the cops asked him why so many people had to die. Davis answered that for some things, you didn't need a reason. The juries never heard that, though. Davis hadn't been read his rights. The juries did hear from Davis' lawyer, the famous Richard "Racehorse" Haynes.

At the first trial, for the murder of Andrea Wilborn, Haynes attacked the witnesses, accusing them of various sexual depravities, drug use, and worse. It worked; Davis walked.

A year later, Davis met an FBI informant who claimed the oilman had tried to hire him to kill the judge in his ongoing divorce proceedings, and others, including Priscilla. The cops faked a picture of the judge's bloody body, put a wire on the informant, and set up another meeting with Davis where the happy millionaire forked over $25,000.

Davis was locked up immediately. This time, it took $2 million and Racehorse's best efforts for two trials. Again, Davis skated away.

Soon after the second acquittal, Davis found religion and made a great show of destroying some of his worldly goods. He went bankrupt in 1986 and could still be tried for the murder of Stan Farr.

Priscilla died of breast cancer in 2001.

Two detailed books have been written about the crimes—*Final Justice* (1993), by Steve Naifeh and Gregory White Smith, and *Blood Will Tell* (1979) by Gary Cartwright. Cartwright's book is the basis for the 1995 TV movie, *Texas Justice*.

DeFeo, Ronald, Jr.

Amityville

There really was a horror in Amityville. It didn't have anything to do with goop on the walls or ghostly pigs. It was about a violent father and son.

Ronald DeFeo worked in his family's car dealership and thought he had finally made it when he was able to buy the house on the river at 112 Ocean Avenue in Amityville, Long Island.

Ronald DeFeo, Jr., called Butch, was the oldest of his five children. Ronald Sr. was said to be quick with his mitts when the kids misbehaved and was hardest on Ron Jr., an apple that didn't fall far from the tree. As a teenager, Junior had violent fights and once even pulled a shotgun on the old man. It was one of several weapons the kid owned.

Junior also liked to indulge in booze, heroin, and speed. His featherbed job at the car dealership kept in him pocket change but it wasn't enough. In the fall of 1974 he and a friend faked a robbery when Ron Jr. was sent to deposit some checks and cash from work. He claimed to have been stuck up on the way to the bank. It didn't fool people for very long, and somehow, it brought all of Junior's discontents into sharp focus.

Early on the morning of November 12, 1974 he loaded up a high powered hunting rifle and slaughtered his parents, two brothers, and two sisters as they slept in their beds. Then he took a nice long shower, packed up his bloody clothes and rifle, and ditched them in a Brooklyn storm drain before he reported to work. Throughout the day, he wondered aloud to friends why no one was answering the phone at his house when all the cars were parked there. Late in the afternoon, he and some acquaintances went over and discovered the bodies. Junior sobbed with uncontrollable grief and told police he feared a hitman was responsible.

The cops cracked his story easily.

At trial, his counsel mounted an insanity defense, but it didn't take. Junior got six consecutive 25-years-to-life sentences.

In April 2006 DeFeo appeared on a televised interview to claim, without any proof, that his sister had actually committed most of the murders. But how did the all-too-real horror become *The Amityville Horror*, and why did the wild-eyed yarn become such a huge hit?

The first part is easy: George and Kathy Lutz bought the DeFeo house at a bargain price a year or so after the murders. When things got tough financially, they had to move out. That's when writer Jay Anson came in. Riding the wave of credulity spawned by William Peter Blatty's allegedly based-on-fact *The Exorcist*, Anson and the Lutzes came up with all sorts of ghosties and ghoulies and things that went ka-ching in the night.

The book did very well and the film with James Brolin, Margot Kidder, and Rod Steiger became a smash hit, spawning no less than six sequels and a remake in 2005.

But the real source of the story's popularity had nothing to do with Ronald DeFeo and very little to do with the town of Amityville, New York. The initial fictions, both on the page and on screen, found their resonance in the economic problems of the middle class in the 1970s: double-digit inflation, skyrocketing gas prices, and monster mortgages. Those *are* profoundly frightening and, as Stephen King notes in his book *Danse Macabre* (1978), the movie plays on those fears so brilliantly it turned Amityville into an unusually long-lived franchise.

Diamond, Jack "Legs"

Legs Diamond was one of the most colorful of the early New York gangsters. With his unfettered libido and reputation for indestructibility, he attracted attention. But he always looked out for himself first, and even in a world where betrayal was the norm, he had a bad reputation.

Some said he got the nickname "Legs" by stealing merchandise from trucks and running away from cops in the crowded streets. Others said he got it from running out on his partners and friends. He

did run out on the Army when he was drafted in World War I, he deserted. When they caught him, they locked him up in Leavenworth for a year and a day. He made connections in the joint that got him work with Little Augie Orgen and **Lepke Buchalter** (in their union rackets and bootlegging) when he got out. He also provided muscle for gambler **Arnold Rothstein**.

Legs demonstrated such proficiency as a shooter that Little Augie ordered him to kill their main rival, Nathan "Kid Dropper" Kaplan. Since the Dropper was known to surround himself with bodyguards at all times, Diamond decided to outsource the hit to Louis Kushner, who was perhaps not the brightest bulb on Little Augie's chandelier.

They filed phony assault charges against the Dropper and were waiting when he showed up at the Essex Market Court on August 28, 1932. With dozens of cops and his own men swarming around him, Dropper left court and got into a police car that was to take him to a second hearing. Before the car could move, Kushner jumped up on the rear bumper and fired his pistol through the rear glass. He wounded two cops and killed the Dropper with a bullet to the head.

Kushner, pleased as punch to be the center of attention, posed for photographers and smiled as they took him away.

The competition now depleted, Little Augie extended his reach and put Legs in charge of beer and dope in a territory stretching from Manhattan to Albany. Legs also bought part ownership in the Hotsy Totsy Club, a Broadway speakeasy. It was rumored he used the back rooms to bump off rival mobsters after he invited them to the club on the pretext of discussing negotiated settlements.

In 1929 Legs and one of his lieutenants exchanged words with Red Cassidy, a low-level mobster. The confrontation escalated and ended with Legs perforating Red, who managed to get out with the help of his pals. Red died a few hours later. Legs took a powder until the heat died down and he could be sure witnesses would keep their mouths shut. It worked. Sometime later, the charges were dismissed.

But while Legs was out of the picture, **Dutch Schultz** moved in and took over a chunk of Diamond's booze biz. Eventually, they met and worked out an arrangement where the Dutchman paid Legs $500 grand for the places he had appropriated. But as Dutch was leaving the hotel where the meeting had taken place, he was ambushed by two men in an alley. One of his men was killed, though he was unhurt. Legs had already scrammed, so Dutch knew who was behind the attempted hit.

After that, full-scale war. It's when the legend of Legs' uncanny ability to absorb bullets and recover from the wounds grew to biblical proportions. He was hit with an incredible number of slugs and buckshot. He was seriously wounded five times over the next two years and survived all of them, to the surprise of his doctors. It all reportedly led Dutch to ask, "Ain't there anybody that can shoot this guy so he won't bounce back up?" according to Robert Jay Nash's *Bloodletters and Badmen* (1973).

Schultz got his wish on December 18, 1931. For years, many people assumed it was the Dutchman's men who caught up with Legs in a rooming house in Albany, and put three bullets in his head, two in his chest. The credit really should go to Albany's finest.

According to writer William Kennedy, who talked to some of the people involved, Diamond was trying to establish a protection racket to shake down the local merchants. But the Democratic political machine controlled all of the major vice and crime in the city, and those guys weren't about to open things up to an outsider. Party chairman Dan O'Connell ordered the police to take care of Diamond and they did the job.

Kennedy tells the story in *Legs* (1976), the first of his Albany novels. Diamond is also the protagonist of Bud Boetticher's wonderfully titled *The Rise and Fall of Legs Diamond* (1960). He's a supporting character in *Portrait of a Mobster* (1961), *Murder, Inc.* (1960), *Hit the Dutchman* (1992), *Mad*

Dog Coll (1992), *The Outfit* (1997), and *Cotton Club* (1984).

Dillinger, John

John Herbert Dillinger was America's greatest criminal, the Elvis of outlaws.

Like the King, he was an average middle-class white kid who skyrocketed to the top of his chosen profession to huge public acclaim and equally huge disapproval, only to die an early death. Then, finally in death, he received the highest degree of celebrity the American public can bestow—the faithful believed he was still alive.

And in Dillinger's case, it might have even been true.

Born in 1903 in Indianapolis, Indiana, little Johnny started getting into trouble early on. His mother died when he was four and his father seems to have been a distant figure. As a teenager Dillinger joined the Navy and quickly deserted. Back home, he grew bored with work but showed real promise as a baseball player. He also had a way with the ladies, and they responded. In 1924, when he was 21, he and an older friend had a few beers and decided to rob a grocer. They made a complete mess of it and were quickly captured. Dillinger's dad told his son not to bother with a lawyer and to throw himself on the mercy of the court. He followed the dubious advice and got 10-to-20 years from a by-the-book judge.

In the reformatory and later in prison, Dillinger's cocky, independent nature made him a poor prisoner. He attempted to escape several times and was often disciplined. He settled down, or appeared to, after he gravitated toward the older inmates, experienced bank robbers like Harry Pierpont, John "Red" Hamilton, and Walter Dietrich, who'd learned his craft from the legendary **Herman "Baron" Lamm**. Dillinger also met the playful Homer Van Meter who would become his friend and partner in crime.

All of the older guys were looking at long stretches. In the early 1930s, Dillinger had the best shot at an early parole so they constructed an elaborate scheme. The more experienced cons taught their eager young acolyte all they knew about the business of bank robbery. They gave him the names of people to contact for help, and told him which banks and businesses offered the best possibilities for big scores. The idea was that when he got out, Dillinger would commit enough jobs to bribe guards, buy guns to smuggle into the prison, and arrange transportation and hideouts. Then they'd bust out and join him. Amazingly, it worked. Well, almost.

Dillinger became a good prisoner and was paroled. He knocked over several banks while working with substandard partners and managed to sneak four pistols back to his pals. But in the meantime, he was picked up by the cops—who had staked out his girlfriend's apartment. While his pals were breaking out of prison, Johnny D. was locked up in Lima, Ohio. When Harry Pierpont learned what had happened, he returned the favor: he and his gang robbed a bank in St. Marys, Ohio, and then went to Lima. In the process of springing Dillinger, Pierpont killed Sheriff Jess Sarber, a man who had treated his prisoner well, and they earned the name "the Terror Gang."

For the next nine months, Dillinger and different gangs ran wild in the Midwest, sticking up banks and raiding arsenals and police stations for weapons, ammunition, and bulletproof vests. Though the gangs had no single leader, Dillinger became the star. He had a signature move, an athletic vault over the counter to impress and intimidate bank employees. Also, he tended to be polite to older women, or so it was reported.

During those dark days of the Depression, banks were often seen as the enemy of the common man. In that light, Dillinger wasn't stealing people's money, he was stealing the banks' money. The gang's exploits became front page news and they were reported to be everywhere. Several traps were set, but Dillinger managed to elude them all, sometimes racing through the streets in his Hudson Terraplane. When things got too hot in the Midwest, the gang decided to spend Christmas in Daytona Beach.

After Florida, they headed west and were hiding out in Tucson when they were recognized by the police and arrested on January 25, 1934. All of the Midwestern states wanted the gang and actually engaged in a bidding war to have them extradited. As it happened, most of the gang went to Ohio, while the Chicago cops got Dillinger. They didn't keep him long.

On March 3rd, Dillinger broke out of the Crown Point jail with the famous wooden gun he had carved and darkened with shoe polish. Or maybe he had a real pistol, or maybe he was unarmed. Choose your favorite version of the story. With that incident, as with so many in Dillinger's life, it's difficult to tell the truth from embroidery from complete fabrication. In any case, Dillinger took several hostages, stole a couple of real Tommy guns, boosted a sheriff's car and calmly cruised away from the prison without a shot being fired.

But, when he drove the sheriff's car across a state line, he committed a federal offense—bringing **J. Edgar Hoover** and his bureau, ravenous for good publicity, into the picture. Innocent Midwestern bystanders were in mortal peril.

With his pals in jail, Dillinger started a new gang that included Homer Van Meter and **Baby Face Nelson**, a psycho who had a stint with the Capone mob on his resume. They moved their base of operations to Minnesota and embarked on another series of bank robberies to raise money for Pierpont's defense. Dillinger was wounded in one encounter with the law, and the gang decided to cool it for a time. They hid out at the Little Bohemia Lodge north of Rhinelander, Wisconsin in April 1934.

They thought they were safe, but the owner's wife tipped the feds. Hugh Clegg, assistant director of the FBI, and famous G-Man **Melvin Purvis** decided to ambush them. A dozen or so federal agents hid in the woods near the lodge and were approaching it as three men came out and got in a car. The tightly-wrapped feds opened fire, wounding two and killing one, all innocent bystanders. The outlaws escaped, though their molls were later found in the basement.

John Dillinger, with two of his little friends. (AP Photo)

Over the next few months, the details of Dillinger's story are even murkier. According to the "official" version, he and Van Meter altered their appearance and fingerprints through plastic surgery. Dillinger, one of the most recognizable men in the country, was so confident in his new look that he freely walked the streets of Chicago and adopted the alias Jimmy Lawrence. He kept company with a new girlfriend, Polly Hamilton, a waitress and part-time hooker who worked for madam Anna Sage.

Anna Sage, who would be the famous "woman in red," ratted Dillinger out to Chicago cop Martin Zarkovich. Zarkovich approached Purvis and the FBI to set up a trap. Anna told them that she, Polly, and Dillinger were going to see one of two movies on the night of July 27th. The feds staked out both theaters and were waiting at the Biograph where the trio went to see Clark Gable in *Manhattan Melodrama*. When they came out, Purvis spotted Dillinger. Agents ordered him to stop and gunned him down. They claimed he had pulled a gun. Only two bystanders were wounded.

Various versions of the "unofficial" version say Jimmy Lawrence was a low level Chicago hood who resembled Dillinger and suffered from a serious heart condition. The doubters point to numerous inconsistencies between the autopsy report and the known facts about Dillinger. They also say that if the FBI had killed the wrong guy—knowingly or not—the truth would have been so embarrassing they would have played along with the deception. And they say that by that point in his career, Dillinger himself knew it was over and he wanted to get out. In short, everyone wanted John Dillinger to go away, and so he went away.

Even for those who don't normally entertain conspiracy theories, there is room for some doubt in this case and it is altogether appropriate for such a legendary figure.

In the wake of his brief criminal career, Dillinger has become a genuine icon of popular culture, equal if not superior to Elvis or Marilyn. The myth about his extraordinary endowment seems to have sprung from a photograph of his sheet-covered corpse where his arm, stiffened by rigor mortis, makes an impressive tent of the sheet. Ever since then, boys have told tales about how the impressive appendage is kept in a jar deep in the vaults of the Smithsonian. Or did J. Edgar Hoover display it on his desk? The variations befit his status.

Of all American outlaws, John D. has fared particularly well in fiction. In the brilliant *Illuminatus!* (1975) trilogy of novels by Robert Shea and Robert Anton Wilson, he is a central character, intimately involved with Marilyn and the assassination of JFK. That's his fictional zenith, but he has also been the subject of novels by Harry Patterson (*Dillinger: A Novel*, 1983), Arthur Knight Winfield (*Johnnie D.*, 2000) and James Carlos Blake (*Handsome Harry*, 2004).

In nonfiction, Dillinger is rediscovered every decade or so. The most interesting contemporaneous account of his eventful life is *Dillinger: The Untold Story* (1994) by Russell Girdarin and Louis Piquett, Dillinger's lawyer. Leading the conspiracists is Jay Robert Nash's 1970 *Dillinger: Dead or Alive?* More recently, Dary Matera's *John Dillinger: The Life and Death of America's First Celebrity Criminal* (2004), takes the more traditional approach. John Toland's *The Dillinger Days* (1963) and Bryan Burrough's *Public Enemies* (2004) look at the Midwestern gangs that flourished in the 1930s.

Naturally, Dillinger's story has been filmed but it didn't happen right away. Immediately after he was shot, Will Hays, President of the MPAA, decreed "no motion picture on the life and exploits of John Dillinger will be produced, distributed, or exhibited" according to Carlos Clarens' book, *Crime Movies* (1980). In those days, the studio system was so monolithic it could issue such a proclamation and make it stick. Nothing was done until 1945 when tough guy Lawrence Tierney made his screen debut in *Dillinger*, a very short biopic that skates over the surface of his criminal career and pays little attention to details or characters.

The All-American outlaw has made at least a dozen more screen appearances from such outré fare as *The Erotic Adventures of Bonnie and Clyde* (1988) to *Young Dillinger* (1965) starring Nick Adams. John Milius' 1970 *Dillinger* is lively, but plays fast and loose with facts to draw parallels between Dillinger (well played by Warren Oates) and Melvin Purvis (Ben Johnson). *The Woman in Red*, written by John Sayles and directed by Lewis Teague is a passionate left-of-center look at the economic, racial and social conditions of the 1930s that drove people to break the law. It actually sticks fairly close to the known facts with a plot built on details of Dillinger's life. Still, it is forced to make the most of a low budget.

The great Dillinger movie—from a Scorsese, a Stone, or a Soderbergh—has yet to be made.

Doolin, Bill

The Doolin-Dalton gang was formed after the original **Dalton Gang** was obliterated in the disastrous Coffeyville bank robbery attempt of 1892.

By then, Bill Doolin had been with the outfit for about a year. An Oklahoma cowboy, he had run afoul of the law when the authorities broke up a keg party he and several friends were attending in Kansas. The cops were within their rights—Kansas was dry—but the guys didn't take it well and two deputies were either wounded or killed.

Doolin joined the Dalton gang, but he did not take part in the Coffeyville disaster. Either his horse came up lame on the morning of the abortive robbery, or he disagreed with Bob Dalton on tactics, or he realized how reckless and doomed the job was. Whatever the reason, later that year, Bob's brother Bill joined Doolin's gang along with such notables as Bitter Creek Newman, Tulsa Jack Blake, Little Bill Raidler, and Dynamite Dick Clifton. They became the "Oklahombres," some of the most popular outlaws of their time.

They robbed trains and banks, and holed up in a part of the Oklahoma badlands called Hell's Fringe. Doolin knew the country intimately, and the guys

were so well-liked that locals tipped them off to approaching lawmen.

Things went so well for about a year that Doolin was able to marry—albeit in secret. Then on September 1, 1893 the gang was hiding out in the wild town of Ingalls, in the Oklahoma Territory, when they were surprised by a posse of marshals. An intense gunfight broke out in the street outside the Ransom & Murray Saloon. The gang escaped after suffering some wounds, and left three lawmen and two bystanders dead.

A few months later, Dalton and some members of the gang split off on their own. They pulled one job on the First National Bank of Longview, Texas. Another bystander was killed in the process and Dalton was gunned down within two weeks by lawmen who had trailed him to his hideout.

Pressures on the surviving members increased as the marshals put higher and higher prices on their heads and local goodwill slowly withered under the harsh glare of dollar signs. Doolin was captured by the famous marshal Bill Tilghman in January 1896, but Doolin engineered a mass escape in July from the Guthrie jail and got out with either 12 or 37 other prisoners (accounts vary).

He was on the loose for little more than a month before he was tracked down by another marshal posse and killed on August 24th.

Doolin and his gang have never enjoyed the popularity of the James brothers. Randolph Scott starred in *The Doolins of Oklahoma* (1949), a film bearing little resemblance to either the truth or the legends ascribed to the Oklahombres.

The names Doolin and Dalton are probably best known now for their role in the Eagles' 1973 album *Desperado*, a "concept" work equating the careers of nineteenth century outlaws with 1970s rock musicians.

Doss, Nannie

Be glad you're not related to Nannie Doss. Be very glad.

Nannie Doss, "rat poison murderess" held in Tulsa, Oklahoma, 1954. (AP Photo)

Born Nancy Hazel in Blue Mountain, Alabama in 1905, she had a hardscrabble childhood on a small farm. She found her only escape in romance magazines. From those, she fantasized an ideal love she never found in real life, not that she didn't try. At 16, she married Charley Braggs and they produced four daughters. In those same years, both she and Charley screwed around flagrantly, and Nannie became famous for her dark moods.

When she turned mean, nobody crossed her. As the marriage disintegrated, Charley realized something was wrong. Exactly what that was became clear in 1927 when their two middle girls died. Food poisoning was suspected in both cases and Charley probably knew how the food came to be poisoned. He fled. (Thereafter, whenever the family talked about Nannie's husbands, Charley would be referred to as "the one that got away.")

In 1929 Nannie married Frank Harrelson, a handsome factory worker and drunk. Theirs was another tempestuous relationship, but Nannie kept herself under control until 1945. Something changed when her eldest daughter, Melvina, who had grown and married, had her second child.

Nannie was there at the hospital with Melvina and her husband during a long and difficult delivery. It's impossible to say exactly what happened, or why. Melvina had given birth to a little girl. She was still woozy from the ether she had inhaled as an anesthetic, and her husband was asleep in a chair. Nannie was holding the baby. Melvina thought she saw or dreamed something unspeakable—her mother stabbing her daughter in the head with a long hat pin.

Whatever happened, the infant was dead and the doctors had no explanation. A few months later, Melvina's other child died while Nannie was taking care of him. Cause of death—asphyxiation, unexplained. At the boy's funeral, Nannie was inconsolable. It was all she could do to cash in the $500 insurance policy she had taken out on the child. Nannie was now ready to move on to adults.

She spiked husband Frank's corn liquor with arsenic. He succumbed, in considerable pain, on September 16, 1945.

Nannie didn't find husband number three until 1947. She met Arlie Lanning through a lonely-hearts column and moved in with him in Lexington, North Carolina.

Like Frank, Arlie was a drunk, and, like Charley, he was a skirt-chaser. Perhaps because Nannie had become infatuated with the modern miracle of television, as had all America, Arlie lasted for three years. Then Nannie made up a special batch of stewed prunes and arsenic. After Arlie's untimely demise and the mysterious fire destroying their house, Nannie briefly moved in with his mother. She too succumbed to some mysterious ailment before Nannie took the insurance money for the house and moved in with her ailing sister Dovie. Dovie expired inexplicably in her sleep in June.

AMERICAN MURDER

In 1952, working through another lonely-hearts club, Nannie met the recently retired and unlucky Richard Morton. They married and she moved into his house in Emporia, Kansas. As it turned out, Morton was not nearly as well off as he had led Nannie to believe. She might have gotten rid of him right away, but things changed in January 1953 when Nannie's father died (she had nothing to do with that one) and her mother moved in with Nannie and her new hubby.

Days later, Mother Hazel was stricken with horrible stomach pains and died. The clock was ticking for Richard. Three months later, Nannie was crying over his grave.

Husband number four was Sam Doss, of Tulsa, Oklahoma. Nannie met him through one of her clubs while Richard was still among the living. They married in June.

Unlike her previous beloveds, Sam was a pillar of moral rectitude, a seriously thrifty man, early to bed, early to rise. He briefly expected his new wife to live the same sort of life, but she chafed under the strict rules and left him. Sam followed like a puppy and promised to make life happier for her. Gave her access to his checking account and took out a couple of big insurance policies. Bingo! Nannie whipped up some more prunes. She had not, however, taken Sam's hardy constitution into account.

She gave him his first dose of arsenic in September. It made him horribly sick and sent him to the hospital for three weeks. He was finally released on Oct. 5th. Back home, Nannie laced his coffee with more arsenic. Sam never saw another sunrise. Unlike her other victims, though, Sam had a doctor who was paying attention and knew something wasn't right. He ordered an autopsy and Nannie was arrested.

As police uncovered her past and connected the dots, she admitted her guilt. Sentenced to life in Oklahoma, she died in the state pen in 1965 of leukemia.

Nannie's story has never been told on screen, though she might have been a small part of the inspiration for Stephen King's Annie Wilkes in *Misery* (1987).

Dunne, Dominick

Dominick Dunne came to crime writing late in life for the most terrible of reasons.

He was born into a wealthy, well-connected family. His brother was novelist John Gregory Dunne. Stephen Sondheim was a college classmate. Dominick palled around with Gore Vidal and had a fling with Anaïs Nin. He got his start in the entertainment business as a producer on *The Howdy Doody Show*. Afterwards, he found moderate professional success in films and television and his career followed the now-familiar trajectory of overindulgence in drink and drugs, a failed marriage, and burnout.

Then in 1982 his daughter, actress Dominique Dunne, was murdered by an ex-boyfriend. It was a particularly brutal and pointless killing. There was no doubt the man had done it—he had abused other women—nor were there any extenuating circumstances. He was simply a vicious thug. But the trial was a revelation for Dunne.

The jury never learned the most important facts about the killer and they bought his side of things. Though he was convicted, he served less than three years in jail and was set free.

Dunne was outraged and poured his anger into the pages of *Vanity Fair* with the article, "Justice: A Father's Account of the Trial of His Daughter's Killer" in 1984. Since then he has gone on to write more articles and books, mostly focused on celebrity crimes, but never losing his sense of genuinely righteous anger.

Dunne's enthusiasm, however, can get him in trouble. Some bizarre things he said about ex-Congressman Gary Condit, suspected in the murder of his aide Chandra Levy, led to an out-of-court settlement and an apology.

Given Dunne's background and experience, he is at his best when writing about the glamorous and rarified celebrity crimes. When he writes about the **Menendez brothers**, for example, he knows it's important they lived in Beverly Hills, but it is more

Dominick Dunne, spurred to action after his daughter Dominique's murder. (AP Photo)

important they lived at one of the best addresses on one of the best streets in Beverly Hills.

Dunne may have reached his widest audience with his coverage of the **O.J. Simpson** trial where he was a constant presence. He has never been shy about using his status for a bully pulpit, as he did with the novel, *A Season in Purgatory* (1993) a thinly fictionalized account of the Martha Moxley murder by Michael Skakel. Dunne often includes himself as a character, and while some might consider that a flaw, he has never claimed complete or even partial objectivity.

First and last, Dominick Dunne is a storyteller. At his best, he is a passionate storyteller. Many of his *Vanity Fair* pieces are collected in the book *Justice* (2001). *Another City, Not My Own* (1997) is his

fictional account of the Simpson trial. Dunne also has a crime series, *Power, Privilege, and Justice* broadcast on Court TV.

Durrant, Theo

Virtually forgotten and unknown, Theo Durrant was one of the most famous murderers of his day. In 1895 millions of newspaper readers from coast to coast followed the breathless details of the trial and execution of the "Demon of the Belfry." Today, it's easy to see him as the first of California's sexual predators—the Golden State equivalent of **Herman Mudgett** and Jack the Ripper—but there is more to his story.

On the surface, William Henry Theodore Durrant was quite a catch. As a promising student at San Francisco's Cooper Medical College, the young man was almost a doctor. A year before, he had nearly died of viral meningitis. Still lived with his parents. His sister Maude had just gone to Germany to study music. He was in the Signal Corps, the nineteenth century version of the National Guard, taught Sunday school, and served as usher and librarian at Emanuel Baptist Church. He was always quick to volunteer to fix anything needing repair at the church, so quick he had a master key.

On April 3, 1895 Durrant visited the church with 18-year-old Blanche Lamont, a shapely high school senior. They rode the trolley and flirted playfully. That afternoon, several more people saw them going into the church building. About three hours later the choir director, Theo's friend George King, came to the sanctuary. As King sat down at the organ, Durrant appeared looking disheveled and flustered. He said he had been upstairs working on the gas jets and had inhaled some fumes. Could George run down to the drugstore and get him a Bromo-Seltzer? Sure.

When Blanche was reported missing to the police, Durrant was one of the first people they interviewed. He wondered if she might have "gone astray" or been kidnapped by white slavers. Given his sterling reputation, the cops bought his story.

Nine days later on Good Friday, April 12, Durrant was with a new girl, Minnie Williams, age 21. They were seen arguing or talking animatedly outside the church that evening, right before they went inside. Two hours later, Durrant showed up at a fellowship meeting in the home of another church member. Again, he appeared confused and upset, but was fine by the time the gathering broke up at midnight. Durrant told his friends he had to go back to the church to check on something, and on Saturday he joined his Signal Corps unit bivouac at Mount Diablo.

While he was off on maneuvers, the Ladies Society got together to plan their flower decorations for the Easter service. As she was getting ready in the library, one of the women opened a cupboard and discovered Minnie's body. The young woman had been horribly slashed and stabbed with a dull table knife, and gagged with underwear crammed down her throat. Cause of death—strangulation.

The cops continued to search the church for Blanche, but a broken lock on the door to the belfry kept them from it until the next day, Sunday. They found the body on an upper landing, naked, but arranged almost respectfully on its back with a wooden block for a pillow. The clothes had been hastily hidden higher up in the rafters. Evidence suggested Blanche had been attacked in the library, then carried up to the second landing and killed there. Services were cancelled and Durrant was arrested with his Signal Corps unit.

The trial for Blanche's murder was the nineteenth century equivalent of **O.J. Simpson**. Print media coverage in the six local papers was exhaustive with William Randolph Hearst's *San Francisco Examiner* leading the pack. The papers essentially convicted Durrant and printed stories about "experts" who argued that the shape of Theo's hands and the size of his earlobes "proved" he was a murderer. Then, as now, the salacious sexual angle was fascinating and readers wanted to know all of the most lurid and intimate details. In the end, though, there was no conclusive evidence either woman had been sexually assaulted.

The trial lasted three weeks. More than 100 people testified. Despite the overwhelming circumstantial evidence, Durrant maintained his innocence, save one curious encounter with reporter Carrie Cunningham where he claimed to have witnessed Blanche's murder. The murderers had put some sort of spell on him, he thought. It wasn't clear to him what he had seen, but he knew the killers had threatened his mother.

His lawyers never mentioned Durrant's wild theory, suggesting that perhaps the pastor, who also had a master key, might be the real killer. It took the jury all of five minutes to disagree. Durrant was sentenced and sent to San Quentin to be hanged.

He kept the appeals process chugging along for three years. At his execution, one of the strangest and most famous tales about the case took place. His parents were there, and, according to the warden at San Quentin, they seemed somehow proud of their boy and still proclaimed his innocence. After the hanging, as they waited for officials to finish work with the body, a prisoner asked them if they would care for something to eat. Why, yes, they answered.

Then, as it happened, the meal and their son's corpse arrived at the same time. With the coffin a few feet away in the same room, the Durrants sat down and tucked in to the beef, fruit salad, and tea with hearty appetites. His mother was heard to say, "Papa, I'd like some more of that roast." The anecdote is usually cited to illustrate the Durrants' coldness toward their son but, even if it is accurate, there's probably more to understand.

By far the most complete modern examination of the murders is found in Virginia McConnell's fine 2001 book, *Sympathy for the Devil*. She makes a reasonably persuasive explanation of Durrant's crimes that fits the known facts beginning with the strange, if not unhealthy relationship Theo had with both his mother and his sister. His father was manic depressive. Theo may have suffered from it, too. A manic high combined with residual brain damage from meningitis could account for an

Durrant, Theo

unprovoked attack on Blanche Lamont, followed by an immediate almost amnesiac denial of it, and a desire to confess.

He might have made a vague confession or statement to Minnie—as he did later to Carrie Cunningham—that he had seen the killers and wanted her help in exposing them. That would explain Minnie's cryptic comment to a friend that she knew too much about Blanche's murder, and how Theo was able to persuade her to go into the church at night with him, and finally, the radically different wounds that killed her.

Whether the explanation is accurate or not, Ms. McConnell tells a complex story that could provide the basis for a good film or miniseries. She also does an excellent job of weighing the validity of the charges in the initial print coverage.

If Theo Durrant has been neglected in popular culture, he has found another kind of literary immortality. William Anthony Parker White, better known as crime writer and critic Anthony Boucher, also used Theo Durrant as one of his several pseudonyms. He also called himself H.H. Holmes and Herman Mudgett.

Ferguson, Paul
Ramon Novarro

Ramon Novarro was one of the biggest stars of the silent screen. He played the title role in the 1925 version of *Ben-Hur*, the most expensive movie ever made at the time. His smoldering Latin looks led some to dub him "the new Valentino." He had been born in Mexico, but his family was forced to leave the country after the 1910 revolution. His father had been a prosperous dentist. Ramon found his way into acting almost by accident, as so many did in the early days of Hollywood.

Though his popularity waned, he continued to work in the sound era and appeared in smaller roles on television. By the 1960s Novarro lived the relatively quiet life of a semiretired star whose work had been largely forgotten. He drank too much and col-

lected unemployment insurance. He was also a closeted homosexual who occasionally paid for the company of young men. In 1968, he chose the wrong one, 22-year-old Paul Ferguson.

After a troubled childhood, Ferguson spent most of his life on the streets. He had been married four times and barely knew his younger brother, Tom, when the kid showed up on his doorstep in LA. Tom was on the run from juvenile authorities back in Chicago. Having just been laid off of his job, Paul was looking for money. As he had done in similar situations in the past, he turned to hustling. A friend who was involved in the business gave him Novarro's number.

The details of what happened on the night of October 30th are not clear because the story has changed several times. We do know the Ferguson brothers went over to Novarro's house and all three of them had a lot to drink. Tom made a long distance call to an old girlfriend in Chicago and told her where they were. Later she would say she could hear screams in the background. Paul, possibly acting alone, tied up the older man and beat him to death. He and Tom may have thought Navarro had $5,000 hidden in the house.

Finally, they took $20 from Novarro's pocket and ransacked the house before they ran away.

It took LA police detectives only a few days to learn of Paul's identity and to track him and his brother down. At first, they claimed Tom had killed Novarro, because they thought as a juvenile, the 17-year-old wouldn't face the death penalty. When the court said he could be tried as an adult, he changed his story. Throughout the trial, each of the brothers claimed the other had committed the murder, they all had been drunk, and Novarro had made unwanted advances. In the end, both were found guilty of murder one and sentenced to life.

Tom was paroled in 1977. Sometime in the 1980s, he was convicted of rape and sent back to prison. Paroled in 1990, he was sent to prison again in 1997 for failing to register as a sex offender.

Paul was paroled in 1978. In 1989, in Missouri, he was convicted of rape and sodomy. He's serving a 30-year stretch.

With the publication of Kenneth Anger's *Hollywood Babylon* (1975), Ramon Novarro's sexual orientation became the source of outrageous stories, one claiming he had been murdered with a sex toy. Details varied in different versions, but the point of the exaggerations was to turn a private, courtly man into a flaming caricature.

Andre Soares' biography *Beyond Paradise* (2002) corrects the lies, and Novarro's films have found a new audience on cable classic movie channels.

Finch, Bernard

The first act could have come straight from a really bad soap opera.

In the Los Angeles of the 1950s, divorce was still something of a stigma. But when Dr. Bernard Finch and his wife Francis discovered they were in love with, respectively, Barbara Daugherty and her husband, Forrest, something had to be done. The two couples unhitched and remarried.

But things did not go smoothly for the good doctor, a socially prominent physician, and his new bride. Arguments turned into fights. He beat her. At work at his clinic, things were no better. He was being sued for malpractice by several patients and he compounded the problem by having an affair with the ex-wife of one of them, Carole Tregoff. If that weren't enough, he then hired her to be his secretary.

In the spring of 1959 Barbara Finch decided she'd had enough and hired a detective to dig up dirt. Under California law in those days, if she could prove adultery or abandonment, she would have been awarded virtually all of Dr. Finch's assets, plus alimony. In short, she could ruin him. The doctor fought back in a series of steadily escalating physical and legal confrontations, ending with her taking out a restraining order against him.

Finch installed Carole in a Las Vegas love nest and they set to work on counter proposals. Plan A involved a smalltime crook named John Patrick Cody. The doctor and his cupcake wanted Cody to sweet talk Barbara into the sack, or, if that didn't work, to kill her. Payment: $1,400 on a down payment of $350. Cody took the money but didn't do the job. Instead, he split for Wisconsin.

Plan B involved a .38 pistol.

On the night of July 18th, coming off of a two-day bender, the unhappy couple drove from Vegas to the doctor's house in West Covina.

Details of the meeting are in dispute, but around 11:00 p.m. Mrs. Finch's maid heard shots and ran to the front door. She found the doctor standing over his wife who was on the floor of the garage. He had a pistol in his hand. The doctor smacked the maid around, and ordered his wife to stand up. She did, then ran out into the night. He gave chase. A moment later, the maid heard a shot. In the confusion, Carole and the homicidal doctor were separated. He stole a car and made it back to Las Vegas before she arrived in her car. Exhausted by their night's labor, they fell asleep. Later that day, they were arrested and charged.

Perhaps the most astonishing part of the story is the whopper Finch told at his trial.

In his version, he and his inamorata had gone there simply to talk. Enraged at the presence of Carole, Barbara pulled the .38. He took the pistol from her and threw it over his shoulder, he said. Somehow, it went off, the bullet hitting Barbara in the back right between the shoulder blades. They had a tender conversation there in the driveway before she expired.

The prosecution clearly demonstrated the fatal wound was fired at her as she was running away. They also had the attaché case the doctor had left on the lawn, the one with the .38-caliber ammunition, the heavy clothes line, the rubber gloves, the hypodermic needles, and the drugs (a murder kit). Nonsense, replied the doctor. He always brought those along on house calls.

Finally, there was Cody's testimony about what they'd hired him to do.

Finch cried when he took the stand and described the terrible accident and his dying wife's last words. As ridiculous as it was, he managed to persuade at least one juror and the first trial ended in a hung jury. So did the second trial.

At the third, Dr. Finch was convicted on first-degree murder, Carole on second-degree, both on conspiracy. She was paroled in 1969; he in 1971.

The trial was an early dry run for O.J. with mobs of press and pseudo-press reporting every breathless detail. It became worldwide front page news. Local LA papers even recruited studio starlets to give their impressions of the proceedings. Even so, the case has largely faded from public consciousness. Perhaps **Sam Sheppard** cornered the market on philandering doctors.

Novelist Eric Ambler wrote an excellent account of the crime and the trial. Originally published in *Life* magazine, it was expanded in his true crime book *The Ability to Kill* (1987).

Fish, Albert

In the spring of 1928 Albert Fish took 10-year-old Grace Budd away from her New York home. Fish was a kindly, grandfatherly gray-haired gent. Using the alias Frank Howard, he told Grace's parents they were going to a birthday party for another girl. Instead, Fish led her to an abandoned cottage in Westchester, New York where he killed her and committed unspeakable atrocities on her body. She was one of probably 15 children he killed, and perhaps another 100 that he harmed.

Born in Washington, D.C. in 1870, Fish was orphaned at five and later would blame the abuse he suffered at St. John's Orphanage for his crimes. His criminal record began in 1903 with grand larceny and continued with lesser crimes, punctuated by stints in mental institutions.

Able to maintain a facade of normalcy, he married at 28. Though the marriage lasted for 20 years and produced six children, it must have been unusual. Fish indulged in brutal self-mutilation with a nail-studded paddle and other instruments. Eventually Mrs. Fish ran off with a halfwit boarder at their home. They took all of the furniture when they left, but returned six months later and asked Fish to take them back. He said she could stay but lover boy had to go. She agreed, but a few days later, Fish discovered she'd secreted her paramour in the attic. They left, never to return, and Fish's madness spun out of control.

In 1927 he kidnapped and murdered four-year-old Billy Gaffney. A year later, he answered a newspaper ad placed by Edward Budd, a teenager who was looking for work, and asked to meet him. The meeting led Fish to Edward's younger sister Grace. Her disappearance remained unsolved for six years, but Detective William King refused to give up.

Hoping to stir up some action, King planted a false lead in Walter Winchell's newspaper column, saying the old case was about to be solved. Ten days later, Grace's mother received a bizarre unsigned letter claiming to be from the killer. The handwriting matched a piece of evidence from 1928, and the letter was written on stationery from a small professional association. Without too much effort, Detective King was able to trace some of the paper to a New York rooming house where one of the tenants matched the description of Frank Howard.

When Detective King confronted Fish on December 13, 1934, the old man pulled a straight razor. He was easily disarmed and confessed immediately and willingly to the Budd murder and many others, all of them rich in perverted details of cannibalism and Fish's own masochism. As he told psychiatrist Frederic Wertham, "I have always had a desire to inflict pain on others and to have others inflict pain on me. I always seemed to enjoy everything that hurt."

He enjoyed it so much he claimed to have stuck needles in his nether regions and left them there.

When Dr. Wertham doubted him, they took x-rays and found at least 29 needles imbedded near his scrotum and rectum.

That might seem to be prima facie evidence of insanity, but the jury didn't buy it as a defense. It took them less than an hour to find Fish guilty. Proving his masochism was no passing fancy, Fish said he looked forward to his date with the electric chair, telling reporters it was the "the supreme thrill, the only one I haven't tried."

On the appointed day, Fish hurried to the chair and helped the executioner fasten the electrodes to his legs. Perhaps because he was still packing so much metal between his legs, when they first pulled the switch, they got nothing more than a bit of blue smoke from a short circuit. It was fixed and second try was successful.

Fish's cannibalism may have been part of the inspiration for Thomas Harris' brilliant creation, Dr. Hannibal Lecter, but his real crimes are too abhorrent to have any place in popular entertainment.

Fisher, Amy

Chances are no one outside the immediate area would even have heard of the "Long Island Lolita" had not tabloid TV been coming into its own in the early 1990s. But cable was expanding, and the new channels and new shows needed more titillating stories to tell, and America was ready to watch.

The verifiable facts of the story are straightforward and certainly salacious enough.

Amy Fisher grew up as the child of prosperous parents in Long Island, New York. For her sweet 16th birthday, her parents gave her a Dodge Daytona. She promptly knocked the exterior mirror off trying to back out of the garage. Hoping to keep the ding a secret from her father, she took the car to Complete Auto Body and Fender where she met Joey Buttafuoco, a slab-sided mullet-head some 20 years her senior. He was married, with two kids. Over the following weeks and months Amy found many reasons to visit Complete Auto, and she and

Amy Fisher and Joey Buttafuoco, together again in another sordid affair (called the Lingerie Bowl) in 2006. (AP Photo)

Joey embarked on a tempestuous affair, knocking off nooners in by-the-hour hot-sheet motel rooms, her place, his boat, anywhere.

Alas, the course of true lust never did run smooth. First, Amy contracted herpes from her hunk-a-hunk-a-burnin' love. Then miffed at her beefy beau, she broke up with him, started stepping out with Paul Makely, his personal trainer, and went to work turning tricks for ABBA Escorts.

Before long, she and Joey patched things up, but by then Amy saw Joey's wife Mary Jo as a problem. If only she were out of the picture, Amy and Joey could find the happiness they so richly deserved. Amy asked around and found that Peter ("Petey G") Guagenti could procure a weapon. She asked; he said yes.

On May 9, 1992 Amy faked cramps for the school nurse and skipped out of JFK High early. Petey G picked her up in a T-bird. He had an automatic in the glove compartment. They drove over to Joey's house where Mary Jo was painting lawn chairs. The young women had a brief talk wherein Amy ratted Joey out, producing a Complete Auto T-shirt as proof of his infidelity. Mary Jo wasn't impressed. Amy shot her in the right temple, and ran.

Neighbors heard the shot and called 911. Miraculously, Mary Jo survived and several days later when she regained consciousness, was able to describe her attacker.

Joey fingered Paul Makely and Amy, who confessed, sort of. After her arrest, her story changed frequently, but she maintained that the shooting had been an accident. She had struck Mary Jo with the pistol and it went off. Right. At about the same time, one of her customers from ABBA sold a sex tape he'd made with Amy to the tabloid TV show *A Current Affair*. Bail was set at a cool $2 million.

Amy raised it on the sale of the film rights to her story.

Joey called the Howard Stern radio show and claimed he'd never done anything untoward with young Amy.

Amy's lawyer tried to cop a plea with prosecutors. She'd get 5 to 15 years if she testified against Joey. Done. But days after the deal was set, another tape, this one made by Paul Makely, hit the airwaves on *Hard Copy*. In it, Amy joked about what she wanted. The judge gave her the full 15 years. A couple months later, Amy testified at Joey's statutory rape trial. Mary Jo stood by her man. Eventually, he, too, pled down and got six months.

In the years since, Joey and Mary Jo divorced. In 1999 Mary Jo appeared before a parole board and requested mercy for the teenager who had shot her. It worked. Amy was released.

Joey flirted with limited fame on cable TV and in movie parts. But when your very name has become a punchline, your career choices are limited.

In 2004 he was found guilty in an auto insurance scam and sentenced to a year in the pen.

Out of jail, Amy had work done to change her looks, married, had a couple of kids, and wrote a book. In 2005, she was working as a newspaper columnist.

Of course, the real significance of this case is not the crime itself but its disproportionate importance in popular culture. How many other crimes have been the subject of made-for-television movies from all three major networks? Those are *The Amy Fisher Story* (1993) with Drew Barrymore, *Amy Fisher: My Story* (1992) with Noelle Parker, and *Casualties of Love: The Long Island Lolita Story* (1993) with Alyssa Milano.

Fleiss, Heidi

At her professional peak, Heidi Fleiss was the most successful madam in Hollywood. She had the most beautiful and expensive girls. Her client list included some of the most powerful men in entertainment and other businesses. It was too good to last.

The daughter of a pediatrician and a teacher, Heidi grew up in an affluent happy family. Her first entrepreneurial efforts involved organizing her preteen girlfriends into a babysitting service. From tiny acorns grow mighty oaks.

Bored with school, Heidi dropped out and worked at an assortment of jobs until, when she was 19, she met Bernie Cornfeld. At 61, Bernie was one of the world's wealthiest men, and he made no secret of his fondness for young women. Lots of young women. He and Heidi got along wonderfully. She worked for him as a secretary and on a more intimate level for several years. Bernie was never faithful to her for very long, but still, they parted amicably and remained close friends until his death.

After they broke up, Heidi dated filmmaker Ivan Nagy (*Trailer Trash Terri*, *Izzy Sleeze's Casting Couch Cuties*, etc.) Sometime in 1988, he introduced her to Elizabeth Adams, a.k.a. Madam Alex, who ran one of the city's most popular call girl rings. Looking toward retirement, Madam Alex brought Heidi in as a sort of executive assistant, albeit an executive assistant who was expected to start work on the ground level, so to speak. Be that as it may, Heidi rose swiftly through the ranks and soon was clearing out the dead wood and recruiting younger, prettier girls.

Business flourished. Heidi was able to buy a $1.6 million house (previously owned by actor Michael Douglas) and to move in with her pal Victoria Sellers, daughter of actor Peter Sellers. Their parties were legendary.

By 1990, however, she and Madam Alex came to a parting of the ways. This time, the split wasn't so amicable. Heidi went into business for herself. She earned a reputation for treating her girls well and for hiring only the best. She prospered until 1993 when she was raided by an LA County Sheriff's Dept./FBI sting operation. They arranged for Heidi to send four of her girls and a stash of cocaine to the Beverly Hills Hilton. Everything that transpired was taped, and the next day Heidi was arrested.

For a time, it was rumored Heidi would go public with her client list. That got everyone's attention, but despite the media spotlight, Heidi did not name names. At the end of a long judicial process, she was found guilty of three counts of pandering—the drug charge was dropped—and sentenced to three years and a $1,500 fine. For those, she served 20 months in a minimum security prison.

She was released in September 1999. Since then, she has been in the news for her combative relationship with actor Tom Sizemore, convicted on various drug charges, and has been the subject of countless tabloid TV features.

Far and away the finest examination of her notorious career is Nick Broomfield's noir-ish 1995 documentary, *Heidi Fleiss: Hollywood Madam*. A year after her arrest, Broomfield arrived in Tinseltown from England with a pocketful of cash. He was prepared to buy the story of anyone who had inside knowledge of the case—anyone from hookers to ex-police chief Daryl Gates, who calmly picked up his payment on camera. Heidi, Nagy, and Madam Alex make appear-

ances. Heidi comes across as a flint-hard chippie and, as a group, the supporting players are about as distasteful a bunch as you'll ever see—Broomfield dives into. He dives into their world with unseemly enthusiasm for his often inconclusive interviews. The vapid story is filled with backbiting, lies, and self-serving evasions. In the end, the only person involved who retains any integrity is porn star Ron Jeremy who neither hides what he does nor tries to make himself more important than he is. Befitting its subject, the film is sordid and utterly compelling.

Floyd, Charles Arthur "Pretty Boy"

Charles Arthur Floyd had a talent for nicknames. As a youth, he was known as "Choc," for his favorite brand of beer, Choctaw. Toward the end of his short life, he was the "Robin Hood of Cookson Hills" and the "Phantom of the Ozarks." But he will always be remembered as "Pretty Boy" and that's the one he really hated.

Charles Arthur grew up on a hardscrabble farm in Akins, Oklahoma. He was a big (6-foot, 2-inch) good looking kid, popular with the ladies; raised some hell on weekends but settled down after he married in 1924. He found it hard to make a living at farming, though, and partnered with a more experienced crook, John Hilderbrand. In 1925 they went to St. Louis where they engaged in a series of small stickups. They hit the big time when they knocked over the payroll of Kroger's Food Store. Choc celebrated by buying a new Studebaker and whooping it up with the missus back in Arkansas. It didn't take the cops long to nail him, and in November, he started a five-year stretch at the Missouri State pen, an overcrowded hellhole where he met his next partner, bank robber Red Lovett.

As soon as Floyd was released in 1929, he met up with Red in Kansas City and picked up the finer points of big city crime. He learned how to use a Tommy gun and began an affair with Juanita Baird, a married hooker. Working with different people, Floyd robbed several banks in Ohio, until he was

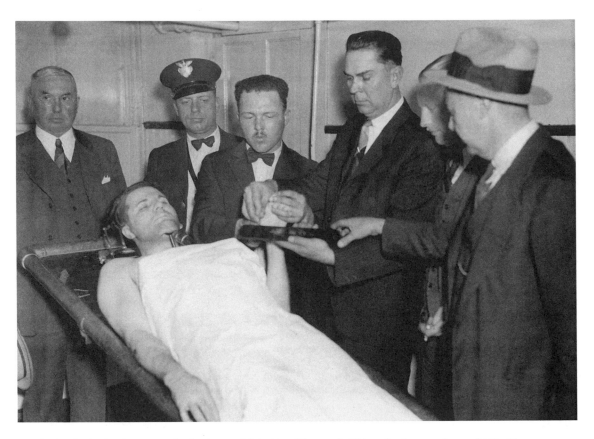

The body of Charles "Pretty Boy" Floyd on a slab in East Liverpool, Ohio, after he was shot and killed in a gun battle with federal agents, October 22, 1934. (AP Photo)

caught in a police shootout in Akron and sentenced to 15 years. That's where his rise to fame really began.

On the way to the Ohio penitentiary, Floyd pulled off a daring escape when he kicked out a bathroom window and leapt from a moving train. He managed to stay several steps ahead of the cops and made it back to Kansas City, but for the rest of his life, Pretty Boy was on the run.

He teamed up with William "Killer" Miller, and they took off with Juanita and her sister Rose. After a couple of quick bank jobs, the four of them were spotted by the cops in Toledo, Ohio. In the shootout that followed, Miller was killed and the two women were wounded.

Choc decided it was time to return home to Oklahoma where he found a new partner and preyed on local banks, where the Robin Hood stories first appeared. Pretty Boy was said to tear up mortgages during his bank jobs before he took the money, thereby liberating honest working folk from the clutches of evil bankers. At other times, he gave the stolen money to the poor he met. It's the stuff of legend, or at least the stuff of folk music, as Woody Guthrie sang in 1939's "The Ballad of Pretty Boy Floyd":

"And as through your life you travel,
Yes, as through your life you roam,
You won't never see an outlaw
Drive a family from their home."

Floyd stayed close to home for the next few years, but in 1933 he ventured out to Kansas City. He and a new partner were there on June 17th, the day of the infamous **Kansas City Massacre**, where four policemen, one an FBI agent, and Frank "Jelly" Nash, the prisoner they were escorting, were all gunned down outside the train station in broad daylight. One witness tentatively fingered Pretty Boy and it was enough to earn him a high ranking on the newly created "Public Enemies" list. State and federal authorities were embarrassed and outraged by the brazen act and swore they would get the killers.

Floyd denied any involvement and it's still doubtful he had anything to do with it. It didn't matter. The heat was hotter than ever.

Floyd went to ground in Buffalo, New York and stayed there for several months. During that time, he may have pulled off one bank job with the Dillinger gang, but it's questionable, too.

Whether he did or not, Pretty Boy was making his way back to Oklahoma when he was involved in an accident on a rural Ohio road in October 1934. The police spotted him but Floyd managed to escape on foot into nearby woods. As it happened, G-man **Melvin Purvis** was in Cincinnati at the time and joined the manhunt. On the evening of the 24th, they spotted Pretty Boy as he was getting a ride in a farmer's Model T. Again he ran for the woods, but was brought down by a sharpshooter and a posse.

They shot him up pretty good, but with his dying breath, he denied to Purvis that he'd had anything to do with the Kansas City business. Even so, opinion has remained divided on Pretty Boy. To the authorities in the 1930s, he was a cold-blooded killer who gunned down policemen who couldn't get to their weapons. To the people whose lives had been destroyed by the Depression, he was Robin Hood. That's how John Steinbeck's Joads describe him in *The Grapes of Wrath* (1939), and generally how he has been seen in the few films made about him. Though he has appeared more often as a supporting character in films about other contemporaneous bank robbers, Floyd was portrayed by teen heartthrob Fabian in the rarely seen *A Bullet for Pretty Boy*. The best biography is Michael Wallis' *Pretty Boy* (1992).

Frank, Leo

It is no coincidence the lynching of Leo Frank occurred during the first flowering of twentieth-century American racism. Though Frank was Jewish, not black, it's easy to shift that kind of hatred to the most visible target, and the people of Georgia were ready to hate.

The state was undergoing a transformation from an agrarian economy to industrial. The National Pencil Company plant in Atlanta was part of the change. It hired many young women at very low wages. Leo Frank ran the plant. Mary Phagan, a 13-year-old from Marietta, worked there. She was a striking young girl, photographs reveal a resemblance to the reigning film star of the day, Mary Pickford.

Early on the morning of Sunday, April 27, 1913, her body was found in the plant basement near the bottom of an elevator shaft. She had been struck on the head and strangled with a cord. She may have been raped. Two notes, written on old order forms, were found near the body. They read:

> "Mam that negro hire down here did this i went to make water and he push me down that hole a long tall negro black that hoo it sase long sleam tall negro i write while play with me."

And, the second:

> "he said he would love me land down play like the night witch did it but that long tall black negro did buy his self."

Suspicion fell on Jim Conley, a black janitor with a history of drunkenness and violence, and on Frank. Like Frank, Conley had been working at the plant on Saturday, Confederate Memorial Day, when Mary had come by to pick up her pay—$1.20. Though traditional Southern bigotry would have fingered the black man, a Jew from Brooklyn could be cast as an equally vile and subhuman villain, particularly when Conley began to tell his wild stories.

> *It is no coincidence the lynching of Leo Frank occurred during the first flowering of twentieth-century American racism. Though Frank was Jewish, not black, it's easy to shift that kind of hatred to the most visible target, and the people of Georgia were ready to hate.*

At various times, Conley said he had seen Frank having "perverse" sexual relations with other girls who worked in the plant, had ordered him to take the body to the cellar, and had dictated the absurd notes. Conley's tales combined with Frank's nervousness at his initial late-night police interrogation led to a grand jury indictment. Other allegations about Frank's licentiousness surfaced, though none were ever proved.

Frank, 28, was married, a graduate of Cornell, and president of the local B'nai B'rith. Even so, newspapers, particularly the Hearst-owned *Georgian*, went on a crusade against him and so did racist politician Tom Watson. Atlanta's ambitious Solicitor General Hugh Dorsey saw the cause as a stepping stone and took charge personally.

The trial was conducted in the hottest part of the summer with a mob sometimes yelling for blood outside the courthouse. The evidence against Frank was unbelievably weak by today's standards. "Experts" with no training or knowledge claimed hair and blood traces found in the plant were Mary Phagan's, and their testimony was accepted. Eye witness testimony concerning Frank's actions at the time of the murder, when he was going home for lunch and was not even in the plant, was discounted. Character witnesses for him

were dismissed as Yankees. At one point, Dorsey even accused him of being homosexual. But the central, incontrovertible point was that Leo Frank was a New York Jew, and Dorsey hammered it home in his summation.

All the while, the crowd outside the courtroom turned uglier, so ugly that everyone, particularly the jury, knew a not-guilty verdict might well cause a riot. With lightning speed, they declared him guilty.

Frank's lawyers worked the appeals process vigorously. They went to the Georgia and U.S. Supreme Courts but were unable to introduce new evidence illuminating the shortcomings of the state's case. The evidence, however, was being made public and "Free Leo Frank" organizations were formed throughout the country. Eventually, it was enough to sway Georgia Governor John M. Slayton. With only weeks to go in his term, he considered the evidence and commuted Frank's sentence to life in prison. In doing so, he effectively ended his political career, just when he had been poised to make a run for the U.S. Senate. He also ordered that Frank be moved to the supposedly more secure prison at Milledgeville.

Around 10:00 p.m. on the night of August 16, 1915, a group of more than two dozen men, many of them pillars of Marietta society, drove in a convoy of cars to the prison and attacked. Overpowering the guards, they hustled Frank into one of their cars and headed back home. It took less than ten minutes without a shot being fired.

They arrived at a grove of trees outside town at dawn and demanded Frank confess to the murder. He refused, saying he wanted his wedding ring to be sent to his wife, and they strung him up. Though the identities of the lynch party were widely known, no one was ever prosecuted.

The men who did it called themselves the Knights of Mary Phagan. Not long afterwards, they would reform themselves as the Ku Klux Klan.

Only months before the lynching, D.W. Griffith's *The Birth of a Nation* (1915, based on Thomas F.

Dixon, Jr.'s novel, *The Clansman: A Historical Romance of the Ku Klux Klan*) had its big premieres in Los Angeles and New York. In both cities, the screenings were preceded by huge parades of horses and men in full Klan regalia riding through the streets.

The film presented the Klan as valiant heroes who saved beautiful little white girls from the clutches of lecherous mulattoes and northern carpet-baggers. The women they could not save chose suicide. One heroine leapt from a cliff rather than submit, and an intertitle card reads "For her who had learned the stern lesson of honor we should not grieve that she found sweeter the *opal gates of death*." (original emphasis)

That is not to say *The Birth of a Nation* inspired the lynch mob. The film simply tapped into the existing emotions and reinforced them. At the time, the epic was on the way to becoming the most popular movie ever made. It played for months, breaking attendance records everywhere, and was regularly reissued over the next decades. Klan membership surged.

In 1982, Alonzo Mann, a 13-year-old office boy at the pencil plant, swore he had seen Conley dragging Mary's body and that Conley had threatened to kill him. In 1986 the state of Georgia pardoned Frank without commenting on his wrongful conviction.

The well-regarded 1937 Mervyn LeRoy film *They Won't Forget* with Claude Rains is based on the Frank case. In 1988 Jack Lemmon, Peter Gallagher, and Kevin Spacey starred in the excellent miniseries *The Murder of Mary Phagan*. The crime was also the subject of the short-lived 1998 Broadway musical, *Parade*.

Frazier, John Linley

Strange days had found Santa Cruz. California in 1970 seemed to be filled with madness on a scale never seen before. Given that climate, John Linley Frazier was at best a minor-league madman. A delusional paranoid schizophrenic, he murdered five people who happened to live nearby.

By all accounts, Frazier's insanity appeared after he suffered head injuries in an automobile accident in May. Until then, he'd been normal enough—married with a son, worked as a mechanic in Santa Cruz. After the accident, things changed. He was taking some drugs at the same time and they may well have exacerbated his condition. Whatever the reason, he started hearing voices. God told him not to drive and that the world needed to be saved from "materialism."

In July he left his wife and moved into a shack on his mother's property. He told anyone who would listen that he'd been ordered to seek vengeance on those who rape the earth. Unfortunately, Dr. Victor Ohta, an eye surgeon, lived right up the hill from Frazier's hovel. Frazier could easily see the well-tended estate, and in his madness, it became the embodiment of the evil he was out to destroy.

On the afternoon of October 19th, Frazier loaded a backpack with supplies, including two pistols, a .22 and a .38. He walked through the woods to the mansion and found Mrs. Ohta home alone. He tied her up with bright silk scarves and waited. When she did not arrive to pick up her sons from school, the doctor and his secretary, Dorothy Cadwallader, in two cars, went for the boys. They reached the house separately; Dr. Ohta and his son Derrick in one car, Mrs. Cadwallader and Taggert in the other.

Because they arrived at different times, Frazier was able to subdue and restrain them all. Then, according to Frazier's somewhat suspect testimony, he began to lecture and argue with the doctor about his delusions. Whatever was said was enough to drive Frazier deeper into his madness. He forced the three adults and two children into the swimming pool where he shot them execution style.

Once they were dead or dying, he went back inside where he typed a somewhat coherent note about his intentions. He left the note on the doctor's car, set fire to the house and, ignoring his previous instructions from God, drove away in Mrs. Ohta's station wagon. He abandoned it in a railway tunnel where it was hit by a switch engine.

When news of the note was published, several members of what was then called the "hippie community" came forward to name Frazier. Police eventually surrounded his place and arrested him a few days later.

At the trial, he pled not guilty by reason of insanity. Despite his obvious mental illness, the jury felt he knew what he was doing and found him guilty. His death sentence was commuted to life in San Quentin when the Supreme Court declared capital punishment unconstitutional.

Frazier might not be remembered at all but his crimes were committed a little more than a year after the Manson family murders in Los Angeles, and they were contemporaneous with fellow Santa Cruz killers **Edmund Kemper** and **Herbert Mullin**. Strange days indeed.

Fromme, Lynette "Squeaky" and Sara Jane Moore

It is inexplicably bizarre such an unassuming president as Gerald Ford should inspire two loony female would-be assassins, but, then, the 1970s were inexplicably bizarre in a lot of ways.

Consider the parallel careers of Lynette "Squeaky" Fromme and Sara Jane Moore. Squeaky got her start with the **Charlie Manson** "family" murders of Sharon Tate and others. Sara got her start with the Symbionese Liberation Army, kidnappers of **Patricia Hearst**.

Squeaky was a true believer in Charlie's insight and brilliance. She thought if she killed the president, Manson would be called to testify at her trial

and everyone would see how wrong they had been about him.

Sara ratted out her pals in the SLA to the FBI. She thought if she killed the president, she would reestablish her bona fides with the radical left.

Squeaky used a Colt .45 semiautomatic. It was loaded but she neglected to jack a bullet into the firing chamber. On September 5, 1975 in Sacramento, California she tried to shoot Ford on the street. The weapon didn't fire but she was so close Secret Service agent Larry Beundorf was able to grab the pistol and prevent her from getting a second try.

Sara used a Smith & Wesson .48 revolver. On September 22, 1975 in San Francisco, California she tried to shoot Ford on the street. Retired Marine Oliver Sipple was close enough and quick enough to hit her arm as she fired. The shot went high and ricocheted, wounding a cabbie.

Squeaky pled insanity. It didn't work and she was sentenced to life; Sara pled guilty. She got life.

Squeaky escaped from Alderson Federal Prison Camp in West Virginia in 1987. She was caught two days later. Sara escaped from Alderson Federal Prison Camp in West Virginia in 1979. She was caught the next day.

Squeaky is now in the Federal Medical Center in Carswell, Texas. Sara is now in the Federal Women's Prison in Pleasanton, California.

Both are minor characters in Stephen Sondheim's musical *Assassins* (1990), but have been largely forgotten.

G, H

Gacy, John Wayne

To the casual observer, he was the most normal of the "normal looking" serial killers, a friendly plump-faced hail-fellow-well-met. But John Wayne Gacy's dark side was close to the surface and seldom stayed hidden for very long.

He was born in 1942 and raised by a violent alcoholic father who called him "dumb and stupid" and questioned his masculinity. As a child, he suffered a head injury and growing up, he attempted to deny his homosexuality. In September 1964 he married and moved to Waterloo, Iowa where his wife's father owned several KFC restaurants. Gacy managed one until 1968 when rumors of his predilection for young boys proved true. He was indicted for sodomy with a teenager, then compounded his problems by hiring another kid to beat up his accuser. It all came out. Gacy pled guilty and was sentenced to 10 years. He earned parole in 18 months. By then, his wife had divorced him and left with their son.

Gacy went back to Chicago and moved in with his mother (his father had died while he was in prison). Within months, she had helped him buy a house and find a job, and he was cruising the bus station looking for boys. In 1972 he claimed his first victim, a pickup whose name remains unknown. He brought the boy to his house, killed him, and buried the body in the crawlspace. The persistent stench was blamed on moisture buildup.

Soon after, Gacy married a divorcee with two young daughters and started a contracting business that employed many teenagers. At the same time, he was a Democratic committeeman and active in volunteer work. Everyone knew him as Pogo the Clown. Apparently, he was not as creepy in person as he appears to be in photographs with his red, white, and blue makeup.

Over the course of the next few years his marriage disintegrated, ending officially in 1976, and he killed dozens of young men. His MO involved isolating them at his home. He used chloroform on the unwilling. Various sexual assaults were followed by strangulation. When the crawlspace filled up, he dumped the bodies in the Des Plaines River.

He was caught in 1978 after becoming a suspect in a disappearance. When police searched his house, they found suspicious evidence, but did not thoroughly search the crawlspace. They were ready to come back when Gacy confessed.

His attorneys attempted a novel defense, claiming Gacy had been temporarily insane 33 separate times. Nobody bought it. He was found guilty in

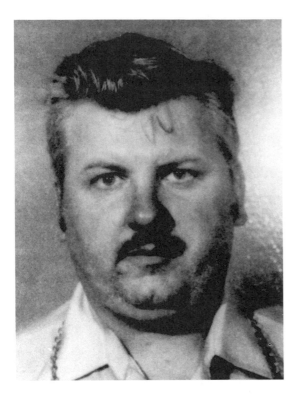

Chicago serial killer John Wayne Gacy from a 1978 photo. (AP Photo)

two hours and executed by lethal injection on May 10, 1984.

Since then, Gacy has become a mid-level celebrity among serial killer aficionados. His crying clown paintings are sought after by collectors, and several rock bands do Gacy songs. He's been the subject of several nonfiction books. The murders were recounted in the low-budget horror flick *Gacy* (2002) and the well-regarded 1992 miniseries *To Catch a Killer* with Brian Dennehy, who received an Emmy nomination for his work.

Gallo, Joey "Crazy Joe"

One version of the story has it that "Crazy Joe" Gallo and his brothers Albert "Kid Blast" and Larry "no nickname" were the hit team that whacked

mobster **Albert Anastasia** in New York in 1957. In another version, Gallo's boss, Joe Profaci, gave him the job and Joey delegated it to underlings.

In either case, the Gallo brothers were street-level hoods for the Profaci gang, later called the Colombo gang. They thought they deserved better treatment and more money for their work. Rather than asking for a raise, they decided to kidnap Profaci's brother-in-law and five members of the gang, and then demanded a bigger cut of the profits as a ransom.

The wily Profaci pretended to agree, but as soon as his men were released, he started murdering Gallo's troops. That bit of business provided the basis for Jimmy Breslin's novel *The Gang That Couldn't Shoot Straight* (1971).

In 1962 Joey was nailed for extortion when he tried to shake down a restaurant in Little Italy. The cops caught him on tape and he got a 10-year sentence. Like many other uneducated crooks, Crazy Joey discovered history, art, and literature in the joint. He became a voracious reader of Hemingway, Sartre, Camus, all the heavy hitters. At the same time, he got to know some of the black inmates. Realizing old racial barriers were disintegrating, he envisioned a future where black dope dealers and white dope dealers could peddle their wares to the same clientèle. He befriended **Leroy "Nicky" Barnes**, who would later go on to become the drug king of Harlem, and made arrangements for black prisoners to find work with his Brooklyn crew, whose ranks were still depleted following the Profaci unpleasantness.

When Crazy Joe got out in 1971, his brother Larry had died of cancer and Profaci had been replaced by **Joe Colombo**. Colombo was at the head of the Italian-American Civil Rights League, and was loudly demanding TV shows and films stop stereotyping Italians as gangsters, and the FBI stop bugging those same gangsters. There was still bad blood between Colombo and Crazy Joe. When Colombo was killed by a black assassin at the Unity Day Rally in 1971, a lot of people thought Gallo had been behind it. The shooter, Jerome Johnson, was killed by Colombo's bodyguards seconds after he struck, so no satisfactory explanation of his actions has ever been given.

Joey claimed he had nothing to do with it. He was, he said, a changed man. Joey got married, moved to Greenwich Village, and was the toast of the show biz world, a true "celebrity gangster." Though he may not have loved the 1971 film made of *The Gang That Couldn't Shoot Straight*, he became a close friend of its star, Jerry Orbach, and his wife Marta.

On the night of April 7, 1972 Crazy Joe threw a birthday party for himself at the Copacabana night club. He and his pals closed the place down at 4:00 a.m. in the morning then set out in search of a late night snack. They wound up at Umberto's Clam House in Little Italy where they were spotted by Joseph Luparelli, a hanger-on with the Colombo mob. Hoping to ingratiate himself to the higher-ups, Luparelli hot-footed it away from Umberto's and found four Colombo soldiers in another restaurant nearby. They called their boss to get permission, then drove back to Umberto's. One of the guys went inside and opened fire.

Crazy Joe slammed out through the front door to Hester Street. The gunman followed and continued to fire. Joey collapsed in the street and bled to death in the emergency room. Though Luparelli eventually told his story to the police, without corroborating witnesses, no arrests were ever made.

Gallo's story was told in the hard-to-find *Crazy Joe* (1974) with Peter Boyle in the title role. Along with **John Gotti**, Gallo can be seen in the character of Joey Zasa in *The Godfather Part III* (1990). He's also the subject of Bob Dylan's song *Joey* (1975).

Gambino, Carlo

Carlo Gambino is widely considered to be the model for Don Vito Corleone in *The Godfather* (1972). There are similarities, but Mario Puzo was creating fiction, not history. He was unconstrained by facts. Don Vito is also similar to **Frank Costello**,

A young Carlo Gambino in a mug shot from the 1930s. (AP Photo)

and Don Vito's son Michael is not unlike Gambino in some ways.

Gambino was born in Sicily in 1902. He made it to New York and hitched his wagon to the up-and-coming stars of his generation, **Lucky Luciano**, **Meyer Lansky**, and **Bugsy Siegel**. He worked as a bootlegger and gunman with Siegel, and impressed Luciano as a guy who had the smarts to go a long way in their business.

During World War II, Gambino and his cousin **Paul Castellano** gained control of the meat packing business in New York. They also had a hand in black market food and gasoline ration stamps. They stole the stamps or bribed workers to steal them, and made millions. After Luciano was deported at the end of the war, Gambino rose to become the number two man in the **Albert Anastasia** organization.

His alignment with the Anastasia-Luciano wing of the Syndicate made him an opponent of the hot-headed **Vito Genovese**, but by the 1950s, Gambino and Genovese were conspiring to get rid of the equally hot-headed Anastasia. Under normal circumstances, Lansky would have sided with Anastasia over Genovese, but "the Executioner," as Anastasia was called, had recently gotten unpredictable and greedy. First, he had ordered a hit on a civilian for no good reason, then he'd tried to horn in on Meyer's Cuban gambling operation. That was too much.

Genovese assured Gambino he would move to the head of the organization and ordered a hit on Anastasia. On October 27, 1957 Anastasia was clipped by two hit men in a barbershop. Gambino took over his rackets, and Genovese tried to crown himself boss of bosses. Unfortunately for him, he chose to have the coronation at the ill-fated Apalachin Conference—the meeting of top mob guys broken up by the New York state police. Not that the humiliation really mattered; by then Gambino was conspiring with Costello, Luciano, and Lansky to get rid of Genovese.

They bribed a drug dealer to testify against him, and had Don Vito locked up for 15 years. Genovese died in prison, leaving the field open for Gambino. Don Carlo ran things for the next decade or so. He disapproved of the drug business and generally kept his people out of it. He may have ordered the hit on Joe Colombo at the Italian American Civil Rights rally in 1971, but it has never been proved. Don Carlo died of a heart attack in 1976 after passing control to Paul Castellano.

Beyond *The Godfather* comparisons, Gambino has appeared as a supporting character in several modern TV gangster films—*Bonanno: A Godfather's Story* (1999), *Between Love and Honor* (1995), and *Boss of Bosses* (2001).

Gein, Ed

Though his crimes were not the most ghastly of their kind in either number or savagery, Ed Gein is the psychopath who became an icon of twentieth century horror. He was a poster boy for serial killers, the monster who hid the unspeakable behind a façade of meek normality. As such, he became the inspiration for some of the most charismatic screen villains.

Physically, he could not have looked less the part. Gein was a childlike, short, effeminate little guy with a crooked grin. Born in 1906 to a totally domineering mother and an alcoholic father, he was the second of two sons. His mom Augusta, a hellfire and brimstone conservative Christian, made some money in the grocery business in La Crosse, Wisconsin and decided to move the family away from the fleshpots surrounding them. Off they went to the little town of Plainfield, Wisconsin where, in 1914, they settled in on a remote 195-acre farm.

Ed's father died in 1940; his brother in 1944 during a brush fire. (Some said little Eddie might have had a hand in it.) After two strokes, his mother kicked off in 1945, leaving Gein alone on the farm with a lot of time on his hands. He didn't have to work the land because he received a subsidy from a government soil-conservation program. His mother had railed against the evils of sex, and Gein developed a warped curiosity about female sexuality. Indeed, with all the publicity about Christine Jorgensen's sex change in 1952, he wanted to become a woman. An operation being impossible for him, Gein stole women's bodies from graveyards in the darkest dead of the night and used them for his own surgical "experiments" and butchery.

He closed off the bedroom and sitting room his mother had used and kept them preserved as she'd left them. He lived in a tiny squalid bedroom and kitchen where he read adventure tales and stories of Nazi atrocities. Over the years, he turned the farmhouse into a chamber of horrors with his collection of preserved skin, skulls, and organs. (One boy saw Gein's grisly collection. When he told people, they laughed it off.)

At some point in the 1950s, Gein's ghoulish necrophilia turned to murder. There were unexplained disappearances in that part of the state but no evidence directly connected them to Gein. His first known victim was 51-year-old Mary Hogan. One night in November 1954 Gein went to the tavern where she tended bar. Finding her alone, he shot her in the head and dragged her body back to his place on a sled.

Three years later, on Saturday, November 17, 1957, Gein killed again. His victim was 58-year-old Bernice Worden, mother of the town's deputy sheriff. He'd spent the week before hanging around the hardware store where she worked and talking to her son Frank. Gein had been particularly curious about when Frank was going hunting. Saturday, he answered. Gein mentioned he would be in to the hardware store that day to pick up some antifreeze.

On Saturday, Gein went into town early. He had a bullet in his pocket. When he and Mrs. Worden were alone, he put the bullet in a rifle that was for sale, and shot her. He locked the front door, dragged the body out back to his pickup, and drove it home.

When Frank discovered the store locked that afternoon, and blood on the floor, he was immediately worried. He also noticed a partial receipt for a half gallon of antifreeze his mother had written. He told his boss, Sheriff Arthur Schley, his suspicions. Sheriff Schley drove straight out to Gein's farm. On a hunch, Worden went over to a place in West Plainfield where he knew Ed liked to eat. He found the little guy there. Gein denied everything, but he acted so odd that Worden took him into custody.

At the same time, Schley made the first of several horrifying discoveries. Bernice Worden's decapitated body had been strung up by the heels, eviscerated and mutilated. Inside the house, bowls made of human skulls, a lampshade of skin, organs in the freezer, a heart in a pot on the stove. It was more than he could bear. When he questioned Gein later that night, he snapped and banged Gein's head into a wall. Guilt and the horror of what he had seen contributed to an untimely heart attack. He died before Gein went to trial.

The doctors who tested Gein's sanity agreed he was schizophrenic and he was locked up in the Cen-

Ed Gein, who looked like a gentleman farmer, on his way to the Central State Hospital for the Criminally Insane, 1957. (AP Photo)

tral State Hospital for the Criminally Insane for the rest of his life. Institutionalization agreed with him; Gein was a model patient and prisoner until his death in 1984.

Naturally enough, his farmhouse became a mecca for the morbid. In March 1958 an arsonist burned it to the ground.

Ed Gein might have been forgotten had he not attracted the attention of writer Robert Bloch. A prolific novelist and short story writer of the old school, Bloch was attracted to the story of a lonely mama's boy. His roots in horror went back to the fantastic tales of his colleague and friend H.P. Lovecraft, but he recognized something more frighteningly immediate and real in Ed Gein, and he was able to transform that horror into Norman Bates in his novel *Psycho* (1960).

Director Alfred Hitchcock had long been fascinated by murders in general, serial murderers in particular in such films as *The Lodger* and *Shadow of a Doubt*. In the late 1950s, he had been making complex big-budget studio films—*Vertigo, North by Northwest, The Man Who Knew Too Much*—and he was tired of them. He was also involved with the television series *Alfred Hitchcock Presents*. He wanted to bring the economical techniques of TV production to a feature film, one that would be made quickly and inexpensively, while at the same time testing the limits of screen violence, sex, and suspense. He was successful beyond his fondest hopes. He produced *Psycho* (1960) himself and made it on a very modest budget. It immediately became his most commercially successful picture, a film everyone had to see. With it, Ed Gein made his first tenuous steps into the mainstream.

Fourteen years later, when Tobe Hooper adapted Gein's story, he took a different tack. Gone were the psychoanalytic explanations. As Hooper put it, *Texas Chainsaw Massacre* (1974) was "a meat movie," grand guignol more explicit and revolting than anything released in conventional movie theaters.

In Hooper's film, Gein is replaced by four homicidal rednecks who spend the entire running time chasing and killing a group of college-aged kids who stumbled upon their isolated farmhouse. The house, filled with rotting flesh and furniture made of body parts, is as important as any of the mostly unsympathetic characters. Add the intense violence and Ed Gein's madness is made real.

Though the film did not come close to Hitchcock's in terms of its cultural importance, it remains a cult favorite that has spawned inferior sequels and dozens if not hundreds of imitators. Another obscure low-budget film, *Deranged*, made the same year, takes a much more realistic approach to Gein's crimes. (The Internet Movie Database [IMDb] lists no fewer than 16 feature films based on Gein.)

In 1988 author Thomas Harris worked with yet another facet of Gein's psychotic personality. Like Gein, the character Buffalo Bill in *Silence of the Lambs* (1991) murders women and strips their skin. By wearing their skin, he hopes to transform himself into a woman. The novel and Jonathan Demme's film are masterpieces of popular entertainment, and Gein's particular brand of madness replaces previous manifestations of horror like Frankenstein's monster or Dracula.

Because of those films, Gein enjoyed (well, he might enjoy it if he were alive) a resurgence of popularity. Another low-budget fact-based film was made about him, as well as two more nonfiction books. His name and madness appear in the work of dozens of hard rock bands from Marilyn Manson to Killdozer.

Genovese, Vito

In many ways, Vito Genovese is the forgotten man among the original gangsters, those Young Turks who took over the most profitable illegal activities in New York in 1931 and created "organized crime."

Born in Italy, Genovese came to America in 1913. He started off with penny ante stuff, and through the judicious application of violence in the right places, became a key figure in **Lucky Luciano's** organization. His particular area of expertise was the importation and distribution of narcotics. When the Castellammarese War broke out between **Joe Masseria** and **Salvatore Maranzano**, Genovese followed Luciano's lead and backed his boss Masseria. As long as the two old "Mustache Petes" had their men fighting and killing each other, business suffered, nobody was making money, and the murders brought unwanted attention from the press and the law.

To end it, Luciano told Maranzano he would betray Joe "the Boss." To spread responsibility for the usurpation, Charlie Lucky proposed a four-man hit team representing the major interests involved: **Joe Adonis**, **Albert Anastasia**, **Ben "Bugsy" Siegel**, and

Genovese. On the afternoon of April 15, 1931 they burst into a Coney Island restaurant and gunned down Masseria while Luciano took an extended bathroom break. A few months later, Luciano hit Maranzano with a different group of killers.

Even though Charlie Lucky then declared there would be no single ruling boss, no *capo di tutti capi*, he and his partner **Meyer Lansky**, known as the "Little Man," were in charge. Genovese worked for them and did very well for himself.

When crusading DA Thomas Dewey turned up the heat on the mobsters and sent Luciano to jail on a prostitution-pandering rap, Genovese was ready. In 1934 he had ordered the murder of Ferdinand "the Shadow" Boccia after Boccia demanded a cut from a rigged card game. Witnesses could connect him with the Boccia hit and Dewey knew about them. In 1937 Genovese learned one of the Boccia witnesses was going to talk. For years, he had been stashing part of his profits in Swiss banks. When the time was right, he simply vamoosed with an entourage befitting a man of his status, and set himself up in Italy.

Genovese made significant donations to Mussolini's fascist party and became chummy with Il Duce himself. A few years later when things went badly for the Italians in World War II, Genovese was on hand to welcome the American liberators and to offer his services as a translator for Army Intelligence. He was also quick to finger the most important black marketeers and make sure they were locked up. Then Don Vito took over their rackets. When the Army brass learned he was still wanted in New York on murder charges, Genovese's star dimmed considerably. He was sent back to face the charges after the war.

No problem. He was able to poison a key witness who was in protective custody, and without his corroborating testimony, there could be no prosecution. Genovese walked on June 11, 1946.

By then, Luciano had been deported to Italy and new power structures were being set up. Genovese tried to solidify his position by ordering wholesale killings of all those who might oppose or testify against him. His main rival was Luciano's man **Frank Costello**.

Don Vito gave the contract to Vincente "the Chin" Gigante. The gargantuan hitman waited for Costello in the lobby of his apartment building and took a shot at him on May 2, 1957. Costello wasn't killed, though the bullet grazed him and he bled profusely from a head wound. And when the cops came, he had to explain the tally sheet from the Las Vegas Tropicana casino he was carrying in his pocket. He said nothing and refused to identify the Chin, so they leaned on him with income tax evasion charges, too. Costello read the writing on the wall and took early retirement.

It appeared that despite missing his target, Genovese had the wind at his back. In October he ordered a successful hit on Anastasia. (Lansky approved that one because Anastasia had been trying to horn in his Cuban gambling operations.) Don Vito decided to consolidate his power and called a meeting of all the bosses in America for November 14, 1957.

The place: the sleepy little burg of Apalachin in upstate New York.

More than 60 bosses from all over the country gathered at mobster Joseph Barbara's country estate. They had barely settled in when one of them noticed road blocks were being set up outside. It turns out all the preparations for the meeting had not gone unnoticed by New York state police Sergeant Edgar D. Crosswell. When he saw all of the luxury cars with their out-of-state plates, he became curious and had the roadblocks ready.

The gangsters panicked. Some ran into the woods; some tried to crash out in their Caddies. The cops hauled them in on completely nonexistent charges. As guilty as the guys certainly were of any number of crimes, they weren't doing anything illegal in Apalachin. But they were brought in, photographed, and booked on obstruction of justice charges. Some of them may have had to explain why they were carrying envelopes full of cash. Don Vito had demanded they bring proof of their allegiance. He didn't get the money and he never recovered from the humiliation.

Luciano, Costello, and Lansky decided it was time to get rid of him, and got the feds to do their dirty work. They bribed a drug dealer who was already in custody to testify against Don Vito, Vincente "the Chin", and several others. The simple plan worked and Genovese was sentenced to 15 years. He died in Leavenworth in 1969.

Vito Genovese has fared poorly on film. His most prominent role is in *The Valachi Papers* (1972), but since it's told from Joe Valachi's point of view—and Valachi was one of the many people Genovese tried to have killed—it is a less than flattering portrait. He is a minor character in *Bugsy* (1991), *Lucky Luciano* (1974), *Gangster Wars* (1981), and the TV productions *Boss of Bosses* (2001), *The Gangster Chronicles* (1981), *Lansky* (1999), and *Bonanno: A Godfather's Story* (1999).

Giancana, Salvatore "Sam," "Momo," or "Mooney"

In some ways, Sam "Momo" Giancana was the archetypal mobster.

He got his start during Prohibition in the 1920s with the **Al Capone** gang and **Frank Nitti** who, on paper at least, succeeded Scarface as the boss. Giancana worked as a driver and hitman and earned the nicknames "Mooney" and "Momo" (derivatives of "crazy") for his hair-trigger temper. His talents ranged far beyond simple strong arm stuff. His rap sheet included assault, bookmaking, conspiracy, bombing, and more than 70 arrests, but he served only three stretches in jail—30 days for auto theft, five years for burglary, four for bootlegging.

When Giancana was drafted in World War II, he admitted he was a criminal and the doctors deemed him a "constitutional psychopath" and not fit to serve.

Momo's real fame came later in life when he claimed in the late 1950s that the CIA hired him to assassinate Fidel Castro. He was also rumored to have worked, more successfully, for Joseph Kennedy in 1960 to deliver votes for his son John Kennedy's presidential campaign.

After JFK was elected, he and Sam shared a mistress, Judith Campbell. At the same time, Attorney General Robert Kennedy was aggressively going after the mob, which led to more rumors that Giancana was involved with the assassination of the JFK in 1963. There was no evidence, however, and life didn't get any easier for Momo.

He continued to hobnob with such celebrities as Frank Sinatra and Phyllis McGuire, but Giancana got into hot water with his coworkers, who thought he was holding out on their fair share of the gambling profits, and the feds, who wouldn't let up on him either. So he took off for Mexico and stayed there until 1974 when the Mexican government, at the behest of the American government, gave him the boot.

Back in Chicago, Giancana was invited to testify before a Senate committee investigating the whole CIA-Mafia-Castro business. But before Sam could talk, on the night of June 19, 1975 somebody with a silenced .22 put seven slugs into the back of his head. Who? Why? No arrests were ever made.

Giancana's story has been told several times, most thoroughly by Seymour Hersh in *Dark Side of Camelot* (1997). Sam and Chuck Giancana, Momo's son and brother respectively, give him credit for all sorts of things in *Double Cross* (1993) as does his daughter Antoinette in 1984's *Mafia Princess* (which was turned into a TV movie with Tony Curtis as Momo). John Turturro played him in the TV movie *Sugartime* (1995), about his affair with Phyllis McGuire.

Giancana is also a supporting character in *The Rat Pack* (1998) and the miniseries *Sinatra* (1992). The more conspiratorial aspects of his story are covered in *Ruby* (1992), *Power and Beauty* (2002), and *Marilyn and Bobby: Her Final Affair* (1993).

Gillette, Chester

Chester Gillette would hardly rate a mention if it weren't for Theodore Dreiser and Elizabeth Taylor.

In 1906 Gillette found himself in a difficult but not uncommon situation. His girlfriend was pregnant.

Gillette came from a curious background. His parents, soldiers in the Salvation Army, moved constantly. Gillette kicked around in college and at various jobs until 1905 when he went to work for his uncle Noah at the Gillette Skirt Factory in upstate Cortland, New York, where he met Grace "Billie" Brown, who had come to the factory to escape life on a farm. She was 19; he was 22.

Chester may also have been seeing other girls who worked there, too, and he had social and professional ambitions that did not include an unsophisticated wife from a poor family. By the spring of 1906, Grace was pregnant and had returned home. Her numerous letters to Gillette urged him to do the right thing. He was evasive until she came back to Cortland. Fed up, she said she would have the baby and name him as the father, crippling his chances for advancement.

In July, Gillette asked her to join him on a trip to the Adirondacks lake country, perhaps promising marriage. They went to three hotels, registering in two as man and wife. At the third, he used an alias; she used her real name. One afternoon, he suggested they rent a rowboat and go out to a remote island on Big Moose Lake for a picnic. Curiously, he brought a suitcase and tennis racquet along. Nobody ever saw Gracie alive again.

That night, still carrying his suitcase and tennis racquet, Gillette swam to shore on the far side of the lake and checked into a fourth hotel.

The next morning, Robert Morrison, the man who had rented the rowboat to the young couple, became worried and set off with a search party. They found the missing rowboat, upturned, and something deeper in the water beneath it. It was Grace's body, her face horribly slashed.

A few days later, Gillette was arrested. He was still at his hotel and had done nothing to cover his tracks. In short order, the police found all of the letters the two had written, and questioned Gillette more seriously. First, he claimed it had been an accident. Grace fell out of the boat. By the time Gillette went to trial, his story had changed slightly. Grace, he said, had panicked when he suggested they tell her parents about her condition, and threw herself from the boat, possibly attempting suicide. And where was his tennis racquet? After unsuccessfully attempting to save Grace, he claimed to have swum ashore and buried the racquet because he feared someone might think he had somehow used it to harm her. As it turned out, he was absolutely right about that part. It took the jury six short hours to find him guilty, and he was electrocuted on March 30, 1908.

Theodore Dreiser reworked the material in *An American Tragedy* (1925) and took all the liberties afforded to any novelist. He used the bare facts of the case as the final part of a much longer story criticizing several elements of American society. The book was first adapted to the screen for director Joseph Von Sternberg in 1931. Dreiser disliked the film and it is rarely seen today.

The story was much more successful in 1951 as George Stevens' *A Place in the Sun* with Montgomery Clift playing the Gillette character, Shelly Winters as the luckless Grace, and a young Liz Taylor at her loveliest as the society babe whose love drives Monty to deep six Shelly.

Not surprisingly, both Dreiser and Stevens made the Gillette character more sympathetic than he actually was and present Grace's death as partially accidental. It makes a more engaging and emotional story, fitting squarely in the tradition of Hollywood's long-running romance with criminals.

Gilmore, Gary

Were it not for Norman Mailer, Gary Gilmore wouldn't even rate a footnote. He was a smalltime

> *When he spotted an attractive woman on the street, he would tail her back to her house or apartment. If she was alone, he'd break in, tie her up, and fondle her. He threatened his victims with a stolen pistol but, during those early formative years, he went no further.*

career criminal who worked his way up from shoplifting as a teenager to armed robbery. His crimes earned him a stiff prison sentence in Indiana in 1964. Paroled in 1976, he quickly returned to theft and burglary. On July 20th, he killed motel manager Ben Bushnell during a robbery in Provo, Utah. The day before, he had murdered gas station attendant Max Jensen.

At the trial, Gilmore offered no defense and was sentenced to death—which is where his story became something different.

In 1972 the U.S. Supreme Court had ruled the death penalty was cruel and unusual punishment. Opponents rallied public opinion for executions and, in 1976, the court essentially reversed itself. When Gilmore refused to appeal his sentence, saying he wanted to be executed, he became the focal point of a political fight between opponents and supporters of capital punishment. That caught the attention of writer Norman Mailer who began writing about Gilmore as the subject of his nonfiction novel *The Executioner's Song*, published in 1979, two years after Gilmore's death.

Gilmore's famous last words were "Let's do it," spoken just before a Utah firing squad carried out his sentence.

Mailer's book was adapted for television in 1982, and the film starring Tommy Lee Jones also became a solid cult favorite on tape in the first days of the home video revolution. A second book, *Shot In the Heart* (1995), by Gilmore's brother Mikal, was adapted by HBO in 2001.

Glatman, Harvey

Even as a child, Harvey Glatman had a thing for ropes. At age four, his overprotective mom Ophelia found him with a string wrapped around his little penis. As he entered puberty, Glatman progressed to autoerotic asphyxiation—the dangerous practice of tying a noose around one's neck, looping the line over a beam and tightening it to the point of passing out while masturbating, thereby getting a double high.

Later, not content merely to abuse himself, Glatman moved on to unwilling girls. Growing up in Denver in the straitlaced 1940s, he was a terribly shy, sort of smart but goofy-looking teenager. He tried to meet girls without actually speaking to them. When he spotted an attractive woman on the street, he would tail her back to her house or apartment. If she was alone, he'd break in, tie her up, and fondle her. He threatened his victims with a stolen pistol but, during those early formative years, he went no further.

Police caught him breaking into one woman's place in 1945. While he was awaiting trial, he kidnapped and fondled another woman and served eight months of a one-year sentence in prison for it.

Paroled, he moved back to New York, where he'd been born, and his assaults on women escalated, becoming tentatively more violent, as he threatened them with a toy pistol and a pocket knife. He was caught and sent to Sing Sing where he served a two-year stretch before he earned another parole. He went back to Denver and moved in with his mother until 1957. Then with her help, Glatman relocated to Los Angeles, where she set him up as a TV repairman.

There, he also indulged in his favorite hobby, photography. It was his entry into the shadowy world of models. For young women hoping to make it in Hollywood, nude modeling was one way to pay the bills until that big break arrived. Glatman bought an expensive Rolleicord camera and started calling himself Johnny Glenn.

He killed his first victim on August 1, 1957, a 19-year-old divorcée named Judith Ann Dull. Glatman told her he had an assignment from a detective magazine. He'd pay $20 an hour to take pictures of her tied up in her apartment. She agreed. Once Glatman had her hands bound behind her back, Henry pulled out a .32 automatic. He raped her repeatedly while he took pictures of her in various fearful poses. That night, he drove out to the desert where he strangled her and shot more film of her body before burying her in a shallow grave.

The next year, on March 8th, Henry did much the same to Shirley Ann Bridgeford. He met her through a lonely hearts club. She thought they were simply going on a date when he drove her out to the Vallecito Mountains and pulled his pistol. The rest was the same.

He met Ruth Mercado (real name Angela Rojas) through a personal ad offering her services as a model in August 1958. She, too, agreed to pose in her apartment. Glatman raped her there, then took her out to the desert.

His luck ran out with Lorraine Vigil. She was another young novice model, but Glatman reached her through a photography studio where the shoot was to take place. He picked her up in his car, and when he drove away from the city, she became suspicious. He threatened her with the pistol, but she fought back. Glatman had stopped by the side of a remote road and was attempting to tie her up when the weapon went off. She was wounded but managed to grab the automatic and scramble out of the car. That's when California highway patrolman Tom Mulligan happened by.

Later that night, Glatman confessed to everything and told the cops where he had hidden his collection of photographs. Sentenced to death, he was sent to the same San Quentin cell that would

later be occupied by **Charles Manson** and **Richard Ramirez**, the "Night Stalker." Glatman was executed in the gas chamber on September 18, 1959.

Though Glatman has not been the direct subject for any motion picture, his story bears some similarities to Michael Powell's brilliant 1960 film, *Peeping Tom.*

Gohl, Billy

Short, thick-bodied, bullet-headed Billy Gohl was a bad man in a bad town. He showed up in Aberdeen, Washington around the turn of the twentieth century. Aberdeen, on Gray's Harbor, was a timber town where unlucky sailors might get shanghaied onto lumber boats.

Gohl knocked around at various jobs, earning a villainous reputation in the process, until 1903 when he became the local agent for the Sailor's Union of the Pacific. As such, Gohl was the guy a newly arrived seaman might turn to if he had a fat pay envelope in his pocket or valuables that needed safekeeping while he made the most of his time ashore. Billy had other plans.

His office at the Union Hall was cantilevered above the fast-flowing Wishkah River. It had a trapdoor in the floor. Should the luckless fellow arrive alone and unnoticed, Billy would measure his potential holdings. If he thought there was sufficient profit to be made, he'd whip out his pistol or his knife and kill the sailor. Then he'd clean the weapon and empty his victim's pockets before disposing of the body through the trapdoor.

It's impossible to say how many men he killed, but between 1903 and 1913 more than 200 bodies turned up Gray's Harbor. There were so many they were referred to as the "Floater Fleet," and Aberdeen was called the "Port of Missing Men" or the "Hellhole of the Pacific." As public outrage grew, Gohl was always one of the loudest voices calling for more effective police action.

He was caught and convicted on two counts of murder in 1913. The first was local cattle rustler

Charlie Hatberg. He crossed Gohl and wound up in Indian Creek with a 25-pound anchor and chain around him and a bullet in his back. The second was sailor Fred Nielssen. When Nielssen visited the Union Hall, he was carrying a gold watch with the name August Schleuter engraved on it. Assuming the watch would be too easily identified, Gohl left it on after he'd killed the man. When the body was discovered, Gohl even identified it as Schleuter. When the investigation turned up the victim's real name, and the cops came for Gohl.

Gohl's luck may finally have run dry but not completely. Washington had abolished the death penalty in 1912, so he got life instead of the noose. (In part because of his crimes, the death penalty was reinstated in 1914.) Gohl died in prison in 1928.

Though he may well have been America's most prolific serial killer, Gohl is largely unknown. He does however retain local notoriety in Aberdeen at his namesake Billy's Bar and Grill.

Gotti, John

Despite the nicknames—Dapper Don, Teflon Don—and the $2,000 suits, John Gotti was strictly Old School, a tough mobster who killed people who got in his way or didn't follow his orders.

Gotti was part of the Gambino crime family in New York and got his first break in 1973 when he and two others clipped James McBratney. McBratney was an Irish mug who had been part of a gang who kidnapped and murdered Don **Carlo Gambino**'s nephew Manny. Gotti served a stretch at Green Haven Prison on a manslaughter conviction for the crime. Not long after he was released, Don Carlo died and named **Paul Castellano** as his successor.

Gotti hated Castellano because he was trying to move the mob into more legitimate and less dangerous enterprises. Beyond their philosophical differences, Gotti thought his patron, underboss Neil Dellacroce, was more deserving of the promotion.

In spite of his contentious relationship with Castellano, Gotti and his crew did well in the late

1970s and 1980s. During those years, Gotti also had to deal with the FBI. They tried to nail him on a variety of charges but Gotti and his attorney always found a way to beat the rap. The trials and Gotti's obvious pleasure at being in the spotlight earned him the Teflon Don moniker, because the charges didn't stick. He became a celebrity, first in New York, then nationwide when he made the cover of *Time* magazine with his portrait painted by Andy Warhol, no less.

Gotti faced trouble on other fronts. In 1980 his young son was killed in a traffic accident when he was hit by a car driven by John Favara. A few months later, Favara was kidnapped while leaving work and was never seen again.

Late in 1985 Neil Dellacroce died. Members of Gotti's crew were said to be suspected of drug dealing, officially forbidden by Mafia rules at the time, but honored more in the breach than the observance. Word was out, however, that Castellano was going to take it seriously. On December 2, 1985 a team of Gotti gunmen clipped Castellano and his top man Thomas Bilotti on the street outside Sparks Steakhouse in midtown Manhattan. It was a blatant, public kiss-my-ass statement and it left Gotti in charge.

He continued to win his court battles until the FBI's wiretaps nailed him. When they hit him with their final RICO (Racketeer Influenced and Corrupt Organization Act) charges, they had 100 hours of incriminating taped conversations. Even so, Gotti might have found a way out yet again had not his fellow mobster **Salvatore "Sammy the Bull" Gravano** decided to cooperate with the feds.

Perhaps it was the way the Dapper Don had bad-mouthed Sammy on the tapes that led Gravano to confess to 19 murders and virtually every other illegal thing he had ever done. For his testimony, Sammy got a slot in the witness protection program, which he screwed up, and Gotti got life.

The Teflon Don died of throat cancer in prison in 2002.

In the years since, his family and children have upheld the family tradition of celebrity criminals. His

Alleged Gambino family crime boss John Gotti (aka. the "Teflon Don") during a break in testimony in New York Supreme Court in Manhattan, January 23, 1990. (AP Photo/Daniel Sheehan)

son John "Junior" Gotti was involved in a long-running trial concerning—among other charges—an attempt to kidnap Guardian Angels founder and radio personality Curtis Sliwa. It ended in 2006 after three hung juries. His daughter Victoria turned her life into a "reality" TV series called *Growing Up Gotti*.

John Gotti's career and eventual conviction have been the subject of several nonfiction books. In TV films, he has been portrayed by Tom Sizemore in *Witness to the Mob* (1998), Anthony John Denison in *Getting Gotti* (1994) and, most memorably, by Armand Assante in the HBO production *Gotti* (1996). Gotti was a partial inspiration for Joey Zasa in *The Godfather, Part III* (1990).

Graham, Barbara

Had the real Barbara Graham been as innocent as the cinematic Barbara Graham (as played by Susan Hayward), a true miscarriage of justice would have occurred. But Babs wasn't that innocent, so she got the gas chamber while Susan got an Oscar.

Barbara was born in Oakland, California in 1923 to the irresponsible young Hortense. When Barbara was two, Hortense was sent to the Ventura State School for Girls. While her mom was in reform school, Barbara was looked after, sort of, by her extended family. Hortense was released a few years later, promptly got knocked up again, and paid little attention to her daughter.

Barbara grew up on the streets where she turned out to be quick, cute, and sexy. By the time she was 13, she'd been sent to Ventura. A few years later, she drifted into casual prostitution working the Oakland navy yard. At the same time, she was ambitious enough to want more, so she went to a business college in hopes of landing an office job. Like many young women in her situation, she found a husband. In short order, they had a couple of children and became financially strapped. When he learned about Barbara's past, he got a divorce and custody.

That did it for Barbara. She moved to Southern California where she applied herself to her original profession more seriously. Her second marriage was to a customer. It was annulled. She relocated to San Francisco where she was caught providing a false alibi in court for a couple of pals, and served a stretch for perjury. She was 28 when she was released and made one more attempt at the straight life, taking a job as a nurse's aide in Tonopah, Nevada.

For a while, it worked. She married for a third time and settled down, but smalltown life just didn't cut it, so she caught a bus to LA and went back to the life. Working out of bars, she met and eventually married Henry Graham, a bartender who wasn't troubled by her line of work. Henry also liked to experiment with drugs and shared them with Barbara. He also suggested she might want to take some of her clients to an illegal gambling joint out in the suburb of El Monte. It was run by an acquaintance of his, a guy named Emmett Perkins. Barbara said yes. At about the same time, she and Henry had a son, and both parents became addicted to heroin.

In 1953 Barbara again abandoned husband and child and moved in with Emmett Perkins, who dabbled in other criminal activities. The footloose filly fell in with Perkins' plan to rob Mabel Monohan, an elderly widow who was rumored to have a safe full of cash in her suburban Burbank home. As it turned out, there was no safe but Mrs. Monohan was still security conscious. She would never open her door to a strange man. But what about another woman… a woman who was having car trouble?

Late on Tuesday, March 10, 1953 Barbara, Perkins, and three other hoods—John L. True, Baxter Shorter, and Jack Santo—forced their way into Mrs. Monohan's house. Barbara pistol whipped the old lady before they tied her up, gagged her, and tied a pillowcase over her head. She died of asphyxiation. The gang tore up the house and found nothing. The brutal killing shocked the city and Mrs. Monohan's daughter offered a $5,000 reward for information about the killers. The reward led a smalltime crook to contact police and tell them he had been involved in planning just such a robbery with four other men two years ago. One of them was Baxter Shorter, reputed to be a top-notch safecracker. Jack Santo was another.

Police picked up Shorter and he agreed to testify against the others if he was given immunity. Though he didn't know the real names of his associates, Shorter told the cops exactly what had happened. At about the same time, John True was arrested. Perkins and Santo realized Shorter had turned on them, so they kidnapped him, took him out to the desert and killed him. That really brought the heat down on them. Barbara, Perkins, and Santo were identified as suspects in both the Monohan killing and the Shorter kidnapping.

Three weeks later, on May 4th, undercover cops spotted Barbara buying heroin and followed her back to a cheap apartment. When they broke the door down, they found Barbara, Perkins, and Santo, all stark naked in mid-gamahuche, and arrested them on the spot.

Barbara was separated from the men and kept in the women's jail where she struck up a relationship with a younger woman named Donna Prow. Barbara turned to Donna when she learned John True had been granted immunity and would testify against her. (Shorter's confession was inadmissible without his testimony in court.) Barbara was distraught, but Donna had a suggestion. She said she knew this guy who, for the right amount of money, might be willing to provide an alibi for her. Barbara said yes, find him.

Donna's friend Sam showed up at the women's jail a few days before the trial. When they talked, he was worried Baxter Shorter might reappear. Barbara said it wasn't a concern; she could absolutely positively guarantee nobody would ever hear from Shorter again, no way, no how. Sam paid two more visits and they concocted a story about being together in an Encino motel on the night of the Monohan murder. On his final visit, Sam made sure there was no chance some other story would surface to conflict with his alibi. No, she said, on the night in question, she was at the Monohan house.

Okay, Sam said, he would bribe a desk clerk to doctor the motel register. They were in business. Barbara was relieved.

The trial began on August, 14, 1953. True, fully immunized, told how the five of them had botched the Monohan job. His testimony was so exact and damaging Barbara told her lawyer she'd had a revelation. Yes, before then, she'd told him she couldn't remember where she had been on the night of the murder, but her old lover Sam had visited her and now it all came back to her. Her attorney was dubious but agreed to listen to Sam.

But, alas, the next morning when Sam showed up in court, he revealed that his occupation was "police officer" and he was going to be a witness for the prosecution. Not only had Barbara been set up by Donna Prow, but Sam had been wearing a wire and her most damning admissions were immortalized on tape. Even so, Babs took one more shot and tried to testify on her own behalf. She said she had been lying to Sam, she claimed, because she was afraid and really didn't know where she had been that night.

Nobody bought it; all three were found guilty. They went to the gas chamber on June 3, 1955, first Barbara by herself, and then Perkins and Santo together.

Normally, that would have been the end of the matter, had not movie producer Walter Wanger decided to use the story to resurrect his troubled career. (In 1951, Wanger had come to believe his

wife, actress Joan Bennett, was having an affair with her agent Jennings Lang. Wanger shot Lang in the balls and served four months in a minimum security facility for it.)

Wanger wisely decided that if Barbara's story was going to work as a major motion picture, she had to be innocent. So he enlisted writers Don K. Mankiewicz and Nelson Giddy and director Robert Wise (who would later make *The Sound of Music*) to clean the girl up. In their hands, Barbara became a spirited young woman who made some bad choices and was led astray by men who used her. (Cue violins.) Susan Hayward grabbed the role and ran with it. In 1958 she copped the Best Actress Oscar for *I Want To Live!*, beating out Liz Taylor's brilliant turn as Maggie in *Cat on a Hot Tin Roof*. The story was retold and Barbara was made even more innocent in a 1983 TV movie of the same title with Lindsay Wagner.

For a more accurate examination, find a copy of reporter Bernice Freeman Davis's 1961 book, *The Desperate and the Damned*. Though she was not fully persuaded of Barbara's guilt either, she creates a portrait of a troubled, self-destructive woman.

Graham, John

John Graham was a troubled young man who progressed from forgery to insurance fraud to mass murder in the space of four short years.

Born in 1932 in Denver, Graham was placed in an orphanage by his mother, Daisie. His father died when he was three years old, and Daisie, a realistic businesswoman, knew she could not provide for the boy. He stayed in foster care for the next ten years until she remarried. Things were still tough financially, but Daisy did well with several businesses, one of them a popular drive-in restaurant.

In 1948 Graham spent a rough year in the Coast Guard. He was often AWOL but when the Guard learned he was under age, he received an honorable discharge. Back home in Denver, Graham found work with a manufacturing company. It ended when he stole and forged company checks totaling several thousand dollars. He bought a new convertible with the money and lit out for Texas. His little adventure ended when he tried to outrun a highway patrolman and crashed into a roadblock. They shipped him back to Colorado where Daisie promised to repay all the money her boy had stolen.

After that episode, Graham settled down for a time. He married and had a couple of kids. Still, he and his wife had to live in his mother's house where they paid rent. The arguments between Graham and Daisie over money were loud and frequent. Then, in 1955, his Chevy pickup wound up parked on railroad tracks and was totaled by a train. Graham collected the insurance and used some of it to repay his mother. At about the same time, there was a suspicious explosion at the restaurant. Again, the insurance company ponied up.

In November Daisie planned a trip to Alaska to visit her daughter, Graham's half sister. Right before he drove her to the airport, Graham gave her a special Christmas present he had wrapped himself. Minutes after United Airlines Flight 629 took off from Stapleton Airport, it exploded in midair. All 44 people aboard were killed.

Airline officials and authorities realized immediately a bomb was probably the cause and found evidence in the rear luggage compartment—a strong odor of gunpowder and traces of chemical compounds associated with dynamite. When they looked into the backgrounds of the passengers, they learned some had purchased flight insurance at a coin-operated machine in the airport. (These machines were ubiquitous in America well into the 1960s.) Graham had bought a $37,500 payout for his mother.

At his first interview with the FBI, Graham denied having given his mother anything to take on the plane. He freely gave the agents permission to search his house. When they did, they found wire matching evidence from the crash site. At his second questioning, Graham admitted he had made a bomb from 25 sticks of dynamite and also found it somewhat amusing that his mother had been carry-

ing a box of shotgun shells. Throughout the process, agents were surprised by the lack of any emotion on Graham's part. Even though he would later recant his confession, Graham never really seemed to care or to be angry about his capture.

His trial was a one-sided affair. The prosecution presented a solidly constructed technical case based on irrefutable physical evidence and Graham's own words. The defense took less than two hours. The jury didn't even need that much time to find Graham guilty. And though the appeals process was automatic in death penalty convictions, Graham said he wanted no part of it. He meant it, and attempted suicide in jail by hanging himself with his socks. Guards found him quickly and he was soon healthy enough for the gas chamber.

Graham's was one of the first cases of airline violence, and it became a key part of the 1959 *The FBI Story*, starring James Stewart. The film is very much an "authorized" view of the agency and so it's no surprise such a simple and efficiently solved crime would be highlighted.

Gravano, Salvatore "Sammy the Bull"

Along with Abe "Kid Twist" Reles and **Joe Valachi**, Sammy "the Bull" Gravano is one of the Mafia's great songbirds.

Throughout the 1980s he was with the New York Gambino crime family. As a soldier and hitman for the mob, his stock rose dramatically in 1985 when he conspired with **John Gotti** to assassinate their boss **Paul Castellano**. With that audacious hit, he and Gotti rose to the top. Always in love with the spotlight, Gotti also became a prime target for the FBI. Like the other bosses, he was under near constant surveillance in the late '80s. The feds managed to bug an apartment where he did a lot of business and talked freely. When Gravano wasn't around, Gotti told some lies about him to another boss. The Bull learned about the tapes and specifically about what Gotti had said when they were in court facing racketeering charges. Until then, Gotti had been the "Teflon Don" because the government's charges never stuck to him, but with the tapes and what he saw as a personal betrayal, Gravano realized it was over for them. The feds knew too much.

And so, as they say, he flipped. In 1991 Sammy agreed to confess to everything he and Gotti had done in return for a reduced sentence and enrollment in the Federal Witness Protection Program. He admitted to taking part in 19 murders and other crimes. The trials and legal matters weren't sorted out until 1995 when his sentence was reduced to time served and he was set free.

In 1997 Gravano collaborated with Peter Maas, author of *The Valachi Papers* (1969), on his story, *Underboss* (1997). It became a bestseller.

After that, you might think Gravano would disappear with a new appearance and new identity somewhere in smalltown middle America, but you would be wrong. Sammy the Bull missed the action and so he started dealing ecstasy in Arizona. The feds caught him. He pled guilty and is now serving a 20-year stretch.

Sammy has been featured in two TV films, *Witness to the Mob* (1998) where he's played by Nicholas Turturro, and *Gotti* (1996) with William Forsythe doing the honors.

In *Underboss*, Gravano described to Maas how the experience of seeing *The Godfather* (1972) had changed everything for him. For the first time, he saw himself and his life on screen. Some years later, he would join that world in a different way. In *The Godfather, Part III* (1990), Gravano is fictionalized as Anthony "the Ant" Squigiliaro, muscle for the John Gotti character, Joey Zasa.

From Sammy the Bull to Tony the Ant is something of a demotion, but, hey, that's show business.

Guiteau, Charles

A lunatic fired the bullets that wounded President James Garfield; the doctors finished him off.

Some of Charles Guiteau's madness can probably be traced back to his abused childhood. Whatever the cause, he was an obnoxious, overbearing crankcase. As a young man in 1860, he joined the Oneida Community in New York. It was a utopian commune with an emphasis on free love. But women who believe in free love still have standards, and when Guiteau didn't get enough love, he left, and threatened to write nasty things about the place unless he was paid off. Then, remarkably, he managed to pass the bar exam in Chicago and promptly failed at his law practice. He was briefly married to a 16-year-old girl, but that failed, too. He became a self-styled preacher and then a self-styled political expert. Throughout, he was in and out of jail, often for debt.

In 1880 Guiteau dashed off a mistake-filled paper in support of the James Garfield presidential campaign. After Garfield won, Guiteau convinced himself he was the cause and moved to Washington. According to letters he wrote to the new president and other officials, he was ready to take over as ambassador to Austria or France, whatever. When it didn't happen and he was told to buzz off, Guiteau went out and bought a pistol—a nice British .44 Bulldog—and stalked the President.

On July 2nd, after having been in office for only nine months, Garfield was planning to take a holiday break. He was at the Baltimore and Potomac train station when Guiteau came up behind him and shot twice. One bullet grazed Garfield's arm. The second lodged near his spine.

Guiteau tried to run but gave up without a fight when stopped.

Medical standards at the time were crude. The President's physician didn't believe in basic sanitation. For weeks, literally, various doctors probed Mr. Garfield's wound trying to remove the bullet. The wound got much more serious and infected. The President developed blood poisoning and died in unimaginable agony 79 days later on September 19th.

Guiteau continued his bizarre behavior at the trial, claiming to have been acting on orders from

> *Belle Gunness may not match today's image of a femme fatale, but she was still one of America's most successful female murderers, a real "Lady Bluebeard."*

God and wandering off in pointless courtroom outbursts. The jury didn't cotton to his insanity defense and quickly found him guilty.

He was hanged on June 30, 1882 right after he treated the assembled crowd to a recitation of his poem *I Am Going to the Lordy*. Stephen Sondheim and John Weidman used part of the work as the basis for the *Ballad of Guiteau* in their musical *Assassins* (1991, 2004). Guiteau has been the subject of other songs, too.

Perhaps the best visual depiction of the man and his crime is Rich Geary's fine graphic novel, *The Fatal Bullet* (1999).

Gunness, Belle

Belle Gunness may not match today's image of a femme fatale, but she was still one of America's most successful female murderers, a real "Lady Bluebeard." And by the standards of her time—the turn of the twentieth century—she could turn heads.

Yes, with properly robust foundation garments, Belle could squeeze her figure down to a shapely 48-37-54, and she knew how to spin a good line. Circumstantial evidence suggests Belle, a Norwegian immigrant, murdered her first two children and husband, and that she burned three houses and one business (all people and buildings insured), before she moved to La Porte, Indiana, and married widower Peter Gunness.

Alas, their happiness was short-lived.

One night in the kitchen, while reaching for a shoe, Peter was struck on the head by a heavy cast iron sausage-grinder that fell from a shelf. Belle's daughter Jennie said she had seen Mama smack him on the head with a cleaver, but nobody believed the kid. Even a special jury bought Belle's preposterous story.

Not long after she moved in, Belle set up a pen out back where she raised and butchered hogs. At the same time, she was placing ads in various publications, including *The Skandinaven*, looking for a husband. Over the next eight years, Belle put quite a dent in the population of the proverbial Norwegian bachelor farmers. Her method was simple: she and her prospects would exchange letters where she would make it clear she wasn't interested in any guy who couldn't bring at least $1,000 or so to the relationship. Once the bottom line had been established, she would invite the unfortunate fellow up to La Porte. Then he'd disappear.

All went swimmingly for Belle and her lover/handyman/accomplice Ray Lamphere until she hooked up with Andrew Helgelian from South Dakota. He, too, came to the farm and vanished, but his brother Asle became suspicious. Realizing she'd run out her string, Belle fired Lamphere and made arrangements to burn her farmhouse. She had another hired hand buy some kerosene. On the night of April 27, 1908 the place burst into flames and was completely consumed.

When people went through the debris in the basement, they made a horrifying discovery—four bodies—Belle's three children and a woman who had been decapitated. Right from the beginning there was strong doubt the headless body was Belle's. It was too small, even considering the shrinkage caused by the fire. And the horror wasn't over, not even close.

They found eight men's watches, human bones, and teeth. Then Asle Helgelian showed up to help uncover evidence. He suggested they dig at the fresh trash pit near the hog pen, where they found the dismembered remains of his brother Andrew and Belle's daughter Jennie, who'd supposedly gone off to college in San Francisco. They kept digging and found more bodies and parts of bodies, between 12 and 14 they thought, but by then things were getting crazy.

As soon as the newspapers picked up the story, it made headlines everywhere and huge crowds thronged to La Porte, as many as 10,000 the next Sunday.

Lamphere was arrested and charged with four counts of murder and one of arson, even though he had a solid alibi for the time the fire started.

By the time the trial began the next fall, La Porte had become politically divided by the crimes. The Republican prosecutor said Lamphere was guilty of all charges; the Democrats said Belle was alive and she had planted the fourth body. Circumstantial evidence continued to pile up against Belle. The day before the fire, she had met with her lawyer and drawn up her will, leaving everything to the Norwegian Orphan's Home. The money her would-be suitors had brought was nowhere to be found. Estimates of the total ranged from $20,000 to $100,000.

There were traces of strychnine in the stomachs of the dead children, but given the careless treatment of the bodies, it was inconclusive. Finally, some neighbors claimed to have seen Belle and a male companion in the area weeks after the fire.

In the end, the jury reached an uncertain verdict, convicting Lamphere of arson but finding him not guilty of the murders. He was sentenced to two-to-20 in the penitentiary. He died of tuberculosis about a year later, still claiming Belle was alive.

Was she?

Prosecutors were able to find a dental bridge plate attached to a tooth. A dentist was able to identify it as Belle's, but it was hardly definitive proof of her death. If, indeed, Belle was a cold-blooded psychopath who had burned, poisoned, and hacked up so many victims, it would be nothing for her to rip out a tooth for false evidence to keep authorities off her trail.

In Los Angeles 1931, a woman named Esther Carlson was accused of murder. She died before she went to trial, but two people who were familiar with Belle claimed that a newspaper photograph of Esther matched Belle. Hardly definitive proof, again, and it certainly doesn't matter now. We'll never have a satisfactory conclusion to the story of Belle Gunness.

Belle remained a local celebrity, however, and a few books were written about her. Lillian de la Torre's 1955 Gold Medal paperback, *The Truth About Belle Gunness*, has a wonderfully evocative, sexy cover that presents Belle as an Anita Ekberg blonde temptress. She has not yet been the subject of a "based on a true story" movie, but she may well have been a partial inspiration for such thrillers as *Black Widow* (1987) starring Theresa Russell.

Hagan, Thomas

(Malcolm X)

Malcolm X was one of the most complicated and contradictory figures in the American civil rights movement.

Born Malcolm Little in 1925, he discovered Islam while in prison. When he got out in 1952, he called himself Malcolm X, rejecting his "slave name" and became a forceful proselytizer for his beliefs. He was so effective he was asked to join the Nation of Islam by its leader Elijah Muhammed.

During the years Dr. Martin Luther King, Jr. was advocating nonviolent protest and integration into mainstream society, Malcolm X called for justice "by any means necessary," armed self defense, and separation from the "white devils" who ran America. At the same time, political conflict within the Nation of Islam was intensifying. Malcolm's popularity but put him at odds with Elijah. Eventually there was a schism when Malcolm formed the Muslim Mosque Incorporated.

In 1964 Malcolm made his hajj or pilgrimage to Mecca where, like Paul on the road to Tarsus, he experienced a deep spiritual rebirth. This led him to a more conciliatory and inclusive stance. Not everyone accepted it.

Late on the night of February 14, 1965 Malcolm's house was firebombed and burned to the ground. He, his wife, and children escaped. No one was ever charged for the arson. A week later, on February 20th, he was to address a large crowd of his followers at the Audubon Ballroom in Harlem.

As he went on to the stage, two diversions occurred. A couple of men began a fight near the front of the hall, and a smoke or stink bomb went off at the back. Malcolm said "Cool it there, brothers," as a man emerged from the crowd and pulled a sawed-off shotgun from beneath his coat. He fired both barrels point blank into the podium and Malcolm's chest. The shooter ran and two men sprang up with pistols. They emptied them into the fallen Malcolm and ran.

In the confusion, two of the assassins escaped. Thomas Hagan, one of the pistoleers, was wounded and caught by the crowd out front. He was being beaten when police took him into custody. Later, Thomas 15X Johnson and Norman 3X Butler were arrested. Both worked for the Nation of Islam. Many said they never would have been allowed into the building by Malcolm's security people.

At trial, Hagan (aka Talmadge Hayer) confessed and said Butler and Johnson were not involved. Still, all three were found guilty. They served their sentences and have since been paroled.

Naturally, other conspiracies involving the FBI and federal forces have been suggested, but no proof has ever been found.

The Autobiography of Malcolm X, cowritten by his friend Alex Haley, was one of the seminal books of the 1960s. It served as a partial basis for Spike Lee's film *Malcolm X.* His carefully choreographed and detailed depiction of the assassination and Ossie Davis' stirring eulogy combine to create a brilliant conclusion.

Hanssen, Robert

Compared to Aldrich Ames he was a second rate spy, but Robert Hanssen was still responsible for the deaths of at least three people, and he may have had a peripheral role in 9/11. But what makes Hanssen so fascinating are the contradictory details. Though he sold secrets to the Soviets, politically, he was a rightwing ideologue. Though he belonged to the ultra-conservative Opus Dei movement within the Catholic church, he loved the company of strippers, wrote porn, and rigged up a hidden camera so his buddy could catch all the action when he and his wife were in bed.

Hanssen grew up the son of a Chicago cop who had worked in the city's "Red Unit," ferreting out local politicos who might have leftward leanings. Hanssen went to college and joined the Chicago Police Department's internal affairs division where he may have begun his career as a double agent, also working for the feds. Early in 1976, he joined the FBI.

He and his wife Bonnie moved to Gary, Indiana and then to New York where he first approached Russian agents and inquired about employment. He made $20,000. When Bonnie found out about it, she hit the ceiling and made him promise, cross your heart and hope to die, that he would never betray his country again. Seemingly contrite, he said he wouldn't and she believed him.

In 1981 Robert was transferred to headquarters in Washington. He didn't do too well within the organization, in part because he was a creep (nickname: "Dr. Death"). He disrespected the women who were then moving up the federal hierarchy, was known to cop a feel, and once even attacked a young woman who left a meeting early.

Hanssen became reacquainted with the Soviet KGB in 1985 when he ratted out three officers who were double agents. They were executed and Hanssen received $50,000. For the next five years, he passed along documents and computer discs to the Russkies, usually using parks in Northern Virginia as drop sites. He made more than $600,000.

The government finally stumbled on the traitorous activities when a Russian mole traded Hanssen's KGB file to the CIA. The feds then put him under heavy surveillance and arrested him as he dropped off a package of classified documents at a park on February 18, 2001.

A few months later, Hanssen, his lawyer, and the FBI made a deal. He'd spill his guts in exchange for a life sentence and the promise that Bonnie and the kids would get his $38,000 a year pension.

There has been some speculation that software he passed to the Russians may have found its way to Osama bin Laden and been used to help him avoid capture. It has not been proved. Hanssen is in the federal prison in Lewisburg, Pennsylvania.

Hanssen's crimes have been the subject of several books. David Vise's *The Bureau and the Mole* (2001) tells the story well. Hanssen was portrayed by William Hurt as a tightly wrapped, unstable figure in *Master Spy* (2002), the excellent miniseries written by Lawrence Schiller and Norman Mailer. It covers Hanssen's entire career. The 2007 theatrical release, *Breach*, focuses on the final months of Hanssen's operations and his relationship with a young FBI agent, Eric O'Neill, who was instrumental in his capture. Chris Cooper plays Hanssen with a quiet, absolutely believable intensity. Neither work attempts to explain why Hanssen did what he did; instead, they focus on the man's contradictions.

Hardin, John Wesley

Though he has never been as well known as some of his contemporaries, John Wesley Hardin was one of the most prolific killers in the Old West. He claimed to have gunned down 44 men. Given the lack of evidence and witnesses, the number is impossible to verify, but Hardin certainly had the mean disposition and the quick hands to give it some credence.

Named for the famous Methodist preacher by his father, who was also a man of the cloth, Hardin started killing at age 15. He was born in Bonham, Texas

in 1853 and his first victim was a black man. In that case, as in all others, Hardin claimed self-defense. He said the man attacked him with a club as he was peacefully riding home from his uncle's farm.

Knowing the Union forces who governed postwar Texas would never believe his story, young Hardin was forced to go on the run. Then he was forced to kill the soldiers who came after him.

For almost ten years, Hardin roamed Texas and the southwest, earning a reputation as a fast gun. He carried his pistols in an unusual but effective rig: he sewed holsters into a vest and positioned them so the gun butts were angled inward, across his chest. The setup afforded him a smoother and faster cross draw than the conventional holster-on-hip arrangement. Must have made it easier to go to the bathroom, too.

Most of his victims seem to have been people who made the mistake of arguing with him over card games. At one point, Hardin claimed to have gotten the drop on Wild Bill Hickok when he, Wild Bill, was Marshal of Abilene. Most historians and experts dismiss the claim as typical braggadocio from his autobiography.

In 1874 Hardin shot and killed deputy sheriff Charles Webb who was trying to arrest him. That got everyone's attention. The state slapped a $4,000 bounty on his head and sent the Pinkertons and Texas Rangers on his trail. Hardin ran and the Rangers caught up with him three years later in, of all places, Pensacola, Florida. Hardin was on board a train when Lt. John B. Armstrong and his men found the outlaw and four accomplices.

Unfortunately, for the desperado, he had overdressed that day and got his pistols hung up in his suspenders. Armstrong gave him a sharp rap on the head and shot one of his companions.

At trial back in Texas, Hardin acted as his own attorney. By all accounts, he was well-spoken and impressive, and so he was only convicted of second degree murder and sentenced to 25 years. In prison, he studied law and was pardoned in 1984. The glory days were long past by then but Hardin still boasted, blustered, and threatened. He spent his last months in El Paso, keeping company with a notorious floozy, Mrs. McRose, whose husband was a cattle rustler.

In the summer of 1895 Mrs. McRose was arrested on drunk and disorderly charges. When Hardin learned what had happened to his beloved, he got mad at John Selman, the cop who had rousted her. Not surprisingly, Hardin and Selman had a long history of bad blood, and so when the gunman said he was going to kill him, the lawman took it as truth. And instead of waiting, he stalked Hardin.

Selman found him in the Acme Saloon and shot him in the back of the head before he had a chance to clear his vest. Though it was certainly a case of murder, the jury bought Selman's claim of self-defense.

Hardin probably reached the height of his limited fame with the release of Bob Dylan's 1967 album *John Wesley Harding* (sic). The title cut is a typically woozy paean to the killer. It begins "John Wesley Harding/ Was a friend to the poor./ He trav'led with a gun in ev'ry hand."

Hardin was a popular guest character on many TV westerns in the 1950s. He was at least a partial inspiration for the character of John Bernard Books in Glendon Swarthout's novel *The Shootist* (1975), though he is less recognizable in the 1976 John Wayne film of the same title.

On film, Hardin was portrayed by Rock Hudson in *The Lawless Breed* (1953), based on his autobiography, and in Larry McMurtry's miniseries *Streets of Laredo* (1995) by Randy Quaid.

Harris, Clara

When a wronged wife catches her no-good two-timing hubby with his floozie at the No Tell Motel and, overcome with anger, runs him down in her Honda Civic, it's not really news. But when the wife and hubby are wealthy respected dentists, the place is a swanky waterfront resort hotel, the car is a shiny new $70,000 S-Class Mercedes Benz and she runs

over him not once but three times—and it's all caught on videotape—well, people are going to take notice.

Clara and David Harris were married in 1992 at the Nassau Bay Hilton in Houston. She was a beautiful Colombian immigrant. They met where they worked as orthodontists at the Castle Dental Center. She later opened her own practice and David founded Space Center Orthodontics. In 1998, twin boys were born (David also already had a teenaged daughter, Lindsey, from his first marriage.) They lived in a small mansion in the trendy suburb of Friendswood. Life was good.

Life was not so good for Steve Bridges and Chuck Knight. In January 1999 they suspected their wives Gail and Julie were having an affair with each other. Yes, they thought these suburban housewives were lesbians. They engaged Bobbi Bacha's Blue Moon Investigations to tail the two soccer moms and find evidence of their secret lives. Ms. Bacha took the case and learned the women were good friends and nothing more. She thought that was the end of it.

Seven months later, Gail Bridges and Julie Knight showed up in her waiting room. They had filed for divorce from their respective husbands and were being threatened with allegations of lesbianism. Julie hired Bobbi to follow her soon-to-be-ex to find out what he was up to. Turned out Chuck was carrying on with Laurie Wells, another friend of theirs who had actually gone to Lamaze class with Gail. The double divorce soon became a triple divorce. (A couple of years later Bobbi would arrange for Gail and Julie to appear in disguise on the *Sally Jessy Raphael Show* to tell their story for the "My Husband Spies on Me" episode.)

Meanwhile, back with the orthodontists, business was booming. David Harris had acquired several other practices and was preparing to construct a huge new office to have room for Clara's practice. In August 2001 he hired Gail Bridges as a receptionist. By then, her divorce had gone through, and she and her three kids lived nearby.

The relationship between David and Gail began as simple and obvious office flirtation. By May 2002 they were sneaking off for afternoon delight at the Nassau Bay Hilton and other places. Everyone who knew them agreed this was not normal behavior for David. Until then, both he and Clara had been driven by work, too driven, perhaps, since it had broken up his first marriage. He and Clara seemed to have things in the right balance. She had a particularly strong relationship with David's parents and his daughter Lindsey. So, at 44, successful in every way, he had a midlife crisis.

On July 17th he confessed all to Clara. She took it bad, not as bad as she eventually would, but bad enough. When she pressed him for the reasons behind the affair, he said Gail was younger, shapelier, and less domineering. Clara then experienced her own midlife crisis. She swore she would change, engaged a personal trainer, and scheduled liposuction and breast enhancement. She also fired Gail.

David swore everything was over, but he needed to meet Gail one more time—just for dinner at Perry's restaurant, to end things on the right note. Clara agreed but was suspicious, so suspicious she paid a visit to Bobbi Bacha at Blue Moon Investigations. Describing the situation, she said she wanted someone to be close enough to the couple during their meal to eavesdrop. After all, Gail Bridges was rumored to be a lesbian—who knew what she might be cooking up.

Bacha later said she didn't realize Clara was talking about the same Gail who had already been involved in two other cases and who had gone with her to New York for the Sally Jessy Raphael show business. So she assigned the stakeout to a relatively inexperienced part-timer, Lindsey Dubec.

Dubec followed David from work. He didn't go to Perry's, instead he met Gail back at their favorite rendezvous, the Nassau Bay Hilton. They chatted in the bar for a time, then went upstairs to a room David had reserved. Dubec retreated to her car and positioned it where she could watch David's car. She got out her video camera and waited.

Smiling Clara Harris, who killed her cheating husband David by mowing him down with a Mercedes, awaits her verdict Friday, January 19, 2007 in Houston, Texas. (AP Photo/Houston Chronicle, Carlos Antonio Rios)

Clara, meanwhile, sensing something was amiss, decided to act. She enlisted David's daughter Lindsey (not to be confused with the Blue Moon Lindsey) and they set out in search of the wayward orthodontist. They didn't find him at Perry's or any of his other usual haunts. A call to Blue Moon told them he was reportedly at a hotel. Clara zipped over to the Hilton with Lindsey in her Benz.

Right off the bat, she spotted Gail's massive Lincoln Navigator and launched into her retaliation: bent the wipers, smashed the lights, gave the paint job some good deep scratches with her keys. At the front desk, she and Lindsey were told a David Harris was not registered. He had used a false name and paid cash. What to do? His cell phone! They called and told David one of his sons was sick; he needed to come home immediately. Then they waited for him in the lobby.

When he and Gail came out of the elevator, Clara lost it big time. The fur began to fly in a classic hair-pulling, name-calling, leg-biting, blouse-ripping catfight. All the while, Lindsey pummeled her father with her purse and screamed that she hated him. Eventually, hotel employees broke it up. A desk clerk escorted David and Gail across the parking lot. A manager forced Clara and Lindsey out of the building and into the Benz.

Instead of leaving, though, Clara fired up the Benz and burned rubber as she roared across the blacktop in search of Gail's Navigator. She found it just as Gail was getting inside. David was beside the SUV. At the last moment, she cut the wheel and slammed directly into her husband, throwing him 25 feet across the pavement. He was still alive when Clara bounced over two medians and roared across the lot to run over him. Before she was through, she nailed him two more times while Lindsey screamed for her to stop. The other Lindsey got it all on tape.

In terms of media circuses, the trial was a two-ring show. Before it started, Clara went to New York to be interviewed on the three major networks. She cried at each appearance. She cried a lot in court, too, and claimed that even though she really couldn't remember exactly what had happened, it was all an accident. Really. Not that it did any good; the jury found her guilty and sentenced her to 20 years, to be served at the Mountain View Unit.

Normally, that might be the end of the story, but Clara continues to cast herself as the victim. In 2005 she did a jailhouse interview with Oprah Winfrey, and the Clara Harris Defense Fund continues to lobby for her release.

The best book about the Byzantine tangle of sexual dalliances and accusations in Houston, the murder, and the trial is Steven Long's *Out of Control* (2004). Before the trial in November 2002, Skip

Hollandsworth wrote a long piece for *Texas Monthly* magazine. It became the basis for the made-for-TV film, *Suburban Madness* (2004). The film treats the material as bleak black comedy and sticks fairly close to the facts. It does glamorize Bobbi Bacha (who receives "consultant" credit along with Skip Hollandsworth) and inflates her importance, but it does a better job of telling an accurate story than most Hollywood "based on a true story" films.

Harris, David Ray

On the night of November 21, 1976, Dallas police officer Robert Woods pulled over a stolen car, a Dodge Cornet, driven by David Harris. Harris pulled out a pistol and killed him. Later, when he was picked up by police, Harris claimed the murder had been committed by Randall Dale Adams, a man he had met earlier in the day when Adams' car had run out of gas. That evening, the two men had gone to the 180 Drive-In where they'd smoked some weed, drank a little beer, and watched *The Swinging Cheerleaders*. Adams, Harris said, had driven back and killed patrolman Woods.

When Adams was picked up, he told a different story. Yes, Harris had given him a ride and, yes, they'd gone to the drive-in, but he didn't like the movie. They had left early, and Harris had driven him back to the motel where he was staying.

Even though Adams, 28, had no record, the cops and the prosecutors decided to pin the killing on him. Why? Because Harris was a local boy? Or because Harris was a juvenile and couldn't be given the death penalty if convicted? Whatever the reasons, they accepted Harris' story despite his rap sheet and how he had bragged to friends about killing a cop, and the dubious reliability of several witnesses.

Adams was tried, found guilty, and sentenced to death—never wavering in his claim of complete innocence.

Eleven years later, filmmaker Errol Morris became intrigued by the case and made it the subject of his groundbreaking "nonfiction" crime film, *The Thin Blue Line* (1988).

Using new interviews with witnesses and key participants, and recreations of important moments, he examined the murder. Piece by unemotional piece, he demolished the state's case. All of the evidence is found to be lacking and the film ends with a genuine surprise.

In no small part because of the film, Adams' conviction was overturned and the state declined to try him again. Harris was found guilty of another murder and was put to death in 2004. On its own merits, the story of Adams and Harris may not seem particularly important, but it was important to Errol Morris and his careful dissection of the Texas justice system remains a remarkable piece of filmmaking.

In 2001 the Library of Congress placed *The Thin Blue Line* on the National Film Registry, a list of culturally significant works.

In a quirky postscript to the story, after he was freed, Adams sued Morris over the film. It had to do with the film's classification—was it a documentary or a commercial release—if the latter, was Adams entitled to money if the film was wildly successful. It wasn't and the matter was settled out of court. Adams told his version of the story in his book *Adams v. Texas* (1991).

Harris, Eric, and Dylan Klebold

Columbine Shooting

It took the two of them 16 minutes to kill 12 students, one teacher, and themselves. They had four weapons—two sawed-offs, a TEC-DC9 semi-automatic pistol, and a 9mm carbine—more than 90 bombs, and a lot of ammunition. They'd been planning the attack for more than a year. Or perhaps they had merely been talking about it and fantasizing until the fantasies became a plan. That's the part no one will ever know.

For Eric Harris and Dylan Klebold, a couple of middle class white kids from stable homes, the signs

of trouble had been there. In 1996 Harris was writing about explosives and violence on his website. A year later, he was using the site to threaten the life of Brooks Brown, a former friend, and others. Cops took it seriously enough to consider asking for a search warrant, but nothing was done. Then in early 1998 Harris and Klebold were caught stealing computer equipment; their sentence was counseling and community service.

On April 20, 1999 the two boys loaded their ordnance into their cars, a BMW and a Honda Civic, and drove to Columbine High School near Littleton, Colorado. On the way in, they saw Brooks Brown and told him to leave the school.

They took a couple of bombs made from propane tanks in duffle bags, left them in the cafeteria, and waited in the parking lot. The bombs were timed to detonate at 11:17 a.m., but they didn't. Harris, 18, and Klebold, 17, then took their guns into the school and opened fire. Many of their victims were in the cafeteria and the library. The two boys walked through the hallways, and fired at anyone they saw and others trying to hide. They also attempted to set off several more improvised explosive devices, but only a few of them worked.

Despite the limited duration of the killings, a rich mythology has been constructed around them. Some claim Christians were targeted and a few of the victims have been transformed into martyrs. Others say the primary targets were the jocks who had bullied the boys. Eyewitness testimony is understandably contradictory but it does seem likely Harris and Klebold were quickly sickened by what they were doing—reportedly saying to each other that shooting people was no longer "fun." Right afterwards, they shot themselves.

It took the SWAT team several hours to clear the buildings. The finger-pointing began soon thereafter.

Heavy metal music, video games, prescription drugs, inattentive parents, ineffective police, negligent school officials, rampant bullying, easy availability of guns and ammunition, "goth" subculture, movies, a national climate of violence. All of them were blamed as the killings themselves became a focal point of the late 1990s culture wars.

Filmmaker Michael Moore added fuel to the fire with his 2002 agitprop documentary *Bowling for Columbine*. He used the massacre as an entry point for a frantic attack on the firearms industry and its apologists in particular, and American capitalism in general.

A year later, director Gus Van Sant took a more thoughtful approach in *Elephant,* a fictionalized version of the events filmed at a Portland, Oregon school. The film is a curiously paced meditation on what it must have been like inside the school that day. Using mostly young nonprofessional actors, Van Sant scrupulously avoids any explanation or political statement. There is a homosexual element to the relationship between his two killers, and some mild harassment is shown, but neither is put forward as a reason for what the boys did.

Van Sant's larger point is that we live in a world of random events. He's right and that's why the word "Columbine" has come to be synonymous with sudden, inexplicable, devastating violence.

Harris, Jean

Jean Harris gunned down Dr. Herman Tarnower at a pivotal moment in American cultural history. In 1980 feminism was in full flower and, as Diana Trilling put it in her book, *Mrs. Harris: The Death of the Scarsdale Diet Doctor* (1981), there was "a great upswelling of feeling" for the woman who was the headmistress of the prestigious Madeira School for girls in Virginia, near Washington, D.C. But once the facts came out and people heard Harris' transparent and all-too-familiar rationalization for murder, things changed.

Tarnower was a successful doctor who'd founded the Scarsdale Medical Center and counted major corporations and the bluest of New York bluebloods among his clients. He lived large on a lavish Westchester estate and became a household name when

his book *The Complete Scarsdale Medical Diet* (1978) surprised everyone by hitting the bestseller lists.

Jean Harris was the divorced mother of two sons. She'd begun her professional career by establishing a kindergarten in her home when the boys were little. She took over the Thomas School in Connecticut in the early 1970s and then moved on to the Madeira School. She and Tarnower became a couple in 1967. Though he had a well-earned reputation as a philanderer, he proposed to Jean. She turned him down, saying she didn't want to move her sons out of their school. Sometime later, when she changed her mind about making their relationship permanent, he was no longer in the mood. Much has been made of Tarnower's freewheeling sexual adventures, and others have labeled him a social climber and professionally ambitious. It may be true, but they're not crimes and the doctor didn't try to hide them. He was unapologetically what he was.

For a time, Harris accepted it. It was when she came to feel threatened by a younger woman who worked with Tarnower that she changed. At around the same time, she was having problems with her charges at Madeira. Four seniors had been given the boot for drug paraphernalia possession: parents were complaining vociferously, fellow students were protesting. And the headmistress was running short on her own drug of choice, Desoxyn, prescription speed, provided by the good Dr. T.

It all came to a head in March 1980. Harris wrote Tarnower a long, bitter rambling letter in which she accused him of a host of sins, including a series of harassing phone calls. She also admitted making the same kind of calls herself. After mailing the intemperate missive, she had second thoughts and, on March 10th, called Tarnower asking him not to open it. She called him again later that day and said she wanted to talk. He was against the idea. She persisted and finally he relented, reportedly saying, "Suit yourself." He should have changed the locks.

Jean packed up a .32 revolver and set off around 5:30 p.m. She got to Tarnower's house after 10:00 p.m. She later said her intention was to kill herself.

Jean Harris, during an interview with Barbara Walters for *20/20*, 1984. (AP Photo)

(Why though, would she drive for five hours on one of the most congested highways in America when she could have done it at home?)

She let herself into the house and found Tarnower, already in bed, asleep, alone. Her version of what happened next is neither original nor persuasive.

She claimed after a brief conversation, she put the pistol to her temple and was about to pull the trigger, to end it all, when Tarnower grabbed her arm and twisted it. The gun went off, thereby explaining the wound in his hand. Then they dropped the gun and wrestled for it, and… and… she blacked out. She couldn't really remember any of what happened next but they both must have

reached for the gun, and somehow, God knows how, it went off. It went off three times, striking Tarnower in the chest, arm, and back. He died of massive internal bleeding.

Harris was charged with second degree murder. (In New York at the time, the charge of first degree murder was reserved for the killing of police or on-duty corrections officers.) She was found guilty by an eight-woman, four-man jury and given a 15-year-to-life sentence. Governor Mario Cuomo commuted that sentence after 12 years and she was freed. During the time she was behind bars, she wrote three books and became pals with journalist Shana Alexander who wrote a sympathetic defense of her own, *Very Much a Lady* (1983).

The Tarnower killing has been dramatized twice, first in the 1981 television movie, *The People Vs. Jean Harris* with Ellen Burstyn and again in 2005 in the HBO film, *Mrs. Harris*, with Annette Bening and Ben Kingsley, based on the Alexander book.

Harvey, Julian

By 1961 Julian Harvey almost certainly had some experience at insurance fraud and murder. Back in 1949 he had managed to survive an accident when his car crashed through a bridge railing near Ft. Walton Beach into a Florida swamp, killing his wife and mother-in-law. At the time, no one suspected anything.

Harvey was an Air Force pilot who'd flown bombers in World War II and would go on to fly jets in Korea. After leaving the service, he became a charter boat captain.

On November 8, 1961 Harvey set sail from Ft. Lauderdale in the 60 foot ketch *Bluebelle*. Aboard were his new bride, Mary Dene, and Green Bay, Wisconsin optometrist Arthur Duperrault with his wife Jean and their children Brian, Terry Jo, and Renee.

As Harvey would later tell the Coast Guard, on Sunday, November 12th, they were off Stirrup Key in the Bahamas when a sudden squall snapped the mainmast. It pierced the hull and collapsed onto the passengers. As the boat sank, it burst into flames. The captain managed to escape in a dinghy and retrieve the body of little Renee. Everyone else was lost. He was picked up several hours later by a tanker, the *Gulf Lyon*.

Later that week after Harvey had made his formal statement, word arrived in Miami there was another survivor. A Liberian freighter, the *Captain Theo*, had found Terry Jo Duperrault floating on a cork raft. She'd been adrift for three days and was suffering from shock, dehydration, and exposure, but her chances of recovery were good. Upon hearing the news, Harvey quickly left the hearing.

Terry Jo's story, when she recovered, was different than Harvey's version. She said she'd been awakened

in the middle of the night by screams. She found her mother and brother dead, in pools of blood, in the central cabin. She climbed the stairs to the main deck where she met the captain. He angrily ordered her back to her bunk. She was trapped there as the boat began to sink. Finally, with oily water rising around her, she made her way out. In the darkness, she could see Harvey. He might have had a rifle or a pistol. A dinghy tied to the ketch came loose and he swam for it. She managed to untie a cork lifefloat just as the *Bluebelle* went down.

On Thursday morning, the second mate of the *Captain Theo* spotted her in a shark-infested sea and was able to bring her aboard. A Coast Guard chopper brought her back to Miami.

By then Harvey had checked in to the Sandman Motel and finished things. He slashed veins in his wrists, legs, and throat. Police called it one of the bloodiest suicides they had ever seen. After his death, authorities learned two other well-insured boats had met with "accidents" under Harvey's command. He had been in financial trouble and had recently taken out a $20,000 double indemnity life insurance policy on his new wife.

Novelist John D. MacDonald became fascinated by the story and used it as the basis for one of his longest and most complex novels, *The Last One Left*, in 1967. The killings provide an entry point examining family, greed, and business in Florida and America in the mid-1960s.

No one has adapted Harvey's story for film or television.

Hearst, Patricia

Seen today by people who don't remember 1974, the Patricia Hearst kidnapping must seem like a bizarre farce—the ridiculously pompous pronouncements, the absurd demands, the results when the demands were met, and finally, the resolution. At the time, though, it was a defining moment in the larger generational and political conflicts that threatened to split the country.

Patty Hearst, aka "Tania," in front of the SLA flag, 1974. (AP Photo)

The story really begins on March 5, 1973 when smalltime crook Donald DeFreeze escaped from jail. He hooked up with a loopy little group of political activists led by Mizmoon Soltysik in Berkeley, California. This bunch decided to call themselves the Symbionese Liberation Army, or, to use the official title the "United Federated Forces of the Symbionese Liberation Army." (Symbionese, by the way, is an invented word meant to imply symbiosis and harmony. Go figure.)

In November 1973 they murdered their first target, Oakland school superintendent Marcus Foster. Like DeFreeze, Foster was a black man, but he advocated school ID cards which made him part of the fascist pig ruling class, or something to that

effect. He was a convenient target who was shot down with cyanide-coated bullets.

SLA member Emily Harris worked in the registrar's office of U.C. Berkeley. She had access to the personal information of one of the school's most prominent students, Patricia Hearst, granddaughter of newspaper magnate William Randolph Hearst.

The nutcases kidnapped Patty on February 4, 1974 from the apartment she shared with her fiancé Steven Weed. Over the following weeks and months, they made a series of demands, including the release of two of their comrades in the slammer and the distribution of millions of dollars in free food to the poor. The Hearst family attempted to meet the second demand. Virtual rioting erupted in

Patty Hearst on trial. (AP Photo)

a few distribution locations. By then, DeFreeze was calling himself Field Marshall Cinque Mtume and had become the group's mouthpiece. Some have theorized Soltysik was the real brains behind the outfit, though the word "brains" has no real meaning in this context.

On April 14th came the first shocker. The SLA knocked over a branch of the Hibernia Bank and there, caught by the security cameras, was Patricia Hearst, now calling herself "Tania" in honor of Che Guevara's squeeze, brandishing a rifle at bank patrons.

How was her transformation from heiress to terrorist accomplished? Some have suggested she was in on everything, including her kidnapping. Others argue her situation was a classic example of the Stockholm Syndrome where hostages take on the views of their captors. She claimed she was locked in a closet for weeks and raped by male members of the

gang. At some time during her captivity, she formed a romantic relationship with one of the guys. Whatever the truth, the image of her in a black beret, holding a rifle in front of the SLA symbol of a seven-headed cobra became an icon of the era.

When things got too hot in San Francisco, the SLA headed for Los Angeles. Bad move. DeFreeze, Soltysik, and several others were trapped in a small house there. Hundreds of cops surrounded the place and on May 17th they were killed in a massive firefight.

Patty and Bill and Emily Harris were not in the house and escaped. They were captured back in San Francisco in September 1975. By then, in the public mind, the kidnap victim had been replaced by the revolutionary and she was charged with bank robbery. F. Lee Bailey led a shaky defense. The prosecutor countered with an expert who focused on her teenaged sexual experience and called her a rebel looking for a cause.

It worked. Patty was convicted and sentenced to 35 years for robbery and firearms charges. She served less than two years before President Jimmy Carter commuted her sentence in 1979. In 2001 Bill Clinton gave her a full pardon.

After her release Patty married Bernard Shaw, her former bodyguard, wrote a book about her experiences, *Every Secret Thing* (1982), and did the talk show circuit. She also used her celebrity to create a niche acting career, primarily in John Waters' outrageous comedies.

Her kidnapping was the subject of Paul Schrader's 1988 film, *Patty Hearst* and the fairly obscure Spanish picture *Secuestro*. It was parodied in Paddy Chayefsky's *Network* (1976). Stephen King has said Donald DeFreeze was a partial inspiration for Randall Flagg, the villain in his epic *The Stand* (1978).

Robert Stone's 2004 documentary, *Guerrilla: The Taking of Patty Hearst*, tells the story through archival TV footage and interviews with the few SLA survivors, but not Ms. Hearst herself. Younger

150

viewers may not fully believe everything they see in it; they should.

Heirens, William

It is possible, even likely, William Heirens never killed anybody, that he was simply a troubled, unlucky teenager. One thing is for sure—if the Chicago cops acted today with an 18-year-old as they did in 1946, he would never even have gone to trial, much less been convicted.

This much we know: Heirens came from a tumultuous home. To escape his parents' arguments, he took long walks, and on those walks, he indulged in breaking and entering—going into other people's houses and apartments for the thrill of it. Sometimes he stole things—books, guns, money, stuff. On June 5, 1945 divorcée Josephine Ross, mother of two, was murdered in her North Side apartment. She had been stabbed several times and the place was ransacked. No sexual assault, no fingerprints, only a small amount of money missing.

Six months later, Navy WAV veteran Frances Brown was killed in the same neighborhood. Both women lived in apartments. Like Ross, Frances had been stabbed, but she'd also been shot. The body had been left in a bathtub. The police found one bloody smudged fingerprint on a doorjamb, and scrawled on a wall in lipstick, the words "For heavens sake catch me before I kill more. I cannot control myself."

One month later, in January 1946, six-year-old Suzanne Degnan was kidnapped from her bedroom on the first floor of her family's house. A ransom note read "Get $20,000 ready and wait for word. Do not notify FBI or police. Bills in $5's and $10's." On the other side, "Burn this for safety."

A ladder that reached the little girl's window was found outside. The police received an anonymous call to check the sewers. They did and found the dismembered pieces of Suzanne's body. With the horrific crime wave spurring them on, the police worked 24/7 on the killings and the politically ambitious State's Attorney William J. Tuohy stayed in the forefront. They got nowhere for another six months, well almost

nowhere. Then they caught William Heirens in an apartment building. He ran, they chased. He pulled a pistol but did not fire it and was quickly incapacitated by three cops, two on-duty, one off-duty.

They took him to the Cook County Jail hospital where they worked him over mercilessly. The beating didn't work. Heirens maintained his innocence. Two psychiatrists, Drs. Grinken and Haines, were brought in. If the cops couldn't beat a confession out of the kid, maybe the shrinks could get it with drugs. They doped Heirens up with sodium pentothal, the "truth serum" of the movies.

According to the prosecutors, Heirens then claimed to have a split personality and his "other" half, George, committed the crimes. We'll never know exactly what was asked or what was answered because no transcript was made of the interrogation—not that any statement made under duress, under the influence of drugs, and without the benefit of counsel (Heirens had not yet been allowed to speak to a lawyer) has any validity in the first place.

The physical evidence was little help. The police claimed one print on the ransom note matched Heirens' on nine points, but the FBI standards called for 12 matches for identification. (Another fingerprint expert said there was no match.) And Heirens' prints did not match the doorjamb print in the Frances Brown murder.

Eyewitnesses at or near the three murders had described suspects who did not resemble Heirens. Handwriting experts said the writing on the wall and the ransom note did not come from the same hand. The one expert who did claim Heirens had written both later changed his opinion. Finally, Heirens passed a police-administered lie detector test (the state's attorney claimed it was inconclusive.)

Despite the flimsy evidence, Heirens was essentially lynched in the press. A false confession was published in a newspaper. If that weren't enough, his three lawyers urged him to accept a plea deal and to confess. Eventually, after even more denials and changes of mind, Heirens did confess before a judge and was sentenced to three life sentences.

Immediately, he retracted his plea and has continued to deny the killings.

Casting even more doubt on Heirens' involvement, another man, Richard Russell Thomas, confessed to the murder of Suzanne Degnan. He was a known child molester who had also been convicted of kidnapping and extortion. But he had moved to Phoenix, Arizona and when Heirens emerged as the main suspect, Chicago lost interest in him.

Heirens was sent up the river and has been the proverbial "model prisoner," earning a college degree. He is now in a minimum security facility.

In 1996 the ABC news show *Prime Time Live* broadcast a reexamination of Heirens' case and focused on the doubts concerning his guilt. Of the books written, Lucy Freeman's *Before I Kill More* (1955) argues that justice was served, while Dolores Kennedy's *Bill Heirens: His Day In Court* (1991) finds the evidence lacking. As of this writing, efforts to exonerate and free Heirens continue.

Hennard, George

But for his depressingly high body count, George Hennard was just another jerkoff loser with a gun. At 35, he had no real friends, and, more significantly, no girlfriend. No surprise there. He was an unashamed racist and misogynist who blamed the world for his many shortcomings.

George had been busted for marijuana in Texas in 1981. When he was caught with more dope in 1989, they kicked him out of the Merchant Marines. (Previously, he had been suspended for racial remarks.) After getting the boot, he sometimes worked in construction, and his countless hatreds festered until they became uncontrollable. He bought a couple of semiautomatics, a Ruger and a Glock.

In June 1991 he wrote a long bitter letter to two young women who lived near him in Belton, Texas. Though he had never spoken to them, he was moved to state, in part, "I found the best and worst in women [here]. You and your sister are on one side. Then the abundance of evil women that make up the

worst on the other side... I will no matter what prevail over the female vipers in these two rinky-dink towns in Texas. I will prevail at the bitter end."

The women were frightened enough to show the letter to the police who could do nothing.

Four months later on October 16th, one day after his 35th birthday, Hennard took his pistols and drove his Ford Ranger pickup to nearby Killeen, the other rinky-dink town he'd discussed in the letter.

At 12:45 p.m., the height of the lunch hour, he crashed the truck through a window in Luby's cafeteria. As patrons rushed to help him and the old man he'd hit, Hennard opened fire. For the next 15 minutes, he carefully and slowly made his way through the cafeteria. With a strange smirky smile, he shot everyone he saw. Almost everyone. He killed Anica McNeil's mother, who was right beside her, and then told Ms. McNeil to take her daughter, four-year-old Lakeichha and leave. They did.

While the killing was going on, auto technician Tommy Vaughn leapt through a large plate glass window. He was severely injured but cleared the way for several other people to follow him to safety. More managed to get through a kitchen door.

Hennard continued to kill, searching out victims who attempted to hide under tables and firing at point blank range. He killed 22 people that afternoon; two more died later and 20 were injured.

Wounded by police when they made their way into the building, Hennard ran back to the men's room where he shot himself in the head.

The pathetic Texan's massacre may have had something to do with the restaurant scene in *Natural Born Killers* (1994), but in terms of popular culture, he is little more than a footnote. Some sources claim a ticket stub for the movie *The Fisher King* (1991) was found in Hennard's pocket. In that film, an offscreen character attacks a nightclub with a shotgun. The story is false, but it remains a favorite among the movies/comic books/rap music/video games-cause-violence crowd.

Warren Beatty & Annette Bening at the *Bugsy* premiere, 1992. (AP Photo)

Hill, Virginia

Virginia Hill probably rose as far through the ranks of organized crime as any woman in America ever has, though it doesn't mean much. She never had any real power, but she was important for two reasons.

First, she was the queen of the celestial gamahuche. In other words, the woman could suck a golf ball through a garden hose. **Joe Adonis**, **Frank Costello**, **Frank Nitti** and, most famously, **Ben "Bugsy" Siegel** could attest to her abilities.

Second, she was smart enough not to steal from those same men and became a trusted bag woman who could move cash from—point A to point B without dipping into the till. She could also be trusted to launder money and transport stolen jewelry.

Virginia got her start when she moved from Alabama to Chicago for the 1933 World's Fair, where she worked as a hooker and accountant for the Capone mob. Later, possibly on Capone's orders, she moved to New York and began an affair with Joe Adonis. In his book, *Bugsy's Baby*, author Andy Edmonds claims while Virginia was with Adonis, Bugsy met her and was smitten. He snuck her away from Adonis and they moved out to California together. Other sources say Virginia and Bugsy met in Hollywood where she was trying to break into the movie business. In either case, she set herself up in a swanky place in Beverly Hills, and she and Bugsy entered into a gloriously tempestuous relationship.

Their fights and infidelities were the stuff of legend. After Siegel had straightened things out in Los

Angeles for his East Coast cronies, he had a vision of a new Xanadu in Las Vegas and started work on his final dream. Rumor has it he named his Flamingo Hotel and Casino after his nickname for Virginia, a tribute to her particular prowess.

Bugsy ran into significant delays in construction. At the same time, Virginia was making a series of transatlantic flights. Bugsy's mob pals, also his investors, came to suspect he was siphoning off funds and she was depositing them in Swiss banks. True or not, she was in Paris on the night of June 10, 1947 when Bugsy was shot and killed in her house.

Three years later, she was called to testify before the Kefauver Committee on organized crime. She played it cool during the televised portions, but in the closed hearings, she told the senators exactly how she had made her mark.

They nailed her on an IRS rap, then she married a ski instructor and decamped to Europe. That was the end for her.

Edmonds says Virginia had kept a diary, noting down the amounts of money she had transported over the years and the people she had worked with. Faced with destitution, she tried to use it to blackmail Adonis, who had been deported by then and was living in Italy. She got greedy and he had her bumped off. The official version of her death is suicide by overdose of sleeping pills.

Had her career followed the same trajectory today, doubtless Virginia would have been offered a TV reality series or a talk show. The über-moll has been portrayed twice on film, first in the 1974 made-for-television *Virginia Hill Story* with Dyan Cannon, and most memorably in *Bugsy* (1991) by Annette Bening.

Hillside Stranglers

They were not the most prolific serial killers, but they were probably the most sadistic. In 1977 and '78, Kenneth Bianchi and Angelo Buono reveled in the most brutal torture imaginable.

Bianchi grew up as the troubled son of adoptive parents in Rochester, New York. He may have been involved with some murders there before he moved to Los Angeles in early 1976 and fell in with his cousin Angelo Buono. Buono, a pimp, had a history of sexual violence. Together, they decided to recreate **Caryl Chessman**'s "red light rapist" MO. Impersonating cops—Bianchi worked as a security guard—they would stop young women on the street or in their cars, and show them fake badges. If they could get the woman into their car, they'd take her to Buono's suburban house where they would rape, torture, and garrote her. The tortures involved electrical shocks and injections with caustic liquids. They dumped the bodies in various places, earning the tabloid nickname "Hillside Strangler."

Their victims were hookers, waitresses, school girls. Once they stopped Catherine Lorre on the street. When they realized she was the daughter of actor Peter Lorre, they let her go, knowing it was too risky to harm a celebrity.

Between October 1977 and February 1978, they killed 10 women. By then, the heat was on and Bianchi left town. He went to Bellingham, Washington. A year later, he was arrested there for the murder of two women he lured with the offer of a house-sitting job.

When authorities linked Bianchi to the LA murders, he denied everything. Then he tried to claim he had multiple personalities and the evil "Steve" had committed the murders. Nobody bought that nonsense, so he finally ratted out his cousin and pleaded guilty.

That wasn't the end of the story. In jail, Bianchi was contacted by young Veronica Lynn Compton, a fellow necrophile. The two sub-geniuses hatched a scheme for her to meet him in prison and smuggle out some of his sperm hidden in a rubber glove. She'd take it back to Bellingham where she would kill a woman and plant Bianchi's seed, as it were, thereby creating the impression the "real killer" was still at large.

The first part of their crackpot plan worked. Compton spirited her precious cargo out of the joint, but she botched a poorly planned attack, was nailed for it, and served time.

Bianchi and Buono's trials were extended exercises in judicial complication filled with more confessions and retractions. In the end, both were found guilty and sentenced to life.

Buono died in prison of natural causes in 2002. Bianchi is locked up in Washington.

Two serious books have been written about the killings, *Two of a Kind: The Hillside Stranglers* by Darcy O'Brien, and *Hillside Stranglers* by Ted Schwartz. The sick cousins have also been the subject of an unusually large number of movies, perhaps more than any other serial killers. No less than five of them have been made, all for television or home video.

Hinckley, John Jr.

Arthur Bremer's memoir *An Assassin's Diary* (1973) begat *Taxi Driver*'s Travis Bickle. Bickle, with an assist from John Lennon's killer **Mark David Chapman**, begat John Hinckley. Though his target was the President of the United States, and though he'd tried to found a white supremacist organization, Hinckley's motivation was really not political.

Hinckley was the troubled son of a prosperous Texas oil family. After graduating from high school, he knocked around, trying college for a time, drifting, and living with other family members sporadically, but always returning to his parents' home, who had moved to Colorado by then. In 1976 Hinckley discovered the movie *Taxi Driver*. After repeated viewings, he became obsessed with the character of Iris, the young prostitute, and with Jodie Foster, the actress who played her. (It is probably not a coincidence Hinckley's blonde mother Jo was sometimes called "Jodie.") In the film, an insane Bickle attempts to "save" Iris from the life after he has failed in an assassination attempt on a politician.

Conflating the film with reality, Hinckley decided to "save" Jodie Foster from the Yale Drama School. He moved briefly to New Haven, Connecticut where he phoned her twice and sent her a series of increasingly deranged and threatening letters. He also wrote to the FBI about a plot to kill the actress.

On December 8, 1980 Hinckley's already fragile mental state took a big hit when his musical idol John Lennon was killed. He wrote to Jodie Foster, "after tonight, John Lennon and I will have a lot in common. It's all for you."

At the same time, Hinckley's emotional instability was further manifested with bouts of hypochondria. He was also seeing a psychiatrist who recommended his parents take a "tough love" approach and kick the kid out. They did.

Hinckley was on a bus back to New Haven when he stopped in Washington, D.C. There he saw that President Ronald Reagan was scheduled to give a speech the next day at the Hilton Hotel. He loaded up his revolver and waited in the area where the president would leave the hotel. When Mr. Reagan waved at the crowd, Hinckley dropped to a shooter's crouch and squeezed off six shots in three seconds.

Police officer Thomas Delahanty and Secret Service agent Timothy McCarthy were wounded. Press Secretary James Brady was hit in the head. As Secret Service agent Jerry Parr tried to shove the president to safety, Hinckley's final shot ricocheted off the waiting limousine's bulletproof glass and hit Mr. Reagan in the left side. His wound was more serious than anyone knew at the time.

At the trial, Jodie Foster's subdued testimony about Hinckley's behavior was part of the reason the jury found him not guilty by reason of insanity. The verdict really frosted Republican pumpkins, though Hinckley's attack actually generated a strong sympathetic reaction with the American public and boosted Mr. Reagan's image.

The attack also led James Brady, who remains in a wheelchair, to become active in the politics of gun control. The Brady Handgun Violence Prevention

James R. Hoffa, right, Midwestern boss of the Teamsters Union, talking with Robert F. Kennedy, in Washington, D.C., August 21, 1957. (AP Photo)

Act, or the Brady Bill, was signed into law in 1993 but was substantially weakened in 1998.

Hinckley is still confined in a mental institution. For a time, his name was something of a punch line. In his musical *Assassins* (1990), Stephen Sondheim pairs Hinckley and **Lynette "Squeaky" Fromme**, who unsuccessfully tried to plug President Gerald Ford, in a duet to Jodie Foster, "Unworthy of Your Love." The book *Breaking Points* (1985), by Hinckley's parents, attempts to explain how they dealt with his illness, the assassination attempt, and what came after.

Today, most people would probably have trouble identifying John Hinckley Jr.

Hoffa, Jimmy

It's really unfair that one of the most important labor leaders of the twentieth century has been reduced to a tired punchline, but nothing in Jimmy Hoffa's life became him like the leaving of it.

Though the final details of Hoffa's fate will probably never be known, it's almost certain he was killed by the mobsters he had palled around with for decades. Hoffa had worked his way up through the ranks to become president of the Teamsters Union, 1.6 million members strong. During his rise, he moved gangsters into positions of power within the union and gave them access to the rank and file's pension fund.

In the late 1950s the Senate's McClellan Committee looked into the relationship. The committee's chief counsel was Robert F. Kennedy, who decided he was going to "Get Hoffa." When he became Attorney General, he did.

In 1962 Hoffa managed to beat a bribery rap with a hung jury, but was later convicted of trying to bribe one of the jurors and got an eight-year stretch. In 1964 he was also convicted for misappropriating $20 million in pension fund loans and was sent to the Lewisburg Federal Penitentiary.

While he was locked up, the mob solidified its position within the union. Hoffa's sentence was commuted in 1971 by President Richard "I Am Not a Crook" Nixon. The Teamsters had broken with tradition and supported the Republican. Hoffa agreed to stay out of union business but quickly started trying to worm his way back in. It didn't sit well in some circles.

On the afternoon of July 30, 1975 Hoffa thought he was going to meet some of his associates for lunch at the Machus Red Fox Restaurant in Bloomfield Township, Michigan to facilitate his reinstatement. At 2:30 p.m., he called his wife and told her it looked like he had been stood up. Soon after, eyewitnesses claimed they saw Hoffa get into the back seat of a maroon Mercury Marquis belonging to the son of a local gangster. He claimed he loaned the car to Chuckie O'Brien, a trusted friend who was virtually a son to Hoffa.

Hoffa's Pontiac was found at the restaurant the next day. Chuckie said he hadn't seen his friend and had alibis lined up for the whole day. Within a week, search dogs traced Hoffa's scent to the back seat and trunk of the Merc. In 2001 DNA tests matched a hair found in the back of the car with one from Hoffa's hair brush. It's about all the hard evidence there is.

Though Hoffa was declared legally dead in 1982, speculation concerning his whereabouts continues. The most popular theories put his remains under one of the end zones at Giants stadium in New Jer-sey's Meadowlands, or in a toxic waste site in Jersey City. Or perhaps he was processed in a fat-rendering plant. More recently, the FBI dug up large parts of a Michigan farm on the word of a jailed mobster. Like everyone else, they found nothing.

The mystery has made Hoffa something of a cult figure. His life was thinly fictionalized in the 1978 film *F.I.S.T.* where Sylvester Stallone played Johnny Kovak, a labor leader who was forced to turn to hoodlums for help in the 1930s.

The well-regarded 1983 miniseries *Blood Feud* dramatized the long struggle between Hoffa, played by **Robert Blake**, and RFK, Cotter Smith. The 1992 film *Hoffa*, from writer David Mamet and director Danny DeVito is a generally laudatory look at the man as played by Jack Nicholson.

Holman, Libby

In 1930 Libby Holman was one of the sexiest women this side of Hollywood. For five years, she had been appearing in Broadway shows and revues. Though the roles tended to be small, Libby attracted considerable attention with her smoldering singing voice and a provocative figure she loved to show off in slinky dresses and minimal undergarments.

She really hit the big time with the show *Three's A Crowd* where she introduced the sultry torch song *Body and Soul*. The show was in pre-Broadway try-outs in Baltimore when she met Smith Reynolds.

He was the troubled youngest son of the Reynolds tobacco family. A true playboy, he zipped around in his own amphibious plane, a Savoia-Marchetti, and habitually carried a .32 Mauser automatic because he feared kidnappers, not without some justification. One look at Libby and he was smitten. He pursued her with all the ardor he could muster and a bottomless checkbook.

At the same time, Libby was having a passionate fling with Louisa d'Andelot Carpenter, daughter of Margaretta du Pont, of Du Pont Chemical. Louisa was a charismatic lesbian who was equally smitten

Libby Holman Reynolds, (left), the belle of the courtroom, circa 1933. (AP Photo)

with the songbird. (Libby was catnip for horny East Coast zillionaires.)

For her part, Louisa seemed to have accepted Smith's passion and didn't object when he and Libby married in 1931. At the time, Libby was 27; Smith was 20.

With considerable reluctance, Libby agreed to take a one-year sabbatical from the stage and live with Smith at Reynolda, the family's sprawling country estate in Greensboro.

Things went poorly from the start. The free-thinking, free-loving Broadway babe was just a wee bit out of place in suburban North Carolina. She invited many of her smart New York friends down

to visit, but she and Smith still had problems. In those pre-Viagra days, he felt he was not all the man he could have been and insecurity aggravated his volatile nature. He was known to threaten suicide at particularly emotional moments of high drama.

On Monday, July 4, 1932 Smith and Libby threw a party for Smith's friend, C.G. Hill, of the Cannon textile fortune. To properly celebrate, they bought a five-gallon keg of the finest 100-proof corn whisky and a tub of home brew. About a dozen friends, including Smith's best bud Ab Walker, were invited and they began drinking in the afternoon. Some of the assembled young funseekers put on swimming suits for a dip in the lake. From that point onward, key details are a little fuzzy.

According to one account, Smith was uncharacteristically abstemious. Barely touched a drop; according to another, he was completely hammered. Libby may have vanished for several hours. She may have been seen kissing Ab Walker by Smith or it may have been a joke. She may have flirted more seriously with other men. They all drank a lot and ate a lot and wandered about the house and grounds. Things began to break up around 9:30 p.m.

Around 12:30 in the morning, Libby and Smith went upstairs to their bedroom. Ab Walker was still there—he was living in the house that summer—and was locking up. At 12:45 a.m, he heard a shot and a few minutes later, he heard Libby yelling his name. Upstairs on a sleeping porch off the bedroom, Smith had shot himself in the head. Ab, Libby, and another houseguest carried him out to Libby's Cadillac and drove him to Baptist Hospital where he died the next day.

In his biography of Libby, *Dreams That Money Can Buy* (1985), Jon Bradshaw claims Ab and Libby were on the sleeping porch with Smith. Enraged at her conduct during the day and evening, Smith started an argument. With Libby drunkenly sprawled on the bed, he took his Mauser from the bedside table and threatened to kill himself. When either Libby or, more likely Ab, tried to take it away from him, they struggled and it went off.

The initial coroner's verdict was suicide, but there were complications. What about the location of Smith's pistol? Different people had searched the sleeping porch three times before it was found—after Ab had been in the room alone. Libby's statements were contradictory, too. First, she said she'd been in the bedroom, then she said she was on the porch with Smith. There were also questions about the angle of the wound.

Enough doubts were raised an inquest returned an "open" verdict, stating that, in their opinion, Smith had been killed by a bullet fired by "a person or persons unknown." The verdict sent the matter to a grand jury and Libby and Ab were indicted a month later.

Then the other shoe fell. Libby was pregnant.

Following the little bombshell came weeks of legal maneuvering on the part of the Walker and Holman families, the Reynolds family, and the state of North Carolina. Libby spent part of the time ensconced in Louisa's mansion. In the end, the prosecutor decided to enter "nol-pros." In other words, he chose not to charge them, though he had the option to do so at a later time. By then, everyone just wanted the matter to go away and it was the least embarrassing course for all concerned.

Libby and her son Christopher received a sizeable inheritance from the Reynolds family. They lived for a time with Louisa and her adopted daughter.

Though she never returned to the stage full time, Libby performed occasional concerts and maintained friendships within the entertainment business, hanging with the likes of Noel Coward, Montgomery Clift, Dorothy Parker, and Elizabeth Taylor. She also appeared in the 1947 experimental film *Dreams That Money Can Buy.*

After World War II, Libby's second husband committed suicide and Christopher was killed in a climbing accident on Mt. Whitney in California in 1950. Libby killed herself by turning on her Rolls Royce in the garage of her Connecticut mansion in 1971.

Naturally, a story packed with such juicy scandal has been dramatized. David O. Selznick's story "A Woman Called Cheap" became the 1935 Jean Harlow film *Reckless.* The picture was made as a straight drama, but then studio heads decided it could be turned into a musical and so new scenes were added and others were reshot. It flopped.

The story was much more successfully adapted in 1956 by Douglas Sirk. *Written on the Wind* turns the tale into a glossy soap opera with Lauren Bacall as Lucy Hadley, unhappy wife of feckless gadabout Kyle Hadley (Robert Stack). Rock Hudson plays his faithful best friend Mitch Wayne. Dorothy Malone won a Best Supporting Actress Oscar for her portrayal of the nymphomaniacal sister Marylee Hadley.

Hoover, J. Edgar

First and last, J. Edgar Hoover was a political animal.

In creating the FBI, he was a bureaucrat. In nurturing its growth, he was a skillful manipulator of the media who, like many of the outlaws he pursued, understood the importance of good press. In public, he chose his battles carefully and usually won. In private, he kept his secrets.

Before Hoover joined the Bureau of Investigation, as it was known in 1924, it was toothless and poorly organized. Hoover set standards for the agents and established a strong management structure. He also made anti-communism one of the Bureau's core principles. He had been active in Attorney General A. Mitchell Palmer's infamous Palmer Raids, and throughout his career, he kept files on all those he saw as possible enemies.

When the crime wave of the 1920s and '30s stunned the country, he presented the FBI as a savior, an American Scotland Yard. In the wake of the **Kansas City Massacre**, where one agent and three policemen were killed, Congress passed nine bills giving the Bureau more power and money. Hoover made sure he and the Bureau became synonymous in the public imagination. If other agents, most notably **Melvin Purvis**, soaked up too much limelight, they were eased out. When **Bruno Hauptmann** was arrested and charged with the Lindbergh baby kidnapping, Hoover dashed to New York for a photo op, even though the FBI had nothing to do with the collar.

Hoover used his friendship with powerful radio host Walter Winchell to good advantage. The radio show *Gangbusters* was based on FBI material. The Bureau got into Hollywood too, with a series of movies beginning in 1935, the most significant of them being James Cagney's *G-Men*. Pulp magazine stories lionized the FBI, as did the *War on Crime* comic strip. Prolific Courtney Cooper wrote grand stories of agents for *American Magazine*, picturing Hoover as a flawless leader whose men were intelligent and brave with miraculous scientific tools at their disposal for the analysis of evidence. (In this regard, they were not unlike contemporary TV forensic detectives.)

Hoover also had bestsellers ghostwritten under his name. In 1958, *Masters of Deceit*, about the ongoing Red Menace, sold more than two million copies and was on the bestseller list for the better part of a year. Don Whitehead's *The FBI Story*, subtitled "A Report to the People," with a foreword by Hoover, was a bestseller in 1956 and became a popular Jimmy Stewart movie in 1959. *The FBI* television series starring Efrem Zimbalist, Jr. enjoyed a nine-year run beginning in 1965.

As Fred Cook put it in *The FBI Nobody Knows*, "Never before, on any level of government, have the American people been subjected to such brainwashing on behalf of any agency."

The facade of perfection didn't show any cracks until the 1970s when the Bureau's numerous illegal wiretaps and electronic surveillances were made public in the wake of Watergate. By then, though, Hoover was dead. Later, details and innuendo surfaced about his lifelong relationship with his close friend and deputy Clyde Tolson, and Hoover's name became a punchline.

For all of his formidable image polishing, or perhaps because of it, J. Edgar Hoover has remained a supporting character in popular entertainment. In films about the 1960s, he is typically a villain or a representative of the forces of repression.

Horn, Tom

His apologists say Tom Horn was framed for a murder he didn't commit, but even if they're right, he was a cold-blooded hired gun who claimed he would kill anyone for the right price.

Born in 1840, Tom left an abusive home early and went west where he worked as a stagecoach driver, Indian scout, lawman, and rodeo cowboy. He also rode with Teddy Roosevelt's Rough Riders (all right, he took care of the pack mules), and was in on the surrender of Geronimo and the capture of the **Dalton Gang**. In all of those jobs, he earned a reputation as a tough customer, but he didn't earn much money.

Horn tried to correct this lamentable situation by hiring himself out as a "range detective" to the wealthy ranchers trying to eliminate their small fry competition in the latter stages of Wyoming's **Johnson County War**. In the decades-long conflict, the cattle barons were aligned with powerful state and federal political forces. They could essentially legalize their assassinations by claiming any individual man or woman was a rustler who had stolen cattle from the open range.

By that time, Horn was not interested in face-to-face confrontations, if he ever had been. He preferred to work from a distance with a rifle. As the story goes, he put a rock beneath the head of each person he killed as a signature.

It ended in 1901 when Horn mistakenly murdered the 14-year-old son of intended victim Kels Nickell. The killing outraged everybody and legendary lawman Joe Lefors, who had led the posse to capture **Butch Cassidy**, went after Horn.

Lefors arranged to share several drinks with Horn in a Denver hotel and rigged up some sort of crude listening device so a hidden stenographer could note what was said. It was a prototype of today's wire. In his cups, Horn admitted to shooting the Nickell boy. Later, Horn denied the accuracy of the transcript, but the "confession" became the primary evidence used at his trial.

Horn was convicted and, to the great relief of the Wyoming cattlemen, went to the gallows in 1903 without revealing the names of his employers. In the years since, Horn has been lionized and demonized by those who have written about him and dramatized his story. William Goldman, writer of *Butch Cassidy and the Sundance Kid*, took a crack at it in the 1979 miniseries *Mr. Horn*, with Keith Carradine in the title role. Steve McQueen starred in the lackluster *Tom Horn*, a year later. It was his next to last film.

Huberty, James

To date, James Oliver Huberty holds the record for the largest number of victims in a single "spree" shooting—the mindless, angry, wholesale murder of strangers.

Huberty, a heavy drug user and gun nut, had a tough life. In 1949 when he was seven, his mother abandoned the family to become a missionary and save heathen souls for Jesus. As a young man in Ohio, Huberty trained to be a mortician but lacked the social skills needed to work with the living public. He was a cranky, bitter guy who loved to argue. Even so, in 1965, he married. He and his wife Etna had a couple of kids and he worked as a welder at the Babcock & Wilcox plant in Canton. Huberty's house burned down in 1971 and he was arrested once for drunk and disorderly. Still, he managed to cope until the plant closed and he was laid off in 1982.

Though he managed to find another job, it didn't last, and the family relocated to San Ysidro, California near the Mexican border. Again, Huberty found it difficult to hold onto a job. He worked briefly as a security guard, but his mental state continued to deteriorate.

Something inside him snapped on the afternoon of July 18, 1984. After paying a traffic ticket in the morning, Huberty put on a black T-shirt and camouflage pants, and armed himself with a 9mm pistol, shotgun, and an Uzi semiautomatic. When Etna asked what he was up to, he picked up a bag filled with ammunition and said, "Society's had their chance. I'm going hunting for humans."

He didn't have to go far to find them.

There was a McDonald's a couple hundred yards down the street from their apartment. Huberty walked into it around 4:00 p.m. and opened fire. Before it was over, he killed 21 people—the youngest eight months old—and wounded 19. Most of them were Mexican or Mexican-American. Huberty apparently blamed them for his personal and professional failings. He fired on men, women, and children for more than an hour before Chuck

Foster, a SWAT team sniper, shot him from the roof of a nearby building.

McDonald's razed the building two months later and donated the property to the city. It's now the site of the San Ysidro Community College and a monument to the 21 victims.

In 1987 Etna filed a $7.88 million suit against McDonald's and Babcock & Wilcox. In a variation on the famous "Twinkie defense," she claimed Huberty had been driven to kill by excessive consumption of Chicken McNuggets. The monosodium glutamate in the nuggets reacted with the lead and cadmium Hubert had absorbed during his years as a welder, she theorized, and triggered his rage. The suit was dismissed.

Huberty's story has not been dramatized or fictionalized directly on film, though he might have been part of the basis for the 1993 film *Falling Down*, starring Michael Douglas. Huberty was the subject of a TV documentary *American Justice: Mass Murderer—An American Tragedy* (2000) and the 1993 video documentary *Murderers, Mobsters & Madmen, Vol. 1.*

J, K

James, Jesse

Both man and myth were products of the Civil War; specifically, the war as it was seen from the South.

Jesse James was from Missouri, a border state where communities and even families were divided by the issues of slavery and secession. The James family had farmed tobacco and owned slaves. Jesse and his older, more even-tempered brother Frank were Secessionists. Frank had served in the Confederate army, but the war in Missouri was not one of big battles like Bull Run or Gettysburg. It was a more personal, internecine matter with poorly organized groups on both sides terrorizing civilians. Jesse joined Frank and mass murderer **William Quantrill** and his Raiders. Jesse was 17 and took part in at least one atrocity while riding with **"Bloody Bill" Anderson**, another psycho in uniform.

At the end of the war in 1865, an amnesty was offered to Southerners. The James brothers, along with their fellow guerrillas, the Younger brothers, were trying to take advantage of it when they were set upon by Union troops who opened fire. Jesse was seriously wounded in the chest. He was nursed back to health by his cousin Zeralda Mimms, who'd been named after his mother. Nine years later, he would marry her.

For a time after the war, Jesse and Frank attempted to work their family farm, but by 1866 they decided to make a career change and became bank robbers. It was a choice with political implications. Many unreconstructed Southerners saw banks as part of the industrialization Northerners were forcing on them.

The first one they hit with the Youngers was the Clay County Savings Bank in Liberty, Missouri. They pulled the job on Valentine's Day and got away with $58,000. On the way out of town, they shot and killed college student George Wymore, who happened to be on the street at the wrong time.

They continued to rob banks for the next four years. In 1872 they hit a fair in Kansas City and wounded a little girl. A year later they derailed a Rock Island train, killing the engineer. Overall, they were so successful the Pinkerton Detective Agency was hired to come after them. In 1875, agents attempted to ambush the brothers at their mother's farm, but they botched the whole thing and succeeded in setting the house on fire, blowing the woman's arm off, and killing her son Samuel, Jesse's half-brother.

When news of the debacle got out, the Pinkertons backed off and public sympathy for the James brothers increased. The gang had always had vocal supporters, first among them John Newman Edwards, editor of the Kansas City *Times*. As part of his campaign to return Southern sympathizers to political office, he published Jesse's letters and editorialized on his behalf.

Things generally went well for the gang until September 1876 when they decided to head north and rob the First National Bank in Northfield, Minnesota. They cased the town for a time, then went to the bank where they found an uncooperative staff.

In their distinctive long-linen dusters—worn to hide their weapons—the gang did not go unnoticed by the townspeople. They were quickly recognized as trouble and the Minnesotans took up arms. With shotguns, rifles, and pistols, they opened fire on the lookouts. Those who didn't have weapons threw rocks.

Inside the bank, cashier Joseph L. Heywood refused to open the vault, even though it was unlocked, anyway. Another employee escaped and was wounded. Frustrated, Jesse fatally shot Heywood in the head as he ran for the front door. Outside, he found his gang under fire. Three were either killed there or died within days. Nearly all of them were wounded as they ran to their horses and fled. The gang broke up outside of town and never reformed. The Younger brothers and Charlie Pitts went one way and were captured two weeks later.

Jesse and Frank were reduced to stealing vegetables from fields as they made their way back to Missouri and then to Tennessee where they could hide out.

That was the end of the original and most famous James gang. Three years later, the brothers attempted a comeback with new associates. By then, though, public sentiment had begun to turn against the outlaws. In the process of robbing banks, trains, and even a stagecoach, more innocent bystanders were killed and a $10,000 reward was posted for the James brothers, dead or alive. Jesse adopted the alias Thomas Howard and moved with Zeralda and their two kids to a small house in St. Joseph, Missouri. He also grew a beard and dyed it black.

The new gang slowly disintegrated and reformed with other members. One of the new guys was young Robert Ford who joined with his brother Charles. They sometimes accompanied Jesse as bodyguards. Robert, though, had gotten word to Missouri Governor Thomas Crittenden that he was ready to collect the reward.

On April 3, 1881 the Fords went to Jesse's house to plan the next job in Platte County. As the story goes, when Jesse stepped up on a chair to adjust a crooked picture on the wall, Robert Ford shot him in the back at point blank range. Jesse was 34.

Frank surrendered later and was acquitted on murder charges. Robert Ford was charged with murder, too, but those charges were dropped by the governor. He took his reward money and moved to Colorado where he was killed in 1892 by one of Jesse's fans. And Jesse did have his fans.

In death, stories of his courage and generosity grew to Biblical proportions—the widows he befriended, the children he looked after. The tales grew and were word spread through nineteenth-century dime novels.

Jesse Jr. played his father in one of the first silent films, *Jesse James Under the Black Flag* (1921). Since then, there have been dozens if not hundreds more, from the unapologetically cheesy *Jesse James Meets Frankenstein's Daughter* (1966) to the more serious. If not the best, then certainly one of the most enjoyable is the 1939 *Jesse James* with Tyrone Power and Henry Fonda as Jesse and Frank. The film was remade in 1957 as *The True Story of Jesse James* with Robert Wagner and Jeffrey Hunter. Maverick director Sam Fuller took a different tack by focusing on Bob Ford in *I Shot Jesse James* (1949).

Despite an element of stunt casting by having real brothers play the James, Younger, and Ford brothers, Walter Hill's *The Long Riders* (1980) does an acceptable job with the material. The 1994 *Frank & Jesse*, with Rob Lowe and Bill Paxton in the title roles, paints them as romantic heroes with really bad Southern accents and makes Allan Pinkerton

The death of Jesse James in 1882, immortalized on the cover of the *New York Detective Library*. (AP Photo)

Brad Pitt as Jesse James, from the movie *The Assassination of Jesse James by the Coward Robert Ford*, 2007. (Kobal)

(William Atherton) the villain. The most recent is *The Assassination of Jesse James by the Coward Robert Ford* (2007) with Brad Pitt in the title role.

Probably the best and least biased modern book is T.J. Stiles' excellent *Jesse James: Last Rebel of the Civil War* (2002).

Johnson, Ellsworth Raymond "Bumpy"

Though he is best known as a heroic figure in the "black Mafia," Bumpy Johnson played a relatively small role in the New York crime scene. He spent the better part of his adult life behind bars, doing three stretches on drug raps. His notoriously short fuse meant he spent a lot of that time in solitary. He became a voracious reader in the pen and later wrote poetry.

Born in 1906, he came to Harlem from Charleston, South Carolina and went to work for Stephanie St. Clair, aka "Queenie." She ran the numbers racket uptown. The numbers, better known now as Pick-Three, was an illegal lottery. Customers placed a small bet of a few cents on the three digits of their choice. The winning numbers came from an arbitrary published figure each day. It might have been the last three digits of a stock exchange total, or a number from race track. The few winners took home a nice piece of cash. The numbers bank raked in a big haul every day. Bumpy provided muscle for Queenie when other gangs encroached on her turf, and also moonlighted as a pimp, drug dealer, and holdup man.

In his day, Bumpy (so named for a big bump on the back of his head) was famous for dressing sharp and flashing fist-sized wads of cash. More important, he was one of the key players when **Dutch Schultz** and the Italian and Jewish gangs decided they wanted a piece of the action. He and Queenie made arrangements with **Lucky Luciano** and **Meyer Lansky**.

Like most of the colorful figures of the time, Johnson was not universally loved. Some said he gave money to local charities and saw him as a Robin Hood figure, while others knew him as a parasite who fed upon his community.

Throughout his life, at least the times when he wasn't incarcerated, Johnson managed to balance his loyalties, working as an enforcer for Luciano and others while maintaining at least the appearance of independence. He died of a heart attack in 1968.

On film, he has been portrayed twice by Laurence Fishburne, first as a supporting character named Bumpy Rhodes in Francis Ford Coppola's *The Cotton Club* (1984) and then as the protagonist of Bill Duke's *Hoodlum* (1999).

Though Duke's underrated film is only loosely based on fact, it contains three superb performances that really capture the characters. Fishburne brings real star power to his role. Tim Roth's Dutch Schultz is properly hot-headed, greedy, and crude. As Luciano, Andy Garcia is a silken charmer, and, for once, he looks right with the drooping wounded eye.

The real Bumpy also provided the spirit for the character of Harlem gangster Bumpy Jonas in Ernest Tidyman and Gordon Parks' *Shaft* (1971).

Johnson County War

Wyoming's Johnson County War could not have been more perfectly tailored for the movies.

The bad guys were stinking rich white cattle barons, the ultimate privileged fat cats. The good guys were hard-working ranchers, God-fearing folk who were simply trying to make a living for their families.

It started in 1892 when members of the Wyoming Stock Growers' Association decided they were losing too many cattle. For decades they had been grazing their cows on open range. Small homesteaders sometimes took an unbranded calf, or maverick, and claimed it as their own. In addition, many members of the Association were absentee landlords and it was not uncommon for their own hired help to dip into the till of livestock to start their own operations.

No one can say precisely what the reasoning was, but members of the Association decided to take matters into their own hands. Their first victim was Cattle Kate Watson, a hooker who accepted cows in lieu of cash. They lynched her and spread a story through the newspapers they controlled that she had been a "bandit queen." After they got away with that murder, they decided to outsource the dirty work. They made up a "death list" of the worst of the offenders—by their standards—and hired a group of about 50 "regulators" or killers to go into Johnson County and get rid of the problem.

They coldly slaughtered two ranchers, Nate Champion and Nick Ray. Word of the murders spread quickly and the regulators soon found themselves outnumbered by a force of 200 armed and angry local ranchers. The killers retreated to a farm where they were surrounded. That's when the cavalry came to the rescue. Literally.

The Association pulled strings reaching as high as the Oval Office to President Benjamin Harrison, and they got the Sixth Cavalry to remove the regulators from the custody of local law enforcement. Eventually, they also had the trial moved to a different location and all charges were dropped.

While the organized part of the Johnson County War ended, the big ranchers continued to hire individual "range detectives" (including **Tom Horn**, the legendary Indian Scout and lawman turned assassin), to intimidate and kill the little guys up into the early twentieth century.

Asa Mercer wrote a book about the cattlemen's efforts at ethnic cleansing, called *The Banditti of the Plains* (1894). Serious and largely successful attempts were made to suppress it—copies were burned, the printing plates were destroyed, and even the Library of Congress copy mysteriously disappeared. The book survived, though, and was eventually reprinted by the University of Oklahoma Press in 1954.

Owen Wister's 1902 novel *The Virginian* is built around a highly fictionalized version of the war. George Stevens' *Shane* (1954) is certainly the finest film version. *Hannah Lee* (1953), Michael Cimino's bloated *Heaven's Gate* (1981), *Tom Horn* (1980), *Mr. Horn* (1979), *The Johnson County War* (2002), and Kevin Costner's *Open Range* (2003) all use a variation of the conflict as a basis for their stories.

Jones, James Warren

The road to Jonestown began in Indiana in 1947 when 16-year-old James Warren Jones took up street corner preaching. Coming from the Pentecostal branch of American Protestantism, he was an early believer in racial equality and social justice.

Privately, he was also a believer in sexual experimentation, both hetero and homo. Those public beliefs were not at all popular in postwar America and Jones was criticized for them. Eventually, the criticism and persecution led to fully blown paranoia. By then, the Reverend Jim Jones had about a thousand brainwashed followers who shared his delusions about the imminent end of the world.

Over the course of his career, Jones was sporadically affiliated with other denominations, but his message of fervent religious socialism remained fairly constant. Like so many true believers of his ilk, he drifted to California in the 1960s. An article he read in *Esquire* magazine persuaded him that Mendocino County, California was going to be a safe haven after the coming nuclear war. He established branches of his People's Temple church in Los Angeles and San Francisco, and also broadcast his ideas on radio.

In 1973 he was busted for lewd conduct at a gay meeting place in MacArthur Park. A year later, he entered into an agreement with the South American nation of Guyana to create a commune on a 3,000-acre parcel of land. To finance "Jonestown," as it was called, he pressured members of his flock to turn all of their worldly possessions over to him. About 1,100 obeyed and moved to the primitive jungle compound.

Conditions were atrocious. People lived in shacks, worked at punishing physical labor seven days a week, and lived on a diet of beans and rice and little else. Armed guards enforced discipline and punished anyone who objected or tried to escape. Of course, word got out to family members. They learned of Jones' increasingly bizarre rants about CIA conspiracies and his threats of mass "revolutionary suicide."

Residents even practiced for it in dry runs called "white nights" where they would be awakened and told mercenaries had surrounded them. Suicide by drinking poison was the only answer. Given cups of colored liquid, they all drank and waited to die until they were told their leader had been testing their faith.

California Congressman Leo Ryan had become interested in such psychological manipulation during the **Patricia Hearst** kidnapping. After hearing from concerned family members, he organized a trip in November 1978 to Guyana with members of his staff, reporters, and American embassy personnel.

After considerable stonewalling from People's Temple officials, Ryan's party flew more than 100 miles from the capital, Georgetown, to Jonestown. Rev. Jones was ready. The group arrived late in the day and saw a sanitized version of the place. They were served dinner and treated to a musical performance before Jones tried to hustle them out. But some of the residents managed to pass notes saying they wanted to leave. The visitors stayed.

The next day, as the party was getting ready to depart, Rep. Ryan was attacked by a man with a knife but was not harmed. Fifteen members of the

Temple were with the party, hoping to make a getaway. One of them, Larry Layton, was a plant.

Rep. Ryan had arranged for two small planes to accommodate the extra passengers. As one plane was preparing to take off, Layton pulled out a pistol and opened fire. At the same time, a tractor and trailer approached the second plane. Armed Temple members jumped out and started shooting. Ryan and four others were killed. Six were wounded. One plane managed to get off the ground and to report the attacks to Guyanese police.

By then, it was too late.

Jones had gathered his congregation and told them they would soon be under attack. The cyanide soft drinks were ready. The people lined up and let the children go first. The youngest ones had the juice squirted into their mouths with syringes. The rest "drank the Kool-Aid" (though it wasn't actually Kool-Aid). Jones died by a gunshot wound to the head, possibly self-inflicted. Some escaped into the jungle, but the final body count was 913, almost a third of them children.

In the years since, several preposterous conspiracy theories have been floated, and the bizarre reality of such a mass suicide is still hard to accept, much less to understand.

Footage of Jones in action has been incorporated into several documentaries, generally of the "mondo" school. The story was slightly fictionalized in the Mexican exploitation film *Guyana: Crime of the Century* (1979) where Stuart Whitman played Rev. James Johnson and Gene Barry is Rep. Lee O'Brian. It's raw-looking and amateurishly staged, but sticks close to the known facts. The 1980 made-for-TV *Guyana Tragedy: The Story of Jim Jones* has a better reputation but is more difficult to find. A new documentary, *Jonestown: The Life and Death of the People's Temple* was released in 2006.

Judd, Winnie Ruth

It's difficult to persuade people you're innocent if you travel from Phoenix to Los Angeles with two

Winnie Ruth Judd in a Phoenix courtroom, 1932, on trial for the murder and dismemberment of Anne LeRoi and Hedvig "Sammy" Samuelson. (AP Photo)

chopped up bodies in two trunks and a valise, but Winnie Ruth Judd managed it to an impressive degree. By all accounts, she could be utterly charming when she needed to be, and at certain times in her life, the quality served her well. At other times...

By 1931 young Winnie had come a long way from her hometown of Darlington, Indiana where she was a preacher's daughter. First, she moved to California and made an ill-advised marriage to Dr. William C. Judd, 22 years her senior and a morphine addict. They traveled to Mexico where he worked with the poor while she suffered two miscarriages and contracted tuberculosis.

Winnie recovered in a California sanitarium and separated from the good doctor, though in letters, she claimed to still love him. He stayed in Mexico.

She moved to Phoenix where she found work as a medical secretary at a private clinic and began an affair with a married pillar of the local community.

At the same time, she became friends with two women, Anne LeRoi, who worked at the same clinic, and Anne's "roommate" Hedvig "Sammy" Samuelson. It's impossible to precisely define the relationship shared by the three women. It has been strongly hinted that Anne and Sammy were lesbians who recruited Winnie. Others claimed all three were sexually adventurous and hosted wild parties for Winnie, her male lover, and his well-heeled pals.

Whatever the case, Winnie moved in with Anne and Sammy, but things didn't work out and she moved back to her rented house pretty quickly. But on Friday, October 16, 1931 Anne and Sammy invited Winnie to spend the night and she accepted. An argument ensued. It may have involved another woman who worked at the clinic. It may have involved Winnie's lover. It certainly involved a .25 caliber automatic.

Winnie was the only one of the three to survive the night. Her version of the fight revolves around that time-honored explanation: "We were both struggling for the gun when it went off." Sammy, she said, attacked her first, snuck up on poor Winnie in the kitchen with the gun. Winnie defended herself. While they were wrestling, Anne attacked her with an ironing board. And then… and then… it was all a blur; she didn't know what really happened, but somehow, inexplicably, tragically, Sammy and Anne were dead.

Details of the rest of the weekend are equally vague, but by Sunday evening Anne and Sammy's bodies had been dismembered and packed up in two heavy trunks and a valise, accompanying Winnie on the Golden State Limited express bound for Los Angeles.

On Monday morning at Union Station, a baggage handler and his boss noticed a red liquid leaking from a trunk. They also noticed a noxious smell and concluded it might contain contraband venison. When Winnie and her brother, who lived in

LA, showed up to claim the bags, they asked her to open them so they could inspect the contents. She claimed her husband had the only key and hotfooted it out of there as fast as she could, but not before the railroad men noted the car's license number. They called the police who picked the trunks' locks.

After the initial shock and after examining the bodies, the police realized some body parts were missing. Those were found in a valise stashed in the ladies' bathroom. There with the valise was a matching hatbox where the cops found a surgical dissecting kit, a .25 caliber pistol, a box of ammunition, a knife, and makeup.

The press dubbed Winnie "The Trunk Murderess" and the hunt was on.

The police quickly deduced that neither her husband nor her brother could have had anything to do with the killings. She had surprised her brother when she showed up in town and asked him to help her with her bags. She skipped out on him soon after they left the station.

Four days later, they found Winnie hiding in, of all places, a funeral home. She went into her "and then we both reached for the gun" routine, and, to prove self-defense, displayed a bullet wound in her hand.

The jury didn't bite. At her first trial, Winnie was convicted and sentenced to hang.

But Phoenix Sheriff John R. McFadden was unhappy with certain inconsistencies and sloppy police work. He was able to persuade a grand jury to take another look at Winnie. Enough doubts were raised—and her winsome beauty had created enough public sympathy—that the governor granted her a sanity hearing. That's where the histrionics really began.

Winnie's mother testified her daughter had been "more or less insane for all her life," and her dad claimed his family tree was full of "loonies." To prove them right, Winnie wailed and loudly threatened to throw herself through a window. It worked. The court agreed she was a certifiable fruitcake, and they shipped her off to the Arizona State Mental Hospital.

But wait, there's more!

Having made her mark as a murderess, Winnie embarked on a new career—escapee. She walked away from the hospital no less than seven times while she was being held there. She was such a charming, cooperative helpful inmate that a friendly nurse gave her a key. Most times when Winnie escaped, she wasn't loose for very long and didn't go far. Twice, she even turned herself in, but, in 1962, the footloose Winnie skipped out and was gone for more than six years.

As Marian Lane, she landed a great job as a companion to the matriarch of a wealthy San Francisco clan. She fit right in, and was so loving and helpful she became a member of the family, and continued to live with them after her charge had died (of natural causes). All would have been fine if the cops hadn't managed to track her down through the DMV, but, in 1969, they did. Winnie, however, had no desire to go back.

She hired a high-priced mouthpiece—famous defense lawyer Melvin Belli—who urged then-Governor Ronald Reagan not to extradite her to Arizona. Alas, the Gipper demurred and they carted her off.

By this time, it was obvious that whatever she'd done or not done, the Trunk Murderess was no danger to anyone. In 1971 she was released. Winnie moved to Stockton, California where she lived a quiet life until she died in her sleep in 1998.

It's easy to understand why such a slight, sweet-looking and often sweet-tempered woman who committed such a grotesque, horrific crime would become a celebrity. Her appearance flies in the face of all our preconceptions about monstrous murderers. It's one thing for male killers to have choirboy charm, but women who kill (and dismember!) must somehow reveal that depravity in their appearance. Winnie simply did not.

Astonishingly, her story has never been dramatized by Hollywood.

Kaczynski, Ted

Unabomber

If Ted Kaczynski had just met the right girl and managed to get laid, we might have been spared the Unabomber. But he didn't, so the insane crank acted on his madness by sending bombs almost randomly to anyone who fit into his crackpot worldview.

Even today, no one doubts Kaczynski is brilliant. As a child he skipped a couple grades but a long childhood hospitalization may have been the cause, at least in part, of his stunted social abilities. He never got along well with anyone outside his family, and his relationships with his mother and younger brother David were troubled. It didn't stop him from graduating Harvard at 20, and going on to the University of Michigan where he earned his doctorate and taught for three years. At the same time, his personal life was a mess. He was such a washout with women he came to doubt his orientation and went to the University Health Center to see about having a sex change operation.

Again, one has to wonder whether a few snips and tucks and hormone shots might have changed things, but he opted to stick with the original equipment.

In 1967 Ted was hired to teach math at the University of California at Berkeley. He didn't fit in there, either, and resigned two years later. Sometime later he moved to a remote little shack in Montana, based on Thoreau's living quarters described in the nineteenth-century classic, *Walden*. For a time, Ted was joined by his brother in the back-to-nature quest, but he opted out and got married.

Ted stayed and stewed, his resentment against technology festering. He acted on it in 1978. He left a package for Professor Buckley Crisp of Northwestern University in a parking lot at the University of Illinois, Chicago, with Crisp listed on the return address. The package went back to Crisp who was immediately suspicious. He called campus police. When Officer Terry Market opened the box, the thing exploded in his hand. He was injured, but not

Former University of California at Berkeley math professor and "Unabomber" Theodore (Ted) Kaczynski escorted into the federal courthouse in Helena, Montana, April 4, 1996. (AP Photo/Elaine Thompson)

seriously since the bomb misfired. Curiously, part of the bomb was made of wood.

A second bomb also injured its recipient. The third was more sophisticated. It was placed aboard American Airlines Flight 444 in Chicago and partially detonated by an altitude-sensitive trigger. The plane made an emergency landing after the cabin filled with smoke. Had the device gone off as planned, it would have destroyed the airplane and killed everyone on board.

That's when the FBI created the name UNABOM, for University and Airline Bomber. It became "Unabomber" in the mainstream media when Kaczynski escalated his activities.

In 1985 a graduate student lost four fingers and an eye, and computer store owner Hugh Scrutton was killed by two of Kaczynski's infernal devices. Before he was through, Ted would kill three people and injure 29.

In 1993, as the bombings continued, Kaczynski sent letters to the *New York Times* and some of his victims. He said the bombs would stop if his 35,000-word manifesto was published. He also wrote to publisher Bob Guccione saying he would consider publication in *Penthouse* magazine but still wanted a more respectable forum.

At the urging of Attorney General Janet Reno and FBI director Louis Freeh, the *Times* and *Washington Post* agreed to publish the semicoherent rant, in the hopes someone would recognize the writer's style.

That's precisely what happened with David Kaczynski. After serious soul-searching and his own investigation, he and his wife Linda contacted the FBI. Their only condition was they not be identified. The feds agreed and promptly leaked their names when they had Kaczynski in custody. David and Linda had also asked prosecutors not to seek the death penalty. Again, the feds agreed and reneged.

Ted Kaczynski was taken without incident at his little crackerbox shack in Montana. After considerable legal wrangling and an unsuccessful jailhouse suicide attempt to hang himself with his underwear, Kaczynski pleaded guilty to all charges. He was sentenced to life without parole and is serving his time at the Florence, Colorado "supermax" facility where he continues to write.

Remarkably, some people have taken the lunatic seriously. They agreed with some of his neo-Luddite ideas and ignore or discount his actions. To date, the only dramatic adaptation of the story has been a TV movie, *Unabomber: The True Story* (1996).

Kansas City Massacre

Four law enforcement officers and one crook were gunned down on the morning of June 17, 1933 in the parking lot of the Kansas City train station. The sheer brazenness of the act caught the nation's attention and eventually helped swing public sympathy away from dashing criminal desperados and toward the FBI. Beyond that, it's difficult to say much of anything definitive about the Kansas City Massacre. To this day, nobody knows exactly who did it or why.

Frank "Jelly" Nash was a career criminal with an impressive record. He started robbing stagecoaches on horseback. Convicted on murder charges, he'd been sent to Leavenworth and escaped in 1930. Afterwards he probably worked with **Al Capone** in Chicago and with the Pendergast machine that ran Kansas City. He'd also been part of the **Karpis-Barker** gang.

By 1933 he and his new wife had moved to Hot Springs, Arkansas another "open city" for criminals where Richard Galatas ran things from his White Front Cigar Store. Galatas and Dutch Akers, the local chief of detectives, made sure the cops and politicos got their cut of the gambling, prostitution, and drug business. Out-of-town crooks knew they were safe in Hot Springs as long as they didn't interfere with the locals.

But two FBI agents, Joe Lackey and Frank Smith, and Otto Reed, the police chief of McAlester, Oklahoma, had the storefront staked out on June 16th and spotted Nash. They picked him up and, knowing they couldn't turn him over to the locals, hustled him to Fort Smith where they caught a train to Kansas City.

Word of Nash's capture got back to his old pal Verne Miller, an ex-sheriff turned embezzler, bank robber, and hitman. Miller recruited two accomplices, either Maurice Denning and William "Solly" Weisman, or **Pretty Boy Floyd** and Adam Richetti. Arming themselves with Tommy guns, they drove down to Union Station to meet the train.

By then, four other lawmen were waiting on the platform to escort Nash and company. The FBI wanted to get Nash back to Leavenworth as quickly as possible. In those days Kansas City, under the control of political boss Tom Pendergast, was as crime-ridden, corrupt, and freewheeling as Hot

Springs. The plan was to hustle Jelly into a car and drive the final 30 miles to the prison rather than stay on the train for the one-hour layover.

Just as the FBI agents and local cops were getting into their cars, Miller got the drop on them. After ordering them to raise their hands, Miller and his associates opened up, riddling the car with bullets. When it was over Chief Reed, Jelly Nash, FBI agent Raymond Caffrey, and police detectives W. J. "Red" Grooms and Frank Hermanson were dead, and two more were wounded.

A second carload of gunmen may have sprayed the agents' car as the first killers made their getaway. Even though the busy parking lot was filled with eyewitnesses, details about the attack were hazy and contradictory.

One person swore the first triggerman was Pretty Boy Floyd. It's true he was in Kansas City that day, but to his last breath, he denied having anything to do with the killings.

What was the purpose of the massacre—to spring Nash or to kill him? The latter seems more likely. Given his involvement in local machine politics, he might well have known something important and had to be silenced. And since the shooters were professionals, it's easier to see the operation as a successful hit than an unsuccessful rescue.

The immediate result of the massacre was a massive investigation and manhunt on the part of the FBI and an abrupt end to the Bureau's unofficial "no weapons" policy. Beyond that, no arrests were ever made.

Five months after the massacre, Verne Miller's body, naked and bearing signs of torture, was found in a ditch near Detroit. Two weeks later, Weisman's body, likewise mutilated, turned up outside Chicago. Denning was never found. Pretty Boy Floyd was gunned down by federal agents in October 1934. Richetti was executed in 1938.

The killings were fictionalized in the FBI-approved movie, *G-Men* (1935), and they were the sub-

> *"Alvin Karpis" simply doesn't have a good ring. Then there was the nickname, "Old Creepy." Not really an improvement. More to the point, Karpis avoided headlines; he didn't want to be famous, he wanted to be rich.*

ject of the 1975 made-for-television movie *Kansas City Massacre.*

Karpis, Alvin

By just about any standard, Alvin Karpis was one of the most successful of the 1930s outlaws, but he has never been as famous as contemporaries **John Dillinger**, **Bonnie and Clyde**, and the rest.

In part, it's the name. "Alvin Karpis" simply doesn't have a good ring. Then there was the nickname, "Old Creepy." Not really an improvement. More to the point, Karpis avoided headlines; he didn't want to be famous, he wanted to be rich.

A Canadian who moved to Kansas as a kid, Alvin knocked around doing nickel-and-dime stuff until he met Freddie Barker, of the **"Ma" Barker** gang, in the Kansas State pen. He and Freddie hit it off immediately. On Karpis' first day in the place, he and Freddie smoked some homegrown marijuana in the yard. Yes, they shared a joint in the joint. After they'd both been released in 1931, they started robbing banks together, then with Ma's pals. They continued to work as a team, knocking over banks and kidnapping wealthy people until 1935 when the gang broke up, and Ma and Freddie were killed in an FBI shootout.

Karpis then shifted gears and decided to resurrect the lost art of train robbery. He thought a $200,000 payroll was going to be on Erie Train No. 622 in Ohio. He and a new gang had carefully planned the job, holding the engineer at gunpoint and breaking into the mail car while the train was stopped in a small town. It all went perfectly except the payroll had been shipped on an earlier train, and they collected only $34,000.

But it was enough. By then, Karpis was the last of the bigtime independent criminals (as opposed to organized criminals) at large. He was Public Enemy Number One, and **J. Edgar Hoover** wanted him behind bars. Hoover, never shy about putting himself and his Bureau in the public eye, had recently been humiliated at a Senate subcommittee hearing when a senator noted he had never personally made an arrest.

The FBI chief sent out an order that when Karpis was located, nothing was to be done until he could get there. In May 1936 they learned Karpis was in New Orleans. Hoover flew down immediately and was, indeed, on hand when Old Creepy was nabbed.

In the book, *The FBI Story* (1959), an official history with a foreword by Hoover, Karpis is described as reaching for a rifle when Hoover literally grabs him. As Karpis tells it in the more entertaining (but equally self-serving) *The Alvin Karpis Story* (1971), the rifles were locked in the trunk of the Plymouth coupe he was sitting in, and he was surrounded by agents with drawn guns before Hoover showed his face.

No matter. Karpis was sent to Alcatraz, and then to the McNeil Island pen in Washington state. In 1969 he was paroled and deported to Canada. His autobiography was published two years later. He moved to the luxurious Costa del Sol in Spain and died there in 1979. Initially, there was some controversy surrounding his death. Sleeping pills were found close at hand, but police later said it was due to natural causes.

Karpis was the subject of the 1974 made-for-TV movie *The FBI Story: The FBI Versus Alvin Karpis, Public Enemy Number One.* Robert Foxworth played the bank robber opposite Harris Yulin's J. Edgar

Hoover. It has never been available on home video and is said to be something of a serious sleeper.

Kehoe, Andrew

Andrew Kehoe was filled with an overpowering anger that mushroomed into madness. The madness may have stemmed from a severe head injury sustained in St. Louis in 1911, but some said he had always been different, even dangerous. After all, there had been rumors he had had something to do with his stepmother's death. She was killed when an oil-burning stove exploded in 1886 when Andrew was 14.

Sometime after the St. Louis accident, Kehoe moved back to his native Michigan and married Nellie Price. They bought a farm in the small town of Bath, near Lansing, and soon found themselves in financial straits. Nellie had medical problems that burdened their limited budget, but Kehoe came to blame the area's taxes for his money problems, particularly the tax for a new school championed by school board superintendent Emory Huyck.

Kehoe was so insistent on the matter he ran for the school board and even served as treasurer. But he held the post only briefly and was not reelected. Instead, in 1926, the board hired him to be a custodian at the school. It might have seemed a logical position for someone who was as handy with machines and electrical equipment as Kehoe. But by then, he'd failed to keep up with the mortgage on the farm and had descended into a kind of quiet insanity nobody recognized.

While pretending to work at his custodial job, Kehoe was actually planting explosives—more than 1,000 pounds—in attics and crawlspaces, all wired to go off at the same time. He bought the stuff in small amounts from different stores over several months and squirreled it away a bit at a time. When he'd finished at the school, he went to work on his farm. He set charges in the house and barn, and hobbled the horses to make sure they'd be killed. Sometime before or afterwards, he beat Nellie to

death and partially dismembered her body. He then filled the back seat of his truck with dynamite, machine parts, scrap metal, and any sort of makeshift shrapnel he could find. Finally, he put his rifle on the front seat.

At 8:45 a.m. on May 18, 1927, a beautiful spring morning, he set off the first explosions at his farm. As neighbors ran to help, they found Kehoe already driving away toward town. That's when the school blew up.

The walls of the northwest wing were blown outward and the roof collapsed into the interior. In that first instant, dozens of children and teachers were killed or injured. People immediately dug through the smoking rubble attempting to rescue the kids they could hear crying inside.

Kehoe pulled his truck to the curb and surveyed his bloody handiwork. Then he saw Superintendent Huyck, who had been teaching a class, working with the rest. Kehoe called out to him. When Huyck was close enough to the truck, Kehoe picked up his rifle and fired at the dynamite. It exploded, obliterating both men and three other people, one of them eight-year-old Cleo Clayton who had survived the first explosion in the school.

By then, local and state police and fire departments were on the scene. They found more than 500 pounds of unexploded dynamite in the basement and other parts of the building. Apparently, only half of Kehoe's charges had detonated as planned. The other half, still attached to wires and timers, was carefully removed without further harm.

The final count was 45 killed, mostly children, 58 injured.

The Bath bombing remains the most serious act of school violence in America and is second only to the Oklahoma City bombing as an act of domestic terrorism. Today, there's a small park and a plaque commemorating the victims where the school once stood.

This kind of horror is not the stuff of popular entertainment, and the true story is not as well known as it might be because it occurred as Charles Lindbergh was making his historic transatlantic flight. The most complete account of the bombing is found on the Web at http://freepages.history.roots web.com/~bauerle/disaster.htm. Creator Ronald D. Bauerle, whose great-uncle died in the explosion, wears his religion and politics on his sleeve, but he has gathered all of the pictures and firsthand accounts—many of them extremely hard to find until now—in one well-organized site. It is a fitting memorial to a largely unknown chapter in American crime, though the mad passion that caused it is still in evidence today.

Kelly, George "Machine Gun"

Despite his threatening moniker, George "Machine Gun" Kelly was the wimpiest of the famous 1930s gangsters.

The whole idea of the machine gun as his signature weapon was the creation of his ambitious wife Kathryn, who was constantly pushing her laidback hubby to greater criminal heights.

For his part, George was happy being a common bootlegger, even though he'd served a year in Leavenworth after being convicted of selling booze on an Indian Reservation. Kathryn considered herself to be from classier stock. Her parents ran a "fugitive farm" on a Texas ranch where, for $50 a night, criminals could hide from the law.

She bought George a Thompson and made him practice shooting walnuts out at the ranch. He did manage to achieve a certain degree of proficiency with his chopper, though there's no solid evidence he ever actually fired it at another human being. Even so, Kathryn trumpeted his exploits as a bank robber to her underworld chums. It's true that "Machine Gun" participated in bank jobs in such backwater burgs as Tupelo, Mississippi and Wilmer, Texas, but in those hard times, the payoff wasn't very good.

Kathryn decided it was time for them to upgrade to kidnapping and pestered George until he and his partner, the equally unambitious Albert Bates,

agreed. They settled on Oklahoma City millionaire Charley Urschel and proceeded with minimal forethought. They burst in on Urschel and friends as they were playing bridge one night.

Problem One: Identifying the victim.

The would-be kidnappers didn't know precisely what their man looked like, and neither of the guys in the house would reveal his identity. George and Albert elected to snatch them both and got several miles down the road before they thought to ask to see some ID. Once they'd sorted it out, they kicked Urschel's friend Walter Jarrett out of the car after stealing $50 from him.

Problem Two: Collecting the ransom.

They stashed Urschel at Kathryn's parents' place and demanded $200,000. But they botched the first payoff because George couldn't start the car. A second face-to-face money transfer was successful. They got the money, in marked bills, and freed Urschel. (Kathryn wanted to kill him but for once George stood his ground.)

Problem Three: Evading the authorities.

Albert headed west for Denver while George and Kathryn dyed their hair to disguise themselves and went on a booze and shopping binge in Chicago. Things then went south fast. Albert and Kathryn's folks were identified and quickly arrested, in part because Urschel had paid close attention to details and gave the cops a lot of help. George and Kathryn hid out with friends in Memphis where they were found one morning—both brutally hung over—by the local police. **J. Edgar Hoover** claimed his agents made the collar and that Machine Gun had pleaded, "Don't shoot, G-Men, don't shoot!" Neither the federal participation nor George's use of the term "G-Men" is accurate.

George spent the rest of his life in Alcatraz and Leavenworth where he died in 1954. Kathryn was released in 1958.

Obviously anything resembling the real facts of Machine Gun Kelly's criminal career is not the stuff of big-screen crime drama, but the name and the myth are irresistible. He makes an appearance in Mervyn LeRoy's propagandistic *The FBI Story* (1959) and in John Milius' *Dillinger* (1973). B-movie auteur Roger Corman took a crack at the story in 1958 with *Machine Gun Kelly* starring a young Charles Bronson in the title role.

Kemper, Edmund

He didn't want anyone to know what he'd done as a child; it's easy to understand why. As a teen, Edmund Kemper killed his grandparents. But, according to the parole board, he'd done his time at the Atascadero State Hospital for the Criminally Insane and was rehabilitated. The psychiatrists and doctors strongly disagreed but the board let Kemper out anyway.

Three years after his release, Kemper had to appear before another board and persuade more doctors he really was a good boy and they should seal his records. It worked. They thought he was cured and sent him on his way. He didn't tell them about the head he had in the trunk of his car.

Born in 1948, Kemper first showed his violent side by chopping the heads off his sisters' dolls. The games the kids played involved some payback because he asked the girls to tie him to a chair and pretend to be his executioners. He later killed the family's pet cats.

All the while, his mother was telling him how rotten and grotesque he was. Kemper eventually grew into an imposing 6-foot 9-inches and 300-plus pounds. When mom could no longer handle him, she shipped him off to live with his father who shipped him off to the grandparents in North Fork, California. In 1964, when he was 15, Kemper shot them. There had been an argument, but he said he wondered what it would feel like to kill his grandmother. Afterwards, he didn't want his grandfather to suffer the loss. Then he called the cops and waited for them on the porch.

Kemper spent the next six years at Atascadero and there was no real followup care after he left the place. He wound up living with his mother, who had moved to Santa Cruz where she worked in the state university's admissions department. He got a job with the California Highway Department, bought a Ford Galaxy, joined the Junior Chamber of Commerce, and took to hanging around with cops at the courthouse and listening to their stories.

At the same time, Kemper was on the prowl, looking for pretty young women who hitchhiked among the various college campuses in the area. Despite his imposing size, Kemper developed a reassuring line to convince girls he was trustworthy.

His real aim was murder and rape, in that order. He was incapable of sexual relations with another person who was not completely compliant. Between May 1972 and February 1973 he claimed six victims. He dismembered and decapitated the bodies, eating parts of them and keeping souvenirs before disposing of the bodies. (At the same time, another insane murderer, **Herbert Mullin**, was also terrorizing the Santa Cruz area.)

On April 21, 1973 Kemper focused his murderous rage on his mother. He bashed her head in with a claw hammer, chopped up her body, and tried to force parts of it down the disposal. He put her head on the mantle and invited her friend Sarah Hallett over for dinner. When she arrived, he killed her, too. He made a half-hearted attempt at escape, getting as far as Pueblo, Colorado before he called the Santa Cruz police to confess. It took several tries before he was able to persuade them to send someone over to check his mom's place.

He finally confessed to all the murders, going so far as to tell the judge that death by torture was probably the more appropriate punishment for him. But California didn't have the death penalty at the time, so he is still serving his time in Folsom Prison.

Kemper's incarceration has proved to be of some value. He is among the most intelligent and lucid of serial killers and he has given experts extensive inter-

> *The noose was tightened snug around his neck. Weights were tied to his ankles and a hood was draped over his face. "Let her rip!" he yelled, and, unfortunately for the people in the first row, that's exactly what happened.*

views. FBI agents John Douglas and Robert Ressler talked to the killer at length when they were beginning their profiling work for the Behavioral Science Unit. Their analysis of his methods, thought patterns, and tactics has been useful in the identification and tracking of other murderers. Those insights have been cited in many serious works of nonfiction. Thomas Harris has borrowed some of Kemper's characteristics for his character Buffalo Bill in *Silence of the Lambs* (1991).

Ketchum, Thomas "Black Jack"

Among Old West outlaws, Thomas "Black Jack" Ketchum was not exactly on the A-Team. If anything, he was one of the worst, but he certainly made a spectacular exit.

Black Jack was emotionally unstable. Some said his problems began when he was rejected by a woman. After reading a particularly brutal "Dear Black Jack" letter, he became so unhinged that he beat himself over the head repeatedly with the butt of his revolver. Afterwards, he was never the same.

Black Jack's gang operated around the same time as **Butch Cassidy**'s and even shared some of the same personnel, but Ketchum lacked Butch's flair. He had, for example, a tendency to rob the same trains and stagecoaches at the same places over and over. But

since he was so proficient at running away, he managed to elude the authorities for some time. When he wasn't robbing trains and fleeing from posses, Ketchum was a nasty drunk who was said to have gunned down several men in barroom altercations.

But they didn't get him for murder.

In 1899 Black Jack finally tried to rob the Folsom, Arizona train once too often. Conductor Frank Harrington recognized the outlaw as he approached and wounded him with a shotgun. Ketchum was arrested the next day and tried on charges of "attempted train robbery." It was a serious offense, punishable by death, and that's what Black Jack got.

Various complications delayed the execution of the sentence until 1901. By then, Ketchum was news, and the *New York Times* sent a reporter to cover his hanging.

Black Jack watched from the jail in Clayton, New Mexico as a gallows was constructed and tested, and loudly maintained his innocence to anyone who would listen. When they took him from his cell on April 25th, he was full of piss and vinegar. He refused to have anything to do with the priest who had come to make things easier, and asked to have a fiddler playing when they strung him up.

As he approached the gallows, he yelled to the crowd and the assembled reporters, "I'll be in hell before you start breakfast, boys!" and quickly hopped up the 13 steps.

The noose was tightened snug around his neck. Weights were tied to his ankles and a hood was draped over his face. "Let her rip!" he yelled, and, unfortunately for the people in the first row, that's exactly what happened.

Perhaps the rope had stretched during the testing process, or perhaps they'd used too much weight. For whatever reason, Black Jack dropped so hard his head was yanked clean off his neck, splattering the closest spectators with gushing blood. The 1956 film *Blackjack Ketchum, Desperado* left out that part.

Kimes, Sante

Sante Kimes' brutal, bizarre life has been filmed twice as black comedy—really the only way it can be presented as entertainment. Sante was a bad apple who spoiled those closest to her and was lethal to everyone else.

The daughter of a prostitute, she was born in 1934 and ran wild in the streets of LA as a girl. As a teenager, she was adopted by a middle class family and seemed to have everything she needed for success—striking good looks, personality, ambition. But she was a creature of overpowering avarice who loved to steal even when she didn't need to. She marched steadily onward from shoplifting to petty theft to grand theft auto to prostitution.

She had burned through a couple of marriages and countless aliases by the time she met millionaire motel magnate Kenneth Kimes in 1971. She got her hooks into him and found he shared her appreciation for the big con. They came up with a crackpot scheme to sell special bicentennial posters to public schools and post offices, and managed to weasel their way into meetings with First Lady Pat Nixon and President Gerald Ford.

They got caught, however, and returned to their life of luxury when the poster scam imploded. A year later, their son Kenny was born.

Kenny grew up in a household where his mother kept Mexican maids locked up as slaves and continued her larcenous ways, stealing minks, or torching her various real estate holdings for insurance, usually staying one step ahead of law enforcement.

Eventually, she was nailed—on a slavery rap, of all things!—and served three years in a minimum security facility. She emerged unrepentant.

After Kenneth died in 1994, Sante pulled Kenny into her increasingly violent schemes. In 1998 they had killed David Kazdin, who had been helping them loot her late husband's real estate properties. Sante and Kenny made their getaway from LA in a brand new Lincoln Town Car purchased with a hot check. In Florida, they learned about wealthy,

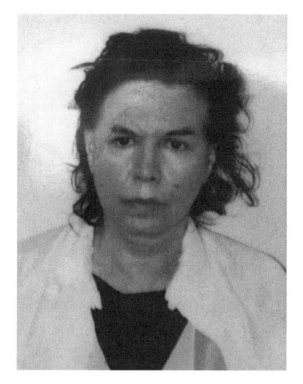

Not so glamorous Sante Kimes, 1998. (AP Photo)

eccentric Irene Silverman who had turned her East Side mansion in New York into luxury suites renting for $6,000 a month. Irene was a free-spirited bon vivant who liked to spice things up and wasn't overly concerned with the particulars.

When Sante and Kenny knocked on her door and claimed an old friend as a reference, Irene agreed to let them have an apartment. They moved in and set their plot in motion straight away. Sante practiced forging Irene's signature. They collected the necessary forms for a real estate sale. Once they had everything in place, they planned to kill the trusting Irene, get rid of her body, and tell everyone she'd sold her house to Sante and headed off on vacation.

Only the first part worked. They shot Irene, hid the body in a trunk, and disposed of it at a New Jersey construction site. But when they came back, they found a confederate—who knew nothing about the murder—had ratted them out to the feds for the Kazdin murder and the hot Lincoln.

Once they were in custody, all their sins caught up with them. In 2000 Sante was convicted on 58 charges. Kenny was nailed for 60. Then they were sent to LA to be tried for the Kazdin killing. (Between trials, Kenny, armed with a ball point pen, took *Court TV* reporter Maria Zone hostage for three hours.) At the next trial, Kenny turned on his mom and they each got a life sentence tacked onto the 100 years they already had.

Several books have been written about the killer Kimes and two television films have been made: *Like Mother, Like Son: The Strange Story of Sante and Kenny Kimes* (2001) with Mary Tyler Moore and Gabriel Olds (based on Adrian Havill's 1999 book *The Mother, the Son, and the Socialite*) and *A Little Thing Called Murder* (2006), starring Judy Davis and Jonathan Jackson. Both stick fairly close to the unbelievable truth because no embroidery is necessary.

Koresh, David

From its bungled beginning to the horrifying conclusion, the government's attempt to remove David Koresh from his Waco, Texas compound was a colossal screwup. All told, 90 people died.

Koresh was born Vernon Wayne Howell but came to think it was not a fit name for the Messiah. In 1993, he was the leader of the Branch Davidians, a splinter group of the Seventh Day Adventists. A charismatic, loquacious fellow, he had several hundred followers who bought his particular brand of baloney. He believed the final days were approaching, and the group financed their activities in part through gun sales which brought them to the attention of the Bureau of Alcohol, Tobacco, and Firearms (ATF), who decided to bring Koresh in. There were also reports of child sexual abuse within the group's Mt. Carmel Center.

Initially, the feds planned a surprise raid on Sunday, February 13, 1993 but Koresh got wind of it. Even after learning they had lost the element of sur-

prise, AFT honchos pressed on. They had over 70 men and Blackhawk helicopters ready to rock-n-roll, and they thought the Davidians locked up their weapons on the Sabbath. Wrong.

The Davidians were armed and waiting when the assault team arrived. No one can say with certainty who shot first, but the "surgical strike" erupted into a huge two-hour gunfight punctuated by concussion grenades.

When the smoke cleared, four AFT men and six cultists were dead. Koresh was wounded in the wrist and abdomen.

Under his increasingly unhinged leadership, the Davidians dug in. Out on the perimeter, the ATF was joined by the bomb squad, Texas Rangers, U.S. Marshals, local cops, and the FBI's Hostage Rescue Team (HRT). For the Davidians, the siege was the fulfillment of Biblical prophecy, and they were prepared with stockpiles of food, water, weapons, and ammo. Several experts predicted a Jonestown-like mass suicide if the feds attacked.

Both sides settled in for a standoff that would last 51 days.

During the standoff Koresh promised repeatedly to come out. After Passover… As soon as he'd finished writing his thoughts on some particularly thorny bit of scripture… When God told him to…

A few of his followers—adults, children, puppies—left or escaped but it became clear most of those who remained inside the compound would not or could not leave. Tactics escalated, and, caught in the archetypal no-win situation, the feds continued to screw up.

They shut off the electricity at regular intervals; they placed harsh lights around the place at night; they emptied the diesel tanks; they played loud bad music; they threatened worse.

Finally on April 19th, they acted. At dawn, two large Combat Engineering Vehicles rumbled up to the buildings, punched through the walls and pumped in tear gas. They were backed up by a tank, more choppers, and fighting vehicles.

The Branch Davidian compound near Waco, Texas, ablaze on April 19, 1993. (AP Photo/Ron Heflin)

Eighty-one Davidians, including leader David Koresh, perished as federal agents tried to drive them out of the compound. **Timothy McVeigh** later used the government's actions at Waco as justification for the Oklahoma City Bombing in 1995.

No one is certain how the fires happened. Some claim government weapons started the blaze. The government says either the fires were deliberately set or kerosene lamps were accidentally overturned. Whatever the source, just after noon on that windy day, several buildings burst into flame.

Only nine people made it out. When the flames had died down, they went in and found the bodies, more than 20 of them children. Koresh was among them. He'd either killed himself or been shot by a lieutenant.

In the years since, several conspiracy theories have been put forth. Whatever the truth of them, it's impossible to defend the government's actions, which served to make a bad situation infinitely worse.

One made-for-TV dramatization of the story was produced in 1993, but the most popular film to come out of the siege is the 1997 documentary *Waco: Rules of Engagement*. It presents Koresh as a misunderstood patriot who exercised his second amendment rights and was attacked by Janet Reno's jackbooted thugs.

The best description of the original confrontation is at the Crime Library website. Retired agent Chuck Hustmyre was there, and he tells the story with immediacy and honesty.

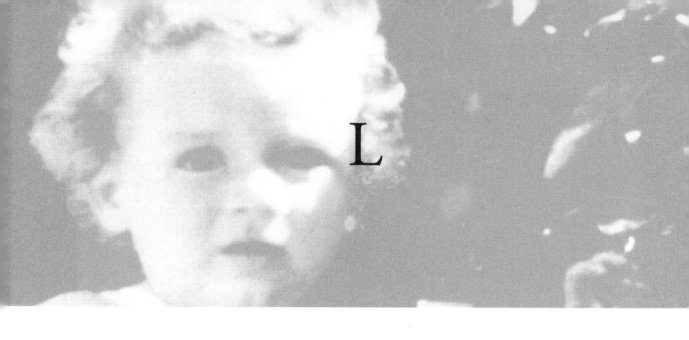

L

Lamm, Herman K. "Baron"

"Baron" Lamm's work has been seen in thousands of movies. Virtually every heist picture contains the big planning scene where the crooks use maps, little models, and props to show how their knockover of the bank or armored car or casino or racetrack, whatever, is supposed to go down. Of course, in the movies, the job never goes according to the plan, but "the plan" is Baron Lamm's contribution to crime and to popular culture.

Lamm—he gave himself the rank of Baron—was a Prussian immigrant. He came to America for the first time at the turn of the twentieth century and worked briefly with **Butch Cassidy**'s Wild Bunch. Sometime before World War I, he returned to Germany to enlist in the Army but was cashiered for cheating at cards.

The Baron hotfooted it back to America where he once again made a living robbing banks and people. Arrested in 1917, he was sent to the Utah State Prison where he had time to reflect and to adapt what he knew of military tactics and organization to the business of armed robbery. The result became known as the Baron Lamm Technique.

The first step was to case the joint, to look it over and draw up a floor plan; to learn who could open the safe; where the guards were stationed; etc. Then he came up with a schedule because time was critically important. When they were committing the robberies, the gang had to leave after a certain number of minutes, no matter much or how little they had collected. Finally, there was the getaway. The Baron favored plain, unobtrusive cars with powerful engines and professional drivers behind the wheel. Escape routes had been carefully researched and maps, called "gits," were kept on the dashboard—in short, a primitive form of Google maps.

After he got out of prison, Lamm put his theories into practice and was a success for several years. On December 13, 1930 his gang hit the Citizens Bank of Clinton, Indiana. Everything went fine until the getaway driver panicked and blew a tire. A comedy of errors followed as the gang stole other mechanically-challenged vehicles and a posse of police and vigilantes closed in on them. The Baron and two other gang members died in the massive shootout that ensued. Two other outlaws, Oklahoma Jack Clark and Walter Dietrich, were captured and sentenced to life at the Michigan City State Prison.

One of the first inmates they met there was a young **John Dillinger**, eager to learn all they could teach him.

Meyer Lansky, under arrest. (AP Photo)

In later years, Johnny D. would be a strong proponent of the Lamm Technique, but all of those wonderful little details—the floor plans, the timetables, the number of steps to the guard station—would find their fullest flower on the big screen.

Lansky, Meyer

The Mafia, Murder Inc.

"The Little Man," as he was respectfully known, was the most successful gangster America has ever produced. Some sources claim he was worth as much as $400 million when he died in 1983. He was 81 years old. Save some youthful indiscretions that led to brief lockups, he did no hard time. Not that the government didn't want him; the feds tried repeatedly to nail Lansky for tax evasion but couldn't make it stick.

He was born Maier Suchowljansky to Jewish parents in Grodno, Poland in 1902. They came to New York where the renamed Meyer Lansky immediately fell in with the wrong crowd. In most versions of the story, Lansky met **Lucky Luciano** when he refused to pay for protection from the older boy and fought back. Another version has young Meyer meeting Luciano and **Ben "Bugsy" Siegel** when he came upon them fighting over a hooker. Whatever the circumstance, the three became fast friends and business partners.

Their first criminal enterprises involved a floating crap game, stealing cars from gangs, then the formation of their own Bug sand Meyer Mob to move booze at the height of Prohibition. The Mob worked as bootleggers and sometimes stole from other bootleggers they'd been hired to protect. They were also available for more specialized violence, specifically murder for hire.

Early on, Lansky fell under the influence of famous gambler **Arnold Rothstein**, the man who fixed the 1919 World Series. He instilled an appreciation of profit over egos in Meyer and Lucky, if not in their friend Bugs. When Rothstein was killed in 1928, they were ready to take the next step.

Their opportunity came in 1931 with the long-running Castellammarese War between crime kingpins **Joe "the Boss" Masseria** and **Salvatore Maranzano**. Luciano worked for Masseria but knew both of the "Mustache Petes" were over the hill. Lansky and Luciano had already had some success at organizing the hoodlums of their generation. Meyer suggested they take a side and kill Masseria, but do it with a hit squad representing different gangs thereby spreading the responsibility. He volunteered his friend Bugsy Siegel to represent him. The others were **Joe Adonis**, **Albert "the Executioner" Anastasia**, and **Vito Genovese**. Luciano lured Masseria to a Coney Island restaurant where the deed was done.

Maranzano crowned himself *cappo di tutti cappi*, boss of bosses, but Lansky and Luciano thought the less-hierarchical organizational structure of the Jewish mobs made more sense. Instead of one boss, there would be several equal bosses. Maranzano remained boss of bosses for about four months before they had him killed.

Afterwards, Luciano was considered to be the first among equals of the New York gangs, but Lansky was always close at hand to advise him. He and Luciano also recruited several members of the old Bug and Meyer Mob to form **Murder, Inc.** in the 1930s, as the enforcement arm of "the Syndicate." The Syndicate was the name the popular press gave to the gangs who controlled gambling, prostitution, loan sharking, drugs, booze, and the union rackets in large cities.

Luciano was busted on a pandering rap—based on perjured testimony, many said—in 1936 by D.A. Thomas Dewey. With Lansky's help, though, he continued to run things from prison. After Luciano's release and deportation in 1945, Lansky continued to let him be the name and face people associated with organized crime while he, Lansky, worked tirelessly behind the scenes to maximize profits for everyone.

It was Lansky who met with Louisiana politician Huey Long, the Kingfish, and arranged to bring slot machines to New Orleans. Lansky also introduced the Kingfish to the joys of numbered foreign bank accounts where he could stash his cut from the one-armed bandits. At the same time, Lansky was moving into other markets too, in Miami and most prominently in Cuba where he and the dictator Fulgencio Batista split the island's gambling profits.

Castro's revolution put a serious kink in the operation, but Lansky wasn't finished. He moved to the Bahamas and created Caesar's Palace casino in Las Vegas with Teamster money.

In 1970 the Justice Department set up a special strike force with the sole aim of getting the Little Man. After they went so far as to try to bust him for a few pills he was carrying without a prescription, he and his wife went to Israel. He tried to claim citizenship there under the Law of Return that grants citizenship to anyone born of a Jewish mother. A long court fight ensued and in 1972 Lansky was forced to return to America.

Old age took its toll with health problems including open heart surgery. Lansky died of cancer in 1983.

Given his reticence, it is not at all surprising Hollywood has been slow to recognize his contribution. In *The Godfather, Part II* (1974), Hyman Roth is a thinly disguised Lansky. He even says the famous line attributed to the Little Man, "We're bigger than U.S. Steel."

Under his own name, Lansky has shown up as a supporting character in most of the fact-based mob movies of recent years, most notably *Havana* (1990), *Mobsters* (1991), *Bugsy* (1991) and *Lost City* (2005).

The 1999 HBO biopic *Lansky* is a bit talky and methodically paced. It doesn't dwell on the horrific violence that was part of Lansky's life, but overall, Richard Dreyfuss makes him a believably serious, fretful character.

Leopold and Loeb

If nothing else, Nathan Leopold and Richard Loeb proved crime ought to be left to those with some natural abilities. Dabblers, even smart gifted dabblers, make stupid mistakes.

Sons of privilege, the young men decided to commit murder, but not as a "thrill kill," as it is often referred. Leopold and Loeb were trying to prove they were Nietzschean supermen, truly superior beings. Wrong.

No one could doubt their intelligence. By the time most teenagers were graduating from high school, they'd finished college. Richard Loeb was the more outgoing, glib and confident. Nathan Leopold was more withdrawn, less comfortable socially. They came from prominent, respected Jewish families.

In the spring of 1924 Leopold was ready to move from his wealthy Chicago suburb to Harvard Law School. He and Loeb had been close friends for years—close emotionally, intellectually, and sexually—and their relationship had developed a sick, secret criminal side. They'd started with petty stuff—shoplifting, false fire alarms, and vandalism.

They graduated to car theft and finally burglary. In November 1923, armed with pistols, they broke into Loeb's fraternity house in Ann Arbor and stole anything they could carry. Afterwards, they decided they were ready for something really serious.

They spent the spring of 1924 planning and practicing a murder of deliberate complexity. They couldn't simply kill a stranger. No, they needed a greater degree of difficulty and so they would begin with a kidnapping. It would have to be someone younger and weaker, and someone with rich parents (like theirs) who could be counted upon to come up with a ransom. First, they had to work through the details of the snatch and payment.

They would need a car, one that couldn't be linked to either of them, and so they developed an elaborate scheme where Leopold registered in a Chicago hotel as Morton D. Ballard, a Peoria salesman, who needed a car. He contacted a rental car agency and, when he was asked for a reference, gave Loeb's number and a false name. Ballard got a glowing recommendation. Add a $50 deposit and a hotel address, and they had a car.

For the ransom payment, they'd send a letter demanding $10,000 be packaged and sealed. They would call the victim's father and tell him to go to a drug store with a public phone. They'd call and send him to a specific train where he would find a letter placed in the telegram slot of a stationery desk in the last car. The letter would tell him precisely where to throw the money from the moving train. They had already practiced that part, too, tossing packages and studying where they landed. To write the ransom note, they used a portable typewriter taken from the Ann Arbor fraternity house loot.

All they needed was a victim. Loeb's neighbor and distant cousin Bobby Franks was the perfect candidate.

They met Bobby on his way home from school and coaxed him into the car. Leopold probably drove. In the back seat, Loeb brained the boy with a chisel and stuffed a gag down his throat, suffocating and killing him. They covered him with a lap robe and drove out of town to wait for nightfall. At a secluded spot, they stripped off his clothes, threw some away, and took the body to a marshy area near Wolf Lake. Leopold was familiar with the place from bird watching trips to the area. They poured hydrochloric acid on Bobby's face to make identification more difficult, and on his penis to hide his circumcision. Then Leopold put on his hip boots, climbed down into the water, and shoved the body into a culvert.

In the darkness, the two truly superior beings left the boy's feet sticking out of the culvert, and Leopold dropped his glasses right next to it.

Later that night, they got rid of the rest of Bobby's things and addressed the ransom letter. They called the distraught Franks and told them their son had been kidnapped and the family would receive instructions.

The next day, Leopold and Loeb cleaned the blood off the back seat of the rental. When the Leopold family chauffeur Sven Englund saw what they were doing, they claimed to be working on a wine stain. He found it curious; he'd never seen either of them work at anything.

Their careful plan proceeded apace. They burned the lap robe outside of town. They pulled the keys from the stolen typewriter and tossed them in a lagoon; the typewriter body in another. Loeb bought a ticket on the Michigan City train and left the note for the Franks in the telegraph slot.

The Franks received the original ransom letter special delivery that morning. Jacob Franks and his friend Samuel Ettelson notified the police and started arrangements for the money. At about the same time, Bobby's body was spotted by a Polish immigrant laborer and was pulled from the culvert by a passing railroad repair crew. They took it directly to the cops. A reporter heard a rumor there had been a kidnapping and made the connection between it and the body. The description of the anonymous child's body did not sound like his son to Jacob Franks, but he sent his brother-in-law to check it out.

While he was gone, Loeb called the Franks house and told Ettelson he was sending a cab. Franks was to take it to a drugstore at 1465 East 63rd Street. Stunned, Ettelson gave the phone to Franks, and Loeb repeated the instructions. Both men were so upset they forgot to write down the address, but before they could do anything, Franks' brother-in-law called and told them the body was Bobby. Leopold and Loeb called the drug store twice before they realized their brilliant plan had gone awry.

After that, things got really crazy.

The next day, Loeb managed to tag along with two newspaper reporters who checked out the drugstore on East 63rd Street. When one of the reporters asked him if he knew the boy, Loeb was quoted as replying, "If I were going to murder anybody, I would murder just such a cocky little son of a bitch as Bobby Franks." Later, he went with them to view the autopsy.

Meanwhile, the cops learned Leopold was a regular visitor to Wolf Lake, and it turned out the glasses they'd found there had a unique feature—the hinges. Only three pairs with those particular hinges had been sold in the Chicago area and one of them belonged to Nathan Leopold. It was a measure of the families' prominence the police decided to question the boys at the LaSalle Hotel, not at headquarters.

The young men were interviewed separately about their activities the night of the kidnapping. At first, there were discrepancies, but the boys were able to smooth those over by saying they'd been out drinking, picked up some girls, you know how it goes. States Attorney Robert E. Crowe, personally in charge of the case and up for reelection in the fall, bought their story, and even took them out to a lavish dinner at the newly opened Drake Hotel. Afterwards, Leopold and Loeb were magnanimous: they told the press they certainly understood how they could have been suspected.

But two reporters learned Leopold was part of a law study group. He usually typed up the notes for everyone in the group, and once he had used a portable typewriter. They got copies of those notes and compared them to the ransom letter. Same typewriter. The cops talked to Leopold's chauffeur who

Bobby Franks, kidnapped and murdered on May 12, 1924, the victim of Nathan Leopold and Richard Loeb's attempt at a "perfect crime." (AP Photo)

told them he'd been working on the car the boys claimed to have used on the night of the kidnapping.

When told what the chauffeur had said, Loeb spilled his guts. When told what Loeb had said, Leopold spilled his guts. The only difference in the gut-spilling was that each claimed the other had actually done the killing. Not that it mattered; they would both swing for it. Or so everyone thought. Initially, the boys confessed and cooperated fully, even enthusiastically with Crowe and the police, revisiting key locations and retrieving evidence they'd hidden. As details were made public, the local papers demanded blood.

Enter the brilliant **Clarence Darrow**. Loeb's father literally fell down on his knees and begged the most famous defense attorney in the country to

Leopold and Loeb in court, awaiting the verdict in their case, 1924. (AP Photo)

represent his son. Darrow agreed, not out of any sympathy with the young killers, but because he was so passionately opposed to the death penalty.

He adopted what appeared at first to be a risky strategy but was really the safest. Everyone assumed he would rely on an insanity defense, but on the first day of the trial, Darrow changed the boys' plea to guilty. By doing so, he eliminated the jury. Instead, the evidence would be presented to a single judge, John R. Caverly, who would decide the punishment. Darrow knew he had no chance with a jury, but he knew Judge Caverly and he knew no one less than 21 years old had ever been executed in Chicago.

He admitted the boys' guilt and did not dispute any of the prosecution's evidence. He saved everything for his closing speech, and the speech—which took three days—is considered the highpoint of his career. It remains an eloquent, heartfelt argument. And it worked. Both Leopold and Loeb were sentenced to life plus 99 years.

That's not the end of the story.

Some claimed later Leopold and Loeb lived luxuriously in the two prisons at Joliet and Stateville where, at various times, they were placed. They had all the books, money, furnishings, booze, and dope they wanted and even private dining in the officers' lounge with specially prepared meals. It may have been the truth while they were being held in Chicago, but things weren't so sweet in the big house.

For Loeb, it ended in 1936. A new inmate, James Day, claimed Loeb attacked him with a straight razor in a bathroom and demanded sex. Miraculously, Day managed to escape the brutal rape, wrestle the razor away from Loeb and inflict 56 wounds, without suffering a scratch himself. The wound that killed Loeb, a slash across the throat, came from behind.

Leopold, with the help of poet Carl Sandburg, was paroled in 1958. He'd been a model prisoner helping other inmates with their education and building the prison library. After his release, he moved to Puerto Rico where he took a job as a lab technician. It paid $10 a month. In 1961 he married Trudi Feldman Garcia de Quevedo. He wrote two books, the memoir *Life Plus 99 Years* (1952) and *A Checklist of the Birds of Puerto Rico* (1963) and was never in trouble with the law again. His wife was by his side when he died in 1971.

Though Leopold and Loeb captivated a nation, their "crime of the century" was completely eclipsed a few years later by the **Lindbergh** kidnapping. They were among the first tandem killers who would become more common later in the twentieth century—Dick Hickock and **Perry Smith**, the **Menendez** brothers, the **Hillside Stranglers**—two people who would probably not have committed murder on their own but somehow were able to talk each other into the act.

Leopold and Loeb also enjoyed extensive press coverage. Meyer Levin, a newspaperman who was tangentially associated with the original case wrote an excellent nonfiction novel about it, *Compulsion* (1956). It was turned into a fine film with Orson Welles as the Clarence Darrow character in 1959. Alfred Hitchcock fictionalized the situation in his experimental suspense film *Rope* (1948) and the material was updated in Barbet Schroeder's *Murder By Numbers* (2002).

None of the film versions, though, have addressed the element of Judaism in the crime. Of course, the killing and the trial reverberated throughout the Jewish community in Chicago and America. How could it happen to their brightest sons? Not so curiously, the fact even the victim was Jewish was seen as something of an ameliorating factor; in the same way years later, Atlantans were relieved there was no racial element in the child murders that took place there.

Lewingdon, Gary and Thaddeus

Nobody knows exactly why Gary and Thaddeus Lewingdon murdered so many people with so much, well, overkill. They stole some stuff, so greed was involved. So were drugs, but given the excessive nature of the killings, chances are the brothers simply enjoyed it.

The story began in November 1977 when they broke into a gun store and stole two .22 caliber Lugers. They fitted the pistols with homemade sound suppressors (silencers) and embarked on a two-man crime wave around Columbus, Ohio. Their first victims were two waitresses who were shot several times as they closed up a café. Right away, a mentally unbalanced young woman made a detailed confession, implicating two other men, and the three of them were arrested.

They struck again two months later, in February 1978, killing a man, his girlfriend, and mother in his suburban home. Again, each victim had been shot repeatedly, and the crime scene was littered with .22 shells.

In April, a man and his four dogs were gunned down in his rural house near Granville, Ohio. Later the same month, a preacher moonlighting as a securi-

ty guard was killed at a private club. By then, the cops had realized something extraordinary was taking place, and had ballistics tests done. They matched.

In May, another man and his wife were slain in their home, both shot in the head several times. Police made the connection with the original murders, the ones they thought had been solved, and realized they were part of the pattern. The three suspects were released. Still, they could find no connection between the victims. They offered a reward but got nothing worthwhile. The killings stopped until December 1978 when a man was shot repeatedly with a .22 while he was working in his garage.

The cops finally caught a break. The last victim's wallet had been taken and his credit card was on the stolen list. On December 9th it showed up at a local department store. Gary Lewingdon, holding the card, was detained until the police arrived.

Taken into custody, he immediately sang loud and long, and ratted out his older brother Thaddeus, who was picked up PDQ and joined Gary in song. It turned out both of them had extensive rap sheets for petty stuff, but nothing to indicate murder.

Within weeks, the brothers were indicted on multiple murder charges and, without much fuss, found guilty on virtually all of them. They were sentenced to several consecutive life sentences.

In prison, Gary went nuts and was transferred to a hospital for the criminally insane. He tried to escape in 1982 but got nowhere. In 1983 he petitioned a court to be allowed to commit suicide. It was denied. Thaddeus died of lung cancer in 1989.

Beyond terrorizing central Ohio, the brothers Lewingdon had no real impact on popular culture—no books, no movies, no heavy metal rock songs. Good.

Lindbergh Kidnapping

It was America's first "crime of the century." H.L. Mencken called it "the greatest story since the Resurrection," and, to this day, people still argue about it. It remains the most important American crime, one that defined a time when gangsters were first being treated as heroes, fascism was on the rise in Europe, and America was entering the darkest days of the Depression.

With the Lindbergh kidnapping, all of the elements fell into place—celebrity, murder, mystery, horror, suspense, solid police work, sloppy police work, a rambunctious trial, a flood of wild revisionism, and a newly-minted media of mass print and electronic communications to feed a steady stream of details to a breathless public. And that public, like the O.J. public, was primed to soak up every word and every rumor.

In 1932 Charles Lindbergh was one of the most famous men on the planet. His 1927 transatlantic flight in the *Spirit of St. Louis* made him an instant celebrity, and when he married stunning blueblood Anne Morrow, they became even more celebrated. With the birth of their son, Charles Jr., they were transformed into a slim, beautiful ideal family. American royalty.

They were never comfortable with their status, however, and quickly learned how dangerous it could be. Anne's sister Constance had been threatened by a would-be kidnapper who demanded $50,000 not to act. The family took the threat seriously enough that Lindbergh spirited her out of town. The police arranged for another young woman to impersonate her and to follow the mailed instructions for a false money drop. Though nothing came of it, kidnapping had become more prevalent on a national scale and the Lindbergh family decided to move out of the public spotlight. They decided to build a large house near the remote central New Jersey town of Hopewell; yet details of their life and the construction of the house were discussed in hundreds of magazine and newspaper articles, radio broadcasts, and newsreels.

At the same time, ex-con Bruno Richard Hauptmann, an occasionally employed carpenter, lived in a Bronx apartment with his wife, Anna. Back home in Germany, Hauptmann, an illegal immigrant, had been a second-story man or burglar who specialized in breaking into houses by climbing to less secure windows on upper floors. One of his convictions was for robbing the home of the mayor of Bernhruch, Germany by using a ladder to get to a window.

Bruno had also robbed two women, at gunpoint, as they pushed baby carriages. After his first incarceration, he'd been arrested again, but before they could lock him up, he stowed away on a ship and made it to America. (Actually, he stowed away three times but was caught twice and sent back.)

On Tuesday, March 1, 1932 Hauptmann found himself at liberty. He was out of work and didn't have to do anything until that evening when he picked up Anna from her job at a bakery/restaurant. He had a car—a green Dodge. He had a ladder he'd constructed in part from lumber in his attic. He may have had a small bottle of ether.

That Tuesday was cold, blustery, and rainy. Hauptmann drove to out to central New Jersey, where the Lindberghs had found they really didn't care for their large new house. They spent weekends there and were planning to move into another mansion, but the baby had a cold and so they decided to stay.

Hauptmann parked on Featherbed Lane near the house. Land around the place had been cleared, and the windows had no curtains so it was easy for him to follow the movements of the people in the house—Mrs. Lindbergh; Betty Gow, the baby's nurse; Ollie and Elsie Whately, the butler and cook; and Lindbergh himself who arrived from New York City about 8:30 p.m., after the 20-month-old baby had been put to bed.

Between 9:00 and 9:30 p.m., Hauptmann carried his ladder to the house, climbed to the nursery window, and opened a faulty shutter. He crawled in, yanked the baby from his crib, left a ransom note, and clambered back down the ladder. At some point in the process, he either fell or dropped the little boy or struck his head and killed him. The detail is relatively unimportant. Hauptmann had always planned to kill the child. One section of a rail split and Hauptmann ditched the ladder about 75 feet from the house. Half a mile farther along, he stripped most of the clothes from the baby's body.

Charles Lindbergh, Jr., shortly before he was kidnapped and killed, 1932.

He drove on back roads for a couple of miles and stopped in the woods north of the little town of Mount Rose. The Lindberghs' house was visible across the valley and, by then, he might have been able to see the lights as they began their frantic search for their son. Hauptmann left the car, made his way through the underbrush, scratched a quick shallow grave and roughly covered the child's body with dirt and leaves. The next day, he mailed his second ransom note to the Lindberghs.

Enter Dr. Joseph F. Condon, a true loose cannon. A retired Bronx teacher, he was deeply moved by Lindbergh's plight when he learned about the kidnapping, and wrote a letter to the *Bronx Home-News* adding $1,000 of his own money to the ransom and volunteering to act as a go-between with the kidnapper. Hauptmann read the letter in the paper and decided to accept the offer, possibly for reasons of proximity. He even wrote Condon's address and telephone number on a closet door frame in his apartment.

On March 9th, Condon received a reply from Hauptmann in the mail. The letter told Condon to contact Lindbergh and to give him a second smaller envelope that was enclosed in the first. Condon telephoned and managed to get through to Lindbergh who sounded unimpressed until the doctor described the curious symbol at the bottom of the letter—two overlapping circles with three holes punched in them. It was the same symbol on the original note. Lindbergh asked Condon to come out to Hopewell immediately.

For the next three weeks, Hauptmann delivered his demands through phone calls and notes, while Condon and Lindbergh placed newspaper ads to answer him. Their remarkable correspondence included increased ransom demands on one side, and proof the child was alive on the other. The first time Hauptmann asked for the money, via a note delivered by a cabbie, it was not ready, and Condon met him late at night in a cemetery to explain. They had a long conversation.

Finally, on April 2nd, Lindbergh had raised the $70,000 ($50,000 in fives and tens, $20,000 in fifties). The bills were gold certificates and their serial numbers were recorded. When Condon met Hauptmann at a second cemetery, the doctor said they had been able to raise only $50,000. Happy he'd been able to save his hero $20,000, Condon turned over the money and Hauptmann gave him a letter saying the baby was on the "boad [sic] Nelly" near Elizabeth Island.

Immediately, Lindbergh and Condon set off in an airplane on a fruitless search to find the imaginary boat "Nelly." Five weeks later, the baby's body was discovered. By then, Hauptmann was already spending the money, spending it carefully. He knew police were monitoring the appearance of the bills, and so he tended to buy small items with individual bills and use the change. (The $20,000 Condon withheld was the $50s, which would have been the easiest to spot.) In April, President Roosevelt took the country off the gold standard. Hoarding of gold was forbidden, though the bills remained legal tender. On the May 1st deadline, Hauptmann cashed in $2,980 at the Federal Reserve Bank using a fake name and address.

Lt. James Finn of the NYPD thought the ransom money was going to be the key to the catching the kidnapper, so he kept track of the bills' appearance on a New York City wall map studded with pins to indicate where the money showed up. He also noticed many of the located bills had curious creases from being folded once lengthwise and then twice more, so they might fit comfortably into a small vest pocket.

At the same time, Arthur Koehler, an expert on wood and trees, was studying Hauptmann's ladder. A detailed examination of the boards told him some had come from one of 1,598 planing mills in operation from Alabama to New York. Eventually, he was able to learn where the lumber had been made and even to pinpoint the store in the Bronx where five parts of the ladder were sold. It was a remarkable piece of scientific detective work.

In the summer of 1932 Hauptmann took a couple of hunting trips, one of them with a guide in Maine. He also decided it was a good time to send his wife Anna to Germany to see if it was safe for him to go back there. She learned the heat was still on for Bruno, and when she returned, she found he was stepping out with young gum-snapping bombshell Gerta Henkel. He told his broker he was ready to leave his wife, but they stayed together. In November, Hauptmann decided to go to the movies.

He saw *Broadway Through a Keyhole* at Loew's Sheridan Square Theater. He paid for his ticket with a $5 bill. Mrs. Cecile Barr was working the booth that night and remembered the way he tossed the folded bill at her. She described the man to Lt. Finn when he checked on the bill the next day.

In 1933 the Hauptmanns took a Florida vacation, the same winter Hauptmann gave his tubercular friend Isidor Fisch a ticket to Germany and $600 to buy reichmarks. By 1934 Hauptmann had run through most of his $5 bills and was dipping into the tens. Lt. Finn decided to concentrate his search on gas stations. After all, they knew the kidnapper had a car.

Lt. Finn sent a letter to all stations asking the pump jockeys to note down the license plate numbers of anyone who paid for gas with a gold certificate. On Saturday, September 15, Hauptmann bought five gallons of ethyl at a Warren-Quinlan station in Manhattan. He paid the 98¢ tab with a $10 gold certificate. Attendant Walter Lyle remembered the letter and wrote "4U-13-41" on the bill. It was identified as part of the ransom money at the

Anne Morrow Lindbergh and baby Charles, Jr. (AP Photo)

bank and the next Tuesday Lt. Finn got a name and address from the Motor Vehicles Bureau: "Richard Hauptmann, 1279 East 222nd Street, the Bronx." That night, cops gathered near the house.

Hauptmann was arrested the next morning soon after he'd left in his car. They found a $20 ransom bill folded in his wallet, and when they searched his house, they discovered new furniture and a $500 console radio. They spent the rest of the day and night interrogating their man and getting handwriting samples from him. They didn't find the bulk of the money until the next day. Hauptmann had hidden it behind a wall in a garage he built near the house. Throughout his questioning, he consistently denied everything until confronted with evidence.

After denying he had any money, he claimed all of the cash had been left to him by his good friend Isidor Fisch last December. They'd been in the fur business together. Fisch had owed him some money, yeah, that was it, and Hauptmann hadn't found this money until just the other day. Had no idea it was there. Fisch had given him a shoebox and he hadn't opened it until it got wet. And where was Fisch? Fisch had gone back to Germany, and, oh, by the way, Fisch died six months ago.

It was a lame, unbelievable story, but it was the only one he had and Hauptmann stuck to it. When he was shown the door frame where he'd written Condon's address and phone number, he couldn't say why it was there, but he did admit to writing it.

Right after his arrest, five witnesses picked Hauptmann out of lineups: the two gas station attendants who'd taken the key ransom bill; the taxi driver who'd delivered the note to Dr. Condon; and a Lindbergh neighbor and a New Jersey student who'd seen a man driving near the house on the day of the kidnapping. The only witness who refused to make an identification one way or the other was Dr. Condon, who, as usual, was enjoying his time in the spotlight and thought he might be able to establish a personal relationship with Hauptmann and persuade him to confess.

Hauptmann had been in custody for a week before the cops got around to searching his attic and found more money, a small pistol, and a short floorboard that matched one rail of the ladder. While he was locked up in a Bronx jail, Hauptmann tried to fashion a shiv and a cell key out of a pewter spoon he pilfered from a meal tray.

The trial began on January 2, 1935 in Flemington, New Jersey, and the hysteria that had been a part of the story from the beginning reached new heights. At the urging of the Hearst newspapers—and with the guarantee of exclusive rights to his story—Hauptmann accepted flamboyant Edward J. Reilly as his attorney. (William Randolph Hearst had longstanding problems with Lindbergh; the pilot had turned down an offer to star in a flying movie with Hearst's mistress Marion Davies, and relations had been strained thereafter.)

In a move that previewed his questionable legal tactics, Reilly immediately printed up stationery with an illustration of the famous ladder. Throughout the trial, he drank heavily, and spent most of his evenings with a series of pulchritudinous babes who claimed to be secretaries there to take dictation. The town of Flemington, of course, was jammed. It was *the* place to be seen. Celebrities like Jack Benny and Clifton Webb showed up. A local restaurant served up Lindbergh Steak and Hauptmann Beans among the other lunch specials. Out on the street, hucksters hawked models of the ladder, locks of the baby's hair, and autographed photos of the parents. Western Electric installed an elaborate teletype that went directly to London, and 168 new telephone lines were fed into the town. At one point, newsreel cameras and microphones were set up surreptitiously in the courtroom, but they were discovered and removed. It wouldn't have been difficult to slip them in. After hours, the courthouse was open and crowds took turns sitting in the participants' chairs.

During the trial itself, New Jersey Attorney General David Wilentz led the prosecution and laid out a solid case based on the witnesses, the money, the ladder, and Hauptmann's handwriting—which may well have been the most damning aspect because the ransom notes, the samples taken by police, and other bits of Hauptmann's writing shared similarities in the shape of letters, repeated misspellings, and such curiosities as his use of a hyphenated "New-York" and placing dollar symbols after numbers. Eight experts testified for the prosecution on the handwriting. One for the defense.

Hauptmann's witnesses were a collection of crackpots—at least one had been institutionalized several times—and ne'er-do-wells who, under cross examination, seldom stayed with their original stories which tended to be pretty flimsy to begin with. After a trial of over 43 days, it took the jury 11 hours to find Hauptmann guilty with no recommendation of mercy.

After the conviction, several people tried to persuade Hauptmann to tell the truth. If he confessed, they argued, his sentence could be reduced to life in prison. He refused. Even at the eleventh hour, when New Jersey governor Harold G. Hoffman (a crook himself, having later admitted to embezzling $300,000)—expressed doubt Hauptmann had acted alone and ordered more investigations—the kidnapper said nothing.

Finally, as the all appeals and subplots played themselves out, radio star Gabriel Heatter set up to broadcast live near the New Jersey State Prison in Trenton where Hauptmann was held. Executioner Robert G. Elliott, who pulled the switch on **Sacco and Vanzetti**, **Ruth Snyder**, and Judd Gray, prepared the electric chair. On April 3, 1936 Bruno Richard Hauptmann was executed.

It was hardly the end of the story.

Lindbergh Kidnapping: The Surrounding Circus

Lindbergh Kidnapping

During and after the investigation of the Lindbergh kidnapping, virtually everyone who was involved became a suspect. Some of those suspicions

were completely legitimate; some were the result of competition among jealous law enforcement agencies; some were simply bizarre. Beyond the official police work, wild fantasies and hoaxes blossomed in fertile conspiratorial soil.

At first, everyone assumed a gang of some kind had pulled off the audacious kidnapping, and it was easily possible they'd had inside help. All of the Lindbergh and Morrow household staffs were thoroughly questioned. Lindbergh himself thought organized crime might be involved, or, if not involved, willing to help find the child as they had the year before in Fritz Lang's cinematic masterpiece *M* (1931).

Understandably, he was open to making overtures to **Owney Madden**, owner of the famous Cotton Club. Lindbergh authorized a couple bootleggers, Salvy Spitale and Irving Blitz, and mid-level mobster Mickey Rosner to make contact with the big time New York gangster. He even gave them a copy of the original ransom note, against the wishes of the cops who thought details might make it easier for hoaxers to impersonate the real kidnapper. Nothing came of it.

At the same time, the intense rivalry between **J. Edgar Hoover**'s Bureau of Investigation (as it was called then) and the New Jersey State Police, led by Col. H. Norman Schwarzkopf (grandfather of the general who led U.S. forces in the first Gulf War) resulted in their withholding evidence from each other.

Swindler and all-round crackpot Gaston Means persuaded gullible Washington socialite Evalyn Walsh McLean that a shadowy criminal mastermind known as "The Fox" was responsible for the crime, and he, Means, could retrieve the child for a mere $100,000. She gave it to him. Later he admitted it was all a lie.

"Commodore" John Hughes Curtis conned an equally gullible group of rich folks in Norfolk, Virginia, into believing the baby was being kept in an offshore boat. He actually went to New Jersey to meet with Lindbergh. In the end, though, he too admitted he'd made it all up.

Violet Sharpe, a maid in the Morrow home, was questioned four times by the New Jersey State Police

Bruno R. Hauptmann, convicted of the Lindbergh kidnapping. (AP Photo)

and told conflicting stories about her conduct right before the kidnapping. Violet drank and slept around even though she was engaged to the Morrows' butler Septimus Banks, which was why she was so evasive. When the cops called and said they were going to conduct a fifth interrogation, she swallowed a dose of cyanide chloride and died immediately.

The Lindberghs themselves were accused of killing their child, supposedly because he was somehow malformed, and then fabricating the kidnap story. Others claimed Anne's sister Elisabeth Morrow killed the child because she was either mad or in love with Charles. Still others said the baby wasn't dead at all. They pointed to the first published posters which stated his height at 29 inches. At autopsy, they said, the body was measured at 33 inches. Both are true; the poster contained a typo—it should have read 2-feet 9-inches.

When Dr. Condon refused to finger Hauptmann after his arrest, the New York police wondered if the two might not be partners and questioned the go-between for several hours.

Famous Burlington County, NJ detective Ellis Parker, miffed he'd been shut out of the investigation by both the feds and state cops, decided Hauptmann was innocent. On the eve of the Hauptmann's execution, Parker kidnapped disbarred lawyer Paul H. Wendel and beat a confession out of him. Of course, Wendel denied the confession as soon as he was free. Eventually Parker and his gang went to jail for it. In fact, they were the first to be convicted under the new federal Lindbergh Law.

The Hauptmann-was-completely-innocent revisionism has continued in waves since the execution. Why would anyone buy such a far-fetched theory in the face of the overwhelming evidence? Partly, it was because Hauptmann never admitted anything, despite all the evidence. And after his execution, Anna became a tireless torchbearer for her departed hubby.

All of the theories and speculations have been grist for a steady stream of books and films. *Scapegoat* (1976) by Anthony Scaduto and *The Airman and the Carpenter* (1989) by Ludovic Kennedy cover the Bruno-was-framed territory pretty well. *The Case That Never Dies* (2004) by historian Lloyd C. Gardner contains the most recent theories, and he had access to many newly released documents.

For my money, though, the two best works on this endlessly complex case are by professor and former F.B.I. agent Jim Fisher. His *The Lindbergh Case* (1994) spins out the whole mad story as a nonfiction novel, and *The Ghosts of Hopewell* (1999), a much shorter book, summarizes key events with admirable brevity, examines the validity of the various theories, and attempts to make some sense of the many contradictions and gaps in the story.

Somewhat remarkably, only two films have been made about the subject, both for television, *The Lindbergh Kidnapping Case* (1976) with Anthony Hopkins as Hauptmann and *Crime of the Century*

(1996) with Stephen Rea. Agatha Christie used a fictionalized version of the crime as the background for *Murder on the Orient Express* (1974).

Doubtless, more books and films will follow because the Lindbergh kidnapping is truly a case that will never die. Like the Kennedy assassination, the idea that a single otherwise unremarkable man could topple a godlike figure flies in the face of our assumptions about the natural order of things. The final truth—that we're all vulnerable—continues to surprise.

List, John

John Emil List became famous not so much for his crimes (appalling as they were), but for his capture—TV got him.

A midlevel executive who had failed at a number of positions, List was also a devout Bible-reading Christian, an upright citizen so respectable he was never seen without coat and tie, even when he mowed his lawn. When financial straits and his wife's serious health problems became too much to bear, List used his religious conviction to concoct a bizarre rationalization. He could not commit suicide because if he did, his soul would be damned to hell. If, however, he were to murder his family, God in his infinite mercy, would forgive him and they would all go to heaven. Problem solved!

In 1971 List was in a difficult situation. Six years before he'd moved his family—wife Helen; kids Patricia, John Jr. and Frederick; and his mother Alma—to the pleasant little burg of Westfield, New Jersey after he had found a good job at the First National Bank. He'd even used his mother's money to buy "Breeze Knoll," a grandiose mansion complete with a ballroom and a Lewis Comfort Tiffany stained glass ceiling. Then he was fired. Again. It had happened before.

For months, List had been pretending to go to work, only to spend the day reading at the train station. Meanwhile, Helen was in terrible health from the combined effects of prescription drug abuse, alcoholism, and recently diagnosed syphilis. Just as important to List, she refused to go to church with

him. Fitting into the spirit of the times, daughter Patricia was rebelling; she was drinking and showing an interest in the occult. Then First Federal Savings & Loan initiated foreclosure proceedings on the house. It was all more than he could bear.

List made careful plans, telling the kids' teachers they were going on vacation. On November 9, 1971 he essentially stalked and killed his family. In the morning, after the children had left for school, he took out his pistol and shot Helen as she ate breakfast in the kitchen. Then he climbed the stairs to his mother's apartment and shot her.

A bit later, Patty called from Duke's Deli and said she wasn't feeling good. Could he pick her up? He drove to the deli and when they got back to the manse, he hurried inside first. Then lurking at the door, he shot her from behind as soon as she came in. He did the same a few hours later with Fred, but John Jr. got home early and surprised his father. The boy put up a fight. It took ten shots for List to kill him. At some point during the day, he also killed the family dog, Tinkerbelle.

Then he sat down and wrote out a full confession addressed to his pastor. The next day, with $2,500 in cash, he drove away. His 1963 Chevy Impala was found in long-term parking at Kennedy airport. As soon as the bodies were discovered (about a month later), New Jersey police began their search for List and a grand jury indicted him on five counts of murder and fleeing across state lines.

But List had planned his getaway as carefully as he'd planned the killings. He vanished.

With the new name Robert P. Clark and a new Social Security number, he moved across the continent to Golden, Colorado near Denver. He lived in a trailer and worked as a nightshift cook at a motel. For a time, as before, he prospered—got a better job, bought a used VW, joined a new church, met another woman, Delores Miller. The years passed. In 1985 he and Delores married and the old patterns reappeared. List was fired from his job, tried to start his own financial consulting business, and failed. More money problems. Delores grew unhappy.

In February 1987 Wanda Flanery picked up a copy of a cheap tabloid, the *Weekly World News*, in the supermarket checkout line. She read an article about the List family murders and thought the killer bore a spooky resemblance to her neighbor Bob Clark, down to the details of the scar behind his ear and his penchant for wearing a coat and tie everywhere. When the enquiring mind showed the piece to her friend Delores, she seemed curious and said she'd ask her hubby about it. But Delores did nothing. Soon thereafter, the Clarks moved east to Richmond, Virginia and a new job for Bob.

The tabloids were not the only ones interested in List. New Jersey police detective Jeffrey Paul Hummel and Captain Frank Marranca still worked the case, though there had been no developments. Through their efforts List was brought to the attention of producers of the new TV show *America's Most Wanted*, where unresolved crimes were dramatized and viewers urged to phone in tips. Not surprisingly, List himself was a regular viewer but he missed the broadcast on May 21, 1989 when he was featured.

Wanda Flanery didn't miss it. Back in Colorado, her suspicions about her ex-neighbor were resurrected and she persuaded her son-in-law to call the show and give them the Clarks' Virginia address. Eleven days later, the FBI arrested List at his job.

In short order he was extradited to New Jersey, tried, convicted, and sentenced to five consecutive life terms in the state penitentiary where, as of this writing, he still resides, an enfeebled old man. In 2002 he was interviewed by Connie Chung on the show *20/20 Downtown*.

List's story was turned into the 1993 TV film, *Judgment Day*, where he was played by **Robert Blake**, who would be moved to desperate straits in his own difficult marriage to Bonny Lee Bakley. List has been the subject of three books, *Thou Shalt Not Kill* (1990) by Mary Ryzuk, *Death Sentence* (1990) by Joe Sharkey, and *Righteous Carnage* (1991) by

Timothy Benford and James J. Johnson. In an epilogue to the latter book, the authors note List had actually been living beneath the solution to his financial problems. The Tiffany ceiling in his New Jersey manse was a masterpiece that could have been sold and covered all of his debts. The ceiling was destroyed when the house burned in 1972.

On film, List's character might have been a partial inspiration for Patrick Bergin's abusive husband in the Julia Roberts vehicle *Sleeping with the Enemy* (1991). Writer Christopher McQuarrie, a New Jersey native, has said List was the basis for the enigmatic and formidable Keyser Soze in *The Usual Suspects* (1995).

The List story was also a springboard of sorts that inspired crime novelist Donald Westlake to write the brilliant script for *The Stepfather* (1987). Westlake takes the idea a step further by imagining his character Jerry Blake as a serial family slayer. The film begins with his List-like elimination of one family then follows his relationship with a new wife and kids. Actor Terry O'Quinn is letter perfect in the role. His physical resemblance to the real List adds another level of creepiness to an already bizarre and frightening horror story.

Longet, Claudine

Claudine Longet's biography could have been written by Jackie Collins.

She was a waif-like French gal with big eyes and a breathy voice who arrived in America to be a dancer in the Follies Bergère review at the Tropicana Hotel in Las Vegas. In 1961 she met singer Andy Williams there and sparks flew. They were married on Christmas. She was 19; he was 34. A year later, his recording of Henry Mancini's *Moon River* went to the top of the charts. It and other hits led to his headlining an easygoing and extremely popular TV variety show. She often appeared with him and their three children. One son, Bobby, was named for their good friend Robert Kennedy.

Longet was a singer, too, with a few light pop hits and albums to her credit. She also appeared in more than 50 television shows in the 1960s and early '70s. Her only notable film role was in Blake Edwards' *The Party* (1968) opposite Peter Sellers.

In 1969 Longet and Williams separated. A few years later, she shacked up with Vladimir "Spider" Sabich, a competitive skier known as much for his looks as his athletic abilities. Longet and the kids joined him in an Aspen, Colorado chalet. But all was not sweetness and light for the golden couple. He had told friends he was ready to move on and for her and the kids to move out. Later, she would say it wasn't true; they were as profoundly in love as ever.

In either case, on the afternoon of March 21, 1976 Sabich returned from a day on the slopes and prepared to take a shower. Longet walked into the bathroom with a .22 pistol. It went off. He was hit in the stomach. Bleeding heavily, he died in the ambulance on the way to the hospital.

Williams joined Longet immediately and stayed with her throughout the ensuing trial.

The prosecution had a difficult case because two key pieces of evidence were ruled inadmissible. The police had demanded Longet, who said she'd been drinking that afternoon, take a blood test. Supposedly, it also revealed cocaine. Then they confiscated the diary in which she described the personal problems she and Sabich were experiencing. But the cops hadn't gotten a court order for the blood test or a warrant for the diary. Neither was mentioned at the trial, so it didn't take long.

Longet was found innocent of manslaughter but guilty of criminally negligent homicide—a misdemeanor. The sentence was a $250 fine and 30 days in the county jail to be served whenever it suited her.

After a Mexican vacation with her defense lawyer Ron Austin—who immediately left his wife and family and moved in with his comely ex-client—Longet served her time, most of it on weekends.

In 1978 the Sabich family filed a wrongful-death suit against her. It was settled out of court with a confidentiality clause that kept her from ever writing a book about the killing.

Claudine Longet (with Peter Sellers from *The Party*, 1968) eight years before the shooting death of Vladimir "Spider" Sabich. (Kobal)

As of this writing, she and Austin continue to live happily ever after in Aspen.

It has been widely reported the Rolling Stones' 1980 *Emotional Rescue* album contained a provocative song entitled "Claudine." It was lawyered out of the album but has been bootlegged extensively. She was also the subject of a *Saturday Night Live* skit, made in 1977 when the show was at its early peak. The title, "The Claudine Longet Celebrity Ski Shoot" says it all.

Lucas, Henry Lee

No one will ever know exactly how many people Henry Lee Lucas killed. It's certainly not the 600-plus he "confessed" to; he only did that to embarrass the police and put himself in the spotlight.

Lucas came from a childhood that sounds like the beginning of a bad joke. With a violent hooker mom and a legless dad, he and his eight siblings grew up in squalid poverty in the southwest Virginia mountains. Later, Lucas would tell nightmarish tales of sexual abuse, bestiality, and starvation. As a teenager, he lost an eye due to his mother's neglect. In 1954 he was arrested for burglary in Richmond. After his release in 1959, he moved in with his sister in Michigan. Creepy Mom showed up there, too, and demanded he come back to Virginia with her.

On the night of January 11, 1960 mother and son went to a bar where they got liquored up and angry with each other. They argued and when they got back to his sister's place, Lucas pulled out his pocket knife and stabbed his mother to death.

Five days later, a state trooper picked him up in Ohio. Lucas confessed to the killing and to necrophilia with the body. After hearing about his upbringing, the court convicted him of second degree murder. Ten years and two attempted suicides later, Lucas was paroled. Immediately, he got into trouble again, was arrested for attempted kidnapping, and was sent back inside.

Released again in 1975, Lucas drifted. Sometime around then he met Otis Toole, a transvestite arsonist. They soon became fast friends. Otis introduced new pal Henry to his retarded young niece Becky Powell. The bizarre ménage a trois lived with Toole's mother until she died in 1981.

Lucas and Becky took off and lived briefly with the elderly Kate Reid in Ringgold, Texas before they moved to a church in Stoneburg, Texas. They stayed there until 1982 when, according to Lucas, Becky became homesick for Florida and left. Not long after, Mrs. Rich disappeared, too.

Ten months later, the Texas cops nailed Lucas on a weapons bust. After being jailed for several days, he confessed to murdering Becky Powell and Mrs. Rich. He said he'd burned the older woman's body in an outdoor stove and buried the girl in a field.

Human remains consistent with his story were found in both places.

At the arraignment for the Rich murder things got really weird—even by Lucas' standards. He told the judge he had murdered 100 women. After he was found guilty at the trial, the confessions continued and he brought Otis Toole into the act. Otis, he said, had helped him find victims on interstate highways. Toole, locked up for arson in Florida, eagerly concurred. Lawmen from sea to shining sea flocked to Texas to see if Lucas might be responsible for any of their unsolved homicides.

Helpful Henry was only too happy to oblige. He was released from his cell to use the phone; he was able to travel—life was good. His claims became even more outlandish. He and Otis added cannibalism to their resume and said they belonged to a satanic cult. Otis also claimed to have killed six-year-old Adam Walsh, son of John Walsh, host of *America's Most Wanted* on television. Nothing came of it. Toole died in prison of cirrhosis of the liver.

Eventually Lucas' confessions led to another Texas murder trial for a girl known only as Orange Socks. In the midst of it, Lucas began to recant. No dice. He was found guilty and sentenced to death.

Before it was all over, Lucas would admit to one writer he'd killed only three people—his mother, Becky, and Mrs. Rich. But by then Henry Lee Lucas had become the stuff of legend. He was the face of our new boogieman, the serial killer. Then-Texas governor George W. Bush commuted his death sentence to life. Lucas died in prison in 2001 of heart failure.

In 1986 filmmaker John McNaughton took the bare bones of the Lucas, Otis, and Becky story and made *Henry: Portrait of a Serial Killer*, a dark and disturbing horror movie (originally given an X rating by the MPAA, it was later released on videotape without a rating). In the title role, Michael Rooker is unnervingly detached but believable. The film has a naturalistic, documentary quality that makes the action all the more impressive.

McNaughton taps directly into our fears of men who appear to be completely ordinary but are really sick sexual predators. The original was followed by an inferior sequel. Whatever the literal "truth" of Henry Lee Lucas' crimes, McNaughton's film remains one of the most cold and frightening cinematic horrors ever made, with an unexpected conclusion.

Lucchese, Gaetano "Tommy," or "Three-Finger Brown"

Tommy Lucchese's importance in the creation of the Mafia far outstrips his notoriety. He never achieved the legendary status of his contemporaries **Frank Costello** or **Lucky Luciano**.

Like them, he emigrated from Italy to New York near the beginning of the twentieth century and essentially became a street kid after his father threw him out. His right index finger was mangled when he had a job in a machine shop, and he gave up on honest labor. A few years later, when he was being booked on auto theft charges, the arresting officer gave him the nickname of "Three-Finger Brown" after a famous major league pitcher. It stuck.

Lucchese joined Luciano and Costello and went to work for **Joe "the Boss" Masseria**. As part of his rackets, he got a cut of all the kosher chickens sold in New York, and was also heavily involved in narcotics and loan sharking in the garment industry. (In the depths of the Depression, particularly usurious "knockdown" loans earned him a cool $5 million a year.) Throughout his career, he made significant donations to both the Democratic and Republican parties.

During the Castellammarese wars of the late 1920s Lucchese joined Luciano in taking Masseria's side against rival don **Salvatore Maranzano**. When Luciano decided to make his move, orchestrating the murder of Masseria in May 1931, Lucchese stuck with him. A few months later, when it was time for Luciano to consolidate his power, he turned to Lucchese to finger rival Maranzano for the Jewish hit team that killed Masseria.

Afterwards, Lucchese became second in command of the Gagliano family. It was one of the five families who shared control of criminal activities in New York. The Gagliano gang was universally considered as the most profitable and peaceful of the five. When Tommy Gagliano died of a heart attack, Lucchese took over in an orderly transfer of power.

Lucchese always maintained a low profile, so low that in 1943 he was able to shepherd a bill through the U.S. Congress that made him a naturalized citizen. Around the same time, New York legislators had Lucchese's criminal record erased. His 1920s convictions for car theft and bookmaking simply vanished, and the parole board gave him a "Certificate of Good Conduct."

Officially rehabilitated, Lucchese prospered and lived respectably in the tony community of Lido Beach on Long Island. He died of cancer in 1967 and had one of the largest funerals, even by gangland standards, anyone could imagine.

Befitting his lifelong desire to avoid the spotlight, Lucchese has been poorly represented in gangster films. He's a minor character in two TV miniseries, *The Gangster Chronicles* (1981) and *Love, Honor, and Obey: The Last Mafia Marriage* (1993).

Luciano, Charles "Lucky"

"Lucky" Luciano was the man who organized organized crime in America. He got rid of the last of the "Mustache Petes"—who'd been running things in New York's Italian gangs in the early years of the twentieth century—and who had mired the business in near-continuous internecine war. Luciano's goal was simple: he didn't want to get mad; he didn't want to get even; he wanted to get rich.

Born Salvatore Lucania in Sicily in 1897, he moved to New York with his family when he was ten. Right away, he started shoplifting and charging the littler kids a penny or two for "protection." As the story goes, one kid refused to fork it over and put up a hell of a fight when Luciano showed him what he needed protection from. The kid was

Reputed mob boss Charles "Lucky" Luciano in Naples, Italy, 1946. (AP Photo)

Meyer Lansky. He became Luciano's lifelong friend and advisor, and he introduced the older boy to the ambitious, wild-eyed **Ben "Bugsy" Siegel.** The three of them went a long way together.

As Luciano grew in wisdom and stature, his criminal enterprises became more lucrative. Working with the Five Points gang, he got into dope peddling, bootlegging, gambling, and prostitution. By the mid-1920s Luciano controlled all of the commercial sex in Manhattan. He collected half of the take from the most expensive courtesans and call girls, and the cheapest hookers.

In the late '20s war broke out between Luciano's boss **Joe Masseria** and the newly arrived Sicilian **Salvatore Maranzano.** Though Luciano claimed to be completely loyal, Maranzano tried to coax him and the other Young Turks to his side. For a year,

the two gangs jockeyed for an advantage, killing off low-level members of each other's organizations. Though Maranzano's position was solidifying, no end was in sight.

Luciano earned the nickname Lucky one night in 1929 when he was taken for the proverbial ride. For years all he would say was that four guys jumped him on a street near the Hudson River and threw him into the back of a big black touring car. For the next few hours, they beat him within an inch of his life. Slashed his face, cut his throat (but missed the jugular), stabbed him with an ice pick. He was dumped on Staten Island near dawn. A beat cop found him and took him to the hospital where he recovered and kept his mouth shut. Thereafter, he was Charlie Lucky.

Decades later when they talked about their lives to writers, Luciano and Meyer said the beating was administered by Maranzano's men at an arranged meeting in a warehouse. When Luciano didn't respond with proper enthusiasm to the Sicilian's overtures, his henchmen came out of the shadows. Maranzano apparently believed he had intimidated Luciano into taking his side. For a time, it appeared he had.

In May 1931 Luciano and Meyer orchestrated the killing of Masseria at a Coney Island restaurant. Luciano took him there and was in the bathroom when four of his associates gunned down the boss.

With his rival gone, Maranzano proclaimed himself the boss of bosses (*cappo di tutti cappi*) and anointed Charlie Lucky his second-in-command. Maranzano wasn't stupid; he knew Luciano was ambitious, and so even while he was promoting the younger man, he hired hitman **Mad Dog Coll** to kill him. Luciano wasn't stupid either, and was quicker than Maranzano. On September 10th Lucky sent four men to the new boss' private offices. They identified themselves as Treasury agents and as soon as they'd isolated their target, they killed him. Mad Dog kept the $25,000 down payment Maranzano had made and did nothing.

Charlie Lucky was then in charge of New York, though he took pains to say he was only one boss, not *the* boss. Working from a luxurious suite in the Waldorf-Astoria Hotel, he consolidated his power by getting the various gangs to cooperate. Until then, the Mustache Petes hadn't trusted the Jewish or Irish gangs and refused to have anything to do with them. Luciano understood there was enough to go around.

The various gangs controlled illegal booze, sex, drugs, gambling, numbers, and union rackets. If they could simply agree on the division of the spoils, they could stop killing each other and concentrate on making money. "The Syndicate" was born (it was the name most often in the popular press; it was also called "the Committee" or "the Combination").

For several years, it worked. They all grew wealthy, or, more accurately, wealthier. But then hotshot prosecutor Thomas E. Dewey decided to get tough on crime, particularly on prostitution. He leaned on the madams and working girls and got some of them to rat out the big guy.

Curiously, at the same time, Luciano may have saved Dewey's life. When he started putting the heat on the mob, **Dutch Schultz** wanted to get rid of him. Even though his Syndicate brethren knew killing such a prominent public figure would be the worst thing they could do, the Dutchman would not be dissuaded. He swore he would take care of Dewey himself. On Charlie Lucky's orders, three of Bugsy's boys popped Dutch in the men's room of the Palace Chophouse in Newark, New Jersey.

Dewey didn't care. He took his evidence to a grand jury and Luciano was indicted on 90 counts. Dewey got his convictions in 1936 and sent Charlie Lucky to Clinton Prison in Dannemora for a 3-50 stretch.

Five years later, providentially for Luciano, Japan bombed Pearl Harbor and America went to war. Early in 1942 the French liner *Normandie* was being converted to a troop carrier in New York harbor. One night, it went up in flames and was utterly destroyed. Officials in Washington didn't know the cause. It might have been an accident or it might have been the work of Axis saboteurs. Whatever the case, the gangs were so powerful on the docks no one could guarantee security but them. If the government wanted to be certain, they'd have to deal with the gangsters. And even though he was in prison, Luciano was still in charge of the gangs. He was the man to see.

When the feds went to Dannemora, Charlie Lucky said he'd feel more talkative in more comfortable surroundings, something like Great Meadow Prison, the country club of penal institutions.

Once he was installed at Great Meadow and granted easier access to his unincarcerated associates, Luciano agreed to play ball. Yes, he said, he would personally see to it everyone on the docks gave 110-percent to the war effort. And a year later, Luciano did all he could to see that his contacts in Sicily helped the Allied invasion of the island.

The irony in all this is that it was Luciano who had ordered the burning of the *Normandie* in the first place. Actually, his pal **Albert Anastasia** came up with the idea and made sure it was carried out, but Charlie Lucky was behind it.

When the war was over, Luciano was paroled on the condition he be deported to Italy and never leave. Lucky agreed, but no sooner had he ensconced himself in Rome's palatial Quirinale Hotel, that he decamped for Havana. In the late 1940s Cuba was Meyer Lansky's playground. He ran the booze and babes, and shared the wealth with dictator Fulgencio Batista.

Luciano called a meeting of American mobsters, and he still had enough power that they all joined him in Cuba. At the time, Bugsy Siegel was stuck in the prolonged and expensive construction of the Flamingo Hotel and Casino in Las Vegas. When Luciano and the rest demanded he repay some of the millions he'd borrowed to build his dream, Bugsy went batty. Yelling, cursing, recriminations— the Bugster left angry. Charlie Lucky ordered the removal of his old friend, and it was done.

Once U.S. officials learned Luciano had left Italy, they hit the ceiling and ordered him back. No dice.

He stayed in Italy for the rest of his life and continued to control heroin traffic with the Corsican gangs and their French connection in Marseilles, though his importance in America waned in the '50s.

In the early 1960s Luciano entered negotiations with film and TV producer Martin Goshe to bring his life to the screen. They ran into problems with Lansky and the other remaining bosses, and so Charlie Lucky put the movie deal on hold and told his life story to Goshe. Those talks became the basis for the book Gosch wrote with Richard Hammer, *The Last Testament of Lucky Luciano*. It was published in 1974, twelve years after Luciano was felled by a heart attack in the Rome airport. He is buried in St. John's Cemetery in Queens, New York.

Lucky continued to be a significant figure in movies and books, second only to Capone among gangsters. In popular entertainment, he is the embodiment of the sleek, sexy gangster—fashionably dressed, erudite, charming most of the time but ready to order murder when necessary. The first dramatization of his arrest and trial was 1937's *Marked Woman* with Bette Davis. Eduardo Ciannelli played gangster Johnny Vanning. Bogie was the DA who brought him down.

Under his real name, Luciano has appeared in more than 20 films and TV shows. Among the most important are Anthony LaPaglia in *Lansky* (1999), Angelo Infanti in *The Valachi Papers* (1972) Gian Maria Volontè in *Lucky Luciano* (1974), Christian Slater in *Mobsters* (1991) and Andy Garcia in *Hoodlum* (1997).

Luetgert, Adolph

Let's be clear about one thing right up front: Adolph Luetgert did not kill his wife and grind her up and package her with his sausage. True, he did dispose of the body in his sausage factory, but there's no evidence the unhappy Mrs. Luetgert ever made it into the bratwurst. Still, that was the rumor in 1897 and sales plummeted.

A German immigrant, Luetgert was a man of vast size and appetites. He weighed more than 250 pounds while Louisa (also called Louise) couldn't top five feet in high heels. She was the second Mrs. Luetgert, and by the time she moved in with Adolph, his sausages were popular throughout Chicago. Unfortunately, the business had run into hard times and his personal life was a mess.

Adolph was screwing around with three other women: May Simmerling was Louisa's niece and also worked in their home; Agatha Tosch ran a saloon with her husband; and wealthy Christine Feldt was his "official" mistress.

Inevitably, Louisa found out and went ballistic. Loud fights between them were commonplace in the neighborhood. Their house was located right next door to the factory. At various times, Adolph was seen choking the little woman and chasing her down the street with a revolver in his paw.

He finished her off on May 1st. A few weeks before, he had bought more than 300 pounds of highly caustic potash and 50 pounds of arsenic. He ordered his workers to melt the potash in a big vat in the basement. On the night in question, he went to the factory and twice told the night watchman to leave and fetch things from a nearby drug store. Around the same time, 10:30 p.m. or so, two people saw Luetgert leading the missus through the alley between home and factory. It was the last anyone saw of Louisa in the flesh, as it were.

A few days later, workers reported a brown, sticky glue-like slime on the basement floor near the big vat. Luetgert told them to clean it up and to throw away any big pieces they might come across.

When Louisa's brother Diedrich Bicknese came to visit that same week, Adolph said the little lady had vamoosed. He had no idea where she was, but, fearing scandal, he'd hired a couple of detectives to track her down.

Bicknese checked with friends she might have turned to, and, when he found nothing, went to the Chicago cops. Police Captain Herman Schuettler knew about the Luetgerts' stormy relationship.

When he learned about the goop at the vat, he ordered a thorough search of the sausage works.

When they drained the vat, they found several bone fragments that later turned out to be human, and two gold rings, one with the engraved initials LL. Both rings were known to be Louisa's, and because the arthritic joints of her fingers had swollen, she'd been unable to take them off for years. Luetgert was charged with murder.

Two of his girlfriends testified against him. Mrs. Feldt did the most damage. She said right before Louisa disappeared, Adolph had given her $4,000 to hold for him, and the day after, he'd presented her with a blood-stained knife.

Despite the overwhelming circumstantial evidence, the first jury could not reach a verdict. At his second trial, Luetgert was found guilty and sentenced to life. He died in Joliet Prison in 1911.

Both trials were front-page news worldwide. Though Luetgert has been largely forgotten today outside of the Midwest, Robert Loerzel tells his story in brilliant detail in *Alchemy of Bones* (2003). For all its macabre details, the case has never been filmed.

M

MacDonald, Jeffrey

Early on the morning of February 17, 1970, six months after the Tate-La Bianca murders, Dr. Jeffrey MacDonald killed his pregnant wife and his two young daughters. It happened in their house in Fayetteville, North Carolina at the Fort Bragg Army base.

As the jury saw it, the Green Beret beat his wife Colette with a club and stabbed her. When his older daughter, Kimberly (age five) tried to intervene, he clubbed her and slashed her throat. Finally, he stabbed two-year-old Kristen with a knife and an ice pick. He may have been in an amphetamine-induced rage. When he was finished, he scrawled the word "pig" on the wall in blood, telephoned for help, and gave himself a few wounds, one puncturing his lung.

McDonald later claimed the family was attacked by four hippies, one a woman, who said, "Acid is groovy. Kill the pigs." When the Army looked into the killings in an Article 32 hearing, roughly the equivalent of a civilian grand jury, they found insufficient evidence to charge the doctor. Privately, Army investigators disagreed.

When Colette's stepfather Freddy Kassab watched his son-in-law's appearance on the *Dick Cavett Show* on December 15, 1970, he was pro-

foundly troubled. Until then, he had believed in MacDonald's innocence and supported him, but when he heard the man complaining about how he had been mistreated and saying nothing about his slaughtered family, Kassab changed his mind.

He and Army investigator Peter Kearns refused to let the matter go and in 1975 MacDonald was indicted by a North Carolina grand jury. Four years of legal wrangling over double jeopardy and the right to a speedy trial followed before MacDonald was finally brought to court in July 1979. During that time, he met writer Joe McGinniss and approached him about writing a book. After much discussion, MacDonald agreed to let McGinniss have complete access to him and his lawyers, and to write a book about the murders and the trial.

At first, McGinnis, like so many others who knew him, was charmed by MacDonald. Here, after all, was an intelligent, well-spoken, attractive Princeton graduate. How could he possibly have committed such unspeakable crimes?

But as the state laid out its case, detailing the patterns of the bloodstains and connecting the fiber evidence, particularly a shirt MacDonald claimed had been wrapped around his hands on the night of the murders, McGinniss was persuaded his subject

Capt. Jeffrey MacDonald at Ft. Bragg, NC, headed to a hearing regarding his murder charges, 1970. (AP Photo)

was guilty. So was the jury. They convicted Mac-Donald on two charges of second degree murder for Colette and Kimberly, and on first-degree for Kristen. They sentenced the doctor to three consecutive life sentences.

More appeals on technical grounds were mounted (MacDonald's case has been before the U.S. Supreme Court more than any other.) His supporters pointed to an unstable young woman, Helena Stoeckley, as a possible suspect. Before she died in 1983, she told several conflicting stories about her activities that particular night in 1970.

McGinniss's book about the subject, *Fatal Vision*, became a bestseller and MacDonald sued him over it. After maddeningly complicated legal maneuvering, described in the epilogue to the 1989 paperback edition, they settled out of court.

Dr. MacDonald remains in prison, still maintaining his total innocence. In March 2006 DNA analysis revealed that a hair found in his wife's hand came from him.

In 1984 McGinniss' book became a television miniseries. Karl Malden won an Emmy for his portrayal of Freddy Kassab.

Madden, Owney "the Killer"

Owney Madden can be seen as the token WASP among the Italian, Irish, and Jewish gangs that flourished in New York in the 1920s and '30s. But ethnicity counted for little back then; Owney was as tough as any of them, particularly in his younger days. His nickname, "the Killer," was for real.

Born in England, he immigrated with his family to the Hell's Kitchen neighborhood in 1903 and became a leader in the Gophers gang as a teenager, knocking down $200 a day through robbery and extortion. His fighting skills with blunt objects—lead pipes, saps, brass knuckles—and pistols were legendary. He was also a horny, jealous kid. He killed William Henshaw, a clerk who made a pass at a girl Owney fancied. He shot the young man on a trolley in plain sight of a dozen witnesses. Henshaw identified him before he died. The witnesses melted away.

As the Gophers grew more powerful, they also became more confrontational with their rivals the Hudson Dusters. Things came to a head in 1914 when Owney and Duster honcho Patsy Doyle fell for the same girl, Freda Horner. When Owney gained the fair maiden's affections, Patsy began ratting out Gopher operations to the cops.

Owney arranged an ambush, getting word to the Duster that Freda wanted to see him at an Eighth Avenue saloon. When Patsy showed up, Owney put three slugs in him. At the murder trial, the faithless Freda turned state's evidence and fingered him. Owney got ten-to-twenty at Sing Sing but was paroled in January 1923.

Upon his release, Owney found a new world. The Gophers' ranks had been depleted and the arrival of Prohibition had changed everything. The joint, however, had given Owney some maturity.

He went into the illegal booze biz and became a bootlegger with **Dutch Schultz**'s outfit. He had some legitimate enterprises, too, including a laundry service and ownership of the legendary Cotton Club in Harlem. He ran the club with his partner Frenchy DeMange.

When the Dutchman went to war with rival bootlegger and full-time head case **Vincent "Mad Dog" Coll**, it was Frenchie that Coll kidnapped and ransomed back to Madden to raise funds for his legal representation. Mad Dog had inadvertently gunned down a five-year-old boy and needed the best lawyer money could buy. After Coll was acquitted, he called Madden. Owney kept him on the phone and had the call traced so Dutch's men could nail him in a phone booth. Good-bye, Mad Dog.

When Prohibition was repealed, Owney and Frenchie got into the fight game. They managed the careers and, when necessary, fixed the outcomes for such luminaries as Primo Carnera, Rocky Marciano and Max Baer. Suspicions arose after Carnera won the heavyweight championship. Madden decided it was time to make another career change and "retired" to Hot Springs, Arkansas. He opened the Hotel Arkansas casino and spa in 1935 and others later. With its *laissez faire* attitude toward men who might have problems with the law in other cities, the town was already a favorite watering hole for all of the mob guys. **Lucky Luciano** and **Meyer Lansky** were invested in it, and Charlie Lucky visited regularly.

Owney made sure the right payoffs were made and kept all of the gears running smoothly. Yes, there was that time when Luciano was extradited from the town to face a New York pandering rap, but, mostly, Hot Springs was a swell place. Owney became one of its more respected citizens. In 1943 he married the postmaster's daughter and became an American citizen. He died a wealthy man, of natural causes, in 1965.

The wild days of Madden's youth have not yet been filmed, though they certainly have all the raw material for a great movie. As supporting characters in Francis Ford Coppola's *Cotton Club* (1984), Owney (Bob Hoskins) and Frenchie (Fred Gwynne) almost steal the show. Owney is also the main character and narrator of Michael Walsh's novel *And All the Saints*, and shows up as Owney Maddox in Stephen Hunter's novel, *Hot Springs* where things turn out quite differently for him.

Mafia, The ("Cosa Nostra," "The Syndicate," "The Commission," Organized Crime)

There are endless arguments about when the Mafia began—nineteenth century, thirteenth, earlier?—and even what the word means. Is it an acronym for "Monte alla Francia Italia anela!" ("Death to the French is Italy's cry!") or does it come from a French soldier raping a young girl in Palermo, her mother screaming "Ma fia, ma fia!" ("my daughter, my daughter!") and the Sicilians taking it up as their battle cry when they rose up in mass revenge?

No matter. Gangs with connections to Sicily were found in American cities in the late nineteenth century. Operating within the Italian immigrant communities, they loaned money at usurious rates, arranged for friends and relatives to come over from the Old Country (at great expense, usually involving more borrowing and endless debt), extortion, gambling, lotteries, hookers, whatever. They were hated, loved, feared, and respected.

The New Orleans mob murdered police chief David Peter Hennessy in 1890. He had been investigating a series of murders and claimed to be ready to expose the Italian secret society behind it when he was gunned down. (His dying words were that "the Dagoes" did it.) Nineteen gang members were indicted by a grand jury for the killing. A year later, some of the men were found not guilty. The public was outraged and a massive lynch mob stormed the Old Parish Prison where the rest of the men were being kept. Eleven men, all Italian immigrants, were shot and/or hanged, sparking an international incident. By the early twentieth century, independent Mafia gangs were established in most major cities.

In May 1929 a meeting of most of the major gangland figures was held in Atlantic City, New Jersey. There, they agreed in principle to work together, but the situation in New York was unsettled.

For practical purposes, what is called the Mafia in America began in 1931 when **Lucky Luciano, Meyer Lansky,** and their fellow young Turks in New York bumped off **Joe "the Boss" Masseria** and **Salvatore Maranzano.**

Those two had been locked in a battle for supremacy in criminal enterprises for years. Their lieutenants and soldiers had been killing each other in what came to be called the Castellammarese War. Masseria and Maranzano were the last of the "Mustache Petes," older guys who operated by a strict code of revenge and honor. Every slight had to be answered, and rigid unquestioning obedience to the rules and the established power structure were more important than making money. It was a closed, clannish, all-male organization, profoundly racist and anti-Semitic. Masseria had been in charge for a long time; Maranzano had been sent from Sicily to take over operations in the New World.

True Americans, Luciano and Lansky were interested in profits. Their mentor had been **Arnold Rothstein,** famous as the man who fixed the 1919 World Series (whether he actually did or not). He impressed upon them that they were businessmen. In the screwily enjoyable 1991 movie *Mobsters,* Rothstein, wonderfully played by F. Murray Abraham asks Luciano (aka "Charlie Lucky"), "What's the secret of America? Money! Everything is money, Charlie, don't ever forget it."

They didn't. Luciano worked for Masseria but was heavily recruited by Maranzano to join his organization. Finally fed up with the pointless conflict, Charlie Lucky agreed to take out his boss, but in his own way. He and Lansky recruited a four-man "dream team" to do the dirty work, thereby spreading the responsibility. **Joe Adonis, Albert Anastasia, Vito Genovese** and **Bugsy Siegel** shot Masseria in a restaurant where he had been dining with Luciano.

Five months later, Luciano put together another group of killers, all Jewish, according to some sources. Impersonating federal agents, they murdered Maranzano in his office.

Luciano, Lansky, Siegel, **Dutch Schultz, Legs Diamond,** and all the rest were young guys who had worked their way up through tough street gangs. Their families had emigrated from poverty-stricken Italy and European ghettos. They made money by selling beer, whisky, dope, and sex, loan sharking, union corruption, and extortion. They stayed out of jail, for the most part, by paying off the police, judges, and politicians. Prohibition was the greatest thing that ever happened to them; it made the gangs incredibly wealthy and turned them into heroes for millions of Americans who liked to take a drink.

When Luciano and Lansky took over, they talked with gang leaders in other cities and all essentially agreed to cooperate rather than kill each other. In New York, five families—the Bonanno, Colombo, Gambino, Genovese, and Lucchese—ran things. Detroit had its **Purple Gang.** The Capone mob ran Chicago, even though Big Al was in jail by then and Paul Ricca was in charge. Some of these men tried to remain anonymous. Some loved the warm glow of the spotlight and became famous or infamous, depending.

This larger organization was sometimes called the Syndicate, in the popular press, or the Commission. The group maintained the structure of the older Mafia, capos or dons were in charge of families (also called *borgatas*) with underbosses, consigliares, and soldiers beneath them. But there was no single boss of bosses, *capo di tutti capi.*

Instead, they would divide up their territories and work out differences among the bosses. They set up **Murder, Inc.,** as their enforcement arm. These were hit men, half from Jewish mobs, half from the Italians, who took care of troublemakers, witnesses, whatever. Well, in theory, anyway.

In truth, they continued to be greedy and violent even though, as Bugsy Siegel so famously said, "We only kill each other."

In the early days, their cause was aided immeasurably by **J. Edgar Hoover**. America's top lawman steadfastly maintained that the Mafia was a myth, and instead devoted his agency's considerable resources to chasing high profile bank robbers like **John Dillinger** and ferreting out communists wherever he might find them. It really wasn't until **Joe Valachi** flipped and went public with the story of his career in the Mafia that the Red Hunter paid any attention.

By then, Luciano had served time for prostitution and, at the end of World War II, had been deported to Italy, though he still kept his hand in.

Bugsy Siegel was creating the first luxury casino and hotel in Las Vegas. The New York families were fighting with each other and Big Al was dead from the clap.

Meyer Lansky ran things behind the scenes. Silky **Frank Costello**, nominally in charge, made sure the right payoffs were made. His main rival was the ambitious **Vito Genovese**. In 1957 Don Vito took out a contract on Costello. Wounded in an attack, Costello decided it was a good time to retire. Genovese then took out another old rival, Albert "the Lord High Executioner" Anastasia, and made ready to declare himself to be *capo di tutti capi*.

Alas, he chose to do it at the Apalachin Conference, which proved to be a massive embarrassment when state cops staked out the meeting in upstate New York and panicked the assembled mobsters. A few escaped but most were arrested and booked. In those pre-Miranda days, it really didn't matter that they weren't doing anything illegal.

Soon after the conference debacle, Genovese was locked up on a bad drug rap that had been cooked up by the other bosses, and **Carlo Gambino** took over. By that time—after the televised Kefauver

Committee hearings on organized crime and Valachi's testimony—the government and the public were well aware of the mob's many activities and FBI surveillance steadily increased.

Before he died of natural causes in 1976, Gambino appointed **Paul Castellano** as his successor. Castellano tried to move the New York families into more legitimate businesses but it didn't sit well with the more "traditional" old school mobsters, particularly **John Gotti**, the Dapper Don.

In 1985 Gotti had Castellano gunned down on a busy Manhattan street and took over as boss. For years, he evaded federal charges but that ended when the FBI wired an apartment where he worked, relaxed, and talked freely. With 100 incriminating hours of audiotape, the feds had Gotti by the short and curlies. Their case was locked up in 1991 when Gotti's right-hand man **Sammy "the Bull" Gravano** decided to cooperate. He confessed to everything they had done, and Gotti went to prison where he later died of cancer.

Since then, law enforcement has continued to harass the mob. As the power of the organized gangs has diminished in the real world, their status in popular entertainment has skyrocketed.

Filmmakers' fascination with urban gangsters goes back to the earliest days of silent films. From then until now, movies and television have reflected society's contradictory views of these characters. On one hand, they're vicious thugs who prey on the innocent and will kill or threaten anyone who stands up to them. On the other hand, they're rebels, rich glamorous outsiders who defy a corrupt establishment. On yet another hand, they may well be "good" gangsters who stand up against the "bad" gangsters who are even more evil and not nearly as attractive.

Hundreds of films have been based on real gangsters. At their worst, they're cheap exploitation; at their best, they're masterpieces of popular entertainment.

D.W. Griffith's 1912 *The Musketeers of Pig Alley* is often wrongly called the "first" gangster movie.

He and others had dealt with the subject before, but it is probably the first important gangster movie.

Promotional material of the day billed it as "Unparalleled drama inspired and played on the streets of the American city—bold—truthful." Some scenes were shot on the streets of New York and even today they have a strong documentary immediacy. The film was inspired by the corruption and murder accusations made against police officer **Charles Becker**. It ends with a brief, intense gunfight.

The main character is the Snapper Kid (Elmer Booth, no relation to Edwin or the famous acting family). At the beginning, he is a villain who steals a young husband's wallet, but he redeems himself a few minutes later when he saves the man's wife (Dorothy Gish) from being drugged and presumably raped by another gangster. At the end of the film, the happy couple provides him with an alibi when the cops try to arrest him.

Public Enemy (1931) made James Cagney a star. Though it's widely considered to be based on **Al Capone**, the character also has elements of Chicago boss Dion O'Bannion, and the famous "grapefruit" scene comes from a story told about gangster Hymie Weiss, his moll, and an omelet. *Little Caesar*, also released in 1931, is another film based in part on Capone and other Chicago hoods, the most important being **Salvatore "Sam" Cardinella**. The role and the film had an equally beneficial effect on the career of a young Edward G. Robinson.

A year later, in 1932, Ben Hecht and William Wellman's *Scarface* took more liberties with Capone's story, mixing in elements borrowed from O'Bannion and Big Jim Colosimo. For their time, all three broke new ground in depictions of violence and sex. They were so controversial they played a large part in the institution of the MPAA's production code, which placed strict limits on the content of studio films and led to a dearth of really good gangster movies later in the decade.

Capone and his mob were rediscovered by television in the 1950s, with *The Untouchables*. Robert Stack starred as Eliot Ness and for four seasons, he and his G-men established new standards of violence for the small screen. The series served as the basis for the 1987 film and a new series in the 1990s.

Several New York gangsters provided the raw material that Mario Puzo crafted into *The Godfather* in 1969. His novel became a phenomenal bestseller. Young director Francis Ford Coppola assembled a near perfect cast and resisted pressure from some at the studio to make the film on a modest budget with a contemporary setting. Instead, they created one of the greatest of American films. Against all odds, they recreated their success two years later with *The Godfather, Part II*, the rare sequel that is equal to or better than the original.

Martin Scorsese's masterpiece *Goodfellas*, based on the book *Wiseguy*, is certainly the most realistic recent Mafia film. It glamorizes the characters, as any Hollywood film does, but it takes pains to show their venal, dishonest sides, too.

Many real gangsters have claimed the two *Godfather* films had a profound effect on how they looked at themselves and what they did for a living. In the book *Underboss*, Sammy "the Bull" Gravano says the first film was a life-changing experience for him, and the movie has been so influential for so many years now that for some mobsters, life imitates art. This is one of the central tenets of David Chase's *The Sopranos*, the HBO series about New Jersey gangsters. Widely regarded as one of television's finest long-form works, the series gave a group of stock characters new depth and humanity.

The formula for all of them, from *The Musketeers of Pig Alley* to *The Sopranos* is the same: mix liberal amounts of sex and violence with a really charismatic nail-it-to-the-floor performance by a relatively unknown actor.

Malvo, Lee Boyd

"D.C. Snipers"

Everyone was looking for a white man in a white van.

Why?

Early in the series of murders that came to be known as the "D.C. Sniper" attacks, someone said he had seen a white van near the site of one of the killings. Given the nature of the crimes—random shootings with a high-powered rifle—it was generally assumed the killer was a deranged white middle-aged gun nut acting alone. Wrong on all counts.

Lee Boyd Malvo was born in Jamaica in 1985. He never really knew his father, and his mother often left him in the care of friends and family. In 1999, on the island of Antigua, young Malvo met John Allen Muhammad.

A divorced American veteran of the first Iraq war, Muhammad quickly became a father figure. He had been involved with Louis Farrakhan's Nation of Islam and may have indoctrinated the boy with his own brand of separatism. Whatever the case, by early 2002 the two were living in a homeless shelter in Bellingham, Washington. People who knew them assumed they were father and son. In Tacoma, Washington they stole a Bushmaster XM-15 rifle from a gun shop where they had also taken target practice.

From there, they became "spree" killers, traveling from state to state, stealing and murdering as they went.

What later became the Washington, D.C. attacks actually began on September 5, 2002 in Clinton, Maryland, where pizzeria owner Paul LaRuffa was killed. His laptop computer was later found in the modified police car that Muhammad and Malvo had acquired. It was a dark blue Chevrolet Caprice with a modified back seat (so a shooter could stretch out in the most stable prone shooting position) and a hole cut in the trunk for firing.

Their second target was a liquor store in Montgomery, Alabama. Malvo's fingerprints were found at the scene where one employee was killed and another was wounded on September 21st.

A week later, Muhammad and Malvo were back in the D.C. area. On the evening of October 2nd, they shot a man in a Maryland supermarket parking lot. The next day, they killed five more people in Maryland and the District of Columbia.

The victims were young, old, black, white, male, female. They were all outside either standing still or moving slowly. Considering the weapon, the shooting platform and the range (50 to 100 yards), the shots were not particularly difficult for a trained marksman. In all, 13 people would be killed, three seriously wounded.

Muhammad left Tarot cards at some of the scenes. On October 19th, when they shot a man south of Washington in Ashland, Virginia, they left a three-page crackpot letter in a plastic bag demanding $10 million and a telephone contact. Earlier, Muhammad had called a hotline to make his demands, but he had been cut short by a staffer who didn't believe him when he said he was the shooter.

When he did finally get through, Muhammad mentioned the Alabama killing, apparently not knowing Malvo's print had been found. Authorities were able to link the two names and learned Muhammad had purchased a Chevy in New Jersey.

By October 23rd, news spread that the cops were interested in a dark colored Caprice. The next day, two people spotted it at a Maryland rest stop and called it in. Muhammad and Malvo, asleep inside, were taken without incident.

Such an essentially random series of murders would put any metropolitan area on edge, but Washington became particularly tense. The 9/11 attack on the Pentagon had occurred just a year before, and everyone was seriously spooked.

Naturally, the cops were criticized for any number of reasons, but the one hero who emerged was Montgomery County, Maryland Police Chief Charles Moose. Even though some of the killings took place outside his jurisdiction, he became the public face of law enforcement during the siege. When the 2003 television movie, *DC Sniper: 23 Days of Fear*, was made, he was played by Charles S. Dutton. Chief Moose wrote a book about the experience, called *Three Weeks in October: The Manhunt for the Serial Sniper*, published in 2003.

Both Muhammad and Malvo were convicted of murder and other charges, and face more. Muhammad was sentenced to death; Malvo to life without the possibility of parole.

Several other books were written about the shootings and the killers were interviewed by scores of psychiatrists and doctors during the lengthy legal proceedings. Some claimed Muhammad was motivated by radical Islamist beliefs. At his trials, on occasion, he acted as his own lawyer and displayed signs of mental instability.

Regardless, it is still hard to find a satisfying answer as to why the man and the boy did what they did.

Manson, Charles

According to the "official" version of the story as popularized by Vincent Bugliosi's bestseller *Helter Skelter*, Charles Manson was a Svengali who could bend others to his will and ordered the Tate-La Bianca murders in hopes of starting an apocalyptic race war.

Others interpret the events surrounding the killings in more prosaic terms. The infamous Manson "family" was simply a group of drug-addled teenagers and young people who hung out together to get high, screw, and generally waste time. Involvement in street-level marijuana dealing led to one failed murder attempt and one spur-of-the-moment murder. The others that followed were a coverup designed to spring a member of the group who had been arrested.

Everyone agrees that until he became associated with the celebrity killings, Manson was a third-rate crook whose only brush with criminal greatness came in the early 1960s when he was a cellmate of famous 1930s bank robber **Alvin Karpis.**

Manson was born in Cincinnati in 1934 to a prostitute mother who was never able to care for him. When she couldn't find a foster home, he was placed in a reform school. He ran away and spent most of his youth incarcerated in other institutions. His crimes were usually nonviolent—car theft, bad checks, pimping—though he was involved in one prison rape.

Released in 1967, Manson headed to San Francisco and fell in with the hippie movement. He and some girlfriends wandered south to Los Angeles where they met and, for a time, crashed with Beach Boy Brian Wilson. (The Beach Boys actually recorded one of Manson's compositions, "Never Learn Not to Love.") Around the same time, Manson also met music producer Terry Melcher, son of movie star Doris Day and boyfriend of Candice Bergen. Melcher heard some of Manson's songs and decided the guy didn't have a future in the business.

Some time later, Manson and his pals, the "family" if you will, were living at the Spahn Ranch in the San Fernando Valley. The rundown place had been a location for western movies. They could stay there, get stoned, and weren't bothered by anyone.

Things started to go bad in July 1969 when Manson's associate Charles "Tex" Watson tried to rip off a black drug dealer named Bernard Crowe. He took Crowe's money and didn't deliver the goods. Crowe took Watson's girlfriend and said he wouldn't release her from his apartment until things were squared. Manson tried to help out but wound up shooting Crowe. He left the place thinking he had killed the dealer—he hadn't—and that Crowe was a high-ranking Black Panther—he wasn't.

A few days later, when another drug deal involving friend and actor Bobby Beausoleil went south, the group was already edgy and fearful. Some bikers claimed Beausoleil had sold them some bad mescaline and demanded a refund. Manson, Beausoleil, and some others went to their source, Beausoliel's ex-roommate Gary Hinman.

Details of the meeting are disputed, but the end result was that Hinman signed over papers to a car and a van to Beausoleil before he was stabbed to death, and the words "political pig" were written on

Sharon Tate, one of the Manson family's victims, as seen in the *Valley of the Dolls* (1967). (Kobal)

Charles Manson clowning in court on murder charges, 1970. (AP Photo)

the walls in blood. (According to some sources, this was meant to point suspicion at the Panthers.) A week or so later, Beausoleil was picked up and arrested. Three days after that, the first of the famous murders took place.

Watson, Susan Atkins, Patricia Krenwinkle, Leslie Van Houten, and Linda Kasabian—presumably on Manson's orders—drove in a borrowed car to the Beverly Hills house where Melcher had lived on Cielo Drive. They cut the telephone lines. On their way in, the gate opened, and 18-year-old Steve Parent drove out. Watson shot him four times. (Parent had been visiting caretaker William Garretson who lived in a guest house, and heard nothing that night.)

Leaving Kasabian as lookout, Watson and the three other women went into the house where they found actress Sharon Tate, eight months pregnant, and Voytek Frykowski, a friend of Tate's husband, director Roman Polanski, who'd asked Frykowski to look after her while he was in Europe. Also present were Frykowski's girlfriend, coffee heiress Abigail Folger, and hairdresser Jay Sebring, Tate's old friend and lover. The four of them were shot and stabbed to death in a frenzy of sadistic violence. When they had finished, one of the women wrote "Pig" on a door in Tate's blood.

The next night, the killers went out again, accompanied by Manson and another man. Manson directed them to a house in another luxurious neighborhood. They found the home of grocery store executive Leno La Bianca unlocked. He and his wife were inside. After they had been tied up, Manson left, and the two were murdered by Watson, Krenwinkle, and Van Houten. Again the violence was excessive and they wrote on the walls, including the famously misspelled "Healter Skelter."

Shortly after those killings, the police raided the Spahn Ranch on an auto theft charge. Manson and company were taken in and then released. Afterwards, Watson split for Texas and Manson and some others moved to the Barker Ranch in the Mojave Desert, where they were arrested later that month.

In jail, various members of the gang talked about what they had done. Eventually, Linda Kasabian became a government witness, and her testimony was the key to convictions on first-degree murder raps for Manson and five others. They were sentenced to death, which was later commuted to life when the Supreme Court ruled the death penalty unconstitutional in 1972.

Whatever the motives of the bunch, there is no question Manson did not actively participate in the murders. How, then, did this two-bit crook become such a Great Satan in the public imagination?

First, prosecutor Vincent Bugliosi created the mythic figure during the trial and later embellished upon it in his 1974 bestselling book. Second, and infinitely more important, Manson played the part perfectly. With his long hair and wild eyes and a cross that became a swastika carved into his forehead, he was the personification of everything an older generation of Americans feared about the younger generation. The peace, love, and happiness of Woodstock were a lie; Manson, evil incarnate, was the dark reality. In short, he was the right monster at the right time.

In the years since, Manson has become almost a brand name. He has inspired dozens of rock songs and albums; even an entire career for Marilyn Manson (real name, Brian Warner).

Several books have been written about Manson and "the family," most of them taking one extreme or the other on the matter of his criminal aptitude. The murders have been dramatized four times to date; first in the dirt cheap *Helter Skelter Murders* (1970), to TV adaptations of *Helter Skelter* (1976 and 2004), and the rarely seen *Book of Manson* (1989).

Bobby Beausoleil is also a 1960s cultural footnote. He appeared in the exploitation western, *The Ramrodder* (1969), filmed at Spahn's Ranch, and two Kenneth Anger short films, *Invocation of My Demon Brother* (1969), with the Rolling Stones, and as the title character in *Lucifer Rising* (1972). Manson supporter **Lynette "Squeaky" Fromme** found her 15 minutes of fame when she tried to aid his cause by attacking President Gerald Ford in 1975.

Maranzano, Salvatore

He wanted to be boss of bosses, and actually held that title for a few brief months, but Salvatore Maranzano is remembered as a catalyst or transitional figure in the history of American organized crime.

An educated, refined Sicilian who had studied for the priesthood before deciding to become a hoodlum, Maranzano arrived in New York after World War I. He made a place for himself and eventually became the chief rival of **Giuseppe "Joe the Boss" Masseria**. Joe the Boss was as rough-hewn as Maranzano was polished and the two men loathed

each other. Their generation of Italian gangsters was known as "Mustache Petes."

The Young Turks, led by **Lucky Luciano** and **Meyer Lansky**, didn't warm to Maranzano either. They had made fortunes as bootleggers during Prohibition and realized the narrow worldview of the Sicilians—who trusted only each other and, grudgingly, some other Italians—would not work in America. They were happy to work with Irish gangs, Jewish gangs, even with white Protestant gangs if the price was right. They were interested in making money, not in maintaining clannish codes of strict obedience and honor.

Even so, Maranzano found recruits for his cause. Back in the Old Country, Benito Mussolini had vowed to get rid of the Mafia, and young Italian gangsters emigrated to America by the hundreds. Many of them, including a young **Joe Bonanno**, joined the courtly Salvatore and listened raptly as he discoursed on Julius Caesar, with whom he felt a special affinity.

By 1928 things had come to head between Maranzano and Masseria, and open conflict broke out as their men ambushed each other. Statistics aren't particularly reliable in this area, but as many as 50 men may have been killed in what has come to be called the Castellammarese War.

They fought to a virtual stalemate. Though Luciano was nominally Masseria's man, Maranzano courted him seriously. When he made a firm offer, Luciano considered it, then put the older man off, telling him it wasn't the right time for him to make such a significant decision. He softened the refusal with a case of good Scotch. It wasn't enough. Maranzano arranged another meeting on Staten Island. When Luciano again demurred, Maranzano's men beat him nearly to death, slicing open the side of his face so that one eyelid drooped for the rest of his life. Amazingly, though, he lived.

For years, Luciano refused to identify his assailants. At the time, he persuaded everyone it had all been some sort of mistake. He had been taken for a ride and lived to tell the tale. From then on, he was "Charlie Lucky."

Luciano finally agreed to help Maranzano. On April 15, 1931 he talked Joe the Boss into taking an afternoon off for a big lunch at their favorite Coney Island restaurant. After the meal, while Charlie Lucky was in the can, four gunmen came into the place and blasted Masseria. They were **Joe Adonis**, **Albert Anastasia**, **Vito Genovese**, and **Bugsy Siegel**.

Maranzano immediately called a meeting of both sides of the conflict. All of the New York Mafiosi were summoned to a Bronx meeting hall where Maranzano held court from a throne-like chair. He divided the gangs into five families and appointed leaders to each of them. He installed himself as *capo di tutti capi*, and graciously accepted tribute, in cash (no checks), from his new commanders.

In private, he ordered the deaths of Luciano, **Frank Costello** and other key figures in New York, along with **Al Capone** in Chicago. Knowing he couldn't trust any Italian hitmen who might have loyalties to one or more of the intended victims, he outsourced the killings to **Vincent "Mad Dog" Coll**.

Luciano and Lansky tumbled to the old man's plans and beat him to the punch. They hired a four-man Jewish hit team who disguised themselves as federal agents. On September 10, 1931 they went to the Park Avenue real estate business Maranzano used as a front and demanded to see him. They needed to look at his tax records, they said. After disarming his bodyguards, they went after Maranzano with knives and pistols. He died in his private office, the one place where he probably felt safest.

Mafia lore has always had it that Luciano followed up on the Maranzano assassination with the wholesale extermination of his followers and friends from coast to coast, the so-called Night of Sicilian Vespers. Three of Maranzano's New York associates were killed later that same day, but there are no records of large numbers of killings elsewhere. Joe Bonanno was given control of Maranzano's operations in a reorganized Mafia.

Even though he was a relatively minor figure, Maranzano has been treated well by Hollywood. In *Bonanno: A Godfather's Story* (1999) Edward James Olmos makes the most of limited screen time. Joseph Wiseman, who also played the titular villain in *Dr. No*, is impressive in *The Valachi Papers* (1972). But the fullest portrait of the man comes in *Mobsters* (1991). There, to ease confusion with Masseria, the name is changed to Faranzano and Michael Gambon makes him a memorable villain in an underrated film. Maranzano also appears briefly in 1999's *Lansky*.

Marin County Courthouse Shootout

George Jackson grew up in Chicago in the 1950s and began his association with the criminal justice system as a child. By 1966 he was in a California prison where he founded a Marxist organization, the Black Guerrilla Family, dedicated to ending racism and getting its members out of the joint.

At roughly the same time, Angela Davis was discovering Communism at Brandeis University and then at UC San Diego where she studied with radical guru Herbert Marcuse. In 1969 she began teaching philosophy at UCLA. When the powers that be learned she was a proud card-carrying member of the Communist Party, she was promptly uninvited. She sued to get her job back and won in court, but then-Governor Ronald Reagan said no.

With an upraised fist and perhaps the most luxuriant and famous 'fro of those hair-politics days, she quickly became a cultural icon, a literal poster girl on dormitory walls everywhere.

At least part of the reason for Governor Reagan's veto was her vocal support for the Soledad brothers, three black inmates who were housed in the maximum security cellblock of Soledad prison for killing a guard. The three were Jackson, Fleeta Drumgo, and John Clutchette.

Locked in solitary 23 hours a day with lots of time on his hands, Jackson wrote two books that became huge bestsellers, *Soledad Brother* and *Blood in My Eye*.

Ms. Davis spearheaded the Soledad Brothers Defense Committee, with considerable help from Jonathan Jackson, George's teenaged brother. As part of her activities, she bought several firearms, completely legally.

On the morning of June 7, 1970 Jonathan Jackson spirited some of those weapons into the Marin County Courthouse. Another prisoner, James McClain, was on trial for a stabbing. Apparently, young Jonathan meant to arm McClain and two other prisoners, William Christmas and Ruchell Magee, who were there to testify. They would then take white hostages who would be traded for his brother's freedom and the revolution would spread like wildfire across the land.

In the midst of the trial, Jonathan stood up, told everybody to freeze, and brandished the weapons, one of them a sawed-off shotgun. Jackson, McClain, and the others took five hostages—three jurors, Judge Harold J. Haley, and DA Gary Thomas. The muzzle of the sawed-off was taped or strapped beneath Judge Haley's chin.

The group of kidnappers and hostages had made it as far as the parking lot when a massive gunfight erupted. It ended with the deaths of Judge Haley, Jonathan Jackson, McClain, and Christmas. Gary Thomas, one juror, and Magee were seriously wounded.

Angela Davis took a powder. For two months on the lam, the flower of the Revolution was featured on the FBI's Ten Most Wanted list until they nabbed her in a New York motel. Charged with kidnapping, murder, and conspiracy, she was whisked back to California.

On August 21, 1971, a few days before he was to go on trial on the original charge of killing a guard, George Jackson was killed in prison. According to officials, he was involved in an escape attempt. Armed with a 9mm pistol, Jackson killed three guards, execution style, and two white prisoners before he was killed by guards who stormed the building.

Some who favor conspiracies claim the cops knew in advance about the weapons in both the courthouse and the prison, but let things go on for their own purposes. Others say internccine politics within the Black Panther Party were behind George Jackson's death.

Angela Davis went on trial for her part in 1972. The government charged she had been involved with the courthouse kidnappings, but the prosecution provided little in the way of proof and she was acquitted by a mostly white jury.

In the years since, the killings have faded from the public memory of those tumultuous times. Angela Davis ran for vice-president and remains a darling to the handful of diehard Communists who are still kicking around.

George Jackson's books are still in print.

Masseria, Giuseppe "Joe the Boss"

"Joe the Boss" Masseria was one of the last of the New York Mafia's Mustache Petes—the old guys who had ties to the **Black Hand** and the other gangs operating in the city at the turn of the twentieth century. Born in Sicily in 1880, Masseria came to America in 1903 and became a member of the Morello gang, New York's best.

He was a short, five-foot two-inch hardass famous for his putrid body odor, black suits, and perpetually spaghetti-stained shirtfronts. He rose through the ranks quickly, often by assassination, and made enemies. In 1922 his main rival Umberto Valenti sent two gunsels after him. They shot his bodyguards then chased the diminutive mobster into a millinery shop. Masseria managed to bob, flinch, and spin away from their attack until they ran out of ammo and retreated, thereby earning a reputation as a guy who could dodge bullets.

Afterwards, he pretended to make up with Valenti by inviting him to lunch at a restaurant on East 12th Street. Dessert was a hail of gunfire: exit Valenti.

Masseria stayed on top until 1927 when Sicilian Mafiosa **Salvatore Maranzano** arrived in the Big Apple and set up shop. He was a direct threat and the struggle between the two camps came to be known as the Castellammarese War.

Masseria thought he had loyal lieutenants on his side, Young Turks **Lucky Luciano**, **Vito Genovese**, and others. But they chafed under the Mustache Pete's old-fashioned ways and his rabid anti-Semitic hatred of their friends **Meyer Lansky** and **Bugsy Siegel**. They also realized the war was hurting profits for everyone and so they decided to end it.

On April 15, 1931 Luciano suggested to Masseria that they indulge in a long leisurely lunch at their favorite Coney Island Italian joint, Nuova Villa Tammaro, and off they went. Joe the Boss wolfed down spaghetti with white clam sauce, lobster, Chianti, pastries, and coffee. His shirt was surely a mess by the time Luciano proposed they cap the afternoon with a friendly game of pinochle. After they had played for awhile, Luciano commented he needed to take a leak—a "long leak" he said later—and went to the bathroom. Immediately, the front door opened and four armed men hurried in—**Joe Adonis**, **Albert Anastasia**, **Vito Genovese**, and **Bugsy Siegel**. They pumped 20 slugs into Joe the Boss and he died face down on the table, the ace of diamonds dangling from the fingers of his right hand.

That, at least, is the famous story. Some say that an NYPD report puts the finger on another underboss and claims the Young Turks did not participate. Within months, Luciano would arrange the killing of Maranzano. On September 10th, gunmen identifying themselves as Treasury agents arrived at Maranzano's private offices, disarmed his bodyguards and stabbed and shot the new boss.

It matters little who actually pulled the trigger on Masseria. Mario Puzo knew the popular version and reworked it for the famous scene in *The Godfather* where Michael Corleone avenges the attempted assassination of his father Don Corleone by Police Chief McCluskey and the villainous Sollazzo. It is one of the most famous scenes in American popular literature. When Francis Ford Coppola was hired to direct the film, he knew how important it was to get it right, and so he created a "promptbook" of the novel.

Coppola literally cut the pages out of the book and glued each page to a hollowed-out sheet of 8.5 x 11-inch paper so he could see both sides, and put the pages in a big three-ring binder. He then used the extra-wide margins to write notes about what each scene meant and how it should be filmed. Coppola used the notebook, not a copy of the script, as he was making the film. Scene 26 was labeled as "The Killing." He called it the "key scene" and "the core." He wanted "to show the killing as terrifying and explicitly as possible having taken the tension to an unbearable degree, to further define Michael's character in regards to his cool, totally calm execution of these men. Pitfalls: rushing this would ruin it. Otherwise, this scene can't be ruined."

He was right, of course. It's one of the great moments in a great American movie.

Massie Case, The

In 1931, Hawaii was a territory, not a state, and the white officers at the Pearl Harbor Naval Base routinely referred to native Hawaiians as "niggers." Within the last year, there had been 40 attacks on native Hawaiian women who required hospitalization. Such overt racism was the norm in America, not the exception. It was institutionalized in the South with Jim Crow laws, and even if it was denied in other parts of the country, it was a fact of life. That attitude explains some of the injustices and outrageous acts that transpired during the various crimes known as "the Massie Case."

Young Thalia Massie was the wife of Lt. Thomas Massie, recently graduated from Annapolis. She was also the niece of inventor Alexander Graham Bell, and the daughter of the politically connected Fortescue family from Washington, D.C., and Long Island.

On Saturday, September 12th, Thalia was kicking up her heels at the Ala Wai Inn, a popular nightspot with Navy personnel. While there, she had angry words with an officer and he may have followed her when she left on foot.

An hour later, face bruised and jaw broken, she told police she had been raped repeatedly by five or six Hawaiian men.

Five young working class men were arrested— Benny Ahakuelo, Henry Chang, Horace Ida, Joe Kahahawai, and David Takai. From the beginning, the evidence against them was weak. Under the influence of painkilling opiates, Thalia identified three of the men as her attackers. But the staff at the hospital where she was treated said there were no signs of rape, and, later, her gynecologist said if he had told all he knew, it would have made everyone look foolish. On top of this, the five suspects had solid alibis.

None of it mattered to an outraged press. The alleged crime touched a deep nerve in the national psyche. Newspapers called the men "degenerates," "fiends," and "thugs" who "forced decent white folks to take up arms to protect the honor of their women." Straightaway, the five were charged with rape and brought to trial. Though each was offered immunity to rat out the others, all maintained their innocence. Despite the racially charged climate, the jury deadlocked and the judge declared a mistrial.

From the mainland, hysterical demands for "justice" were redoubled. Suspect Horace Ida was taken by a group of white vigilantes who beat him unconscious. Admiral Yates Stirling, the highest ranking Naval officer on the island, said, "Under our own democratic form of government the maintenance of white prestige had become increasingly difficult." While all of this was going on, some of Lt. Massie's fellow officers began intimating that perhaps his wife was not as completely innocent as she claimed to be.

So, to preserve "white prestige" or something more personal, Lt. Massie, his formidable mother-in-law Grace Fortescue, and two sailors, E.J. Lord and A.O. Jones, kidnapped Joseph Kahahawai. They snatched him off the street and drove him to Mrs. Fortescue's rented bungalow. Later, they

claimed they wanted to force a confession at gunpoint. Massie said he asked Kahahawai if he had attacked Thalia. The Hawaiian answered yes and, enraged, Massie shot him, or something to that effect. The cops caught the quartet of kidnappers as they were trying to dispose of the body. When questioned, they all claimed not to remember who shot Kahahawai or how it happened because they were in a group "daze."

Realizing the weakness of their position, Mrs. Fortescue opened her checkbook and brought out the big guns.

At 74, Clarence Darrow had been retired for four years and was flat broke, devastated by the Depression. For $25,000 (not an inconsiderable sum in 1932), he agreed to represent them and mounted a completely shameful defense. Even though no jury had convicted them, the five men were guilty, he argued. And so whatever Massie and anyone else might have done was justified and even honorable. And, besides, they had been temporarily insane.

Prosecutor Jack Kelley was not afraid of the famous Darrow and forcefully argued against the disgraceful strategy. A representative jury—three native Hawaiians, two Chinese, one Portuguese, and six white Americans—unanimously judged the defendants guilty of manslaughter. Conviction on the more serious charge of second-degree murder might well have resulted in rioting, so the verdict was probably the fairest anyone could have expected. Even so, it was too much for the establishment. Some 103 congressmen of both parties sent Territorial Governor Judd a telegram urging he pardon the murderers. Then President Herbert Hoover contacted Judd and a "compromise" was made.

Judd called the killers into his office and reduced their sentences from ten years to one hour. They called for cocktails and 60 minutes later were free to go. Mrs. Fortescue, the Massies, and Darrow caught the next boat home.

Two years later, the Massies divorced. He stayed on in the Navy. The rest of Thalia's life was troubled. She attempted suicide several times and succeeded in 1963. The case was an ignominious conclusion to Darrow's career.

Initially, Hawaiian authorities tried to downplay the entire matter. They knew how incendiary the case could be and feared, with some justification, that it might bring about the imposition of martial law and the loss of the limited self-government the islands enjoyed. When the story did reach the national stage, it revealed the ugliest side of America—the unvarnished, unapologetic racism that pervaded almost all levels of society. Perhaps because of that, it took decades for the killing to make any impact in popular culture.

In 1984 Norman Katkov turned the Massie Case into a potboiling melodramatic novel, *Blood and Orchids,* adapted into a TV miniseries in 1986. In 2005 Professor David Stannard took a much more serious look at the case in his nonfiction book, *Honor Killing: How the Infamous 'Massie Affair' Transformed Hawai'i.* It is by far the most detailed account of the entire business, really a significant true crime book. It also served as partial basis for a fairly thin PBS *American Experience* documentary, *The Massie Affair.*

Matasareanu, Emil and Larry Eugene Phillips

Conventional wisdom holds that Emil Matasareanu and Larry Phillips were inspired by the end of the movie *Heat* to rob the Bank of America in North Hollywood. But their real motivation may have been closer to **Eric Harris** and Dylan Klebold. Like the Columbine High School killers, they wanted to go out in a brilliant hail of gunfire.

Matasareanu, a Romanian immigrant, and Phillips were ex-cons with violent records. On February 8, 1997 they loaded up three assault rifles they had modified (illegally) to fully automatic fire. The weapons would fire as long as the trigger was depressed and the bullets were in big circular magazines. They also carried a pistol and more than a thousand rounds of full metal jacket armor-pierc-

ing military ammunition. Their torsos were protected by body armor. Homemade bulletproof Kevlar was wrapped around their arms and legs. With ski masks and black clothes, they were ready for their closeup.

Clearly, they had something more than a quick smash-and-grab in mind when they entered the North Hollywood branch at 9:15 a.m. in the morning. After ordering the patrons to the ground, they shot out the plexiglass doors separating the lobby from a more secure area. They had gathered more than $300,000 in cash when the cops and the television helicopters showed up.

What followed was a 44-minute shootout between the bank robbers and LAPD broadcast live nationally. Most of it took place on the streets right outside the bank, well within range of the local stations' airborne cameras. The bad guys wounded 11 officers and six civilians, several of them seriously. Their ammunition punched right through the cops' protective gear while their own bulletproofing was effective against handgun rounds.

Before it was over almost 400 cops, including SWAT teams, were engaged in the gun battle. Police were able to bring heavier weapons to bear. Phillips was wounded 11 times; Matasareanu 29 times. It's unclear whether Phillips killed himself with his pistol or if he fired involuntarily when a police bullet severed his spine.

Matasareanu attempted to steal a pickup truck but was foiled by a cutoff switch installed by its owner. He surrendered when he ran out of ammo and bled to death from his wounds before an ambulance arrived.

Astonishingly, that last detail was the subject of some controversy and a wrongful death suit. Matasareanu's estate sued two officers, claiming they had violated the crook's civil rights by delaying medical attention. Years later, the case ended with a mistrial and an out-of-court settlement.

The TV news footage was the basis for two documentaries. It was also featured on several websites.

222

The story was dramatized in the 2003 made-for-television film *44 Minutes: The North Hollywood Shootout,* which recreated the most famous images but was riddled with continuity errors.

McCall, Jack "the Coward"

Cross-eyed punk Jack McCall killed James Butler Hickok. That's about the only thing in Wild Bill's remarkable life everyone agrees upon.

Beyond that, legend and fact are often contradictory.

Hickok was born in Illinois to a family active in the underground railroad. As a boy, he helped slaves escape. As a teenager, he may have belonged to the antislavery "Redleg" forces that fought in Kansas. He worked as a stagecoach driver and became friends with William "Buffalo Bill" Cody years before either of them were famous.

Early in his life, eastern writers found Hickok fascinating and tales began to appear in print. In 1861 a *Harper's Monthly* piece described his taking care of the entire "McCanles Gang." Other versions of the story say David McCanles had a disagreement with Hickok. The subject was either McCanles' mistress, who had been seeing Hickok, or money owed to McCanles by Hickok's employer, a stage line. On June 12th, an angry McCanles, who may have had his 12-year-old son in tow, went to Hickok's cabin and called him out. Hickok refused. McCanles said he would drag him out and went inside. He may have been armed; Hickok certainly was. He killed the visitor and also shot the two men who had accompanied him.

During the Civil War, Hickok fought for the Union. He got the name "Wild Bill" then, either to differentiate him from his brother Lorenzo, "Tame Bill Hickok," or when he single-handedly stopped a lynch mob.

After the war, in 1865, he took part in what has come to be called the first Old West gunfight with his friend Davis Tutt. Again, motivation is in question. The disagreement between them was either over a gambling debt or a woman, but the upshot was that the two men agreed to meet at the Market Square of Springfield, Missouri at 6:00 a.m. on the morning of June 21, 1865.

They faced off on opposite sides of the square and walked toward each other. At about 75 yards, Tutt pulled his pistol and fired a wide shot. Wild Bill steadied his pistol with his off hand, the classic shooter's three-point stance, and put a bullet through Tutt's heart. He turned himself in immediately, was tried and acquitted on manslaughter charges.

He also worked as an army scout for General George Custer. In 1869 he was elected sheriff of Hays City, Kansas, a notoriously tough town. Some say he left after cleaning it up; some say he was thrown out for graft. Afterwards, he became marshal of Abilene, where he came up against gambler and gunfighter Phil Coe. Again, important details vary, but one night in 1871 on a crowded street, Coe and Hickok faced off and Hickok killed him.

Immediately, his deputy and friend Mike Williams burst through the crowd. Not realizing who he was, Hickok shot him. Williams died three days later. Some say it was the last time Wild Bill fired at another man and that he went into a profound depression because of it. Whatever the reason, after that, he joined a couple of Buffalo Bill's Wild West shows, but his heart was never it in.

In 1876 Hickok was in the mining town of Deadwood, in the Dakota Territory, with his friends Charlie Utter and Calamity Jane. He spent most of his time gambling, drinking, and being famous in Nuttal and Mann's Saloon No. 10—where the coward Jack McCall found him. Like so many other American assassins, he wanted to make a name for himself by killing a celebrity. Hickok was his ticket to immortality.

After losing more than $100 to Wild Bill, McCall came back to the No. 10 and found Hickok still playing poker around 4:00 p.m. in the afternoon on August 2, 1876. Though Wild Bill famously refused to sit with his back to a door, he broke his rule that day. McCall stepped up behind him and shot him in the back. Wild Bill was holding a pair of aces and a pair of eights, and thereafter it has been known as "a dead man's hand."

And this is where the story really gets strange: not being part of a state, Deadwood had no functioning government and so a hastily assembled court was convened the next day with a prosecutor, judge, defense attorney, and jury. McCall claimed he had been exacting vengeance because, years before in Abilene, Hickok had killed his brother. A credulous jury bought it.

McCall slammed out of town as quick as he could. He made it as far as Wyoming where he got drunk and boasted he had killed Wild Bill in a fair fight. He was promptly arrested again and sent to Yankton, South Dakota for a new trial. Since the first trial had had no legal standing, double jeopardy was not an issue.

At the second trial, McCall was found guilty.

President Ulysses Grant refused to act on his behalf and the little weasel was strung up on March 1, 1877. He was buried in an unmarked grave.

Wild Bill's treatment on film goes back to the days of silent movies when the first great western star, William S. Hart, played him in *Wild Bill Hickok* (1923), Gary Cooper in *The Plainsman* (1936), Roy Rogers in *Young Bill Hickok* (1940), Forrest Tucker in *Pony Express* (1953), Jeff Corey in *Little Big Man* (1970), L.Q. Jones in *Wild Times* (1980). The popular kids' TV show, *The Adventures of Wild Bill Hickok* (1951–58) starred Guy Madison and Andy Devine.

In recent years, filmmakers have tried to find the real man and have been pretty successful. Jeff Bridges is excellent in *Wild Bill* (1995) as a man who can't escape his own legend. Much of the film is set in Deadwood, as was a 1964 television production, *The Great Adventure: Wild Bill Hickok—the Legend and the Man,* starring his father, Lloyd Bridges.

The story of those last days was told in fullest detail in the first season of David Milch's HBO series

Deadwood (2005) with Keith Carradine as a memorable Wild Bill and Garret Dillahunt as McCall.

McCarty, Henry ("Billy the Kid")

He was the archetypal American outlaw—young, brash, cocky, good-looking, rebellious—the bad boy we all know and love. That was the image of Billy the Kid; the reality is Henry McCarty. Doesn't have quite the same ring, does it?

But then, the literal historical truth of Henry/ Billy is comparatively unimportant. "The Kid" is a central part of our American mythology and it's fair to say he was an impetuous, emotional young man who was on his own in a relatively lawless place where firearms and alcohol were readily available. He was caught up in larger conflicts that forced more mature and cautious men to take sides.

He was born around 1859, probably in New York City, and moved west with his mother who died in Santa Fe, New Mexico in 1874. The 15-year-old soon got into petty scrapes with the law. By 1877 he was working in Camp Grant, Arizona where he ran afoul of blacksmith and bully Frank "Windy" Cahill. According to some versions of the story, they were in a saloon when Cahill called the Kid a pimp and smacked him. McCarty pulled a pistol and killed the larger man with a single shot. They locked him up, but, as he was to do time and again, McCarty escaped from jail and went on the run.

Sometime later, he was back in New Mexico, first stealing cattle from and then working for English rancher John Tunstall. At the time, Tunstall was smack in the middle of the Lincoln County War. It was a fight for political and economic power between the interests of the merchants and the ranchers. Even though Tunstall was only a few years older than McCarty, he became a strong father figure. When Tunstall was gunned down in cold blood by Sheriff William Brady and a bunch of gun thugs he had deputized, the Kid joined a group of "regulators" on the other side.

William McCarty, aka Billy the Kid, in the famously reversed ferrotype from circa 1880. (AP Photo)

McCarty was involved in the killing of three men, including Sheriff Brady, who had taken part in the Tunstall murder. Depending on who's telling the story, the regulators' actions were either executions, ambushes, or fair fights. This chapter of his life ends with McCarty on the run again, and under indictment for Brady's killing.

In 1879 retired Union General Lew Wallace, who was then in the process of writing *Ben-Hur*, became the Territorial Governor. To end the conflict, he offered amnesty to everyone who had been involved in the Lincoln County War, but only those who hadn't been indicted. In the spirit of compromise, he agreed to meet with McCarty to work something out. They decided the Kid would be arrested, then go through the motions of a trial and tell all he knew before he would be released. Again, key details of what was said and done are at odds, but in the end, the deal broke down and the Kid escaped.

More gunfights followed—including the one with Joe Grant where the Kid surreptitiously unloaded his rival's revolver—and more miraculous escapes as McCarty and his pals made their living rustling cattle. It's impossible to say exactly how many men he killed during that time, but it's certainly not the 21 attributed to him in dime novels.

In 1880 when the Kid's old friend Pat Garrett was elected Sheriff in Lincoln County, Governor Wallace put a $500 bounty on McCarty's head. On December 21st, Garrett cornered the Kid and his gang holed up in a deserted farmhouse near Stinking Springs. After a two-day standoff that cost the life of his good friend Charlie Bowdre, McCarty surrendered.

He was sent to jail in the town of Mesilla to wait for his trial. During his incarceration, he gave several newspaper interviews and the legend of the dashing young outlaw began to take shape. In short order, he was tried and convicted of the killing of Sheriff Brady, and sent to Lincoln to hang. But on April 28, 1881, while Garrett was out of town, the Kid pulled off his most audacious escape. Possibly on the way to the privy, he got hold of a pistol and

killed Deputy J.W. Bell. He then loaded a shotgun and waited for Deputy Robert Ollinger, who had been across the street and would have heard the first shot. As the Deputy ran toward the jail, the Kid stepped onto a second story balcony and let him have it with both barrels.

He then got rid of his manacles, stole a horse, and rode out of town. Garrett gave chase and caught him on the night of July 14th at the Maxwell ranch near Fort Sumner. Again, the story is told in different ways.

One version has the Kid in bed with his Mexican girlfriend and Garrett waiting until he stumbles, happy and defenseless, from the sack. Another has Garrett in Maxwell's bedroom asking about the Kid's whereabouts, when the Kid comes in, pistol in hand. In both, the result was the same. Garrett shot McCarty in the chest and killed him. And from that moment to this, the life and death of Billy the Kid have been rich material for storytellers of every stripe.

Garrett himself, with the assistance of ghostwriter Marshall Ashmun Upson, was one of the first to write a book, with the seemingly endless title of *The Authentic Life of Billy the Kid: the Noted Desperado of the Southwest, Whose Deeds of Daring and Blood Have Made His Name a Terror in New Mexico, Arizona & Northern Mexico*. From this beginning, the two sides of the mythological Kid emerged, the smiling happy young man and the cold-eyed remorseless killer. In the following decades, an element of Robin Hood-like altruism would become part of the legend.

The Kid has been portrayed so often in every form of media—from Aaron Copland's ballet to the cheeseball exploitation flick *Billy the Kid vs. Dracula*—that a full list is impossible. He was subject of more than 40 films including King Vidor's *Billy the Kid* (1930); Howard Hughes' *The Outlaw* (1943, famous for Jane Russell's cleavage in the promotional material); and Sam Peckinpah's *Pat Garrett and Billy the Kid* (1973). (The Peckinpah film was initially released in a somewhat comprehensible version reedited by the studio. It was restored to something approaching the director's intentions on DVD where it is a showcase for many of the great character actors who appeared in the westerns of the 1950s and 1960s.)

Gore Vidal worked with the Kid's story twice in *Gore Vidal's Billy the Kid* (1989) starring Val Kilmer and in *The Left-Handed Gun* (1958) with Paul Newman. The latter film takes its title from the mistaken belief the Kid was a southpaw. People assumed he was a lefty because the famous tintype photograph of the Kid showing him with a holster and pistol on his left side. But tintypes were a reversed image and a closer examination reveals the Winchester rifle he was holding has the loading port on the left side. All model 1873 Winchesters had the port on the right.

Robert Utley's excellent 1989 book, *Billy the Kid: A Short and Violent Life*, separates the real story from the many legends. So does Michael Wallis' *Billy the Kid: The Endless Ride*, a fine popular biography published in 2007.

In 2006 French director Anne Feinsilber made the documentary *Requiem for Billy the Kid*. In it, she found parallels between McCarty and the poets Rimbaud and Verlaine. Go figure.

McConaghy, Robert

Though murderer Robert McConaghy's story became nationally famous through a bestselling pamphlet in the nineteenth century, it has never been filmed. If it was, it would have to be a black comedy.

Pennsylvania, May 30, 1840: in a fit of madness or uncontrolled anger, McConaghy murdered his family—his wife, his mother-in-law, and four of her children. Only his father-in-law, William Brown, survived the attack. Even though there was no doubt as to McConaghy's guilt, he maintained complete innocence at his trial. It didn't wash with the jury; he was convicted and sentenced to death.

On November 6th in Huntington, a huge crowd gathered to watch his hanging. McConaghy was brought out. He mounted the gallows. The noose was tightened around his neck. The trap was

opened, his body fell... and the rope broke. McConaghy hit the ground unharmed physically but in a state of complete mental shock.

While a new and better rope was located, a shaken McConaghy was returned to the scaffold. There he began to babble and, finally, made a full confession.

The second rope held.

William Brown remarried and raised a second large family in the house where the murders occurred. He died there in 1965.

McGurn, Jack "Machine Gun"

Jack McGurn is much more deserving of the moniker "Machine Gun" than the more famous George Kelly. **Machine Gun Kelly** was really just a happy-go-lucky bootlegger who had to be shoved up the ladder of criminal success by his grasping wife Kathryn.

McGurn was a gangster of the old school, and the brains behind one of America's most famous crimes.

He was born James Vincenzo De Mora in Chicago's Little Italy in 1904. As a teenager, he boxed under the name "Battling Jack McGurn" and showed promise as a welterweight. His career ended when his father, a grocer, was murdered by the Genna gang in 1923. De Mora-McGurn vowed revenge. He taught himself how to shoot and went to work for **Al Capone**, the Gennas' primary adversary. While "Scarface" Capone was establishing himself in Chicago, he had avoided direct competition with the Gennas, but that didn't last.

Given the kid's personal involvement and his skill with firearms, Capone assigned him to nail the Genna brothers' men. McGurn was good at it. Within weeks, he had shot and killed six of their top guys. Each time he got one, McGurn would put a nickel in the dead man's hand. Why? He had heard the guys who killed his father had dismissed him as a "nickel and dimer." After that, Machine Gun rose through the ranks of Big Al's soldiers to become one of his most trusted gunfighters, second only to bodyguard Phil D'Andrea.

McGurn invested his earnings in jazz joints. Fancying himself to be a Rudolph Valentino type, he sported flashy clothes and slicked back his hair. The babes loved it.

In 1927 up and coming comedian Joe E. Lewis was working at the Green Mill cabaret when McGurn acquired partial ownership of the place. Then the rival New Rendezvous offered Lewis a raise to $1,000 a week. He took it and was a smash hit. McGurn was not pleased. He threatened the comic but Lewis refused to be swayed. A few days later, three of McGurn's thugs forced their way into Lewis' hotel suite. They pistol whipped him, cut his throat and tongue, and slashed his face.

It took Lewis years just to learn how to talk again and a decade to get back to his career. Even Capone was appalled at McGurn's actions, and gave Lewis $10,000 to help with expenses while he made his recovery. But, hey, if his boy McGurn had been a bit too enthusiastic, well, that wasn't necessarily a bad thing.

A year or so later, when Big Al turned his attention to rival Bugs Moran, he gave McGurn the job of eliminating him. It was McGurn who came up with the idea of luring Moran into a sweet business deal and then disguising hitmen as cops. On February 14, 1929 a black Cadillac that appeared to be a police car pulled up in front of the Moran mob's headquarters. A bunch of guys got out and went into the place. A few minutes later, seven men were dead in the **St. Valentine Day's Massacre**. Moran, as it happens, was not among them.

McGurn was the prime suspect but chorine Louise Rolfe swore he had been with her all day. That was the famous "blonde alibi." When it proved to be false sometime later, McGurn married Louise so she couldn't testify against him. Though he was charged with the killings, he was never brought to trial.

When Capone was busted on tax charges and sent to jail, McGurn's fortunes declined. His clubs closed during the Depression and he was reduced to small time drug dealing.

Someone from his past caught up with Machine Gun on February 13, 1936 on the eve of the seventh anniversary of the St. Valentine's Day Massacre. That night in a bowling alley, five gunmen cut him down. They left a nickel and a comic valentine in his hand.

It read:

You've lost your job,
You've lost your dough,
Your jewels and handsome houses,
But things could be worse, you know.
You haven't lost your trousers.

No one was ever charged with his murder.

McGurn's revenge/rags-to-riches story has provided the template for countless gangster and action movies. He was a supporting character in *Capone* (1975), *The Verne Miller Story* (1987), and *The St. Valentine's Day Massacre* (1967). The Joe E. Lewis incident is dramatized in *The Joker Is Wild* (1957) with Frank Sinatra.

McMartin Family (Virginia; Peggy McMartin Buckey; and Ray Buckey)

In hindsight, the story is so ludicrous as to be laughable. Or it would be if so many lives hadn't been destroyed by it.

What would become known as the McMartin case began in 1983 in Manhattan Beach, California a little town south of Los Angeles. That's where Judy Johnson, an alcoholic paranoid schizophrenic, became convinced her two-year-old son Matthew was being sexually abused at his daycare center, the McMartin Pre-School. She decided 28-year-old Ray Buckey, a teacher there, was a pedophile and contacted police who told her to have the boy examined at the Children's Institute International (CII) at UCLA.

The first person to look at the kid was a new intern who agreed there was evidence of abuse. From there, Mrs. Johnson went to another center for abuse victims where her stories escalated dramatically to include child murder. Manhattan Beach police began an investigation of the McMartin school. On September 7th, they arrested Ray Buckey, and then released him for lack of evidence. The cops also contacted some 200 families who had had children at McMartin and asked them if they had noticed anything unusual about their kids.

Sometime around then, the matter came to the attention of LA District Attorney Robert Philibosian who turned it into a political issue by assigning Assistant DA Joan Matusinka to spearhead an independent investigation. As part of the project, parents were urged to send their children to see her friend Kee McFarlane, a social worker and grant writer at CII.

Various researchers and self-styled "experts" went to work on the kids, urging them to tell stories about the adults who worked at the school and to name other children who might know something. They used anatomically correct dolls and heavy-handed interrogation techniques to get the answers they wanted to hear. Before it was over, the children reported they had seen Ray Buckey killing giraffes and horses and babies; there were secret tunnels beneath the schools; there were mutilated corpses; and that actor Chuck Norris was involved in these evil schemes.

At no time during the entire process was a single piece of real evidence of physical abuse ever discovered. But it didn't matter. The wheels of justice were grinding forward. The DA's office spent millions and they had to have something to show for it.

By the spring of 1984 CII claimed to have found 360 instances of child abuse, largely based on the "repressed memories" pried loose by the intensive questioning. Using this bizarre reasoning, a child who claimed to be happy and normal was refusing to admit he or she had been subjected to acts of unspeakable violence. The teachers who appeared to be the friendliest and most caring were really the most dangerous.

School founder Virginia McMartin, Peggy McMartin Buckey (her daughter), Ray Buckey (her grandson), his sister, and three other teachers were charged with more than 200 counts of child abuse and arrested. Over the next two years of preliminary hearings, the prosecution presented a case based on ritual satanic abuse. News stories about the suspected satanism in Manhattan Beach mushroomed into theories of a nationwide network of evil.

As the hearings went on in 1984, one lawyer resigned from the DA's office and said he thought the defendants were being railroaded. The original accuser, Judy Johnson, died from complications of her alcoholism. In 1986 charges were dropped against everyone except Peggy McMartin Buckey and Ray Buckey.

The trial itself began in April 1987 and lasted for three years. At the end of it, Peggy Buckey was found not guilty. The jury could not reach a verdict on 13 counts against Ray Buckey, but found him innocent on the other 39. A second jury could not reach a verdict either. Buckey was finally freed after having been denied bail for five years.

The charges were based on the children's bizarre lies and exaggerations and highly questionable photographs of genital "scarring." After $16 million had been spent and hundreds of lives had been affected, real pedophiles were still quietly going about the fulfillment of their sick fantasies. The lasting importance of the McMartin case is that its hysteria set back legitimate efforts to stem child sexual abuse.

The story was dramatized in the excellent 1995 HBO film *Indictment: The McMartin Trial.* It was nominated for several awards and won three Emmys. Though the action is necessarily compressed, the film sticks close to the facts and realistically portrays the hysteria the McMartin family had to face. It drives home the point that in today's culture, as it was in the 1980s, the accusation of child sexual abuse is essentially equal to a conviction.

McVeigh, Timothy

Oklahoma City Bombing

Like **Eric Rudolph**, Tim McVeigh was a right wing gun nut whose love of firearms grew to

The aftermath of the Oklahoma City Bombing—the husk of the Alfred P. Murrah Federal Building in downtown Oklahoma City, April 1994. (AP Photo)

include bombs. Unlike Rudolph, who attacked the 1996 Atlanta Olympics, McVeigh created a weapon of mass destruction to become one of America's most brutal murderers.

His upbringing in western New York state was unremarkable. Most of his neighbors and classmates remember him as a happy, outgoing child. After high school, he enlisted in the army and served with distinction in the first Gulf War. An expert gunner in a Bradley fighting vehicle, he was awarded a Bronze Star. But after the war, he tried to realize his longtime goal of joining the Green Berets. Possibly exhausted by his tour of duty, he failed the rigorous physical tests and left the service.

Disappointed and bitter, he worked briefly as a security guard. At the same time, he became involved in some of the more extreme areas of conservative politics. He haunted gun shows. His entertainment favorites included the idiotic fantasy film *Red Dawn*, where armed white teenagers save America from invading communists, and *The Turner Diaries*, a racist screed about an armed uprising against the government.

McVeigh drifted into a rootless existence, hanging out with Terry Nichols and Michael Fortier, a couple of buddies from his time in the service. McVeigh's conspiratorial fantasies grew through the government assault on Randy Weaver and they found a focal point in the standoff between **David Koresh**'s Branch Davidians and the ATF. When that ended in slaughter on April 19, 1993, McVeigh was incensed and began to apply himself seriously to bombmaking. It was time, he decided, to teach America a lesson.

With Nichols' help, he bought and stole the necessary materials—blasting caps, ammonium nitrate (fertilizer), and nitromethane (high powered racing car fuel). Nichols helped McVeigh leave his car, a piss-yellow 1977 Mercury Marquis, in downtown Oklahoma City. They removed the license plate and left a note saying the battery was gone. The next day, they picked up a Ryder rental truck and loaded it with 7,000 pounds of their homemade explosives in 55-gallon drums.

On the morning of April 19, 1995 McVeigh parked the truck in front of the Alfred P. Murrah Federal Building, lit a fuse, and walked away. Minutes later, it exploded. The blast was so massive, so powerful, it disintegrated the front side of the nine-story building. The building's day care center was so close to the truck that the children there were almost certainly killed instantly, and never knew what happened. Others were less lucky.

More than 500 were wounded, many grievously; 168 were killed.

A couple hours later on I-35, Oklahoma state trooper Charlie Hanger stopped a piss-yellow '77 Marquis without plates. McVeigh couldn't produce registration or insurance papers, either. When the patrolman saw a bulge under McVeigh's jacket, he drew his own weapon and took McVeigh's Glock 9mm. The bomber protested he had the right to bear arms. Trooper Hanger cuffed him and called his dispatcher to run a check on McVeigh's license. Suspicious, but without any additional information, he charged McVeigh on minor matters and had him jailed.

Meanwhile, commentators and authorities were talking about dark complexioned, Semitic-looking men who had been seen in the area. Even today, some claim McVeigh was in league with Islamic extremists. The evidence says otherwise. McVeigh

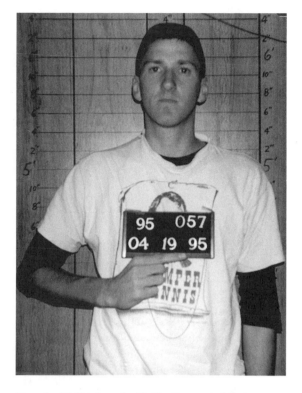

Timothy McVeigh at the Noble County Jail in Perry, Oklahoma, booked on a firearms charge just hours after the Alfred P. Murrah building was blown up, April 19, 1995. (AP Photo/HO/File)

didn't try very hard to hide his involvement. He used his own name and a few aliases during his preparations. His name came up on a federal computer list days after the bombing while he was still in jail. After that, the pieces fell into place.

At the trial, his lawyers tried to create some doubt about others who might have been involved, most prominently "John Doe #2," a figure who was seen by some witnesses with McVeigh before the bombing. But the witnesses against McVeigh were so persuasive the jury had little trouble arriving at a guilty verdict and then a death sentence.

For their parts in the conspiracy, Michael Fortier got 12 years and Terry Nichols got life without parole. An unrepentant Timothy McVeigh was executed by lethal injection on June 11, 2001.

No one has attempted to dramatize his atrocity. He is the subject of two well-researched books, Richard Serrano's *One of Ours* (1998) and *American Terrorist* (2001) by Lou Michel and Dan Herbeck. Michel and Herbeck, reporters for the *Buffalo News*, interviewed McVeigh extensively before his execution and provide the closest thing we'll ever have to a firsthand account of his actions and some insight into his motivations.

Menendez Brothers

Erik and Lyle Menendez might be more famous today had their double celebrity LA murders not been so thoroughly eclipsed just a few years later by **O.J. Simpson.**

Jose Menendez was a refugee from Cuba who became a successful—some said ruthless—businessman with the Hertz car rental company and RCA Records. In 1986 he moved his family—wife Kitty and sons Lyle and Erik—from Princeton, New Jersey to California where he was hired by LIVE home video to run the company. He did it well and a year later they moved to Beverly Hills. Their mansion was on Elm Street, a classy address in a classy neighborhood. In the past, the joint had been rented to the likes of Elton John.

The boys were typically spoiled rich kids who been getting into various kinds of trouble since puberty. Lyle had been kicked out of Princeton for plagiarism. Then he and his younger brother started breaking into homes in Los Angeles and stealing cash and jewelry to the tune of $100,000. After they were caught with stolen property and arrested, their dad pulled some strings—as he always did—and got them off with counseling and community service.

Around the same time, Jose was doing so well with LIVE that the company took out two "keyman" life insurance policies on him, $15 million for the company and $5 million for the family. At home, things were not going so well. According to

Dr. Jerome Oziel, the therapist who had counseled the boys, they were narcissistic sociopaths completely lacking in consciences. Perhaps because of this, Jose was talking about cutting them out of his will.

The boys decided their only course of action was murder. Using stolen IDs, they bought two Mossberg 12-gauge shotguns in San Diego. On Sunday, August 20, 1989 they told their parents they were going to the movies. They left and came back early, sneaking in through the French doors of the TV room where their parents were dozing. They slaughtered them with the kind of excessive violence usually found in bad movies. Five point-blank blasts for their dad; nine for their mom. The bodies were virtually destroyed. Even so, the boys were so self-possessed they collected all 14 shells and disposed of them with the guns. Then they called 911.

Not long after the funeral, they learned the $5-million policy was not in effect because their father had not taken a second physical for it. Still, they weren't without resources. First, they had the home computer with the potentially contentious will erased by professionals. Then they went on an extended spending spree that included a new Porsche for Lyle, a Jeep for Erik, fancy condos for both, a tennis coach, and Rolexes. They were burning through their inheritance at a record-setting pace. But while Lyle was holding up well, Erik was wracked with guilt and spilled his guts to therapist Dr. Oziel.

Eventually, Oziel's girlfriend, Judalon Smyth went to the cops and told them that both Lyle and Erik had confessed to the doctor and he had tapes and notes on all of it. Lyle was arrested on March 8, 1980. Erik, who was playing tennis in Israel, was booked three days later.

Defense lawyers employed the now familiar childhood sexual abuse defense for the young men. Jose and Kitty were so brutally demonized by their sons' attorneys that the first trial resulted in a hung jury. The strategy didn't fly at the retrial where the brothers were found guilty on all charges and sentenced to life without parole in separate facilities.

Erik and Lyle Menendez face the music after being convicted of murder, 1990. (AP Photo)

A number of books were written about the young killers in the aftermath of their prolonged trials, and two movies were made for television in 1994: *Menendez: A Killing in Beverly Hills* and *Honor Thy Father and Mother: The True Story of the Menendez Murders*. Neither made much of an impression and, given the nature of the case and the tenor of the defense, it's no surprise people just want to forget about this one.

Metesky, George

George Metesky was a nut with a grudge.

He planted his first bomb at the Consolidated Edison building in Manhattan on November 16, 1940. It was a simple little pipe bomb in a wooden box with a note that read "Con Edison crooks, this is for you." It didn't go off. Given the note, that may have been the point. His second bomb, found one year later, didn't explode either. A few months later, after Pearl Harbor, the police got a letter saying there would be no more bombs for the duration of the war, but afterwards, the power company Con Edison would pay for its "dastardly deeds."

The third bomb, another dud, showed up on March 29, 1950 in Grand Central Station. The bomb squad recognized the construction and the workmanship. The fourth bomb worked. It blew up in a phone booth in the New York Public Library. Ditto the next

Actor Sal Mineo (shown in August 1957), arrives at LaGuardia airport in New York. (AP Photo)

one in Grand Central Station. Before it was over, the "Mad Bomber," as he was dubbed in the press, planted 30 bombs in public places—Madison Square Garden, Penn Station, movie theaters. Though he didn't kill anyone, a porter in Penn Station was permanently crippled and 15 people were injured.

Psychiatrist James Brussel was instrumental in putting together a profile of the bomber. After examining the bomber's letters, Brussel deduced the man was insane and, given the intensity of his hatred of Con Edison, he was probably an ex-employee. If the company would examine its records more fully, they would probably find the man's name. (They had already done that, but the power company had been created by combining several small utilities in the 1902s and '30s, and preconsolidation records were disorganized and incomplete.)

Brussel suggested the bomber actually wanted to be caught and if the police publicized the profile, they might engage him in a correspondence where he would give something more away.

It worked. A Con Ed clerk found the records of a George Metesky who had been injured in a plant accident and blamed his tuberculosis on it. The company hadn't agreed. At about the same time, the bomber mentioned the date and location of that injury. D'Oh!

When police paid him a visit, he confessed on the spot.

He fit Dr. Brussel's profile with uncanny accuracy. Though this was not the first time such conjecture had been applied to an unknown subject, it highlighted the value of the technique now widely used.

George Metesky was found to be criminally insane and committed to the Mattawean Asylum. He was declared to be cured in 1973 and was released. He died in 1994.

It is believed Metesky's career inspired the likes of Unabomber, **Ted Kaczynski**, **Timothy McVeigh**, and other psychopaths. Hollywood has not been as receptive.

Mineo, Sal

Sal Mineo will always be thought of with his two live-fast-die-young costars, James Dean (car crash at 24) and Natalie Wood (fell off a yacht at 43). They made permanent impressions as "Plato," Jim and Judy, the beautiful and sexually ambiguous young heroes of 1955's *Rebel Without a Cause*.

Mineo was nominated for an Oscar for his work. The rest of his professional career followed the bumpy path typical of Hollywood. He received his second Oscar nomination for *Exodus* in 1960, but by the middle of the decade, the fickle industry seemed to have little use for his talents.

Perhaps acknowledging his budding bisexuality, Mineo took unconventional roles to say the least—a gay stalker in *Who Killed Teddy Bear?* (1965); a prison rapist on stage in *Fortune and Men's Eyes*, which he also directed; and, in his final stage appearance, a gay burglar in *P.S. Your Cat Is Dead.*

On February 12, 1976 Mineo was returning to his West Hollywood home from a rehearsal for *P.S.* when he was stabbed to death. He had just gotten out of his car when he was attacked. Some suspected a sexual or drug angle to the murder, but career criminal Lionel Ray Williams had a simpler motive: money. More than a year later, he confessed to his cellmate in the Calhoun County jail in Michigan, where he was pulling a stretch for forgery. It had simply been a mugging that went bad. He panicked when Mineo screamed after he had been stabbed. Guards overheard the story and bugged the cell.

A Los Angeles jury found Williams guilty of second degree murder. He was sentenced to life and paroled in 1990. Since then, he has been locked up again on parole violations, and Sal Mineo has become a minor icon in the pantheon of Hollywood bad boys. Doubtless, he would be ranked more prominently had his killer not been so prosaic.

Molineux, Roland

Like **Harry Thaw**, Roland Molineux proved the old jailhouse axiom, "Rich men never burn."

In New York's Gilded Age, Molineux was the pampered son of a wealthy family. A good looking kid, at 15 he had been named as the correspondent in a divorce suit. Though his nominal job was at the family's New Jersey dye factory, Roland spent much of his time at the snobby Knickerbocker Athletic Club in midtown Manhattan. There he was known as a whiner who constantly went to the board of directors demanding other members be disciplined or thrown out for whatever they might have done to piss the young master off.

One such member was Henry C. Barnet who was involved with the delectable debutante Blanche Cheeseborough. Roland also had his eye on the toothsome Miss C.

In October 1898 Barnet suddenly and inexplicably died. The initial explanation was diphtheria, but

there were mutterings something darker had transpired. Wasting no time, Roland put the moves on the presumably distraught Blanche and they wed. A couple weeks later, the club's athletic director Harry Cornish had the temerity to defeat Molineux in a weight-lifting contest.

Rolly went to the board with an ultimatum: either Cornish was to be sacked or he would resign. Cornish stayed. Rolly walked. On December 23rd, Cornish received a bottle of Bromo-Seltzer in the mail at the club. Thinking it was a joke from a friend about over-imbibing during the holidays, he took it home to his rooming house.

Five days later Cornish's landlady, Mrs. Katherine Adams, came down with a crushing headache. Cornish offered her some of his Bromo. She drank some and said it tasted bitter. He tried a bit and said it seemed fine to him.

She finished her dose and died in unspeakable agony moments later. Cornish was sickened, too, but managed to get to the club and the doctor there. He recovered several days later. The doctor, meanwhile, remembered that Barnet had mentioned something about receiving a bottle in the mail. He analyzed the Bromo-Seltzer and found it had been laced with the deadly cyanide of mercury. Then he called the cops.

They found the mailing wrapper for the Bromo in Cornish's office, and compared the writing on it to the club's members. Straightaway, they fingered our boy Rolly.

The trial was a sensation. Molineux claimed complete innocence. The prosecution proved that before the Barnet murder, he had rented two mailboxes, one in the name H.C. Barnet, the other using the name Harry Cornish. Under Barnet's name, he had ordered an amount of Kutnow's Stomach Powder from Cincinnati. They also found he had ordered cyanide of mercury, ostensibly for the dye plant.

The jury said guilty. Molineux was sentenced to the chair and sent to Sing Sing. Then, in Roland's darkest hour, when all seemed lost, Daddy rode to the rescue. His phalanx of lawyers argued testimony about Barnet's death should not have been allowed, since the lad was on trial for the Adams murder. While sweating out the appeal, Rolly wrote a book, *The Room With the Little Door*. It was well received and started the rehabilitation of his public persona.

By the time he went to trial again in 1902, people had forgotten what a repellant slug he was and set him free. Afterwards, he actually covered some murder stories for newspapers and wrote a play. But a few years later, Blanche divorced him and he died in an insane asylum in 1917.

A major book about Molineux is in the works. So far, his story has not made it to the screen.

Monroe, Marilyn

When Marilyn Monroe died in 1962, there was virtually no controversy or curiosity about the cause. The troubled actress, whose career was at its lowest ebb, had taken an overdose—perhaps accidentally, perhaps on purpose.

But, in later years, as details of President John Kennedy's sexual adventures emerged, things changed. By then, Marilyn was becoming a cultural icon and she was drawn into the conspiratorial orbit still surrounding the Kennedy family. Her life, both personal and professional, had been unstable. A troubled childhood and doubts about her abilities as an actress made her unusually insecure.

Her acting career was almost ruined as it was beginning when nude photographs were made public. But an apology and an explanation that she had posed for the pictures when she was broke won over public opinion. Whatever her talent as an actress, her screen presence could not be denied. At her best, she radiated a sweet natured but supercharged sexuality that was transmitted directly through the camera to the audience. She was a movie star.

There were also the high-profile marriages to baseball star Joe DiMaggio and playwright Arthur Miller. At the same time, she appeared in some good films—*Niagara*, *Some Like It Hot*—and many

duds. She was also hitting the booze and the pills so hard she became notoriously unreliable and difficult to work with. In the summer of 1962, production on her final feature, *Something's Got to Give*, was shut down because the studio lost faith in her.

At that time, in many ways, she was dependent on her psychiatrist Dr. Ralph Greenson and Eunice Murray, a live-in nurse/companion he had engaged for her. Both were involved on the night of August 5th, when she was found dead from an overdose of Nembutol and chloral hydrate. The Nembutol had been prescribed by her personal physician, Dr. Hyman Engelberg, who actually called the LAPD to report her death. Beyond that, the details—exact time of death, who found the body and when, how the drugs were administered—are hard to nail down.

Some have claimed Robert Kennedy, then Attorney General, and his brother-in-law Peter Lawford visited Marilyn's house that night. But as far as RFK is concerned, it's virtually impossible. He and his wife were with friends in Gilroy, California that weekend. This has not deterred the conspiracy theorists. They hint at long-term sexual relationships involving the star, the President, his brother, organized crime, **Jimmy Hoffa, J. Edgar Hoover,** Frank Sinatra… the list goes on. No one has ever produced a single piece of proof that anyone else was involved.

Books and articles about the various theories abound. On film, Larry Buchanan's 1989 *Goodbye, Sweet Marilyn* is a tasty slice of feverish low-budget schlock that rounds up all the usual suspects.

Morrell, Ed

It's remarkable the story of Ed Morrell and the California Outlaws has not been translated into film or television. Perhaps the political aspects smack too much of radicalism, or perhaps the prison abuses so central to the conclusion are too grotesque for popular entertainment. Even so, these guys were archetypal nineteenth century American Robin Hoods.

The Outlaws were formed to fight the mighty Southern Pacific Railroad. The railroad had the

Marilyn Monroe in *The Seven Year Itch* **from 1955. (Kobal)**

power to condemn land in its right-of-way, to pay the owners a small amount and drive them off, using as much force as needed or desired. According to its opponents, the railroad also used more corrupt methods to drive farmers off their land in the San Joaquin Valley. In 1880 the conflict exploded with the "Slaughter at Mussel Slough." On that day, thinking a number of the farmers were going to be at a picnic, the railroad sent out a gang to repossess their homesteads. But the settlers tumbled to the plot and confronted the railroad men. The following gunfight ended with five settlers and one railroad man dead.

The violence escalated into a form of open warfare as the locals banded together against the rail-

road. The Outlaws were led by Chris Evans and the brothers George and John Sontag. Their primary tactic was train robbery, but they claimed never to take anything from passengers or to touch the U.S. mail. Instead, with each job, they broke into the company safe in the express car, then melted back into the population. The conflict lasted for years. On one side, the Southern Pacific had its own detectives and the Pinkertons who tried to infiltrate the Outlaws' many sympathizers in local communities. For their part, the Outlaws did the same thing, placing ne'er-do-well Ed Morrell within the office of railroad detective "Big Bill" Smith.

Gradually, the railroad won the war of attrition and the Outlaws' numbers were greatly reduced.

George Sontag was captured and sent to prison. In 1893 both Evans and John Sontag were seriously wounded and captured in the Shootout at Stone Corral. John died about a month later. When George heard the news in Folsom Prison, he started a riot and was shot. Chris Evans was locked up in the Fresno jailhouse where Ed Morrell worked.

Accounts differ on key details about what happened next. Either Big Bill Smith had organized a plan to have Evans killed while trying to escape, or Morrell conned Smith into believing another train robbery was imminent. Whatever, the result was that Morrell broke Evans out of jail and they escaped into the mountains. Again lawmen, railroad dicks, and bounty hunters gave chase. Again, the escapees had so much local support they were able to elude their pursuers, yet still found the opportunity to grant interviews to sympathetic newspaper reporters. Evans and Morrell stayed on the loose for several months before they were caught and summarily sentenced to life.

Both were sent to Folsom, a notoriously brutal institution where Morrell was to become one of the most famous inmates. Inside, he maintained his activist attitude and was subjected to extreme mistreatment. Among the Folsom favorites were "the derrick," a device that held prisoners with their hands bound behind them and only their toes touching the floor, and the "lime cell," a small room coated with lime and hosed down so the lime would be suspended in the spray and burn the inmate's throat and lungs with every breath.

After they had done their worst to Morrell at Folsom, he was transferred to San Quentin where he wore the infamous "San Quentin overcoat," an elaborate and extremely painful straightjacket. His years of torture earned Morrell the nickname of "Dungeon Man." He managed to withstand the horrors by devising a form of self-hypnosis. He survived inside until 1908 when corrupt administrators had been thrown out and honest prison officials recommended his release. The acting governor granted Morrell a pardon.

Upon his release, Morrell wrote of his time in prison in his autobiography, *The 25th Man* (1924).

It became a popular hit and put Morrell at the head of national efforts for prison reform. Several states enacted new laws against corporal punishment of inmates, and Morrell advised Congress on the matter. His book attracted the attention of Harry Houdini and Jack London. London's novel *The Star Rover* (1898) is based on Morrell's self-hypnosis techniques and the "astral projection" he allegedly achieved while in that state. On a more realistic level, Frank Norris' 1901 novel *The Octopus* is based on the Slaughter at Mussel Slough.

Morris, Frank

Conventional wisdom has it no one ever escaped from Alcatraz Island while it was a prison. Frank Morris may be the exception.

An intelligent lifelong criminal whose career peaked with armed robbery, Morris was shipped to the Rock on January 20, 1960. There he met brothers John and Clarence Anglin and Allen West. Over two years, they devised and executed an elaborate escape plan. It involved digging through the rear vents of their cells to gain access to a utility corridor. From there, they could get to a roof and then to the rocky beach and San Francisco Bay.

West did not participate in the actual escape. Morris and the Anglin brothers made their attempt on the night of June 11, 1962. They had constructed an inflatable raft of raincoats and paddles from plywood. They placed homemade realistic dummies in their beds.

They were never seen again, though remnants of the raft and paddles were found later on nearby Treasure Island. Because no vehicles were reported stolen that night or the next day and the men were not rearrested, the FBI concluded they had drowned in the bay.

But did they?

In 2003 the Discovery Channel show *Myth-Busters* addressed the question. Hosts Jamie Hyneman and Adam Savage made a raincoat raft. They chose a time when tide conditions were the same as they had been on that night back in 1962. They made it to the mainland near the north tower of the Golden Gate Bridge in about 40 minutes.

The 1979 Don Siegel film *Escape from Alcatraz* dramatizes the events with Clint Eastwood as Morris and the Elgin brothers played by Fred Ward and Jack Thibeau. Filmed on the island, it is one of the most engrossing and detailed prison escape pictures ever made.

Moseley, Winston

The Kitty Genovese case is famous for the wrong reasons.

Early on the morning of March 13, 1964 Winston Moseley, a budding serial killer, spotted Kitty as she was coming home from work to her apartment in Kew Gardens, Queens, New York.

After she had left her car, he chased her and stabbed her twice in the back. She fought back and screamed. One neighbor shouted for him to leave her alone. Moseley ran away on foot but returned in his car minutes later. By then, Kitty had crawled into a hallway at the back of her building. Moseley knifed her again and attempted to rape her dead body. Necrophilia was part of his pathology, as he admitted to the cops when they picked him up six days later as he was stealing a TV set. He freely admitted what he had done to Kitty Genovese, and to Barbara Kralik, 15, and to Mae Johnson, 24.

Moseley was 29, married, had two kids. Why had he murdered and raped? A compulsion came over him, he said. But the killer was not the focus of public attention.

Two weeks after the killing, Martin Gansberg wrote a piece that appeared in the *New York Times* under the headline "Thirty-Eight Who Saw Murder Didn't Call the Police." The first sentence read "For more than half an hour 38 respectable, law-abiding citizens in Queens watched a killer stalk and stab a woman in three separate attacks in Kew Gardens."

> *Two weeks after the killing, Martin Gansberg wrote a piece that appeared in the* New York Times *under the headline "Thirty-Eight Who Saw Murder Didn't Call the Police." The first sentence read "For more than half an hour 38 respectable, law-abiding citizens in Queens watched a killer stalk and stab a woman in three separate attacks in Kew Gardens."*

Virtually none of it was true. Some people did call police; others yelled out; no one heard or saw everything; many thought it was a lover's quarrel or argument that had spilled out from a nearby bar.

But, as is so often the case, the initial misinterpretation of the facts became the story. It wasn't a story about a young woman savagely attacked by a psychopath. It was a story about public apathy and alienation. The catch phrase became "I didn't want to get involved." Countless breast-beating articles and books were written about Kitty Genovese. Her case became the inspiration for Harlan Ellison's award-winning short story "The Whimper of Whipped Dogs," the famous comic book series *The Watchmen*, and the well-regarded but rarely seen 1975 made-for-TV film *Death Scream*.

The real cultural importance of the killing came from improved telephone reporting to police in New York—there was no 911 emergency number in 1964—and increased interest in neighborhood watch programs.

Mountain Meadows Massacre

Why were 120 people in the Baker/Fancher wagon train slaughtered in southwest Utah in 1857?

Some claim the Mormons in the area believed they were about to be attacked by the United States army and thought the California-bound emigrants from Arkansas and Missouri had something to do with it. Others claim church leader Brigham Young ordered the murders to show the federal government he was in charge. Still others say the impoverished Mormons simply wanted to steal wagons, farm equipment, money, cattle, and horses from the unusually well-stocked settlers.

Evidence suggests the third answer, though it's difficult to believe there was no involvement by church officials. The emigrants had been threatened and treated poorly ever since they had entered Mormon-controlled territory. No one would sell or trade with them for necessary supplies, and in Salt Lake City, they were falsely told the southern route, via Mountain Meadows, was safer than the northern route to California.

They were camped between two hills at Mountain Meadows when they came under rifle fire from both hills early on the morning of September 7th. The first assault came either from Paiute Indians, who had few firearms, or from Mormons disguised as Paiutes. The siege had begun.

It was led by John D. Lee, a Mormon Bishop and major in the militia. He apparently had second thoughts about the atrocity he was committing and communicated his uneasiness to his superiors. They sent three wagonloads of well-armed reinforcements under the command of Maj. John Higbee.

The next day, September 11th, Lee rode into the Baker/Fancher camp and told the people he had managed to insure their safety against the marauding Paiutes. The men and women, who were virtually out of ammunition, simply had to surrender their weapons and allow his men to lead them to safety. After considerable discussion, they reluctantly agreed. Flanked by their newly arrived protectors, they left their belongings and walked away.

About a mile out, Higbee yelled out the order, "Do your duty!" and his men opened fire. Seventeen children—all younger than six—were spared and sent to live with Mormon families. The rest were killed. Some were buried in mass graves; some were left where they fell.

As early as 1859 a federal warrant was issued for Lee, but the church moved him to remote areas of the territory. He was kept out of custody until 1874 when he was excommunicated and turned over to federal authorities. At his first trial in Utah, the jury deadlocked. A second convicted him and Lee was executed by firing squad in 1877. No one else was ever charged.

When word of what had happened finally got out, all but one of surviving children were picked up by the army and returned to their relatives. At the same time, Mormon leaders were destroying documents and doing their best to make the whole thing go away. Considering the enormity of the crime, the church did an exemplary job of minimizing its involvement for almost a century.

The first nonfiction book on the subject, Juanita Brooks' *Mountain Meadows Massacre*, wasn't published until 1950. It was followed by William Wise's *Massacre at Mountain Meadows* in 1976, Will Bagley's *Blood of the Prophets* in 2002, and Sally Denton's *American Massacre: The Tragedy at Mountain Meadows* in 2003. Wise and Denton place the blame squarely on Brigham Young.

The Mormon church cooperated with Richard Turley on his more sympathetic 2004 book, *Tragedy at Mountain Meadows*. He claims to have seen documents relating to an investigation the church instigated in 1892. Astonishingly, the church concluded Lee had acted alone and exonerated itself.

More recently, several novels have been written about the atrocity. The heavy-handed 2007 film, *September Dawn*, with Jon Voight and Terrance Stamp, fingers Young.

Mudgett, Herman Webster

H.H. Holmes

H.W. Mudgett, popularly known by his alias H.H. Holmes, defies definition. Murderer, thief, rapist, bigamist, sadist, liar—he was all of them. How many people did he kill? Between 27 and 200, possibly, though others put the body count in the 40 to 100 range. Why did he kill? For money and for fun.

Mudgett was born around 1860 in Gilmanton Academy, New Hampshire. He appears to have started, as so many young psychopaths do, with a father who beat him often and fiercely. Mudgett's first victim may well have been a childhood friend who died in a fall while they were playing in an abandoned house. At the same time, young Mudgett was torturing small animals—kittens, puppies, rabbits—under the guise of "scientific experiments."

By the time he had reached college age, Herman had learned how to bilk insurance companies by taking out policies for fictitious individuals and then provide bodies to match the names. He stole cadavers from the University of Michigan's medical lab until he was caught.

Mudgett was a practiced and facile liar. Using his famous alias, Dr. Holmes showed up in Chicago in 1886 and went to work for Everett Holton, who owned a drugstore. Within a year, Holton had died and his wife had vanished. Mudgett told anyone who asked that Mrs. Holton and her daughter were visiting family in California, and asked him to take over the day-to-day business of running the pharmacy. He did well at the drugstore and with other scams, so well that he invested those profits in the construction of a huge, three-story 100-room building across the street. It would become the infamous "Murder Castle," a bizarre labyrinth of tiny windowless rooms that could be turned into gas chambers, hidden staircases, false ceilings, and chutes for delivering bodies to the cellar with its vat of acid, oven, lime pit, and dissecting table.

When asked why he was building such a large place, Mudgett would answer that the upcoming Chicago Fair of 1893 would attract large numbers of visitors and he intended to rent rooms.

He also used the building to attract young women with the promise of jobs and/or marriage. Many made inquiries; few left. During the next four years, Mudgett sold several human skeletons to nearby medical schools. No one knows how many women Mudgett killed during that time, or what horrors they were subjected to. Perhaps the last of them was Minnie Williams, a wealthy Texas heiress. She stayed at Mudgett's Castle and had apparently accepted his proposal of marriage, but hesitated when asked to turn over her inheritance. Her sister Nannie, also called Nettie, became involved, too, and at some point, they learned Holmes also had a wife in Wilmette. Soon thereafter, the Williams sisters went missing.

Perhaps realizing his time was running out, Mudgett put the torch to the Castle. Of course, he returned to his old scam and tried to collect the insurance, too. He also went back to another form of his insurance fraud with a partner named Ben Pitezel. Muggett sent Pitezel, along with his wife and kids, to Philadelphia to establish himself as a patent attorney and take out a fat life insurance policy. Then Muggett would join him in the City of Brotherly Love where they would procure a cadaver, disfigure it, and pass off as Pitezel.

In the meantime, Mudgett made a little side trip to Texas where he tried futilely to get his hooks into the Williams sisters' money. When it didn't work out, he stole a horse and took off. He got as far as St. Louis where he was arrested on a separate matter. While he was being held in jail, he discussed the Pitezel con with his cellmate, train robber Marion Hedgepeth. He also asked Hedgepeth for the name of a good attorney and promised to pay $500 for the recommendation. Hedgepeth provided a mouthpiece who sprung Mudgett, but Mudgett reneged on his side of the deal and took off for Philadelphia.

Justifiably honked off, Hedgepeth wrote to the insurance company and ratted out Mudgett.

By then, Mudgett had already put his plan in motion. But he had actually killed Pitezel and taken off with his three kids. (Mrs. Pitezel was at a loss as to their whereabouts.) With this information, the insurance company sent out Pinkerton detectives, and the outlines of Mudgett's vast criminal career began to emerge.

The detectives caught up with their man in Boston on November 16, 1894 as he was preparing to flee the country. Locked up, Mudgett freely admitted to insurance fraud and embarked on a series of lies that changed as circumstances dictated. First, he claimed he and Pitezel had used a cadaver and that Pitezel had taken the children and left. Weeks later, he claimed Pitezel had committed suicide. And the kids? The kids were with Minnie Williams in England.

In June 1895 Mudgett pled guilty to insurance fraud. His sentencing, however, was delayed, and Philadelphia police detective Frank Geyer embarked on a search for the Pitezel children. It turned out to be an astonishing piece of police work. Geyer's wife and daughter had been killed in a fire a short time before, and the loss gave him an extra incentive to find the missing kids. He set out to retrace Mudgett's recent past with dogged persistence and an understanding nothing Mudgett said could be trusted.

Geyer went first to the Midwest, using photographs of Mudgett and the kids and Mudgett's known aliases to learn if anyone remembered them. It was a complex trail leading from city to city. Finally, in Toronto, Geyer located a house Mudgett had rented, and there in the dirt floor of the cellar was a fresh shallow grave. It contained the bodies of Pitezel's two daughters.

By July Geyer's search was making headlines. He returned to the Midwest, searching in Chicago, Indianapolis, and smaller towns. Finally in August, in Irvington, Indiana, he found another house Mudgett had rented. He also found a large coal stove, and inside were the burned remains of Pitezel's son. It was August 27th.

The wheels of justice soon turned with a speed unknown today. Mudgett went to trial for the murder of Benjamin Pitezel. He loudly proclaimed his innocence and briefly acted as his own attorney, but the evidence was overwhelming. Five days later, he was sentenced to hang in May.

With the promise of $10,000 from the Hearst newspapers and another chance to put himself in the spotlight for a little while longer, Mudgett wrote a "full" confession. At first he claimed 100 victims, then adjusted the figure to 27 (police determined he was lying until the end, claiming to have killed people who were still alive). Whatever the number, he denied the killings were really his fault because the devil made him do it.

Fittingly, prison officials botched Mudgett's hanging. They misjudged his weight and so when they sprang the trap on the gallows, his neck was not broken. Instead, Mudgett was left twisting and twitching for 15 minutes before he strangled to death.

For more than a century, Mudgett/Holmes was relatively unknown. Wide public knowledge of his crimes came with Erik Larson's 2003 bestseller, *Devil in the White City*. It is an excellent look at Mudgett and Chicago at the end of the nineteenth century. Harold Schechter's *Depraved: The Shocking Story of America's First Serial Killer* also earns a solid recommendation, as does Rick Geary's graphic book, *The Beast of Chicago*.

Mudgett's criminal career is given a Ken Burns-like documentary treatment on the DVD *H.H. Holmes: America's First Serial Killer*. Writer/producer/director/editor John Borowski uses old photographs, newspaper headlines, and rudimentary dramatic recreations to tell the awful story. As of this writing, Tom Cruise's production company had purchased an option on the film rights to Larson's book, but no solid plans have been announced.

Mullin, Herbert

Soon after Herbert Mullin graduated from high school in 1965, his life fell apart. He had come from a prosperous, solid middle class Santa Cruz family with no signs of abuse. He was popular, played football, had a girlfriend, and was voted "most likely to succeed" as a senior. But when his best friend was killed in a car accident, the first signs of paranoid schizophrenia appeared. He heard voices, hallucinated, and came to believe his April 18th birthday had cosmic significance because it was the anniversary of the 1906 San Francisco earthquake and Albert Einstein's death. By 1969 Mullin had become so ill, his family urged him to commit himself to a mental institution. He did, but checked himself out before he got any real help.

At the same time, he was compounding his problems with LSD, booze, and marijuana. He then drifted to Hawaii and San Francisco, in and out of different facilities, constantly deteriorating. One day he would declare himself to be a Conscientious Objector to the war in Vietnam; the next day he would try to enlist in the Marines.

He bottomed out in the fall of 1972 when the voices told him to kill. For the next four months he obeyed the voices, claiming later his victims wanted to die. He clubbed a homeless man to death with a baseball bat; eviscerated a hitchhiker; stabbed a priest in the confessional; shot a friend and his wife; shot another acquaintance, a woman, and her two small sons; shot four teenaged boys who were camping; shot a retiree in his driveway. There were witnesses to the last murder, and Mullin was quickly arrested.

Though he clearly demonstrated mentally illness if not insanity, during his questioning and trial the jury found he did not meet the legal standards and found him guilty on two counts of first degree murder. He was sentenced to life and will be eligible for parole in 2025.

The jury foreman caused something of a stir at the time of the verdict by claiming in an open letter Governor Ronald Reagan bore at least some of the responsibility for the murders because he had closed so many mental hospitals.

Given the random nature of Mullin's crimes, he has been reduced to something of a footnote in the overall madness of California crimes in the late 1960s and early '70s.

Murder, Inc.

Lucky Luciano, **Meyer Lansky**, **Vito Genovese** and the rest of their cutthroat pals created a national crime Syndicate or Commission in the early 1930s. It was based on the idea that the various gangs would divide up their illegal enterprises—gambling, booze, sex, drugs, loan sharking, rackets—and cooperate rather than compete with each other. Everybody would make more money and live longer.

In theory, it was rock solid, but these guys tended to be quick-tempered, ruthless, and greedy, and so they knew there had to be some mechanism to maintain the new order. They came up with "Murder, Inc.", as it was called in the popular press.

Actually, these enforcers were an outgrowth of the old Bug and Meyer Mob from Siegel and Lansky's early days together. Murder, Inc. was made up mostly of mid-level hoodlums, about half of them Jewish and half Italian, who could be trusted to kill strangers. Most of the victims were other mobsters who had broken the rules or potential witnesses to Syndicate crimes. Murder, Inc. personnel would also perform assassinations for outsiders if they were cleared by the brass.

The killers prided themselves on being able to work with a wide variety of tools beyond the conventional pistol—bomb, ice pick, piano wire—and to either make the murder as splashy as possible to make a statement, or to get rid of the body so it would never be found.

The going rate was $1,000 to $5,000 per hit. The killers were brought in from out of town and often left before the local cops even knew what had happened. Estimates of the number of murders they committed range from 400 to 700.

The first boss was **Joe Adonis**. Later **Albert Anastasia**, the Lord High Executioner, and **Louis**

"Lepke" **Buchalter** ran things. True sadists through and through, they were naturals for the job.

Probably the most famous victim was mobster **Dutch Schultz**. He was so incensed over crime-busting DA Thomas Dewey that he wanted to have the lawman killed. But it was against the rules. The top gangsters knew killings of cops, reporters, or politicians caused more problems than they solved, and so they were off limits. When the Dutchman refused to be dissuaded, Lansky, Luciano et al. took out a contract on him, and that was that.

Things began to unravel in 1940 when crusading New York DA Burton Turkus got a break with hitman Abe "Kid Twist" Reles. While locked up, Reles learned he had been marked for death by his bosses. He asked Turkus for immunity in exchange for a full confession. For two years, he shared his remarkable memory for the names, dates, and details of more than 200 killings. His testimony sent several of his fellow killers to the chair, most prominent among them Lepke himself.

Reles was in the midst of another trial on November 12, 1941. At 7:00 a.m. in the morning, while he was in police protective custody, accompanied by six officers at the Half Moon Hotel on Coney Island, Brooklyn, he went out a sixth floor bedroom window. Some knotted sheets were found in the room. They provided a figleaf explanation he was somehow trying to escape his protectors or playing a trick on them. Years later, Luciano said **Frank Costello** had shelled out $50,000 to corrupt cops so he could get rid of Reles. Even though Reles's testimony was not enough to get to most of the top guys, he opened people's eyes to what was going on within the mob.

The first film version of the story was the 1951 pseudo-noir *The Enforcer* with Humphrey Bogart as the crusading DA who uses an informant to ferret out the secrets of a group of freelance killers. The Byzantine story is told through flashbacks within flashbacks. Viewers today may be surprised by the cops' naiveté. At the time the film was made, the gangland definitions of such terms as "contract" and "hit" were unknown to moviegoers and so they had to be explained.

The 1960 *Murder, Inc.* is more straightforward, based on a book of the same title by Burton Turkus and Sid Feder. In it, Henry Morgan is the crusading DA with Peter Falk as Reles. The performance earned Falk his first Oscar nomination. His most intense moments of hair trigger anger might have been the inspiration for Joe Pesci's work in *Goodfellas* and *Casino*. The film uses some of the known facts as a framework, but spends too much time on an overwrought subplot.

Murrell, John

John Murrell was:

a) America's most brutal mass murderer with more than 500 victims.

b) A master criminal and revolutionary who planned to lead a slave rebellion to take over New Orleans.

c) A petty thief who knew how to spin a good yarn.

In all likelihood, the answer is c), but Murrell (or Murrel or Murel as the name is sometimes spelled) was certainly a colorful character, and he found a biographer who shared his predilection for embellishment.

Murrell was born in 1794, the son of a modest circuit preacher. He and his brothers were either horse thieves or wealthy plantation owners. (Hey, there are a lot of stories.) Murrell became a habitué of New Orleans finest whorehouses and gambling joints where he would target wealthy ne'er-do-wells from out of town. He would then waylay and kill them on their return trip along the Natchez Trace, steal their valuables and sink their corpses in the river using a particularly gruesome technique: he disemboweled the bodies and filled them with sand to weigh them down. At the same time, he may have been stealing and reselling slaves, or he may have been stealing and arming slaves for the great rebellion. Or he may have been a common outlaw who had organized like-minded fellows into some sort of gang.

Whatever the degree of Murrell's lawless ambitions, in 1834 he met a young fellow named Virgil A. Stewart, and they traveled together for some time through wild country. During the trip, Murrell told Stewart many equally wild tales. A year later, Stewart published these stories in a pamphlet with the imposing title, *A History of the Detection, Conviction, Life and Designs of John A. Murel, The Great Western Land Pirate; Together With his System of Villainy and Plan of Exciting a Negro Rebellion, and a Catalogue of the Names of Four Hundred and Forty Five of His Mystic Clan Fellows and Followers and Their Efforts for the Destruction of Mr. Virgil A. Stewart, The Young Man Who Detected Him, To Which is Added Biographical Sketch of Mr. Virgil A. Stewart.*

In his wide-eyed little fiction, Murrell claimed to be amassing an army of slaves who would attack New Orleans. Once the city had been secured as their base, they would take over Louisiana and Mississippi! And while all this was going on as a diversion, Murrell and the Mystic Clan criminals would spread their evil tentacles into Nashville and Memphis, and would turn that part of the Mississippi into an independent criminal nation.

Yeah, right.

The upshot was that Murrell was arrested in 1835 and served 10 years in a Tennessee prison. The charge was horse-stealing. All of Murrell's other alleged crimes involve a large amount of speculation, but it only adds to his standing as a folk hero, the embodiment of the antebellum Southern outlaw. And he did have that reputation. Ten years after his death and release from prison, his body was disinterred and parts were sold off and treated as relics. His skull is still unaccounted for, but one thumb remains in the holdings of the Tennessee State Museum.

Whatever fame Stewart's pamphlet brought to Murrell, his lasting place in literature was secured by Mark Twain, a man who knew a good story when he heard one and seldom let the facts get in the way. Murrell makes an appearance in Twain's *Life on the Mississippi* (1883). He is also the subject of John Wray's 2005 novel *Canaan's Tongue.*

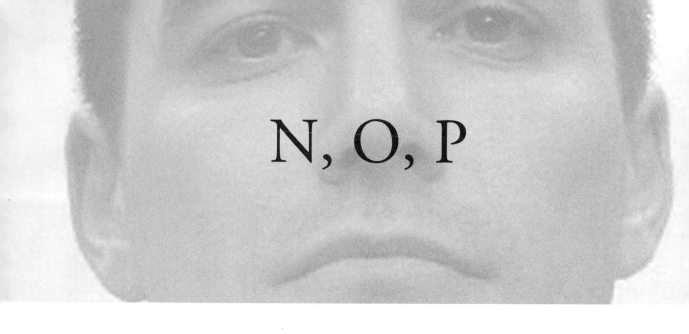

N, O, P

Nash, Jay Robert

Jay Robert Nash began his professional career as an editor of serious literary journals and professional magazines in Chicago in the 1960s.

His first effort in true crime writing was *Dillinger: Dead or Alive?* in 1970. Focusing on the inconsistencies in the appearance of the corpse and other curious details, he concluded that someone else was fingered by the famous Lady in Red and killed by FBI agents in 1934, and Dillinger lived on. The idea has found great popularity among conspiracy theorists and even those who are more skeptical find it hard to resist. Next came *Citizen Hoover* (1972), one of the first books to take a critical look at the FBI.

In 1973 came *Bloodletters and Bad Men,* Nash's *chef d'oeuvre,* a one-volume compendium of American crime. Along with Carl Sifakis' *Encyclopedia of American Crime* and Richard Hammer's *Playboy's Illustrated History of Organized Crime,* it is one of American crime's standard reference guides. Any librarian will tell you it is also one of the most popular; Nash's book was revised and expanded in 1995. Some of the same material is covered in his *Encyclopedia of Western Lawmen and Outlaws* (1989, 1994).

Nash has also written and edited *Spies* (1997), *Terrorism in the Twentieth Century* (1998), *World*

Encyclopedia of Organized Crime (1993), *Look for the Woman* (1981), *World Encyclopedia of Twentieth Century Murder* (1992), *Murder Among the Rich and Famous* (1988), *Murder Among the Mighty* (1984), and *Almanac of World Crime* (1981, 1987).

Nash has also published fiction, poetry, and nonfiction in other fields.

National Police Gazette

"We offer this week a most interesting record of horrid murders, outrageous robberies, bold forgeries, astounding burglaries, hideous rapes, vulgar seductions, and recent exploits of pickpockets and hotel thieves in various parts of the country."

All that and much much more (including ads for erectile dysfunction remedies) were yours for only a nickel. That's what the *National Police Gazette* promised to deliver for more than a century beginning in 1845. In its heyday, it was a combination of the *National Enquirer, America's Most Wanted, Playboy* and *Sports Illustrated,* and as such, it was hugely popular.

Other publications called the *Gazette* had existed earlier in England. The American version was created by George Wilkes and Enoch Camp. Camp soon retired and Wilkes sold the paper to former New York City police chief George Washington Matsell. The new publisher promptly lowered his sights and added racy woodcut illustrations featuring busty young women (usually several busty young women) drinking and cavorting, being victimized by criminals, smoking tobacco or opium, and wearing low cut dresses and nighties with daring décolletage. (Editorially, the paper was disingenuously appalled by such behavior from busty young women who did not know their place.)

Matsell sold out in 1866 and the *Gazette* declined until 1877 when Richard Kyle Fox took over. He made the content even more scandalous and offered cut-rate subscriptions to bars, barbershops, taverns, and hotels—anyplace where groups of men were likely to congregate. He also started printing the *Gazette* on pink paper to distinguish it from its competitors, and to publish photographs of boxers and burlesque stars.

At the height of its popularity, the *Gazette* was read by millions and charged advertising rates comparable to such "legitimate" publications as the *Ladies Home Journal*. It counted among its readers Thomas Edison, James Joyce, and Jesse James. James even submitted pictures of his gang to the paper.

Since the *Gazette* pushed as many limits as it could, it was roundly condemned by upright citizens everywhere. The state of Texas tried to impose a specific tax on the paper, but was shot down in court. The *Gazette* faced even more serious criticism from the other end of the social spectrum. Particularly in its early years, the paper was hated by the criminals whose crimes it reported. Some of them tried to retaliate after they'd been released from jail, by gathering their friends and colleagues into mobs and physically attacking the New York editorial offices.

While refined sensibilities might question the *Gazette*'s choice of subject matter, the writing could actually be quite good—simple, vivid, and immediate; exactly what its readers wanted. The *Gazette*'s description of the murder of **Bill "the Butcher" Poole** is particularly strong.

Richard Fox died in 1922. His crew published the paper for another decade or so before they sold it. Circulation fell as other more specialized magazines siphoned off readers, and mainstream tabloid newspapers became more like the *Gazette*.

Today, the *Police Gazette* survives as the working title of the third volume of James Ellroy's *Underworld USA* trilogy. The first two books are *American Tabloid* and *The Cold Six Thousand*.

Nelson, Earle

The papers dubbed him the "Gorilla Killer" and the "Dark Strangler." Both were horribly accurate. Earle Leonard Nelson was a psychotic sexual predator who killed more than 20 women, girls, and children in the 1920s. He was a monster who never had a chance.

Before he was a year old, both of his parents had died from syphilis. He was raised in San Francisco by his grandmother, an evangelical Christian who already had two children and wasn't prepared to deal with a troubled boy. To use today's terminology, Nelson exhibited bipolar tendencies early on, swinging between exuberance and dark depression. He drenched his meals in olive oil and gobbled his food like a starving animal. Given to long solitary walks, he often returned home wearing different, inappropriate clothes. He picked up his grandmother's religion and obsessively read the Bible, particularly the Book of Revelation.

As a teenager, he visited whores with equal zeal. He developed a violent, fearsome temper. He occasionally talked to imaginary figures and was caught shoplifting. A hulking figure with massive mitts, he suffered a violent head injury as an adolescent when his bike was hit by a trolley car, and then a few years later, another one when he fell from a ladder.

At 18, Nelson was sentenced to San Quentin for burglary. Upon his release, he succumbed to the patriotic fever sweeping pre–World War I America and joined the Army. In short order, he deserted and then enlisted in the Navy. That lasted for a month.

He then deserted again in San Francisco and signed up for the Medical Corps. That didn't work out either, so he went back into the Navy briefly before his mental problems became so serious he was committed to the Napa State Mental Hospital.

Nelson escaped from Napa State three times in the year he was there. After the third escape, the various authorities involved threw up their hands and wrote him off with a military discharge and a note in his file that he had improved.

After his final escape, Nelson fetched up near San Francisco working as a janitor at St. Mary's Hospital, where he met and married Mary Martin. An older woman, Mary was deeply religious like his grandmother. Nelson appears to have treated her more as a mother than a wife as his mental state continued to deteriorate. His clothing habits became even more curious. He sometimes tried to cut Mary's clothes to fit him. He became more possessive and angry, and finally attacked her when she was in the hospital recovering from an illness. That did it; she refused to accompany him when he demanded they move.

Shortly after, on May 19, 1921 Nelson gave in to his violent demons and attacked 12-year-old Mary Summers as she played in her basement. (He had pretended to be a plumber searching for a gas leak.) The girl fought him off, and Nelson fled but was captured a few hours later on a trolley. At a competency hearing, he was judged to be dangerous and sent back to Napa, the facility he had already walked away from three times. He would escape again—twice—in the four years he stayed there until his release. That's when the "Dark Strangler" first appeared.

Nelson's first victim was Clara Newmann, a 62-year-old widow who ran a boarding house in San Francisco. One morning in February 1926 Nelson inquired about a room. She took him upstairs where he strangled her, then raped her dead body. Two weeks later, he did the same thing to another matronly landlady, Laura Beal, in San Jose.

Newspapers noted the similar horrific details of the murders and called the strangler the "Gorilla Killer" because the brutality of the killings were reminiscent of Poe's story, "The Murders in the Rue Morgue." Nelson hit the road and continued to follow his pattern of killing back in San Francisco, then again in Santa Barbara, Oakland, and twice in Portland, Oregon.

Nelson's brazen MO varied little. He located middle-aged or elderly women running boarding houses, asked about a room, and, after determining they were alone, attacked them. He made only cursory attempts to hide the bodies and sometimes stole jewelry and money. After staying in Portland for several days, he headed east—Kansas City, Philadelphia, Buffalo, Detroit, Chicago—and, for more than a year, continued to kill.

Finally, Nelson went to Canada and something changed. He found a room at a boarding house in Winnepeg, but his first victim there was Lola Cowan, a teenager who was selling paper flowers. After enticing her back to his room, Nelson killed her and hid the body under his bed. His next victim was another change from his routine: Emily Patterson was a wife and mother who was cleaning her house when Nelson somehow managed to talk his way in. Her husband discovered her body under their son's bed that night.

The two brutal murders electrified everyone in the area and a $1,500 reward was offered for the killer. Winnipeg wasn't that big and suspicion immediately settled on strangers. Nelson was headed out of town when he was first arrested and taken to the Killarney jail. Claiming to be a good Christian boy named Virgil Wilson, he was so persuasive the guards left him alone in his cell. Again he escaped, apparently believing he could still bluff his way out of the country. He was recaptured the next day without putting up any resistance.

Before his trial, a steady stream of witnesses came north from the United States to finger Nelson and detail his involvement with earlier murders. He steadfastly maintained his complete innocence as a media storm gathered and swirled around him. At the trial, the evidence against him was so massive, his defense was based only his troubled background and irrational behavior. The jury didn't go for it: it took them less than an hour to find him guilty. Still proclaiming his godliness and innocence, Earle Nelson was hanged by the neck until dead on January 13, 1928.

In the end, though Nelson was suspected of several more murders, he was officially connected to 22 killings, one of them an 8-month-old baby he strangled with a diaper. The world was better off without him.

America had seen serial killers before (though no one used the term at the time), but Nelson was the first whose brutal murders were reported in newspapers, national magazines, and on the new medium of radio. The attention he attracted in the media would be repeated with the **Leopold and Loeb** case and the **Lindbergh** baby kidnapping.

Earle Nelson's murders provided part of the basis for Alfred Hitchcock's 1943 masterpiece, *Shadow of a Doubt*. In it, Joseph Cotten plays Uncle Charlie, the Merry Widow Murderer. The character is a silky psychopath whose true nature is discovered by his namesake niece (Teresa Wright) while he's hiding out with her family in the little town of Santa Rosa, California. Nelson's story is told much more fully in Harold Schechter's *Bestial: The Savage Trail of a True American Nightmare* (2004).

Nelson, George "Baby Face"

"Baby Face" Nelson was the most violent of the famous 1930s bank robbers. Where **John Dillinger** or **Alvin Karpis** would carefully plan a job to minimize physical force, Nelson loved to barge in, Tommy gun blazing, and kill anyone who didn't cooperate quickly enough. It wasn't a particularly profitable technique, but Baby Face loved it.

Born Lester Joseph Gillis, he grew up around the Chicago stockyards and learned early on that a little fellow like himself—he never topped five-feet five-

inches—had to be the toughest kid on the street to survive. He started out stealing cars then joined the Capone mob as a "convincer" who kept labor union men in line. But he was so enthusiastic in his work that he kept killing people who were only supposed to be beaten up. He was asked to leave, and so may have been the only person kicked out of **Al Capone**'s gang for being *too* violent.

About the same time, he married the equally diminutive Helen Wawzynak and started sticking up jewelry stores to support her. He was caught in January 1931 and sent up to Joliet. A year later, as he was being transported back from a pretrial hearing for another crime, he knocked out a policeman and escaped from a commuter train. Helen was waiting in a car. They hightailed it to California where Baby Face went to work for bootlegger Joe Parente. That's where Nelson met John Paul Chase, who would become his friend and partner in crime.

Having risen as high as they could in the Golden State booze biz, Chase, Helen, and Baby Face left in 1932 and settled in St. Paul, Minnesota, one of the most corrupt cities in the Midwest in those days. With a couple of new recruits, they hit banks in Wisconsin, Nebraska, and Iowa.

During John Dillinger's brief incarceration in the Crown Point jail, his pal Homer Van Meter approached Nelson and they agreed to join forces. Once Dillinger had busted out, the combined gang knocked over two banks in Sioux Falls, South Dakota and Mason City, Iowa. Both jobs involved heavy gunfire and relatively meager payoffs.

Nelson and Helen were hiding out with what was left of the gang at the Little Bohemia Lodge when **Melvin Purvis** and his G-men attempted their ill-fated ambush. The feds killed one bystander and wounded two more while the gangsters flew the coop. Nelson was separated from the others but managed to steal a car from three federal agents, killing one and seriously wounding the others in the process.

After that mess Baby Face, Helen, and Chase went back to California where they learned

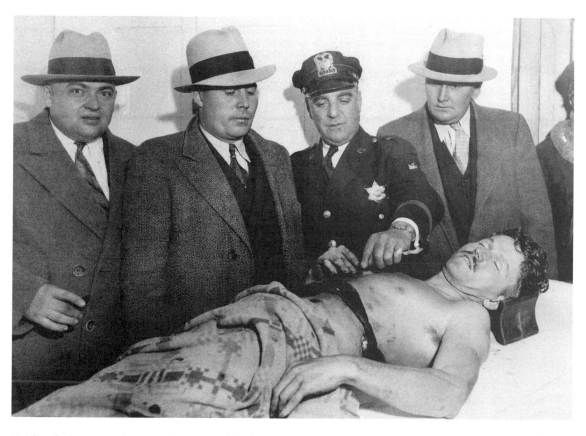

Unidentified agents and police officer around the body of "Baby Face" Nelson in a morgue near Chicago, November 28, 1934. (AP Photo)

Dillinger had been killed in Chicago. His death (if he died) meant Baby Face had moved from Number Two on the Public Enemies List to the coveted Number One spot, but his joy was short-lived when he realized the reward for his capture had not been increased. Even as Numero Uno, he was worth only half as much as Johnny D. in his prime (and Dillinger had been taller, too.)

Nelson vowed to change all that; he'd show them! He'd rob a bank a day for a month! Baby Face, Chase, and Helen returned to the Midwest where they found nobody was interested in joining his grandiose scheme. But the feds learned they were back, and were on the lookout.

On September 27, 1934 two agents spotted the trio in their car and gave chase. Baby Face crashed into a ditch. Agents Herman Hollis and **Sam Cowley**, both armed with machine guns, closed in. Baby Face wasn't impressed. To the amazement of nearby witnesses, the tiny gangster pulled out his own Tommy gun and walked straight into the G-men's crossfire.

They hit him several times, but Nelson stayed on his feet and returned fire. He got Cowley first and then turned on Hollis. When the last shot had been fired, both G-men were dead and Nelson was mortally wounded. Helen and Chase took him away. The next day, his naked body—stripped to delay identification—was found in a ditch. A fitting end for a tiny thug who never deserved any sympathy.

Baby Face's tarnished image kept him from achieving any real prominence in popular culture. On screen, he has often appeared as a supporting character, played most notably by a squirrelly Richard Dreyfuss in John Milius's 1973 *Dillinger*. Nelson was also the protagonist of two films, both titled *Baby Face Nelson* where he was portrayed by Mickey Rooney in 1957 and C. Thomas Howell in 1995.

New Orleans Axeman

There are three possible explanations for the unsolved New Orleans Axeman killings of 1918-19:

1) A lone maniac attacked Italian grocers (mostly) and their wives.

2) Several people were inspired by the first attacks and adopted the technique for their own purposes.

3) A Mafia enforcer terrorized the Italian community.

It's difficult to describe the murders in any detail. Normally reliable sources disagree about the basics. Were the killings a second wave to a series that had occurred in 1911? Some say yes, some no. In either case, early on the morning of May 23, 1918 Joseph Maggio and his wife Catherine were found by his brothers on a blood-soaked bed. Both had been attacked with an ax and a straight razor. A door panel had been chiseled open, though it may not have been large enough to admit a grown man.

A couple weeks later, grocer Louis Besumer and his mistress Anna Harriet Lowe were attacked. Both survived, at least initially. Anna, more seriously wounded, was taken to the hospital. Before she died, she claimed Besumer had attacked her—and that he was a German spy! (World War I was still going on.) Besumer, a Pole, denied everything and was arrested. (He was later tried and acquitted.)

Then in August, the pregnant Mrs. Edward Schneider was attacked. She had a serious gash in her head and some teeth had been knocked out, but she and her unborn child survived. Later she said she had been taking a nap and had awoken to find a dark figure standing over her with an ax. That's all she remembered.

Five days later, Joseph Romano was the victim of an ax-wielding assailant. Where Mrs. Schneider had been neither Italian nor connected with the grocery business, Romano was an Italian barber. He did not survive the attack.

The killings then ceased until March 10, 1919. They began again in Gretna, across the river. The victims were Charles and Rosie Cortimiglia; they survived but their two-year-old daughter Mary did not. When she recovered, Rosie claimed her neighbors and rival grocers Frank and Iorlando Jordano had done it. They were arrested.

A few days later the *New Orleans Times-Picayune* received a letter allegedly written by the Axeman. In florid, fevered prose he boasted of his supernatural powers and promised to return on the next Tuesday. But, like an angel of the Lord, he would bypass any house where jazz was being played. That was enough to cause residents of the Big Easy to throw raucous parties where the freshly penned *Mysterious Axeman's Jazz* was the most popular musical number. There were no attacks.

They resumed on August 10th, when sleeping grocer Steve Boca was brained with an ax. He survived. So did 19-year-old Sarah Laumann (neither Italian nor grocer) who was attacked in September.

The final victim was Mike Pepitone. He was killed on October 27th, and his wife said she saw the attacker or attackers (there may have been two) but she could provide no useful identification. That's when the New Orleans killings ended, but not the story.

In December, Rosie Cortimiglia recanted. She said she had lied when she accused the Jordanos. A saint had appeared to her and told her to make a clean breast of it. Both Jordanos were released.

Also in December, the widow Pepitone traveled to Los Angeles. Dressed in black, she sought out one Joseph Mumfre. Lurking in a shadow, she shot and killed him, then waited for the police. After her arrest, she claimed Mumfre was the man she had seen in her husband's room.

Mumfre did have an extensive criminal record. Between 1911 and 1919, he had been in and out of prison, and all the killings had during his unincarcerated periods. Some claim he was a **Mafia** hitman, or perhaps associated with the **Black Hand**, an Italian extortion operation. But it certainly doesn't account for all of the killings, nor does it explain them. Still, the ax murders stopped. Mrs. Pepitone served three of a ten-year stretch and was released. Nothing more is known of her.

As a figure in popular culture, the Axeman has never really spread beyond the New Orleans area. There he is part of the city's colorful supernatural heritage, along with voodoo and Anne Rice's baroque tales.

Ng, Charles, and Leonard Lake

Charles Ng and Leonard Lake were such sick monsters they have not found much of a following. Even serial killer aficionados who soak up the smallest details of Gein and Bundy don't care about these guys. In terms of pop culture, they simply don't register. Their names are largely unknown outside of northern California, and that's a very good thing.

Lake was born in 1946 in San Francisco. His troubled childhood was marked by early sexual fantasies involving bondage and women as slaves, and violent disagreements with his younger brother, Donald. Lake joined the Marines in 1966 and served in Vietnam, without seeing combat. His psychiatric problems became more severe there, and he was in therapy for two years before his 1971 discharge.

Ng (pronounced "Ing") came from a wealthy Hong Kong family. Born in 1961, he became a compulsive but incompetent shoplifter and thief as a boy. He was sent off to an English boarding school

but quickly got the boot for stealing. As a teenager, he came to America on a student visa but dropped out of college in California after one semester. More run-ins with the law followed. In 1979, claiming to be an American citizen, he enlisted in the Marines. He was, he said, a ninja warrior. Two years later he and two others were caught stealing military weapons on a base in Hawaii.

Ng managed to escape custody and returned to northern Calfornia where he met Lake, who fancied himself a survivalist. Within a few months, Ng had moved in with Lake and his wife. Five months later, both men were busted on a federal weapons charge.

Lake skipped out on his bond, but deserter Ng faced a court martial. He was convicted and served 18 months at Leavenworth. Released in 1983 he went straight to Lake who had moved to a cabin near Wilseyville, California. That's where their crimes became more serious.

With the help of neighbors—some of whom eventually disappeared—Lake had built a large concrete bunker, complete with secret rooms, next to the cabin. The first victim appears to have been brother Donald who came by for a visit in July 1983 and was never seen again. Most of the other victims were people who were simply unlucky enough to come across the two psychos. There was the guy who was trying to sell a used Honda to Lake, and the family who had some audio-visual equipment for sale. They vanished, along with many others.

It all fell apart on June 2, 1985 when Ng tried to shoplift a bench vise from a south San Francisco lumber yard. A clerk saw him and called the cops. As they arrived, Ng took a powder, leaving Lake in the stolen Honda with the vise in the trunk. Right away, the police learned the tags didn't match the car's registration. And there was the .22 revolver (complete with silencer) in the car. Lake also appeared older than 26, the age on the stolen driver's license he carried.

He was arrested on the spot and taken to a police station where Lake admitted he was a fugitive. He

FBI SAN FRANCISCO
CHARLES
CHAT
NG
52A NEW
APRIL 30 1982

Charles Ng, charged with 12 murders from 1984–85, in an FBI photo from 1982. (AP Photo)

asked for a glass of water and used it to wash down cyanide capsules he had hidden in his clothes. Four days later, after convulsions and what we can only hope was unspeakably agonizing pain, Lake was dead.

By then, the cops were uncovering the chamber of horrors he and Ng had created in the bunker. The place was filled with blood-stained mattresses, shackles, bullet holes, and a broken bench vise. They also found videotapes of Lake and Ng torturing and raping women, and diaries describing what they had done in detail. There were also bone fragments and other human remains. In the end, they had evidence of 25 bodies, some of them children.

Ng, meanwhile, had made it as far as Chicago and then into Canada. After more than a month on

the lam, the stealthy ninja warrior was caught shoplifting in Calgary, Alberta. He put up a fight and even shot a security guard in the hand before they got him under control. Once he was in custody, Ng and his lawyers began some masterful manipulation of the Canadian and American legal systems.

Ng served time in Canada for the crimes he had committed there, but fought extradition to America and managed to put it off until 1991.

During those years, he studied law and when, finally, he was returned to California, he used every delaying tactic available—filing hundreds of motions, hiring and firing attorneys, representing himself at times. Jury selection didn't begin until 1998. Before it was over, the trial cost more than $20 million, mak-

Officers around the body of Frank "the Enforcer" Nitti, gangster and reported chief of the Capone syndicate, found near a railroad embankment in Riverside, Illinois, 1943. (AP Photo)

ing it the state's most expensive prosecution. But it took the jury only 50 minutes to find Ng guilty on 11 counts of murder on May 3, 1999.

The jury decided life without the possibility of parole was not a sufficient punishment and the judge agreed. Ng is now on death row in San Quentin.

Nitti, Frank "the Enforcer"

Frank Nitti was never the top-drawer gangster he was made out to be in either the original *Untouchables* television show or the 1987 film.

But since everyone knows his boss **Al Capone** was jailed for tax evasion and died enfeebled and

unhinged by syphilis, another good strong villain was needed for fact-based Midwest crime stories. With his nickname "the Enforcer," Nitti fit the bill.

The truth is considerably less exciting.

Nitti was born in Sicily in either 1883, 1884, or 1888. As a young man, he emigrated to New York and then to Chicago where he became a barber. He also became a fence for stolen goods. As such, he was well known to Mafia boss Johnny Torrio and his successor, Capone.

Given Nitti's connections and organizational skills, Capone put him in charge of liquor distribution during Prohibition. Like his boss, Nitti pulled a stretch on tax evasion charges, but his sentence was short. Capone was still locked up when he was sprung. Nitti then became the public face of the Chicago mob, but when **Lucky Luciano** and **Meyer Lansky** set up the national syndicate in 1931, they didn't discuss it with him. They went to Paul, "the Waiter" Ricca who was really in charge in Chicago. The dapper Ricca avoided publicity as assiduously as Capone courted it, and was content to let Nitti be the figurehead.

In 1932, two rogue cops, possibly acting on orders from the newly elected mayor Anton Cermak, burst into Nitti's office and shot him. Though severely wounded, Nitti survived. A year later, when Cermak was sharing a convertible with Franklin Roosevelt, he was not so lucky. Wanna-be assassin **Joseph Zangara** took a shot at the President but missed and plugged the mayor. Cermak died three weeks later.

In the 1940s Nitti and Ricca were involved with a group of mobsters who made an attempt to put the squeeze on movie studios through threatened strikes by the projectionists union. When it all fell apart and several of them were charged, Ricca ordered Nitti to take the fall for the rest. Afraid of another prison sentence and perhaps dying of cancer, Nitti killed himself on March 19, 1943.

Failing to extort Hollywood executives hardly puts one in the same league with Scarface. It was left to the creators of *The Untouchables* series to do that. They transformed Nitti into Eliot Ness's main nemesis. In episode after episode, he was Public Enemy Number One. In the 1987 *Untouchables* film, writer David Mamet, director Brian DePalma, and actor Billy Drago turned Nitti into a dandified psychopath who was almost but not quite as fearsome as Robert DeNiro's Capone.

In *Road to Perdition* (2002), Stanley Tucci's Nitti is a much more polished and urbane gangster. Given his larger-than-life reputation, Nitti has been embraced by the most recent wave of gangsters, or gangstas in the rap and hip hop community.

O.K. Corral

In the violent history of the American West, the actual events that took place at the O.K. Corral on the afternoon of October 26, 1881 barely deserve a footnote. But, if a popular writer tells the story from your point of view, and if you make the right friends in Hollywood, then your footnote becomes a central element of western mythology. That's what Wyatt Earp did.

Along with his brothers James, Morgan, and Virgil, Wyatt moved from Iowa to California after the Civil War. (He was too young to serve, but James fought for the Union and was seriously wounded.) Wyatt worked as a teamster and stagecoach driver. His first experience in law enforcement was as a constable in Lamar, Missouri. He left there under a cloud, possibly for pocketing some of the fines he collected. He worked again as a deputy in Wichita and Dodge City, Kansas. Some of his biographers claim he built a strong reputation as a courageous, tough-minded peace officer; others say he was a nobody in those days.

In either case, he was a tall strikingly handsome man, and it was during this time that he became close friends with Doc Holliday, the tubercular dentist, gambler, and gunfighter.

In 1879 Wyatt's older brother Virgil was appointed deputy U.S. Marshal in Tombstone, Arizona. Wyatt and James went with him. A year later Morgan and Doc Holliday joined them.

By this time, the Clanton family and the McLaury brothers (sometimes spelled McLowery) were well established in the area. Both were associated with the Cowboys (sometimes spelled Cow-Boys), a loosely organized gang of rustlers and thieves under the leadership of Curly Bill Brocius and John Ringo. In Tombstone, opinions were divided about the Cowboys and the Earps along roughly political lines. Some saw the lawmen as favoring the interests of the town and the business leaders over those of the ranchers. To them, the Cowboys were high-spirited young men who occasionally went a little too

256

far. Others saw the Earps as legitimate peacemakers who were trying to bring order to a place rapidly evolving from a frontier settlement to a real town.

Beyond those disagreements, two things are certain: first, Tombstone had a strict no-guns-in-town policy; second, the Clantons and the Earps hated each other and didn't try to hide it. Tension between them heated up with a stage robbery in March 1881. Wyatt believed blowhard Ike Clanton was involved. Clanton claimed the job had been pulled off by Wyatt and Doc Holliday. At least, that's what Doc's squeeze Big Nose Kate Elder said. (Later, she took it back, saying she had just been drunk and mad at Doc.)

On Tuesday, October 25th, Ike Clanton and Tom McLaury drove into Tombstone to get supplies. In Clanton's case that meant whisky and he went on a bender. Late that night, he ran into Doc Holliday, who was also drunk. They had words. Wyatt had been deputized some months earlier but was not currently on the force. Still, he broke things up before they became violent. Virgil then spent the rest of the night playing cards with Clanton and McLaury who were unarmed.

The next morning, after the game, Virgil turned in, but Ike, a notoriously mean-tempered drunk, kept hitting the sauce and mouthing off about what he was going to do to the Earps. He also fetched his guns. Around noon, Virgil and Morgan confronted Ike. They pistol whipped the drunk, took his weapons and had a judge fine him $25 plus court costs.

At about the same time, two other things happened: Tom McLaury showed up and Wyatt saw him; Thinking he might be armed, Wyatt gave him a beating, too. Then Ike Clanton's younger brother Billy (19) and Tom McLaury's brother Frank arrived in town and learned what was going on. With that, the stage was set for the famous gunfight.

By mid-afternoon Ike and Billy Clanton, Tom and Frank McLaury, Billy Claiborne, and several horses were hanging out in a dusty vacant lot behind the O.K. Corral. Believing the men were illegally carrying weapons, Virgil, Morgan, Wyatt, and Doc

Holliday walked down Fremont Street with the goal of disarming them. They carried revolvers and a short double-barreled shotgun. It's unclear precisely how the Cowboys were armed or, in some cases, whether they had any weapons. Key details are contradictory, depending on who's telling the story.

Still drunk but not stupid, Ike Clanton made a quick exit as soon as he saw what was going down. So did Billy Claiborne. Later, both would claim to have been unarmed.

Virgil yelled, "Throw your hands up. I want your guns!" Then the shooting started. Some say the Earps fired first; some say the McLaurys. When it was over about 30 seconds later, Billy Clanton and Frank and Tom McLaury were dead or dying. Virgil and Morgan Earp had been wounded; Doc Holliday had been grazed by a bullet. Wyatt emerged unscathed.

Eventually, various charges would be filed against all of the survivors but no one was ever indicted. A few weeks later, Virgil was shot by unknown assailants and was so severely wounded he completely lost the use of his left arm for the rest of his life. Three months after that, Morgan was assassinated in a similar ambush.

In March 1882 Wyatt and Doc Holliday went after some of the suspects in Morgan's murder and killed Frank Stilwell, "Indian Charlie" Cruz and Curly Bill Brocius. These, probably, are the bare facts of the matter. Doc Holliday died of tuberculosis in 1887. Wyatt Earp lived until 1929 and was always reluctant to talk about those days. But he went back to California where he became peripherally involved with the movies. By the early twentieth century he was a minor celebrity, due largely to the tales told about him by his friend Bat Masterton, and his friendship with such Hollywood luminaries as director John Ford and actors Tom Mix and William S. Hart.

Twice, Wyatt attempted to collaborate on an autobiography with writers, but both projects floundered. Toward the end of his life, he talked extensively with writer Stuart Lake who used the

Gunfight at the OK Corral, **Hollywood-style, with Burt Lancaster (Earp) and Kirk Douglas (Holliday), 1956.**
(AP Photo)

interviews, his own research, and a vivid imagination to create *Wyatt Earp, Frontier Marshal*. The book became a national bestseller in 1931 and rose to even greater popularity when it was serialized in the *Saturday Evening Post*.

With the serialization, the book cemented the image of the Earps as tall, stern men in black frock coats and ties who defeated the rawboned primitive Clantons. Within that story is the friendship between two radically different but appealing personalities—Wyatt, the fearless lawman, and Doc, the doomed Byronic gunman. The characters struck a strong chord with 1930s readers who were experiencing an alarming increase in criminal activity with rampant kidnappings, bank robberies, and gangsters machinegunning each other in the streets.

Director John Ford brought that version to the screen in 1946 in *My Darling Clementine*, with Henry Fonda and Victor Mature as Wyatt and Doc. The film is more notable for the striking Monument Valley locations and Fonda's performance than for any fealty to the truth.

In the mid-1950s Hugh O'Brien portrayed Wyatt as a rock-jawed barrel-chested hero in the popular television series *The Life and Legend of Wyatt Earp*. As the theme song said, "long live his fame and long live his glory and long may his story be told."

In 1957 John Sturges made *Gunfight at O.K. Corral* with Burt Lancaster and Kirk Douglas as Wyatt and Doc. The film heightens the contrast between the straight-arrow Wyatt and his ne'er-do-well friend.

The Tombstone story is fictionalized in Edward Dmytryk's 1959 *Warlock*, with Fonda, again, and Anthony Quinn. Sturges returned to the material in 1967 with *Hour of the Gun*, which begins with the O.K. Corral and focuses on Earp's vendetta with James Garner and Jason Robards, Jr.

In 1971's *Doc*, director Frank Perry and writer Pete Hamill tried to use the Earp story as a metaphor for the Vietnam war with Harris Yulin as a homosexual Wyatt standing in for President Lyndon Johnson, and Stacy Keach as Doc, presumably standing in for Secretary of Defense Robert McNamara.

Kevin Reynolds' 1994 *Wyatt Earp* is a sobersided three-hour biopic with Kevin Costner in the lead. Alas, Dennis Quaid as Doc, enters late and leaves early.

Far and away the most enjoyable screen version of the story is the 1993 *Tombstone*, written by Kevin Jarre and directed by George Cosmatos. It's an ambitious adventure built around historical fact and unusually scrupulous attention to period detail. For my money, Kurt Russell's Wyatt and Val Kilmer's Doc are as fine as any who have appeared on screen. The supporting characters are strong, too, particularly Dana Delaney as Josephine Marcus, the woman Wyatt loved and lived with for most of his life.

The gunfight is presented fairly accurately. Action that takes place before and after it are compressed and exaggerated to heighten the mythic elements of the tale. Historically true? Hardly. Exciting? Definitely.

Of the many books written on the subject, Allen Bara's 1998 *Inventing Wyatt Earp* is an exemplary piece of popular history.

Osama bin Laden

Osama bin Laden has many reasons to hate the United States and Western popular culture. As the son of an incredibly wealthy and religiously conservative Saudi Arabian family, he was raised to believe in the superiority of his particular brand of Wahabbi Islam over all other faiths, philosophies, and people. It is violent, narrow-minded, anti-Semitic, and profoundly misogynistic.

In 1982, when he was in his mid-20s, bin Laden traveled to Pakistan and saw the results of the Russian invasion of Afghanistan firsthand. Thousands of refugees streamed across the border, and Osama came to sympathize with the Mujahedeen rebels who were fighting the Soviets. He returned to Saudi Arabia and raised millions for them. Then he went to Afghanistan himself, helped build roads, and to fight with the resistance. His operation there came to call itself "al Qaeda," or "the base."

After the Russians finally pulled out in 1989, bin Laden kicked around Saudi Arabia and the Gulf states where he continued to attract followers and make connections with like-minded Islamists. At the time, one of his primary enemies was Saddam Hussein of Iraq. When the secular Hussein invaded Kuwait in 1990, Osama bin Laden was quick to volunteer his group to defend Saudi Arabia. The country was Hussein's natural and obvious next target, and so bin Laden, the local boy, was mightily pissed off when Saudi King Faisal told him to shut up and, instead, turned to America for protection.

For bin Laden, that was the worst possible scenario. His religious patriotism had been insulted and it meant American troops—including armed women and the hated Jews—would be stationed in Islam's holiest cities and sites. His ratty little beard quivered with righteous wrath.

The Saudi government put him under house arrest but he managed to obtain permission to go to Pakistan on business. From there, he made his way to the Sudan where he could operate more freely. The first terrorist act he helped to sponsor was the February 26, 1993 truck-bomb attack on the World Trade Center. Six died and more than a thousand were injured. The attack was led by Ramzi Yousef; Yousef's uncle Khalid Shaikh Mohammed, was also peripherally involved.

In 1996 bin Laden moved back to Afghanistan and organized the attack on the Khobar Towers Air Force barracks in Dhahran, Saudi Arabia, killing 19 American soldiers. Some months later, he announced his official declaration of war or "jihad" against America and Israel.

In 1998 bin Laden was behind the August 7th bombings of American embassies in Nairobi, Kenya, and Dar es Salaam, Tanzania, killing more than 200 people and injuring thousands. Only 16 of the dead were Americans, though it mattered little to the bombers. The bombings received the attention bin Laden wanted and proved to Khalid Shaikh Mohammed that he, bin Laden, was serious. Mohammed joined al Qaeda, and began making plans for the 9/11 atrocities.

But the next attack, in 2000, was on the *USS Cole*, a Navy destroyer anchored in the port of Aden, Yemen. Seventeen American sailors were killed, 37 more were injured. While the CIA and American forces tried unsuccessfully to nail bin Laden with a Cruise missile, Shaikh Mohammed sent a group of young Muslim fanatics, led by Mohamed Atta to America. Atta, a grim square-headed guy, was an Egyptian college student who shared his bosses' hatred of Americans and Jews.

Atta was in charge of about 20 revolutionaries who moved into a series of apartments and attended flight school in Florida. They learned how to pilot jet airliners and crisscrossed the country on commercial flights to familiarize themselves with air travel.

On the morning of September 11, 2001 Atta and 18 others boarded four airplanes: American Airlines Flight 11 from Boston to Los Angeles; United Airlines Flight 175 from Boston to Los Angeles; American Airlines Flight 77 from Washington Dulles to Los Angeles; and United Airlines Flight 93 from Newark, New Jersey to San Francisco. They had first-class tickets placing them close to the pilots. Less than an hour into each flight, they attacked and killed flight attendants using box cutters, knives, and some sort of aerosol pepper spray. They overpowered or killed the pilots and took control of the planes, two Boeing 757s and two Boeing 767s.

Telling the passengers they had bombs and were going to land, they turned the planes around. At 8:46 a.m., AA 11 smashed into the North Tower of the World Trade Center. At 9:03 a.m., US 175 hit the South Tower. At 9:37 a.m., AA 77 crashed into the Pentagon near Washington, D.C.

Using cell phones, passengers aboard UA 93 learned about what was going on with other planes and attacked the hijackers in the cockpit. At 10:03 a.m., the plane crashed into a field in Shanksville, Pennsylvania. Its target had been the United States Capitol Building in Washington, D.C.

The South Tower collapsed at 9:59 a.m., the North at 10:28 a.m.. The final death count was 2,986—including the murderers. As horrible as the events of 9/11 were, they would have been incalculably worse had Flight 93 destroyed the Capitol. Beyond the human cost, the symbolic significance of that image would have been even more devastating.

Osama bin Laden retreated deep into the mountains on the border between Afghanistan and Pakistan. His death, by various means, has been reported several times but no solid proof exists. He remains unpunished.

In 2002 fellow al Qaeda terrorists killed more than 200 people when they bombed a nightclub in Bali. On March 11, 2004 bombs left in knapsacks on commuter trains in Madrid, Spain killed 190. A little more than a year later, four suicide bombers killed 56 on the London bus and subway system; more than 700 were injured.

Khalid Shaikh Mohammed was captured near the Pakistani capital, Islamabad, in 2003 and is in American custody.

Naturally, following an event of 9/11's magnitude, conspiracy theories have been put forward. They range from fantastic constructions involving missiles and hidden explosives to the conventionally anti-Semitic to a more plausible collusion of government and intelligence officials who knew about the plot and did nothing to stop it—a completely unprovable conspiracy of omission. All are discussed in Gore Vidal's 2002 *Dreaming War* and David Griffin's 2004 *The New Pearl Harbor*. The documentary *The 9/11 Press for Truth* (2006) examines government actions before and after the attacks and finds many disturbing gaps in official responses.

Reactions to 9/11 in popular art and culture have been a very mixed bag. Bruce Springsteen's 2003 album *The Rising* finds redemption and forgiveness in the horror.

Art Spiegelman's book *In the Shadow of No Towers* (2004) details his horror at the attack and then his anger at the government's response. *New York Times* reporters Jim Dwyer and Kevin Flynn tell the stories of some survivors who were inside the towers in their fine book *102 Minutes* (2005). In his 2006 novel *Blow the House Down*, retired CIA agent Robert Baer suggests Iranian involvement in the planning of the atrocity and a CIA-Khalid Shaikh Mohammed connection.

The first feature films released about 9/11 are focused on the passengers who rebelled over Pennsylvania. The made-for-television *Flight 93* (2006) plays up the pathos and hammers home the emotional side. Paul Greengrass' theatrical release, *United 93* (2006), takes an almost documentary approach to the same material and is infinitely more moving.

The documentary *9/11* is based on the work of two French filmmakers, Gédéon and Jules Naudet, who were videotaping New York firefighters and captured their reactions throughout the long day. It's a superb serendipitous piece of work.

Michael Moore's 2004 film *Fahrenheit 9/11* is unapologetic political propaganda.

The "official" story is set out simply and eloquently in *The 9/11 Commission Report*. In 2006 it was adapted as a propagandistic TV miniseries placing most of the blame on Bill Clinton. Oliver Stone's theatrical release *World Trade Center* (2006) really had nothing to say about the causes of the attack. It's a standard-issue Hollywood feel-good rescue picture.

Oswald, Lee Harvey

The assassination of President John Kennedy on November 22, 1963 has been examined more thor-

oughly than any event in modern history. It was captured on film by Abraham Zapruder. Hundreds of people watched it happen. Experts and amateurs of every stripe have weighed in on it. Countless words have been written and theories put forth, and still no one has produced a single piece of evidence to show that anyone other than **Lee Harvey Oswald** pulled the trigger.

The banality of evil has never been so clearly illustrated.

Oswald was a smirking screwup whose unhappy childhood produced a troubled adult. His widowed mother put him in orphanages from time to time as she remarried and moved. Nowhere did the boy fit in. When he was 17, he wrote to the Socialist Party of America that he was a dedicated Marxist. Less than month later he enlisted in the Marines, where he continued to screw up. He did manage to qualify as a sharpshooter there. After two court-martials and a nervous breakdown, he was discharged. He traveled to the Soviet Union where he tried to defect; when he was rejected by the Reds, he attempted suicide. After a stint in a Russian psych ward, he was allowed in.

It didn't take long for him to sour on life in the glorious People's Republic and to complain about it bitterly. He did meet his wife Marina there, and in 1962 they came back to America and ended up in Dallas. He couldn't hold down a job and wound up living apart from her. It was pretty much a hand-to mouth existence for them and their small child. Still, he managed to scrape together enough for a couple of mail order weapons—$29.95 for a Smith & Wesson .38 revolver and $21.45 for an Italian Mannlicher-Carcano rifle with scope.

On the night of April 10, 1963 Oswald took the rifle out and tried to kill prominent Dallas right-winger Edwin Wallace. He took a shot through a window and missed, grazing the man's head. (Later tests on the bullet fragments would suggest that it came from Oswald's Carcano though the round was too badly damaged for an exact match.)

Around the same time, Oswald tried to find a way to get to Cuba, but received no help from the

A mortally wounded Lee Harvey Oswald, shot by Jack Ruby, November 24, 1963. (AP Photo)

Soviet embassy in Mexico City. Finally, in October, he was hired to work at the Texas Schoolbook Depository. A few weeks later, officials announced the president and first lady would be visiting the state to boost prospects for his upcoming reelection campaign.

The motorcade was going to pass right by the Book Depository. At this point in the route, the president's open car was traveling at a stately 11 mph. From a corner window on the sixth floor, Oswald had a clear line of fire. By stacking up book boxes around the window, he made a sniper's nest shielded from his fellow workers.

At 12:30 p.m., he fired three shots. Exactly which ones hit their target has been a subject of great debate. The result was not: one shot hit the president in the neck. Another hit him in the head. Texas governor John Connolly, sitting in the front seat, was wounded too. The motorcade sped to Parkland Hospital where Kennedy was declared dead.

Oswald hid his weapon and strolled out of the building. He had been seen in the window and a bare-bones description of the suspect was already being circulated. At 1:15 p.m., veteran Dallas patrolman J.D. Tippit stopped Oswald on Tenth Street. As he got out of his car, Oswald pulled his .38 and killed the officer. He hurried away and ducked into a shoe store. The sound of sirens grew louder as police converged on the area. From the shoe store, Oswald ran into the Texas Theater where cops cornered and arrested him. Later, he was charged with the murders of Patrolman Tippit and President Kennedy.

Oswald was questioned for 12 hours by the Dallas police, FBI, and Secret Service. No tapes were recorded; no notes were taken. Throughout, Oswald denied any involvement with either killing.

On Sunday, November 24th, police planned his transfer from the Police and Courts Building to the more secure County Jail. It was no secret. All of the broadcast and print media had been invited. In the basement of the building, Oswald was flanked by cops when **Jack Ruby** stepped out of the crowd and shot the assassin once in the stomach. It was broadcast live on NBC and caught on film in famous still photographs. Oswald was taken to the same trauma unit where the president had been treated two days before. He died there, too.

The second killing, carried out in such an inexplicable manner before the cameras, was almost as shocking to the nation and the world as the first had been.

From the moment the news of the first assassination broke, the three television networks stopped running their regular programming and commercials to concentrate on events nobody could really comprehend. Like the atrocities of 9/11, the Kennedy assassination was so unexpected, at first, it did not seem completely real. A kind of numbness set in. When everyday reality finally resurfaced, the conspiracy theories blossomed, and the assassination became a cultural watershed. The most popular suspects are the CIA, the **Mafia**, and the Cubans. Just about everyone else, from the Illuminati to the Rotarians have been fingered, too.

Of the thousands of books published, the original *Warren Commission Report* (all 26 volumes) and Gerald Posner's *Case Closed* (1993) lay out the evidence and conclude that both Oswald and Ruby acted alone. The book and CD *President Kennedy Has Been Shot* (2003) attempt to recreate the timeline of events as they were reported from many sources.

Mark Lane's 1966 *Rush to Judgment* was the first to posit a conspiracy. Jim Garrison's *On the Trail of Assassins* (1988) was the inspiration for Oliver Stone's brilliant crackpot propaganda film *JFK* (1991). In 1979 the film of Richard Condon's novel *Winter Kills* took the conspiracy in an entirely new direction. Robert Dyke's ambitious low-budget *Timequest* (2002) has a time traveler arriving from the future on November 21, 1963 to try to change history.

A more realistic approach is taken in the excellent 1964 documentary, *Four Days in November* from producer David L. Wolper. The film doesn't go into details, real or suspected, of the assassination but in terms of emotion, it is absolutely accurate. It captures the confusion and sense of dislocation everyone felt at the time better than any fiction.

Packer, Alferd (or Alfred)

In November 1873 Alferd Packer led a group of 20 luckless greenhorns from Provo, Utah in search of gold in the Colorado Rockies. Things went bad quickly.

Starving, they struggled through nasty weather as far as the camp of Chief Ouray in Colorado. The chief strongly advised they stay with his people until spring or go back to Utah. Ten of the would-be prospectors took his good advice. It's unclear what happened to four others, but five—Shannon Bell, James Humphrey, George Noon (or Moon), Israel Swan, and Frank Miller—elected to follow Packer farther into the mountains. Chief Ouray gave them provisions and a warning to stay close to the river, and off they went.

Within weeks, they were lost and starving again. The six men finally found shelter in an abandoned trapper's hut. Exactly what happened in the hut is problematic. Packer was the only one who came out alive.

In April 1874 he walked into the Los Pinos Indian Agency near Gunnison. He claimed his companions had abandoned him, but Chief Ouray observed, "You too damn fat." Authorities agreed.

Some months later, search parties found the five bodies. Four of the skulls had been crushed. One had been shot. All were missing most or some of their flesh. Packer changed his story. He first claimed one man had died of starvation, Bell had killed the others, and he had killed Bell in self-defense.

When he came to trial, the jury didn't go for it. They convicted him of murder and cannibalism and sentenced him to 40 years. Wonderful stories, most of them apocryphal, swirl around Packer. The trial judge supposedly said, "Packer, you depraved Republican son of a bitch, there were only five

Democrats in Hinsdale County and you ate them all!" Then there's the matter of his name. It's listed as "Alfred" on some documents. One story has it that after a possibly dyslexic tattoo artist misspelled it as "Alferd" on his arm, Packer changed it.

Packer confessed and was jailed, but escaped and was on the loose for several years until he was spotted in either Cheyenne, Wyoming or Salt Lake City. (Details about the later part of his life are contradictory.) He was paroled in 1901 and is said to have become a vegetarian before he died in 1907.

Trey Parker, who would go on to create the TV series *South Park*, wrote a play about Packer when he (Parker) was a student at the University of Colorado. In 1993 he adapted it for the screen as *Cannibal: The Musical*. It is cheesy, cheeky, and cheerfully tasteless. The 1999 horror film *Ravenous* contains elements of Packer's story.

Alferd also inspired several songs, including C.W. McCall's "1999 Comin' Back for More."

Packer's story is often confused with the Donner Party, a wagon train trapped by winter snows in the Sierra Nevada Mountains in 1846. Of the 89 people who set out, 45 survived and some of them resorted to cannibalism. Lewis Keseberg was cast as the villain and tried for murder. At trial, he was so persuasive in describing the horror of what he was forced to do to survive, he was found not guilty—and so Packer remains the West's only convicted cannibal.

Pancoast, Marvin

Vicki Morgan was sweet seventeen when she met Alfred Bloomingdale in 1970. He was 54 and loaded. Bloomingdale's department store, Diners Club credit card—those were his.

Vicki was a knockout, though even at that tender age she had some mileage including a young son from a failed relationship and an older husband. But those didn't matter to Alfred. He was smitten and he wanted Vicki to join in his indulgence for kinky games. He liked to tie up prostitutes and whip them with his belt. Even more, he liked Vicki to watch.

Vicki agreed and Bloomingdale set her up in a little love nest not too far from his Beverly Hills mansion. Everything was ducky for a time. His wife Betsy palled around with Nancy Reagan, wife of then Governor Ronald Reagan. Alfred fooled around with Vicki and whomever, and promised he would make sure she was always well taken care of.

In 1982 Alfred died of cancer and Betsy decided Vicki would *not* be well taken care of. Vicki hired attorney Marvin Mitchelson, who had made a name for himself prying a tidy sum loose from actor Lee Marvin when he tried to leave his girlfriend. The payment came to be known as "palimony," and Vicki hoped Mitchelson could do something similar for her; They filed a $5 million suit, but it went nowhere; the judge threw it out.

Miss Vicki responded by announcing she was going to write a tell-all book that would embarrass all of the movers and shakers who had joined in Albert's little games. After all, hadn't he been a member of President Reagan's kitchen cabinet?

She engaged a writer but things were still tight financially so she sublet a room in her apartment to Marvin Pancoast, a paranoid schizophrenic gay man who had undergone a series of electroshock treatments to alleviate his homicidal fantasies. He was obsessed with killing his entire family. Vicki and he had met in a mental hospital at one of his many commitments (she was in for depression and drug use).

Why would she have allowed such a character into her home? Because, more than anything else, Vicki feared being alone, and despite his problems, in his own way Marvin cared for her. Cared for her too much.

They were on the verge of eviction when he went nuts. Angered that she was sleeping late and fooling around with her writer, Marvin went into her bedroom on the night of July 7, 1983 and beat her to death with a baseball bat. He then drove over to the North Hollywood police station and admitted

Ex-model Vicki Morgan, pictured in 1982, was found beaten to death with a baseball bat in North Hollywood on July 7, 1983 by mild-mannered friend Marvin Pancoast. (AP Photo)

exactly what he had done. He told the cops he had killed her because she wouldn't shut up, but their relationship was complicated and volatile. Conflicted about his orientation, Marvin had convinced himself he was in love with Vicki but knew she could not or would not reciprocate.

Right afterwards, hotshot attorney Robert Steinberg made an extraordinary claim. He said the proverbial "mystery woman" had appeared in his office on the day Vicki was buried and had given him three videotapes. They contained footage of orgies that included the aforementioned rich and powerful Pooh-bahs of the Reagan administration. But before anyone could get a look at them, the tapes vanished as mysteriously as they had allegedly appeared. A year later, Steinberg was indicted by a grand jury for filing a false report.

Despite some attempts to conjure up a conspiracy, Pancoast's confession stood and he was convicted of first degree murder. He died in Vacaville prison of complications related to AIDS.

Vicki Morgan was the model for the main character in Dominick Dunne's novel, *An Inconvenient Woman* (1998), and the 1991 film of the same title.

Panzram, Carl

In the early twentieth century Carl Panzram was a remorseless, unapologetic murderer and rapist. Driven by rage and resentment, he drifted across America, terrorizing anyone smaller or weaker who was unlucky enough to meet him. He may have killed as many as 21 men and boys—and he claimed to have raped 1,000—but mere numbers cannot do him justice.

Born in Minnesota in 1891, Panzram was constantly beaten by his five older brothers. His father deserted the family when he was seven. By the time he was 11, he had been convicted on burglary charges and sent to the Minnesota State Training Facility where the beatings continued as part of the "Christian training" he received. It's also where he was first subjected to rape and sexual abuse. He retaliated by burning down a workshop and learning to play the game. He hid his anger and in 1905, the school declared him to be reformed and set him loose. For the next five years Panzram was a hobo, riding the rails across the Midwest. His most memorable experience in those years was a gang rape by four older bums in a freight car.

Panzram continued to steal and was caught again in Montana. By the time he escaped from that state reform school, he weighed 180 pounds. At 15, he was as big and strong as a grown man. His anger against Christians was still strong and he stayed on the move, burning churches as he passed through little towns, and breaking into houses.

In late 1907, drunk in a Helena bar, he fell for the pitch of an Army recruiter and enlisted. He was charged with insubordination on his first day in the service and was never out of trouble during his short military career. After four months he was court-martialed for theft, found guilty, dishonorably discharged, and sentenced to three years hard labor at the federal pen in Leavenworth. Back in the day, "hard labor" was not a euphemism.

A 50-pound ball was chained to Panzram's leg. Every day he had to load his ball, an 18-pound sledgehammer, crowbar, pick, and shovel into a wheel barrow. He pushed it three miles from the prison to the quarry where he busted rocks for ten hours. He did it every day for three years. When they let him out in 1910, Panzram was bigger, stronger, angrier, and more vicious than ever. Using a series of aliases, he drifted across the country to California and back, burglarizing homes, always on the lookout for guns, raping any man he encountered, and burning unattended buildings.

He did stretches in the Montana and Oregon State Prisons where he was regularly beaten, tortured, and locked up in solitary. He escaped in 1917, was quickly recaptured, then escaped again in May of 1918. He then found work as a merchant seaman and traveled to South America, Panama, and Europe before he turned up in New Haven, Connecticut in 1920. Turning his sights on the more comfortable bluebloods, Panzram found an impressive looking house to break into. It turned out to be the home of ex-President William Howard Taft. Panzram made off with a small fortune in jewelry, bonds, and a .45 automatic.

He used the money to buy the yacht *Akista* and moved his base of operations to the lower east side of Manhattan where his MO changed. Panzram cruised bars looking for sailors. When he found one who was flush, he'd offer him an easy job and a soft berth aboard the *Akista*. Once he had the man out on the boat, he'd get him drunk, rape, and shoot him. After stripping the valuables, he would weigh the body down with a stone, put it in his skiff and row out into

Long Island Sound where he dumped it. Panzram boasted later he had killed 10 men that way.

The *Akista* was wrecked in a storm on the New Jersey coast. After more trouble with the law, Panzram stowed away on a ship bound for Africa where he found work with an oil company. He raped and killed children there. At least, he claimed to; he also boasted of killing six African men and feeding their bodies to crocodiles. True or not, by 1922, he was back in America and looking for another boat to steal.

July 18, 1922 found Panzram in Salem, Massachusetts. That afternoon, he happened upon 11-year-old Henry McMahon. Panzram persuaded Henry to go with him on the trolley to a remote, lonely part of town where he beat, raped, and killed the boy. It's one of the few instances where the victim's name is known and the circumstances of the crime can be verified.

About a year later Panzram stole a yacht in Providence, Rhode Island and sailed down to Long Island Sound and up the Hudson to Yonkers, New York. Along the way, he changed the name on the boat and picked up a young accomplice and catamite, George Walosin. After Panzram stole some fishing nets, Walosin jumped ship and went straight to the cops. Nyack police nabbed Panzram on charges of sodomy and robbery.

A helpful lawyer arranged bail after Panzram offered his boat as payment. By the time the lawyer learned the yacht was stolen, his client was long gone. Panzram went back to New York City, finding the opportunity to rape and murder another young boy along the way, then went up to the prosperous little burg of Larchmont, where he was caught attempting to steal from baggage left at the train station. He was sentenced to five years at Sing Sing, but almost immediately he was transferred to Clinton Prison, also called Dannemora, considered at the time to be the most brutal institution in America.

On his first escape attempt Panzram fell 30 feet from a prison wall, breaking both legs and ankles and injuring his spine so severely he was in pain for much of the rest of his life. Good. Better still, he received no treatment for his injuries for 14 months when doctors decided to operate and only removed one of his testicles.

Unfortunately, they let him go in July 1928 even though Oregon authorities had been in contact with New York about Panzram's crimes under other aliases.

Heading south, he committed another child murder in Philadelphia and a string of burglaries in Baltimore before he was caught by police breaking into a house in Washington. They threw him into the D.C. jail. There, finally, something changed and the monster was possessed by a need to confess. It may have been the result of a small kindness showed to him by a new guard, Henry Lesser. The young man gave him a little money for cigarettes, food, pencil and paper so he could write down the story of his life.

Panzram produced a graphic 20,000-word autobiography describing every crime he had committed and perhaps some he'd only fantasized about, with no apologies and no regrets. He claimed to have learned early on that might makes right and he had spent the rest of his days searching out the weak, harmless, and unsuspecting, and subjecting them to the pain he had suffered.

As word reached the public of his many crimes, Panzram was charged in the Henry McMahon killing and the more recent Philadelphia murder. But before he could be tried on these counts, he had to face the Washington burglary charges. Acting as his own attorney, he was so threatening in court as he admitted his guilt that he got another 25 years in Leavenworth.

Panzram arrived for his second visit to Leavenworth on February 1, 1929, his rage undiminished, promising to kill anyone who crossed him. That promise came true in June when he attacked Robert Warnke, a civilian who ran the laundry where Panzram worked. He bashed in the man's head with a 20-pound iron bar then went berserk, attacking the other inmates in the laundry. He had virtually destroyed the place before guards were able to surround it. When he realized they were there,

California Dept. of Corrections mug shot of Scott Peterson, accused of murdering his wife Laci and their unborn son (2005). (AP Photo)

Panzram dropped the bar and went back to his cell quietly and without incident.

The trial that followed was really a part of Panzram's elaborate suicide. His execution on September 5, 1930 was the final act.

Panzram spent a few months on Death Row with **Robert Stroud**, who would later be known as the Birdman of Alcatraz, before his date with the hangman. He went to the gallows unrepentant and as filled with self-loathing as ever. After demanding the courtyard be cleared of all preachers and clergymen (his actual term was "Bible-backed cocksuckers"), his last words to the executioner were "Hurry it up, you Hoosier bastard, I could've killed a dozen men while you're fooling around."

Panzram's autobiography was the basis for Thomas Gaddis' 1970 book *Killer: Journal of a Murder* and the 1996 film starring James Woods. It's a typical whitewash that softens the real Panzram to unrecognizability.

Peterson, Scott

Scott Peterson first came to public attention at Christmas 2002, when he claimed his pregnant wife Laci was missing, and pleaded for help finding her. Four months later, he was arrested for her murder.

Every step in the process was followed by the communications media, from the most serious print news publications to the sleaziest tabloid TV.

Though the exact means were never determined, Peterson killed his wife and dumped her body in the ocean near the Berkeley Marina. He claimed to be fishing at the time. The body of an infant boy, with the umbilical cord attached, washed up in San Francisco Bay on April 14th. The next day, a female torso was found.

Three days later, the cops caught Peterson down in La Jolla, near the Mexican border, with $15,000 in cash, camping equipment, a map to his mistress' workplace, a pistol, and a stash of Viagra. The mistress, Amber Frey, had been cooperating with police and had even attempted to finagle a confession out of Peterson during taped telephone conversations. He might have known about her duplicity, so it is unclear whether the pistol or the Viagra was meant for her.

Never one to let the grass grow, Amber cranked out a bestselling book, *Witness* (2005), published while Peterson's trial was underway. Even though the evidence against him was circumstantial, it was persuasive, and a jury found him guilty of first degree murder for his wife and second degree murder for his unnamed son. He was sentenced to death by lethal injection and awaits it now in San Quentin.

Amber Frey's book was hustled into a made-for-television movie broadcast in May 2005. Even at the time, it seemed somehow unnecessary because the theatrics of the real case had been so exhaustively documented and discussed as they occurred.

Pierce, Bruce

Alan Berg

Just a few years ahead of his time, Alan Berg was a popular radio talk show host with a strong political bent. In the 1970s and '80s, before the AM airwaves came to be ruled by conservative wingnut wackos, he was an opinionated, confrontational, articulate liberal. More to the point, Alan Berg was a liberal Jew who loved nothing more than to shine the spotlight on American neo-Nazis and white supremacists. He also talked about sex, religion, and race. He was so good at his job that one year, he won awards for being both Denver's most loved and most hated media personality.

He worked KOA, 850 AM, a powerful 50,000-signal station that reached 200,000 listeners. Berg himself was a wiry bolt of energy, one of those skinny guys who was fueled by nicotine and caffeine. In 1984 he was 50 years old.

On the night of June 18th, Berg was gunned down when he came home. His killers were neo-Nazis Robert Matthews, Bruce Pierce, and David Lane. They had been financing their political extremism by counterfeiting and robbing banks throughout the west. Having tracked Berg's movements, they waited outside his condominium. Pierce shot him with a machinegun as he got out of his Volkswagen.

Pierce and Lane were caught after an extensive federal manhunt and eventually convicted of violating Berg's civil rights. Matthews was killed in an extended siege after being trapped in a house on Whidbey Island, Washington.

Berg's career and murder provided the inspiration for Eric Bogosian's play *Talk Radio* (1987) and its 1988 adaptation by director Oliver Stone. The film is also based on Stephen Singular's book *Talked to Death* (1987), but it pays scant attention to the facts of Berg's death. Instead, it focuses on the curi-

> *The Hotel Pierre robbery was the biggest jewel heist ever pulled off in America.*

ous relationship that exists between radio host Barry Champlain (Bogosian) and the unseen audience. Like Berg's fans, they are angered, shocked, and outraged by his performance, but they listen and are moved. Some are moved to action.

Pierre Hotel Robbery

The Hotel Pierre robbery was the biggest jewel heist ever pulled off in America.

At about 3:45 a.m. on January 2, 1972 a small group of guys led by Bobby Comfort arrived in a limo and forced their way into the office of the Pierre, a classy joint overlooking classy Fifth Avenue on the classy upper east side of New York.

Some of the guys were wearing rubber noses and fake beards. Despite their appearance, they knew what they were doing. In short order, the staff was herded into the executive offices, handcuffed, and blindfolded with adhesive tape. A few guests who happened onto the knockover got the same treatment. The targets were the 208 safe deposit boxes in the cashier's office.

The Pierre's clientele was (and remains) well-heeled. The residents had all sorts of loot stashed in the boxes, and despite impressively thick doors, they also had exterior hinges vulnerable to hammers and chisels. The thieves, who had pulled off just this sort of job before in other New York hotels, had remembered their hammers and chisels. They spent two hours cracking open about half the boxes and left with a huge haul.

The most conservative estimate was $4 million in jewels, securities, and cash. Others said it might easily have been twice that amount. Though the gang had threatened one security guard with a pistol, not a single shot had been fired.

Public reaction was overwhelmingly positive. As Pete Hammill wrote in the *New York Post*, at the time, "The holdup at the Hotel Pierre was beautiful. Nobody got hurt. The pre-war amenities were scrupulously observed. The robbers got away with something like ten million dollars, and maybe more; and when it was over everybody in New York felt better, except the people who got robbed."

Nevertheless, a joint task force of New York's finest and the FBI sprang into action. The first job was to find out exactly what had been stolen. That turned out to be tricky. Despite the amount of swag lifted, some of the owners cared little about its return. Hell, they were insured and had weightier financial matters to worry about. (Richard Nixon's New York campaign had its headquarters in the hotel. It may have been the source of more than $800,000 in small bills the gang had taken.) Whatever their reasons, many of the hotel's guests were not interested in cooperating with the cops.

But, the cops did catch a break.

An FBI snitch was contacted by the gang about taking some of the ill-gotten gains off their hands. He got in touch with his contact at the Bureau and arranged a meeting between Bert Stern, one of the gang members, and an agent posing as a fence. At the meeting, Stern brought some of the securities from the Pierre and parted with them for $700. Stern said he'd call to set up a larger sale of jewels. Police attempts to follow Stern and two people he spoke with after the meeting were inconclusive. A second meeting took place in a hotel where Stern and two other gang members were arrested with a little more of the Pierre loot. Then Bobby Comfort was nabbed at his hotel.

Leads developed from a separate investigation of a jewel theft several months earlier from actress Sophia Loren pointed to a fifth gang member in the Bronx. The upshot of all the arrests was very little because the DA, who had not been notified before the first arrests, said they didn't have proper probable cause, and so all the evidence was inadmissible. In fairness, it was more complicated than that because the FBI snitch couldn't or wouldn't testify. The bottom line: Comfort and a few others plea bargained, and most of the booty was never recovered. The statute of limitations is now long past.

The kind of story where bad guys who aren't really bad because they don't hurt anybody is catnip to Hollywood. Bobby Comfort's mother told him stealing was wrong but killing was evil, and he believed her. He was the last of the gang to leave the Pierre, and his last act was to slip $20 into the pocket of each staff member who had been handcuffed.

The story has been filmed once as the well-regarded made-for-cable *Cool Money* (2005), with several more ambitious projects are in different stages of development. Such diverse talents as John Cusack, directors Tony and Ridley Scott, and even Woody Allen have recently been "attached" as they say, to a Hotel Pierre project.

For now, the best sources of information are two books, Robert Daley's *Target Blue* (1973, in the chapter "The World's Greatest Jewel Robbery") and Ira Berkow's excellent nonfiction novel *The Man Who Robbed the Pierre* (1987).

Pino, Anthony "Fats"

Brink's Job

The 1950 Brink's job was thoughtfully planned and perfectly executed. Afterwards, it pretty much all fell apart. What was at the time the biggest robbery in American history brought nothing but pain to the guys who pulled it off.

Anthony "Fats" Pino was the brains. He cased the Brink's Building in Boston, Massachusetts for two years, and recruited eight more guys including his brother-in-law Vincent Costa and Joseph "Specs" O'Keefe. They figured out how to break into the place at night and even pulled the cylinders from the door locks. Then they took the cylinders to a locksmith who agreed to work after hours to make keys for them.

They studied the building, noting which rooms were lit at particular times, so they would know how many people were working and when the largest amounts of cash were passing through. On January 17th, they made their move. First, they dressed in standard Hollywood heist outfits—dark clothes and caps, Navy pea jackets, rubber soled shoes, Halloween masks. They got in through the ground floor and unlocked doors that took them to the back of the building and up to the second-floor counting room where they got the drop on five Brink's workers and tied them up. The haul was $1.2 million in cash; $1.5 million in checks, securities, and money orders; and four pistols from the Brink's guys. They were in and out in about 30 minutes.

After they had gotten away in a truck stolen for the job, they paid off some of the guys but hid most of the loot with the idea they wouldn't touch it for six years until the statute of limitations had expired. Then they scurried away to establish alibis.

A few months later, O'Keefe was busted on another burglary in Pennsylvania and was sentenced to three years. He told Pino he needed his share to pay for his appeal. He didn't get it.

Still miffed after his release, O'Keefe kidnapped Vincent Costa and again asked for his share from Pino as ransom. Pino bought him off for relative chicken feed, and decided to fix the problem permanently.

He hired hitman Elmer "Trigger" Burke to whack O'Keefe. The normally reliable assassin muffed the job. O'Keefe escaped a famous 1954 shootout with serious gunshot wounds and agreed to turn state's evidence.

In 1956 the surviving gang members went on trial and were convicted. All but O'Keefe got life sentences. The same year, about $50,000 of the stolen money was found in a cooler that had been sealed up in a wall in a Boston office building. To this day, more than $1.15 million in currency is still missing.

In 1978 director William Friedkin and writers Noel Behn and Walon Green made *The Brink's Job*, a very nice little comic caper with Peter Falk and Warren Oates in the lead roles.

Poole, William

In his wonderful 1927 book *The Gangs of New York*, Herbert Asbury introduced William "Bill the Butcher" Poole by saying he "was commonly held to be the champion brawler and eye gouger of his time, and not even the ferocious mayhem experts of the Five Points and the Fourth Ward dared engage him in combat."

In Martin Scorsese's 2000 film of the same title, he became Bill Cutting and was played with villainous glee by Oscar-nominee Daniel Day-Lewis. That character, however, bears only a passing resemblance to the real Bill the Butcher.

Bill was a Bowery gang leader and sworn enemy of the Tammany Hall mob, who ran the city. Bill provided muscle for the Know-Nothing Party, and at a fearsome six-feet, 200 pounds, he loved nothing more than to give some other guy a good thumping.

In Scorsese's film, Bill Cutting is killed during the draft riots of 1863. The real Bill Poole was killed eight years earlier in a legendary confrontation.

On the night of February 24, 1855 Bill and a couple of pals went into Stanwix Hall, a fancy new saloon, looking for a fight or a drink. Around midnight, three Tammany toughs—Lew Baker, Paudeen "No Nose" McLaughlin, and Jim Turner—slipped in and locked the door behind them.

Crowding up against the Butcher at the bar, McLaughlin called him a black-muzzled bastard and either spat on him or threw a drink in his face. At the same time, Turner pulled a long-barreled Colt from beneath his coat and took a shot at Bill. But, attempting to steady the heavy piece on his elbow, he was jostled and shot himself in the arm. He fell but fired again and got Bill in the leg.

The Butcher collapsed. Baker stepped up, pulled his pistol and fired twice, hitting Bill once in the chest and once in the stomach. Miraculously, Bill heaved himself up off the floor, grabbed a carving knife from a handy table and advanced on Baker. "I'll cut your heart out," he screamed and everybody believed him until he fell again.

The Tammany guys vanished into the night.

Even more miraculously, Bill hung on to life for another two weeks, despite a bullet lodged in his heart. With his last breath, he sat bolt upright in bed and declaimed, "Good bye, boys. I die a true American."

Baker attempted to flee by ship but was caught and brought back. After several politically charged trials, he was acquitted.

Bill Poole's funeral was one of the first massive gangster sendoffs, attracting more than 5,000 people, carriages, and marching bands. The sidewalks of Broadway were packed as the cortege passed.

Bill's final words inspired several quickly written dramatizations for live New York performances: some cheap melodramas already in production were rewritten so at the closing curtain, the hero could literally wrap himself in the flag and say "I die a true American."

The lesson has not been lost on generations of politicians, preachers, and pundits.

Prohibition

From 1920 until 1933, the Volstead Act and the 18th Amendment made it illegal to make, sell, or transport beer, wine, and intoxicating liquors in America. It was meant to strengthen family values, to end the scourge of public drunkenness, increase productivity, and, in general, to make us all better people. As Michael A. Lerner puts it in *Dry Manhattan: Prohibition in New York City* (2007), "Never before had the federal government attempted to regulate the private lives of adults to the degree that Prohibition did, and never before had the Constitu-tion been used to limit, rather than protect, the personal liberties of individuals."

Once the Amendment went into effect, the Law of Unintended Consequences came back to bite the country with a vengeance. Prohibition created a perfect storm of criminality.

First, it turned millions of Americans who happened to enjoy the occasional toddy into lawbreakers. And because Prohibition was seen by many as rural religious conservatives imposing their narrow attitudes on more educated and sophisticated city dwellers, alcohol became a fashionable forbidden fruit. The Roaring '20s were an era of massive cultural changes and advances in individual personal freedom with the introduction of affordable automobiles and mass communication media. Radio, movies, newsreels, newspapers, and national magazines all made the forbidden fruit seem that much sweeter.

Second, urban gangs were revived. Used by the big city political machines for muscle, the gangs had been declining in numbers and power until Prohibition made illegal alcohol an attractive new market for them. In Chicago, gangster Big Jim Colosimo refused to see the potential of the ban on alcohol. In short order, he was murdered by his lieutenant Johnny Torrio who, along with his new partner **Al Capone**, soon became one of the most powerful men in the city.

Capone and his gang made incredible profits. One study concluded that between 1916 and 1928, the price of whiskey skyrocketed 520 percent! A barrel of Prohibition beer that cost $5 to produce might fetch $50. With such tax-free windfall profits, the balance of power between the gangs and the politicians was reversed. The gangs were able to bribe government officials and to equip themselves with the fastest cars and the best weapons. In short, if they couldn't buy them off, they could outrun them and outgun them.

In the larger cities, Prohibition was essentially unenforced. There were roughly 200,000 speakeasies (illegal bars where the right softly spoken

Beer barrels destroyed during Prohibition by federal agents, January 1920. (AP Photo)

word opened the door) in the country, 32,000 in New York City alone. The Treasury Department was charged with enforcing the ban but was severely understaffed with largely untrained agents, many of them political appointees. They did virtually nothing to stem the rising tide of imported booze smuggled across the borders and brought in by ship, and homemade "bathtub" gin.

In 1930 the Treasury Dept. sent an undercover agent into the U.S. Senate to find out who was supplying our august elected officials. The Senate was naturally outraged when they learned of it and demanded to know who had given the order. The director answered it had come from the White House. The President's people clammed up and said nothing.

In 1932 the Democratic Party called for the repeal of Prohibition. Franklin Roosevelt won the White House, and on February 20, 1933 Congress passed the 21st Amendment, repealing the 18th. By then, though, well organized criminal activity had become firmly rooted in American culture.

Puente, Dorothea

It was a scene straight from a Gahan Wilson cartoon—the Victorian gingerbread mansion, the kindly old grandmother who ran a boarding house there, the bodies buried in the backyard.

But Dorothea Puente was hardly a kindly old grandmother, unless Grannie was directly related to

Lucretia Borgia. She was a skilled predator who chose her victims carefully and stole from them even after she had killed them.

Born Dorothea Gray into a large family in Redlands, California in 1929, she had a tough childhood. She was just a child when her parents died within a year of each other, and the kids were shipped off to different homes. By the time she was 16, Dorothea was turning tricks in Olympia, Washington. Even then, she was fond of inventing new identities for herself, spinning tales about her past and spending lavishly on clothes.

She was married long enough to have a couple of kids but she lost them—or gave them up—when she and her husband broke up. Before she was 20, Dorothea had served a stretch for forgery. She was married a second time to a merchant seaman, and worked as a hooker while he was away. She was busted for prostitution in 1960 in Sacramento. By 1976 she had burned through a few more husbands and was running a boarding house on F Street, where she began to figure out her main scam, stealing and forging checks from her tenants. Caught in 1978, she was sentenced to five years probation.

That didn't even slow her down. In 1982 Puente murdered her first tenant, Ruth Monroe, who thought she was going to be a partner in another of her landlady's interests. But soon after she moved into the F Street house, she died of a codeine-Tylenol overdose. The death was judged a suicide even though, a mere month later, Dorothea was arrested and convicted of drugging four elderly people to steal from them. She got five years in the California Institute for Women at Frontera, but was released after three with the provision she stay away from old people and not handle government checks.

Dorothea, of course, readily agreed and did not tell the authorities she had already struck up a penpal relationship with 77-year-old Everson Gillmouth. When they let her out of Frontera in 1985, poor Everson was there to drive her back to F Street. She killed him right away and dumped the body in a crude coffin in the Sacramento River where it was

found by fishermen. It would be years before he was identified.

In the meantime, Dorothea got down to work. She moved into the top floor of the house, put color TVs in the downstairs bedrooms and rented them out at reasonable rates. Provided two hot meals a day and did not allow alcohol. To social workers trying to find places for the homeless, she was perfect. They didn't know her MO. Once she got to know her tenants, Dorothea forged their signatures on disability and Social Security checks. She killed them with Dalmane, sleeping pills she received from three different doctors. As long as the feds thought her charges were still among the living, the checks kept coming every month. From time to time, Dorothea would have to ask local handymen to help her by digging a hole—a big hole—for a tree she wanted to plant, or whatever.

Many of her clients had drug and alcohol problems and were not readily missed after she had slipped them their last Mickeys. But it wasn't always the case. People wondered what had become of Alberto "Bert" Montoya after Dorothea claimed he'd gone back to Mexico. So she hired a guy at a halfway house to pose as Bert's brother-in-law and to call his social worker with the tale that Bert had moved in with another family. The social worker didn't buy it and called the cops. On December 11, 1988 Detective John Cabrera came by the F Street house to look around. When he and his colleagues dug in the backyard, they found a human foot in a shoe.

Dorothea was aghast. What could that be? As the officers continued to search the next day, she asked if it would be all right if she went down to a nearby hotel for a cup of coffee. Certainly, they said, and kept digging. A few hours later, the body count was up to four and Dorothea was on her way out of town.

Bert was there, along with Leona Carpenter, Benjamin Fink, James Gallop, Vera Faye Martin, Dorothy Miller, and Betty Palmer. They ranged in age from 51 to 78 and had suffered from a variety of ailments that left them vulnerable to Dorothea's tender mercies.

With $3,000 in her purse, Dorothea caught a bus to LA. A few days later, she sidled up next to 59-year-old Charles Willgues as he was sipping a cold one in the Monte Carlo Tavern. Her husband had just died, she said, and she'd come to the City of Angels for a fresh start, but the cabbie had taken off with her luggage, and, by the way, how much money do you make? Before the afternoon was over, Donna Johansson, as she called herself, had suggested they move in together. Charles demurred, but agreed they'd meet again the next day.

That night, Charles decided Donna might be the woman he had heard about on television. He contacted a local TV station and they sent the cops to Dorothea's motel. She gave up without a fight, knowing it wasn't over and began her defense on the flight with police back to Sacramento. She claimed, yes, she had cashed the checks, but she hadn't killed anybody. Those seven people died of natural causes!

Her trial was one of the longest and most expensive in a state famous for long, expensive trials. On March 31, 1989 she pleaded not guilty to nine counts of murder. It took four years of preparations and the trial didn't begin until February 1993, the venue changed to Monterey. It lasted for months. The jury saw more than 3,000 pieces of evidence, heard more than 150 witnesses.

In the end, Dorothea was found guilty on three counts, a mistrial was declared on the other six; and she was sentenced to life without the possibility of parole at the Chowchilla Women's Facility.

To date, no enterprising Hollywood producer has attempted to put an *Arsenic and Old Lace* spin on Dorothea's story.

Purple Gang

Though they were never as famous as **Lucky Luciano** or **Bugsy Siegel**, Detroit's Purple Gang had essentially the same beginnings.

The founders were immigrant kids, mostly Jewish, who grew up on the rough ghetto streets at the beginning of the twentieth century.

As criminals, they progressed steadily from such penny ante stuff as shoplifting and bullying other kids to vandalism and extortion of local merchants. The latter is said to be the source of their name.

As the story goes, two shopkeepers were complaining to each other about the gang's depredations. One said they weren't like other kids; the other replied he was right, they were rotten and off-color, the purple of spoiled meat. So, under the leadership of Abe Bernstein, they became the "Purple Gang."

They came into their own a few years ahead of the rest of the country in 1917 when Michigan enacted its own statewide **Prohibition** on the sale of alcohol, the Damon Act, and went dry. The Purples and other local gangs immediately began field testing the various bootlegging techniques soon used nationwide. They moved booze from neighboring Ohio and from Windsor, Canada directly across the Detroit River. In 1919 the gang took a break when the Damon Act was declared unconstitutional, but a year later, the Volstead Act became the law of the land and the Purples were back in business.

Thousands of speakeasies or "blind pigs," as they were called in that part of the country, sprang up. Much of the booze sold in these joints came from Canada and as much as three quarters of that illegal hooch may have been smuggled through Detroit. The Purples had their paws on a lot of it. Their specialty was hijacking loads of liquor in transit, and they were so brutal with other gangsters they encountered that they developed a fearsome reputation.

Part of their reputation came from their early use of the **Thompson submachine gun**. They didn't shrink from the wholesale destruction that could be inflicted with the choppers, and they became so well known for their proficiency that **Al Capone** and **Machine Gun Jack McGurn** hired brothers Phil and Harry Keywell from the Purples when they went after Bugs Moran in the **St. Valentine's Day Massacre**. Bernstein also provided the two loads of whiskey used to lure

Moran into Capone's trap. (Moran, of course, escaped the massacre.)

The Purples thrived throughout Prohibition, though they were never as tightly organized as their counterparts in Chicago and New York. They branched out into jewel theft, vice, and gambling. Success, as it always does, took its toll. Rivalries and disagreements within the gang weakened it. In 1931 three key members were convicted on murder charges and sentenced to life without parole. The remaining mugs were absorbed by the national Syndicate Lucky Luciano was setting up at the time.

Only one film has been made about these guys, the hard-to-find *The Purple Gang* (1960) with bad boy **Robert Blake** as the psycho killer "Honeyboy" Willard.

Purvis, Melvin

In the early days of the FBI, there was room for only one star and it wasn't Melvin Purvis. It was his boss, **J. Edgar Hoover**.

Purvis was the Special Agent in Charge of the Chicago office and was intimately involved with the Midwestern crime wave of the 1930s. He had a hand in its most spectacular failure—the Little Bohemia raid—and its successes—the killing of **John Dillinger** (if he was killed) and **Pretty Boy Floyd**. But Hoover was never one to share credit and the two could not work together.

For example, press releases that came out of Washington and the other regional offices began with the words "J. Edgar Hoover announces…" Those coming out of Chicago read "Melvin Purvis announces…" Purvis' eventful career with the Bureau lasted from 1927 to 1935, but in his final years, he was quietly replaced by Samuel Cowley, a more experienced and capable administrator.

After Purvis left the Bureau, the bickering with Hoover continued in print. Purvis' book about his years in the FBI, *American Agent* (1936) barely

mentions Hoover. Hoover's *Persons in Hiding* (1938) leaves out Purvis. Purvis is mentioned, albeit only in passing, in Don Whitehead's "official" history, *The FBI Story* (1956), but his name is nowhere to be found in the otherwise excellent index.

Some have claimed that Hoover had Purvis blacklisted from any other work in law enforcement after he left the Bureau. He did, however, stay in the public eye with the Melvin Purvis Junior G-Men Club for Post Toasties cereal, the "Law and Order Patrol." In 1937 Purvis was still a celebrity and engaged to marry beautiful would-be actress Janice Jarratt, but that ended when she kept him waiting in public once too often and he walked out.

During World War II, Purvis worked with the Army War Crimes Office. After the war, he returned to his native South Carolina and practiced law. On February 29, 1960, in poor health, he committed suicide. Legend has it he used the pistol he had killed John Dillinger with; in truth, he didn't fire a shot that night outside the Biograph Theater in Chicago. The weapon in question was the nickel-plated .45 he had been given when he left the Bureau.

Some dismiss Melvin Purvis as a prima donna who quit in a huff when he didn't get enough attention. Others say the Chicago office was simply unable to deal with the all-star lineup of criminals it faced while under his leadership. There's probably a kernel of truth to both, but it's also true that like every other law enforcement officer in those bloody days, he was working against determined opponents who were often better armed and better liked by the public. It wasn't an easy job.

Purvis appeared in many of the gangster films set in the 1930s. Dan Curtis, producer of the *Dark Shadows* horror soap opera, made two TV films starring square-jawed Dale Robertson, *Melvin Purvis: G-Man* (1974) and *The Kansas City Massacre* (1975). In John Milius' *Dillinger* (1973), Purvis, well played by Ben Johnson, is seen as sort of a mirror image of the gangster he hunted.

Melvin H. Purvis, left, federal investigator behind the capture and slaying of John Dillinger. Purvis is congratulated in 1934 by William Stanley, acting attorney general, and J. Edgar Hoover, head of the agency that became the FBI. (AP Photo)

Q, R

Quantrill, William

William Quantrill was a second-rate horse thief and cattle rustler who saw the outbreak of the Civil War in 1861 as a chance to improve his station. While the large armies of the Confederacy and the Union fought in the east, the fighting in the west was done by smaller, poorly organized groups. Kansas had its pro-Union Jawhawkers; in Missouri, pro-slavery forces were Bushwhackers. The two groups fought each other and attacked towns and farms where opposition sympathizers lived. Terrible things were done on both sides, but everyone agreed the worst offenses were carried out by the Bushwhackers, and Quantrill's Raiders were the worst of the worst.

The group began with no more than a dozen or so members. **William "Bloody Bill" Anderson** joined, so did the Younger brothers and Frank James. His little brother Jesse signed on near the end of the war.

The outfit was nothing like a regular army unit, there was little formal discipline. Instead, it attracted thieves, rapists, drunks, and killers. Quantrill went to Richmond, Virginia in 1864 and was commissioned as a captain, but he was essentially acting on his own.

The most infamous incident was Quantrill's 1863 attack on Lawrence, Kansas. Senator James Lane, famous for his fiery opposition to slavery, lived there. Quantrill reasoned that if his men attacked with sufficient savagery, the citizens would realize it was the presence of Lane that had brought on their suffering and would get rid of him. And there were also money, liquor, food, and the fact that the local Union troops had been called away.

Around 5:00 a.m. on the morning of August 21st, Quantrill and his men fell upon the unprotected town with the goals of shooting every man and boy they found, stealing everything of value they could carry, and burning the rest. Upon hearing the attackers' rebel yells, Senator Lane realized what was happening and hid out in a cornfield.

Meanwhile, Quantrill's orders were carried out. Some 200 unarmed men and boys were rounded up and executed. When it was over at 9:00 a.m., Quantrill retreated and spent the winter hiding in Texas.

As word of the atrocity got out, Quantrill was branded as a common outlaw and even regular Confederate troops would have nothing to do with his outfit. His men deserted in increasing numbers and by the end of the war, his Raiders had been reduced to a handful of the faithful, including Frank James.

Dennis Rader (date unknown), the self-named "BTK" murderer in Kansas. (AP Photo)

After Lee's surrender at Appomattox, amnesty was offered to Southerners if they surrendered, but Quantrill knew he would be locked up and executed if he tried to give himself up in Missouri or Kansas. He made it as far as Smiley, Kentucky where Union troops ambushed his group in May 1865. Quantrill was wounded in the gun battle and, as he tried to flee, was shot in the spine and paralyzed. He died a few weeks later in unspeakable pain.

Quantrill still has his defenders among Southern apologists, but not in Hollywood. John Wayne went up against a loony Quantrill, thinly disguised as William Cantrell (Walter Pidgeon) in *Dark Command* (1940). Audie Murphy did much the same as **Jesse James** against veteran heavy Brian Donleavy's Quantrill in *Kansas Raiders* (1950). Ang Lee's *Ride*

With the Devil (1999) presents the conflicts in more blatantly political terms and captures the emotional tenor of the times much more accurately than other Hollywood films. Quantrill isn't a character in Clint Eastwood's *The Outlaw Josey Wales* (1976), though the film looks at that part of the war and its aftermath from a Southern point of view. Slavery is ignored.

Rader, Dennis

BTK Killer

Given the length of his murderous career, Dennis Rader, aka "BTK," must be considered a successful serial killer. For more than 30 years, he stalked and slaughtered his Wichita neighbors.

In appearance and background, he was a thoroughly ordinary, unremarkable white guy. There appears to have been none of the abuse, estrangement, or family violence so often seen in the childhood experiences of other mass murderers. Born in 1945, he grew up in a middle class family, the oldest of four brothers. He admitted to sexual fantasies about Annette Funicello on *The Mickey Mouse Club*, but virtually every male of his generation did too. He also killed pets and indulged in bondage and cross-dressing at an early age. He served in the Air Force from 1966 to 1970, married, had a couple kids, and graduated from Wichita State University with a degree in Administration of Justice.

Rader worked for ADT home security systems, then as a supervisor for the Park City Compliance Department. The position has been described as a "glorified dog catcher," where Rader was responsible for animal control, zoning, permits, etc. He was also active in his church and volunteered as a Cub Scout leader.

At the same time he dubbed himself the "BTK killer" for Bind, Torture, Kill. After identifying potential victims, he would pack up his "hit kit"—a bowling bag or briefcase loaded with a pistol, knife, rope, tape, handcuffs, and spare clothes—then sneak into their houses.

His first victims were the Otero family. He broke into their home thinking that only the mother and her daughter were there. Finding the husband and son, he killed them, too. Though no sexual assault took place, he masturbated over the bodies.

Nine months later, Rader called a newspaper reporter and told him to look inside a particular book in the public library, where his first letter was found. He took credit for killing the Oteros and claimed to be unable to control himself. By then, he had already killed another woman, Kathryn Bright.

It was three years before Rader killed again. He locked Shirley Vian's three kids in a closet while he did his brutal work on her. More letters followed to newspapers and TV stations demanding recognition and publicity. In April 1979 he broke into a house and waited for the woman who lived there to come home. When she didn't, he impatiently wrote her a poem and left. Then he stopped killing, again.

Nothing until 2004 when Rader again wrote to the *Wichita Eagle* to take credit for a 1986 murder. He included proof, a photocopy of victim Vicky Wegerle's driver's license and photos of her body.

The correspondence continued and became more frequent using classified ads, eventually leading to Rader sending in a computer floppy disc. The police examined it and found it contained the words "Christ Lutheran Church" and "Dennis," though Rader was probably unaware it. With those clues and DNA evidence supplied by his daughter, the police closed in on Rader. Surrounded by cops on the way home one day, he put up no fight and confessed to the murders. Talking to the arresting officers and later in court, he seemed almost offhand in describing what he had done, and pleased to finally be the center of attention.

He's now serving ten life sentences.

Several books were rushed to publication after Rader's capture and a television movie about the murders, *The Hunt for the BTK Killer*, aired in 2005. It's formulaic and restrained in its depiction of the killings. Gregg Henry is believable as Rader,

particularly in the interrogation and confession scenes—which seem so accurate they may have come from transcripts or tapes. Another nano-budgeted exploitation flick, *BTK Killer* (2005), went straight to video.

Ramirez, Richard

Night Stalker

After he had been sentenced to death for multiple murders, kidnappings, rapes, and other atrocities, Richard Ramirez, the "Night Stalker," brushed it off saying, "Big deal, death always comes with the territory. I'll see you in Disneyland."

Born in 1960, Ramirez grew up in El Paso, Texas and moved to Los Angeles when he was 18. By then, he was already an experienced pothead. Some have claimed Ramirez's cousin showed him graphic Polaroids of murders and rapes committed in Vietnam, and later shot his wife in the young man's presence—whetting his appetite for violence. Perhaps; but even if the stories are true, it doesn't explain what he became.

In LA, Ramirez turned to burglary to support his growing drug habit. He became proficient at stealing cars and breaking and entering. At the same time, he earned a long rap sheet for drug possession, traffic tickets, and auto theft.

On the night of June 28, 1984 the breaking and entering became rape and murder. Ramirez went through an open window and stabbed and slashed 79-year-old Jennie Vincow to death. He continued to attack at night, sometimes using a gun. He wasn't picky about his victims. They ranged in age from children to women in their 80s. Given time, he would mutilate the bodies or draw satanic pentagrams on them. The few who survived an encounter with the "Night Stalker," as he came to be called, described his long dark hair, gapped rotting teeth, and foul breath. In the spring and summer of 1985 the pace of his LA attacks increased alarmingly. He briefly relocated to San Francisco, and both cities were terrorized.

Late in August, LAPD forensics was able to get a good fingerprint at one of the Night Stalker's crime scenes and police were finally able to put a name to their suspect. His picture was distributed everywhere and it did the trick. The next day, Ramirez tried to steal several cars in a Hispanic neighborhood and was attacked by an angry mob. They chased him down and turned him in.

Though he spontaneously confessed to one of the cops who arrested him—"I did it, you know. You guys got me, the Stalker"—the trial was lengthy and expensive. It lasted more than a year, cost millions, and made Ramirez a celebrity with that weird strain of women who are attracted to the vilest murderers. Eventually, in 1996, he married one of them.

Ramirez was convicted on all 45 counts against him and sentenced to death. As of this writing, he is still in San Quentin waiting for the sentence to be carried out.

Many have noted Ramirez's obsession with satanic heavy metal music, particularly AC/DC's album *Highway to Hell* and the song "Night Prowler." Several books have been written about him and he was the subject of the 1987 low-budget effort, *The Night Stalker,* with B-movie veteran Charles Napier as the tough detective. The story also inspired a made-for-television movie, *Manhunt: Search for the Night Stalker* (1989).

Ramsey, JonBenet

Someone killed six-year-old JonBenet Ramsey in December 1996. The case probably wouldn't have generated national attention had her parents not entered the little girl in several children's beauty pageants. Dozens of photographs and videos were distributed of this blonde child all dolled up to look like a glamorous young woman. To many observers, the images added an element of sexual exploitation that made the whole story doubly sickening.

John and Patsy Ramsey were a well-heeled couple who lived in a 15-room house in Boulder, Colorado with JonBenet and her brother Burke, age 9. On December 26th, Patsy Ramsey claimed she discovered a curiously worded three-page hand-written ransom demand. JonBenet was not in her bedroom. The Ramseys called police and friends. A quick search of the house revealed nothing.

Later that day, JonBenet's body was found in a wine cellar. She'd been struck on the head with a hard object and throttled with a garrote made from a length of nylon cord and a paintbrush handle. Some experts later said she had been sexually assaulted.

Initial suspicion fell heavily on the parents, but the evidence was far from conclusive.

Though the paper used for the ransom note came from a pad the Ramseys owned, it held no fingerprints. The best experts could say was Patsy Ramsey *might* have written the note. Footprints not matching the Ramseys were found in and around the house. In the end, a grand jury declined to indict them.

This left three possible scenarios:

1) Mr. or Mrs. Ramsey or their son killed JonBenet, perhaps accidentally, and faked the other evidence.

2) A predatory pedophile made his way into the house, killed the girl, moved her body, then wrote a long ransom note before he left.

3) At some earlier time, the perpetrator gained entrance to the Ramsey home and stole the notepad. He returned on December 26th intending to kidnap the girl and was overcome by murderous lust.

Several books have been written about the murder with experienced professionals and experts taking opposite positions on the Ramseys' guilt or innocence. In 2000 two movies were made for television: *Getting Away With Murder: The JonBenet Ramsey Mystery*, and *Perfect Murder, Perfect Town: JonBenet and the City of Boulder.*

Patsy Ramsey died of ovarian cancer in June 2006. Two months later, in August, John Mark Karr, a troubled man with a history of sexual prob-

John and Patsy Ramsey meeting with reporters about the murder of their daughter, JonBenet, on May 1, 1997 in Boulder, Colorado. (AP Photo/Denver Post, Helen Davis)

lems, confessed to the murder. After a brief frenzy of publicity, it was revealed to be a hoax.

Ray, James Earl

James Earl Ray killed Dr. Martin Luther King, Jr. He confessed before a judge, and later, when he tried to deny that confession, he failed two polygraph tests. The remaining questions, then, are why he did it, and who else was involved. The answers are not so clear cut. Dr. King was a controversial man with many enemies.

By the spring of 1968 King had won the Nobel Peace Prize and delivered his famous "I Have A Dream" speech in Washington, D.C. His work with the Southern Christian Leadership Conference had been instrumental in the passage of the Voting Rights Act and other court decisions bringing an end to state-sponsored racial segregation. He had angered many, including FBI director **J. Edgar Hoover,** a diehard Red-baiter who saw connections between equal rights for blacks and international communism. As early as 1962, Hoover and Attorney General Robert F. Kennedy had bugged Dr. King's phones and placed him under surveillance.

James Earl Ray was a two-bit racist redneck crook with a record of petty crime including armed robbery. Hardly a master criminal, he dropped his wallet at one job and fell out of his car while escaping from another. But he was industrious enough to squirrel away a tidy bankroll by selling drugs while locked up in the Missouri State Prison. Simply put, he had the combination of cunning and stupidity that keeps so many small timers in jail but may, on occasion, lead to success, particularly when the small timer is cranked up on meth. Ray escaped from the pen in 1967.

For the next few months he moved around, working at odd jobs and stealing stuff wherever he could. He made it as far north as Canada and as far south as Mexico where he was probably moving drugs. At the same time, one of his brothers was involved with a white supremacist group and the George Wallace presidential campaign. Within the racist community, word was out that certain like-minded wealthy individuals were willing to pay $50,000 for the murder of Dr. King.

Ray may have believed he could collect it, or his motivation may have been more conventional—he simply wanted to be famous for killing someone important. Whatever the reason, by the spring of 1968 Ray was following Dr. King's movements. On March 29th, he stopped in Bessemer, Alabama to buy a .243-caliber hunting rifle with a telescopic sight. Later the same day, he called the store and said he had changed his mind, he needed a more powerful weapon. The next day, for another $5, he traded it in on a Remington .30-06 and more lethal soft-point bullets.

Dr. King was in Memphis to lend support to a sanitation workers strike. He was staying at the Lorraine Motel. On April 4th, Ray checked into a cheap rooming house nearby.

From his room—the one he'd requested after being given another with the wrong view—Ray could see the door to Dr. King's room some 66 yards away. A nearby bathroom actually provided a better line of fire. As Dr. King and some of his associates gathered on the balcony outside his room around 6:00 p.m. that evening, Ray locked himself in the bathroom. With the rifle at that particular angle at that distance, it was an easy shot, even for an inexpe-

rienced marksman. The bullet hit Dr. King in the jaw. Doctors pronounced him dead an hour later.

Ray's carefully planned getaway unraveled moments after he left the rooming house when he saw a police car down the street. Panicked, Ray tried to stash the stuff he was carrying in a doorway. He dropped his suitcase and a box containing the rifle, and tried to cover them with a blanket before he got into his Mustang and drove away. The weapon was found moments later.

Ray abandoned his car in Atlanta and headed north to Toronto where he obtained a Canadian passport under an alias. (In those times, it wasn't difficult—all Ray needed was a fake birth certificate. With such documentation, travel agents routinely obtained passports for their clients.)

The assassin flew to London and then to Lisbon where he hoped to find work as a mercenary. When it didn't pan out, he returned to London. It was, after all, easier to steal where you knew the language. He was on his way to Belgium where he still hoped to find mercenaries, when Scotland Yard picked him up in Heathrow Airport.

From the moment of his arrest, Ray turned jailhouse lawyer and tried to work the system, first refusing to waive extradition. But the physical evidence against him was overwhelming. He'd left his prints on the rifle and in the car. Many witnesses saw him in Memphis. Ray invented a fictitious character he called Raoul and claimed he had been following Raoul's orders since they had met in Montreal. It was Raoul, not Ray, who had shot Dr. King.

It was a pathetically weak defense and days before his trial in 1969, his lawyer persuaded Ray to plead guilty. It was, he argued, the only way to be certain to avoid the death penalty. Ray agreed and was sentenced to 99 years. Days later, he reverted to type and recanted.

In the late 1970s the House Select Committee on Assassinations reexamined the evidence and concluded Ray had killed Dr. King and probably had help from his brothers.

Then in 1993, HBO and England's Thames Television sponsored a mock "trial." Throughout the broadcast proceedings, Ray continued to spin his tales and was joined by a small army of conspiracy theorists who embraced his lies and soared to even greater heights of fantasy. Even some members of Dr. King's family fell for the nonsense.

Ray died in prison in 1998 from complications associated with kidney disease.

Because Martin Luther King, Jr. has become such a respected, even venerated figure, the story of his murder has not often been dealt with in popular entertainment. The only mainstream treatment is Abby Mann's 1978 miniseries *King*.

The best books on the subject are William Bradford Huie's *He Slew the Dreamer* (1968) and Gerald Posner's *Killing the Dream* (1998).

Rees, Melvin

"The Sex Beast" is the forgotten serial killer of the 1950s. Though Melvin Rees' crimes were numerous and horrifying, they were not as nightmarish as his contemporary **Ed Gein's**, and he lacked **Charlie Starkweather's** bad-boy outlaw image.

Rees first came to the attention of authorities in 1955 when he was a student at the University of Maryland. He attempted to drag a young woman into his car. Later, she refused to press charges and the matter was dropped. After all, he came from a good family—father worked for C&P Telephone, mother for the Department of the Interior—and everyone knew him as an intelligent young man and a talented musician. Details of his more serious crimes vary maddeningly among normally reliable sources, but these are the bare facts.

While Rees was a student he killed four teenaged girls in Maryland—Mary Shomette, Ann Ryan, Mary Fellers, and Shelby Venable. Rees admitted to two of the murders, though he was never convicted of them; prosecutors thought they had stronger evidence in other cases.

In June 1957 Rees attacked a couple parked in a lover's lane near Annapolis, Maryland. After forcing his way into the car, he killed the woman, Margaret Harold. Her unidentified lover escaped and contacted police. When they returned, they found the body had been stripped and raped. Nearby was a cinderblock building. The basement was filled with pornographic and morgue photographs. Among them was a yearbook picture of a University of Maryland coed. When questioned, she had no idea who might have kept the picture or put it there.

On January 11, 1959 the Jackson family—Carroll and Mildred and their children Susan (age 5) and Janet (18 months)—disappeared near Fredericksburg, Virginia (about 70 miles from Annapolis). They probably stopped on a rural road to help Rees, whose car appeared to be disabled. Rees tied up Carroll with his own necktie and shot him in the head. He threw little Janet into a ditch and dropped her father's body on top of her. She suffocated. Rees then drove Mildred and Susan back to Maryland where he raped and murdered both of them. He buried them in a shallow grave.

Carroll and Janet's bodies were discovered on March 4th; Mildred and Susan were found a week later. Their bodies were close to the cinderblock building, close enough that the police wondered if there might be a connection to the Margaret Harold murder.

As news of the Jackson killings spread, Glenn Moser talked it over with his friend Melvin Rees. Hopped up on bennies, Rees launched into an existential defense of murder in general. There were no absolute rights and wrongs, etc. When Moser asked him directly if he had killed the Jacksons, Rees would not deny it. His answers troubled Moser so much that he sent an anonymous letter to the police, fingering his pal and saying the guy might also have been involved with Margaret Harold's death.

When the cops investigated Rees, they learned he had once dated the coed in the yearbook photograph. They had their suspect, but he had moved, with no forwarding address.

Nothing happened for a year, then Rees contacted Moser again and said he was living in Hyattsville, Arkansas. Moser took the information to the police, in person. Since Rees had crossed state lines, they brought in the FBI. The feds nabbed Rees in June 1960 and searched his rooms. They found a .38 revolver inside a saxophone case, and handwritten notes describing sadistic sexual acts in details that matched the Jackson killings, along with a newspaper photo of Mildred Jackson. The pistol matched the bullet that killed Margaret Harold.

Rees was convicted of Harold's murder and got a life sentence. He was also found guilty in Virginia and sentenced to death. In the appeals process, though, he was found to be incapable of assisting in his defense and his sentence was commuted to life. He died of heart problems in the U.S. Medical Center for Federal Prisoners in Springfield, Missouri in 1995.

Though his psycho-on-lovers-lane MO has appeared in any number of horror films, Rees' story has not been brought to the screen.

Remus, George

Bootlegger George Remus is said by some to have been the model for Jay Gatsby. Okay, if *The Great Gatsby* had not ended with the hero fatally shot and floating on a raft in his pool, and if Scott Fitzgerald had decided to make the conclusion a farce, maybe so. Beyond that, the only real similarities are lavish parties in a big bootlegger's house.

Remus' family emigrated from Germany to Chicago around the turn of the twentieth century. George became a pharmacist, then a criminal defense lawyer. When Prohibition kicked in and Remus saw some of his clients becoming majestically wealthy, he decided it was time to cash in himself. By using loopholes in the Volstead Act, he was able to buy distilleries and sell the alcohol to himself, then steal it from himself, and distribute it through speakeasies.

Remus was so successful he moved into a mansion in Cincinnati's swanky Price Hill neighborhood. His soirees were notable for his tendency to give outlandish gifts. On two occasions, with Elvisian largesse, he presented brand new automobiles to all the women who came to his parties.

But the law caught up with Remus, and he was given a two-year stretch in Atlanta for bootlegging. When he got out, his wife Imogene sued for divorce. Certain she had been unfaithful, Remus gunned her down in front of their daughter. That should have been the end of it, but at trial, Remus elected to serve as his own attorney. True, he had been disbarred, but so what? He was pleading insanity anyway.

His antics in the courtroom were front page news nationwide for a month. It took the jury only 19 minutes to acquit him. The prosecution then tried to have him committed to a state asylum, but four months later, Remus walked out, a free man.

Fitzgerald's ending is better.

Ridgway, Gary

Green River Killer

At some point, numbers become meaningless. Gary Ridgway, the Green River Killer, confessed to the rape and murder of 48 young women in Washington state. Some experts believe he may have slaughtered twice that many. Most of the women were prostitutes who worked the streets where Ridgway picked them up. He disposed of many of the bodies in and around the Green River near Seattle. The case frustrated law enforcement for decades, to the point that they asked advice from jailed serial killer **Ted Bundy**.

An unexceptional, ordinary looking man, Ridgway was a Bible-thumping Christian misogynist who had trouble relating to women. He'd always been drawn to prostitutes, though he would loudly proclaim his hatred of them to anyone who'd listen. In 1982 he began to take out the anger he felt toward all women on them.

His MO was virtually identical to **Joel Rifkin**, the New York murderer. Ridgway would meet hookers on the infamous Sea-Tac Strip, usually in a pickup with a camper top. During some of his killing years, he lived alone in a single-family home where he preferred to take them. He killed by strangulation during or after sex. He often hid the bodies in clusters that he would revisit later. The prosecutor's summary of Ridgway's necrophilic sexual practices is so deeply revolting it's hard to read (a link to it is available on the Wikipedia website.)

Several of the bodies were discovered soon after Ridgway began to kill, and a massive police task force was created. In 1983 they actually interviewed him in connection with the disappearance of one young woman. He claimed to have had nothing to do with her, and they believed him. A year later, in 1984, he was picked up for the solicitation of an undercover policewoman posing as a hooker. He was released after he passed a polygraph. Two years later, he passed *another* lie detector test.

Still, his name was in police records, and when the killings continued and connections to other missing and murdered women showed up, police obtained a warrant and searched his house. Ridgway cooperated and even gave a saliva sample by chewing on a piece of gauze. At the time, 1987, testing was limited and there was little to be done with such samples.

In the late '80s, the pace of the killings slowed and the task force was disbanded in 1990.

It wasn't until 2001 that a new task force took a fresh look at the mountain of accumulated evidence. DNA testing had become much more sophisticated, and samples taken from the first murder victims were sent to a lab and compared with Ridgway's 1987 sample. On September 10, 2001 they got a match. Ridgway was arrested and, when confronted with the DNA evidence, spilled his guts. He finally confessed to the 48 known murders and provided information on the location of the bodies in exchange for a life sentence. Some still believe another killer may have been at work in the same area at the same time, but Ridgway's arrest put an end to one of the longest and most involved police investigations in the history of American crime.

To date, the killings have been the subject of one A&E television documentary, *The Riverman*, a well regarded made-for-TV 2004 film and an obscure 2005 film, *Green River Killer*.

Rifkin, Joel

Despite the large number of his victims, Joel Rifkin will always be thought of as a fairly pathetic serial killer—literally more a punchline than a monster.

Rifkin grew up on Long Island in the 1960s, one of those boys who somehow inspires or incites abuse from others. In elementary school, he was picked on mercilessly. In high school at East Meadow, it got worse. A poor student, Rifkin failed at everything he tried, and was ignored, ostracized, and bullied. That's when his sexual fantasies of rape, bondage, and female combat began to form. He had no real relationships with girls his own age.

After graduation in 1977, he enrolled in and dropped out of a couple of local colleges. The only areas where he showed any aptitude were horticulture and photography. More than once, he tried to get away from home by renting an apartment, but he always came back.

In 1987 his chronically ill father committed suicide. A few months later, Rifkin was nailed for soliciting sex from an undercover policewoman. By then, sex with prostitutes was the driving force in his life and his sexual urges were becoming more violent.

He acted on them in March 1989 while his mother was out of town. Rifkin cruised the East Village in Manhattan one night and picked up a crackhead whore he knew only as Susie. Back at his house they had sex. When Susie asked him to help her find more drugs, he beat her with a howitzer shell, then strangled her to death. After a refreshing nap, he dismembered the body, packed up the pieces in various containers—the head fit in a paint can—and drove to New Jersey to get rid of them.

Susie has never been identified. Rifkin's pattern was forming, but it was more than a year before he went after his second victim, another prostitute, in late 1990. Then he picked up the pace, killing again in July 1991 and again in September. If his mother was away, Rifkin took the women to his home. If not, they went to motels or used his car. His method of beating followed by strangulation remained the same, but he dumped the bodies in trunks or 55-gallon drums.

Since he chose his victims from society's lost and cast-off, they were not missed, and few missing-person reports were filed with police. In all, Rifkin slaughtered 17 women.

He was finally caught on June 28, 1993 when he was spotted driving a pickup without a rear license tag. New York state troopers tried to stop him, and Rifkin led them on an early morning high-speed chase that ended when he crashed into a telephone pole. In the bed of the truck, under a blue tarp, was the decomposing body of Tiffany Bresciani.

When police searched Rifkin's bedroom, they found a horde of souvenirs—ID cards, jewelry, wallets, drivers licenses—a record of his kills. In his initial interrogation, Rifkin admitted everything and even drew maps to help the police find the bodies not yet located. Later, he would try to recant it all, saying he had been denied contact with a lawyer. It didn't fly.

After several trials, Rifkin was found guilty and was sentenced to 203 years in prison. He is now held in solitary at the Clinton facility in Dannemora.

Though he is New York's most prolific serial killer, he has never found a real place in the public imagination. His most lasting fame may come from a memorable episode of *Seinfeld* where Elaine worries about the implications of her new boyfriend's name, Joel Rifkin.

Rogers, George W.

September 8, 1934: three days out of Havana, bound for New York, the luxury liner *Morro Castle* was steaming toward disaster.

The lifeboats were leaky and drills had been cancelled. Fire drills had been stopped, too, and

hydrants had been capped on an earlier voyage after a passenger broke her ankle on a wet deck during a drill. The weather was turning bad and the smoke detector system had been turned off so passengers wouldn't be bothered by the noxious smell of a shipment of raw hides in the hold.

And, there was a full blown psychopath on the loose.

His name was George White Rogers, a suety, pear-shaped puke. He had been diagnosed with Fröhlich's Syndrome as a child, a pituitary disorder that produced excess body fat, genital underdevelopment and, not surprisingly, mental problems. In short, Rogers was one sick puppy.

He had been placed in charge of the ship's radio, having conned the previous chief radio officer into resigning through a series of anonymous letters. He knew it was coming to an end; in the short time he'd been on the job, he had been caught in thoroughly pointless petty thefts and told he would be fired as soon as the ship reached port.

Somehow, in his twisted reasoning, Rogers had convinced himself the ship's captain, Robert Wilmott, was responsible and on the previous voyage, Rogers had tried to poison him. The unsuccessful attempt only made Wilmott more careful and suspicious, but on the night of the September 8th Rogers somehow got it right. At 7:45 p.m., the captain was found in his bathroom, half on the toilet, half in the tub, pants around his knees. Nobody will ever know exactly what killed him—a doctor said it was a combination of heart failure and indigestion—because a few hours later, the ship was ablaze.

As the ship headed into a nor'easter, Rogers started the fire with a small incendiary device hidden in a closet filled with uniforms, directly below the storage area for a Lyle gun, a device used to fire a line to someone who's gone overboard. It was powered by a 25-pound explosive charge.

As for the ship itself, the *Morro Castle* was a party-hearty boat where the patrons could cruise from New York to Cuba, whooping it up with legal

Morro Castle on fire (1934), the handiwork of George Rogers. (AP Photo)

liquor and all the hanky panky they could handle. The *Morro Castle* was also used to run guns to the Cuban dictator who was fighting communist rebels.

Chief Officer William Warms was appointed acting captain. When he first learned of the fire, he thought it was a minor incident and treated it as such. The ship plowed on through high winds that fanned the flames and soon they were beyond control. Conditions deteriorated with passengers and crew helpless to do much. Throughout the panic, a few people noticed how Rogers seemed to be enjoying himself. Finally, the *Morro Castle* turned toward shore off Asbury Park, New Jersey where it ran aground and was consumed by the flames. Before it was over 134 people, passengers and crew, were dead.

Initially, Rogers was portrayed as a hero who stayed at his post even as he was threatened by the conflagration. He even appeared briefly on Broadway to relate his valiant deeds. He did suffer some superficial burns and blamed Warms and the chief engineer for the disaster. Even though some suspicions were raised about his role in the disaster, he had been publicly crowned as a good guy and walked away.

The porcine pyro went back home to Bayonne, New Jersey where he opened a radio repair shop. Again, not surprisingly, he couldn't make a go of it, and the place burned mysteriously while he was on break one day. A few years later, he managed to land a job on the police force as assistant to Vincent Doyle, who was in charge of the radio bureau.

Before long, Rogers wanted Doyle's job and tried to kill him by boobytrapping an electric pump.

This time, there was no question who was guilty. In the investigation, many of the details of Rogers' criminal record and involvement in the *Morro Castle* were uncovered by the DA. But rather than complicate their open-and-shut case in the Doyle murder attempt, they kept those facts secret. A psychiatrist diagnosed Rogers as a full-blown psycho, and he got a 12-to-20-year sentence at the state pen in Trenton.

When World War II came along, radiomen—even psychotic radiomen—were at a premium and so Rogers was paroled. The armed services disagreed about their need for card-carrying fruitcakes and turned Rogers down. He remained free however and landed a job on a ship. That ended when he was arrested—nobody's quite sure for what—in Darwin, Australia.

Rogers made it back to New Jersey where he managed to function for the next decade, but in 1953 he had a disagreement over money with his neighbor William Hummel, age 83. Hummel had been trying to recover $7,500 Rogers owed him. Hummel was preparing for a Florida retirement and had $2,400 in cash at his home when Rogers showed up. Rogers bashed in the old guy's head with a footstool, then used it to kill Hummel's daughter, 58, who was also in the house.

Rogers then started spending like the proverbial drunken sailor and was soon arrested. Sent back to the state prison, he died of a brain hemorrhage a few years later.

George White Rogers might have been remembered as a tragic, deeply flawed hero if Gordon Thomas and Max Morgan Witts hadn't become interested in the *Morro Castle* disaster. Their excellent 1972 book, *Shipwreck*, reveals how Rogers managed his bizarre crimes. It also provided much of the basis for a 2002 A&E documentary about the events.

Of more immediate importance to Americans in the 1930s, the destruction of the *Morro Castle* led to changes in passenger ship safety features including flameproof furniture, fire patrols, and emergency gear.

Rogers, Mary Cecelia

She was America's first famous murder mystery, and Mary Cecelia Rogers' case remains unsolved. Given the state of police investigations in New York in 1841, it's no surprise.

Cops—called leatherheads or roundsmen in those days—were part-time freelancers, amateurs who earned very little in the way of wages or the rewards they might get from robbery victims.

By all accounts, Mary Rogers was a bright attractive young woman. For several years, she worked in a tobacco shop, and was extraordinarily popular with the clientèle. She counted James Fenimore Cooper, Edgar Allan Poe, and much of the New York legal and newspaper community among her customers. She was such a hit in the store that when she went missing for a time in 1838, it caused a minor sensation. When she returned, after reportedly visiting relatives in Brooklyn, the store was jammed. Everyone made such a to-do that Mary swooned. Apparently, the attention did not agree with her and she resigned a few months later to work in her mother's boarding house.

The city of New York was going through one of its regular growth spurts in those years and attracted many ambitious young men. Several of them passed through Mrs. Rogers' place, and Mary seldom lacked male companionship. In the summer of 1841 she was ardently pursued by two of her mother's roomers, law clerk Alfred Crommelin and cork cutter Daniel Payne.

In June, perhaps reluctantly, Mary decided to marry Payne. Angered, Crommelin moved out, but didn't go far; only a few blocks and he didn't cut off all contact.

On Sunday, July 25th Mary set off, saying she was going to visit an aunt who lived in the city. It was the last anyone saw of her. She didn't show up at her aunt's house; no one there even knew she had been coming. On Wednesday, her body washed up on the other side of the Hudson River near Hoboken, New Jersey.

During the time she was missing, her fiancé searched diligently for her and published a missing person item in a local newspaper. When the jilted Crommelin learned of her disappearance, he, too, joined the search. He was actually in Hoboken when the body was brought ashore, and identified his ex-squeeze.

A hasty coroner's inquest was held where it was determined Mary had been abducted and murdered. He face and neck were bruised and it appeared her hands had been tied. She was buried that evening.

At the same time, one of the men who had discovered the body went to Mrs. Rogers' boarding house to give her the sad news. Curiously, neither she nor Mr. Payne, the previously frantic fiancé, seemed surprised.

Public interest in the murder was kept alive by a vigorous newspaper war. No fewer than seven papers covered the story. The competition among them for the juiciest, freshest detail made sure inquiring minds didn't forget about Mary. Of course, New Jersey officials wanted New York to handle the matter, while the New Yorkers claimed it was New Jersey's problem since the body was found there.

Eventually, a reward was offered, Mary's body was disinterred and moved, and New York took over the investigation. Several theories and suspects were put forward but nothing came of them. Interest was flagging when, a month later, two boys found women's clothing and personal items in a heavily wooded thicket in New Jersey, about a mile from where the body had been picked up.

One of the boys was the son of Frederica Loss who ran a popular tavern. She said a young woman who might have been Mary had been at her place during the key time when she was missing. Some came to suspect that Mrs. Loss had been involved in helping Mary obtain an abortion. It might even

have been performed at her place. Again, though, there was no proof.

Finally, in October, fiancé Daniel Payne left New York for Hoboken. Drunk, he asked directions to the thicket. He was seen writing something near it. That night, he continued to drink. He also finished off a bottle of laudanum, tincture of opium. He was found dead near the river the next morning with a suicide note in his pocket.

That might have been the end of it, but a year later, Poe thought the story of Mary Rogers would make an excellent subject for the sequel to his popular short story, "The Murders in the Rue Morgue." (In that tale, his brilliant French detective, C. August Dupin deduced that a double murder had been perpetrated by an orangutan.) For the sequel, Mary Rogers became Marie Roget, New York became Paris, the Hudson became the Seine. Dupin sorts it all out with his customary genius.

"The Mystery of Marie Roget" was published in three parts in *Snowden's Ladies' Companion*. Since then (and before), countless writers, playwrights, and filmmakers have taken similar liberties, reshaping the known facts of any familiar story to meet the demands of their fictions while their audience's interest is at its peak.

On a more practical level, two years later, the city of New York formed the first full-time professional police department in America. Boston, Philadelphia, and others followed.

Today, the best versions of the real story are Rick Geary's graphic book, *The Mystery of Mary Rogers* (2001) and Daniel Stashower's richly detailed *The Beautiful Cigar Girl* (2006).

Rolling, Daniel

His childhood could serve as a blueprint for the creation of a killer. His father, a cop, brutalized the entire family, particularly his son Danny. As a teenager, Daniel Rolling "experimented" with alcohol and drugs. Suicide attempts, voyeurism, house breaking, armed robbery, eight years in the pen, parole.

Danny Rolling, perpetrator of the Gainesville slayings, in court, 1994. (AP Photo)

Between the parole and his arrival in Gainesville, Florida, Rolling had it out with his dad and shot him in the head—the old man lived—and he killed three other people in Shreveport, Louisiana. (He was never charged with those murders but he did confess to them later.)

By Friday, August 24, 1990, Rolling had traveled to Gainesville and was camping out in a small wooded area. That night, he broke into an apartment where University of Florida students Christina Powell and Sonja Larson lived. He bound them with duct tape, raped, murdered, and mutilated them with a hunting knife.

The next night, he broke into Christa Hoyt's place. She was a student at Santa Fe Community College who was working as a records clerk for the county Sheriff's Office. Rolling's attack on her was

even more savage. She was also eviscerated and beheaded.

Early on Tuesday morning, Rolling broke into a third apartment, one shared by friends Manuel Taboada and Tracy Paules. They probably thought they were fairly safe because Manuel was a 6-foot 2-inch jock. But Rolling caught him while he was asleep. Judging by the defensive wounds on his arms, Taboada was able to fight back for a time. Rolling killed them both, but was interrupted before he could do more.

Later that day, he and accomplice Tony Danzy robbed the First Union National Bank. Police spotted them as they were returning to their makeshift campground. Danzy stopped when ordered to; Rolling ran. Danzy was arrested and their stuff was taken as evidence—evidence of the robbery. Police had already identified a local mentally disturbed man as the primary murder suspect and paid no attention to anyone else.

Rolling stole a car and headed east and south, breaking into more houses and sticking up convenience stores. He was caught about a week later as he attempted to knock over a Winn-Dixie grocery store in Ocala. He was locked up but, still, no one suspected he had anything to do with the Gainesville murders until authorities finally noticed the strong similarities between them and the earlier killings in Shreveport.

When the evidence they had collected at Rolling's campsite was examined closely, the cops found conclusive physical and DNA evidence.

Against his lawyer's advice, Rolling pleaded guilty. The abuse he had suffered as a child played a large part in his defense. It wasn't enough to outweigh the horrors of the five Gainesville murders and he was sentenced to death. He was executed by injection on October 25, 2006.

Two nonfiction books have been written about his crimes, *The Gainesville Ripper* (1994) by Mary Ryzuk and *Beyond Murder* (1994) by John Philpin and John Donnelly. They've never been filmed as such, though the basic madman-attacks-students plot has been seen in countless slasher films.

Rothstein, Arnold

"A.R.," as he was known to his associates, was the most civilized of the great American gangsters. His most lasting contribution to his chosen field, though, came with the young men he influenced.

Born a math prodigy to a respectable middle-class Jewish family in New York in 1882, Rothstein was drawn to pool halls, poker tables, and crap games. His image, though, was always of the well-dressed soft spoken gentleman. Didn't smoke. Didn't drink. Devoted husband.

Understanding numbers as well as he did, Rothstein realized that with gambling, it was more profitable to run the game than to play the game. Vastly more profitable. He still placed bets on virtually anything throughout his life, but it was for fun, not to make a living. More important, he developed strong contacts within the Tammany Hall political machine that ran New York, and worked with both politicians and gangsters, and loaned them money. He became known as the man to see, the man who could fix anything in New York.

From managing bets on sports and politics and loan sharking, he branched out to "bucket shops" as the stock market heated up at the beginning of the new century. They were gambling dens dressed up as securities markets that catered to suckers. Rothstein mostly provided the muscle that backed them up.

He was also heavily involved with the theft of Liberty bonds from the messengers who transported the easily negotiable securities between banks and brokerage houses. Between 1918 and 1920 about $5 million in the bonds was stolen, almost all of it carefully arranged with cooperative messengers who knew when and where they would be robbed.

When **Prohibition** reared its ugly head, Rothstein was briefly involved in bootlegging. For a time, he cornered the market in the best English and Scottish booze, but he came to realize the liquor business was too big for him control and too violent for his personal taste, so he got out. Later in life, he would invest in the new narcotics trade. To a large degree, though, Rothstein's criminal pursuits—gambling and bookmaking—are either legal or considered relatively unimportant today.

Of course, A.R. will always be most famous as the man who fixed the 1919 World Series, the Black Sox Scandal, though he was probably not the brains behind it. Eight members of the heavily favored Chicago White Sox let it be known in certain circles they would be willing to throw some games against the Cincinnati Reds if the price was right. They were motivated by the team's legendarily parsimonious owner Charles Comiskey.

Two gamblers agreed to the scheme and asked Rothstein to bankroll them. Later, testifying before a grand jury, A.R. said he turned them down. Realizing a fix that big would certainly be found out, he wanted no part of it, and claimed even to have lost money on his own bets. He produced a $25,000 canceled check to prove it. He did not mention the $350,000 he had won.

During the same years, A.R. was a mentor to the next generation of gangsters, particularly **Meyer Lansky**, "the Little Man", and **Lucky Luciano**. He impressed upon them the importance of profits over rigid ideas and warfare between gangs. There was plenty to go around, and so cooperation was a smarter strategy than cutthroat competition.

Rothstein's life ended badly. In 1928 he suffered some undefined health problems that compromised his judgment. He lost heavily in a marathon poker game organized by gambler George McManus, then refused to pay up, claiming the other two players had cheated. When word got out that A.R. was welshing on a bet, everyone knew something was wrong. A week after the game, McManus called and asked for a meeting at the Park Central Hotel. Rothstein went up to room 349 and somebody shot him in the stomach. He refused to tell the cops who did it, and died two days later.

In the popular imagination though, Arnold Rothstein will always be known as the man who fixed the series. The reputation was cemented as early as 1925 with the publication of F. Scott Fitzgerald's *The Great Gatsby*, where A.R. was a supporting character under the name Meyer Wolfsheim, "the man who fixed the World Series back in 1919."

Rothstein was also the inspiration for Damon Runyon's loveable gangster Nathan Detroit in *Guys and Dolls* (1950). One of his epic pool games provided, at least in part, the basis for the Minnesota Fats character played by Jackie Gleason in *The Hustler* (1961). (Rudolf Wanderone began calling himself Minnesota Fats after the film was released.)

In *The Godfather II* (1974), Hyman Roth claims to have based his name on Rothstein.

A.R. is an important supporting character in *Mobsters* (1991) where he's wonderfully played by F. Murray Abraham. He's also in *The Rise and Fall of Legs Diamond* (1960), *Lansky* (1999), and *Gangster Wars* (1981). John Sayles places him at the center of the Black Sox scandal in *Eight Men Out* (1988). In the rarely seen 1961 *King of the Roaring 20's*, Rothstein is the hero. David Janssen, television's *The Fugitive*, did the honors in the film.

Ruby, Jack

Lee Harvey Oswald

He was born Jacob Rubenstein but changed his name to Jack Ruby in 1946 when he started a mail order business with his brothers in Chicago. He had grown up on the streets working at whatever came to hand—selling novelties, scalping tickets to Cubs games, newspaper subscriptions.

After his brothers bought him out of the mail order outfit, he moved to Dallas where his sister Eva ran a nightclub, his entrée into the business. Over the following years, he ran a series of strip joints, nightspots, and bars. In 1964 Ruby was in charge of the Carousel Club, a downtown burlesque house popular with cops. Ruby was something of a police groupie, who was known to hang around headquarters. He was also a flag-waving patriot, famous for his short fuse. He was quick to fight whenever he heard anti-Semitic or racial slurs. That temper had gotten him in trouble; during his years in Dallas he had been arrested on charges of disturbing the peace, concealed weapons, assault, and liquor violations.

Like everyone else in Dallas and America, he was shocked and stunned when President Kennedy was assassinated. Unlike everyone else, he had the means to act on his outrage. When Dallas police made a media event of Lee Harvey Oswald's transfer from the Police and Courts Building to the County Jail, Ruby had little trouble slipping in among the writers, photographers, and broadcasters. As Oswald appeared, Ruby stepped out of the crowd and shot him in the abdomen.

When asked why, he said he didn't want to put Mrs. Kennedy through the distress of a public trial and, besides, he wanted to show everybody that Jews had guts. Many have claimed Ruby was acting on orders to get rid of Oswald before he talked—orders from the Mafia, the CIA, the FBI, Castro—insert your favorite sinister force here.

For his part, Ruby steadfastly denied he was working for or with anybody. He succumbed to a stroke in 1967 at Parkland Hospital, the same place where the President and Oswald died.

On film, the 1978 made-for-television *Ruby and Oswald* follows the known events. *Ruby*, made in 1992, is one of the most far-fetched assassination films imaginable. The producers take such liberties with history that they add a postscript admitting much of the film, including one of the central characters, is fictional. It ends up being an attempt at a Unified Conspiracy Theory with no evidence and precious little drama.

Rudolph, Eric

Eric Rudolph is the logical, violent extension of far right-wing political thought. He believes women should not be allowed to have abortions, and homo-

Jack Ruby (center, second row) in cuffs, after a battery of psychiatric tests to determine his competency to stand trial in the murder of Lee Harvey Oswald (1964). (AP Photo)

sexuality is a sickness that cannot be tolerated in public. He doesn't like the Beatles, either, particularly John Lennon. But while other namby pamby Dittoheads sat around and whined about those things, he acted.

The high school and college dropout grew up in the mountains of North Carolina and fancied himself a survivalist, but was kicked out of the army for smoking weed. He found a target for his various complaints in the 1996 Atlanta Olympics. To him, the games were a celebration of "the ideals of global socialism."

Rudolph put together a backpack bomb filled with explosives and shrapnel and placed it near a sound tower at a rock concert in the Centennial

Park. The event had drawn a good-sized crowd and Rudolph might have gotten a much higher body count if not for security guard Richard Jewell.

Jewell spotted the unattended knapsack around 12:30 a.m. Saturday, July 27th. He brought it to the attention of his supervisor and the Georgia Bureau of Investigation. They were clearing the area when the bomb went off about 1:20 a.m. More than 100 people were hurt. Alice Hawthorne, of Albany, Georgia was killed, and TV cameraman Melih Uzunyol suffered a fatal heart attack as he ran to record the explosion.

In the days that followed, the FBI tried to pin it on Jewell, leaking his name to the press and turning a search of his apartment into a full-blown media event in the hopes he would confess. Instead, Richard Jewell hired a lawyer and passed a polygraph. Eventually, Attorney General Janet Reno was forced to make a public apology, and several news organizations settled with Jewell out of court, but it's still a particularly shameful episode for the Bureau.

Rudolph, in the meantime, was not idle. In January 1997 he set two more bombs at the suburban Northside Family Planning Clinic. The first damaged the building, the second, designed to get the police who investigated, wounded seven.

A month later, Rudolph placed two more bombs at the Otherside, a lesbian nightclub. Five people were injured in the first explosion. The second bomb was defused.

Almost a year later in January 1998 he planted a bomb at an abortion clinic in Birmingham, Alabama. It killed Robert Sanderson, a police officer moonlighting as a security guard, and permanently disabled and blinded nurse Emily Lyons.

As Rudolph was skulking away from the clinic, a witness saw him pulling off a blond wig and noted down the license of his pickup. Police ID'ed him from the plate number, and the manhunt was on. Rudolph went to ground in western North Carolina and managed to elude capture for five years. Some of the locals who shared his politics probably helped him.

Rudolph was caught as he was dumpster-diving behind a Sav-A-Lot supermarket in Murphy, North Carolina. He was arrested without incident by rookie officer Jeffrey Postell.

Rudolph was charged with six counts and could have received the death penalty but the Bush administration Justice Department reached a plea agreement. In return for his revealing the location of a dynamite stash, they gave him life without parole. He now spends his days at the Florence, Colorado "supermax" facility. His story has not inspired Hollywood, but it was told in deep detail by Maryanne Vollers in her excellent book, *Lone Wolf* (2006).

Rule, Ann

Could any true crime writer ask for a better break than to work with the most infamous murderer of the day? That's precisely what happened to Ann Rule. Her personal association with Ted Bundy began while they were both working nights at a suicide hotline in the Seattle Crisis Center in the early 1970s. At the time, he was a college student and she was eleven years older, with children, going through a difficult divorce. She was struggling to start a career as a writer, often working with police, and volunteering at the center.

Between phone calls, they became good friends talking over their most personal problems—her brother's suicide, his illegitimacy. When her shift ended at 2:00 a.m., Bundy would walk her to her car and make sure she was locked in and the engine turned over before he went back inside.

When a serial killer went to work in the area and clues pointed toward a young man named Ted who drove a light-colored VW, as Bundy did, she reluctantly became suspicious and told a police officer colleague what she feared. Three other people also voiced their doubts about Bundy to the cops. Nothing came of it.

At the time, she was working closely with police. From childhood, Rule had close family ties with law enforcement—an uncle and a grandfather who were sheriffs in Michigan, another uncle a medical examiner, a cousin who was a prosecutor. She had worked as a policewoman in Seattle until her superiors found out how nearsighted she was.

So when Bundy was revealed to be a sociopathic monster, Rule was able to write about him and his apprehension from the ultimate insider's point of view. The result, *Stranger Beside Me* (1980), became a huge bestseller and fundamentally changed true crime writing.

Where Truman Capote's *In Cold Blood* (1966) focused on the two killers, how their lives had led them to murder, and what happened to them after, Rule's sympathies were squarely on the side of the victims and the police who were trying to find a killer. The 20-plus books and hundreds of articles she has written since follow the same course. Unlike her first success, most of her other work has been about less sensational crimes.

Rule has written about interesting cases, not the celebrity trials: a mother who shot her children, a girl who confessed to murdering her stepmother, a man who killed his mistress and tried to pin it on another mistress. She has also written several volumes of her "crime files" series, addressing lesser-known cases in chapter-length treatments.

In all of her work, Rule is sensitive to the people who have suffered. She never exploits her material or dwells on descriptions of their inherent horrors. She still works extensively with law enforcement organizations and with crime victims' groups.

To date, five of Rule's books have been adapted as TV films or miniseries: *Stranger Beside Me* (2003), *Every Breath You Take* (2003), *And Never Let Her Go* (2001), *Dead by Sunset* (1995), and *Small Sacrifices* (1989).

Russell, George

In the pantheon of modern serial killers, George Russell is known for the psychotic ferocity of his attacks and his deep-seated misogyny. He killed three young women. Doubtless, he would have murdered more had it not been for solid police work across three jurisdictions.

Russell's troubled upbringing included two abandonments by his birth mother that left him in the care of relatives and, as a teenager, of his stepfather, a dentist. Otherwise, this handsome young black man grew up in affluent Mercer Island, Washington, near Seattle. He displayed a talent for trouble early on, dropping out of high school and embarking on a youthful criminal career of breaking and entering, burglary, trespassing, vandalism, and drug sales.

His stepfather kicked him out at age 17. Russell moved to the suburb of Bellevue in 1975. For the next 15 years, he drifted through an active singles scene, moving often, usually crashing with friends and acquaintances. Though no one knew it, he made his living as a cat burglar, stealing and selling jewelry. He was a familiar face at all the hottest bars, a charming guy who had a way with the ladies.

But something changed on the night of June 22, 1990 when he met Mary Ann Pohlreich at Papagayo's Cantina. Her naked body was found the next morning in an alley behind a nearby restaurant. She had been brutally raped, sodomized, and beaten. One blow had ruptured her liver. Cause of death was blunt instrument trauma to the head, but many of the more grotesque injuries had occurred after death. The body had been twisted into a tortured contortion and "decorated" with found objects.

A month later, his second victim was Carol Ann Beethe. Like Pohlreich, she was a pretty, flirty woman who liked her nightlife. After hanging out at the Keg, she went home, checked on her two daughters and went to bed. The doors of her house were unlocked. Russell had no trouble getting in. Again, blunt instrument trauma to the head was the cause of death. Russell must have surprised her so suddenly that she was unable to scream or defend herself.

A daughter found her bloody body in bed the next morning. Again the savagery of the attack was remarkable, as was the staging of the body, impaled on a shotgun (hers).

The third victim was Andrea "Randi" Levine. Like the first two women, she was well known in the "yuppie bars," as they were called back in the day, as something of a tease. She was found in her apartment stretched across her bed. Same vicious head wound, same rape, more than 200 slash wounds, a copy of *The Joy of Sex* placed in her hand. Bruise marks indicated that a ring might have been forced from her hand.

Detectives from King County, Bellevue, and Kirkland worked on the investigation and found two common threads connecting the three women. They went to the same bars, and all of them knew a George Russell. The Seattle police knew him, too.

They were already looking for him on suspicion of burglary.

They caught him on the night of September 12, 1990. After getting a report of a suburban prowler, the area was flooded with patrol cars and Russell was picked up on the street. It turned out the woman who had reported the prowler was a close friend of Andrea Levine, and a habitué of the same bars.

Once the investigation focused on Russell, the pieces fell into place. A friend had loaned him a pickup on the night of the first killing. When Russell returned it, the truck smelled bad and the seat was stained. Those stains proved to be blood matching Mary Anne Pohlreich's. DNA testing on sperm samples taken from her body matched Russell. Jewelry he had sold to several people was also traced to the victims. The physical evidence was enough to convict Russell on three charges of first degree murder. He was sentenced to life.

John Douglas examines Russell in his book *Journey Into Darkness* (1997).

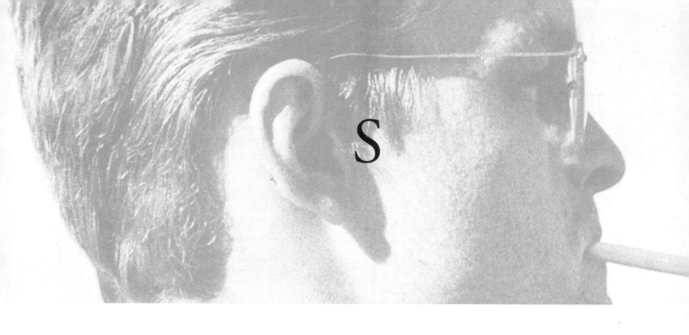

Sacco, Nicola, and Bartolomeo Vanzetti

It's barely possible that Nicola Sacco and Bartolomeo Vanzetti actually committed two murders and a robbery. Some still think they did it, but it's unlikely. It's much more likely they had nothing to do with the crimes.

It is absolutely certain they had the wrong politics (anarchist), the wrong nationality (Italian), and the wrong religion (none). In the end, they were punished not for what they might have done, but for what they believed and for who they were.

The two immigrants were accused of taking part in the 1921 robbery of almost $16,000 from a South Braintree, Massachusetts shoe factory payroll. Paymaster Frederick A. Parmenter and guard Alessandro Berardelli were gunned down in the knockover. Five men were involved.

A couple of weeks later, Sacco and Vanzetti joined two acquaintances at a garage where they had gone to pick up a car belonging to one of the other men, Mike Boda (some have fingered Boda for the 1921 Wall Street bombing.) The car had been left for repairs, and the local police wrongly suspected it might have been the getaway car. The cops asked the garage owner to let them know when the owners showed up.

While the garage owner's wife tipped off the cops, her husband made an excuse to keep the car. Sacco and Vanzetti were arrested a little later on a trolley. Both were carrying pistols and both had "anarchist" literature. Even though they had clean records—no convictions, no arrests—and the robbery bore all the signs of a professional job, they were charged for the crimes.

It was clear from the beginning of the trial that Judge Webster Thayer had decided the defendants were guilty and he was going to make an example of them. Just two months earlier, another anarchist, Sergei Zabraft, had been before Judge Thayer for breaking U.S. Attorney General Mitchell Palmer's infamous Red Scare laws, and the jury had found him not guilty.

Thayer, a hidebound member of the moneyed conservative elite, wasn't about to let it happen again. The strongest evidence against Sacco and Vanzetti involved ballistics, but it was highly suspect. One "expert" testified one of the bullets could have been fired from Sacco's automatic, but he couldn't even disassemble it. The state's other expert was later found to have manipulated his testimony in other trials if he agreed strongly enough with the prosecution, and there is reason to believe the incriminating bullet was planted.

Eyewitness testimony was important, too, but it really meant little because Sacco was a ringer for local gangster Joe Morelli. Later, Celestino Medieros, a member of Morelli's mob, actually confessed to the crime, exonerating Sacco and Vanzetti. When he was arrested, Medieros was carrying a wad of cash that roughly equaled one fifth of the Braintree payroll haul. (No money was ever found in the possession of Sacco and Vanzetti.)

But nothing cut any ice with Judge Thayer. In private conversations, he referred to the defendants as "dago bastards" and "sons of bitches," and in his instructions to the jury, he virtually ordered them to find the defendants guilty. The jury followed his instructions.

Sacco and Vanzetti immediately got new lawyers and appealed, but in Massachusetts at the time, Thayer handled all of the appeals. They dragged on for six years and during that time protests in support of the two men became more numerous and energetic. Felix Frankfurter, not yet a Supreme Court Justice, wrote a passionate defense published in *Atlantic Monthly*. Huge demonstrations took place in Switzerland, England, South America, Germany, and many other countries. All useless.

Massachusetts Governor Alvin Tufts Fuller appointed a commission to study the case, but it was merely the government's final fig leaf. The commission was cut from the same cloth as Thayer and backed him up despite the evidence.

On August 23, 1927 Sacco, Vanzetti, and Medieros went to the electric chair. Six months later, a bomb went off at the executioner's home (no one was hurt). The same happened to Thayer five years later with the same result.

In 1977 Governor Michael Dukakis exonerated the pair.

Perhaps more than any other figures of their time, Sacco and Vanzetti came to represent the sharp divisions splitting the country. To the wealthy law-and-order establishment, they personified an assault on American values and morality. To the artistic and journalistic communities, they were victims of political repression, and this is where their names have endured. They have been the subject of artists in every medium from Ben Shahn's famous illustrations to Upton Sinclair's nonfiction novel *Boston* (1928). Virtually every writer of that age commented on the case in poetry, drama, or prose, but perhaps the most moving portrait is found in the two men's *Collected Letters* (1928).

The story has been filmed several times. Maxwell Anderson's play *Winterset* (1935) has been adapted twice, first in 1936, and for television in 1945. Guliano Montaldo's 1971 French/Italian production *Sacco e Vanzetti* is well-regarded, but the most intriguing is Sidney Lumet's 1960 TV miniseries *The Sacco-Vanzetti Story* with Martin Balsam and Steven Hill. In 2007 Peter Miller's documentary *Sacco and Vanzetti* was released. For the most part, it's a calm film that lets the facts speak for themselves and avoids more emotional appeals. Miller has worked with filmmaker Ken Burns and takes the same careful approach.

Saldana, Theresa

There was never any question that Arthur Jackson was crazy; he had the Section 8 discharge papers from the army to prove it. A resident alien from England, he had also threatened to kill President John Kennedy—that got him deported back to Blighty. But after he saw the film *Raging Bull* (1980), his obsessions focused on actress Theresa Saldana, who played Jake LaMotta's sister.

In 1982 Jackson returned to America and began to stalk Saldana. He tried to get her address by hiring a private detective who found her through the DMV. On the morning of March 15, 1982 Jackson waited at her West Hollywood apartment. When she came out, he attacked her with a knife, stabbing her ten times.

Water deliveryman Jeffrey Fenn was close at hand and managed to restrain Jackson. He was arrested and hospital personnel were able to save Theresa's life. Her horrific attack and rehabilitation are the subject of the TV film *Victims For Victims* (1984), also the name of the organization she founded. Saldana starred in the film and has gone on to have a successful career on television.

Jackson is in a mental institution in England where he will spend the rest of his miserable life.

Perhaps the most important cultural outcome of this atrocity was the passage of California's Drivers Privacy Protection Act. It was created in reaction to the attacks on Saldana and Rebecca Schaeffer, another young actress who was murdered by an insane fan in an almost identical attack in 1989.

Salem Witch Trials

The historical truth of the events that took place in Salem, Massachusetts in 1692 has to do with a theocratic government and simmering disputes between neighbors in a poisonous small town. In popular culture, the witch trials have become a lens through which successive generations have examined their own concerns.

Salem was founded in 1626 and became a haven for Puritans, pious and opinionated folk who liked their Christianity hard and uncomplicated. As the place grew more populous, it divided into two groups, the people who lived in town and the farmers who lived nearby. The church levied taxes and called the shots.

By 1672 the farmers were known as Salem Village and they wanted their own church. They got it, but it didn't solve their problems. The community was so fractured and rancorous that preachers simply didn't last. Reverend Samuel Parris, who came from Barbados, was the fourth. He brought his family and a slave named Tituba whose religious beliefs seem to have included some sort of paganism or animism.

Arthur R. Jackson, escorted by unidentified deputy after his 1982 arraignment for stabbing actress Theresa Saldana. (AP Photo/Wally Fong)

One of Tituba's duties was to look after the minister's daughter Elizabeth and other young girls. By all accounts, Tituba was an accomplished storyteller who enthralled her young audience of 10 adolescent girls with divinations and mystical claptrap. Fortune-telling was involved, too, though it's unclear whether it came from the older woman or the girls themselves. Whatever the source, the kids sucked it all in.

At least they did until Elizabeth had some sort of fit, an arm-flapping, foaming-at-the-mouth moment of high pubescent drama. A mystified doctor diagnosed Satanic possession. A spell had been cast on the young girl. But who was the witch that had cast it?

Two magistrates were brought in to sort things out. Tituba promptly confessed, naming Sarah Good and Sarah Osborne as her teachers and confederates.

The inquisitors did not stop with those three. More accusations followed and an accusation was all it took. By their reasoning, a witch would deny she (or he) was a witch. And if any of the young accusers recanted and said she had just made up the story, that, too, was seen as proof she had been bewitched. It was simple. Before the madness was over, Sarah Good's five-year-old daughter Dorothy would be imprisoned in chains after being fingered. So would former minister George Burroughs, and Bridget Bishop, who was young and attractive and haunted the dreams of the Salem menfolk.

In all, 19 people were hanged and one old man, Giles Corey, was pressed to death. When he was accused, Corey refused to answer the charge. The penalty for failure to plead was *peine forte et dure*, with the victim stretched out naked on one board with a second board placed on his chest. Heavy stones where then slowly stacked on the upper board until the suspect either entered a plea or died. The only words Corey said were "More weight."

Beyond the 20 who were executed, three died in prison and several escaped.

It took six months from the first fit and pointed finger to the final execution and by then, even the most devout believers were having doubts. The forces of reason and enlightenment could not ignore the killings, either. A letter from a member of the Royal Society of Science questioning the fairness of the trials was read throughout the colony, and the governor soon shut down the Salem trials. When other courts handed down witchcraft verdicts, the governor immediately issued pardons.

Five-year-old Dorothy was released after her mother was executed. Tituba went back to the Parris household after more than a year in the slammer. The immediate reaction was a prolonged bout of public soul-searching as the religious leaders came to realize how seriously things had gotten out of hand. The previously zealous preacher Increase Mather made his famous pronouncement that it was better that ten guilty witches go free than one innocent be executed.

A century later in 1868 poet Henry Wadsworth Longfellow took up the story in the second part of his long dramatic poem "New England Tragedies, Giles Corey", a critique of Puritanism. At the time, Longfellow was one of the most popular writers in the country.

The most famous dramatic recreation of the trials is Arthur Miller's 1953 play, *The Crucible*. In it, he equates the Salem witch hunts with the anti-Communist hysteria rampant in postwar America. The play was adapted for television in 1959, and as a feature film with Daniel Day-Lewis and Winona Ryder in 1996. Two other dramatizations were made as a miniseries in 2002 and a PBS *American Playhouse* production in 1985.

Tituba has gained more cultural currency following the publication of Maryse Condé's novel *I, Tituba* (1992). Though accurate information about her background is unknown—she may have been South American, African, or Native American—she has come to symbolize resistance to the white European males who were the source of all evil.

Finally, the trials continue to be a rich source of tourism for Massachusetts, where witchcraft has been so commercialized it's a virtual cottage industry. That facet of the story is the basis for the 1993 Disney comedy *Hocus Pocus*.

Schmid, Charles Howard "Smitty"

Charles Howard Schmid served as a sort of prototype for **Charles Manson**. Driven by an uncontrollable energy that ranged between eccentricity and dark madness, he was able to attract a following of easily-led young men and women and persuade them to join him in senseless killing.

In mid-1960s Tucson, Arizona, Smitty, as he was called, tried to cut an Elvisian figure as he cruised the Speedway, the curiously named main drag. He sported dyed black, slicked back hair, bespoke cowboy boots stuffed with filler to elevate his diminutive 5-foot, 3-inch frame to a towering 5-foot, 7-inches, and a homemade putty facial mole to complete the "tough" look ensemble. Ridiculous, yes, but combined with a $300 a month allowance from his wealthy adoptive parents—not an inconsiderable sum back in the day—a new car, motorcycle, and his own crash-pad cottage out in the desert, Smitty was a cool cat. He hung out with a few guys who'd already been in trouble with the law and targeted teenage girls.

By then, he was in his twenties and was able to spin outrageous tales about his encounters with the **Mafia**. The kids bought it. He also bragged about all the girls who worked for him, as many as 100 in some tellings.

On May 31, 1964 Smitty decided grandiose lies weren't enough. He wanted to kill somebody. It would have to be someone smaller, weaker, and easily persuadable. He and his friends Mary French and John Saunders settled on Alleen Rowe, a 15-year-old high school sophomore. Mary knew her and was able to talk her into sneaking out of her house after her mother, a night nurse, had gone to work. The four of them drove out into the desert where Schmid and Saunders walked Alleen to a dry wash and smashed her head in with a rock. They buried her in a shallow grave.

Alleen's mother reported her disappearance to the Tucson police. When Smitty, Saunders, and Mary French were questioned, they said they hadn't seen her that night. Alleen was listed as a runaway. Later that year, Saunders enlisted in the Navy and left town. Richie Bruns then took over as Smitty's sidekick, and Smitty continued to cruise the strip for teenyboppers.

In July 1964 Smitty met 16-year-old Gretchen Fritz. Like him, she was a troubled kid from a well-to-do family. At the time, Schmid was sort of engaged to Mary and another girl, but it didn't slow him down. Not surprisingly, though, when Gretchen found out about all the other girls, she was miffed. Then she stole Smitty's diary where he described how he had killed a boy and buried him in the desert. Their fights escalated for a year until

both Gretchen and Mary claimed to be pregnant and demanded marriage.

On August, 16, 1965 Gretchen and her 13-year-old sister Wendy went out to the Cactus Drive-In to see Elvis in *Tickle Me*. Afterwards, they went out to Smitty's shack where he killed them both. His mental state was probably deteriorating by then; he later claimed the killing was getting easier and he really didn't care if he was caught. He didn't even bother to hide or bury the bodies.

Gretchen's father, a doctor, reported his daughters' disappearance and hired a private detective to help find them. The detective found their car and questioned Smitty and Richie, but got nothing. Sometime later, Smitty admitted to Richie what he'd done. Since everyone knew Richie and Gretchen didn't get along, Richie was afraid he would be a suspect, should the bodies be discovered. Smitty then decided it would be good time to hide the evidence. He took Richie out to the desert again where they buried the rapidly decomposing corpses of the Fritz sisters.

Both later claimed to have been questioned by members of the "Tucson Mafia" around that time and Schmid said they forced him to go to San Diego. He was arrested there for impersonating an FBI agent, after he was picked up on the beach asking questions about Gretchen and showing her picture to people.

The guilt was getting to Richie, too. He came to believe that Smitty was going to kill his girlfriend next, and he began hanging around her house to protect her. For his part, Smitty had decided to settle down. He married 15-year-old Diane Lynch.

The pressure was too much for Richie. He confessed everything; told the Tucson police about Alleen Rowe and took them to the bodies of the Fritz sisters. Smitty was arrested immediately, and the Tucson cops went to Connecticut to pick up Saunders. They found Mary French in Texas. As soon as she learned Smitty had married, she joined Richie in full confession. So did John Saunders. The only problem—they couldn't locate Alleen Rowe's grave.

No matter. The D.A. had more than enough to proceed on the Fritz murders; once the trial was finished, they'd move on to Alleen.

In the first trial, the prosecution built a strong case and easily knocked down Smitty's alibi for the night of August 16th. The jury took a little more than two hours to find him guilty. For the second trial, Smitty decided he needed better counsel and hired hotshot F. Lee Bailey, fresh from appealing Dr. **Sam Sheppard**'s case before the Supreme Court.

Bailey agreed to take Schmid's case, basing his decision on the amount of pretrial publicity and the lack of a body. He soon had cause to reconsider and recommended Smitty plead to second degree murder. After a series of confessions and retractions by the volatile Schimd, he was found guilty a second time. Two weeks later, he led police to Alleen's grave.

While Smitty was awaiting execution in the Arizona state pen, the death penalty was abolished by the Supreme Court. He tried to escape three times and made it out once in 1972 but was recaptured.

His life sentence ended in March 1975 when he was attacked by a couple of fellow inmates. He died with some 20 stab wounds to the head and chest.

At the time of his crimes, Schmid gained nationwide notoriety from stories written in *Life* and *Time* magazines. Those attracted the attention of Joyce Carol Oates who fictionalized Smitty's lethal attraction to teenaged girls in her famous story "Where Are You Going, Where Have You Been?" (1966). The story was the basis for the 1985 film *Smooth Talk* with Treat Williams and Laura Dern.

Schultz, Dutch

Of all the ruthless, violent men who rose to prominence in organized crime in the 1920s and '30s, Dutch Schultz was the most ruthless and violent. And probably the craziest.

He was born Arthur Flegenheimer to German Jewish parents in the Bronx in 1904. When he was 14, his father deserted the family and young Arthur never got over it. A tough kid, he dropped out of school and turned to burglary to support his mom. (Curiously, the principal of the school he dropped out of was none other than Dr. J.F. Condon who became famous years later as "Jafsie," the screw-loose go-between in the **Lindbergh** baby kidnapping.)

Arthur started out with petty crimes and like his contemporary **Meyer Lansky**, he really found himself under the tutelage of gambler **Arnold Rothstein**. But Arthur never took to heart Rothstein's core lesson that profits are more important that ego. Arthur always did things his way and it was what finally got him killed.

Arthur took the name "Dutch Schultz" from a deceased hoodlum who was notoriously tough with his dukes. After establishing himself as a bootlegger, Schultz took over other speakeasies and soon had to hire muscle to keep things in order. That's how he met **Vincent "Mad Dog" Coll** and **Legs Diamond**. They didn't stay together for very long, though. Legs went out on his own and soon became a competitor, such a serious competitor that a full-scale war broke out between him and Dutch. It ended upstate in December 1931 when Albany cops pumped Legs full of lead. Relations with Coll came to a similarly fatal conclusion a few months later in February 1932. Some of Schultz's men shadowed Mad Dog. When he stopped to make a call from a phone booth on 23rd Street, they opened up with a Tommy gun and virtually cut him in half.

Around the same time, Dutch decided to branch out from the illegal hooch business and cut himself a slice of Queenie St. Clair's Harlem numbers racket. The game was essentially a Pick-Three lotto where people placed a small bet on a three-digit number determined by a figure published daily—a stock market figure or a betting total from a race track, something supposedly random. But Dutch and his associate Otto "Abbadabba" Berman figured out a way to place bets at the end of the day to influence the number, skewing the already astronomical odds even further in their favor.

Schultz's empire was expanding so rapidly it worried **Lucky Luciano** and Lansky. It also worried Special Prosecutor Thomas Dewey who came after the Dutchman on income tax evasion charges in 1933. The evidence against him was overwhelming, but Dutch managed to get a deadlocked jury at his first trial. When the second trial was moved to upstate New York, Dutch hid his true nature and put on a massive charm offensive. He showed up everywhere as a regular kind of guy and made large donations to all the local charities. It worked and he walked.

But while Dutch had been gone, the other bosses carved up his holdings and Dewey wasn't finished. As soon as the acquittal was delivered, Dewey responded by announcing he had made Schultz his prime target. With that news, Mr. Nice Guy disappeared and the old foaming-at-the-mouth Dutch came roaring back. He called a meeting of the bosses and demanded they do something about Dewey. He wanted the man killed; they wouldn't go for it. It was just too dangerous to hit a high profile public figure. Dutch went nuts and said he was going to take care of it himself within 48 hours.

That cut it.

The bosses quickly arranged for a **Murder, Inc.** hit team headed up by Charlie "the Bug" Workman to take care of the situation. They snuck up on Dutch at his favorite restaurant, the Palace Chophouse in Newark, New Jersey, on October 23, 1935.

The Bug and company caught the Dutchman in the can. They put a .45 slug in his gut and then opened fire on his crew, including Abbadabba Berman.

Dutch didn't die that night, saving perhaps the strangest part of his mad life for the last. The bullet had really torn him up. Doctors operated at Newark City Hospital. They patched him up but could do nothing about the peritonitis he contracted. So they doped him to the earlobes with morphine and called a priest to give him last rites. (Dutch's wife had recently persuaded him to convert.) Then they brought in police stenographer F.J. Lang to take down anything the Dutchman said, perhaps something to incriminate his pals or give them a clue to his killer.

Instead, they got more than 20 hours of free association that added immeasurably to Dutch's status in popular culture. Those rambling, vaguely coherent babbles have inspired a host of writers. Beat icon William S. Burroughs, no stranger to drug-fueled ramblings himself, created *The Last Words of Dutch Schultz: A Fiction in the Form of A Film Script* (1969). Robert Shea and Robert Anton Wilson place the Dutchman prominently in their *Illuminatus!* trilogy (1975), while E.L. Doctorow made Dutch one of the main characters in *Billy Bathgate* (1989) with Dustin Hoffman playing him in the 1991 film.

Schultz shows up as a supporting character in many gangster films. He's the main guy in the rarely seen *Portrait of a Mobster* (1961) with Vic Morrow, and the brashly foolish *Hit the Dutchman* (1992) with Bruce Nozick. Tim Roth played him brilliantly in *Hoodlum* (1977). Burroughs' interpretation of his famous last words formed the basis for a short 2001 Dutch film. And the documentary, *Digging for Dutch* (2001), focuses on the folks who believe Schultz left $7 million and change buried in the Catskills.

Scottsboro Case

There is no good evidence the nine young black men commonly referred to as "the Scottsboro boys" committed any crime.

On March 25, 1931 they had hitched a ride on a freight train in Alabama. It was the height of the Depression and a lot of people had been reduced to hoboing. A fight broke out, and most of the guys in one car jumped off the slow-moving train. Somebody alerted the cops and at the next stop, in Paint Rock, Alabama, a deputy sheriff with armed assistants boarded the train.

Nine young black guys—Olen Montgomery, Clarence Norris, Haywood Patterson, Willie Roberson, Charles Weems, Eugene Williams, Andrew Wright, and Leroy Wright—were arrested. The deputy

Deputy Sheriff Charles McComb and attorney Samuel Leibowitz conferring with seven of the nine "Scottsboro Boys," May 1, 1935. (AP Photo)

sheriff also found one white guy, Orville Gilley, and two white women dressed as men, Ruby Bates and Victoria Price. The women said they had been raped.

Five days later the black men, aged 13 to 20, were indicted by a grand jury. They went to trial in Scottsboro on April 6th and on April 8th they were convicted and eight of the nine were sentenced to hang; 13-year-old Leroy Wright got life.

Throughout the trial, the courthouse was surrounded by a mob. (It was only the presence of the National Guard—with machine guns mounted on rooftops—and the number of defendants that kept the massed peckerheads from lynching them.) Legal representation for the accused was a joke: two lawyers were assigned only moments before the trial began. One was drunk; the other was so old he was virtually retired. Even so, he managed to request a change of venue. It was denied.

The appeals were handled by famous New York attorney Samuel Leibowitz.

As their case became an international cause célèbre, involving Albert Einstein among many others, Leibowitz was able to get the convictions overturned by the U.S. Supreme Court a year later. Many retrials followed. The alleged ring leader, Haywood Patterson, was convicted and sentenced to 75 years. He later escaped, but was recaptured and died in prison in 1948.

Ruby Bates admitted there had never been a rape, but it still took more trials, jail sentences, pardons, and paroles before the rest were freed. The long case highlighted the inequities of the American justice system. The events were dramatized in the 1976 television movie *Judge Horton and the Scottsboro Boys.* In 2000 the PBS series *American Experience* produced the documentary *Scottsboro: An American Tragedy.*

The case's most lasting cultural significance came from Harper Lee. The climatic third act of the trial in *To Kill a Mockingbird* (1960), where Atticus Finch defends Tom Robinson against a false rape charge, was inspired by Scottsboro.

Shakur, Tupac, and Notorious B.I.G.

It is difficult for those not familiar with the world of hip hop to keep things straight. As the legitimate heirs to America's great outlaws, gangsta rappers carefully cultivate their images as tough violent heavily-armed men who live by their own rebellious rules and defy authority. Such personas are built on confrontations with police and conflict with other parts of the larger rap community. That's why the murders of Tupac Shakur and Notorious B.I.G. (aka Biggie Smalls, born Christopher Wallace) have not been solved and probably never will be.

Conventional wisdom holds that the deaths were part of an East Coast-West Coast "war." This is the breakdown:

In Southern California, Marion "Suge" Knight formed Death Row Records. Tupac was his hottest selling artist. Knight was associated with the Bloods gang, particularly the Mob Piru Bloods.

In New York, Sean "Puffy" Combs (aka Puff Daddy and P. Diddy) formed Bad Boy Entertainment. Notorious B.I.G. was his hottest selling artist. Combs was associated with the Crips gang and sometimes used them for security.

Members of both groups routinely traveled and worked with large well-armed entourages. Clashes

Tupac Shakur, 1994, on his way to a court date. (AP Photo)

between them, often involving the theft of their gaudy expensive jewelry ("bling"), were common.

Tupac and B.I.G. had been close friends. But after Tupac was shot and seriously wounded in a 1994 robbery, he came to believe B.I.G. was behind the attack. It put a chill in the relationship, and Tupac's career soared, in part because he survived five bullets. B.I.G. always denied any involvement.

On September 7, 1996 Tupac, Knight, and company were in Las Vegas for the Mike Tyson heavyweight fight at the MGM Grand Hotel. As they were leaving, they were involved in a fight with a young man said to be associated with the Crips. The altercation was caught on a security camera and ended in less than a minute. The Death Row group left the hotel in a convoy of expensive cars and headed for a party. Knight drove the lead car. Tupac was beside him in the passenger seat.

Around 11:15 p.m., they stopped for a light on Flamingo Road. A white Caddy pulled up on their right and someone inside opened fire. Tupac was hit four times. Knight was slightly wounded by a bullet or broken glass. They rushed to the hospital where Tupac died six days later.

Six months later on March 9, 1997 B.I.G. and Sean Combs were at a party celebrating the Soul Train Music Awards at the Peterson Automotive Museum in Los Angeles. When the affair broke up after midnight, they left with their entourage. B.I.G. led the way in a Chevy Suburban. Combs was in a similar SUV right behind him. They were stopped at a stop sign when a Chevy Impala pulled up on the right of B.I.G.'s vehicle. The driver opened fire and killed him.

Virtually everyone who works in rap has been accused of complicity in one or both of the murders. As the most popular theories put it, the boss of one label ordered the hit on the other label's star, and/or he ordered the hit on his own star to reap the benefit of the posthumous hits. (Both Tupac and B.I.G. probably sold more records after they were killed than during their relatively brief careers.)

Whatever the truth, B.I.G. was certainly one of the most influential forces in the business. Tupac Shakur's film work showed he had the talent to have been a major star. He made a strong impression in his second film, *Juice* (1992), where, prophetically, his character idolized Jimmy Cagney's charismatic Cody Jarrett in *White Heat* (1949), and loved the film's fiery suicidal conclusion.

British documentarian Nick Broomfield looked at the complications involved with both murders in *Biggie and Tupac* (2002). He found evidence of police complicity, high-level coverups, resignations, vague connections, and a veritable mare's-nest of accusation and suspicion. Most viewers will come away from the film believing some sort of conspiracy was involved, but they'll have no clear idea of

exactly who was behind the killings or why they were committed.

Shawcross, Arthur

To hear him tell it, Arthur Shawcross was the sickest serial killer America has ever produced. He claimed that as a lad, he was introduced to incest, sodomy, fellatio, and bestiality by his immediate family. The troubled teen was then drafted, sent to Vietnam in 1968, and became a psychotic killing machine who burned a village, and raped, murdered, and ate two Vietnamese women. Back home in upstate New York, he suffered Post Traumatic Stress Disorder and became a murderer.

Not so, according to his mother, brother, sister, and neighbors. Artie had a normal childhood; no sexual abuse, animals were safe around him. And the Army said he had never been in combat. Nobody in his unit really remembered him, at all. But even if the excesses are lies invented after the fact to shore up an insanity defense, the verifiable truth is bad enough.

In May 1972 after returning from Vietnam, Shawcross murdered 10-year-old neighbor Jack Black. He probably sexually assaulted the boy, as he did with his next victim, eight-year-old Karen Ann Hill, killed four months later. Both bodies were hidden. After they were found, he became a suspect and confessed when confronted by police. Even so, he somehow managed a plea bargain with prosecutors, and was charged only with manslaughter in the death of Karen Ann Hill. No charge for Jack Black. For Hill, he got a 25-year sentence and was released on parole in 1987, after serving only 15 years.

You read it right, they let him go. (The only good that came out of this case was it helped lead to a reconsideration of sentencing and parole practices.)

A year later, in March 1988, Shawcross began attacking prostitutes in the Rochester area. He picked them up in a car where he strangled, beat, and raped them, then dumped the bodies in the Genesee River Gorge. Over the course of the next two years, he killed 11 women. FBI profilers were able to give an accurate if vague description of the suspect, which led local police to believe he might come back to take a second look at the bodies.

In January 1990 they used helicopters in aerial searches for the missing women. They got lucky. A chopper spotted a woman's body on a frozen creek. A man was standing by his car on a bridge near the body. He seemed to be urinating—actually he was masturbating—before he drove away. The helicopter followed and alerted patrol cars. A day later Shawcross confessed and was arrested.

At his televised trial, he was found guilty and sentenced to 250 years in jail. All of the media attention spawned several books, television specials, and jailhouse interviews. It was in those talks that Shawcross claimed his own unsubstantiated childhood abuse and his most horrific crimes.

The best works about Shawcross are Jack Olsen's book, *Misbegotten Son* (1993), and Mark Olshaker's 1992 PBS special for NOVA, *The Mind of a Serial Killer*.

To date, no one has attempted to bring his story to the big screen.

Sheppard, Sam

Dr. Sam Sheppard was tried for the murder of his wife by four different juries, criminal and civil. Three found him guilty. The case remains controversial more than half a century later for two reasons: first, it helped establish important legal points about pretrial publicity; and second, it morphed into a landmark of popular culture.

In 1954 Sheppard, his wife Marilyn, and young son Samuel Reese seemed like the ideal young family. He worked at a successful hospital with his father and brothers and lived in the pleasant Cleveland suburb of Bay Village, with a nice house on the shore of Lake Erie. Drove a Lincoln Continental and a Jag. Lovely Marilyn was four months pregnant. But early on the morning of July 4th, a Sunday, someone beat her to death in her bedroom.

The Sheppards had had friends over earlier. Dr. Sam had fallen asleep on the sofa downstairs while watching the late show, *Strange Holiday*, wherein Claude Rains returns from a fishing trip only to learn America has become a fascist dictatorship.

Sheppard claimed he was awakened by his wife calling his name. He dashed upstairs and saw someone he could not identify. They struggled. He was knocked unconscious. Sometime later, he came to and found Marilyn dead on the bloody bed. His son was still asleep. Sheppard then heard a noise and ran downstairs. He saw a "bushy-haired" man running toward the lake, and followed, chasing the man down wooden stairs to the beach where again they struggled, and again Sheppard was rendered unconscious for an indeterminate amount of time.

Eventually, he staggered back to the house and called his neighbor and friend Spencer Houk, the mayor of Bay Village. Houk and his wife Esther drove over immediately. They called the police at 5:57 a.m. Realizing how serious the matter was, the local cops brought in Cleveland homicide detectives and the Scientific Investigation Unit. A Cuyahoga County detective showed up, too.

In those first confused minutes, Sheppard's brother Steve took him to the hospital to treat his injuries—cuts and bruises on his face, chipped teeth, cracked vertebrae in his neck. Mayor Houk dashed back to his house, too, to lock it up, and young Samuel Reese was awakened. Things got even crazier as reporters and neighbors trooped through the house. The police enlisted the aid of local boys to search the yard. Dr. Sam's bag was found near the beach. So much traffic through the house compromised the physical evidence that would become much more important decades later.

By some reports, the police decided that night Sheppard had killed his wife. Why had he waited so long, almost three hours as estimated from the time of death, to call the Houks? There appeared to be no sign of a break-in. (Some evidence, however, of that would surface later.) How could young Samuel Reese have slept through such violence?

Marilyn Sheppard murder scene (from 1954), partially obscured for a jury in 1998. (AP Photo)

Those questions and others bothered the editor of the *Cleveland Press*. As the investigation proceeded over the next weeks and months, the paper ran front page editorials under such headlines as "Someone Is Getting Away With Murder," that all but convicted Sheppard. Perhaps the central key leading to his indictment was Dr. Sam's statement to the police that his marriage was not in trouble and he had been faithful. Both were untrue. He had been carrying on a lengthy affair with Susan Hayes, first in Cleveland, and then in Los Angeles.

All of this was churned up by the print press, television, and radio. By the time the trial began in October, Sheppard had been found guilty in the court of public opinion. In the real trial, Sheppard's attorneys, led by William Corrigan, tried to keep the focus on the physical evidence while the prosecution highlighted the gaps in the timeline and Sheppard's infidelities. The jury obviously found it difficult to sort through. After more than 100 hours of deliberation, they found Sheppard not guilty of first degree murder, but guilty of murder in the second degree in 1954.

The verdict took a terrible toll on the Sheppard family. A few weeks later, Sam's mother committed suicide; soon after, his father died from a hemorrhaging gastric ulcer.

Sheppard's lawyers' attempts to overturn the verdict were swift and constant over the course of the next ten years. When Corrigan died in 1961, the family brought in the then-unknown F. Lee Bailey. He got unexpected help from a popular book, *The Sheppard Murder Case* (1961) by Paul Holmes, and an even more popular television series, *The Fugitive* (1963–67). Holmes' book laid out the evidence and found it lacking. On the TV show, millions of Americans watched as the handsome and passionate Dr. Richard Kimble—who had escaped from police custody to find the mysterious "one-armed man" who had killed his wife—eluded the grim and humorless Lt. Gerard.

In 1964 District Court Judge Carl Weinman ruled that Sheppard had not had a fair trial and ordered him released. Round Two was about to begin. After an appeals court reinstated Dr. Sam's conviction, Bailey took his appeal to the Supreme Court. It ruled in his favor, saying the "massive" publicity had prevented Sheppard from getting a fair trial.

The second criminal trial began on November 1, 1966. Bailey came out swinging and hinted in his opening statement that he would identify the real killer. The second time around, Sheppard's extra-curricular sex life was barely mentioned, and Bailey brought in his own expert, Dr. Paul Kirk, who concluded one piece of blood evidence came from a third party—not Sam or Marilyn. It, or something, provided the reasonable doubt the jury needed. In just a few hours, they found Sheppard not guilty.

And who was Bailey prepared to finger as the real killer? He said later he had a witness who would swear he had seen Marilyn kissing her friend, Mayor Spencer Houk. But Houk wasn't the only other "real killer." There was also Richard Eberling, a con man and convicted murderer who claimed to have worked as a window washer at the Sheppard home on that fateful 4th of July weekend. Moreover, he claimed to have cut his finger and gone down to the basement to wash it.

In the late 1990s when the adult Sam Reese Sheppard embarked on an attempt to finally and fully exonerate his father, Eberling was his number one suspect. And Eberling certainly was a very bad

Dr. Sam Sheppard. (AP photo)

guy. By the time he and Sam Reese had begun communicating, Eberling was in prison for the murder of Ethel Durkin and forging her will (which left him her estate). Eberling was also a practiced liar. He told so many tales about the Sheppards it's impossible to accept any of them.

Eberling claimed Esther Houk killed Marilyn because her husband Spencer was gay and he and Dr. Sam were having an affair. (Eberling was gay.) On another occasion, he said he had killed Marilyn while wearing a bushy wig. (Eberling was bald.) Further confusing things, another window washer claimed he, not Eberling, had been working at the Sheppard house that weekend.

In 1995 Samuel Reese tried to use the new "revelations" in a civil suit to have his father officially declared innocent of his mother's murder. Innocent, not merely "not guilty." Round Three. This time, despite the age and uncertainty of the evidence, DNA testing was to play a part. The case became embroiled in Ohio party politics and went on for years. It didn't really begin until 2000 and lasted for almost a month. In the end, the jury found Sam Sheppard "not innocent."

But wait, there's more.

Sam Reese took one more shot with a wrongful imprisonment suit in 2002, but that jury, too, said his evidence did not meet the burden of proof.

As for the other participants, Richard Eberling died in prison in 1998.

After his release in 1966, Dr. Sam Sheppard married a wealthy German divorcee who had become a pen pal during his incarceration. The union ended with a 1968 divorce and bitter accusations about his drinking and drug use. Sheppard resumed his practice but was sued for malpractice after the death of a patient. Later, for a time, he became a professional wrestler. His gimmick—the nerve hold.

Sam Sheppard was found dead on April 6, 1970; the cause, liver failure. Two fifths of the hard stuff every day will do that.

Was he guilty?

In the two criminal trials—where the threshold of proof was "beyond a reasonable doubt"—he lost one and won one. In the two civil trials—where the standard is much lower—he lost twice. It's as close to a definitive answer as anyone is going to get. More important, his initial trial was one of the first to take place under a media spotlight, and the Supreme Court ruled that when the coverage reaches a certain intensity, said coverage distorts the judicial process. Since then, every high profile criminal case has taken media coverage into consideration.

Sherman, Lydia

Lydia Sherman was the **Susan Smith** of the nineteenth century, a woman who murdered her children and became an infamous celebrity.

Lydia Danbury, an orphan at nine raised by an uncle, was only 17 when she married Edward Struck in 1842 in New Brunswick, New Jersey. He was 40, a widower with six children. She'd trained to be a tailor, but settled into the role of stepmother and housewife and had seven children of her own. Struck worked as a carriage blacksmith. The family moved to New York City.

In 1857 Struck landed a position with the new Metropolitan Police. Things went well for the family until 1863 when Edward was involved in an altercation in a Manhattan hotel. Actually, he was *not* involved and that was the problem. A drunk attacked a hotel bartender. Patrons yelled for help, and the aggressive inebriate was brought down by a passing police detective. Struck said he was several blocks away when he learned of the whole business, and jumped on a streetcar and got there as quickly as he could.

Not so, said hotel employees, Struck had been right outside when the commotion began. He turned and ran when he saw the guy had a knife. (In those days, New York cops were armed only with billy sticks.) Struck was fired before he had a chance to tell his side. The reason for his dismissal, he insisted, was his corrupt superiors wanted to get rid of him for what he knew about them.

Whatever the truth, Struck became despondent or in today's terminology, clinically depressed. He refused to leave the house, couldn't sleep, was suicidal, finally wouldn't even get out of bed.

Lydia didn't know what to do. Struck's older children had grown and were on their own. She had six mouths to feed—one young child had died recently—and no income. She found her answer in an ounce of arsenic. It was only a dime over the counter at the drugstore. A few grains of the powder were enough to kill a fully grown adult. She mixed a bit into Struck's oatmeal. After a night of absolute agony—burning vomit and diarrhea, convulsions and cramps—Struck died on May 24, 1864. Cause of death: consumption.

But that still left Lydia a widow with six kids. She knocked off the youngest first: Martha Ann, six; Edward Jr., four; and William, nine months. The deaths were chalked up to fever and bronchitis.

As long as 14-year-old George was working steadily as a painter's assistant and bringing home a regular paycheck, his prospects were solid. But he had to quit after contracting "painter's colic." He stayed home for a week and showed no signs of improvement, so his mother helped him along with a cup of her special tea. Fatal painter's colic.

Remarkably, with one husband and four children recently deceased, Lydia went to work with her local physician, Dr. Rosenstein. She became his nurse. Nothing is known about the prognoses of his patients while she was part of the practice.

Even with the money Lydia was earning, her frail, sickly 12-year-old Ann Eliza was a trial. She succumbed to typhoid fever. Two years later, in 1866, her oldest daughter, also named Lydia, was similarly stricken.

Finally free of all family responsibilities, Lydia moved. While working at a new job, she met James Curtiss. He was looking for a nurse companion for his ailing mother up in Stratford, Connecticut. Lydia moved in with Mrs. Curtiss, and, just as quickly, moved out when she sniffed a better deal.

Dennis Hurlburt was a wealthy tight-fisted 80-year-old farmer. A recent widower, he was in the market for a live-in housekeeper. Lydia took the position. Within weeks, the job description was rewritten to include wife. A day later she was Mrs. Hurlburt and the lovestruck Dennis was drawing up a new will. He lasted a year until Lydia fixed up a batch of her special clam chowder. It took him three agony-filled days to die. Official cause of death: cholera morbus.

He left Lydia a wealthy woman with $10,000 in cash and twice that in real estate.

Had she been killing strictly to find financial and emotional independence, Lydia could have stopped right there. But even if her methods weren't as open-ly violent as those of **Ted Bundy** or **Carl Panzram**, Lydia was a true predatory psychopath. She'd come to enjoy killing. She loved the power she had over those who trusted her.

So she set her sights on Horatio Sherman, a party-hearty widower with four children and a mother-in-law. Why not? On September 2, 1870, she became Lydia Danbury Struck Hurlburt Sherman.

Two months later, she poisoned Sherman's youngest son, four-month-old Frankie. A month later, daughter Ada, age 14. Horatio took the deaths of his children hard. He wandered off on an epic drunk and was gone for days. When he finally came back, Lydia met him with a soothing mug of hot chocolate. When the debilitating symptoms struck, Sherman called in his regular family doctor, Dr. Beardsley. Familiar with his patient's drinking habits, Beardsley knew he wasn't dealing with a typical hangover. He prescribed a little morphine, mercury, brandy, and water.

Returning the next day, he found Sherman near death, barely breathing. He died that morning. Beardsley immediately requested a post mortem; three weeks later he got the results: arsenic.

By then, Lydia was gone, back to New Brunswick. She was kept under surveillance while the bodies of her other recent victims were exhumed and examined. More arsenic was found and she was arrested.

Her trial became an early media sensation, providing a preview of the **Lizzie Borden** murder trial that would take place up the road in Massachusetts 20 years later. Newspaper and magazine readers followed all the harrowing details as they were revealed in testimony. Lydia's lawyers tried to claim perhaps her last husband had been accidentally poisoned or had committed suicide. It didn't work.

Lydia was found guilty of second-degree murder and sentenced to life in the Wethersfield state prison. She died of cancer there in 1879.

In her day, Lydia received precisely the same kind of treatment she would enjoy today. Quickie books about her were cranked out. After her conviction, she wrote out a confession that was rushed into print as a pamphlet and became an instant bestseller. Along with other "angels of death" like **Jane Toppan**, she came to embody public fears of women's growing independence and demands for political power.

Beyond the catchy *Ballad of Lydia Sherman* by the Mockingbirds, her story has not found dramatic expression.

Sherrill, Patrick

Thanks to the actions of Patrick Sherrill and a few other deranged civil servants, the phrase "going postal" has entered our vocabulary.

Sherrill—nicknamed Sandy and, more accurately, "Crazy Pat"—followed the pattern established by **Howard Unruh** and other spree or mass murderers. As a youth, he was an indifferent student, reclusive with poor social skills. But he loved guns and demonstrated real skill with firearms in the military. Beyond that, however, he did not do well in the Marines and left after two years. Moved back in with his mother in Oklahoma. Tried college and dropped out. Worked at a series of jobs including a stint with the postal service, but he couldn't stay with any of them, primarily because he was so cranky and unpleasant. Nobody wanted to work with him.

In 1985, after his mother had died and left him her house, he landed a second job at the post office as a full-time substitute letter carrier. Again though, his rude behavior offended everyone he came in contact with, and he was suspended. On August 20, 1986, fearing disciplinary action or another firing, Sherrill loaded up two .45 automatics and several hundred rounds of ammunition in his bag.

He slipped in through the back door of the Edmond Post Office and shot the first people he saw, two of his supervisors, killing them both. Then with a pistol in each hand, he made his way through the building and shot everyone he saw. Every insult, every criticism, every snub, every imagined slight he

had ever suffered, was answered with a bullet. Fifteen minutes and 14 victims later, his spasm of violence was over. The story ended, as these so often do, with his turning a weapon on himself. A series of less serious incidents involving post office workers and firearms occurred later in the 1980s and 1990s, and "going postal" became a cliché.

Not surprisingly, Hollywood has not found it necessary (or potentially profitable) to dramatize the story of Sherrill or his fellow nutjobs. The closest the film business has come is the Joel Schumacher-Michael Douglas 1993 film, *Falling Down*.

Short, Elizabeth

The Black Dahlia

The mystery of the Black Dahlia will never die.

The case may have been solved, but speculation about who killed Elizabeth Short and why she died is not going to stop. It's too much a part of our view of Los Angeles as the Bad Place where the American Dream went wrong.

Elizabeth Short (she preferred to be called Beth) was born in Massachusetts in 1924. He father abandoned the family and moved to California in 1930. When she was 19, she went west and briefly stayed with him. They didn't get along. She moved out and got a job at Camp Cook where her dark good looks earned her the title "Camp Cutie." Like most young women of her age, she wanted to get married and for a time, she was engaged to a pilot. He was killed in a crash overseas.

Afterwards, Beth tried to get into the entertainment business but really just stayed on the fringe. She had done some modeling, and had some professional pictures taken. She hung around nightclub and showbiz folks. That was about it. She certainly never made any money.

She did have an exotic look: pale skin and long, full, flowing black hair, and she enhanced it by dressing in black. In 1946 the popularity of the film *The Blue Dahlia* led to the variation that became her nickname. The moniker and the look led to the assumption in some circles that she slept around, or perhaps even worked as a hooker. There is no evidence she ever did.

On January 9, 1947 she'd been out with a salesman. He left her at the Biltmore Hotel where she said she was going to meet her sister. Six days later, her body was found in a weed-choked vacant lot. She had been beaten and slashed. Her body had been sliced in half at the waist, the two parts drained of blood and carefully cleaned before they were dumped.

Given the horrific nature of the crime, it became the LAPD's most extensive investigation to date with hundreds of cops chasing down thousands of leads. One of those was a letter and package sent to the *Los Angeles Examiner*. It contained her Social Security card and other personal items, including her address book, minus several pages. All of the items had been washed with gasoline to remove any fingerprints. Then, nothing, at least not immediately.

In the years since, interest in the case has varied but never completely faded. Many suspects have been fingered, ranging from the utterly ridiculous—Woody Guthrie and Orson Welles—to the more serious.

In 1995 Janice Knowlton claimed "repressed memories" had revealed that her dead father had done murdered Short. In 2003 former LAPD detective Steve Hodel made the same claim but with more evidence. He had found photographs of a woman who resembled Short in an album belonging to his father. His father, a doctor, had briefly been a suspect in the original investigation. Others have questioned the validity of the pictures and his theory.

Perhaps the most plausible suspect is John Anderson Wilson. His story is laid out in John Gilmore's book *Severed* (1998). Wilson, an alcoholic cripple with a record of sex offenses, made a bizarre "confession" on tape in 1981. He said he'd been told this story by a friend who turned out to be an invented character. Wilson said this person described the murder in so much detail it sounded completely believable. He said he had picked up

Elizabeth Short (left) enjoying finer days with friend Marge Dyer (circa 1944). (AP Photo)

Elizabeth Short and offered her a place to stay. He attacked her at his house, beat her, and cut her with several knives. After she was dead, he put the body on boards placed across a bathtub where he cut it with a large butcher knife and let the blood drain out. He cleaned it and wrapped it before he drove to the vacant lot.

Gilmore gave the tape to the police but before they could interview the man, Wilson died in a fire he had started himself. Fell asleep in bed with a cigarette.

Is the story true? It fits the facts and Wilson was also a suspect in the similar case of socialite Georgette Bauerdorf, who was murdered a few years before Short was killed. (The two women had known each other, too.) Whatever the extent of Wilson's involvement, it does nothing to change the Black Dahlia as a cultural icon.

In 1977, John Gregory Dunne turned her into "the Virgin Tramp" in his fine novel *True Confessions*, using the case to examine connections between the Catholic Church and the police force in various areas of corruption. It was filmed in 1981 with Robert De Niro and Robert Duvall. Novelist Max Allan Collins combined the Dahlia and the **Cleveland Torso Killings** in his novel *Angel in Black* (2002).

Elizabeth Short was a muse to James Ellroy in his long-running exploration of the deepest darkest corners of his own past. He first discovered her in Jack Webb's book *The Badge* (1958) when he was 11 years old. The case became inextricably linked to his own mother's unsolved murder which had happened a few years before. He called it "the sole forming trauma that shaped my imagination." It was the direct inspiration for his novel *The Black Dahlia* (1987).

A more stylized variation on the crime is also a key element in Ellroy's *LA Confidential* (1990). The 2006 Brian DePalma adaptation of *The Black Dahlia* is beautifully incoherent, and really has nothing to do with the actual case beyond actress Mia Kirshner's eerie resemblance to Elizabeth Short. *Ulli Lommel's Black Dahlia*, poorly made exploitation, went straight to DVD in 2006.

In 1975 *Who Is the Black Dahlia* was made for TV with Lucie Arnaz. It really does not do justice to the story.

Siegel, Ben "Bugsy"

Virginia Hill, The Mafia

Conventional wisdom has it that Ben "Bugsy" Siegel was a compulsive womanizer who couldn't stay focused on business. But in the film *Bugsy* (1991), written by James Toback, Siegel's friend **Meyer Lansky** sees him differently. "Ben has only one problem," he says, "he doesn't respect money." History bears him out, but whatever the truth, Siegel was certainly the flashiest and sexiest of the old school gangsters.

He was born in Brooklyn to poor Jewish parents in 1906. By the time he was 14, he was extorting money from street vendors by selling them protection. Not long afterwards, he became close friends with Lansky. As the story goes, they bonded when Meyer refused to pay the older boy a penny and fought back. Who knows? It might even be true. They did form the Bugs and Meyer Mob, a notoriously tough gang that stole cars, ran booze, and murdered anyone who got in their way.

Their mentor, gambler **Arnold Rothstein**, always stressed the importance of profits over violence, but Bugsy, as the hated nickname suggests, enjoyed fighting and killing. When it came time for his generation to take over the larger gangs, Siegel had a pistol in his hand.

In the 1920s Bugsy and Lansky were tight with **Charles "Lucky" Luciano**, who was second in command to **Joe Masseria**, one of the Mafia's last Mustache Petes. Masseria was involved in a torturous power struggle with his fellow boss **Salvatore Maranzano**. When Luciano arranged for Masseria to be killed, Lansky volunteered Siegel to be one of the gang-of-four who shared responsibility for the controversial hit. Bugsy appears not to have been involved with the murder of Maranzano that took place a few months later.

Under Luciano's leadership, the eastern gangs consolidated their spheres of influence in what came to be called the Syndicate. In the late 1930s they sent Bugsy to Los Angeles to take over the operations run by bookmaker Jack Dragna and mobster **Mickey Cohen**.

The moment Siegel arrived in Hollywood, he knew he was in his element. For openers, his childhood friend George Raft was one of the movies' most popular stars. With his introductions, Bugsy was soon partying with the likes of studio boss Jack Warner, Clark Gable, and Gary Cooper. Siegel had the money, the good looks and, as long as he held his temper, the charm to fit right into their world. His reputation as a gangster simply made him that much more exotic.

Bugsy Siegel, at his Beverly Hills home, gets rubbed out by fellow mobsters in 1947. (AP Photo)

If a third of the stories and rumors are true, Bugsy never lacked for female companionship. Even after his wife Esta and daughters moved west, he maintained a revolving door harem including actress Marie "the Body" MacDonald and the Countess Dorothy Dendice Taylor DeFrasso. (According to one wild story, Bugsy and the Countess met some guy who claimed to have invented an atomic bomb and they tried to sell it to Benito Mussolini before the war. But the dingus turned out to be a dud at a test demonstration.)

Bugsy's real work in Los Angeles involved setting up gambling joints and establishing a wire service to connect the East Coast with California horse race-tracks. He was also instrumental in the creation of

the first shipment routes of heroin and opium from Mexico, not to mention more bootlegging, and his gambling ship, *The Rex*, operated outside of the 12-mile limit.

Through it all, the most important woman in his life was mob moll **Virginia Hill**. They had a tempestuous sexual relationship and she was involved with his Las Vegas business dealings.

In the popular version of the story, Siegel stopped in the little one-horse Nevada town as he was driving east from LA and, like Coleridge, had a mystical vision of a stately pleasure dome in the desert. He then took that dream to his pals and persuaded them to invest millions in what would become the Flamingo Hotel and Casino. In a more prosaic version, Lansky asked him to take a look at the town where gambling was already legal, and Bugsy gradually warmed to the idea.

The source of the inspiration is not particularly important; the result is. Bugsy threw himself into the project and was unable or unwilling to change things when costs skyrocketed to more than $6 million. At the same time, his personal life was falling apart. Esta divorced him in 1946 and Virginia Hill may have been skimming money from the project and flying it to Switzerland.

When Luciano, Meyer, and the rest expressed reservations, Bugsy assured them he was merely experiencing temporary setbacks. If they'd just be patient, they would get their money back and more. He almost made it work.

The unfinished hotel opened in December 1946. It wasn't quite the stellar occasion he had promised because some of his Hollywood pals were by then becoming leery of him. Before long, the Flamingo closed and reopened in March 1947. It was turning a profit, but by then, it was too little too late.

On the night of June 27, 1947 in Beverly Hills, as he sat reading a newspaper on Virginia Hill's sofa, someone outside fired an M-1 carbine and shot him in the eye. Bugsy had lived fast, died young, and left a nasty looking corpse.

Amazingly, the movies have not done nearly as much as they could with such rich material.

True, the Barry Levinson-James Toback *Bugsy* (1991) is one of Hollywood's classiest gangster pictures. Siegel and Virginia Hill were never more glamorous than when portrayed by Warren Beatty and Annette Bening. Bugsy also shows up as a supporting character in *Mobsters* (1991), *Lansky* (1999), and *The Gangster Chronicles* (1981).

The character of Moe Green in *The Godfather* (1972) is loosely based on Bugsy. Harvey Keitel played Siegel in the 1973 TV movie, *The Virginia Hill Story*, with Dyan Cannon. Kietel also played Mickey Cohen in *Bugsy*.

Simpson, O.J.

If nothing else, the O.J. Simpson trial proved it is easier for a camel to go through the eye of a needle than for a rich man to go to prison.

To be sure, race was the deciding factor in the verdict, but poor men do not assemble a "dream team" to defend them. Simpson's high-powered attorneys were able to deliver an acquittal in his criminal trial. A civil court found Simpson responsible for the deaths of his ex-wife Nicole Brown Simpson and her friend Ronald Goldman.

Orenthal James Simpson first gained fame as a football player. He won the Heisman Trophy as a running back at the University of Southern California, then went on to a record-setting career with the Buffalo Bills of the AFL and NFL. He parlayed it into modest success in the movies—most notably the *Naked Gun* police comedies—and on television commercials where he ran through airports, shilling rental cars for Hertz.

He was 30 years old, married with a family when he first met Nicole Brown. She was an 18-year-old waitress. They married in 1985, had a couple of kids, and divorced in 1992. He was fond of smacking her around, and the police were called several times. In 1989 he pleaded no contest to spousal battery and was sentenced to community service and probation.

On June 12, 1994, a Sunday, their daughter Sydney had a dance recital. Nicole went with her family and friends. O.J. was there, too, but had no contact with them. After the recital, the family went to the Mezzaluna Trattoria for dinner. Ronald Goldman worked there as a waiter. Later that night, Nicole's mother Juditha realized her glasses were missing. They were found outside the restaurant. Nicole called Goldman, and he said he would drop them by her condo on Bundy Drive after his shift was over.

The same evening, after the recital, Simpson had gone to dinner at McDonald's with Kato Kaelin, a young man who was a houseguest at Simpson's Rockingham Avenue mansion. They took the Rolls

O J SIMPSON **NICOLE BROWN SIMPSON** **RON GOLDMAN**

O. J. Simpson (left), charged in the June 1994 murders of Nicole Brown Simpson (center), and Ron Goldman. (AP Photo/File)

through the drive-in window. Simpson also had a white Bronco, provided by Hertz. Back home later that night, Kato went to his bungalow.

Around 10:15 p.m., Nicole Simpson and Ron Goldman were stabbed and slashed to death in the entranceway to her condo. They were attacked from behind. Her throat was cut so deeply she was nearly decapitated. Both were stabbed repeatedly. Later, her mother's glasses were found by the bodies. Also nearby were a single bloody glove and a knit cap.

About 10:25 p.m., limousine driver Alan W. Park arrived at the gate outside Simpson's Rockingham Avenue address. He was to pick up O.J. for a late flight from Los Angeles to Chicago. He tried to contact someone in the house via the gate phone but got no answer. Around 10:45 p.m., Kaelin heard a noise outside the bungalow.

At about the same time, Park saw a man in dark clothing hustling up the driveway to the house. The next time he called, Simpson answered and said he had been asleep. A few minutes later, he and Kaelin

loaded his bags into the limo. Sweating heavily, Simpson asked that the air conditioning be kept on high all the way to LAX.

The bodies were discovered later that night by neighbors who were alerted by Nicole's worried dog. LAPD arrived at 12:13 a.m., and the investigation began. In the months that followed, much would be made of those first hours—how evidence was gathered and processed, how people were treated, which leads were followed—and despite the shrill claims of lawyers, it was mostly handled well and professionally. Mostly.

Simpson was contacted that morning and returned to Los Angeles around noon. Police were in his house. He was briefly handcuffed there before they took him downtown, where he was questioned and released. They noticed and asked about a deep cut on his right hand.

Two days later, Robert Shapiro signed on as Simpson's attorney. On Thursday, Simpson went to Nicole's funeral; on Friday he was charged with her

Mug shot for O.J. Simpson from June 17, 1994 after surrendering to authorities at his Brentwood estate in Los Angeles. (AP Photo/Los Angeles Police Department)

murder. Through Shapiro, he agreed to turn himself in, but didn't show up at the appointed time.

When police went to Simpson's house, they found a "to whom it may concern" letter that appeared to be a suicide note with Simpson referring to himself as a "lost" person. Later that day, Simpson was spotted riding in a white Bronco (not his Bronco) with his friend Al Cowling.

Patrol cars and TV news choppers leapt into action and the famous low-speed chase was on! Millions watched the live television footage as cheering spectators lined the roads and the distraught widower threatened suicide. Eventually, Cowling drove back to the Simpson estate where the ex-star was arrested. Inside the car, they found more than $8,000 in cash; a .357 magnum revolver; family pictures; fake goatee, mustache, and glue to apply them; and passport.

Right afterwards, the race card made its first appearance. Both *Newsweek* and *Time* magazines used Simpson's mugshot (left) on their covers that week, but *Time* darkened the image, making Simpson's familiar sunny face appear more brutish and menacing.

Six months later, before a predominately black jury, the trial began. It was the media circus to end all media circuses. Many have been highly critical of the TV coverage, and the channels that went all-O.J. all the time, but the truth is the broadcasters were simply providing what their viewers wanted to see. This was a story that immediately mainlined itself into the American psyche. It became an important part of our culture as it was happening and was impossible to ignore.

The people involved became as familiar as family during the seemingly endless 10-month trial:

- Lead prosecutor Marcia Clark—brittle and intense
- Prosecutor Christopher Darden—academic, tightly wrapped
- Judge Lance Ito—seemingly dwarfed by his robes and out of his depth even before he was lampooned on the *Tonight Show* by Jay Leno's "Dancing Itos"
- Defense attorney Johnnie Cochran—the swaggering counterpuncher with a preacher's sense of oratory
- F. Lee Bailey—the ex-champ who had botched Patricia Hearst's defense and was looking to go out with one more win under his belt
- Barry Scheck—the smartest kid in class who relentlessly attacked the blood evidence

The prosecutors actually had an unusual problem—an embarrassment of riches in terms of incriminating evidence. Eyewitness testimony, blood, and fibers found at the scenes combined to create a tightly woven storyline that had Simpson leaving his home in his Bronco, driving to his wife's condo about two miles away, and killing her and Ron Goldman.

He dropped his cap and glove at the scene and drove back home where he was late for his limo.

Key blood samples matching all of the participants were found at the condo, in and on the Bronco, at Simpson's house, and on his clothes. He could not satisfactorily account for his actions while the killings were taking place. Footprints matching rare Bruno Magli shoes in his size were found at the condo.

The defense depended, as it does in most criminal cases, on "reasonable doubt." The lawyers attacked the handling of the evidence, noting it had been in an unsecure area for three days when it could have been altered by other police personnel. Some of the blood evidence had not been discovered until July 3rd. Why hadn't it been noticed for two weeks? Couldn't it have been planted?

One of the most dramatic moments took place on June 15—the famous trying on of the gloves. Standing before the jury, O.J. had trouble pulling on the blood-soaked gloves. Johnnie Cochran leapt up with the famous rhyme, "If it doesn't fit, you must acquit!" Prosecutors claimed the gloves had shrunk and later had Simpson try on a new pair of identical gloves, and those fit perfectly, but the damage had been done.

Then there was the question of Mark Fuhrman.

He was an LAPD detective who had been called to a domestic disturbance between O.J. and Nicole years before. He'd also been at the murder scene, and was one of the first police officers to go to Simpson's home. That's where he found the famous second glove. The defense claimed he was a racist, that he found both gloves at the condo, and then had planted one at Simpson's mansion.

The farfetched charge might not have stuck, but after Fuhrman swore under oath on the stand he had not used the word "nigger" in the past ten years, the defense produced an audiotape of interviews he'd given to an aspiring screenwriter. In them, the jury heard him use the word repeatedly and also that he sometimes planted evidence.

In his summation, Johnnie Cochran compared Fuhrman to Hitler, claiming he wanted to exterminate all black people.

On October 3rd, after only three hours of deliberation, the jury acquitted Simpson. The TV and radio audience was massive, between 140 and 150 million. Reaction divided clearly along racial lines. Black viewers generally felt vindicated. After decades of abuse at the hands of the cops and the courts, one of their own had finally beaten the system. To white viewers, the black jury knew the black defendant was guilty and let him off anyway. Conservative white commentators went particularly nuts at the verdict.

O.J. vowed to find the real killer.

Two years later, Simpson was found guilty in a wrongful death trial brought by the Goldman and Brown families. The trial lasted for four months and the jury deliberated for six days. The families were awarded $33.5 million they knew they would never see. Simpson was broke. His only income was a $20,000 per month NFL pension that couldn't be touched by the judgment.

A couple of movies were made for television about the murders and the trial, but they could hardly capture everything that happened or all it meant. Virtually everyone connected with the first trial wrote a book about it, most focusing on how badly everyone else had screwed up. Two of the best are Dominick Dunne's essays first published in *Vanity Fair* magazine and collected in *Justice: Crimes, Trials and Punishments* (2001), and *Evidence Dismissed* (1997), by Tom Lange and Philip Vannatter (as told to Dan Moldea). Lange and Vannatter were the two lead LAPD detectives.

In the years since the trial, defense lawyer Alan Dershowitz has gone on to write several more books, usually aligned with the political left. Mark Fuhrman has done the same on the political right.

Johnnie Cochran died in March 2005.

On the eve of the tenth anniversary of his acquittal, O.J. Simpson took a break from his search for the

Simpson and Manson: "Bad Company" according to a billboard put up by a Denver, Co radio station (1995). (AP Photo)

real killer to appear in Los Angeles at NecroComicon, a horror comic convention, where he signed sports memorabilia. His autograph went for $95 a pop.

Then in November 2006, editor Judith Regan put together a deal in which Simpson would talk about the case in two television interviews with her and write a book (through a ghostwriter), titled *If I Did It*, about how he might have committed the murders. The book was written; copies were shipped to warehouses and the interviews were taped.

When the project was made public, reaction was overwhelmingly negative and it became even more so when Regan claimed she had been abused by her ex, and tried to cast the whole sleazy stunt as a courageous blow for victims' rights. After several

Fox affiliates announced they would not broadcast the O.J. interviews, the book was withdrawn, the interviews were shelved, and Regan was fired.

A year later, the book was published by Ron Goldman's family and became a bestseller. To date, no one else has attempted to revive the matter.

Sirhan, Sirhan Bishara

Though Robert Kennedy is perhaps the most unambiguous of the 1960s assassinations, committed at close range before a large crowd, conspiracy theorists still embrace it.

On June 5, 1968 Kennedy had taken an important step toward winning the Democratic Party presidential nomination. Three months before, Senator Eugene McCarthy had challenged sitting President Lyndon Johnson and done well in the New Hampshire primary. Kennedy, previously attorney general for his brother Jack, had been elected senator from New York. He decided to enter the presidential race, but his campaign had been sputtering until it reached California. He won the primary there and in South Dakota on June 4th, and was in a strong position for the convention to be held later in Chicago.

That night, RFK made a victory speech to supporters in the Embassy ballroom of the Ambassador Hotel. His next appearance was a press conference in another room. To get there, hotel security and a hired guard from Ace Security guided the candidate through a pantry or food preparation area. It was a smallish room, filled with restaurant equipment and about 77 people hoping to catch a glimpse of the senator. Palestinian immigrant Sirhan Sirhan was in the crowd. Behind a rolled up campaign poster, he held an Iver-Johnson .22 revolver.

When Kennedy was close, Sirhan raised his arm and opened fire. He hit Kennedy three times before he was subdued by athletes Rafer Johnson, Roosevelt Grier, and writer George Plimpton. Mutual Radio reporter Andrew West, who had been conducting an on-the-fly interview with the candidate, switched his tape recorder on.

Two of the wounds were not serious but one bullet hit Kennedy in the back of his neck below the right ear, and lodged in his brain. He died the next day. Five other people were wounded.

When police searched Sirhan's room they found notebooks and other writings staring "RFK Must Die." Raised as a Christian, Sirhan had dabbled in other religions but remained firmly anti-Semitic and objected to Kennedy's strong support of Israel during the Six-Day war.

Sirhan was diagnosed as psychotic by the prosecutor's psychiatrist and confessed at his trial. He was found guilty and sentenced to death. The sentence was commuted to life in prison when California

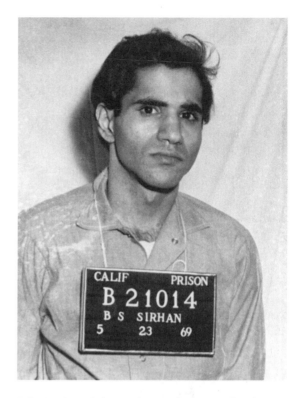

Palestine-born Sirhan Bishara Sirhan's mug shot from San Quentin prison on May 23, 1969. (AP Photo)

abolished the death penalty. He remains incarcerated in the state prison at Corcoran.

Despite the evidence, the eyewitnesses, and common sense, conspiracists have raised questions about the number of bullets fired, marks in a doorframe that might have been bullet holes, the relative position of assassin and victim, a mysterious woman in a polka dot dress, and dozens of other details. Some claim there was another gunman; others say Sirhan had been hypnotized or somehow manipulated into committing the murder. All of the theories, from the lucid to the bizarre, are dealt with in Dan Moldea's definitive book *The Killing of Robert Kennedy* (1995).

RFK has come to figure prominently in the legends and scandals surrounding the Kennedy family. He has been depicted on screen in several films, mostly notably *Thirteen Days* (2000), *The Missiles of*

October (1974), and in several TV miniseries. Emilio Estevez turned the day of the assassination into the multiple character-driven drama *Bobby* in 2006.

Smart, Pamela

On one level, the Pamela Smart case is not at all extraordinary. She persuaded her young lover to murder her husband. It has happened before.

But the crime quickly became a cultural touchstone—an act that fascinated and divided observers. The murder investigation provided the basis for countless television stories and documentaries, and the televised trial was a preview of the madness that would cyclone around the O.J. Simpson case a few years later. The fictional incarnations of Pamela Smart's story are even more interesting, casting her as either a treacherous seductress or a somewhat sympathetic victim who was forced to do what she did. Quite a lot of baggage for one little chippie with porn starlet hair.

The basics are pretty simple.

Pame (her nickname, pronounced Pammy) Wojas grew up in an upper-middle class Florida home. No drugs, no abuse, no divorce. She was an overachieving cheerleader who graduated from Florida State University in three years. She and Gregory (nicknamed Gregg) Smart shared a love for heavy metal music, but soon after they married, he trimmed his shoulder-length hair and got a respectable insurance salesman haircut.

The couple moved to Derry, New Hampshire for his new job and to be close to his parents. There Pame became more career-oriented, too. She wanted to be the next Barbara Walters and took several jobs involving the electronic media. The most promising for her future in broadcasting was as a high school media services director in Hampton. At 22, she didn't look much older than the kids she was working with and they got along terrifically.

A few months into their life together, Gregg admitted he'd had a brief affair. At that point, Pame might have demanded a divorce and claimed their condo on Misty Morning Drive. She had something more creative in mind.

Enter Billy Flynn, a strapping 15-year-old sophomore with an earring, flowing hair, and dreams of becoming a rock guitar god. One look at little Pame and he was hooked. Cecelia Pierce, another 15-year-old, also fell into Pame's orbit as an intern in media services. It's not difficult to understand how this little group—along with Billy's close friends—became a clique with Pame as the alpha female at its center. She solidified her position one weekend in March 1990, while Gregg was out of town.

Pame invited Billy and Cecelia over to watch videos. First feature, the erotic bondage thriller *9½ Weeks* with Mickey Rourke and Kim Basinger getting hot and heavy. Before the night was over, Pame and Billy were recreating key scenes upstairs in the bedroom while Cecelia walked the dog.

Before long, Pame was telling Billy that divorce was out of the question; Gregg would never allow it. If Billy wanted to continue the fun and games—and would any hormonally charged heterosexual 15-year-old guy *not* want to continue the fun and games?—then they would have to get rid of Gregg. It could be done; she'd show Billy how.

On May 1, 1990 while Pame was off at a school meeting 35 miles away, Billy and his friend Pete Randall snuck into Pame's condo. (She had left the back door open.) They had a .38 revolver taken from the father of another friend, J.R. Lattime. Billy and Pete tossed the place to make it look like a robbery and locked Pame's precious pooch in the basement where it wouldn't be hurt. When Gregg came home that night, the kids jumped him, and Billy shot him in the head.

From the moment they began their investigation, Derry police smelled a rat. No sign of forced entry or of a struggle. Execution-style murder by a burglar when burglars almost never carry weapons. Break-in at night when burglaries typically occur during the day. Even though Pame's alibi was watertight, she was a suspect. Her initial reactions struck many of her neighbors as false. A few days after the killing, she met with the police at the condo, which was still closed off as a crime scene. While talking to them there, she repeatedly stepped on the large blood-stained spot on the carpet where Gregg had died. Even after her mother covered it with a towel, Pame continued to walk all over it.

A week or so later, the cops got an anonymous phone call saying Cecelia Pierce knew all about the killing and Pame had planned it with three teenagers. About the same time, J.R. Lattime's father turned in his .38 and told police he thought it might be the murder weapon.

Eventually Cecelia told them what she knew and agreed to help. The police set up two phone intercepts on calls between her and Pame, and Cecelia wore a wire to record two face-to-face conversations. They got what they needed and arrested Pame on August 1, 1990.

At the trial, all the kids admitted their guilt. Most observers agreed Billy Flynn's graphic recreation of the killing and the Cecelia Pierce tapes were the most damaging to Pame. For her part, she admitted having an affair with Billy but denied any involvement in the murder. She tried to explain away the tapes by claiming she was only pretending to admit her part in the plot in hopes of furthering the investigation.

Nobody bought it. She was sentenced to life without parole on three counts—accomplice to first-degree murder, conspiracy to commit murder, and witness tampering. Flynn and Randall got 40 years; their friend J.R. Lattime, 30.

Much of the reason the case attracted so much attention came from its being the first televised trial in America. Cameras were allowed in the courtroom, and the whole business attracted international attention that didn't end with the verdict.

Pame's story became the basis for two excellent novels. In Marge Piercy's 1994 *The Longings of Women*, she is transformed into a believably ambitious lower-middle class girl who marries into a wealthier family and is forced to kill her lazy no-

Pamela Smart playing the part of seductress (1990), used as evidence in her murder conspiracy trial. (AP Photo)

good rotten husband before he can change the beneficiary on his life insurance policy and divorce her. Joyce Maynard's *To Die For*, published a year later, casts her as more cravenly ambitious. The latter book was filmed as a pitch-perfect black comedy directed by Gus Van Sant in 1995. Nicole Kidman's intelligent starring performance set her firmly on the road to international stardom. Pame was also played by Helen Hunt in the made-for-TV *Murder in New Hampshire* (1991).

Smart has been the subject of two nonfiction books, *Deadly Lessons* (1991) by Ken Englade and *Teach Me To Kill* (1991) by Stephen Sawicki.

Smart is at the Bedford Hills Correctional Facility for Women in Bedford Hills, New York, where she maintains her innocence.

Smith, Perry and Dick Hickock

In June 1959 Floyd Wells began serving a three-to-five stretch for breaking and entering at the Kansas State Penitentiary in Lansing. His cellmate was Dick Hickock, who was about to be paroled after serving three years for passing bad checks.

As the two men talked, Wells mentioned a time back in 1948 when he had worked for a man named Herbert Clutter out in the little western town of Holcomb. Clutter hired him as a picker and treated him right—wages, room, and board, and a $50 bonus when the harvest was done. Wells said Clutter kept a safe in his home office, and was able to pay out $10,000 to his workers. After hearing that, Hickock bragged once he was out he would meet up with his old friend and cellmate Perry Smith, who'd been paroled in June. Together they would knock over the Clutter place and kill anyone they found there.

Wells thought it was just talk.

Hickock was paroled on August 13th, and moved back in with his parents in Olathe, Kansas. He wrote to Smith that he had a score lined up, and Smith showed up on November 12th, having skipped parole in Las Vegas. On Saturday, the 14th, they stowed Hickock's 12-gauge shotgun in the back of a '49 Chevy and took off. They stopped in Emporia to buy rubber gloves and nylon cord, and then in Great Bend for duct tape.

They arrived at the Clutter farm in Holcomb about 12:30 a.m., Sunday. As they prepared to pick the lock on the front door, they found it was open. Inside were Herb Clutter, his wife Bonnie, and their two youngest children, Nancy, 16, and Kenyon, 15. (Their oldest Eveanna was married and their other daughter Beverly was in Kansas City studying to be a nurse.)

When Hickock and Smith couldn't locate the safe, they went after Mr. Clutter first. He swore there was no safe, no $10,000. They didn't believe him and tied up everyone—Nancy and Mrs. Clutter in their rooms upstairs; Mr. Clutter and Kenyon in the basement. Once the family was immobilized,

Smith and Hickock started to argue. Hickock wanted to rape Nancy and it angered Smith. Some have speculated they had been lovers in the pen, and Smith became violently jealous. Whatever the cause, he went to the basement and slit Mr. Clutter's throat, then finished him with a shotgun blast to the head. Not wanting to leave witnesses, Smith killed the others with the shotgun and carefully collected the four spent shells.

They left the house with $40-50 and a Zenith transistor radio.

On Monday, November 15, 1959, young Truman Capote read about the crimes in the back of the *New York Times*. Though his literary reputation had been formed on fiction, he wanted to try something different. The story of the Kansas murders engaged him and he persuaded Wallace Shawn, editor of the *New Yorker*, to subsidize his research and writing. Initially, the project was to be an article about the effects of the killings on the town. Capote and his friend Harper Lee, who had just finished writing *To Kill a Mockingbird*, went out to Kansas, and set about talking to everyone connected with the case.

One of the most important interviewees was Alvin Dewey, who headed things for the Kansas Bureau of Investigation. He was also a close personal friend of Herb Clutter, and he realized early on that two people had probably been involved. They had found two important clues at the house—distinctive boot prints, one with a diamond shaped pattern, and one with the Cat's Paw logo.

Meanwhile, Smith and Hickock were plastering Kansas City with bad paper. They wrote hot checks for cameras, suits, TVs, anything easily exchanged for cash before they took off, traveling to Florida and Mexico.

In December, about a month after the killings, Floyd Wells came forward and told the KBI about his old cellmate Hickock's wild talk. They believed him and put out a bulletin on the two ex-cons. They were picked up in Las Vegas on December 30th when cops spotted them in a stolen Chevy.

Dewey and other KBI agents wasted no time getting to Vegas for the first interrogations. Hickock broke first, confessing that Smith had done all the killing. On the ride back to Kansas, Perry Smith told his version of the story to Dewey.

Later, they led police to the other evidence they had buried—the shotgun shells, rope, and tape—and so the trial was essentially cut and dried. It lasted less than a week and the jury took all of 40 minutes to reach a guilty verdict on all counts. They were sentenced to death on May 13, 1960, but after the first trial, new lawyers aggressively worked the appeals process. The sentence wasn't carried out until April 14, 1965 when Smith and Hickock were hanged in Lansing.

During those years, Capote had not been idle. He called his work a "nonfiction novel," a long dense narrative using the tools and techniques of fiction to describe real events. The result was his masterpiece, *In Cold Blood* (1965). It was an instant and influential bestseller, a book everyone read and talked about. It transformed a crime that would otherwise been ignored into an enduring part of the American cultural landscape.

The author was transformed from a respected serious writer into a celebrity who appeared on TV talk shows and magazine covers. A big-screen adaptation was inevitable and the bidding for it was fierce. Famous agent Irving "Swifty" Lazar was in charge of the negotiations. Short-fused producer-director Otto Preminger confronted Lazar in the famous 21 Club and said he had been promised the rights. Lazar disagreed and brained Preminger with a water glass. It took 50 stitches to close his scalp.

The film was made by Richard Brooks in 1967. It's fairly accurate in tone and bleak black-and-white detail, but is marred somewhat by a psychologically contrived ending. **Robert Blake**, who would have his own share of legal problems later, plays Perry Smith. (Coincidentally, he also has a small role in *Treasure of the Sierra Madre*, the real Perry Smith's favorite film.) Hickock is played by Scott Wilson, who is also a victim in *Monster* (2003), about serial killer **Aileen Wuornos**.

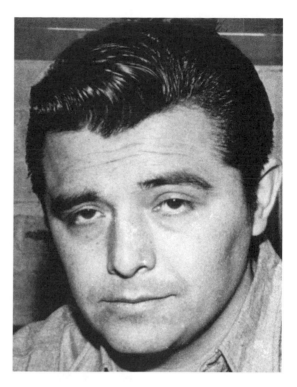

Perry Smith, on trial for the murder of the Clutter family, 1960. (AP Photo)

Bennett Miller's 2005 film *Capote* is about the birth and construction of the book, how it turned Capote into something of a monster and the heavy toll it took on him emotionally and physically. Philip Seymour Hoffman won an Oscar for his portrayal of the writer. Douglas McGrath's *Infamous* (2006) covers precisely the same ground, but focuses more on the relationship between Capote (Toby Jones) and Perry Smith (Daniel Craig). Both are excellent.

Smith, Susan

A deeply disturbed, narcissistic young woman voted "Friendliest Female" as a high school senior became an instant celebrity for the worst reasons imaginable.

On the night of October 25, 1994 Susan Smith ran onto the front porch of Rick and Shirley

Portrait of Smith's two young sons: Michael, age 3, and Alexander, 14 months, shortly before their deaths in 1994. (AP Photo)

McCloud's house in Union County, South Carolina. Hysterical, she cried that a black man had stolen her car, a Mazda, with her two young sons inside. The boys, Michael (age 3) and Alexander (14 months), were strapped into their car seats in back. The black guy had forced his way into the car with a gun at a stoplight, kidnapped her, and ordered her to drive around. Finally, near the McCloud's house, he told her to get out and drove away with her sons.

Almost from the beginning, Sheriff Howard Wells doubted her story. Her description of the carjacker was sketchy and the crime made no sense. Neither Susan nor her family was wealthy, there was no ransom demand, and the car had vanished. He ordered divers to search John D. Long Lake near the McCloud home.

The story of the kidnapped boys, who looked so innocent and appealing in a widely distributed photograph, immediately became a national sensation. Camera crews from all the networks and cable news shows descended upon Union. Susan and her husband David, who were in the middle of a sordid divorce, appeared together time and again on news and talk shows to plead for the safe return of their children.

But as the days passed with no leads or clues, police became more suspicious. David Smith passed a polygraph test. Susan's results were inconclusive. Police applied more pressure. Finally, nine days later, Susan Smith admitted it was all a lie. She'd killed her sons by driving out onto a boat ramp at the lake, releasing the emergency brake, and letting the car roll out into the water. Because it had been going so slowly, the car actually floated far from the shore before it sank. That's why the divers hadn't located it in the murky water.

But why had she done it?

It turned out Susan's personal life contained enough drama and infidelity for a dozen soap operas. She'd come from a family where divorce, suicide, and untimely death were almost commonplace. As a high school student, she'd initiated a sexual relationship with her stepfather. After charging him with abuse, she'd continued the affair as an adult.

While still in high school, she worked at the local Winn-Dixie grocery store where she had affairs with two coworkers, one married. Friendliest female, indeed. The results were an abortion and a suicide attempt. When she came back to work, she met David Smith, a stock boy. She became pregnant again and they married on March 15, 1991. They separated for the first time in March 1992; got back together long enough for a second pregnancy, though both of them were involved in various affairs.

After the birth of their second son, Susan went to work for Conso Products as an assistant secretary to the boss, J. Carey Findlay. She also started dating his son, Tom Findlay, in early 1994. She thought the relationship would be the one that would lead

Drowning reenactment at John D. Long Lake in South Carolina during Susan Smith's murder trial, 1995. (AP Photo)

to something more permanent, but those hopes were crushed on October 17th, when young Tom Findlay sent her a detailed letter saying he wanted to break things off.

Two things bothered him: first, he did not want to become father to another man's children, and second, at a party he had recently thrown, he'd caught Susan and a married man naked, kissing and fondling each other in his hot tub. Somehow, Susan just wasn't what he was looking for in a wife. If that weren't enough, Tom didn't know she was still fooling around with her stepfather, and with *his* father.

At the trial, the prosecution argued Susan had drowned her sons in hopes that, without them, Tom would take her back. Her lawyers claimed she was emotionally ill and had killed the kids as part of a failed suicide attempt. The jury first found her guilty of murder, then in the penalty phase of the trial, rejected the prosecutor's recommendation for death, and sentenced her to life in prison.

The Susan Smith case was the second in five years where the killer claimed "a black guy" had committed the crime. (The other was **Charles Stuart** in Boston.) In the Smith case, though, local authorities were more skeptical about the claim than the national media. Perhaps because of so many of the national figures were embarrassed by their part in the lie, when the truth was revealed, Susan Smith was demonized and vilified even more than she might otherwise have been.

After the first small flurry of books, the story dropped off the cultural radar, save the occasional tabloid update. In 1998, however, novelist Richard Price used the barest bones of the plot—a woman claiming her car and child had been stolen—as the basis for his dense novel *Freedomland*. He changed the setting from South Carolina to a more racially charged New Jersey and used the crime to examine complicated, incendiary issues. It was filmed in 2006.

Snyder, Ruth

Ruth Snyder was an unlikely muse, but she inspired some of America's best crime writers and filmmakers to their finest work. The slightly overweight but still voluptuous bottle-blonde and her diminutive corset-selling paramour provided the prototypes for America's most famous hardboiled murderous lovers.

In this case, though, the truth is closer to farce than to tragedy or even to pulp melodrama.

At the height of the Roaring '20s, Ruth Snyder chafed at her role as wife of Albert and mother of nine-year-old daughter Lorraine. She saw herself as a flirty flapper, a free-spirited, independent young woman who did what she pleased. Her dreams—some of them, anyway—were answered when she met Henry Gray, a dapper little dude who was immediately smitten. They consummated their relationship on the day they met in 1925.

The affair continued for two years with a series of bibulous nooners in hotel rooms. When a babysitter was unavailable, young Lorraine cooled her heels in the lobby while Mommy and Henry frolicked upstairs. At the Waldorf-Astoria, their favorite place, they kept a suitcase in a hotel locker. It was stocked with the necessities—jammies, hooch, condoms, etc. In their boozy post-coital conversations they eventually came up with the idea of getting rid of the inconvenient Mr. Snyder.

Truth be told, Albert did not make it terribly difficult. Ruth had conned him into buying three life insurance policies by claiming the original (and cheapest) had to be signed in triplicate. The most expensive had a double indemnity clause that paid out $90,000 should Mr. Snyder meet with an accidental death.

Ruth labored earnestly but fruitlessly to arrange just such an accident. She disconnected the gas line twice while he was napping. He woke up both times and suspected nothing. While he was changing a tire on the family Buick, the jack "slipped" and the car crashed down, but Albert was unharmed. Another time, he was knocked unconscious by the Buick's starter crank. A third time while he was working on the car in the garage, Ruth brought him a whiskey and he fell asleep, only to awaken and find the engine running and the door was closed. Again, a nick of time escape. Twice more Ruth tried to poison him by putting bichloride of mercury in his booze. He said it tasted terrible and vowed to find a new bootlegger. When he was ailing, she spiked his medicine with narcotics but Albert survived that, too.

Finally, in desperation, Ruth enlisted Gray's assistance and they hatched a plan. (Later, each would claim the other thought it up.) One Sunday night, the Snyder family went to a neighborhood bridge party. Ruth left the side door unlocked. Gray was in Syracuse on a sales trip. He used a coworker to set up a weak alibi at their hotel, and took a train back to New York City. From there, he made his way, drinking heavily, to the Snyders' home in Queens, where he hid in a closet and went to work on his second bottle.

The Snyders returned at 2:00 a.m. Albert, pretty well snockered himself, crashed. Ruth put Lorraine to bed and found time for a closet quickie with Gray before they went to work. Again, each blamed the other for what happened next, but the result was that before daybreak, Albert was dead, his head bashed in with a sash weight and strangled with picture wire. They then ineptly tried to fake a robbery, but rather than actually "stealing" anything, they hid Ruth's jewelry under a mattress and Gray loosely tied her to a chair.

Gray then tried to sneak stealthily back to Syracuse. But the bumbler was noticed at various points on his surreptitious journey by a cop, a cabbie, a conductor, and a Pullman porter.

Meanwhile, back in Queens, Lorraine, who must have been one very heavy sleeper, was awakened by her mother's piteous cries. She ran to the neighbors who had no trouble freeing the widow and called the cops. Ruth claimed she'd been assaulted by two men who "looked Italian" and had stolen her jewelry and killed her husband.

They found her jewels right away. They also found a $200 check made out to Gray and a suspiciously friendly letter from him to Ruth in the day's mail. When they took her downtown for questioning, one of the officers asked about Henry Gray. "Has he confessed?" she blurted out. Oops!

It was steep straight downhill ride from there.

The lethal lovers immediately became America's favorite villains. A newspaper circulation war was going on, and no detail was too sordid to share with an eager public. Both were roundly and soundly condemned but Ruth wound up taking most of the public heat because the flapper was seen as a threatening new form of feminine power and sexuality. Ruth was labeled "The Tyger Woman" who ruled "The Putty Man" with her voracious sexuality.

At the trial, they were represented by separate attorneys who vainly attempted to portray their respective clients as the innocent victim of a scheming villain. The jury didn't care and both were sentenced to the chair.

It was at her Sing Sing execution that Ruth achieved another kind of celebrity immortality. <i>New York Daily News</i> photographer Thomas Howard strapped a small camera to his shin and snuck it into the prison. He finagled a front row seat. At the moment they hit the switch, he crossed his legs, pulled up his pant leg, and snapped the shutter. He got a notorious Kodak Moment of Ruth's death spasm, which scandalized a nation.

The first artistic interpretation of the case came the next year in the play <i>Machinal</i> (1928) by Sophie Treadwell, who covered Ruth and Gray as a reporter. The play is still revived regularly, but in the hands of novelist James M. Cain, Ruth Snyder and Henry Gray were fully transformed into Cora Papadakis and Frank Chambers in <i>The Postman Always Rings Twice</i> (1934). The title refers to Ruth's request, asking her mail carrier to always ring twice so she could intercept insurance bills before Albert saw them.

Double Indemnity (1936) told another version of the story, calling the characters Phyllis Nerdlinger and Walter Huff. Walter Huff was renamed Walter Neff in the 1944 Raymond Chandler/Billy Wilder film starring Barbara Stanwyck and Fred MacMurray, one of the most faithful and atmospheric adaptations of a major novel that Hollywood has ever produced. That film was remade for TV in 1973 with Richard Crenna taking over the Walter Neff role. Crenna then closed the circle in 1981 when he played unlucky husband Edmund Walker in Lawrence Kasdan's homage to Cain, Body Heat (1981).

Postman was filmed in 1946 with Lana Turner and John Garfield, and remade in 1981 with Jessica Lange and Jack Nicholson. Neither version is as successful as first Double Indemnity, and neither is the 1942 Ossessione where director Luchino Visconti transplants the story to fascist Italy.

In all of them, and in countless lesser variations, the archetypes remain the same—the smart, beautiful, ruthless woman and the dopey guy who lets himself be sucked into her scheme. Interestingly, in many of the more modern versions, the woman prevails.

Spangler, Jean

She was the Black Dahlia of Missing Persons. In 1949, two years after the **Elizabeth Short** murder, another Hollywood beauty simply vanished.

Jean Spangler had had only limited success breaking into the entertainment business. She'd modeled clothes, worked as a dancer, and as a bit player in movies and television. Professionally, she was a struggling starlet, emphasis on struggling. On the personal side, however, she maintained an active social life. By age 27 she was divorced with a child. She and her daughter shared a house with her mother, brother, and sister-in-law.

On the evening of October 7th, Jean told her sister-in-law she was going to see her ex, Dexter Benner, about child support payments and afterwards would head for a night film shoot. Later, a clerk at a local market would say he saw Spangler and she appeared to be waiting for someone.

When she hadn't shown up the next morning, her sister-in-law reported her as missing. The next day, an employee at Griffith Park found her purse near a park gate. The strap was broken, suggesting a struggle, but the contents were intact including the famous note:

"Kirk, can't wait any longer. Going to see Dr. Scott. It will work best this way while mother's away."

Friends revealed Jean was three months pregnant. Actor Kirk Douglas, who had met her on the set of his movie *Young Man With a Horn* (1950) quickly volunteered that he hardly knew Jean. He said he had heard about her disappearance through friends and had actually contacted Deputy Chief Thad Brown, who'd investigated the Black Dahlia, before the police tried to reach him.

As for the rest of the brief note, Jean's mother had been away visiting family in Kentucky. "Dr. Scott" might have referred to a shadowy figure rumored to perform abortions (still illegal at the time). He was said to be an ex-medical student known as either "Doc" or "Scotty." But there was also an Air Corps lieutenant named Scotty in Jean's past. They'd had an affair while her husband was stationed in the South Pacific and he had threatened to kill her if she left him, but her former lawyer said the affair had ended in 1945 and there had been no contact between the two since.

When the police looked into Jean's story about her plans for the night, Dexter Benner, backed up by his new wife, said he had not seen her that night, and none of the studios had had a night shoot.

As the LAPD learned more about Jean's private life, they discovered she liked to walk on the wild side. She had recently told actor Bob Cummings, the star of what would be her last film, *The Petty Girl* (1950), that she had a new romance. Nothing serious, she said, but fun.

She might have been referring to Johnny Stompanato. He'd been so taken with Jean that he'd once followed her to Las Vegas. Stompanato worked for gangster **Mickey Cohen** and would become famous in 1958 when he was stabbed to death by **Cheryl Crane**, daughter of his lover Lana Turner. But Stompanato wasn't Jean's only connection with the criminal community—she'd also gone out with Mike Howard, who kept Mickey Cohen's books. She'd also been hot and heavy with David "Little Davey" Ogul, another "known associate" of the Mickster.

Little Davey had just been indicted on a conspiracy rap and so perhaps it was no coincidence he disappeared two days before Jean. Connected or not, neither has been seen since.

Jean Spangler never found a place in popular culture the way Elizabeth Short has; her story lacks the grotesque, lurid details. Instead, she's just another part of the postwar Hollywood Big Nowhere James Ellroy has described so memorably in his books.

Spanish, Johnny

Johnny Spanish was a New York gangster whose most productive years were early in the twentieth century, before the mobs achieved the levels of power they enjoyed during Prohibition. Though he was never as famous as the generation who followed him, he was every bit as violent and vicious.

Born John Weyler in 1891, he killed his first man at 17 and turned to robbery and, later, labor racketeering to make his livelihood. He was famous for always being well-armed. On a normal day he wore two pistols; if he thought things might get interesting, he carried two more in his coat pockets, and when he had a really big job planned, he'd have a henchman or gun bearer loaded down with several more weapons.

In 1909 Spanish partnered up with Kid Dropper (Nathan Kaplan). They became fast friends but parted ways violently when the Kid made a play for Johnny's girl. They fought it out with knives. Spanish barely escaped with his life but thought he had kept his squeeze. When he recovered, he moved in on the "stuss games," a form of faro, on the Lower East Side. He was involved in a gunfight over one of the games and mistakenly shot an eight-year-old girl. Even in those wild days, killing a kid was too much, so he had to leave town until things cooled down. When he returned, he found his girlfriend was pregnant with the Kid's child.

Enraged, Spanish kidnapped her. He took her out to a rural part of Long Island where he tied her to a tree and shot her repeatedly in the stomach. Amazingly, both mother and child survived, though the kid was missing three fingers.

They nailed Spanish on the attack and sent him up for seven years in 1911. As luck would have it, Kid Dropper was nabbed at about the same time. When they were both released in 1917, they tried to patch things up and to work together as labor sluggers. In those days, the labor organizers used thugs to intimidate strike breakers and to persuade workers to join the unions. The bosses used the same muscle to attack strikers' picket lines and to bust up union meetings. High clover for sluggers.

But there was too much bad blood between Spanish and Dropper. Their gang split up and more violence ensued. Each faction tried to get rid of the other and the result was part of the Labor Sluggers War with dozens of casualties.

It ended for Johnny Spanish on the evening of July 29, 1919, when he made the mistake of dining alone, without his customary bodyguards and gun bearer, at a Second Avenue beanery. As he was leaving, three gunmen opened up on him. Kid Dropper was charged with the murder but was never brought to trial. He was assassinated four years later by another rival.

The name Johnny Spanish has been appropriated in a few films, but the character has never appeared on screen. Kid Dropper showed up in an episode of a little-known TV series, *The Lawless Years* that ran from 1959–61. He was portrayed by Jack Weston.

Speck, Richard

Richard Speck is remembered for the horrendous slaughter of eight student nurses in Chicago, 1966. But they were probably not his first victims.

Born in 1942, the seventh of eight children, Speck grew up to be a functional illiterate alcoholic. His father died when he was six. Richard's stepfather, also a boozer, moved the family to Texas and beat the boy regularly. Speck had "Born to Raise Hell" tattooed on his left arm and he lived up to it with 37 arrests. He was married briefly and divorced in January 1966 after his wife said he threatened her with a knife and raped her.

To avoid a Texas burglary rap, Speck headed for Illinois and wound up in the small town of Monmouth where he had lived as a boy. While there, one woman was attacked in her home. She said her assailant had a knife and a strong Southern accent. He cut her housecoat into ribbons, tied her up with them, and raped her. Eleven days later, a barmaid was killed. Someone struck her so viciously her liver was ruptured. Speck was questioned about the murder but managed to talk his way out and disappeared before the police could contact him again.

Speck wound up in Chicago where he found work aboard a Great Lakes freighter, the *Russell.* He was fired in June for fighting. On July 10th, he went to the National Maritime Union hiring hall and tried to get a berth on any ship headed for New Orleans. There were none. He left his bags at a local gas station and set out to do some serious drinking. Three nights later around 11:00 p.m., blasted on booze and dope, he wandered up to a two-story brownstone on East 100th Street. The building was a residence hall for student nurses at the South Chicago Community Hospital. Speck knocked on the door, pulled a knife and a pistol, and got horribly lucky.

Gerhard Richter's work *Eight Student Nurses: 1966*, on display at the Art Institute of Chicago, Thursday, June 20, 2002. The piece memorialized the eight young women murdered by Richard Speck. (AP Photo/Aynsley Floyd)

The door was opened by Corazon Amurao, a nurse from the Philippines, and two of her housemates. Speck threatened them with his weapons but assured them he didn't want to hurt anybody, he just wanted money. They acquiesced. He herded them to an upstairs bedroom where he found three more women. He told them to lie on the floor and tied all of them with strips cut from a bed sheet. Around 11:30 p.m. another nurse returned from a date and got the same treatment. At midnight, two more returned and were subdued and taken to the bedrooms.

Then the nightmare really began. Over the next few hours, Speck methodically slaughtered Valentina Pasion, Pamela Wilkening, Suzanne Farris, Patricia Matusek, Mary Ann Jordan, Nina Schmale, Gloria Davy, and Merlita Gargullo. One by one, he took them to other rooms where they were stabbed and strangled. He tried to rape Gloria Davy. As the young women realized what was happening, they tried to hide under beds. Only Corazon Amurao was successful. She stayed hidden until the terrible sounds stopped. At 5:00 a.m. the next morning she was able to crawl outside onto a narrow ledge and cry for help.

The police arrived quickly and found a crime scene so grotesque and horrific even veteran cops and reporters threw up.

Corazon Amurao was able to give a description— tall, blond, 160 lbs., Southern accent—and the manhunt was on.

Speck simply returned to his bender. Crashed in a flophouse and found a couple new drinking buddies, Shorty Ingram and One-Eye Lunsford. At the same time, the cops caught a couple breaks. They learned that a man matching the description had left his stuff at a gas station, saying he had missed his ship. This led them to the hiring hall where they found a name to go with the description—Richard Speck.

The killer continued to drink, wander, and tell wild tales to anyone who would listen. He finally wound up in a cheap fleabag, the Starr Hotel. On the night of July 19th, he bought a pint of rotgut, smashed the bottle, and tried to slit his wrist with the broken glass. At about the same time, One-Eye was trying to turn him in to police, but the ambulance got to the Starr first and took Speck to Cook County Hospital. Leroy Smith, an emergency room doctor, recognized his patient from newspaper pictures and alerted the cops.

The trial took two weeks. The jury took 49 minutes. The judge gave Speck a death sentence. Then the U.S. Supreme Court changed its mind about capital punishment and Speck's sentence was reduced to 400 to 800 years. He had a massive heart attack on December 5, 1991 and died in prison.

That should have been the end of the story, but five years later, TV newsman Bill Kurtis came into possession of a bizarre videotape starring Speck. The tape was made at the maximum security Statesville Correctional Center, probably in 1988 by two other inmates, and may have been used by Speck to pay off a debt. He appears in blue bikini briefs with hormonally enhanced female breasts. Another inmate sodomizes him and Speck appears to snort from a mound of cocaine. He boasts of his lack of remorse or any feeling for the women he killed, and claims to be having a wonderful time in prison. Portions of the tape were broadcast on WBBM-TV during the May ratings sweeps.

Some officials were understandably upset by the tape, but since the sick puke dodged the death penalty, it seems appropriate he was reduced to such squalid debasement.

Richard F. Speck, accused in the murder of eight student nurses, in court in Chicago, December 19, 1966. (AP Photo/Paul Cannon)

The story has been dramatized in one low-budget film, *Speck* (2002) and is part of the PBS documentary, *Great Trials and Crimes of 20th Century* (1996). The two most complete books are *Crime of the Century: Richard Speck and the Murder of Eight Student Nurses* (1993) by Daniel L. Breo and William J. Martin, and *Born to Raise Hell: The Untold Story of Richard Speck* (1967) by Jack Altman and Marvin Ziporyn.

Spooner, Bathsheba

Think *Body Heat* in powdered wigs and knee breeches.

In Revolutionary War-era Massachusetts, Bathsheba Spooner was quite the femme fatale, a passionate thirty-something who was trapped in a loveless, possibly even abusive marriage. Even worse, she had the wrong politics. She was the daughter of Brigadier General Timothy Ruggles, a wealthy and prominent Loyalist who, in 1776, wisely relocated to Nova Scotia. While he waited to see how the war turned out, his land was seized. Bathsheba might have joined him but she was married to Joshua Spooner, an older wealthy merchant and a mean drunk. She was not happy.

Then, in March 1777, salvation literally arrived on the doorstep of her Brookfield home in the person of a tired and ailing soldier from Washington's Continental Army. Ezra Ross was 16, handsome, and in need of Bathsheba's tender care. She gave it. A year later, he came back for a second visit. Then, as the *Massachusetts Spy* later put it, she followed the "blind impulses of wicked and unchaste desires."

For a time, everything went swimmingly. Joshua was happy to have a soldier from the right side in his house to deflect local suspicion about his wife's Loyalist leanings, and Bathsheba was getting what she wanted. You know what happened next. Yes, she found herself pregnant, and in those days, her options were limited. Adultery was considered a serious crime with serious punishment. Divorce was unheard of.

As she saw it, the only course was to kill her husband Joshua. Alas, her feckless boy toy didn't have the stomach for murder. What to do? Again, providence provided an answer.

James Buchanan and William Brooks were veterans of the British army. They, too, happened by the Spooner home, and Bathsheba recruited them into her scheme. She offered good food and drink, a toasty fire, and the promise of more wicked and unchaste rewards in the future if they could help her rid herself of her husband.

One night, as a drunken Joshua stumbled home from nearby Cooley's tavern, the three ex-soldiers set upon him and beat him to death. They stole his money, his monogrammed silver shoe buckles, his snuff box and watch, and threw the body down a well.

It was discovered the next morning when a maid filled a bucket there and found it covered with blood.

The trio of guilt-ridden sub-genius killers might have had a chance of getting away with the crime had they not worn the victim's stuff in public. But they did and were arrested forthwith.

The Spooner household servants came forward with stories of whispered conversations among Bathsheba and the three men. Faced with such powerful evidence, Bathsheba confessed everything and said she was with child.

The case became the first criminal trial held in the newly independent Massachusetts. It was heard by state Supreme Court Chief Justice William Cushing who would later be appointed to the U.S. Supreme Court. Prosecutor Robert Treat Paine had signed the Declaration of Independence. Bathsheba's lawyer, Levi Lincoln, would become Thomas Jefferson's Attorney General. He attempted a novel defense, arguing the crime had been so ineptly planned and executed that Bathsheba must have been insane. The jury didn't buy it. They also didn't believe Bathsheba was pregnant.

But Rev. Thaddeus McCarty did believe her, and at his urging, the Massachusetts Council stayed her execution until she could be examined by "two men midwives and twelve discreet lawful matrons" to determine her condition. Bathsheba's Loyalist sympathies certainly influenced their decision. Without dissent, all fourteen stated she was not pregnant. A second panel assembled by Rev. McCarty disagreed but by then it was too late. The four were hanged on July 2, 1778 before a crowd of 5,000.

Bathsheba's post-mortem revealed she carried a five-month old male fetus.

To date, the only dramatization of Bathsheba's case was on the radio series *Suspense* in 1953. Her story has also been told by Deborah Navas in the well-researched and involving book *Murdered by His Wife* (1999). As a figure in popular culture, though, Bathsheba has been a reflection of the various era's views of women and their roles. In her

The Infamous St. Valentine's Day Massacre, 1929. (AP Photo)

own time and for the next century or so, Bathsheba was seen as absolutely evil. Early feminists, however, saw her as a heroine and tried to deny her involvement with the murder—the angle Esther Forbes took when she fictionalized Bathsheba in her 1938 novel *The General's Lady*.

St. Valentine's Day Massacre

Al Capone, George "Bugs" Moran

Al Capone was consolidating his position as Chicago's most powerful bootlegger in 1929. For years he had been competing and cooperating with other gangs as circumstances warranted. After all, there was plenty of money to be shared, but people got greedy.

The last thorn in Capone's paw was rival George "Bugs" Moran who had taken over Hymie Weiss' mob after he was killed by Capone's men. Capone gave the Moran job to one of his most trusted associates, **"Machine Gun" Jack McGurn.** McGurn assembled his team, probably including Fred "Killer" Burke, Freddie Goetz, Capone torpedoes Albert Anselmi and John Scalise, WWI veteran Joseph Lolordo, and from the Detroit **Purple Gang**, Harry and Phil Keywell.

Working through an intermediary, McGurn got word to Moran that he had hijacked two truckloads of good bonded whiskey and was looking to unload them. He was offering a limited-time blue-light special. The first transaction went off smoothly, and Moran agreed to accept delivery of the second personally at the S.M.C. Cartage Company on February 14th.

That morning, seven men were inside the brick building. Brothers Pete and Frank Gusenberg, speakeasy boss Al Weinshank, bootlegger Adam Heyer, safecracker John May, bank robber James Clark, and Dr. Reinhart Schwimmer, an optometrist and occasional gangster groupie. Also on hand was May's German shepherd Highball.

A little after 10:30 a.m., a big black Cadillac pulled up to the curb and five men got out, three in police uniforms, two in the trench coats often worn by detectives. They sauntered inside and whipped out Tommy guns. Later, neighbors would say they heard "pneumatic drills."

The visitors left, with the men in uniform holding their guns on the others as if they were under arrest. The Caddy drove slowly away and Highball began to howl.

When the real police arrived, they found the seven men had been lined up facing a wall and shot in the back. Six were dead. Only Frank Gusenberg survived and he refused to talk. He died at 1:30 p.m. that afternoon.

Bugs Moran had been late for the promised delivery and had actually seen the killers arrive. Thinking they were cops and he was seeing a real bust, he waited nearby and took off when the shooting started. For a time, some believed it really had been a rogue police operation, but as outrage grew at the cold-blooded executions, it hardened public opinion against Capone.

No one was ever convicted for the killings.

Being one of the centerpieces of American gangster lore, the massacre has been featured in many films, most prominently in *St. Valentine's Day Massacre* (1967), and even further fictionalized in Billy Wilder's comedy, *Some Like It Hot* (1959).

Starkweather, Charles

To understand Charlie Starkweather and Caril Ann Fugate, you've got to forget all of the roman-

ticized young thrill killers seen in the movies. Don't think about Brad Pitt, Patricia Arquette, Woody Harrelson, Sissy Spacek, Martin Sheen, and all the rest. There was nothing glamorous about Charlie and Caril Ann. They were an immature couple who killed out of boredom and pure meanness, not rebellion. But they did look good on camera—took a nice picture—and in this country, that can count for a lot.

Charlie fancied himself a James Dean type—leather jacket, tight jeans, well-lubricated duck's ass pompadour, cowboy boots to make his five-foot, two inch physique a bit more imposing. In mid-1950s Lincoln, Nebraska he was a poor kid from a big family. He had bad eyes but he was quick, strong, and well-coordinated.

In 1956, when he was 16, Charlie dropped out of high school and started dating Caril Ann Fugate, then 13. Like him, she was a poor student, bored at school, unhappy at home. Both of their families were against the relationship and, of course, it only drove them closer together.

Nothing was easy for them. Charlie got fired from his job in a warehouse and went to work as a garbage man. Caril Ann wrecked Charlie's car, partly owned by his dad, and it caused such hard feelings Charlie moved out. With his minimum-wage job there was never enough money. Late one night at the beginning of December 1957, Charlie stole a shotgun and used it to stick up a service station. The attendant, Robert Colvert, didn't have the combination to the safe so Charlie got about $100 from the register, much of it in change. Perhaps angry at the paltry take or perhaps just angry, he forced Colvert to drive out a deserted county road and shot him in the head.

The killing was big news, but Charlie was not a suspect. For the next two months, life was fairly normal for the young couple. Charlie did get fired again but they still had each other. Then, on January 21, 1958 Charlie borrowed a .22 rifle and went to the house—little more than a squalid hovel, really—where Caril Ann lived with her mother and stepfather. When she came home from school, an argument broke out.

In Charlie's version of the story, Caril's parents attacked him and he was forced to kill them in self-defense. He killed their two-year-old baby—Caril Ann's half sister—because she wouldn't stop crying. He dumped the bodies of the woman and the little girl in the outhouse, and dragged her stepdad out to the chicken coop. What happened next is all but impossible to believe.

With the three corpses freezing outside, Charlie and Caril Ann spend the next week holed up in their little love nest. They bought milk and food from the milkman and grocery store, and warned visitors away with a hand-lettered sign on the front door "Stay a way Every Body is sick with the flu."

Several members of Caril Ann's extended family, friends, and associates came by during the next week. She managed to persuade them all to leave without coming inside, though they were suspicious enough to send the police around. The cops bought the flu story, too, without entering the house or looking around the yard. When the family was finally able to get the authorities to take them seriously, Charlie and Caril Ann were on the run in Charlie's broken-down Ford.

The bodies were found by Caril Ann's brother-in-law. By then, they were hiding out with Charlie's friend August Meyer, a 72-year-old bachelor who lived on a farm 20 miles from Lincoln. Charlie killed him, too, and managed to get his Ford stuck in the mud twice. Armed with the .22 and a sawed-off .410 shotgun, they abandoned the car and hitched a ride. Teenagers Robert Jensen and Carol King were unlucky enough to happen upon them. Jensen recognized Charlie as someone he'd seen around town and stopped.

Charlie forced them to drive back toward Meyer's farm and to climb down into an abandoned schoolhouse storm cellar where he killed them both and sexually assaulted Carol King. (Later, both he and Caril Ann would claim the other was responsi-

Charlie Starkweather, cool spree killer, shortly after being apprehended by the police in Nebraska (1958). (AP Photo)

ble for that particular bit of brutality.) They stole Jensen's Ford and wandered around.

The next day, the bodies of the most recent victims were found. That morning, Charlie and Caril Ann broke into the house of C. Lauer Ward. Ward, president of Capital Bridge and Steel companies, was already at work. His wife Clara and their maid Lillian Fencl were at home. The starcrossed lovers barged in and before the day was over, the two women were dead, Mrs. Ward stabbed and shot, Ms. Fencl stabbed. That evening when Ward returned, they killed him, too. After loading Ward's Packard with everything they thought might be valuable—including some of Mrs. Ward's clothes that Caril Ann wore—they drove away, planning to get to Charlie's brother in Washington state. They made it as far as Wyoming.

Caril Fugate, 14-year-old monster or victim of Charlie Starkweather, as seen in 1958. (AP Photo)

By the next day, the bodies at the Ward house had been discovered and the police were out in force looking for the couple. And not just the police. Ward had been a friend of Nebraska Governor Victor Anderson. He called out the National Guard.

Charlie and Caril Ann were near the little town of Douglas, Wyoming by then. They knew the Packard was hot and were on the lookout for a new ride when they came across Merle Collinson, a traveling shoe salesman who had pulled over to take a nap in his Buick. Charlie shot him nine times with his .22. Caril Ann got in the back seat. Only then did Charlie discover he couldn't release the Buick's emergency brake.

Seconds later, geologist Joe Sprinkle drove past. Seeing the two cars, he thought they'd been involved in an accident and stopped to help. Charlie

threatened him with the .22 and demanded help with the brake. Sprinkle grabbed the rifle and fought back. As the two men were struggling, Deputy Sheriff William Romer pulled up. Caril Ann then sprang from the Buick and ran to the patrol car. When Charlie realized the law was closing in, he let go of the rifle, jumped back into the Packard and roared off.

Romer radioed in the situation and a roadblock was set up in Douglas, where police chiefs Robert Ainslie and Earl Heflin caught up with the speeding Packard as it got mired in traffic. Charlie made it through town and was topping 100 mph when Chief Heflin unlimbered his .30/30 and shot out the Packard's back window. A piece of glass nicked Charlie's ear. Thinking he was bleeding to death, he stopped in the middle of the road and surrendered.

Once in custody, Charlie and Caril Ann spun out several stories about the murders. The various confessions were often contradictory. At first, Charlie took all the credit (or blame) and said Caril Ann had been a hostage. Later, when she distanced herself from him during the legal proceedings, he claimed she had killed Carol King and Lillian Fencl.

At trial, Charlie's court-appointed attorneys went for an insanity defense. It didn't take and the jury recommended death. Caril Ann's trial was later. At the time, she was the youngest woman ever to be tried for first degree murder. Her lawyer opted for the helpless hostage defense. It didn't work either, but the jury took her age into consideration and sentenced her to life.

Charlie was executed in the Nebraska state pen on June 24, 1959.

Caril Ann Fugate served 17 years at the Nebraska Center for Women. She was paroled in 1976 and her parole was "discharged" in 1981. Her whereabouts are unknown.

Obviously, the horrific crimes Charlie and Caril Ann committed against helpless, blameless victims are not the stuff of great drama or even of good escapism, but their image—two beautiful teenagers in love, defying all authority, on the run, rocking across the American desert in a big fast car—has proved irresistible for Hollywood. Films like *Natural Born Killers* (1994), *True Romance* (1993), *Wild at Heart* (1990), and *Kalifornia* (1993) have, with different degrees of success, turned the characters into bizarrely exaggerated archetypes.

Terrence Malick's *Badlands* (1973) sticks closer to reality, but in doing so, the filmmaker deals in carefully calculated dishonesty. He leaves out the most serious crimes and sidesteps others that place his protagonists in anything but a favorable light. Bryan Werner's *Starkweather* (2004) is more accurate but suffers from a threadbare budget and is psychologically suspect.

Perhaps the most insightful interpretation of the couple is Bruce Springsteen's song "Nebraska" (1982). His lyrics are an absolutely accurate reflection of Charlie's voice and attitudes as they revealed in his many confessions.

William Allen's 1976 book *Starkweather: The Story of a Mass Murder* tells the story without embellishment and carefully notes the details of what was done and what was said.

Stratten, Dorothy

According to virtually everyone who knew her, Dorothy Stratten was a sweet-natured young woman who was treated badly by older men.

Born Dorothy Ruth Hoogstraten in Vancouver, British Columbia, she was 16 when she met creepy Paul Snider. He was ten years older and urged her to send photographs of herself to *Playboy* magazine. Three years later, she became Miss August and then Playmate of the Year in 1980.

By then, Dorothy and Snider were hitched and living in California. He was running off the rails with gambling debts and obsessive jealousy. She wanted a career in the movies and eventually made five negligible but not embarrassing films. Actually, she was moving up the food chain more swiftly than most Playmates. She and Snider separated, and soon

Dorothy Stratten, Playboy Playmate of the Year, in front of a poster of herself, 1980. (AP Photo)

she was keeping company with director Peter Bogdanovich, whose affinity for nubile young blondes had been established when he made his first film, *The Last Picture Show* (1971), with Cybil Shepard.

Dorothy was working with him on *They All Laughed* (1981, released after her death) in New York when Snider called and asked for one last meeting. She agreed, thinking this would finish things, and flew to California. She met him at their old apartment. Snider killed her with a shotgun, then sexually assaulted her body before he blew his own head off. She was 20 years old.

Adding a final kink to the lurid tale, a few years later, Peter Bogdanovich married and divorced Dorothy's younger sister, Louise, also an actress.

The story of Dorothy Stratten's short life and brutal death has been adapted twice for the screen.

On television in *Death of a Centerfold* (1981), she was played by Jamie Lee Curtis. Mariel Hemingway starred in Bob Fosse's grim *Star 80* (1983), opposite Eric Roberts as Paul Snider.

Bogdanovich told his version in the book *The Killing of the Unicorn* (1984).

Stroud, Robert

He should have been called the "Birdman of Leavenworth," where Robert Stroud did the work that made him famous. His crimes were unremarkable.

In 1908 Stroud was a teenager in Alaska. He was either a pimp for or a good friend of Kitty O'Brien. Their acquaintance Charlie Dahmer either sexually assaulted Kitty or refused to pay for an evening's fun. The different relationships and motivation depend on whose account you choose to accept. Whichever, Stroud killed Dahmer and drew a 12-year stretch at the McNeil Island pen in Washington state. In 1912 he was transferred to the newly opened Leavenworth penitentiary.

Throughout his long incarceration, Stroud was a difficult, troublesome prisoner, prone to arguments with other inmates and a host of physical ailments. He also worked hard to further his third grade education through correspondence courses. Then on March 26, 1916, he killed guard Andrew Turner by stabbing him with a shank.

After a short trial in May, he was found guilty of first-degree murder and sentenced to death by hanging. With the help of his mother, Stroud appealed the decision, a lengthy process that went to the Supreme Court twice, and resulted in two more trials and two more guilty verdicts and, finally, another death sentence.

Conventional legal means exhausted, Stroud's mother took the case to Woodrow Wilson. At the urging of his wife, the ailing president granted a petition of Executive Clemency and changed the death sentence to life in prison.

Stroud was assigned to a solitary cell in the isolation ward where he found the unusual source of his inspiration. After a storm, he came across a sparrow's nest that had been knocked down. He nursed the fledglings back to health in his cell, and then set about learning all he could about birds. That knowledge led him to specialize in canaries and, over the years, to write two books on the birds and their diseases. He actually raised and sold canaries from his cell and developed a treatment for a form of canary fever. The work made him something of a celebrity within the bird-loving community, and it spread.

In those years, Stroud continued to work for his release and anger prison officials with his unorthodox activities. In 1942 they transferred him to Alcatraz, effectively ending his avian studies. Without the birds, he became something of a jailhouse lawyer, writing a massive history of the American penal system—he found it lacking—and filing more petitions with the Supreme Court.

He was transferred to a minimum security prison hospital in 1959 and died there in 1963. It's doubtful anyone would remember him today if he hadn't been the subject of so many favorable articles and books, and, of course, the famous John Frankenheimer-Burt Lancaster film, *The Birdman of Alcatraz* (1962)—yet another popular work making its protagonist much more appealing than he actually was.

Stuart, Charles

It could have been a scene from any TV cop show, fiction or reality. Actually, it was: a 911 call came through on October 23, 1989. The man says he and his wife have been kidnapped and shot. He's in his car; doesn't know where he is. A black guy did it; black running suit with red stripes. Raspy voice. Forced them to drive to a rough neighborhood, the Mission Hill district of Boston, where he stole her purse and disappeared.

She was shot in the head. He was shot in the stomach. She was seven months pregnant, they had just come from a Lamaze class at a city hospital when it all happened. The woman was Carol Stuart. She died that night after the baby was delivered by C-section. The baby died two weeks later.

Husband and father Charles Stuart was seriously wounded but recovered. His call was recorded on tape, and a film crew with the show *Rescue 911* happened to be in the ambulance that first picked him up. It made for great television and Boston was outraged. The cops went through the neighborhood questioning virtually every ambulatory black man they could find. William Bennett, an ex-con who was picked up for a video store robbery, became their prime suspect. Charles Stuart identified a photograph and, when he saw Bennett in a lineup, said yes, he could be the killer.

Then it all started to unravel.

There had been no raspy voiced black guy. For reasons no one will ever fully understand, Stuart wanted to get rid of his wife. Perhaps he had wanted her to have an abortion. Perhaps he wanted insurance money to go into business for himself. Perhaps he had a lover. Whatever, he stole a revolver from the furrier where he worked and enlisted the help of his brother Matthew, telling him he was taking part in an insurance scam.

That night in the car, he killed his wife, shot himself, met Matthew, and gave him the purse containing her jewelry and the pistol, and told him to take it home. Then he drove around and called 911.

But when Matthew realized an innocent man might die for what he and his brother had done, he decided to do the right thing. On January 4, 1990 he went to the police.

On January 5th, Charles committed suicide by jumping off the Tobin Bridge.

The whole affair revealed the racial divisions and stereotypes still existing in Boston and America. The story of a young black criminal kidnapping a well-to-do white couple found a ready audience in cops, the news media, and the general public. It was a lie people—virtually all white people and probably many black people—were ready to believe. It fit perfectly with their assumptions, assumptions created by thousands of stories they'd heard and read.

In the aftermath of Stuart's suicide, people pretended to be shocked at the wave of book proposals and potential film deals that surfaced. But after the initial furor subsided, producers realized Stuart's story was not the sort of thing anyone wanted to relive. To date, only a few books have appeared. A made for TV movie, *Good Night Sweet Wife: A Murder in Boston* (1990) starred Ken Olin and Annabella Price as the Stuarts.

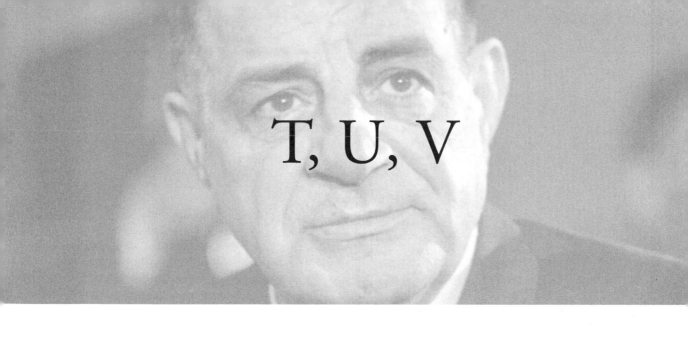

T, U, V

Taborsky, Joseph "Chin"

In 1957 Joseph "Chin" Taborsky and his dim-witted partner Arthur "Meatball" Culombe were labeled Connecticut's "Mad Dog Killers." It wasn't much of an exaggeration. In a series of smalltime stickups they were needlessly brutal, and, for Taborsky, it was the second time around.

A career criminal from age 5, first incarcerated at 14, Joseph was convicted of liquor store owner Louis Wolfson's death during a robbery in 1951. His younger brother Albert was in on the job, too. Plagued by guilt, Albert confessed voluntarily and testified against his older brother. Albert was sentenced to life; the Chin got the chair. He spent more than four years on Death Row working the appeals process. In 1955 the Connecticut Supreme Court overturned his conviction on the grounds that Albert was insane. By then he had been transferred to an asylum and was completely unable to testify at a second trial. Joseph Taborsky was set free and promised to be a good boy.

That lasted for about a year until he met up with his old pal Meatball. Their crime spree began at Thanksgiving 1956 with a hotel stickup and two more liquor store robberies. In all three cases, the clerks were viciously pistol whipped or beaten with a blackjack. Things escalated on December 15th: their first target that evening was Nickola Leone's tailor shop in Hartford. During the robbery, they shot Leone in the face. The bullet lodged in his neck. Incredibly, he survived.

An hour later, Chin and Meatball stopped at a gas station owned by Edward Kurpiewski. They forced him into a bathroom and executed him with a shot to the back of the head. Soon thereafter, Daniel Janowski stopped for gas. He was taken into the garage and killed the same way. Taborsky and Culombe ignored his young daughter who was found asleep in the car a little later by a bus driver.

On December 21st, they robbed a Coventry grocery store. Elderly owner Arthur Vinton and his wife escaped with pistol whipping. Five days later, Taborsky murdered Samuel Cohn when he and Culombe hit his package store.

Their next target was Frank Adinolfi's shoe store in North Haven. Chin asked to see something in a size 12 before Meatball took Adinolfi into a back room and beat him until he was unconscious. While he was busy with that, Bernard and Ruth Speyer came into the store. Taborsky made them kneel on the floor and executed them. When Adinolfi recovered and told his story, State Police Lt. Sam Rome

Portrait of Hollywood director William Desmond Taylor, shortly before his murder, 1922. (AP Photo)

noted the detail of the size 12 shoe, and requested a list of Connecticut inmates with that size foot. Taborsky's name was on it, and eventually Adinolfi identified a photograph of Taborsky and Culombe.

The information didn't come in time for John Rosenthal. Taborsky hit his Hartford drugstore on January 16, 1957 and shot him in the chest. Rosenthal's son Henry was working in the basement at the time. He surprised Taborsky as he was emptying the register and chased him into the street. That was his last killing.

Lt. Rome picked up Chin and Meatball about a month later. Culombe made a full confession and blamed everything on Taborsky. After being pressured by his mother, Taborsky confessed too, both to the recent murders and the original killing of Louis

Wolfson. Both were convicted and sentenced to die, but the U.S. Supreme Court finally said the cops' aggressive tactics had gone too far with Meatball. He pled guilty a second time and got a life sentence.

Taborsky could have appealed his conviction too, but chose not to. After his first release, he'd talked about the horror of living on Death Row. He called it the "supreme agony in the living grave of a death cell." Perhaps he knew with his record, he had no future outside of prison. Whatever the reason, he was electrocuted on May 17, 1960.

Reporter Gerald Demeusy of the *Hartford Courant* wrote about Taborsky for the paper and also helped Taborsky with his memoirs for *Inside Detective* magazine in 1955. Years later, after he'd retired, Demeusy finished the story in his book *Ten Weeks of Terror: A Chronicle of the Making of a Killer* (2002). To date, it has not been adapted for the screen.

Taylor, William Desmond

On the night of February 1, 1922 somebody plugged movie director William Desmond Taylor.

He was not a household name and he was killed at the height of the **Roscoe "Fatty" Arbuckle** unpleasantness, so the mystery surrounding his untimely departure never generated wide public interest or curiosity. Within the film community, though, it continues to be a fascinating subject for discussion, gossip, and juicy speculation.

Taylor was born William Deane Tanner. He was a distinguished-looking Irishman who had come to America around 1890 and found work as an actor in New York, which led to his marrying into a wealthy family. He abandoned his wife and their daughter in 1908 when his efforts in business were unsuccessful. He changed his name, headed west, and fetched up in Hollywood. He landed a lot of bit parts and a starring role in *Captain Alvarez* (1914).

He soon moved behind the camera and became a director specializing in such literary adaptations as *Tom Sawyer* and *Anne of Green Gables*. In 1917 he headed up the Motion Picture Director's Association and kept his digs in the swanky Alvarado Court bungalows.

In short, he had it made.

So, who visited him that February night and put a .38 slug into his chest? And why?

Among the suspects—

Mabel Normand: Comedienne and frequent costar of Arbuckle. She was the last to see Taylor alive. She left his place around 7:45 p.m., right when neighbors thought they heard a shot.

Edward Sands: Taylor's ex-valet, who had stolen money and jewelry from his boss. Taylor had turned him in; some have suggested Sands was actually Taylor's brother.

Mary Miles Miner: Taylor's protégé. She swore eternal love for him… no, not that kind of eternal love, she protested. He was a father figure; pay no attention to the monogrammed lingerie found in his closet or the note that read "I love you—I love you—I love you XXXXXXXXXXXXX."

Charlotte Shelby: Miner's mother, who was said to have had the hots for Taylor herself.

Henry Peavey: Taylor's current valet, a black guy with a fondness for golf clothes. It was rumored he procured young girls and boys for his boss.

An unnamed professional hitman: Taylor had been active in his opposition to drug use within the industry. Suppliers may have put out a contract on him, and a stranger was seen around that afternoon asking directions to the Alvarado address.

There was frustratingly little physical evidence to work with. Peavey had discovered the body, and Taylor's neighbors called his bosses at Paramount. They'd cleaned out any embarrassing material—illegal booze, letters, and who knows what else—before the police arrived. A neighbor said she heard a shot and saw a young man leaving the place the night before, but the neighbor also thought the young man might well have been a woman in disguise.

In the weeks after the murder, no fewer than 300 people confessed, but nothing came of them. As details and rumors were leaked and amplified in the papers, they added to the growing public sense that Hollywood was a den of iniquity and the Hays Office was formed to "clean up the movies."

There was a dubious deathbed confession in the 1960s by actress Margaret Gibson, who was never a suspect and had worked with the director early in his career, but no one really knows who killed Taylor. It hasn't stopped writers from speculating. The murder inspired several books—fiction and non—and "Taylorology," a wonderful web-based newsletter devoted to all facets of the enigmatic case. It has never been the subject of a feature film, though Billy Wilder's *Sunset Boulevard* borrows Taylor's name for Norma Desmond.

Thaw, Harry

It was a lewd, tawdry, violent story that shocked the young twentieth century. Nobody could get enough. The murderer was a spoiled, rich, crazy, cokehead sexual sadist. His victim was a larger-than-life rogue with a fondness for young chorus girls.

The woman they both loved—or at least lusted after—was a beautiful little gold-digger.

Harry Thaw's daddy made his millions in railroads and coke (the coke from coal, not the drug). Young Harry moved from Pittsburgh to New York to sample the highlife. He kept an apartment in a bordello and was fond of tying girls up and taking a whip to them, and using coke (the drug).

Architect Stanford White, who had designed 50 New York buildings, including the Washington Square Arch and the new Madison Square Garden, had a much more palatial bachelor pad, decked out with the gaudiest furnishings of the gaudy Gilded Age, including a red velvet swing.

Evelyn Nesbit, the object of Harry Thaw's murderous affections. (AP Photo)

Evelyn Nesbit met White in 1901 when she was appearing as a chorus girl in the play *Floradora*. The play had opened in 1900 and the six *Floradora* girls were major sex symbols of their time. All of the original sextette had married millionaires. Evelyn, who had already posed as a Gibson Girl, realized *Floradora* was a way out of poverty, so she, her mother, and brother moved from their humble Pittsburgh digs to the Big Apple.

White made nice with both mother and daughter. He paid to have Evelyn's teeth fixed and arranged for her little brother to go to private school. When Evelyn's mom wanted to travel back to Pittsburgh, White encouraged her and promised to look after Evelyn while she was gone. Did he ever.

Later Evelyn would recount different variations on her story, but it boiled down to this: she visited White's lavish apartment on 24th Street where he plied her with a fancy dinner and champagne and had his way with her. As she retold the story of the fateful evening over the years, her degrees of enthusiastic cooperation or steadfast resistance to his advances varied according to the needs and expectations of her audience. But the fact remains that a wealthy, worldly older man seduced a teenaged girl. Whatever degree of coercion was involved at the beginning, Evelyn and Stanford settled into an affair, and neither of them was faithful to the other. White saw other showgirls and Evelyn had a fling with actor John Barrymore that led to an abortion in New Jersey.

At the same time—despite the warnings of her friends who knew of his kinky predilections—Evelyn was seeing Harry Thaw. He wooed her with gifts and flowers as White's interest waned.

In 1903 Thaw persuaded Evelyn and her mother to accompany him on a European vacation. They visited all the hotspots until Mom decided to stay in London while Harry and Evelyn traipsed off to Holland and Germany, no longer maintaining the facade of a chaperone. He claimed he and Evelyn were married and since he was rich enough to rent an entire Austrian castle, complete with servants, nobody disagreed and nobody asked to see a license.

It was at said castle that Harry's dark side surfaced. One morning after breakfast, Thaw produced a leather whip and attacked Evelyn. It was three weeks before she was able to get out of bed. They traveled on to Switzerland where Harry traded in the whip for a rattan switch. That's also where Evelyn discovered Harry was shooting up cocaine.

Thaw's insane rage was motivated in part by his hatred of White. The bad blood between the two predated Evelyn's appearance, but Thaw was particularly incensed and consumed by jealousy over her relationship with the architect.

When they returned to New York, Evelyn went to White and told him about her treatment. At his urging, she filed a legal affidavit with attorney Abe

Hummell detailing what Thaw had done to her. The document was meant to protect her from any retaliation by Thaw and his domineering mother. Evelyn used the threat of it to pry loose an unspecified sum from Thaw.

Over the following months, White was noticeably less enamored of her, and the unhinged Harry came back with even more expensive gifts. Then Harry's mom showed up and said her son was ready to change his ways. All his wild oats were sown, she claimed. It was time for the lad to settle down with a wife and Evelyn was just the girl. Mom's pressure was so intense Evelyn finally agreed. She returned to Pittsburgh where, on April 4, 1905, she became Mrs. Harry Thaw.

Alas, things did not work out in Pittsburgh. Evelyn had no friends there and despite Thaw's wealth, they weren't able to find a place in the social scene. Another European vacation was just the ticket, so in the spring of 1906 they returned to New York for a two week jaunt before their ship departed. During their stay, Thaw was moody, plagued by his obsession with White, an obsession Evelyn may have encouraged.

On the night of June 25th, they decided to take in the musical *Mam'zelle Champagne* at the Madison Square Garden rooftop theater. Though it was a warm evening, Thaw wore a heavy overcoat. He and Evelyn were accompanied by a pair of young hangers-on. Stanford White was there, too, seated at his usual stageside table, and though Thaw meandered through the crowd, White either did not see or chose not to notice him.

The show started, and the singer was belting out "I Could Love a Million Girls" when Thaw stepped up to White, pulled a Smith & Wesson, and shot him three times at point blank range, two bullets into his shoulder, one through his left eye.

In the confusion that followed, Thaw stepped outside and was arrested. At the time, his mother was in Europe, but she sped home and orchestrated what can only be described as a brilliant piece of spin control. The defense team, led by California

Harry K. Thaw, petitioning for release from a sanitarium, circa 1923. (AP Photo)

mouthpiece Delphin Delmas, had two complementary strategies. First, Harry was insane and therefore not guilty; second he had been driven insane by Stanford White's violation of his wife.

It all worked. As details of White's secret life were revealed, the forces of righteousness fell in line behind Thaw. Even the nation's most famous prude, Alfred Comstock, president of the Society for the Suppression of Vice, joined in. So did the major newspapers. They roundly condemned White while milking the story for all it was worth in their ongoing circulation wars (tickets for the trial fetched $100 for scalpers).

On the stand, Evelyn performed admirably, painting White as a rapacious monster, even when the prosecutors entered her affidavit as evidence (she claimed White pressured her to create it). The first jury couldn't reach a decision. Nine months later, a second jury found Thaw not guilty by reason of insanity and he was carted off to an asylum in Matteawan, New York.

Mom immediately set out to prove Harry cured or to have him moved to a more luxurious facility. After all, when Thaw had been locked up in the New York jail, his meals had been catered by Delmonico's, the Big Apple's best beanery. In 1913 Harry's patience ran out and he escaped to Canada. That didn't last long but he was judged sane and freed in 1915.

The first thing he did was divorce Evelyn. A year and a half later, Thaw was back in court after he urged 19-year-old Frederick Gump, Jr., to meet him in New York, and then attacked young Mr. Gump with a whip. Evidence strongly suggested he had made similar overtures to other young men. Eventually, Thaw's family paid off the Gumps and sent Harry back to Matteawan. He was released in 1922 and spent the next 25 years throwing tantrums and getting into various scrapes.

Evelyn parlayed her notoriety into a brief show-biz career that went nowhere. She continued to tell stories about Thaw and White, changing the facts and emphasis to suit her purposes at different times. She had a child during Harry's first incarceration and claimed it was his, saying they'd bribed a guard to sneak her into Matteawan for a night of connubial bliss. She died in Hollywood in 1967.

Thaw's was the first of several "Trials of the Century" and it remains one of the most important. Part of the defense rested on what was referred to as "Dementia Americana," a condition that essentially viewed wives as a possession and gave husbands the right to defend their property by any means necessary. The trial was also about America's definition of itself as a place of innocence and morality in contrast to European sexual depravity. The interlocking ironies of a situation that found the proponents of "family values" defending the actions of a sexual sadist were a key part of E.L. Doctorow's masterpiece *Ragtime* (1981). Milos Foreman's film adaptation takes the

expected liberties with the story. The murder was also the subject of the rarely seen 1955 *The Girl in the Red Velvet Swing*.

For almost half a century, White's name remained tarnished. His public rehabilitation began with Gerald Langford's fine 1962 book *The Murder of Stanford White*.

Thompson Submachine Gun

Brigadier General John Taliaferro Thompson had a dream.

A veteran of the Spanish American War who had specialized in ordnance and small arms, he believed the brutal trench fighting of the Great War could be brought to a speedier conclusion if Allied soldiers were armed with rapid-fire weapons. In those days, fully automatic machine guns—a weapon that fired repeatedly as long as the trigger was pulled—were so large they were usually mounted on bipods, tripods, or wheels. Thompson envisioned something more like a rifle that could be carried by one man.

In 1915 he started to work on his creation. The next year, he and some partners founded the Auto-Ordnance Corporation. Their first problems involved the breech mechanisms that shuttled bullets into the barrel and ejected the empty shell casings. Rifle bullets made the various devices unreliable. They jammed or exploded. Eventually they found that the .45 caliber Colt Automatic Pistol round (a bullet Thompson had helped to develop years before) worked well but in a smaller weapon.

Fine, Thompson said. They revised their design and by 1918 had a working model incorporating all the features that have become so familiar—the pistol grips fore and aft, the round drum magazine. Unfortunately for the young company, the first shipment of prototypes bound for the front was delivered to the New York docks on November 11, 1918, Armistice Day. Peace had broken out in Europe.

Even so, Auto-Ordnance went to work and the first mass-produced Thompson machine guns rolled off the assembly line in March 1921. By then, Prohibition was more than a year old, and millions of Americans were drinking illegal alcohol. The hooch was provided by aggressively competitive, ruthless bootleggers and gangsters who were looking for massive firepower in a compact package. Thompson's product was perfect for their needs, and it was available at fine sporting goods and hardware stores everywhere, not to mention mail order sales (retail price: $225 plus tax). Curiously, though, the weapons were so popular with criminals they could go for as much as $2,000 on the black market (machine guns would not be regulated until the 1934 National Firearms Act).

Sales to military and law enforcement organizations were slow in those years, and at first, the company pitched their product to everyone. One famous print ad showed a cowboy mowing down a gang of Mexican bandidos and their horses.

The Tommy gun quickly captured the public fancy. Of course, outlaws like **John Dillinger** were photographed with their choppers, but so were **J. Edgar Hoover** and Winston Churchill. In fact, it was the Thompson's powerful impact on the American imagination—more than the actual damage caused by the outlaws who favored the weapons—that led to the creation of the FBI as a national crimefighting organization.

Dramatic machine-gun killings filled the newspapers. When people read about the **St. Valentine's Day Massacre** or the **Kansas City Massacre** or the child who was killed in New York when gangster **Vincent "Mad Dog" Coll** opened up on hitman Joey Rao, they demanded that Something Be Done! Hoover responded with a "war on crime" that bears remarkable similarities to the more recent "war on terrorism."

Hollywood filmmakers were also quick to realize how powerful and photogenic the Tommy gun was. No gangster movie was complete without at least one shot of a guy ripping off a long burst from the hip—and the sexual connotations of the image are so blatant further comment is unnecessary.

Thompson, Gerald

Gerald Thompson lived quietly with his grandmother in Peoria, Illinois. He worked at the Caterpillar Tractor company and was known to donate money to any good cause. He bragged that he raped a woman a week for more than a year.

He was able to get away with it for so long because in the mid 1930s, he had realized how much privacy an automobile could afford to an industrious young sociopath. In effect, he turned his car into a mobile torture chamber.

By all accounts, he was not particularly prepossessing, but he learned to turn on the charm persuasively enough to entice young women into his sedan at night. That was all he needed. The passenger side door handle was wired to the battery and delivered a painful shock. Once he had used it to intimidate victims who tried to escape, he'd attack them with a pair of sharp scissors, cutting off their clothes and raping them. To keep them quiet, he also had a camera with a timer-activated shutter. He'd force them to pose in his favorite sexual positions in the glare of the headlights, and take photographs he threatened to use as blackmail material.

His final victim was restaurant hostess Mildred Hallmark.

On the night of June 16, 1935 she had been out on a date and was waiting for a streetcar when Thompson found her. He went through his normal MO and coaxed her into the car, but she vigorously fought back. Police later found Thompson's skin under her nails. He beat her so severely that he broke her neck and stabbed her with the scissors and her own fountain pen. Later, he dumped her body near the Springdale Cemetery where it was discovered.

The viciousness of the killing galvanized the community and the police. At the Caterpillar plant, they took up a collection for Mildred. Her father John worked in the toolmaking shop with Thompson, who made a generous contribution.

As the cops were rounding up suspects, they were also fielding dozens of calls from young women describing an attacker who had electrified his car and had been preying on women for years. It was an anonymous tip, probably from one of them, that led to Thompson.

He confessed during an interrogation on June 22nd. A search of his grandmother's place turned up plenty of physical evidence—bloodstained trousers and seat cushions covered in Mildred's blood type, a diary listing 16 victims complete with descriptions of those encounters, along with hundreds of pornographic photographs from Thompson's stash.

As the details leaked out, the mood in Peoria grew ugly. Mobs gathered downtown and things got so dangerous Thompson was taken away for his own safety. Given the overwhelming amount of evidence, he was convicted quickly and sent to Joliet State Penitentiary where he was electrocuted—a nice touch, that—on October 15, 1935.

As a serial rapist, Thompson was ahead of his time and so he never attracted lasting national attention. While they were fresh in the public memory, his crimes were too sadistic and sick to be transformed into mainstream popular entertainment.

Tirrell, Albert

It is easier for a camel to pass through the eye of a needle than for a rich man to go to prison in America for killing a poor person. Albert Tirrell proved it in 1845 with a defense that, even today, is breathtaking in its imagination and sheer chutzpah.

Though he was married with children, Albert—of the Weymouth, Massachusetts Tirrells—still had a lot of wild oats to sow. The family business, Tirrell's Triumphant Footwear, gave Albert ample opportunity to indulge in his two favorite pastimes, drinking and whoring. He often did both with Maria Bickford.

After meeting her in New Bedford, he installed her in a love nest out on Cedar Lane in Boston. Their assignations were loud and destructive, involving copious amounts of liquor, screaming matches,

and heartfelt make-up sessions. For Albert's wife and family, his flagrant behavior was the last straw.

They had him arrested and charged with adultery. In the middle of the nineteenth century, it was a serious matter—he might have been jailed for several years if convicted—and Albert took it seriously. At least he took it seriously long enough to tell everyone he had seen the error of his ways and would sin no more. His wife and relatives wrote glowing letters about him to the county prosecutor. Albert posted bond on October 20th and was released. The next day he showed up on Cedar Lane with a jug of rum and a rocket in his pocket. For the next week, Albert and Maria followed their drink-bellow-fight-make up pattern, much to the consternation of the downstairs neighbors.

It ended on October 27th when Albert drunkenly slashed Maria's throat with his straight razor, tried to cover it up by setting the bed on fire, and fled, leaving his bloody shirt with her body. A coroner's jury had no trouble deciding Albert had committed the murder, but by then he was in Canada. Family members had helped him escape and, in early November, he wrote to them saying he was going to sail to Liverpool from Montreal. Weather forced the ship to return.

Albert found his way to New York where he caught a second ship bound for New Orleans, but somebody ratted him out and he was arrested and shipped back to Massachusetts in February 1846. By then, the facts of the case were widely known and everyone assumed the trial was a mere formality. But the Triumphant Tirrells weren't going to give up. They hired famous orator and lawyer Rufus B. Choate, and he came up with a bizarre but brilliant defense.

Yes, Albert killed this immoral "Spanish girl" who was "coarse, strong and masculine," but it wasn't his fault because Albert did it while he was sleepwalking! Yes, indeed, chimed in the Tirrells as they trooped to the witness stand to tell stories about how Albert had been a somnambulist since boyhood. Friends and doctors backed them up and the jury bought it.

It took less than two hours to find him not guilty. Albert was tried a second time on arson and adultery charges. Again, Choate's courtroom theatrics carried the day on the arson count. He even suggested Maria had committed suicide by slitting her own throat, but he couldn't make it fly on the adultery rap. For that Albert served three years.

But the sleepwalking defense was established, and others have tried to use it. Tirrell's crimes and trial have largely escaped notice in popular entertainment, though it is possible Wilkie Collins heard of his somnambulism and used a variation on it as a key plot point in his famous 1868 novel, *The Moonstone*, the first true mystery.

Todd, Thelma

As "Hot Toddy, the Ice-Cream Blonde," she was one of the silent screen's most popular stars. Her smoky voice and ribald sense of humor made for a smooth transition to the talkies. But Thelma Todd's fame today comes from her unexplained death.

On Monday, December 16, 1935 her body was found behind the wheel of her V-12 Lincoln convertible. It was in a closed garage with the ignition switch on, gas in the tank. The engine was not running. The actress was wearing the evening clothes she'd had on at a fancy party the previous Saturday night. There was blood on her face and dress; exactly how much blood is in dispute. So was the position of her body. The maid who found her said she had been moved by the time police arrived.

The garage was high above her restaurant, Thelma Todd's Sidewalk Café in Malibu's Palisades. Her apartment was there, too. She shared it with her sometime lover, director Roland West, who was also her partner in the bistro. The garage was a dizzying 270 exterior steps up a cliff from their place. Though his story changed from time to time, West claimed Thelma came back from a party around 2:30 a.m. Sunday morning and he refused to let her in. Perhaps she staggered up the stairs and drunkenly started the car to keep warm.

Others, however, claimed to have seen her driving with an unidentified "dark man" later that Sunday. He might have been her ex-husband Pasquale DiCicco, or it could have been someone else. DiCicco was known to pal around with New York gangsters, and **Lucky Luciano** was trying to establish himself in Los Angeles. Luciano had been pressuring Toddy to let him open a gambling operation on the third floor of her café—she said no. Could he have contracted a hit on her?

Further muddying the waters, at the Saturday night party Thelma had told her friend, actress Ida Lupino, that she'd just embarked on an affair with an important San Francisco businessman whom she could not name. She was going to see him soon, maybe later that night. Who was he? Did she see him? Nobody knows.

All the Hollywood moguls simply wanted the matter to go away. The last thing they needed was another scandal. Todd's death was declared a suicide but there were too many unanswered questions to simply leave it be. A second inquest was held and a grand jury came to the accurate but useless conclusion that her death was due to carbon monoxide poisoning.

Whether the poisoning was a result of suicide, accident, or murder, it ended Roland West's sputtering career. He never worked again and Thelma Todd's death remains officially unsolved. Perhaps because the story still embarrasses the film community, it has never been mentioned in movies.

Toppan, Jane

In turn-of-the-century Massachusetts, she was the psychopath with a smiley face. Jane Toppan, née Honora Kelly, was a cheerful nurse by day, angel of death by night. She admitted to killing 31 people; the real count is probably closer to 100 and, if so, it would make her America's Number One Female Serial Killer.

She was born in Boston in 1857 to poor parents. Her mother died while Honora was still a baby, leaving her and her sister in the care of their drunken, violent father. He held onto them for six years

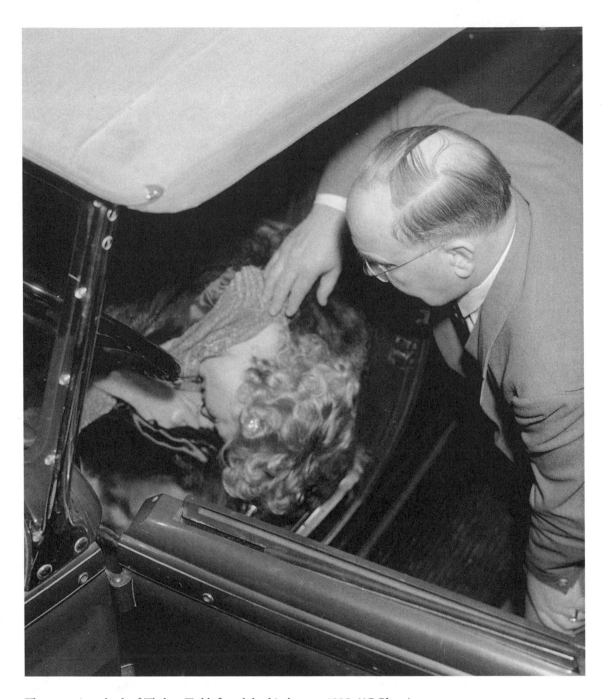

The mysterious death of Thelma Todd, found dead in her car, 1935. (AP Photo)

before giving them to the Boston Female Asylum and vanishing. Two years later, Honora was taken in by Mrs. Abner Toppan, a widow, and her family. There, she took the name Jane Toppan, though she was not legally adopted, and, apparently, the family never fully accepted her. She grew up feeling alienated, not really a part of any group or institution. Still, the face she presented to the world was sunny, friendly, and competent. She went to the training school of the Columbia Hospital where she was considered an excellent student nurse, though one who was perhaps a bit too intrigued by autopsies. She was also a vicious gossip and, like many psychopaths, she was also a pyromaniac.

Still, her professional reputation was so strong that for a time she worked as head nurse at Massachusetts General Hospital, until they learned she had not actually graduated from nursing school and had forged her certificate.

She then became a private nurse and continued to use the dark techniques she had developed. Jane was a poisoner with an inventive MO. Whenever doctors suspected a patient had died of morphine poisoning, they checked the pupils of the victim's eyes. If the person had been poisoned, the pupils would be contracted. Jane mixed atropine with the morphine so the pupils of her unfortunate patients would be dilated, and their deaths would be considered a result of their illness.

Working late at night, she killed dozens of them, and later admitted to getting a heady erotic rush at the act. She'd sometimes get into bed with her victims at the moment of death. She administered her lethal cocktails slowly, just a little dose each day to her patients until they'd had enough.

The nature of her work kept her on the move and she managed to avoid serious suspicion for many years. But her compulsion to kill became even stronger and she lost whatever control she might have had. It all ended in the summer of 1901 when she was vacationing with the Alden Davis family in Cape Cod. During the six weeks they were there, she killed Davis, his wife, and their two married daughters.

The husband of the last victim suspected something wasn't right with Jane, and ordered an autopsy on his wife. The poisons were discovered and police were able to trace the prescriptions forged by Jane. She ran away to Amherst and attempted suicide, but was "saved" (if that's the right word) by medical intervention.

At her trial, her lawyers would admit to only 11 killings (*only* 11!) but Jane didn't really help her case when she said, "This is my ambition: to have killed more people—more helpless people—than any man or woman has ever killed."

She probably didn't realize her sick ambition, but nobody can say she didn't give it her best shot. She was finally declared not guilty by reason of insanity after her attorneys swore she would never apply for parole or release, no matter how sane or nuts she might be adjudged in the future. She spent the rest of her days and nights at the State Hospital in Taunton, where she died, 81 years old, in 1938.

Jane has not been found to be a suitable (i.e. profitable) subject for popular entertainment. Her name, however, was appropriated for the low-budget horror film, *American Nightmare* (2002), where B-movie diva Debbie Rochon's character is a vengeance-seeking serial killer.

Torresola, Griselio and Oscar Collazo

The assassination attempt on President Harry Truman is not widely remembered, and most who do recall it tend to dismiss it as no big deal. They're wrong, it was quite serious.

Griselio Torresola and Oscar Collazo were fervent supporters of Puerto Rican independence. In the fall of 1950 their fellow revolutionaries mounted an armed coup. It failed badly and bloodily, but leader Albizu Campos got word to Torresola in New York that the planned assassination of the American president was to go forward. Torresola and his confederate Oscar Collazo armed themselves with 9mm semiautomatics and took a train to Washington,

D.C. Originally, their mission was to take place at a different time with more men, but events on the island had forced their hand.

On the evening of October 31, 1950 they booked rooms at the Hotel Harris. The next morning they caught a taxi and asked to be taken to the White House. The helpful cabbie told them it was being remodeled. The President, he said, was living across the street at Blair House. Torresola and Collazo quickly cased the place, then went back to their hotel to plan an assault and arm themselves. That afternoon, they went back.

There were guard houses at both ends of the building, manned by plain clothes police and Secret Service. Torresola came at Blair House from the west; Cellazo from the east. They reached the guard stations at about the same time and opened fire. The ensuing gunfight lasted less than 40 seconds. Police officer Leslie Coffelt was seriously wounded but managed to return fire and to kill Torresola before he died. Collazo and officers Donald Birdzell and Joseph Downs were wounded. The gunfire awoke President Truman from his nap in a second floor bedroom. At the height of the action, he went to a window and looked out. Given the ferocity of the engagement and the position of the assassins, Mr. Truman might easily have been hit or killed.

Collazo was tried, convicted, and sentenced to death, but Truman commuted it to life. Collazo was a model prisoner. In 1979 President Jimmy Carter pardoned him and Collazo returned to Puerto Rico where he died in 1994.

This moment of dramatic violence has never been filmed. It has, however, been recreated in remarkable detail by Stephen Hunter and John Bainbridge Jr., in their excellent book, *American Gunfight* (2005). It would make a hell of a movie.

Tracy, Harry

Though he has been mostly forgotten today, in 1902 Harry Tracy was front-page news coast to coast. One of the last of the old time outlaws, he went out on his own terms.

Harry was born in either New York or Wisconsin sometime around 1876. He grew up in Boston where he earned a reputation as a tough kid. In the mid-1890s, he took Horace Greeley's famous advice and went west where he met David Merrill. First arrested for stealing geese, they aimed higher and embarked on a life of crime. In 1897 Tracy escaped from a Utah prison. Then, according to some sources, he joined **Butch Cassidy**'s Wild Bunch. Other sources say he joined Merrill with another gang at Robber's Roost, a Colorado hideout used by Butch and others. The latter seems more likely because Tracy probably would not have fit in with the famously easygoing Cassidy. His temperament was darker, angrier, and meaner. His nickname was Mad Dog and photographs reveal a grim, beetle-browed visage.

During his time at Robber's Roost, Tracy was captured repeatedly by the law but always found a way to escape.

By 1902 Butch had relocated to Bolivia, and Harry and Merrill were locked up in the Oregon State Penitentiary in Salem. On the morning of June 9th, they staged a daring escape. Armed with a short-barreled Winchester rifle, almost certainly smuggled in for them, Tracy opened fire killing two guards and wounding two more and another prisoner. Tracy and Merrill used the wounded guards as a shield to retreat into the woods.

Immediately, the alarm was raised and a posse gave chase. The resourceful escapees found or stole new clothes, food, and horses, and rode north toward Washington state. Two days later, they were surrounded by a 50-man posse but managed to elude their pursuers. A company of the Oregon National Guard joined the effort to no avail.

The desperadoes found a farmer with a small boat and forced him at gunpoint to row them across the Columbia River to Washington. They were hiding out in a barn when Tracy happened upon a Portland newspaper that claimed Merrill had been the one who ratted him out to Oregon authorities in the first place. Details vary as to what happened next. Tracy either shot Merrill in the back when he cheated during a formal back-to-back duel with pistols, or he strangled him as he slept. In either case, as he admitted later, it was cold-blooded murder.

Striking out on his own, Tracy commandeered a launch and forced its captain to take him up the Puget Sound from Olympia to Seattle. From there, he went northwest toward Bothell where he encountered another posse led by Sheriff Edward Cudihee. Tracy killed one deputy and wounded two others before he slipped away again.

He holed up in the Van Horn farmhouse where he held the family hostage and supplied himself with dry clothes and a hot meal. Mrs. Van Horn managed to alert a grocery delivery boy to her predicament, and when Tracy left an ambush was waiting. Again, the lawmen weren't quick or resourceful enough and their trap backfired. Tracy killed two more and disappeared into the forest.

Heading south, he stopped in the small town of Renton where he took three women as hostages in a farmhouse, though he swore he would never actually do them any harm. Again, the place was surrounded. Again, Tracy got away. He stole another horse and rode east, eluding posses and militias for almost two months. All of his exploits had been covered by newspapers everywhere.

On August 9th, he was trapped at a ranch near Creston in Lincoln County. Late in the afternoon, a five-man posse caught up with him. Tracy tried to run for a wheat field to hide, but was wounded twice in the leg by rifle fire. He managed to find cover behind a large rock but, knowing his time was up, Harry Tracy decided to end it himself and put a bullet through his head.

Some newspapers lionized his courage and ignored that he had murdered several good cops who were simply doing their jobs. Harry's story has been filmed twice, first as the 1928 silent film *Tracy the Outlaw*, and in the 1982 Canadian film *Harry Tracy, Desperado* with Bruce Dern in the title role.

Trafficante, Santo Jr.

Hundreds of rumors and stories float around Santo Trafficante. Facts are harder to come by.

He was born in Florida to a Sicilian family. His father, Santo Trafficante Sr., was a powerful mobster who brought several smaller gangs together. When he died, his son took over, running the business in Tampa and Miami. As a boss, he was tight with **Tommy Lucchese** and **Meyer Lansky** in New York and he worked extensively with Lansky in his Cuban gambling operations. Trafficante attended the famous 1946 meeting **Lucky Luciano** called in Cuba, and he was also at the notorious Apalachin gathering.

Santo was running the show for Lansky in 1959 when Fidel Castro and his guys kicked out dictator Fulgencio Batista. Trafficante didn't run, thinking Castro was just another corrupt dictator who would be willing to play ball once he realized how much money could be made. But Fidel had him thrown in jail then deported.

Not long after, Trafficante said the CIA contacted him and hired him to assassinate Castro. The mobster and his colleague John Roselli cooked up several schemes to grease the inconvenient Communist, from bombs to poisons, but none of them worked out. Roselli suffered the most: in 1976 his legless corpse was found in a 55-gallon drum in the ocean near Miami.

All of it led to speculation Castro learned of Trafficante's actions and sent Cuban assassins to Dallas to kill President Kennedy. Some conspiracy theorists point to Trafficante's connections to labor boss **Jimmy Hoffa**, who had reasons of his own for disliking the Kennedys, and to **Jack Ruby**, who killed **Lee Harvey Oswald**. Trafficante's longtime friend and lawyer Frank Ragano said Santo confessed to involvement in the assassination just before he died in 1987, during heart surgery. No evidence has ever been found to back the alleged confession.

On film, Trafficante has appeared briefly in *Donnie Brasco* (1997) and *Bonanno: A Godfather's Story*

(1999). He will remain a bright star in the hazy firmament of conspiracies.

Trepal, George

Thallium is really nasty stuff.

It's an element often used as rat poison. If a human being ingests enough of it—only a small amount—death is preceded by intense, burning pain. That's what George Trepal used on his neighbors, the Carrs, in 1988.

They lived next door to each other in rural Alturas, Florida. Trepal worked at home on computers. His wife, Diana, was a doctor. They had no kids. The Carrs had five children and grandchildren in their blended family living in the house and the apartment they created in a garage. George and Diana, both members of the Mensa "genius" club, didn't get along with the downhome Carrs. They argued over noise, dirt bikes, etc. George sent an unsigned threatening letter telling them to move.

A small community in the middle of citrus groves, Alturas is the kind of place where people boast they never lock their doors. That made it easy for Trepal to wait until he knew the Carr house was empty, get inside, and leave an eight-pack of poisoned Coca-Cola.

Back in the 1970s Trepal had worked as a chemist in a crank lab. He'd been arrested and served time for it. Thallium happens to be one of the byproducts of methamphetamine production and Trepal had some familiarity with it.

Peggy and two of the kids got sick after drinking the doctored Coke. Eventually, Peggy fell into a coma and died. When investigators examined materials from the Carr house to find the source of the poison, traces of thallium showed up in empty and full bottles.

The cops were suspicious of Trepal, but did not have enough evidence against him to do anything. Officer Susan Goreck of the Polk County Sheriff's Office then went undercover. Adopting the name

Sherry Guin, she met Trepal at a Mensa Murder Mystery weekend gathering he had organized. Over the next several months, she stayed in contact and gained his friendship.

She told him she was going through a rough divorce and when she learned Trepal and Diana wanted to sell their house, she arranged to see it on the pretext she might be interested in buying.

After several visits, she actually rented the house, giving the police the opportunity to make a thorough search. Among the stuff they found was a small bottle of thallium nitrate in a workshop in Trepal's garage. Further searches turned up chemistry texts and a bottle-capping machine.

It was all they needed to build a good circumstantial case against Trepal. He was convicted of murder and sentenced to death in 1991. He remains in prison in Florida.

Susan Goreck tells her side of the story in the somewhat hyperbolic book *Poison Mind* (1995). Trepal's case has yet to be filmed but it was the subject of an A&E *American Justice* documentary.

Turner, Nat

More than a century after his famous rebellion, Nat Turner remains a hero to some, villain to others. To a degree, though, he has been vindicated in popular culture. Mention of his name conjures up an image of justified resistance to inhumane conditions, not of mass murder.

By all accounts Turner was a complex, intelligent, charismatic man. Born a slave in Southampton, Virginia in 1800, he taught himself to read and became a preacher and foreman to other slaves. At 21, he ran away but a vision from above ordered him to return.

He had other visions, too, darker and more violent. In 1831 he interpreted two celestial occurrences—an eclipse and something that turned the sun bluish-green—as orders to mount a rebellion. He persuaded a few closely trusted friends to join him, and early on the morning of August 22nd, they crept into the house of his owners, Mr. and Mrs. Joseph Travis. They killed the whole family, adults and children, as they slept.

Moving on to other plantations, they killed all of the white people they found and urged their fellow slaves to join the revolution.

Such rebellions had happened before and white Southerners feared them. Turner and his followers intentionally refrained from using firearms, to maintain the element of surprise, and moved as quickly as they could on horseback. Still, word spread swiftly.

When Turner and his men neared Jerusalem, the closest town, they were met by a militia and scattered. Turner tried to mount another attack but failed. The remaining rebels where finished off in one more skirmish with state and federal troops. The uprising lasted for two days. About 55 people had been killed.

It wasn't over.

Turner escaped and stayed hidden in the area for several months. In that time, more than 200 black people, many of them completely innocent, were killed by white mobs in Virginia and nearby North Carolina.

Turner was captured on October 30th. Less than a week later, he was tried, convicted, and sentenced to death. After he was hanged, his body was skinned, beheaded, and quartered.

Before he was executed, Turner dictated his famous "Confessions" to his court-appointed lawyer Thomas Gray. Like so many others who have been associated with the infamous over the centuries, Gray published a book based on his experiences. Though its historical accuracy is suspect, it did provide the basis for the most important book on the subject, William Styron's 1967 Pulitzer prize-winning bestseller *The Confessions of Nat Turner*.

The book immediately became a lightning rod for controversy. The very idea of a white writer telling the story was an affront to some black critics.

It was roundly condemned by partisans, most notably in *William Styron's Nat Turner: Ten Black Writers Respond* (1968), which took Styron to task for considering Turner's lust for a white woman as a possible motivation.

At different times over the following years, attempts were made to bring the story to the screen. James Earl Jones would star; Sidney Lumet would direct; no, it would be Norman Jewison. Decades later, it was to be a Spike Lee film. None came to fruition and it is really not surprising for a controversial literary work of limited commercial appeal.

To date, the only dramatization has been a rarely seen PBS docudrama, *Nat Turner: A Troublesome Property* (2003).

Unruh, Howard

"I'm no psycho. I have a good mind." This from the man who had just killed 13 people—neighbors, children, passing strangers—in 12 minutes.

Howard Unruh was the proverbial walking time bomb, a deeply frustrated, angry, alienated man who'd been superbly trained to act upon his madness. In World War II, Unruh served as a machine gunner with a tank crew in Europe. His unit fought its way up the boot of Italy, into France and finally to Bastogne and the Battle of the Bulge.

Throughout the campaign, Unruh kept a detailed journal, listing every enemy soldier he'd killed and, whenever he could get a close look at the bodies, their physical appearance in death. Strange, obsessive behavior, yes, but it was his business. To the Army, Unruh had served honorably and, like thousands of GIs, he'd returned home a decorated hero who tried to resume his life.

But life before the war hadn't been easy. Unruh had been raised in a strictly religious household; read the Bible every day and didn't socialize much. Upon his return to Camden, New Jersey, he moved back in to a small house with his mother. (His father was estranged from the family.) He briefly dated a girl he'd known before the war, but the rela-

Mass murderer Howard Unruh (center) with police after his capture in Camden, New Jersey, September 6, 1949. (AP Photo)

tionship ended. Hoping to become a pharmacist, he used the GI Bill to enroll in Temple University in nearby Philadelphia, but that didn't work out either.

Instead, Unruh became even more withdrawn, stopped going to church but still read the Bible daily. He set up a shooting range in the basement and worked on his marksmanship. He continued to keep his journal and noted down every slight—real and imagined—he had suffered. A particular sore spot seems to have been a gate owned by his neighbors the Cohens. It provided access to Unruh's door and they complained about him leaving it open. Eventually, he built a fence, a large fence with another more elaborate gate.

On the night of Monday, September 5, 1949 Unruh went to the movies across the river in Philadelphia at the Family Theater, open 24 hours. He sat through a double feature of *I Cheated the Law*, about a tricky attorney, and the Barbara Stanwyck vehicle, *The Lady Gambles*. He watched both of them three times and didn't get back until the early hours of Tuesday morning. When he arrived home, the new gate was gone. Someone—surely one of the Cohens— had stolen it. Before he went to sleep, Unruh vowed to kill whoever had done this to him.

The next morning, his mom fixed his usual breakfast of cereal and eggs. Unruh put on his best tropical worsted suit, white shirt, and carefully knotted striped bow tie. Before he went out, he loaded his favorite Luger, dropped a couple of extra clips and loose bullets into his pockets and set out for revenge. It was 9:20 a.m.

The first person he saw was a bread deliveryman. Unruh fired at him and missed. The bread man pulled two kids into his truck for protection and drove for help. Unruh's next stop was John Pilarchik's shoe repair shop. He killed Mr. Pilarchik with two shots and walked next door to Clark Hoover's barbershop. There, he killed Hoover and his six-year-old customer Orrie Smith. As Orrie's mother Catherine screamed in horror, Unruh moved on to a nearby tavern. He fired two bullets into the locked door with no results, so he turned to Cohen's drug store on the corner. At the door, he encountered insurance agent James Hutton who was coming out. Unruh said "Excuse me" then killed him.

Maurice and Rose Cohen realized something was terribly wrong and retreated to their apartment upstairs. Unruh followed. He killed Rose where she hid in a closet, then shot Maurice's mother Minnie as she tried to call the police. Maurice managed to hide his 12-year-old son in another closet before he climbed out a window to a porch roof. Unruh shot and wounded him there. Maurice fell to the street. Unruh dashed back downstairs and finished him off.

His next victim was Alvin Day, who had stopped his car to help James Hutton. He turned and fired at another car, killing two women and wounding a boy. He wounded several others there, too, when he fired into a grocery store.

Next on his list was Zegrino's tailor shop where he found Helga Zegrino, who'd been married to her husband for all of three weeks. She died screaming. Unruh went back out to the street and headed home. Along the way he spotted two-year-old Tommy Hamilton peeking out his front window. Tommy was his last victim. It was 9:32 a.m.

After 12 minutes Unruh had run out of ammunition, so he barricaded himself inside his house and waited as police armed with machineguns sur-

rounded the place and a crowd estimated at more than a thousand had gathered round. By then, the press was onto the story. Philip W. Buxton, assistant city editor of the Camden *Evening Courier* looked up Unruh's number in the book and gave him a call. Unruh answered.

"Is this Howard Unruh?" he asked.

"Yes, this is Howard." He sounded far too calm for a man who'd been slaughtering his neighbors. "What's the last name of the party you want?"

"Unruh."

"Who are you? What do you want?"

"I'm a friend. I want to know what they're doing to you." Buxton could hear gunfire.

"Well, they haven't done anything to me yet, but I'm doing plenty to them."

"How many have you killed?"

"I don't know yet. I haven't counted them. But it looks like a pretty good score."

"Why are you killing people?"

"I don't know. I can't answer that yet. I'm too busy. A couple of friends are coming to get me," Unruh said, though there were no friends on the way. Then he hung up. Tear gas canisters had been shot through the windows. As the house filled with gas, he surrendered and walked out. One of the waiting cops asked what was the matter and wondered if he was a psycho.

An indignant Unruh replied he was no psycho. "I have a good mind."

Doctors disagreed. After months of tests, Unruh was declared legally insane and sentenced to life in what is now the Trenton State Hospital for the insane. For years, the only person he would speak to was his mother. Since her death, he has not spoken to anyone. No one has seen the need to dramatize his story, though he is considered to be the first of the "modern" mass murderers or spree killers.

Mobster Joe Valachi tells all before the Senate Investigations Subcommittee in Washington, DC, 1963. (AP Photo)

Valachi, Joe

For most of his life, Joe Valachi was an unimportant gangster. He was muscle, a "button man" who did the dirty work of killing rivals for his bosses.

Born in New York in 1903, he joined the "cosa nostre," as he called it, during the Castellammarese War between **Salvatore Maranzano** and **Joe "the Boss" Masseria**. In 1935 Valachi started working with the Harlem numbers racket after **Dutch Schultz** was killed (Dutch had threatened to murder D.A. Thomas Dewey, so **Lucky Luciano** and the other top New York mobsters had him whacked). Valachi also dealt dope and, during World War II, made a killing by selling ration coupons and stamps. He was in and out of prison for relatively short stretches during those years.

But in 1959, he was nailed on a serious narcotics beef and sentenced to 15 years in the Atlanta federal pen. Boss **Vito Genovese** was also a guest in Atlanta at the time. He came to believe Valachi was going to rat him out, so he put out a contract on the underling. At least that's how Valachi saw it, and he was probably right. Don Vito was famous for taking out contracts on anyone who pissed him off.

Believing he was a marked man, Valachi attacked another inmate, Joe Saupp, with an iron pipe and killed him. He had mistaken Saupp for Genovese's man Joseph De Palermo.

With the new murder rap hanging over his head and Genovese still threatening him, Valachi turned to the feds and agreed to tell all he knew.

In October 1963 he appeared before Arkansas Senator John McClellan's congressional committee on organized crime. Valachi's testimony was carried live on radio and television and was extensively reported in the print media. Valachi had been such a low-level soldier he didn't always get his facts straight when he talked about the higher-ups, but the hearings riveted the American public. Here was organized crime in the flesh. Viewers, listeners, and readers ate it up.

Five years later, in 1968, Peter Maas' book *The Valachi Papers*, based on the mobster's unpublished memoirs, became a bestseller. Valachi died in prison in 1971, two years after Vito Genovese, also in prison, died.

Maas' book was filmed in 1972 with Charles Bronson in the title role. It's a juicy slice of escapism notable for being one of the first to portray famous mob moments using real names—like the murders of Maranzano, Masseria, and **Albert Anastasia**, and the infamous Apalachin conference raided by New York state troopers.

Valachi was also the inspiration for the character of Frank Pentangeli in *The Godfather, Part II*.

Von Bülow, Claus

After Claus Von Bülow's first trial, William Wright wrote a book about the man and his coma-

Claus Von Bülow and Alan Dershowitz outside a Providence, RI courtroom, 1985. (AP Photo)

tose wife, Sunny. *The Von Bülow Affair* paints a portrait of Claus as an evil murderer—not quite the image most people have now.

Claus Von Bülow will forever be associated with Jeremy Irons' brilliant Oscar-winning portrayal in *Reversal of Fortune* (1990). The film is based on Alan Dershowitz's book about his involvement with Von Bülow's appeal and his *second* murder trial. Not surprisingly, Dershowitz and Wright disagree on almost all important points. In any telling, the story contains all the right elements—wealth, sex, jealousy, generational conflict, drugs, and duplicity.

It begins with Von Bülow's marriage to Martha "Sunny" Crawford in 1966. He was from a well-to-do German family; she was worth millions. With

three children, two from her first marriage and one together, they lived in a gaudy oceanfront mansion among other mansions in Newport, Rhode Island. Theirs was not a particularly happy marriage. He had a mistress; she had health problems. According to some of her acquaintances (including author Truman Capote), she was given to self-medication, injecting herself with various concoctions. Others said she would never have even considered such a thing.

Claus and Sunny had been talking of divorce in 1982. On December 21st, Sunny was found unconscious on the floor of her bathroom. She had lapsed into a coma, almost certainly induced by an overdose of insulin. The same thing had happened a year before and she had recovered. This time, she did not.

She was taken to Columbia Presbyterian Hospital in New York City where she remains to this day.

Claus was charged with attempted murder, tried, and convicted. That's where Dershowitz came in. He brought together a team including lawyer Susan Estrich and several Harvard law students to argue for a new trial before the Rhode Island Supreme Court.

They marshaled an impressive case, hammering the handling of the evidence, inconsistent testimony, and, most important, a syringe encrusted with insulin. The prosecution had presented it as the instrument that led to Sunny's condition. Dershowitz's team argued that if the needle had been used to inject insulin, the act of piercing the skin would have cleaned the exterior. For the needle to have been coated with insulin, someone must have dipped it and left it to dry.

The court agreed with their reasoning. The first verdict was overturned and a second trial was ordered. At the second one, Von Bülow was found not guilty.

The film of Dershowitz's book, by writer Nicholas Kazan and director Barbet Schroeder stays within acceptable limits of fictionalizing and compressing action to shape real events into a satisfying if extremely complex plot. Von Bülow is presented as an icy, contradictory, and not particularly likeable figure. The film is most effective in showing how elusive any objective "truth" can be. It ends with two interpretations of precisely the same evidence, interpretations that arrive at radically different conclusions. Such wisdom is rare in crime writing, and virtually nonexistent in Hollywood movies—*Reversal of Fortune* is one of the very best.

W, Y, Z

Waite, Dr. Arthur Warren

At first blush, Arthur Waite was quite the catch. A tall, handsome, athletic doctor, he was everything a mother could want for her daughter.

Except the doctor was also a ruthless avaricious psycho killer. More to the point, he was an *incompetent* ruthless avaricious psycho killer.

In early twentieth-century New York, Dr. Waite was known as a fine amateur tennis player and a renowned researcher with a fully stocked bacteriological lab at his disposal. All that was lacking in his life was a million dollars. As luck would have it, his wife's parents, Mr. and Mrs. John Peck, had that million. Mr. Peck had earned it in his drug business.

But they showed no signs of dying and leaving it to their daughter, dammit.

At Christmas 1915 the evil Dr. Waite decided to see what he could do to hurry things along.

First, he took his mother-in-law for a drive in the rain with the windshield open (back in the day, windshields on some cars could be tilted open to enhance the wind-in-the-face experience). He was hoping for pneumonia. It didn't happen. Then he tried marmalade laced with ground glass. Nada. To help ease her irritated throat, he dosed her with

aerosol sprays of anthrax, influenza, strep, and other nasty bugs. Still nothing! One of them must have worked because she succumbed on January 30, 1916. Before anyone could examine the body, Waite claimed his mother-in-law's final request had been that her body be cremated.

It was.

Her husband came next and he proved to be even more intractable than his wife. The doctor took another crack at pneumonia with wet galoshes and soaked bed sheets when the old guy came for a visit. No good. Then Waite released chlorine gas in the guest bedroom. Nothing. He snuck some diphtheria germs into Mr. Peck's diet with no results. Typhoid, zip; influenza, zip; tuberculosis, zip.

In desperation, Waite finally gave his father-in-law a massive dose of the old poisoner's standby, arsenic, but even that did not achieve the desired result. In the end, he—a brilliant physician—was reduced to smothering the man with a pillow. Success at last!

The doctor was so overjoyed that he took his mistress out for a well-deserved night on the town where they were spotted by a woman he knew. Appalled at his unseemly behavior when he should have been in mourning, she fingered him to the cops in an anonymous letter.

> *Charles Gillem (aka J.P. Watson) cast himself as a turn-of-the-twentieth-century chick magnet. In assorted publications, he advertised his availability for matrimony… He didn't mention he was a serial killer.*

An examination of Mr. Peck's body turned up evidence of arsenic and the police were able to connect the poison to Waite. He spilled his guts and was sent to the chair at Sing Sing on May 24, 1917.

Wall Street Bombing

On September 16, 1920 a bomb went off near the intersection of Wall and Broad Streets, close to the J.P. Morgan Building and the U.S. Assay Office.

The explosives were probably hidden in a safe in a horse-drawn wagon. It blew up at noon when the area was jammed with the usual lunchtime crowd, blasting 500 pounds of shrapnel in all directions. Thirty-nine people were killed, about 40 wounded.

Immediately, the New York Stock Exchange was closed and key financial districts were shut down in other major cities. Armed guards patrolled the estates of J.P. Morgan, John Rockefeller, and the other princes of industry and robber barons. The assistant U.S. Treasurer called for troops to be stationed in the Wall Street area.

There was some suspicion the bomb might have been part of an aborted robbery. A large number of gold ingots had been transferred from the subtreasury to the Assay Office that day. Perhaps the wagon

had been delayed by traffic and the thieves had abandoned their plan. Political motivation was more likely. Earlier that day, someone had dropped papers containing strident radical statements in a nearby mailbox. One read:

> Remember we will not tolerate any longer.
>
> Free the political prisoners.
>
> Or it will be sure death for all of you.
>
> American Anarchist Fighters.

The bomber or bombers were never found, but two writers have fingered anarchist Mario Buda, aka Mike Boda. In his book, *Buda's Wagon: A Brief History of the Car Bomb* (2007), Mike Davis claims Buda was motivated by the arrest a few months before of **Sacco and Vanzetti**, and that he went back home to Italy after the bombing. Davis cites Paul Avrich's 1991 book *Sacco and Vanzetti: The Anarchist Background* as his source.

The parallels between the Wall Street bombing and **Timothy McVeigh**'s attack on the Oklahoma City Federal Building and the September 11 atrocities are easy to see.

Watson, J.P.

Charles Gillem cast himself as a turn-of-the-twentieth-century chick magnet. In assorted publications, he advertised his availability for matrimony. He described himself as neat, nicely mannered, and comfortably well-heeled with substantial savings and high-powered corporate connections.

He didn't mention he was a serial killer.

Born in Arkansas in 1870, he grew up with a possibly abusive stepfather after his biological dad abandoned the family. One source claims he was a hermaphrodite, with two sets of reproductive organs, male and female. If so, it still doesn't really explain anything.

Charles ran away and was on his own by age 12. He probably killed his first victim in 1893 when a girlfriend became inconveniently pregnant. It appears that for a time he limited his criminal activities to bigamy. He was living in St. Louis with his second wife in 1912 when he was indicted for fraudulent accounting. Charles flew the coop on his advertising business and fled to Canada where he rechristened himself J.P. Watson, and continued with his own form of serial polygamy.

At first, he simply abandoned the women he enticed into matrimony and moved on to British Columbia, to Winnipeg, to Calgary, shedding spouses along the way. All the time, he harbored violent thoughts and fantasies, but didn't act on them.

His first married victim was probably Marie Austin. He married her in Canada in 1918 and moved to Idaho. He crushed her skull with a rock and got rid of the body in a lake near Coeur D'Alene. A few months later he married again in Seattle, and they were still on their honeymoon when he killed her on impulse, or so he said later.

More wives and victims followed throughout the west, though some of them survived. Watson's murders seem to have been a result of rage and opportunity, not premeditation. At least one of the women was sexually mutilated.

Things went brilliantly for the multiple widower until 1920 when the current Mrs. Watson became suspicious of her hubby. Thinking he was two-timing her, she hired a private detective to look into his background.

A suitcase surfaced, filled with marriage licenses and diamond rings of different sizes. The cops arrested Watson, initially on bigamy charges. While he was in custody, an unidentified woman's body was dug up near Plum Station, Washington.

Fearing it might be one of his wives, Watson decided to cut a deal with the Los Angeles D.A. He agreed to a full confession of all his crimes and to show them where he'd buried one body in the immediate area, in return for a life sentence. He owned up to seven killings and 19 wives. But he admitted to a poor memory and others have guessed a more accurate figure may be 25 victims and 40 wives.

Whatever his real body count, Watson spent the rest of his life in San Quentin where he died in 1939. And, as it turned out, the woman they found at Plum Station was not a Mrs. Watson.

Weaver, Randy

What happened to the Weaver family was a tragedy in the classic sense. It was destroyed—some family members were killed—when the parents' dogmatic religious beliefs came into conflict with a dogmatic, bungling government that refused to admit its mistakes.

Randy and his wife Vicki Weaver were fundamentalist Christians with a strong anti-Semitic and racist streak. In 1984 they moved with their children to a remote part of the Idaho mountains to prepare for the end of the world and to have as little as possible to do with what they saw as the "Zionist Occupied Government." They lived in a hand-built cabin without electricity or running water, but with a lot of weapons.

Randy had some connections with the Aryan Nation's white supremacists, though he carefully calls himself a "white separatist." This association brought him to the attention of the Bureau of Alcohol, Tobacco, and Firearms. Agents paid him to saw off the barrels of two shotguns. They then attempted to use that trifling illegal act to force him to become an informant.

Randy refused, loudly, and retreated to his home. The government decided to ratchet up the pressure. In 1990 he was indicted on a federal firearms charge. (Weaver has always denied he shortened the guns to an illegal length.) The feds threatened to use the rap to take Weaver's land, thereby thoroughly solidifying his resolve to stay on it. After another confrontation with armed agents and a letter from the government giving him the wrong date for his trial, an arrest warrant was issued.

By this point, the Weavers and Kevin Harris, a young friend who lived with them, had decided to hole up on their property. The children—Sam, Rachel, Sara, and the baby Elisheba—were with them. They stayed there for more than a year until U.S. Marshals created a Special Operations Group (SOG) to deal with them.

At 2:30 a.m. in the morning of August 21, 1992, a heavily armed team of six SOG men moved onto Weaver's land for surveillance. Exactly what happened after sunrise is a matter of considerable dispute. Everyone agrees the Weavers' dogs started barking at the lawmen and they shot one of the dogs. Randy Weaver, 14-year-old Sam, and Kevin Harris armed themselves and went out to look around.

The government men claimed they identified themselves as U.S. Marshals and fired only in self-defense when they were spotted. Randy Weaver said they simply opened fire. In any case, Sam Weaver was shot in the back and killed, and Kevin Harris killed U.S. Marshal William Degan.

Everything escalated. More government forces came in and surrounded the Weaver house. Crowds gathered at the perimeter and angrily took the Weavers' side.

The next day, FBI sniper Lon Horiuchi set up a nest about 200 yards from the cabin. Late in the afternoon, Randy, his oldest daughter, and Kevin came out. As they headed for the shed where Sam's body had been placed, Horiuchi took his first shot and wounded Randy. The three ran back toward the house and Vicki opened the door for them.

Horiuchi's second shot hit Vicki in the head as she stood there holding her infant daughter. The bullet also wounded Harris.

The siege continued until August 31st. It ended with the help of Col. Bo Gritz, a retired Green Beret and political activist who was generally trusted by right wing extremists. He persuaded Randy Weaver to surrender before the feds attacked again.

Weaver and Harris were charged with murder and several other serious charges. At their trial, they were virtually exonerated. Weaver was found guilty of failure to appear in court on the weapons charge; Harris was innocent on all counts. Randy Weaver

then filed a wrongful death suit against the government and received more than $3 million.

A few of the feds were censured and suspended; nothing more. Idaho state officials indicted sniper Horiuchi on involuntary manslaughter charges. Those were dismissed in federal court. Later, Horiuchi was involved in the standoff with David Koresh and the Branch Davidians.

One film has been made for television, *The Siege at Ruby Ridge* (1996). It's more accurate than most, but the real cultural impact of the incident was more concrete.

The government actions against the Weavers became an early flashpoint in political reaction against what was generally referred to as the New World Order in the 1990s. **Timothy McVeigh** was particularly moved by what happened, and acted on his anger by blowing up the Alfred P. Murrah federal office building in Oklahoma City in 1995.

Webster, John White

If only his father had taught him more about money management, John White Webster argued, he would not have been forced to brain Dr. George Parkman with a chunk of wood and dismember the body. Even Harvard professors have gaps in their education.

In 1849 Webster taught chemistry at the Harvard Medical College. Apparently, he was not a very popular teacher. He'd had problems in private practice as a doctor, too, but he did enjoy hobnobbing with the Cambridge Brahmins. He also had four daughters who were about to make their debuts into high society, so he was experiencing something of a cash flow problem.

It was solved, for a moment, by a loan of several hundred dollars from Dr. George Parkman, a fellow Harvard man. But on November 23rd the doctor arrived at Webster's lab and pressed him for payment. The meeting did not go well. Apparently Webster had sold some materials that were to be held as collateral for the loan, and Parker got angry.

Webster responded by cracking his skull and killing him. He acted quickly to cover up the crime by slicing up the body and burning part of it in an assay furnace. But what to do with the rest?

Initially, no one doubted Webster when he claimed Parkman had met him that day and he had paid his debt. Quite possibly, the doctor had been set upon later by thieves who were after the cash.

Ephraim Littlefield, the Medical College janitor, didn't buy it. He knew the assay furnace was seldom used and it was exceptionally hot. Suspecting what had happened, he realized the only place Webster could have hidden the body was in the vault beneath his office privy. Yes, in those days before indoor plumbing, waste was handled that way. Littlefield took it upon himself to break through the vault wall. His excavation revealed parts of the missing doctor's lower body. Littlefield notified police who took a second look at the lab. They found more body parts in a tea chest and part of Parkman's dentures in the assay furnace.

A few weeks later, Webster's was the first "trial of the century" in New England. (**Lizzie Borden** would attract considerably more attention 42 years later.)

At first Webster claimed he was being framed by the custodian, but the circumstantial evidence was overwhelming and he was convicted. He confessed later, possibly hoping for clemency from the governor. It didn't work and he was hanged on August 30, 1850.

The crime and trial have been the subject of several books, both nonfiction and novels. Perhaps the best and certainly one of the most enjoyable is Helen Thomson's *Murder at Harvard* (1971). More recently, the Webster case was the basis for an episode of the PBS series *American Experience* in 2003 based on Simon Schama's book *Dead Certainties* (1991).

Weiss, Carl

Though Dr. Carl Weiss is known as the killer of Senator Huey Long, he certainly doesn't fit the pro-

file of a political assassin and, given the circumstances, it's easily possible he was innocent.

Weiss had been opposed to the popular Long when he was governor of Louisiana. The Kingfish, as he was called, had many enemies and in 1935, Weiss' father-in-law was about to lose his position as a judge. But would that have been enough to move a prominent physician to murder? After all, Weiss had a busy practice, and he was married with a three-month-old son.

On the night of September 8th the senator and his bodyguards were walking down a corridor in the State Capitol building. Weiss was waiting behind a pillar. The guards claimed later that as they passed, he stepped out and shot Long in the side. They immediately pulled their weapons and unloaded on the doctor. He was cut down by a reported 61 shots.

Long was spirited away to a hospital. Exactly how he got there and who drove him are somewhat unclear. Doctors operated on him and thought they had repaired the damage, but they missed a wound to an artery and Long died two days later.

Some have speculated Weiss was unarmed that evening. They say he struck Long, but that the fatal shot was fired by one of the guards. Considering the walls and floor of the corridor were made of marble and the guards' overreaction to Weiss' appearance was so excessive, it's not difficult to imagine the senator was hit by a ricochet or a poorly aimed shot. If it were the case, someone might also have provided the .32 caliber automatic said to be Weiss' weapon. The caliber of the bullet that killed the Kingfish was never determined; his widow refused to allow an autopsy.

Though Long was a major political figure in his time, his fictional incarnation is perhaps more well known today. In *All the King's Men* (1946), Robert Penn Warren based his Willie Stark on Long. Dr. Weiss becomes Dr. Adam Stanton, and the messy unknowable details of historic truth are transformed into a tidy conclusion to one of the great American novels.

West Memphis Three

In 1993 in West Memphis, Arkansas, three 8-year-old boys were killed. Christopher Byers, Steve Branch, and Michael Moore were beaten and tied up. Branch and Moore died by drowning. Byers was beaten more severely and castrated. Their bodies were found on May 6th in a drainage ditch in a wooded area near a truck stop. They had been missing since the night before.

Police handled the evidence and the crime scene so ineptly that almost nothing else can be said with certainty about the crimes themselves: not the time, not the weapon, not even the exact location. Given the lack of blood at the scene, it's likely the boys were killed somewhere else and dumped there.

Police quickly settled on 18-year-old Damian Echols as the primary suspect. The reason seems to have been that he favored a dark "goth" look and had an aloof demeanor. Neither sat well with the conservative religious community. Echols also had an unsettled family life and minor brushes with the law, but nothing serious. Based on these "facts"—and absolutely no physical evidence—the police came to believe the murders had something to do with a Satanic cult.

About a month later, the cops brought in 16-year-old Jessie Misskelley for questioning. They claim they read him his Miranda rights, but since he was a minor, they needed a written waiver from his parents. They did not get one. Jessie was questioned for 12 hours without a lawyer. Less than one hour was recorded. During this time, he confessed, though he got important details wrong or changed them. Misskelley, who had an IQ of 72, immediately retracted his statement. Even so, he, Echols, and Jason Baldwin, age 16, were charged with murder.

That might have been the end of the story but it attracted the attention of documentary filmmakers Joe Berlinger and Bruce Sinofsky. They had just made the well-regarded *Brother's Keeper* about an old man in central New York who was wrongly charged with murder.

As the boys went to trial, Berlinger and Sinofsky began interviewing various interested parties and following the proceedings. The end result is the excellent but flawed film, *Paradise Lost: The Child Murders at Robin Hood Hills*, that became a surprise hit on home video, HBO, and DVD. It creates a compelling portrait of West Memphis as a place of interstate highways and trailer courts, Bible-thumping religion, fear of the occult, and TV newspeople who reduce every human emotion to a brainless soundbite.

That part of the story is also a heavy-handed indictment of Southern society. Virtually everyone connected with the crimes comes from generations of broken families. They're crude, vindictive, and fearful. Their lives are a numbing succession of cigarettes, soft drinks, and bad teeth (probably the most eloquent plea for dental hygiene ever put on film).

The three teens are shown as essentially shy outsiders who liked heavy metal music and favored black clothes, while the victims' families are presented as hysterical rednecks. And at least one of those family members may not be so innocent.

When the focus shifts to the trial, the case doesn't involve reasonable doubt; it involves a mountain of doubts. The police admit they totally botched a key part of the investigation that occurred immediately after the murders. It took them months to come up with the central piece of physical evidence, and they ignored another suspect who was brought to their attention before the bodies were found. At every turn, serious questions are raised, and the prosecutors either cannot answer them or choose not to.

It wasn't enough to sway the jury, though. The boys were found guilty in January 1994. Misskelley and Baldwin were sentenced to life in prison; Echols got death but remains in prison.

In 2000 Sinofsky and Berlinger made a sequel, *Paradise Lost 2—Revelations*, casting even more serious doubts on the convictions. So have the books *Devil's Knot* (2003) by Mara Leveritt and *Blood of Innocents* (1995) by Guy Reel.

Several bands, musicians, and artists have taken up the cause of the West Memphis Three, raising money for their defense funds. The appeals process is being actively pursued, along with new tests of DNA evidence. In 2007 lawyers filed new evidence based on analysis of a hair found in the shoelace that bound one of the boys. The West Memphis Three Support Group operates a website (www. wm3.org) on their behalf.

White, Dan

"The Twinkie Defense" is commonly misunderstood to refer to a legal strategy claiming a crime was committed because the perp was under the powerful influence of too much sugar or caffeine or cold medication, whatever. In short, it's a last gasp effort by the scoundrel to avoid punishment.

It was created by Dan White's lawyers and they had something else in mind.

In 1978 White, a former policeman and fireman, had been elected as a San Francisco supervisor. He was a law-and-order guy, openly homophobic. Harvey Milk, also a supervisor, was openly gay—the first openly gay man to be elected to public office in the city. The two disagreed, particularly on gay rights legislation.

White found it impossible for he and his wife to live on the $9,600 part-time salary, and so he resigned. Pressured by constituents, he changed his mind and asked Mayor George Moscone to reinstate him. The mayor declined.

On the night of November 27th, White returned to City Hall. He didn't use the front door where he would have had to pass through a metal detector. Instead, he crawled through a basement window and made his way to Moscone's office. Again, he asked to be reappointed. When Moscone refused, White shot him five times. After reloading his .38, White went to Harvey Milk's office and shot him, too.

White surrendered and immediately confessed. At the trial, his attorneys used the videotaped confession to argue White was not fully responsible for

Murder suspect Dan White, undated. (AP)

his actions. They claimed White's consumption of Twinkies and other junk food was evidence of his depression, not a cause of it. (Previously, White had been an advocate of health food.)

The jury bought it. They convicted White of voluntary manslaughter, not premeditated murder. The San Francisco gay community was justifiably outraged and mass demonstrations turned violent. Cops reacted by moving into the Castro District and cracking heads. More than 160 people were hospitalized in what were called the "White Night Riots."

White was paroled in 1983, but his life was in ruins. His marriage fell apart and he committed suicide on October 21, 1985 by starting the car in the closed garage.

The murders are an important milestone in the political struggle for gay rights. They are the subject of two films, the 1985 Oscar-winning documentary *The Times of Harvey Milk*, and *Execution of Justice* (1999), a made-for-cable feature.

Whitman, Charles

On August 1, 1966 about two weeks after Richard Speck had slaughtered eight nurses in Chicago, Charles Whitman barricaded himself on the observation deck of the Texas Tower and set about to kill as many people as he could. Along with the recent assassination of John Kennedy, these acts of savagery ushered in a new kind of random, pointless violence.

Unlike Speck—a drunken, drug-addled jailbird—Whitman was the archetypal All-American boy. Blond, handsome, Eagle Scout, wealthy family, Marine, pretty wife. But beneath the clichés, Whitman's life was tortured.

He grew up in Lake Worth, Florida where his father, C.A., had turned a plumbing business into a small fortune. While C.A. Whitman gave his wife Margaret and three sons all of the material things they could want, he was also quick with his fists and beat his wife and kids whenever he got mad. C.A. got mad a lot.

Charles enlisted in the Marines as soon as he turned 18, right after a particularly violent bout with the old man. His military career began splendidly at Guantanamo Naval Base in Cuba. Young Whitman scored 215 out of a possible 250 on the sharpshooter's test. He was particularly adept at long distances and moving targets. Overall, Whitman did so well he earned a spot in the Naval Enlisted Science Education Project. In the program, the Marines would pay for a college education—tuition, books, and $250 a month. After graduation, Whitman would go on to Officer Candidate School.

Whitman enrolled at the University of Texas at Austin in September 1961 and everything fell apart. He got into trouble over gambling and poaching deer, and his grades were poor. He married his girlfriend Kathy Leissner about a year later and things

briefly improved, but not enough. The Marines revoked his scholarship and he was returned to active duty early in 1963.

Stationed at Camp Lejeune, North Carolina while Kathy stayed in Texas, Whitman was desperately unhappy and got into more trouble. In November, he was court-martialed for gambling and other matters. Found guilty, he was given hard labor and demoted. By then Whitman was so dissatisfied with the military that he was reduced to the humiliation of asking for his father's help. Strings were pulled and he received an honorable discharge in December 1964.

Determined to make a fresh start, Whitman reenrolled at the University of Texas with a new major. He worked as a bank teller and found time to volunteer with the Boy Scouts as a scoutmaster. By then, Kathy had graduated and was working as a high school teacher. Her earning more than he did was one source of irritation according to the journals he kept. Generally, his life and marriage were unhappy. Kathy urged him to look for help, and eventually he did, but not before he had lashed out physically at her, just like his father.

By the spring of 1966 his mother Margaret had had enough of C.A.'s abuse. Despite C.A.'s strong objections, she filed for divorce and moved from Florida to Austin. Whitman was caught between his parents as his father hectored him to persuade his mother to return.

Within Whitman, the violent urges increased. He saw a psychiatrist, Dr. Maurice Dean Heatly, at the university health center, and talked about his overwhelming anger. He said he had fantasized about shooting people from the tower. Then he admitted he'd been thinking those thoughts for a long time and had never done anything. Dr. Heatly didn't take him seriously and told him to come back the following week. Whitman didn't.

Instead, Whitman worked on a heavy schedule of classes and another job as a research assistant. He used Dexedrine to stay up at night and listened to his father talk about his mother.

When it all finally became too much and he surrendered to his demons, Whitman did not snap into uncontrollable rage. He laid out his plans logically and methodically, and took time to note exactly what he was doing in his journals.

On July 31st he bought binoculars and a Bowie knife. He picked up his wife who was working for the summer as a telephone operator. They took in a movie and a late lunch with his mother. They saw some friends before Whitman took Kathy back for the evening shift at 6:00 p.m. He went home and started typing a note to explain what he was planning. He stopped writing when other friends dropped by, then picked up Kathy at 9:30 p.m.

Back home, Whitman called his mother to see if they could come over and cool off from the oppressive 90-degree-plus heat in her air conditioning for a while. Kathy decided to turn in early and Whitman went by himself, around midnight.

His mother met him in the lobby of her building. They went up to her apartment where Whitman strangled, beat, and stabbed her to death. He left a note on her door for the houseman asking not to be disturbed. Around 2:00 a.m. he went home and stabbed his sleeping wife fives times in the chest.

He continued his letter of explanation in longhand. He then made preparations for the day to come. He pulled out his old Marine footlocker and loaded it with supplies: two hunting rifles (one with a scope), three pistols, three gallons of water, transistor radio, gasoline, compass, notebook, pen, hatchet, hammer, flashlight, batteries, knifes, cigarette lighter, alarm clock, pipe wrench, matches, extension cord, gloves, ear plugs, glasses and case, clothes line, wire, sandwiches, Spam, Salted peanuts, raisins, fruit cocktail, toilet paper, and Mennen deodorant spray. He also called Kathy's supervisor and said she wouldn't be in that day.

Around 7:00 a.m., he drove out and rented a dolly to move the heavy footlocker, cashed some checks, and bought more ammunition and weapons—an M-1 carbine and 12-gauge shotgun. At home, he sawed off the shotgun barrel and stock,

Charles Whitman, age 24, not long before his meltdown and massacre at the University of Texas, 1966. (AP Photo)

put on blue coveralls and loaded up the car. At 11:30 a.m. he checked in with campus security and got a loading zone parking permit. A few minutes later, he was moving his stuff into the tower elevator. The final note he'd written said: "I never could quite make it. These thoughts are too much for me."

On the 28th floor observation deck, he clubbed the receptionist with the butt of a rifle and hid her behind a couch. Edna Townsley was still alive then, but died a few hours later. Two people came down from the deck. Whitman let them leave then blocked the door to the reception area with a desk. Within minutes, more would-be sightseers arrived. Two boys pushed the door open. Whitman leveled the sawed-off at them and killed one. As the others fled, he chased them into a stairway and continued

Smoke from Whitman's sniper rifle as he shot victims from the University of Texas tower in 1966. (AP Photo)

to fire, killing a woman and wounding two others. Word that something was happening spread across the campus as Whitman unpacked his footlocker.

Then he settled in to do what he'd come to do. From the 307-foot tower, the sharpshooter had a wide field of fire (for comparison, the Washington Monument is 555 feet). Whitman could cover a large portion of the campus and a heavily traveled street that bordered it. His victims included an 18-year-old pregnant girl (she lived, her baby did not), professors, students, police officers. One man was more than 500 yards away. Over the next hour and a half, Whitman shot 46 people and killed 14. Given the design of the parapet, he had excellent cover and the police couldn't tell how many people were in the tower. City and campus cops returned fire. So did armed citizens.

In the end five men, police officers Ramiro Martinez, W.A. Cowan, Jerry Day, Houston McCoy, and civilian Allen Crum made their way up to the tower and into the reception area. Avoiding gunfire still coming from the ground, they flanked Whitman. Officers Martinez, with a service revolver, and McCoy, with a shotgun, managed to get close enough to take aim. Both shot and Whitman was killed.

In his final letter, Whitman asked that an autopsy be performed on his body to determine if there were any physical causes for his uncontrollable anger. Doctors did find a small tumor in his brain and when it was announced in 1966, many people wanted to believe it explained what Whitman had done. But even then, they knew it didn't; there is no single, simple explanation—as we have seen in the years since in the all-too-numerous cases when malcontented postal/factory/office workers arm themselves and take their anger out on anyone within range.

Whitman's case was one of the first in the modern era. It served as the basis for Peter Bogdanovich's excellent 1968 debut, *Targets*. In the film, Bobby Thompson kills his wife and mother and then picks off random victims with a hunting rifle.

At the same time, aging actor Byron Orlok (Boris Karloff in his last major role) is in town promoting a cheap horror film. When the two finally meet at a drive-in theater, old-fashioned movie horror pales in the face of the new real horror of a madman with a rifle. It's an inspired ending. The film was produced by Roger Corman's company and was seen by many viewers during its initial release at a drive-in. So when Bobby shoots at patrons in their cars, the violence has a double meaning. That confluence of popular art and reality continues at the film's conclusion when Bobby is confronted by both the real Orlok in person and the image of Orlok on screen. It's an inspired screen moment that questions the meaning and place of "classic" horror in a world where "real" horror reaches so easily into everyday reality.

Wilder, Christopher

Christopher Wilder began his killing career in the **Ted Bundy** mold and ended it with a rolling rampage from the **Charlie Starkweather** playbook. In both modes, he conformed to all of the public's preconceptions about charismatic serial killers—a smooth-talking, outwardly normal guy who can charm beautiful women before he attacks them.

Wilder was connected with the disappearance or murder of eight women in 1984. He was charged with and convicted of sexual offenses involving several others. His killings in America may have begun as early as the late 1960s; no one will ever know exactly how many women he killed.

He was born in 1945 to an Australian woman and an American naval officer. The family was wealthy. There is some evidence of early health problems involving convulsions or a seizure. As a teenager, he was involved in a gang rape and was sentenced to psychiatric care involving electroshock therapy.

In 1969, he moved to America and adopted a playboy lifestyle in Florida—bachelor pad, sports cars, the works. He also became a photographer and used his studio to entice women into posing for him. Those sessions sometimes ended in forced sex. The sex sometimes led to charges and convictions, fines, a little jail time, and more psychiatric counseling.

On a visit to Australia in 1982, Wilder was accused of kidnapping two teenaged girls and forcing them to pose for pornographic pictures. His family came up with $350,000 bail and got him out of the country before the trial.

Back in Florida in 1984 Wilder lost what little control he had over his compulsions to kidnap and enslave women. It began in February when Rosario Gonzales disappeared from the Miami Grand Prix where Wilder raced a car. Two months later, teacher Elizabeth Kenyon disappeared from Coral Gables. A private detective found a connection between Wilder and Kenyon, and Wilder became a suspect in the police investigation.

Swearing he wouldn't let himself be taken alive, Wilder bought a 1973 Chrysler New Yorker, a massive land yacht, and put his dogs in a kennel. He withdrew a big wad of cash from his bank account, stole his business partner's credit card, and hit the road.

Wilder's MO was to approach an attractive young woman in a public place, often a shopping mall, and ask her if she would model for him. If he could get her to go to his car, he'd threaten her with a pistol. He'd then take her to a remote lonely spot or motel room where he would either sexually abuse, rape, or murder her. During his final orgy of indulgence, Wilder's personality was disintegrating.

He killed one woman in Indian Harbor, Florida; then kidnapped a Florida State University student in Tallahassee. He drove the FSU student to a hovel in Georgia where he tortured and raped her repeatedly, and even glued her eyes shut. But when she yelled and fought back and banged on the walls, he ran. She survived.

A few days later, Wilder killed a woman in Beaumont, Texas, then others in Oklahoma City, Grand Junction, Colorado and Las Vegas. By then, the FBI realized what he was doing and on April 3, 1984 Wilder hit the Ten Most Wanted list.

The next day, Wilder kidnapped 16-year-old Tina Marie Risico in Torrance, California. He went east, staying in motels where he raped her and managed to enlist her cooperation and assistance in finding more victims. She helped him grab another teenaged girl in Gary, Indiana. For two days, he raped and tortured the second victim. When he tried to kill her outside Rochester, New York, she pretended to be dead and survived.

Wilder and Risico kidnapped one more woman in upstate New York. Wilder shot her in the back and then took Risico to Logan Airport in Boston. He gave her money for a plane ticket to California and cab fare.

On April 13th, a Friday, he tried to kidnap one more girl but she realized something was wrong after she got in his car and jumped out when she had a chance. Later that day, Wilder was stopped at a gas station in Colebrook, New Hampshire when he was spotted by two state troopers, Wayne Fortier and Leo Jellison. As they approached his car, Wilder reached for a .357 in the glove compartment. Jellico jumped him and the magnum went off twice. One bullet went through Wilder and hit Jellico. The second went straight into Wilder's heart and killed him.

Wilder has been the subject of one book-length study, Bruce Gidney's *The Beauty Queen Killer* (1984), and he was mentioned on the History Channel's *History's Mysteries: Infamous Murders* (2001). Tina Marie Risico's experiences provided the basis for the hard-to-find 1986 TV film *Easy Prey*, starring Shawnee Smith as Tina Marie and Gerald McRaney as Wilder. Though his methods and choice of victims have been fodder for countless movies, good and bad, Wilder's crimes have not "inspired" any cinematic retelling.

Williams, Wayne

Did Wayne Williams murder more than 20 black children in Atlanta?

A jury said yes, based on blood, hair, and fiber evidence and eyewitnesses. Conspiracy theorists suggest racial motivation and Ku Klux Klan involvement. Williams maintains his innocence.

The victims ranged in age from 7 to 27. Most were boys and young men. Many were asphyxiated but blunt force trauma, gunshots, and strangulation were also listed. In some cases, the cause of death could not be determined. The killings "officially" began in July 1979. By autumn, four young men had been murdered. A pattern was emerging and national attention was being focused on Atlanta.

The killings resumed in March 1980 and the pace accelerated. Every two weeks or so, another child would disappear, another body would be discovered. Elected officials pointed fingers. Law enforcement agencies squabbled. Celebrities donated money.

In the end, the case was broken by conventional police work. Since victims had been turning up in

bodies of water, cops were stationed near key bridges at night. On May 22, 1981 a rookie under a bridge on the Chattahoochee River heard a splash and the sound of a car engine. He alerted officers on the bridge and they stopped a car driven by Wayne Williams. Two days later, they pulled a body out of the river.

Williams was arrested in June and charged with only two of the more recent killings.

Proving motivation was tough for the prosecution. They painted Williams as bright, spoiled, gay, and somewhat immature. At 23, the dropout still lived with his parents. He was a kind of police groupie and billed himself as a music promoter who was particularly interested in interviewing and helping young hopefuls. He held other black people in contempt and sometimes used harsh bigoted language to describe them.

The strongest part of the case was the physical evidence—hair, fibers, and blood evidence linking Williams to the victims. In February 1982 a jury of nine women and three men, eight black and four white, found him guilty and he was sentenced to two life terms.

In May 2005 the DeKalb County Police Chief reopened the cases of four boys killed in Atlanta. Williams remains in prison and killings fitting his alleged pattern ceased after his arrest.

Several books have been written about the murders, many supporting Williams' innocence. So does the 1985 TV miniseries *The Atlanta Child Murders* written by Abby Mann. Williams has also been the subject of several television and video documentaries, most notably *Serial Killers: Profiling the Criminal Mind* (1999).

Wuornos, Aileen

"I'm one who seriously hates human life and would kill again." That's what Aileen Wuornos told the Florida Supreme Court and she wasn't lying.

The woman who was wrongly dubbed "America's first female serial killer" by the electronic and print media really did despise people. As bitter and crazy as she was, it's still hard not to feel a small degree of empathy with her. From the very beginning, Aileen Wuornos was dealt a bad hand.

Her teenaged parents divorced before she was born. Dad was a psycho child molester who died in prison; mom abandoned Aileen and her older brother Keith when they were kids. They were adopted by maternal grandparents, the ineffectual grandmother Britta and the drunken granddad Lauri. At age six, while she and Keith were setting fires with lighter fluid, Aileen was burned and her face was painfully scarred. Even so, Aileen, called Lee, started screwing around early and had a son at age 14. Lucky for him, she put him up for adoption.

In the next few years, Britta died of liver failure, Keith with throat cancer, Lauri by suicide.

Aileen hit the road, hitching and hooking, boozing and doping. Under numerous aliases, she was often arrested for everything from forgery to car theft. One suicide attempt, one quickie marriage that was annulled.

The only lasting relationship she had began in 1986 when she met Tyria Moore at a gay bar in Daytona, Florida. They managed to get by on the money Aileen made turning tricks at truck stops, moving from one fleabag motel to another for three years. All the while, Lee's anger at the world grew.

In December 1989 she met a kindred spirit in Richard Mallory. He too was a misanthropic boozer with a taste for commercial sex. He and Lee went for a ride in his Caddy. She put three .22 slugs in his chest, wrapped the body in a carpet runner, and dumped it off a dirt road. (Later she would claim Mallory raped her, but there's no evidence and Lee claimed she had been assaulted whenever it suited her purposes.)

Her next victim was David Spears. Then Charles Carskaddon, Peter Siems, Eugene Burress, Dick Humphreys, and Walter Gino Antonio. The MO was virtually identical for all of them. Killed with a .22, body dropped in one location, car stolen and abandoned in another location. One of the cops' big

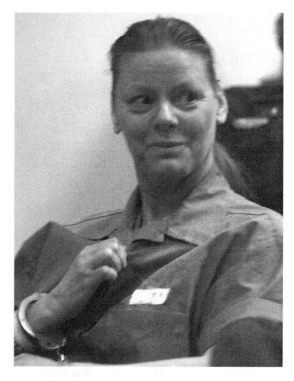

Aileen Wuornos at a 2001 arraignment. (AP Photo)

breaks came when Aileen and Ty wrecked Peter Siems' car. They were drinking and arguing when they ran off the road, and Lee left a bloody palm print on the trunk. Witnesses described the two quarrelsome women.

When police realized the Florida murders were connected and a woman was involved, they were led to Lee's false identities. She pawned a camera and radar detector stolen from Mallory, and Florida law required her to leave a thumbprint on the receipt. The data was sent to the National Crime Information Center and the name Aileen Carol Wuornos was revealed.

Cops began their search for her in early 1991 at the rough joints she was known to frequent. They nabbed her at the Last Resort, a biker bar. By then Ty had split and moved in with her sister, which is where prosecutors found her. Ty had to admit she'd

Nick Broomfield's *Aileen* documentary screening, 2004. (AP Photo)

been aware of what Lee was doing but claimed she didn't want to know any of the details. Despite her don't-ask-don't-tell defense, the authorities persuaded her to help. Ty called Lee in jail and agreed to let the cops record the calls—they got the confession they were looking for.

Lee maintained all the murders had been self-defense. All the men, she said, had threatened to beat or rape her. Over the course of her trials, her statements became more self-serving, and she became more unstable.

After the first guilty verdict Wuornos screamed at the jury, calling them "scumbags of America"— the day before the same jury would decide her penalty. In the end, she received six death sentences.

By then, of course, the media storm was at full force. She and her lawyers signed a movie deal. Arlene Prall, a self-described born-again Christian, said Jesus had told her to contact Aileen. After they met, Prall became an ardent spokesperson for Lee on TV talk shows. Eventually, she and her husband even adopted the multiple murderess. At the same time, some of the detectives who had worked on the case hired a lawyer to handle their potential deals with Hollywood.

Wuornos fired her attorneys and was executed by lethal injection on October 9, 2002 at the Florida State Prison.

Nick Broomfield—who immortalized Heidi Fleiss on celluloid—made two documentaries about Lee, *Aileen Wuornos: The Selling of a Serial Killer* (1992) and

Aileen: Life and Death of a Serial Killer (2003). Though the films are flawed by his repeated efforts to portray the murders as self-defense, they provide a frighteningly vivid portrait of a deeply troubled woman and a political-judicial system that finds her useful.

The Aileen Wuornos most people know, however, comes from the film *Monster* (2003). Glamour babe Charlize Theron tried to prove she was a Serious Actress when she packed on the pounds, spackled on ugly makeup, and stuck nasty false teeth in her mouth. It worked. She won an Academy Award. The film is more accurate than most based-on-a-true-story confections. Surely the producers knew what they were doing when they cast Scott Wilson as Aileen's final victim. He also played **Dick Hickock** in *In Cold Blood* (1967).

Younger Brothers
(Cole, Bob, Jim, and John)

Despite their undeniable success as bank-robbing desperados, the Younger brothers will always be known as sidekicks to the more charismatic **Jesse James.**

The three older brothers—Cole, Jim, and John—met Frank and Jesse when they rode with Quantrill's Raiders in Missouri during the Civil War. Like the Jameses, the Youngers were Southern sympathizers and active participants in the brutal guerrilla war fought in the west. They took part in the killings of unarmed citizens and soldiers that would be considered war crimes or atrocities today, but such acts were all too common on both sides of the bitter struggle.

After the war, political wounds healed slowly, and when the James-Younger gang was formed with brother Bob to rob banks and trains, the crimes were rationalized as part of the struggle against Northern industrialism.

It's uncertain exactly which brothers were involved in which robberies, but by 1868 Cole had been part of a bank job in Russellville, Kentucky, and was considered one of the gang's leaders.

In 1874 John was killed and Jim was wounded in an encounter with Pinkerton detectives. Jim

escaped and returned to the gang. Two years later, the three remaining brothers took the worst of it when the gang made its ill-fated attempt to rob a Northfield, Minnesota bank.

Jesse and Bob were inside the bank, trying to deal with stubborn employees who refused to open the safe. Cole and Jim were lookouts on the street when the townspeople realized what was happening and fought back. They opened fire on the outlaws who were not accustomed to any resistance. It was often enough for them simply to yell "Get inside!" to keep people at bay while they rode away with the loot. Not in Minnesota.

Jesse wounded one cashier and killed another, and as they were all trying to escape, the Youngers were seriously wounded. Cole was hit in the shoulder. Bob's horse was shot out from under him and his elbow was shattered by a bullet. A good part of Jim's jaw was blown away.

The battered outlaws managed to get out of town and regroup briefly before they split up. The Youngers took off on their own and were trapped and captured after another shootout a couple of weeks later.

All three were sentenced to life. Bob became a model inmate. He studied medicine and died of tuberculosis in prison in 1889.

Cole and Jim were paroled in 1901. Jim committed suicide a year later. Cole was pardoned in 1903. For a time, he and Frank James toured with a Wild West show. Later Cole became a traveling preacher warning against the temptations of a life of crime.

On film, the Youngers show up in support in most of the Jesse James films. They are most prominent in *The Long Riders* (1980) and *The Great Northfield, Minnesota Raid* (1972). Cole took the lead in the rarely seen *Cole Younger, Gunfighter* (1958).

Yousef, Ramzi

As terrorist bombers go, Ramzi Yousef was a fairly ineffectual klutz. His 1993 attack on the World Trade Center actually killed far fewer people than

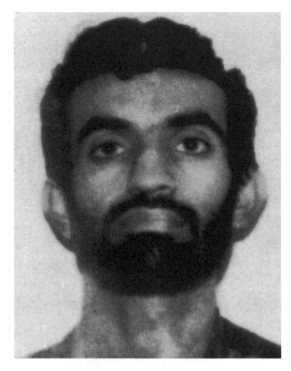

Ramzi Yousef, suspected mastermind of the February 1993 World Trade Center bombing, precursor to the events of September 11, 2001. (AP Photo/File)

the 1920 Wall Street bomb that claimed 30 lives. Yousef did, however, point the way to the future.

He was probably born in Pakistan, son of a Pakistani father and a Palestinian mother, raised in Kuwait and educated in Wales. In the 1980s he became a radical Islamist and joined al-Qaeda where he became a bomb designer (his uncle, Khalid Shaikh Mohammed, was once **Osama bin Laden**'s right-hand man). Yousef came to America, claiming political asylum, in September 1992 and immediately set to work. He met with the butt-ugly blind Sheikh Omar Abdel Rahman, who had been urging his followers to kill Jews and anyone else who disagreed with his nutball ideas.

Working with Mohammed Salameh, a dim-witted Jordanian, and other coconspirators, Yousef plotted to blow up the World Trade Center with an improvised explosive device. It was a 1,200 lb. bomb made of nitroglycerine, ammonium nitrate, hydrogen tanks, and sodium cyanide. The idea was to place the bomb at the southern corner of the parking garage beneath the towers so when it detonated, one tower would collapse into the other. They hoped to kill as many as a quarter of a million people, a number that, in Yousef's mind at least, equaled the suffering of the Palestinians.

While they were still in the planning stages, Yousef and Salameh—who had failed his driver's test four times—were involved in three traffic accidents. One was so serious Yousef was hospitalized. He actually checked on some of the bombmaking materials from his sick bed.

By February 26, 1993 they had assembled the explosive ingredients and had rented a Ryder van in New Jersey. On that snowy morning, the van and two cars drove to New York. Around noon, they parked the van under the towers, lit four fuses, and hightailed it out of the garage.

The device went off a few moments later. It killed six people, injured more than a thousand, and was felt blocks away. It blasted through six stories, all the way down to the PATH train station, and created a 200-foot-wide crater. But the building remained standing.

Yousef caught the next flight out and scampered back to Pakistan.

Miraculously, the first FBI team to investigate the bomb found a piece of the van's differential housing with the VIN (vehicle identification number). It was immediately traced to Ryder and to the specific rental agency. When Salameh went there and tried to get his $400 deposit back, claiming the van had been stolen, they were waiting for him. (He needed the money to buy his own plane ticket out of the country.)

Yousef plotted bombings in other parts of the world and figured out a way to smuggle small amounts of nitroglycerine onto airlines. A test run of his technique killed a Japanese passenger on a flight to the Philippines.

The American government put a $2 million-bounty on Yousef's head and, in 1995, it paid off. A fellow radical who was wasn't quite so committed ratted Yousef out. He was in Islamabad, Pakistan. The feds managed to cobble together a team of in-country agents who worked for the FBI, the DEA, and the State Department's Bureau of Diplomatic Security. They snatched Yousef from a motel and spirited him out of the country and back to America.

On September 6, 1995 he was sentenced to life without parole and will spend the rest of his miserable days at the Supermax prison in Florence, Colorado. Salameh got a 240-year stretch in the Lewisburg, Pennsylvania federal facility.

A reflecting pool was built at the Towers to honor those who died in Yousef's attack. It was destroyed in the 9/11 atrocity.

Zangara, Joseph

There are two theories about Joseph Zangara's 1933 assassination attempt on then President-elect Franklin Roosevelt in Miami.

The first, for which there is zero evidence, posits Zangara was under the control of Chicago gangsters, and his real target was the other passenger in Roosevelt's Buick, Chicago mayor Anton Cermak. Cermak, you see, wanted to get rid of the Capone mob and replace them with his own gangsters. Given that Cermak's nickname was "Ten Percent Tony," for his standard cut of kickbacks and payoffs, he might well have been in competition with Big Al. And, as he was dying, Cermak claimed he was the victim of a mob hit.

The second theory holds that Zangara was an ill-tempered little radical with a $4 pistol and what he hoped was going to be an easy target.

Joseph, born Giuseppe in Italy, had a long history of hatred for authority figures. It began with his father and then was transferred to King Victor Emmanuel III, Calvin Coolidge, Herbert Hoover, and finally Roosevelt.

Zangara had knocked around New Jersey and California before settling in Miami in 1926. As the

Depression worsened, Zangara's resentment simmered and finally bubbled over. When he learned Roosevelt was coming to town, he bought his pistol.

Fortunately, the diminutive shooter (he barely topped five feet in heels) had not counted on the massive crowd who had gathered to hear Roosevelt's short speech. He hadn't counted on the President-elect's polio, either. Because he could not stand easily, Roosevelt made his speech from the backseat of his convertible.

Zangara tried to force his way through the throng, but realized he wouldn't be able to reach the car. Instead, he attempted to stand on a rickety wooden chair, and blazed away while screaming, "There are too many people starving to death!" A quick witted woman in front of him struck his gun hand with her purse. Still, Zangara managed to wound five people, one of them mortally. That was Cermak who was hit in the stomach. As the car sped to the hospital, Roosevelt held Cermak and tried to comfort him.

Throughout the incident, Roosevelt never flinched or showed any sign of fear. His cool composure under fire underscored his image as a strong, steady commander. Zangara's attempt to get rid of a leader only made him more popular.

When Cermak died three weeks later, Zangara was charged with murder.

Zangara was tried and sentenced to death and sent to Raiford Prison where on March 21, a mere five weeks after the shooting, he was led to the electric chair. His last defiant words were, "Lousy capitalists! Goodbye, *addio* to the world. Go ahead, push the button."

They did.

In the pantheon of presidential assassins, Zangara ranks fairly low, somewhere above Squeaky Fromme who botched her shot at Gerald Ford, but well below Booth, Oswald, and the others who accomplished what they set out to do. Like them, he is a character in Stephen Sondheim's musical *Assassins* (1990).

Zodiac victims Paul Stine, Cecilia Shepard, and Bryan Hartnell, from 1968–69. (AP Photo)

Zodiac Killings

They are America's most famous unsolved murders. And the most frustrating—it's difficult to say anything definitive about them.

The man who called himself Zodiac in 1969 may have begun killing with Cheri Jo Bates in 1966. She was a student at Riverside Community College in California. One night while she was studying in the library, he removed the distributor cap from her car. When she was ready to go home and it wouldn't start, he offered help. Instead, he dragged her behind some bushes and savagely murdered her with a knife.

Later he wrote letters to local newspapers claiming he would kill again. Those were the first of 21 letters credited to the killer who dubbed himself "Zodiac" and used the symbol of a cross and circle in a gunsight arrangement.

In December 1968 near Vallejo, Betty Lou Jensen and David Faraday were shot dead on a lover's lane.

The weapon used was a .22 pistol. The next July, Darlene Ferrin and Michael Margeau were attacked while they were parked. This time, the weapon was a 9mm. Margeau survived. Right after the attack, Vallejo police received an anonymous call sending them to the crime scene and taking credit for the earlier shootings.

More letters were sent to Bay Area newspapers giving details only the killer could know. Three of them contained a cryptographic code, and the killer demanded it be published. It was and the code was solved by a high school teacher, though nothing of any importance was learned. The letters, filled with misspellings, claimed Zodiac was killing to collect slaves who would serve him after death.

Two months later, he attacked again. Bryan Hartnell and Cecilia Shepard were picnicking when a man wearing a hood threatened them with a pistol, tied them up, and stabbed them. Before she died, Shepard provided a description including a zodiac symbol on his chest. Hartnell survived.

Zodiac notes and symbols, as viewed by Robert Graysmith, in 2007. (AP Photo)

Zodiac wrote the dates of his crimes on the door of Hartnell's car.

A few weeks later, Zodiac shot cabbie Paul Stine and sent a piece of his bloody shirt in more letters to the *San Francisco Examiner* and other newspapers. In March 1970 a man who may have been Zodiac attempted to abduct a woman and her young daughter. He disabled her car and persuaded her to get into his, but she and her little girl escaped. Afterward, she identified her attacker as Zodiac based on the police sketch of a wanted poster.

Letters, claiming as many as 37 victims, continued to arrive until 1978. It is impossible to say exactly what Zodiac did, how many people he killed, or how much of his correspondence was sheer fantasy.

Because of the lack of concrete information, competing theories abound, and within the community of Zodiac aficionados there is rampant disagreement. Some finger Arthur Leigh Allen, a teacher who died in 1992 and was a suspect. Others put the blame on a radio engineer. The most popular books on the subject are *This Is the Zodiac Speaking* (2001), by Michael Kelleher and David Van Nuys, and *Zodiac* (2002) by Robert Graysmith.

On film, Zodiac provided the inspiration for Andrew Robinson's unforgettable villain in *Dirty Harry* (1971). *The Limbic Region* (1996) and *The Zodiac Killer* (1971) are the most straightforward cinematic fictions. *The Zodiac* (2006) turns the story into a conventional police drama. *The Exorcist III*

(1990) has a character named Gemini based on Zodiac. *Curse of the Zodiac Killer* (2005) is an obscure low-budget horror about a copycat murderer.

David Fincher's 2007 *Zodiac*, based on Graysmith's book, uses the case to examine the nature of obsession. Jake Gyllenhaal plays Graysmith and Mark Ruffalo plays the role of real detective Dave Toschi, who worked on the case. (Toschi was also the model for Steve McQueen's character in *Bullitt*.) Real crimes are seldom handled with as much complexity and sensitivity on screen. Fincher's film is one of the very best.

Zodiackiller.com is a site devoted to the many complexities of the case.

Bibliography

Adams, Randall (with William Hoffer and Marilyn Mona Hoffer). *Adams v. Texas: The True Story Made Famous by the Highly Acclaimed Film* The Thin Blue Line. New York: St. Martin's, 1991.

Adler, Warren. *American Quartet*. New York: Arbor House, 1981.

Alexander, Shana. *Very Much a Lady: The Untold Story of Jean Harris and Dr. Herman Tarnower*. Boston: Little, Brown, 1983.

Allen, William. *Starkweather: The Story of a Mass Murderer*. Boston: Houghton Mifflin, 1976.

Ambler, Eric. *The Ability to Kill: True Tales of Bloody Murder*. New York: Mysterious Press, 1960.

Aptheker, Herbert. *Nat Turner's Slave Rebellion*. New York: Humanities Press, 1966.

Asbury, Herbert. *The Gangs of New York*. Knopf: New York, 1927, 1928.

Badal, James Jessen. *In the Wake of the Butcher: Cleveland's Torso Murders*. Kent, OH: Kent State University Press, 2001.

Bailey, F. Lee, with Harvey Aronson. *The Defense Never Rests*. New York: Stein and Day, 1971.

Barra, Allen. *Inventing Wyatt Earp: His Life and Many Legends*. New York: Carroll & Graf, 1998.

Baxter, John. *The Gangster Film*. New York: A.S. Barnes, 1970.

Beaver, Ninette, Ripley, B.K., and Patrick Trese. *Caril*. Philadelphia, PA: Lippincott, 1974.

Behn, Noel. *Big Stick-Up at Brink's*. New York: Putnam, 1977.

Bellesiles, Michael A. *Arming America: The Origins of a National Gun Culture*. New York: Knopf, 2000.

Berkow, Ira. *The Man Who Robbed the Pierre: The Story of Bobby Comfort and the Biggest Hotel Robbery Ever*. New York: Atheneum, 1987.

Betenson, Lula Parker (as told to Dora Flack). *Butch, Cassidy, My Brother*. Provo, UT: Brigham Young University Press, 1975.

Bishop, Jim. *The Day Lincoln Was Shot*. New York: Harper, 1955.

Blake, James Carlos. *The Pistoleer: A Novel of John Wesley Hardin.* New York: Berkley Books, 1995.

Bledsoe, Jerry. *Bitter Blood.* New York: Dutton, 1988.

Bloch, Robert. *Once Around the Bloch.* New York: Tor Books, 1993.

Blum, Howard. *Gangland: How the FBI Broke the Mob.* New York: Simon & Schuster, 1993.

Bock, Alan W. *Ambush at Ruby Ridge: How Government Agents Set Randy Weaver Up and Took His Family Down.* Irvine, CA: Dickens Press, 1995.

Bonanno, Bill. *Bound by Honor: A Mafioso's Story.* New York: St. Martin's, 1999.

Bonanno, Joseph (with Sergio Lalli). *A Man of Honor.* New York: Simon & Schuster, 1983.

Bradshaw, Jon. *Dreams That Money Can Buy: The Tragic Life of Libby Holman.* New York: William Morrow, 1985.

Breslin, Jimmy, and Dick Schaap. *.44, A Novel.* New York: Viking, 1978.

Bryan Howard. *Robbers, Rogues, and Ruffians: True Tales of the Wild West.* Sante Fe, NM: Clear Light Publishers, 1991.

Bugliosi, Vincent. *Helter Skelter: The True Story of the Manson Murders.* New York: Norton, 1974.

Burrough, Bryan. *Public Enemies: America's Greatest Crime Wave and the Birth of the FBI, 1933-34.* New York: Penguin, 2004.

Burroughs, William S. *The Last Words of Dutch Schultz: A Fiction in the Form of a Film Script.* Viking, 1969.

Cantor, George. *Bad Guys in American History.* Dallas, TX: Taylor Publishing, 1999.

Capote, Truman. *In Cold Blood.* New York: Random House, 1966.

Carter, Rubin "Hurricane." *The Sixteenth Round: From #1 Contender to #45472.* Viking, 1974.

Cartwright, Gary. *Blood Will Tell: The Murder Trials of T. Cullen Davis.* New York: Harcourt Brace Jovanovich, 1979.

Chaiton, Sam, and Terry Swinton. *Lazarus and the Hurricane.* New York: St. Martin's Griffin, 1991, 1999.

Clarens, Carlos. *Crime Movies: An Illustrated History.* New York: Norton, 1980.

Clarke, Gerald. *Capote.* Simon & Schuster, 1988.

Clarke, John Henrik, ed. *William Styron's* Nat Turner: *Ten Black Writers Respond.* Boston: Beacon Press, 1968.

Corwin, Miles. *Homicide Special: A Year with the LAPD's Elite Detective Unit.* New York: Henry Holt, 2003.

Crane, Stephen. *Maggie: A Girl of the Streets.* New York: Fawcett, 1893.

Davis, Bernice Davis (with Al Hirshberg). *The Desperate and the Damned.* New York: Thomas Y. Crowell, 1961.

Davis, Mike. *Buda's Wagon: A Brief History of the Car Bomb.* New York: Verso, 2007.

DeFord, Miriam Allen. *Murderers Sane & Mad: Case Histories in the Motivation and Rationale of Murder.* London: Abelard-Schuman, 1966.

Denton, Sally. *American Massacre: The Tragedy at Mountain Meadows, September 1857.* New York: Knopf, 2003.

Dershowitz, Alan M. *Reversal of Fortune: Inside the Von Bülautlow Case.* Random House, 1985.

Doctorow, E.L. *Ragtime.* Random House, 1974.

Doss, Rodger. *The Killing of a Court.* 1994.

Douglas Ann. *Terrible Honesty: Mongrel Manhattan in the 1920s.* New York: Farrar, Straus and Giroux, 1995.

Douglas, John, and Mark Olshaker. *The Cases That Haunt Us.* New York: Scribner, 2000.
———. *Journey Into Darkness.* Scribner's, 1997.

Drago, Harry Sinclair. *The Legend Makers: Tales of the Old-Time Peace Officers and Desperadoes of the Frontier.* New York: Dodd-Mead, 1975.

Draper, Allison Stark. *The Assassination of Malcolm X.* New York: Rosen Group, 2002.

Dray, Philip. *At the Hands of Persons Unknown: The Lynching of Black America.* Random House, 2002.

Dunne, Dominick. *Another City, Not My Own: A Novel in the Form of a Memoir.* New York: Crown, 1997.
———. *Justice: Crimes, Trials and Punishments.* Crown, 2001.
———. *The Way We Lived Then: Recollections of a Well-Known Name Dropper.* Crown, 1999.

Dwyer, Jim, and Flynn, Kevin. *102 Minutes: The Untold Story of the Fight to Survive Inside the Twin Towers.* New York: Times Books, 2005.

Eberle, Paul and Shirley. *The Abuse of Innocence: The McMartin Preschool Trial.* Amherst, NY: Prometheus Books, 1993.

Edmonds, Andy. *Bugsy's Baby: The Secret Life of Mob Queen Virginia Hill.* New York: Birch Lane Press, 1993.

Eisenberg, Dennis, Dan, Uri, and Eli Landau. *Meyer Lansky: Mogul of the Mob.* London: Paddington Press, Ltd., 1979.

Ellison, Harlan. *Harlan Ellison's Watching.* Los Angeles: Underwood-Miller, 1989.

Eyman, Scott. *Print the Legend: The Life and Times of John Ford.* Simon & Schuster, 1999.

Fenster, Mark. *Conspiracy Theories: Secrecy and Power in American Culture.* Minneapolis, MN: University of Minnesota Press, 1999.

Fisher, Jim. *The Ghosts of Hopewell.* Carbondale, IL: Southern Illinois University Press, 1999.
———. *The Lindbergh Case.* New Brunswick, NJ: Rutgers University Press, 1994.

Fitzgerald, F. Scott. *The Great Gatsby.* New York: Scribner's, 1925.

Freeman, Judith. *Red Water.* New York: Pantheon, 2002.

Gardner, Lloyd C. *The Case That Never Dies.* Rutgers University Press, 2004.

Gardner, Rufus L. *Courthouse Tragedy.* 1992.

Garfield, Brian. *Western Films: A Complete Guide.* New York: Rawson Associates, 1982.

Garrett, Pat F. *The Authentic Life of Billy, the Kid, the Noted Desperado of the Southwest, Whose Deeds of Daring and Blood Made His Name a Terror in New Mexico, Arizona and Northern Mexico, A Faithful and Interesting Narrative.* Norman, OK: University of Oklahoma Press, 1954.

Geary, Rick. *The Beast of Chicago: An Account of the Life and crimes of Herman W. Mudgett, Known to the World as H.H. Holmes.* New York: NBM, 2003.

———. *Bloody Benders*. NBM, 2007.

———. *The Borden Tragedy*. NBM, 1997.

———. *The Fatal Bullet: The Assassination of President James A. Garfield*. NBM, 1999.

———. *The Murder of Abraham Lincoln*. NBM Books, 2005.

———. *The Mystery of Mary Rogers*. NBM, 2001.

Gerald, Marc, ed. *Murder Plus: True Crime Stories from the Masters of Detective Fiction*. New York: Pharos Books, 1992.

Gilmore, John. *Severed: The True Story of the Black Dahlia Murder*. Los Angeles: Amok Books, 1994.

Gilmore, Mikal. *Shot in the Heart*. New York: Doubleday, 1994.

Goldman, William. *Adventures in the Screen Trade: A Personal View of Hollywood and Screenwriting*. New York: Warner Books, 1983.

Good, Jeffrey, and Susan Goreck. *Poison Mind: The True Story of the Mensa Murderer— and the Policewoman Who Risked Her Life to Bring Him to Justice*. William Morrow, 1995.

Gosch, Martin A., and Richard Hammer. *The Last Testament of Lucky Luciano*. Boston: Little, Brown, 1974.

Griffin, David Ray. *The New Pearl Harbor: Disturbing Questions About the Bush Administration and 9/11*. Northampton, MA: Olive Branch Press, 2004.

Guest, Judith. *The Tarnished Eye*. New York: Scribners, 2004.

Hamilton, Stanley. *Machine Gun Kelly's Last Stand*. Lawrenceville, KS: University Press of Kansas, 2003.

Hammer, Richard. *Playboy's History of Organized Crime*. Chicago: Playboy Press, 1975.

Hansen, Ron. *The Assassination of Jesse James by the Coward Robert Ford*. Knopf, 1983.

Hardy, Phil, ed. *Overlook Film Encyclopedia: Horror*. Woodstock, NY: Overlook Press, 1995.

Hasday, Judy L. *Columbine High School Shooting*. Berkeley Heights, NJ: Enslow Publishers, Inc., 2002.

Haskins, Jim. *The Cotton Club*. New York: New American Library, 1977.

Havill, Adrian. *The Mother, the Son, and the Socialite: The True Story of a Mother-Son Crime Spree*. New York: St. Martin's Paperbacks, 1999.

Heimann, Jim . *All-American Ads 1920s*. Cologne, Germany: Tashen, 2004.

———. *All-American Ads 1930s*. Tashen, 2004.

———. *All-American Ads 1940s*. Tashen, 2004.

———. *All-American Ads 1950s*. Tashen, 2004.

———. *All-American Ads 1960s*. Tashen, 2004.

Helmer, William J. *The Gun That Made the Twenties Roar*. Highland Park, NJ: Gun Room Press, 1969.

Hersh, Seymour M. *The Dark Side of Camelot*. Little Brown, 1997.

Higham, Charles. *Murder in Hollywood: Solving a Silent Screen Mystery*. Madison, WI: University of Wisconsin Press, 2004.

Hill, Henry (as told to Gus Russo). *Gangsters and Goodfellas: The Mob, Witness Protection, and Life on the Run*. New York: M. Evans, 2004.

Hinckley, Jack and Jo Ann, with Elizabeth Sherrill. *Breaking Points.* Grand Rapids, MI: Chosen Books (Zondervan Publishing), 1985.

Hodel, Steve. *Black Dahlia Avenger: The True Story.* New York: Arcade Publishing, 2003.

Horan, James. *The Desperate Years: A Pictorial History of the Thirties.* New York: Bonanza Books, 1962.

Horn, Tom. *Life of Tom Horn, Government Scout and Interpreter.* New York: Jingle Bob/Crown, 1977. ((c) 1904 John C. Coble)

Hornberger, Francine. *Mistresses of Mayhem: The Book of Women Criminals.* Indianapolis, IN: Alpha Books, 2002.

Horwitz, Sari, and Michael E. Ruane. *Sniper: Inside the Hunt for the Killers Who Terrorized the Nation.* Random House, 2003.

Huie, William Bradford. *He Slew the Dreamer: My Search for the Truth About James Earl Ray and the Murder of Martin Luther King.* New York: Delacorte, 1968; Montgomery, AL: Black Belt Press, 1997.

Hunter, Evan. *Lizzie.* Arbor House, 1984.

Hunter, Stephen, and John Bainbridge, Jr. *American Gunfight: The Plot to Kill Harry Truman—and the Shoot-Out That Stopped It.* Simon & Schuster, 2005.

Hunter, Stephen. *Hot Springs.* Simon & Schuster, 2000.

———. *Violent Screen: A Critic's 13 Years on the Front Lines of Movie Mayhem.* Baltimore, MD: Bancroft Press, 1995.

Jeffers, H. Paul. *Gentleman Gerald.* St. Martin's, 1993.

Junger, Sebastian. *A Death in Belmont.* Norton, 2006.

Kauffman, Michael W. *American Brutus: John Wilkes Booth and the Lincoln Conspiracies.* Random House, 2004.

Kennedy, Ludovic. *The Airman and the Carpenter.* Random House, 1989.

Kennedy, William. *Legs.* Coward, McCann & Geoghegan, 1975.

———. *O Albany! An Urban Tapestry: Improbable City of Political Wizards, Fearless Ethnics, Spectacular Aristocrats, Splendid Nobodies, and Underrated Scoundrels.* Viking, 1983.

Kent, David. *Forty Whacks: New Evidence in the Life and Legend of Lizzie Borden.* New York: Yankee Books, 1992.

———. *The Lizzie Borden Sourcebook.* Boston: Branden, 1992.

King, Jeanne. *Dead End: The Crime Story of the Decade—Murder, Incest and High-Tech Thievery.* M. Evans, 2002.

Kirchner, L.R. *Robbing Banks: An American History 1831-1999.* Rockville Center, NY: Sharpedon, 2000.

Kurland, Michael. *A Gallery of Rogues: Portraits In True Crime.* New York: Prentice Hall, 1994.

Lacey, Robert. *Little Man: Meyer Lansky and the Gangster Life.* Little Brown, 1991.

Landay, William. *The Strangler.* New York: Delacorte, 2007.

Lange, Tom, and Phillip Vannatter (as told to Dan E. Moldea). *Evidence Dismissed: The Inside Story of the Police Investigation of O.J. Simpson.* New York: Pocket Books, 1997.

Langford, Gerald. *The Murder of Stanford White.* Bobbs-Merrill, 1962.***

Lardner, James, and Thomas Reppetto, *NYPD: A City and Its Police*. New York: Henry Holt, 2000.

Lavergne, Gary M. *A Sniper in the Tower: The Charles Whitman Murders*. University of North Texas Press, 1997.

Lawes, Lewis E. *Twenty Thousand Years in Sing Sing*. New York: Ray Long & Richard R. Smith, Inc., 1932.

Lawson, Kristan, and Anneli Rufus. *California Babylon: A Guide to Sites of Scandal, Mayhem, and Celluloid in the Golden State*. St. Martin's Griffin, 2000.

Lerner, Michael A. *Dry Manhattan: Prohibition in New York City*. Cambridge, MA: Harvard University Press, 2007.

Lessard, Suzannah. *The Architect of Desire: Beauty and Danger in the Stanford White Family*. New York: Dial Press, 1996.

Loerzel, Robert. *Alchemy of Bones: Chicago's Luetgert Murder Case of 1897*. Springfield, IL: University of Illinois Press, 2003.

Long, Steven. *Out of Control: The Clara Harris Murder Case*. St. Martin's, 2004.

Maas, Peter. *Underboss: Sammy "The Bull" Gravano's Story of Life in the Mafia*. Harper Collins, 1997.

McCarty, John. *Bullets Over Hollywood: The American Gangster Picture from the Silents to The Sopranos*. Cambridge, MA: Da Capo Press, 2004.

McConnell, Virginia A. *Sympathy for the Devil: The Emmanuel Baptist Murders of Old San Francisco*. Westport, CT: Praeger, 2001.

MacDonald, John D. *The Last One Left*. Doubleday, 1967.

McDougal, Dennis, and Mary Murphy. *Blood Cold: Fame, Sex, and Murder in Hollywood*. New York: Onyx (Penguin Books), 2002.

McGinnis, Joe. *Fatal Vision*. Putnam, 1983.

Mailer, Norman. *The Executioner's Song*. Little, Brown, 1979.

———. *Oswald's Tale: An American Mystery*. Random House, 1995.

March, Joseph Moncure. *The Wild Party (Drawings by Art Spiegelman)*. New York: Pantheon, 1994.

Marks, Paula Mitchell. *And Die in the West: The Story of the O.K. Corral Gunfight*. William Morrow, 1989.

Matera, Dary. *FBI's Ten Most Wanted*. New York: Harper Torch, 2003.

Maynard, Joyce. *To Die For*. New York: Dutton, 1992.

Mayo, Mike. *VideoHound's Horror Show*. Detroit, MI: Visible Ink Press, 1998.

———. *VideoHound's Video Premieres*. Visible Ink Press, 1997.

Michel, Lou, and Dan Herbeck. *American Terrorist: Timothy McVeigh and the Oklahoma City Bombing*. New York: Regan Books, 2001.

Milto, Joyce, and Ann Louise Bardach. *Vicki: The True Story of Vicki Morgan and Alfred Bloomingdale and the Affair That Shook the Highest Levels of Government and Society*. St. Martin's, 1986.

Moldea, Dan E. *The Killing of Robert F. Kennedy: An Investigation of Motive, Means, and Opportunity*. Norton, 1995.

Monroe, Judy. *The Sacco and Vanzetti Controversial Murder Trial: A Headline Court Case*. Berkeley Heights, NJ: Enslow Publishers, Inc., 2000.

AMERICAN MURDER

Mooney, Michael MacDonald. *Evelyn Nesbit and Stanford White: Love and Death in the Gilded Age.* William Morrow, 1976.

Moose, Charles A., and Charles Fleming. *Three Weeks in October.* Dutton, 2003.

Naifeh, Steven, and Gregory White Smith. *Final Justice: The True Story of the Richest Man Ever Tried For Murder.* Dutton, 1993.

Nash, Jay Robert. *Bloodletters and Bad Men: A Narrative History of American Criminals From the Pilgrims to the Present.* M. Evans, 1973.

———. *Citizen Hoover: A Critical Study of the Life and Times of J. Edgar Hoover and His FBI.* Chicago: Nelson-Hall, 1972.

———. *The Dillinger Dossier.* Highland Park, IL: December Press, 1970, 1983.

———. *Look for the Woman: A Narrative Encyclopedia of Female Poisoners, Kidnappers, Thieves, Extortionists, Terrorists, Swindlers and Spies from Elizabethan Times to the Present.* M. Evans, 1981.

Nash, Jay Robert, and Ron Offen. *Dillinger: Dead or Alive?* Chicago: Regnery, 1970.

National Commission on Terrorist Attacks Upon the United States. *The 9/11 Commission Report.* Norton, 2004.

Navas, Deborah. *Murdered By His Wife.* Amherst, MA: University of Massachusetts Press, 1999.

Newseum. *President Kennedy Has Been Shot: The Inside Story of the Murder of a President.* Naperville, IL: Sourcebooks Media Fusion, 2003.

O'Brien, Darcy. *Two of a Kind: The Hillside Stranglers.* New American Library, 1985.

O'Brien, Joseph, and Andris Kurins. *Boss of Bosses: The Fall of the Godfather—The FBI and Paul Castellano.* Simon & Schuster, 1991.

Olshaker, Mark. *The Mind of a Serial Killer.* (Video) PBS: Nova, 1992.

Oney, Steve. *And the Dead Shall Rise: The Murder of Mary Phagan and the Lynching of Leo Frank.* Pantheon, 2003.

Orth, Maureen. *Vulgar Favors: Andrew Cunanan, Gianni Versace, and the Largest Failed Manhunt in U.S. History.* Delacorte, 1999.

Parish, James Robert. *The Hollywood Book of Scandals.* New York: McGraw Hill, 2004.

Patterson, Richard. *Butch Cassidy: A Biography.* Lincoln, NE: University of Nebraska Press, 1998.

Paul, Raymond. *Who Murdered Mary Rogers?* Prentice-Hall, 1971.

Peary, Danny. *Cult Movies 3.* Simon & Schuster, 1988.

———. *Cult Movies.* New York: Delta Books, 1981.

Perry, Hamilton Darby. *Libby Holman: Body and Soul.* Little, Brown, 1983.

Philbrick, Nathaniel. *Mayflower Madam.* Viking, 2006.

Piercy, Marge. *The Longings of Women.* New York: Fawcett Columbine, 1994.

Pileggi, Nicholas. *Wiseguy: Life in a Mafia Family.* Simon & Schuster, 1985.

Pipes, Daniel. *Militant Islam Reaches America.* Norton, 2002.

Posner, Gerald. *Case Closed.* Random House, 1993.

———. *Killing the Dream: James Earl Ray and the Assassination of Martin Luther King, Jr.* Random House, 1998.

Puzo, Mario. *The Godfather.* Putnam, 1969.

———. *The Godfather Papers and Other Confessions.* Putnam, 1972.

Raab, Selwyn. *Five Families: The Rise, Decline, and Resurgence of America's Most Powerful Mafia Families.* St. Martin's, 2005.

Rabinowitz, Harold. *Black Hats and White Hats: Heroes and Villains of the Old West.* New York: Metro Books, 1996.

Ramsland, Katherine. *The Human Predator: A Historical Chronicle of Serial Murder and Forensic Investigation.* New York: Berkley, 2005.

Reeve, Simon. *New Jackals: Ramzi Yousef, Osama Bin Laden and the Future of Terrorism.* Boston: Northeastern University Press, 1999.

Rhodes, Bernie, and Russell Calame. *D.B. Cooper: The Real McCoy.* Salt Lake City, UT: University of Utah Press, 1991.

Robbins, Trinia. *Tender Mercies: Women Who Kill.* Newburyport, ME: Conari Press, 2003.

Roberts, Gary L. *Doc Holliday: The Life and Legend.* New York: John Wiley & Sons, 2006.

Ronson, Jon. *Them: Adventures With Extremists.* Simon & Schuster, 2002.

Rule, Ann. *Stranger Beside Me.* New York: Norton, 1980.

Sanders, Ed. *The Family.* New York: Thunder's Mouth Press, 2002.

Scaduto, Anthony. *Scapegoat.* Putnam, 1976.

Schama, Simon. *Dead Certainties.* Knopf, 1991.

Schechter, Harold. *The Serial Killer Files.* Ballantine Books, 2003.

Schickel, Richard. *D.W. Griffith: An American Life.* Simon & Schuster, 1984.

Schuster, Henry, with Charles Stone. *Hunting Eric Rudolph: An Insider's Account of the Five-Year Search for the Olympic Bombing Suspect.* Berkley Books, 2005.

Schwarz, Ted. *The Hillside Strangler: A Murderer's Mind.* Doubleday, 1981.

Scott, Gini Graham. *Homicide: 100 Years of Murder in America.* Los Angeles: Loswell House, 1998.

Sennett, Ted. *Murder on Tape: A Comprehensive Guide to Over 1,000 Murder and Mystery Movies on Video.* New York: Billboard Books, 1997.

Serrano, Richard A. *One of Ours: Timothy McVeigh and the Oklahoma City Bombing.* Norton, 1998.

Shea, Robert, and Wilson, Robert Anton. *Illuminatus! Trilogy (The Eye in the Pyramid, The Golden Apple, Leviathan).* Dell, 1975.

Shirley, Glenn. *Law West of Fort Smith: An Authentic History of Frontier Justice in the old Indian Territory.* Henry Holt, 1957.

Sifakis, Carl. *The Encyclopedia of American Crime.* Facts on File, 1982, 2001.

Singular, Stephen. *Talked to Death: The Life and Murder of Alan Berg.* New York: Beach Tree Books, 1987.

Soares, André. *Beyond Paradise: The Life of Ramon Novarro.* St. Martin's, 2002.

Sorrentino, Christopher. *Trance.* New York: Farrar, Straus and Giroux, 2005.

Spiegelman, Art. *In the Shadow of No Towers.* Pantheon Books, 2004.

Spignesi, Stephen J. *In the Crosshairs: Famous Assassinations and Attempts from Julius Caesar to John Lennon.* Franklin Lakes, NJ: Career Press, 2003.

Stahl, Jerry. *I, Fatty.* New York: Bloomsbury, 2004.

Stannard, David E. *Honor Killing: How the Infamous "Massie Affair" Transformed Hawai'i.* Viking Penguin, 2005.

Stashower, Daniel. *The Beautiful Cigar Girl: Mary Rogers, Edgar Allan Poe, and the Invention of Murder.* Dutton, 2006.

Stiles, T.J. *Jesse James Last Rebel of the Civil War.* Knopf, 2002.

Styron, William. *Confessions of Nat Turner.* Random House, 1966.

Sullivan, Robert. *The Disappearance of Dr. Parkman.* Little, Brown, 1971.

Swanson, James L., and Daniel R. Weinberg. *Lincoln's Assassins: Their Trial and Execution.* Santa Fe, NM: Arena Editions, 2001.

Swanson, James L. *Manhunt: The 12-Day Chase for Lincoln's Killer.* HarperCollins, 2006.

Thomson, Helen. *Murder at Harvard.* Houghton Mifflin, 1971.

Time-Life Books. *Mass Murderers.* New York: Time-Life Books, 1992.

Tofel, Richard J. *Vanishing Point: The Disappearance of Judge Crater, and the New York He Left Behind.* Chicago: Ivan R. Dee, 2004.

Toland, John. *The Dillinger Days.* Random House, 1963.

Trilling, Diana. *Mrs. Harris: The Death of the Scarsdale Diet Doctor.* Harcourt Brace Jovanovich, 1981.

Truffaut, François. *Hitchcock, Truffaut.* Simon & Schuster, 1983.

Turkus, Burton B., and Sid Feder. *Murder, Inc.: The Story of the Syndicate.* Da Capo Press, 1951, 1992.

Utley, Robert M. *Billy the Kid: A Short and Violent Life.* University of Nebraska Press, 1989.

Van Every, Edward. *Sins of New York as "Exposed" by the* Police Gazette. New York: Frederick Stokes, 1930.

Vidal, Gore. *Dreaming War: Blood for Oil and the Cheney-Bush Junta.* New York: Thunder's Mouth Press/ Nation Books, 2002.

Vise, David A. *The Bureau and the Mole: The Unmasking of Robert Philip Hanssen, the Most Dangerous Double Agent in FBI History.* New York: Grove Press, 2002.

Vollers, Maryanne. *Lone Wolf: Eric Rudolph—Murder, Myth, and the Pursuit of an American Outlaw.* HarperCollins, 2006.

Walker, Dale L. *The Calamity Papers: Western Myths and Cold Cases.* New York: Forge, 2004.

Wallis, Michael. *Billy the Kid: The Endless Ride.* Norton, 2007.

———. Pretty Boy: The Life and Times of Charles Arthur Floyd. *St. Martin's, 1992.*

Walsh, Michael. *And All the Saints.* Warner Books, 2003.

Warren, Robert Penn. *All the King's Men.* New York: Harcourt, Brace & World, 1946.

Watkins, Maurine. *Chicago.* Southern Illinois University Press, 1997.

Weddle, David. *"If They Move… Kill 'Em"—The Life and Times of Sam Peckinpah.* Grove Press, 1994.

Wilson, Colin, ed. *The World's Greatest True Crime.* New York: Barnes & Noble Books, 2005.

Wilson, Colin. *A Casebook of Murder: The Changing Patterns of Homicidal Killings.* New York: Cowles, 1969.

Winkler, H. Donald. Lincoln and Booth: More Light on the Conspiracy. *Cumberland House Publishing, 2003.*

Wise, William. *Massacre at Mountain Meadows: An American Legend and a Monumental Crime.* Thomas Y. Crowell, 1976.

Wolf, Marvin J., and Katherine Mader. *Rotten Apples: True Stories of New York Crime and Mystery 1689 to the Present.* New York: Ballantine Books, 1991.

Woodrekk, Daniel. *Woe To Live On.* Henry Holt, 1987.

Wray, John. *Canaan's Tongue.* Knopf, 2005.

Wright, Lawrence. *The Looming Tower: Al-Qaeda and the Road to 9/11.* Knopf, 2006.

Wright, William. *The Von Bülow Affair.* Delacorte, 1983.

INDEX

Notes: **Boldface** refers to main entries and the page numbers
on which those entries appear; (ill.) indicates photos and illustrations.

Amy Fisher: My Story, 114
The Amy Fisher Story, 114
Anastasia, Albert, **7–9,** 8 (ill.)
 Adonis, Joe, 4
 Buchalter, Louis "Lepke," 49, 50
 Gallo, Joey "Crazy Joe," 122
 Gambino, Carlo, 123–24
 Genovese, Vito, 126–27
 Lansky, Meyer, 184
 Luciano, Charles "Lucky," 203
 Mafia, 210, 211
 Maranzano, Salvatore, 218
 Masseria, Joe "the Boss," 220
 Murder, Inc., 243
 Valachi, Joe, 362
Anastasio, "Tough" Tony, 7
And All the Saints (Walsh), 209
And Never Let Her Go (Rule), 297
Andersen, Dutch, 65, 66
Anderson, "Bloody Bill," 163, 279
Anderson, Josephine, 9
Anderson, Mary, 9
Anderson, Maxwell, 300
Anderson, Victor, 340
Anderson, William, **9**
Andrews, Franklin, 13
Angel in Black (Collins), 316
Anger, Kenneth, 111, 217
Anglin, Clarence, 238, 239
Anglin, John, 238, 239
Annan, Albert, 10
Annan, Beulah, **9–10**
Annie Oakley, 53
Another City, Not My Own (Dunne), 108
Anselmi, Albert, 57, 58, 337
Anson, Jay, 100
Antonio, Walter Gino, 377
Apalachin Conference, 124, 127, 211, 362
Arbuckle, Roscoe "Fatty," **10–12,** 11 (ill.), 346, 347

Archer, James, 12
Archer-Gilligan, Amy, **12–13**
Armstrong, John B., 141
Arnall, Ellis, 56
Arnaz, Lucie, 316
Arnold, Samuel, 40
Arnold, Stephen, **13**
Arquette, Patricia, 338
Artis, John, 61
Asbury, Herbert, 271
Assante, Armand, 133
Assassination attempts
 Ford, Gerald, 120
 Reagan, Ronald, 155–56
 Roosevelt, Franklin D., 381
 Truman, Harry, 355–56
The Assassination of Jesse James by the Coward Robert Ford, 166
Assassinations
 Cermak, Anton, 381
 Evers, Medger, 28
 Garfield, James, 137
 Kennedy, John, 261–64
 Kennedy, Robert, 322–24
 King, Martin Luther, Jr., 283–85
 Lennon, John, 66–67
 Lincoln, Abraham, 39–42
 Long, Huey, 369
 Malcolm X, 139–40
 McKinley, William, 93
 Milk, Harvey, 371
 Moscone, George, 371
Assassins
 Beckwith, Byron de la, 28
 Booth, John Wilkes, 39–42
 Chapman, Mark David, 66–67
 Czolgosz, Leon, 92–93
 Guiteau, Charles, 137–38
 Hagan, Thomas, 139–40
 Oswald, Lee Harvey, 261–64
 Ray, James Earl, 283–85
 Sirhan, Sirhan Bishara, 322–24
 Weiss, Carl, 369

 White, Dan, 371
 Zangara, Joseph, 381
Assassins, 42, 93, 120, 138, 156, 381
An Assassin's Diary (Bremer), 49, 155
Astor Place riot, 52
Atherton, William, 166
Atkins, Susan, 216
The Atlanta Child Murders (Mann), 376
Atlanta murders, 376
Atta, Mohamed, 260
Atzerodt, George, 40, 41
Austin, Marie, 367
Austin, Ron, 199
The Authentic Life of Billy the Kid (Garrett and Upson), 226
Auto Focus (Schrader), 84
The Autobiography of Malcolm X (Haley), 140
Auto-Ordnance Corporation, 350
Avrich, Paul, 366

B

Baby Face Nelson, 252
Bacall, Lauren, 159
Bacha, Bobbi, 142, 143, 144
Bad Boy Entertainment, 307
Badal, James Jessen, 72
The Badge (Webb), 316
Badlands, 341
Baer, Max, 209
Baer, Robert, 261
Bagley, Will, 240
Bailey, F. Lee, 46, 150, 304, 311, 320
Bailey, Harvey, **15–16**
Bainbridge, John, Jr., 356
Baird, Juanita, 115, 116
Baker, Lew, 271–72
Bakley, Bonny Lee, 36–38, 48, 198
Baldwin, Jason, 370
Ball, Joe, **16–17**

AMERICAN MURDER